Mastering Human Resource Management
Version 1.0

Derek Crews

978-1-4533-9707-7

Mastering Human Resource Management
Version 1.0

Derek Crews

Published by:

FlatWorld
292 Newbury Street
Suite #282
Boston, MA 02115-2832

Gen: 202102261936

Brief Contents

Contents

About the Author

Dr. Derek Crews

Derek Crews (EdD Nova Southeastern University) is Associate Professor of Management in the College of Business at Texas Woman's University. Derek teaches undergraduate and graduate courses in human resource management and talent development. Derek is a Past President of the North Texas Society for Human Resource Management; Past Vice-President for Membership, Texoma Human Resource Management Association; a Senior Certified Professional of the Society for Human Resource Management (SHRM-SCP); a Senior Professional in Human Resources (SPHR) of HRCI; Master Trainer, AchieveGlobal; and Master Trainer; Development Dimensions International. He is also a graduate of Harvard University's Institute for Management and Leadership in Education. Prior to his academic career, Derek served in various managerial and supervisory roles, including Vice-President, Finance and Administration, for Texas Parcel Service.

Derek has consulted with organizations as diverse as the Texas Workforce Commission, Workforce Texoma, Texas A&M, Barbour County Economic Development, Gwinnett Technical College, Black & Decker, Alcoa, Texas Instruments, Tyson Foods, and Walmart. Derek's scholarly publications include articles published in *International Journal of Productivity and Performance Management*, *International Journal of Human Resource Studies*, *International Journal of Business & Social Sciences*, and *Leadership & Organizational Management Journal*.

Source: Provided by Derek Crews.

Acknowledgments

My sincere thanks to the reviewers of this textbook. Their valuable suggestions and feedback have vastly improved the quality of the finished product.

- Dr. Jalane Meloun, Barry University
- Karen Landay, University of Alabama
- Justin A. DeSimone, University of Alabama
- Michael Dutch, Guilford College
- Yi Liu, Trinity University
- Yifeng Fan, Georgia Institute of Technology

I would also like to thank the HR professionals who agreed to interviews and are the focus of the "HR Talk" features in each chapter. Their insights and experience lend a practical, real-world focus to the text:

- Lauren Billings
- Cindie Melton
- Bruce Waller
- Rodney Klein
- Karen Hopkins
- Beth Gottfried
- Justin Dorsey
- Mike Coffey
- Mark Hacker
- Brent O'Bannon
- Drew Dunsmuir
- Ashlie Bagley
- Qiara Suggs
- Steve Larsen
- Evelyn Walter
- Cara Carroll
- Dr. Louis Carfagno
- Marisa Gonzalez
- Wendy Padgett

I am also grateful to the many undergraduate and graduate students at Texas Woman's University who assisted in writing cases and reviewed draft chapters of the book. Their feedback was invaluable in producing a concise book that engages the learner. Kiaa Haynes, my Graduate Assistant, provided assistance with research and proofreading, and her editorial background enabled her to provide extremely helpful input.

I appreciate the staff at FlatWorld for their expertise and support throughout this process. I especially wish to acknowledge Sean Wakely for helping to shape the vision for this book, and Nikki Ross for her dedicated support (and for graciously extending deadlines whenever I needed, which was most of the time). I also want to thank the many people working behind the scenes at FlatWorld for their tireless efforts to produce quality textbooks at affordable prices.

The person to whom I owe the most gratitude to is my wife, Tricia Crews. She has spent unknown hours proofreading, assisting with research, and writing cases. Her expertise in education and curriculum development has been crucial to the completion of this project, but her greatest contribution has been her understanding while I worked many evenings and weekends, and her constant encouragement and moral support.

Dedication

To my father, Irving (Jack) Crews, Jr., for inspiring me to a lifetime of learning and teaching, and to Tricia, my wife and best friend.

Preface

Mastering Human Resource Management is primarily intended as a survey text for instruction of undergraduate majors and minors in Human Resource Management, Business Administration, and related fields. It may also be appropriate for use as a basic introduction at the master's level. Talent analytics, employee engagement, and alignment with the Society for Human Resource Management (SHRM) Curriculum Guidebook are the unifying, central themes of the book.

I wrote *Mastering Human Resource Management* with the rapidly evolving work environment kept firmly in mind. My key goal is to provide learners with the state-of-the-art knowledge and skills needed to successfully recruit, develop, and retain top-performing talent. Many textbooks for the human resource management course were first published in the last century. By comparison, I strove to distinguish this first edition with a fresh and practical approach to contemporary work situations I have not seen other books fully address. *Mastering Human Resource Management's* key themes of talent analytics and employee engagement, combined with its explicit alignment with the SHRM and Human Resource Certification Institute (HRCI) curriculum guidelines, support a contemporary and professional competency from day one. Plentiful theory-into-practice exercises ensure learners understand how to implement best practices. Pertinent and reliable expert scholarship supports the realistic, nuanced, and challenging case studies that are found throughout the text, some of which are drawn from my own private-sector work experiences. The result is a distinctive blend of research and practice that ensures students understand when to apply the right HR strategies.

Each chapter includes at least one "HR Talk" feature, based on an interview with a practicing HR professional. This will help students make the transition from textbook learning to how the concepts are applied in the real world of HR. The goal of the book is to provide a learning resource that covers the theory that students need to know about the HR profession, in a concise, easy-to-read, and well-organized format. Students will be prepared to enter the industry with state-of-the-art knowledge, skills, and abilities.

There are three major trends in the field of human resource management that impacted the development of this book:

1. **Increased interest in data analytics and artificial intelligence.** The technology for talent recruitment, onboarding, compensation, performance management, and talent development continues to accelerate. This includes Human Resource Information Systems (HRIS), Applicant Tracking Systems (ATS), and Learning Management Systems (LMS).

2. **A shift away from human resource management solely focused on the employer perspective**, to a more balanced approach that focuses on employee engagement and work-life balance, while also achieving organizational goals for competitive advantage, productivity, and profitability. The National Study of the Changing Workforce, conducted by Families and Work Institute and SHRM, is a major study of the U.S. workforce that takes a comprehensive look at employees' lives both on and off the job. The study examines components of the work environment that benefit employers and employees, and has led to the development of SHRM's Effective Workplace Index, which consists of the following seven components: Job Challenge and Learning Opportunities; Supervisor Support for Job Success; Autonomy; Culture of Respect; Trust, and Belonging; Work-Life Fit; Satisfaction with Wages, Benefits, and Opportunities to Advance, and Co-Worker Support for Job Success. Each of these seven aspects of employee engagement is addressed in the textbook.

3. **The skills gap continues to constrain business expansion, and human resource professionals will face challenges in finding qualified employees.** Business location decisions today increasingly are made based on the presence of a workforce with the appropriate skills. A sur-

vey of company executives by *Area Development* magazine found that availability of skilled labor has become the most important factor in site selection. Studies indicate that eight out of ten HR professionals report that high-demand technical and soft skills are in short supply, and it is imperative that the skills gap be closed. If employers can't find talent with the skills required for job openings, they must build the talent by investing in employee training and partnering with educational institutions to develop talent pipelines to ensure individuals are prepared to enter the workforce.

Features and Benefits

Throughout the text, these three major themes are developed: Talent analytics, employee engagement, and alignment with SHRM and HRCI guidelines. The following chart summarizes the major features and benefits of the text.

Features and Benefits of *Mastering Human Resource Management*	
Features	**Benefits**
Focus on talent analytics	Conveys the knowledge necessary to utilize talent data in recruitment, onboarding, compensation, performance management, and talent development. This will prepare them to use Human Resource Information Systems (HRIS), Applicant Tracking Systems (ATS), and Learning Management Systems (LMS).
Balanced approach that focuses on employee engagement while also achieving organizational goals for competitive advantage and profitability	Highlights and techniques to enhance recruitment, retention, and performance in an environment of labor shortages and skills gaps. They will be prepared to create a culture of respect and autonomy, which is important to millennials, and to create an effective workplace in a diverse environment.
Alignment with SHRM Body of Competency and Knowledge (SHRM BoCK™) and HRCI's HR Body of Knowledge (HRBoK™)	Provides students with in-depth knowledge of current and relevant HR concepts. This will also prepare students for the SHRM Certified Professional (SHRM-CP) and/or Professional in Human Resources (PHR) exams.

Learning Objectives and Outcomes

The learning outcomes for the text are geared toward the Society for Human Resource Management (SHRM) Competency Model. SHRM is the world's largest HR professional society, representing 300,000 members in more than 165 countries. The SHRM Competency Model covers nine areas of expertise:

1. Human Resource Expertise (HR Knowledge)
2. Ethical Practice
3. Leadership and Navigation
4. Business Acumen

5. Consultation

6. Critical Evaluation

7. Communication

8. Global and Cultural Effectiveness

9. Relationship Management

   The learning outcomes expected for a student using this text are how to:

1. Accurately assess the role of human resource management in creating organizational competitive advantage through alignment with business strategy.

2. Comply with the legal regulations that apply to the terms and conditions of employment.

3. Create a culture of employee engagement that values diversity and mutual respect.

4. Appropriately utilize talent analytics in recruitment, onboarding, compensation, performance management, and talent development.

5. Develop effective communication, consultation and relationship management skills for working collaboratively with management, employees, and vendors.

Organization

Each chapter includes the following sections and features to support learning:

- Chapter-level Learning Objectives
- Opening Case with Discussion Questions
- Feature Strands:
    - "Talent Analytics" features demonstrating real-world use of data analytics in HR
    - "HR Talk" features providing theory in practice from interviews with HR professionals
    - "HR in the Real World" features highlighting stories from HR professionals
- Section-level Learning Objectives, Key Takeaways, and What Do *You* Think questions
- Key Terms throughout the chapter
- Chapter Conclusion
- Chapter End Matter including the following:
    - Theory-in-Practice (TIP) Exercises
    - Case Study with Discussion Questions
    - Resources

Supplements

Mastering Human Resource Management is accompanied by a robust supplements program that augments and enriches both the teaching and student learning experiences. I wrote all supplements to ensure accuracy and to ensure full alignment with the book's narrative. Faculty should contact their FlatWorld sales representative or FlatWorld support at support@flatworld.com for more information or to obtain access to the supplements upon adoption.

Instructor's Manual

The instructor's manual (IM) includes Learning Objectives and an outline for each chapter. The IM also features possible responses to case discussion questions which encourage students to more deeply engage with course material.

PowerPoint Slides

PowerPoint lecture slides provide a concise but thorough outline for each chapter and include relevant tables, figures, and images from the text to enliven lectures and stimulate class discussions. These PowerPoint slides also include a list of Learning Objectives by chapter. Instructors can use the slides as composed to support lectures or customize and build upon them to suit their particular teaching needs.

Online Quizzes

Quiz questions for student self-evaluation are available by section and by chapter in the online version of this text. Students can use the quizzes to test themselves on their comprehension as they move through the different sections of the text or once they have completed a chapter.

FlatWorld Homework

Accompanying FlatWorld Homework for this text is provided in an easy-to-use interface. Multiple choice, fill-in-the-blank, matching, and other question types are available for use and are all auto-gradable. Students who utilize the homework questions should see their performance improve on examinations that are given using the Test Item File questions provided to adopters via Word documents or LMS packages.

Test Item File

The Test Item File (TIF) includes more than fifty questions per chapter in multiple-choice, fill-in-the-blank, and essay-question formats. All answers are provided, including possible responses to the essay questions. The items have been written specifically to reinforce the major topics covered in each chapter and to align with FlatWorld Homework and in-text quiz items. The Test Item File questions are also available in pre-formatted form for easy export into popular learning management systems such as Canvas or Blackboard.

Test Generator—Powered by Cognero

FlatWorld is pleased to provide a computer-generated test program powered by the leading assessment provider Cognero to assist instructors with selecting, randomizing, formatting, loading online, or printing exams. Please contact your local FlatWorld representative or FlatWorld support (support@fwk.com) for more information or to request the program.

Sample Syllabi

Sample syllabi based on either 16-week or 10-week terms provide useful templates that help new adopters transition from their current course textbook to *Mastering Human Resource Management*. Faculty can download the syllabi from the FlatWorld website (https://catalog.flatworldknowledge.com/catalog/editions/mastering-human-resource-management-1#supplements) or they can be obtained by contacting your local FlatWorld representative or FlatWorld support (support@fwk.com).

Human resource management professionals have always been key contributors to an organization's success, but even more so in the constantly shifting and rapidly evolving work environment that seems to have become the norm. In recognition of this accelerating trend, I grounded *Mastering Human Resource Management* in engaging real-world and research-based information to ensure students are well-prepared for the many and various situations they may encounter. I trust you will also find this book to be a useful companion and supportive resource to your classroom instruction. If you have any feedback or input on how I can improve this book, I would be delighted to hear from you.

If you are a faculty member, thank you for considering or adopting *Mastering Human Resource Management* for your course. If you are a student, I hope this book excites you to learn about human resource management and how to leverage that knowledge to make a positive difference in the lives of your work colleagues and organization's goals.

Sincerely

Derek Crews

dcrews@twu.edu

CHAPTER 1
Human Resource Management: Challenges, Emerging Issues, and Roles

Learning Objectives

After reading this chapter, you should be able to do the following:

1. Describe the impact of human capital on organizational success.
2. Identify the challenges that HR managers must address as a result of business, economic, and social change.
3. Recognize the emerging issues and trends that impact human resource management.
4. Compare and contrast the responsibilities of HR managers and line managers.
5. Discuss the career options available in HRM and the competencies necessary for these roles.

Human resources (HR) is often thought of as a department in an organization that hires, does payroll, manages employee benefits such as health insurance and retirement plans, and handles the termination process when an employee separates from the company. As you will discover, effective management of human resources is key to creating a successful and thriving organization. This chapter describes the impact of human capital on the success of the organization, and it presents an overview of the challenges and emerging issues that managers should consider when designing the policies and practices that affect the employees in an organization. The various responsibilities of HR managers and line managers are then discussed. The chapter concludes with an overview of the various opportunities available to those interested in HR as a career field, along with suggestions for gaining the necessary competencies and skillsets for a career in HR.

1.1 Opening Case: Googleyness and Googlegeist

Google provides bikes for employees to use for transportation around its campus. As you can see from the picture, the bikes have Googleyness.

Source: Asif Islam / Shutterstock.com

Google is one of the greatest inventions in modern human history. Within seconds, Google searches allow us to find the answers to almost any question. However, Google's success is due to more than technological innovation. It's also a great place to work. They landed the top spot for six years running on *Fortune's* list of Best Companies to Work For. In 2019, Comparably awarded Google fifteen of their Best awards, including Best Company for Diversity, Best Company for Women, Best Company Culture, Best Company Perks & Benefits, Best Company Compensation, and Best Company Happiness.

Google knows that to have the best available product for the consumer, they need to recruit qualified applicants who not only have excellent technical skills, but also are likely to make a positive contribution to the organization. As part of the interview process, applicants are asked questions to determine their Googleyness, which some describe as the ability to thrive in an environment of ambiguity, uncertainty, and change.

Once employees are hired, Google strives to keep them happy and engaged. The tech titan is famous for perks like free gourmet food, haircuts, and laundry services. Some might think that the company is just awash in money and can afford to pamper employees. But Google also takes a rigorous analytical approach to morale. Google calls its HR department People Operations, which most people in the firm refer to as POPS. They conduct an annual employee survey, referred to as the Googlegeist. It boosted its parental-leave policies, for example, after finding that mothers were leaving at higher rates. The result was a 50% reduction in attrition rates for working moms.

Google's HR department has also taken an interest in organizational behavior and found that mid-level managers are vital to the success of the company. POPS determined this by looking at manager feedback surveys. They found that the highest-scoring managers had the best retention and performance rates because they were good at communicating and driving good outcomes without micromanaging. The low-scoring managers are sent to training, and feedback scores have improved as a result.

The HR department even analyzed the eating patterns of their employees in the cafeterias. POPS found that employees preferred the lunch lines to take between three to four minutes so that they could get their food quickly and also have time to interact with other employees they typically would not see. POPS also found that employees wanted long lunch tables so that people would be forced to talk to each other rather than just socializing within their own friend circles. To increase the health of their employees, POPs placed eight-inch lunch trays next to twelve-inch lunch trays because when analyzing the eating habits of their employees, they found that people were likely to eat smaller and healthier lunches when seeing the different-sized trays side by side.

Google understands that to maintain their dominance and innovation, they have to hire and retain the best employees because of the ever-growing competition between similar technology firms. They developed an excellent employer brand that attracts individuals around the world. People want to be part of the organization, its continuous innovations, and the highly talked about work environment. In addition, Google's executive team recognizes and understands that organizations are more successful when they put their employees first and treat them like they matter. Elodie Lhuillier, the head of HR at Google Switzerland, says:

> We're very conscious of how big a role work plays in people's lives and the importance of meaning within it. We want to be known as a company that genuinely values our people and gives them the freedom to amaze. Research tells us that organizations are more successful when they put people first, trust them and treat them like owners. It also shows that freedom-based organizations perform better than fear-based ones.[1]

 ### Google Wants to Know How a Candidate Thinks

Googlers Jodie and Kelsey share details about the general-cognitive-ability aspect of the Google interview process, Googleyness, and a sample Google interview question.

View the video online at: http://www.youtube.com/embed/elMR82oO2Dc?rel=0

Case Discussion Questions

1. Do you think Google's success could have been achieved without engaged employees?

2. How might the employer brand impact your decision whether to go to work for a particular organization?
3. If you were interviewing for a position at Google, how would you respond to a question about your Googleyness?
4. Can Google's approach to perks be applied to all companies? For example, if a company is strapped for cash, what innovations might they implement without increasing expenses?

1.2 Introduction to Human Resource Management

Learning Objectives

1. Define human capital and human resource management.
2. Explain the impact of human capital on organizations, specifically in terms of organizational culture and competitive advantage.
3. Describe how the management of human resources has evolved from scientific management to the modern era of employee engagement.

What Is HRM?

Before defining human resource management (HRM), it is helpful to first define the context within which HRM occurs. Every organization, regardless of size, industry, or motive, exists to accomplish a mission. This applies to for-profit companies as well as nonprofit entities such as educational institutions and government agencies. Organizations accomplish their missions and seek to create a competitive advantage by combining various types of resources (also referred to as capital) to create a product or service in a way that adds value for the customer.

organization

A collection of people working together to achieve a common purpose.

human capital

The knowledge, skills, competencies, and attributes embodied in individuals that facilitate the creation of personal, social, and economic well-being.

An **organization** is a collection of people working together to achieve a common purpose. Organizations collect and combine various types of capital, such as buildings, equipment, vehicles, investments, and loans that are needed to produce their product or service. Organizational leaders and other experts in the field have come to recognize that the most vital type of capital in any organization is the human assets.[2] **Human capital** is defined by the Organisation for Economic Co-operation and Development (OECD) as the knowledge, skills, competencies, and attributes embodied in individuals that facilitate the creation of personal, social, and economic well-being.[3]

Human capital differs from other types of resources in significant ways. Buildings, land, and equipment can be bought and sold. Improvements can be made, which will result in a return on investment when the asset is sold. However, individuals have human rights and cannot be bought or sold like other assets. They can be leased or contracted with, but the individual can terminate the arrangement because they, and not the organization, own their own human capital. If an employee leaves the organization, any investment that the company has made in the individual (e.g., education, training, development, or coaching) is lost. The opening case about Google illustrates the importance of attracting and retaining human talent, and how analytics and innovation play an important role in creating an employer brand.

Every employee has a responsibility to understand and comply with organizational core values and principles. How can HR reinforce the core values?

Source: © Shutterstock, Inc.

The human resources of an organization also differ from other assets in that they have the capability to think, to learn, and to analyze situations. These assets are often referred to as knowledge-based workers.[4] Competitive advantage is created by attracting, developing, and retaining human resources with superior knowledge, skills, and abilities than those at competing organizations.[5] As information and technology continue to grow, the human resources of a firm will become even more important. As David Bloom stated in *The Creative Society of the 21st Century*, "The value of knowledge...has continued to rise. It is fundamentally different from other forms of capital. As it becomes more abundant, it may be further expanded more easily and cheaply, in turn creating especially lucrative returns."

As the importance of human resources to organizations has grown, so has the importance of a system for managing these resources. **Human resource management** is the set of policies and practices that attract, develop, and retain a qualified workforce, in ways that result in engaged employees who contribute positively to organizational performance.

human resource management

The set of policies and practices that attract, develop, and retain a qualified workforce in ways that result in engaged employees who contribute positively to organizational performance.

The Impact of Human Capital on Organizations

What makes a workforce unique? Why do some companies have motivated, highly skilled, and happy employees who value customer service, while others seem to have employees that are grumpy, do not know their jobs well, and do not treat customers well? Does this just happen by coincidence, or is it the result of an effective human resource management strategy (or lack of one)?

This is a good starting point as you begin your study of human resource management. Think about what makes one workforce different from another. What comes to mind? Perhaps some of the following characteristics:

TABLE 1.1 Workforce Characteristics

Workforce Characteristics
Productivity
Skill level
Education level
Attitudes (toward customers, management, and co-workers)
Quality of work
Knowledge, skills, abilities, and other characteristics (collectively called KSAOs in the HR field)

Give some thought to the role of human resources in the overall competitive advantage of a firm. A workforce that exhibits the above characteristics is likely the result of a proactive human resource strategy. In other words, these characteristics do not happen by accident...they are the result of decisions made by management. The role of HR is to develop the type of workforce that is necessary to accomplish organizational goals and objectives. The main point here is that human resource management is not just a functional area concerned with things such as government compliance, payroll, employee benefits, etc. Rather, HR is a vital component to a competitive business strategy.

Many businesses worry about the ability to grow and compete because they cannot find workers with the right skills. At the same time, many Americans continue to struggle with unemployment and underemployment and finding full-time work that pays a competitive wage. A growing skills gap has created a mismatch between the demand and supply of skills. The skills gap is especially critical in middle-skills jobs, in which sixty-nine million people in the U.S. currently work, representing roughly 48% of the workforce.[6]

If the presence of a large pool of cheap, unskilled workers once helped attract industry, today it will discourage rather than attract businesses.[7] Business location decisions today increasingly are made based on the presence of a workforce with the appropriate skills. A survey of company executives by *Area Development* magazine found that availability of skilled labor has become the most important factor in site selection.[8] In the same publication, site consultant Phil Schneider explains:

> *But throughout this ever-shifting landscape of corporate site selection needs, there is one common denominator that the vast majority of companies and site selection projects demand: the need and expectation for a superior workforce. The availability, quality, sustainability, flexibility, and cost of the workforce is the most common critical location factor; it may not always be the number one factor in the decision model, but it is nearly always in the top five.*[9]

At the beginning of 2019, the unemployment rate in the United States was at a forty-nine-year low of 3.7%.[10] The low number of individuals seeking employment, along with severe skill shortages, has amplified the importance of creating an environment that attracts qualified employees, and one in which employees are engaged and want to stay with the organization. Throughout this text, you will learn theories and techniques to enhance recruitment, retention, and performance in an environment of labor shortages and skills gaps. Upon completion of this course, you will be prepared to create a culture of respect and autonomy and to create an effective workplace in a diverse environment.

organizational culture

The beliefs, philosophies, values, assumptions, attitudes, and expectations of an organization.

You will find it useful to consider the concept of **organizational culture** and its relationship to HRM. Organizational culture is the beliefs, philosophies, values, assumptions, attitudes, and expectations of an organization. The culture represents the type of behavior that is acceptable and expected. It includes conduct, skills, and attitudes. How do new employees become familiar with the corporate culture? How are they indoctrinated? This has implications for orientation, training, and development. What type of behavior does the reward system encourage? This has implications for the compensation policy of the firm. Does the company value cutting-edge technology? This would have implications for training also. As you embark on your study of HRM, consider how human resource policies and practices impact the organizational culture, and how the culture subsequently impacts competitive advantage.

Evolution of HRM

Human resource management has evolved through several major eras or schools of thought. Those eras are Scientific Management, Unionization, and the Human Relations Movement.

The Scientific Management era began around the 1880s, during the Industrial Revolution. Frederick Taylor is often called the father of scientific management. Taylor was a supervisor at the

Midvale Steel Company in Philadelphia. An engineer by training, he began to conduct time and motion studies of employees in an effort to find ways to increase productivity. Taylor's idea of scientific management revolved around three concepts: work rules, work methods, and standardized times. Scientific management involved creating work performance standards and established routine operating procedures that employees were expected to adhere to. Can you think of any modern companies where scientific management is prevalent today? How about McDonald's, or UPS, or the U.S. Postal Service? The main criticism of this school of thought is that it led to repetitive, monotonous jobs, and treated employees like machines to be programmed. In other words, it ignored the human elements of performance such as motivation and creativity.

The Unionization movement began during the 1930s and peaked around 1960. The growth of unions began with the passage of the National Labor Relations Act in 1935. We will be studying unions, labor relations, and collective bargaining in Chapter 12. The union movement had both positive and negative consequences. Many of us enjoy job benefits such as vacation pay, forty-hour work weeks, weekends off, and health insurance, largely because unions negotiated these benefits. Nonunion employers eventually had to offer similar benefits to attract good employees. On the other hand, the union movement sometimes creates an adversarial relationship between labor and management and can hamper productivity and competitiveness if union wage and benefit demands are unreasonable.

The Human Relations era began with the Hawthorne Studies in the 1920s. The movement did not really begin to take hold until the 1960s, but the Hawthorne Studies are generally credited with being the first research into the human element of human resource management. The Hawthorne Studies involved a university research project conducted at the Chicago Western Electric plant from 1924 to 1927. The purpose of the experiment was originally to determine what the optimum illumination level was. At what lighting level would employees be the most productive? The researchers set up two groups: a control group and an experimental group. The illumination level remained constant for the control group, but was altered for the experimental group. The researchers were confused when they found that productivity increased when they increased the lighting levels, but productivity also increased when they decreased the lighting levels. Productivity did not decline until the lighting reached moonlight levels.

The Hawthorne effect refers to the inclination of some people to work harder and perform better when they are being observed as part of an experiment.

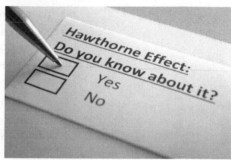

Source: © Shutterstock, Inc.

They then entered a second phase of the experiment by altering changes in hours and working conditions. It seemed that no matter what they did, productivity increased. The researchers then brought in Elton Mayo from Harvard University to assist them. They decided to conduct a third phase of experiments, which were plantwide interviews. The researchers found that the increases in productivity occurred because of the human element of productivity, rather than as the result of the physical work environment. The following is a summary of the four phases of the Hawthorne Studies:

TABLE 1.2 Four Phases of the Hawthorne Studies

1st Phase: Illumination Experiment
• Control group and experimental group • Studied effect on productivity • Increased/decreased lighting

2nd Phase: Relay Assembly Test Room Experiment
• Changes in hours and other working conditions (e.g., breaks, refreshments, temperature)

3rd Phase: Employee Interviews
• Researchers postulated that the human element had a greater impact on productivity than the technical or physical aspects of the job. • They summarized that the increase in output could not be related to any change in their physical conditions of work, but "it could, however, be related to what can only be spoken of as the development of an organized social group and a peculiar and effective relation with its superiors." • They proposed that the work group as a whole determined the production output of individual group members by enforcing an informal group norm.

4th Phase: Bank Wiring Observation Room Experiment
• To test premise of Phase 3 • Instituted group piecework incentive pay plan • Group put pressure on "rate-busters" and "chiselers." In other words, the group put pressure on other team members to not work too fast or too slow. • The work group developed a production output norm. • Found no relationship between productivity and intelligence, dexterity, and other skills. • Determined that group acceptance was more important in determining an individual's output than the wage incentive plan.

The Hawthorne Studies prompted managers to think about the importance of the individual in organizational structure and job design. These experiments eventually caused managers to think more about the people factor in helping to create a company with a competitive advantage. From the 1990s to the present, there has been a shifting emphasis from viewing employees as resources to be managed, toward viewing them as valuable assets that should be respected, valued, and developed.

Key Takeaways

- An organization is a collection of people working together to achieve a common purpose.
- Human capital is defined by the OECD as the knowledge, skills, competencies, and attributes embodied in individuals that facilitate the creation of personal, social, and economic well-being.
- Human resource management is the set of policies and practices that attract, develop, and retain a qualified workforce, in ways that result in engaged employees who contribute positively to organizational performance. Business location decisions today increasingly are made based on the presence of a workforce with the appropriate skills.
- Human resource management has evolved through several major eras. The Scientific Management era began around the 1880s, during the Industrial Revolution, and revolved around three concepts: work rules, work methods, and standardized times. The Unionization movement began during the 1930s and peaked around 1960. The Human Relations era began

with the Hawthorne Studies in the 1920s. The movement did not really begin to take hold until the 1960s, but the Hawthorne Studies prompted managers to begin thinking about the importance of the individual in organizational structure and job design.

What Do *You* Think?

1. As an HR manager, what steps would you take to make sure that employees do not leave for better-paying jobs after your company has invested in training them?
2. Think of a company that you currently work for, or have in the past. What made the work-force different than that of the competitors, and did these differences result in a competitive advantage or disadvantage?
3. Are there skills shortages in the region that you live in? If so, what is being done to close skills gaps?
4. What was the most useful lesson learned for HR managers from the Hawthorne Studies?

1.3 The Changing Landscape of Human Resource Management

Learning Objectives

1. Describe the challenges for HR managers created by the changing demographics and diversity of the modern workforce.
2. Explain how technologies such as applicant tracking systems and human resource information systems are changing the practice of HR.
3. Consider how the recruitment, management, and retention of talent differs in a multinational enterprise.
4. Define the term knowledge economy and recognize how it impacts HRM, especially in regard to recruiting, training, and development of the workforce.

Workplace Demographics and Diversity

The changing nature of the workforce is a major challenge facing HR managers and other business leaders. The population of the United States has undergone significant changes in the past few decades, and projections indicate these trends will continue in the future. There is no longer a typical worker in organizations, as diversity in terms of gender, ethnicity, and religion abounds within organizations. Demographic trends happen gradually, but over time they create major changes in the workforce. The trends indicate that the future workforce will be multigenerational, older on average, more racially and ethnically diverse, and more female.[11] Let's briefly examine each of these trends and the impact upon HRM.

generation

A social grouping of people born within a defined time period who share similar cultural traits, values, and preferences.

When considering the age of the workforce, it can be helpful to look at the generations that comprise the general population. A **generation** is a social grouping of people born within a defined time period who share similar cultural traits, values, and preferences. Generations can be divided into cohorts, which provide a method for analyzing changes over time. Cohorts provide a way to understand how different formative experiences (such as world and economic events, technology, and social changes) interact with the life cycle and aging process to shape people's views of the world.[12] There is no one definitive source for the names and birth years that define generations. For purposes of this textbook, we will use the generational names and years as shown in Figure 1.1.

FIGURE 1.1 The Generations in the U.S. Workforce

Silent Generation (born from 1928-1945)
Age in 2021: 76 and older

Baby Boomers (born from 1946-1964)
Age in 2021: 57 to 75

Generation X (born from 1965-1980)
Age in 2021: 41-56

Millennials (born from 1981-1996)
Age in 2021: 25-40

Post-millennials (born 1997 to present)
Age in 2021: 16-24 (*age eligible to work)

Source: © Shutterstock, Inc.

Rising Above Generational Stereotypes in the Workplace

Dr. Michael G. Strawser offers suggestions for employees and employers to navigate traditional generational characteristics.

View the video online at: http://www.youtube.com/embed/z8faXxpQyFg?rel=0

More than one in three American labor force participants are millennials, making them the largest generation in the U.S. labor force, according to a Pew Research Center analysis of U.S. Census Bureau data.[13] Millennials are the most racially and ethnically diverse adult generation in the nation's history, and the next generation (post-millennials, born since 1997) is even more so.[14] Many millennials entered the workforce during an economic decline, and their lifestyle choices and attitudes toward work are influenced by coming of age during a recession. They also grew up in a wired world and are used to being always connected. The events that shaped their world view are reflected in their attitudes concerning work-life balance, the desire to be involved in meaningful social causes, and a high degree of autonomy and independence.

Although the millennials comprise the largest cohort in the workforce, employers still must be aware of the needs of older workers. It may be surprising, but the average age of the U.S. worker is still rising. This is partly because of low birth rates and the facts that many people are working longer and millennials themselves are getting older.

The workforce will continue to increase in racial and ethnic diversity. By 2024, less than 60% of the U.S. labor force is likely to define itself as "white non-Hispanic," while as recently as 1994, over 75% of the workforce fell into that category.[15] Hispanics are expected to comprise 20% of the labor force by 2024, while African Americans will rise to 12.7% (up from 12.1% in 2014), and Asians will rise to 6.6% (from up 5.6% in 2014).[16] As racial and ethnic diversity increases, employers will see a rise in diversity of dress, religious practices, holiday celebrations, and other cultural differences.

Women are expected to continue to become a larger proportion of the U.S. workforce, rising from 46.8% to 47.2% in 2024. The labor force participation rate of women aged 25 to 54 is projected to rise from 73.9% to 75.2%, while the rate for men in the same age cohort is expected to decline from 88.2% to 87.3%.[17] While the percentage of women in the workforce continues to increase, they are still significantly underrepresented in leadership roles. For example, women make up less than 5% of CEOs of Standard and Poor's 500 (S&P 500) companies.[18]

HR managers play a crucial role in building awareness of diversity and creating a culture of inclusion. As will be discussed further in Chapter 3, compliance with Equal Employment Opportunity (EEO) laws by preventing discrimination and harassment is certainly necessary, but companies should be proactive in eliminating barriers to employment and advancement for minorities.

Technologies

Advances in technology are rapidly changing the way HR professionals do their jobs. Digital technology is impacting virtually every aspect of HR including recruiting, hiring, training and development, and benefits administration. For example, the development of the applicant tracking system has transformed the way in which recruitment is conducted. An **applicant tracking system (ATS)** is a software program that manages the recruitment and hiring process, including job postings and applications. As the name implies, an ATS tracks each candidate through the application process and automates much of the process, saving labor time for the HR department and keeping applicants informed of their status. The days of HR staff reading every resume are quickly disappearing, as ATSs are used to electronically screen applications for relevant keywords. In fact, 98% of *Fortune 500* companies, along with an increasing number of small and mid-sized businesses, filter resumes through an ATS.[19]

The development of **human resource information systems (HRIS)** has also changed the way in which human resource processes and recordkeeping are handled. An HRIS is a software or online solution that is used for data entry, data tracking, and the data information requirements of an organization's HR management. An HRIS typically integrates with a payroll system and tracks paid time off (PTO), attendance, compensation history, positions and pay grades, disciplinary actions, training, development, and other types of data.

The Forbes Human Resource Council, composed of successful human resource executives, has identified the following ways that technology has streamlined their HR processes:[20]

1. Digital interviews save time and money.
2. Everyone can connect through social media, allowing employees to be more open and connect with others in the workplace.
3. Paper records are now digital, helping HR staff to locate needed data quickly.
4. More focus can be placed on relationship building, providing HR professionals to do what humans can do better than machines, which is interact with employees (giving them opportunities to positively impact the culture of the organization).
5. Geographical boundaries are eliminated, which allows even small companies to access a global talent pool.

Globalization

Recruiting, managing, and retaining human resources at a firm with extensive global operations is especially challenging. For example, German firm Siemens has more than 400,000 employees in 190 countries. Volkswagen, Nestle, IBM, Unilever, Walmart, McDonald's, and Matsushita each has more than 150,000 employees outside the firm's home country.

Global business is expanding rapidly, as trade agreements (such as the United States-Canada-Mexico Agreement, or USMCA, and the European Union) are reducing tariffs and other barriers to trade. This is resulting in an increased number of employees who are temporarily assigned to work in another country. Working in another culture poses significant challenges for employees, managers, and the HR department.

Chapter 14 will cover global HR in much more depth, but as you study the text, begin to consider some of the following challenges that international human resource management (IHRM) poses:

1. International staffing policy: Activities directed at recruiting, selecting, and placing employees.

2. Preparation and training of international employees: Onboarding, training and development, and preparing employees for international assignments.

3. International performance appraisal: Providing feedback for employees' professional development.

4. Compensation of employees: Includes formulation of benefit packages that can vary greatly from country to country.

5. International labor relations: Managing relationships with unions and collective bargaining processes.

6. Diversity in an international workforce: The challenges of differences in country cultures, religion, and attitudes toward women and minorities.

The Knowledge Economy and the Nature of Work

Advances in technology and a better-educated workforce have led to what is often referred to as the **knowledge economy**. The knowledge economy is a system of production and services based on knowledge-intensive activities that contribute to an accelerated pace of technical and scientific advance as well as rapid obsolescence.[21] The production of goods and services, and the jobs that this entails, are heavily based upon knowledge and education. Companies strive for competitive advantage by becoming better than their competition either in terms of providing a higher-quality product or service, or doing so at a lower cost, and achieving high levels of productivity. This competitive advantage is increasingly reliant upon a workforce with a high level of knowledge, skills, abilities, and other characteristics, which collectively are referred to as **KSAOs.**

We will examine the role of KSAOs in several chapters of the text, especially Chapter 4 on job analysis and design, and Chapter 7 on talent development. However, since KSAOs are such an important aspect of HRM, let's define each of these terms now. **Knowledge** is the state of having a correct idea or understanding of something or the possession of information about something. It refers to theoretical application, or what sometimes might be referred to as head knowledge or book learning. **Skill** is the capability of accomplishing something with precision and certainty. It refers to practical application of theoretical knowledge. Skills can also be distinguished among three categories: basic, advanced, and expert. An **ability** is a quality in a person or thing which makes an action possible. It refers to an innate capacity that enables a person to develop a skill.

knowledge economy

A system of production and services based on knowledge-intensive activities that contribute to an accelerated pace of technical and scientific advance, as well as rapid obsolescence.

KSAOs

Knowledge, skills, abilities, and other characteristics.

knowledge

The state of having a correct idea or understanding of something or the possession of information about something.

skill

The capability of accomplishing something with precision and certainty.

ability

The quality in a person or thing that makes an action possible.

A potential long-lasting effect of COVID-19 is an increase in the number of employees in the knowledge economy who work from home, at least part of the time.

Source: © Shutterstock, Inc.

Advances in technology are fundamentally changing the nature of work in many industries and creating an imperative for continual lifelong learning. Basic skill levels were once the prerequisite to finding gainful employment, but advanced levels are becoming the norm. Many companies in developed countries are seeing a shortage of skilled workers for increasingly complex jobs.[22]

The knowledge economy is impacting many areas of HRM including recruitment, training, and development. For example, one area of shortage is industrial maintenance technicians for advanced manufacturing plants. In the past, the KSAOs required for these types of workers (which were referred to as industrial maintenance mechanics) involved knowledge of mechanical functions such as hydraulics, what some have called wrench-turning skills. However, these jobs today require knowledge of computer technology including hardware and software, as advanced manufacturing operations increasingly use electronic and automated processes. Recruitment of knowledge workers has been difficult in these types of industries due to outdated perceptions of the nature of the work.

Key Takeaways

- The changing nature of the demographics and diversity of the workforce is a major challenge facing HR managers and other business leaders.
- More than one in three American labor force participants are millennials, making them the largest generation in the U.S. labor force.
- By 2024, less than 60% of the U.S. labor force is likely to define itself as "white non-Hispanic," while as recently as 1994, over 75% of the workforce fell into that category.
- Digital technology is impacting virtually every aspect of HR including recruiting, hiring, training and development, benefits administration, and others.

- Recruiting, managing, and retaining human resources at a firm with extensive global operations is especially challenging.
- The knowledge economy is a system of production and services based on knowledge-intensive activities that contribute to an accelerated pace of technical and scientific advances, as well as rapid obsolescence.

What Do *You* Think?

1. Which generation do you belong to, and how do your attitudes toward work differ from other generations?
2. How might you leverage technology to become more effective in your job, in particular by automating routine tasks?
3. Are you open to taking an HR assignment in another country? If so, how would you prepare yourself for the assignment?
4. What is the difference between a knowledge, a skill, and an ability?
5. Has your impression of manufacturing changed after reading this section of the chapter?

1.4 Emerging Issues and Trends in HRM

Learning Objectives

1. Explain why the HR industry is moving toward a balanced approach that focuses on employee engagement, while also achieving organizational goals for competitive advantage, productivity, and profitability.
2. Recognize how a societal interest in sustainability and corporate social responsibility impacts HR practices.
3. Describe how advances in data analytics and artificial intelligence are improving decision-making in HRM.
4. Discuss the skill-shortage problem in the U.S. and other developed countries and the impact on business location decisions.

Employee Engagement

The HR industry is undergoing a shift from focusing solely on the employer perspective, to a more balanced approach that focuses on employee engagement and work-life balance, while also achieving organizational goals for competitive advantage, productivity, and profitability. The National Study of the Changing Workforce, conducted by Families and Work Institute and SHRM, is a major study of the U.S. workforce that takes a comprehensive look at employees' lives both on and off the job. The study examines components of the work environment that benefit employers and employees, and has led to the development of SHRM's Effective Workplace Index (2018), which consists of the following seven components: job challenge and learning opportunities; supervisor support for job success; autonomy; culture of respect, trust, and belonging; work-life fit; satisfaction with wages, benefits, and opportunities to advance; and co-worker support for job success.[23]

One of the features of this book is a balanced approach that focuses on employee engagement while also achieving organizational goals for competitive advantage and profitability. You will learn theory and techniques to enhance recruitment, retention, and performance, and will be prepared to create a culture of respect and autonomy, which are important in creating an effective workplace in a diverse environment.

 Catbert: The Evil HR Director

A humorous take on the role of HR in supporting employee development.

View the video online at: http://www.youtube.com/embed/0fLNqZQaclg?rel=0

HR in the Real World: The Case of Billy Bad

Human resources is not only the realm of people with HR in their job title. Anyone who has people reporting to them does some HR. One of the most challenging aspects of management is holding them accountable for performance expectations and compliance with work rules or procedures while doing so in a way that treats them with dignity and respect.

In a previous position as vice-president for finance and administration, I was responsible for all of the office staff, including individuals who handled inbound calls from customers and vendors. The work hours were 8 to 5, and it was critical that these employees be at their desk, ready to work and start answering calls at 8:00 sharp. I had one employee who had a habit of show- ing up about five minutes late. Then it became ten minutes late, then fifteen, and then twenty. I counseled the employee and put her on a three-strike process, the official company policy for handling employee disciplinary actions. The first strike (in this case, an incidence of being tardy) resulted in an oral warning, the second strike would lead to a written warning, and the third strike would result in immediate termination. The employee eventually was late a third time. She rode a local bus to work, and had fallen asleep on the bus. She called me to let me know what had happened, and I advised her to take the next bus back to the company, and then to come to my office. She finally arrived to work at 11:30 and came to my office. I had already gone to the pay- roll department and had her final check prepared. I told her that in keeping with the three-strike policy, she was terminated immediately. I then escorted her to her work area, where she put her personal belongings into a box, and she was escorted out of the building. I later found out that some of the employees were referring to me as Billy Bad, which I was not exactly proud of. But it did send a message that the company was serious about being at your work area and ready to work when your shift begins, and no one showed up late for at least a year.

But there is more to the story. As she was walking out of the building with her box of belongings and getting ready to walk back to the bus stop (which was five blocks from our building, and on a hot summer day), something didn't seem right to me. I didn't want her to have to walk that far, carrying her things, so I gave her a ride to the bus stop. I had been coaching this employee for some time and had developed a positive rapport with her. We talked about how this could be a learning experience for her. I also emphasized that we all make mistakes. The important thing is to learn from them. Before she got on the bus, she turned back and gave me a hug. Perhaps the moral of the story is that you can hold people accountable, and send a message when you need to, but at the same time treat people with dignity. One of my favorite quotes on managing human resources is from Anne M. Mulcahey, former chairperson and CEO of Xerox Corporation:

> *Employees who believe that management is concerned about them as a whole person—not just an employee—are more productive, more satisfied, more fulfilled. Satisfied employees mean satisfied customers, which leads to profitability.*[24]

Sustainability and Corporate Social Responsibility

The word sustainability has come to have many different meanings. Sustainability has become a popular buzzword among the business sector, government, and the nonprofit entities, and business leaders find themselves wondering if this is just the latest management fad or a concept that will fundamentally change how businesses are managed and measured. **Sustainability** is a business approach that creates long-term shareholder value by embracing opportunities and managing risks deriving from economic, environmental, and social developments. Simply put, when a business adopts a sustainable approach, they are not just driven by business profits but consider the human and environmental impacts of their actions.

The Brundtland Commission (World Commission on Environment and Development, United Nations, 1987) is generally credited with introducing the word sustainability in their report Our Common Future.[25] The report states that humanity has the ability to make development sustainable—to ensure that it meets the needs of the present without compromising the ability of future generations to meet their needs. Thus, the term originally was coined in reference to sustainable development, and the purpose was to encourage development that had a dual focus on reducing poverty and taking into consideration long-term ecological impacts. The concept has expanded since 1987 and now includes a focus on economic profits, social impact, and the environment. The term triple bottom line, or TBL, was coined for this tertiary focus by Elkington (1998) in his book Cannibals with Forks: The Triple Bottom Line of 21st Century Business.[26] Elkington also refers to the triple bottom line as the three P's: People, Profits, and Planet.

Organizations are no longer assessed only on traditional metrics such as financial performance, or the quality of their products or services. Rather, organizations today are increasingly judged on their relationships with their employees, customers, and communities, transforming them from mere business enterprises to social enterprises.[27] As more companies, nonprofit organizations, and government agencies implement sustainable solutions to the problems of society, it is apparent that the notion of sustainability and corporate social responsibility is more than a fad, but rather is creating a permanent shift in the way that businesses view their responsibilities to stakeholders.[28]

In the context of HR, social responsibility includes creating and maintaining a workplace culture that respects everyone equally, and in which all individuals and groups are treated with

sustainability

A business approach that creates long-term shareholder value by embracing opportunities and managing risks deriving from economic, environmental, and social developments.

dignity and respect. This means that the workplace should be free of any type of harassment or discrimination, and decisions regarding any of the terms and conditions of employment (hiring, promotions, compensation, etc.) should be made fairly and justly.

A socially responsible organization ensures that all employees conduct themselves in an ethical manner and maintain high standards of integrity. HR managers play a crucial role in making sure that new hires understand the organizational code of ethics and values, and providing a process whereby potential violations of ethics or harassment can be reported.

Talent Analytics

Increased capabilities in data analytics and artificial intelligence are transforming the practice of HR by automating many of the mundane functions and providing the tools for HR managers to make data-driven decisions. The technology for talent recruitment, onboarding, compensation, performance management, and talent development continues to accelerate. This includes human resource information systems (HRIS), applicant tracking systems (ATS), and learning management systems (LMS).

Talent analytics are introduced in more depth in Chapter 2 Section 5.

Because talent analytics has become such an important component in almost every aspect of modern HRM, each chapter in this text will include a feature box that illustrates an example of how data and analytics are used in the real world by actual HR managers.

FIGURE 1.2 Ten Trends in Talent Analytics

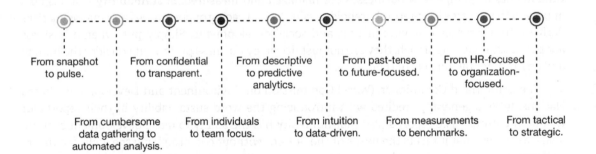

Key Takeaways

- The HR industry is undergoing a shift away from human resource management solely focused on the employer perspective, to a more balanced approach that focuses on employee engagement and work-life balance, while also achieving organizational goals for competitive advantage, productivity, and profitability.
- Sustainability is a business approach that creates long-term shareholder value by embracing opportunities and managing risks deriving from economic, environmental, and social developments.
- In the context of HR, social responsibility includes creating and maintaining a workplace culture that respects everyone equally and in which all individuals and groups are treated with dignity and respect.

- A socially responsible organization ensures that all employees conduct themselves in an ethical manner and maintain high standards of integrity.
- Increased capabilities in data analytics and artificial intelligence are transforming the practice of HR by automating many of the day-to-day functions and providing the tools for HR managers to make data-driven decisions.
- Business location decisions today increasingly are made based on the presence of a workforce with the appropriate skills.

What Do *You* Think?

1. How do you feel when you work for a company or an individual who does not seem to care about your work-life balance or your personal well-being?
2. What companies do you think do a good job of being socially responsible? What are these companies doing that gives you this impression?
3. How has technology impacted the way that you learn new knowledge and skills?
4. Have you ever quit a job, and if so, what was the reason?
5. What company initiatives and programs make you want to stay with a company?

1.5 Responsibilities and Roles in HRM

Learning Objectives

1. Identify the responsibilities of HR managers.
2. Explain the unique challenges faced by solo HR practitioners.
3. Compare and contrast the HR responsibilities of line managers and HR managers.

Responsibilities of HR Managers

In this section, we will first look at the overall responsibilities of HR managers in regard to managing the employee life cycle. Next, we will identify the areas that HR is usually tasked with that are broader in scope. Then we will look at the unique requirements for those individuals who have all of the HR responsibility for a small firm, or as it is sometimes referred to, an HR department of one. Finally, we will explore the HR responsibilities of line managers.

Three of the most significant roles of HR managers have to do with talent: attracting, developing, and retaining individuals with the right talents.

Source: © Shutterstock, Inc.

Employee Life Cycle (ELC)

A model that portrays the journey of a typical employee from the time they first learn about an opening at the organization, through the recruitment and hiring process, until their employment ends.

The **Employee Life Cycle (ELC)** is a model that portrays the journey of a typical employee from the time they first learn about an opening at the organization, through the recruitment and hiring process, until their employment ends. The nine stages of the ELC are: recruitment, selection, onboarding, training, development, coaching, performance appraisal, benefits administration, and separation. These nine stages can also be grouped under three overall categories of talent acquisition, talent development, and talent retention, as shown in Figure 1.3. Let's now look at the HR responsibilities during each phase of the ELC.

FIGURE 1.3 Employee Life Cycle

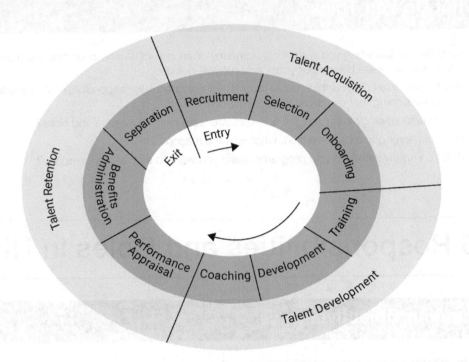

Talent Acquisition

HR managers are responsible for overseeing all phases of the employee life cycle. During the talent acquisition phase, the focus is on attracting a qualified pool of applicants and then selecting the individuals that represent the best potential for success for each position. This includes responsibility for the following activities:

- **Development of a staffing plan.** This is based on a workforce forecast which anticipates future needs and should be driven by organizational strategy and projections, including revenue expectations, product development, market fluctuations, and other environmental changes. In this particular phase, it is crucial that HR managers work in collaboration with operational and financial managers of the organization to ensure that the staffing forecast is in alignment with company plans and strategies.

- **Conducting a job analysis.** Before recruiting individuals for hire, a thorough analysis should be conducted of the exact functions of the position and the skillsets that will be required to be successful. Job descriptions should be prepared for each position, summarizing the essential job functions and the qualifications, including the experience, educational background, and KSAOs that successful job holders should possess.

- **Recruitment.** A qualified pool of applicants should be recruited through multiple recruitment channels, which might include online job postings, social networking, college recruiting, employee referrals, and others.
- **Selection.** The best candidates should be chosen from the pool of applicants. This stage involves applicant pre-screening, assessment, interviewing, and negotiating compensation packages.

Talent Development

Once an employee has been hired, then the talent development process begins with onboarding. However, training, coaching, and other forms of development should continue as long as the employee is with the organization. The management of talent development includes:

- **Onboarding.** This is the initial orientation that the employee receives and should include job procedures, organizational policies and values, performance review processes. Another important aspect of onboarding is to help the employee to become adjusted to the setting and to feel a sense of belonging. Thus, the social aspect of onboarding (meeting other employees, mentoring, etc.) is also the responsibility of HR.
- **Job skills training.** This refers to the skills that new employees need to perform the functions of the job. During the recruitment process, the KSAOs needed for the position should have been identified, and the employees that are hired should possess those KSAOs. However, no matter how qualified the applicant, there are always specific job procedures, equipment types, computer program differences, etc. from one company to another, even within the same industry.
- **Policy and legal training.** This includes training in equal employment opportunity, sexual harassment, ethics, workplace health and safety, cybersecurity, etc. These types of training are necessary to ensure that employees are following laws and regulations and also to mitigate various types of risk.
- **Performance management.** The design of a system whereby each employee's performance is evaluated usually comes under the responsibility of HR.
- **Team-building activities.** Teams that are cohesive, collaborative, and can manage conflict in positive ways are higher performing than those that do not work together well. Team-building activities typically focus on communications, trust, and conflict resolution.
- **Coaching and mentoring.** These development approaches are one-to-one development, as opposed to group training. While coaches and mentors are most often experienced individuals working in the same line of work as the employee, HR managers are often responsible for designing and managing coaching and mentoring programs.

Talent Retention

Retention refers to motivating employees to stay with the organization. Compensation is certainly one method, but research indicates that it is not the top motivator. One of the most effective tools in employee retention is to focus on employee engagement, thus increasing commitment to the company.[29] Talent retention methods include:

- **Compensation.** HR managers should analyze compensation policies to ensure that they are competitive with other employers and distributed fairly among the workforce. Compensation includes anything of value that employees are given in exchange for their work. It includes pay, paid time off (PTO), contributions to retirement plans, health benefits, and tuition reimbursement.
- **Benefits administration.** Employee benefits are a form of compensation, but since they represent an important value to employees and require specific expertise to administer, the category

is treated as a separate discipline within HR. Benefits may include health, dental, and vision insurance, disability insurance, health savings accounts, flexible spending accounts, employee wellness programs, and employee assistance programs (EAPs).

- **Supervisory training.** Research studies show that the number-one factor in retention is the employee's relationship with their supervisor.[30] It is sometimes put this way: People do not quit their jobs, they quit their supervisor.

In addition to managing the events that occur as part of the ELC, HR managers often are responsible for a variety of organizational functions that are not directly related to talent acquisition, development, or retention. These may include:

- **Labor relations.** In companies where the employees are represented by a union, HR is responsible for compliance with the laws that regulate the organization's labor policies and practices, including collective bargaining and handling grievances. These concepts are explained in detail in Chapter 12.

- **Workplace health, safety, and security.** The human resources of an organization deserve to be protected. HR is responsible for ensuring that workers are not exposed to an unsafe work environment or to unnecessary risks. This includes protecting them from on-the-job injury, sickness, and physical or emotional harm that might be inflicted on them by co-workers, individuals outside of the organization, or acts of nature. These responsibilities are explored in Chapter 13.

Talent acquisition, development, and retention activities vary widely across industries. This is one aspect of the HR profession that is appealing to many people who like variety in their work. As the HR Talk feature with Lauren Billings illustrates, HR staff need to be flexible, as one never knows what they might be asked to do.

HR Talk: Lauren Billings

Vice President of Operations

Billings Productions, Inc., dba The Dinosaur Company

Our company has about 40 employees, so we are not large enough to have a full-time HR person. Of course, we do HR because every company with employees has to do HR. But here it can get confusing because HR is split between three people. One of my roles in HR is employee relations. I go out to the employees and let them to know if they need anything to contact me. However, I also have responsibilities in regard to compliance with wage and hour laws.

Our company is unique because we are the only company in the U.S. that makes animatronic dinosaurs. We can't go look at our competitors to see how they are doing things; We just have to figure it out and build it from scratch. So that is our company culture and I think we see that in HR too. I spend a lot of time reading employment law and on the Department of Labor website and to find out what we can and can't do. For example, I wanted to know if we could hire teenagers and I found out that we can't and why we can't. Our field technicians are a very unique situation because they are nonexempt employees, but often fly to where our dinosaurs are located (zoos, museums, etc., around the U.S. and even around the world). I needed to create a policy regarding how much of their travel time should be compensated and had to conduct my own research to figure out the legal requirements. It also gets complicated because they are often flying across time zones and that has to be figured into the calculations as well.

We do have a lawyer that we consult on employee policy issues. One area that is important is confidentiality agreements through which we prohibit employees from sharing our proprietary information. For example, even after someone leaves the company, they are not allowed to post any pictures of our dinosaurs or processes online. I have a bachelor's degree but it is in Family Studies. I worked in HR at GameStop for a short time, and that's where my initial HR knowledge was gained. But for the most part, my HR education has been self-taught. It is very difficult for me to get away during a workday to attend a seminar. I was scheduled to go to a seminar recently and I had to miss it because I had an employee shove another employee and I had to stay here to take of that situation. I have been to a few HR seminars such as employment law, but for the most part it is things that I can read or view on my own time, such as prerecorded webinars.

As a small business, our top three HR priorities are: First, payroll because if something goes wrong there, people notice it. Second is benefits because many people need help understanding how their benefits work. Third is employee relations because that impacts people's feelings and keeping everyone happy. When we have turnover, we can't just go hire someone from a school that trains people on how to manufacture and maintain animatronic dinosaurs, because that does not exist. We have to train them on the job, so employee relations, retention, and employee engagement are crucial to our success.

Solo HR Practitioners

In many small businesses, there is only one individual that is responsible for all of the HR functions. In these situations, individuals are often stretched beyond their capacity to deal with a wide variety of issues, regulatory requirements, training needs, etc. The solo HR practitioner is pulled in many directions and does not have the time or expertise to adequately address all of the responsibilities previously described.

SHRM recently polled small-business HR professionals and asked them to identify the top issues they face.[31] Employee engagement was the number-one issue. One respondent said: "It is a challenge to engage employees across multiple generations and retain high performers to keep them motivated." Their second most important issue was talent acquisition, which has become more difficult recently due to the low unemployment rate. Third, they cited effective leadership, and specifically that being a department of one, they often feel stuck doing day-to-day tasks that have to be done and do not have time to focus on the strategic aspect. These issues were followed by employee relations and the struggle to communicate effectively with employees and other organizational leaders.

So how should the solo HR practitioner handle the demands of their time? You may find it interesting to note that their top concerns have to do with engagement, acquisition, leadership, communications, and relations. With the exception of acquisition, these are all strategic or big-picture concerns. They did not cite doing payroll, managing health insurance benefits, or other day-to-day tasks as their major concerns. If you find yourself in a position as an HR department of one, then you might consider outsourcing some of the day-to-day tasks, freeing yourself up to focus on communications, leadership, engagement, and employee relations. Fortunately, there are many companies that specialize in providing these types of HR services.

HR Responsibilities of Line Managers

Who is ultimately responsible for managing human capital, and for implementing effective human resource management practices and procedures? Which managers within an organization bear the most responsibility for talent recruitment, development, and retention? Is it the **line manager**, who actually supervises the employee, or is it the human resources staff? First, let's distinguish between line and staff managers.

A line manager is a person who directly manages the employees and operations of an organization that create products and services. In a for-profit organization, these are the revenue-producing activities. Line managers are responsible for day-to-day supervision, motivation, and performance management of their direct reports. They are accountable for the results of their unit, including production and profit goals, employee turnover, and other key performance metrics. They get the praise if the team performs well, and they get the blame when things go awry. Thus, the line manager has a vested interest in almost every aspect of human resource management,

line manager

A person who directly manages the employees and operations of an organization that creates products and services.

including recruiting and selecting the most qualified employees, onboarding, training, performance management, and disciplinary actions.

A **staff manager** is a person who manages a department that serves the line managers in a support or advisory capacity by providing information and advice and ensuring compliance with government laws and regulations. Human resources, accounting, marketing, and customer service are examples of staff departments.

Line managers and HR managers should share the responsibility for talent recruitment, development, and retention. Table 1.3 summarizes some of the key HR duties of line and HR managers.

staff manager

A person who manages a department that serves the line managers in a support or advisory capacity by providing information and advice and ensuring compliance with government laws and regulations.

TABLE 1.3 The Roles of HR and Line Managers

Role of the HR Manager	Role of the Line Manager
Provide advice (serve as a consultant to line managers)	Involved in the selection process
Provide support to line managers by assisting with HR functions (recruiting, testing, training and development, administering employee benefits, etc.)	Conduct training and development (with assistance from HR)
HR policy and implementation	Ensure productivity
Dispute resolution	Supervision
	Motivation
	Performance appraisal
	Employee discipline/discharge

You can see from these two lists that there is much overlap between the HR responsibilities of line versus staff managers. In companies with successful human resource practices, the line and staff managers have learned that they both have some responsibility for HR management and have learned to support each other to implement effective HR practices and procedures. Ideally, there is a synergistic relationship between HR and line managers. If the HR managers see themselves as strategic business partners, and they do not have an adversarial relationship, then this can free up line managers to focus on their operations and increasing revenue and productivity.

Key Takeaways

- The employee life cycle (ELC) is a model that portrays the journey of a typical employee from the time they first learned about an opening at the organization, through the recruitment and hiring process, and all of the stages the employee progresses through until their employment ends. The nine stages of the ELC are: recruitment, selection, onboarding, training, development, coaching, performance appraisal, benefits administration, and separation.

- During the talent acquisition phase, the focus is on attracting a qualified pool of applicants and selecting the individuals who represent the best potential for success for each position.

- Once an employee has been hired, then the talent development process begins with onboarding and then continues with ongoing job skills training, policy and legal training, performance management, team-building activities, and coaching and mentoring, as long as the individual is employed with the organization.

- One of the most effective tools in ensuring that employees stay with an organization in the long run is to focus on employee engagement, thus increasing commitment to the company.

- If you find yourself in a position as an HR department of one, then you might consider outsourcing some of the day-to-day tasks, freeing you up to focus on communications, leadership, engagement, and employee relations.

- Line managers and HR managers should share the responsibility for talent recruitment, development, and retention.

What Do *You* Think?

1. Why are you studying human resource management? How do you plan to utilize the knowledge to be more effective in your chosen profession?
2. Think of a time when you first started working in a new company. How would you describe the onboarding experience? What did you like about it, and what would you suggest they do differently?
3. If you found yourself being a solo HR practitioner, what steps would you take to help juggle the many responsibilities and time demands?
4. How should a line manager and an HR manager work together to improve recruiting, development, and retention?

1.6 Careers in HRM

Learning Objectives

1. Identify the types of positions and career options that are available in the HR profession.
2. Explain how to best prepare for a career in HRM.
3. Describe the skillsets and competencies necessary for an individual to perform well in an HR career, in accordance with the SHRM Competency Model.

Positions and Career Options in HR

Human resources is one of the fastest-growing professions, and the demand for highly skilled HR professionals will continue to increase. An organization cannot exist without people, so all organizations have a need for someone (or a team) to manage their human capital. Within HR, there are many different functions, and therefore a wide variety of positions within the field. In fact, there are over 130 different HR job titles![32] Positions within HR fall into three broad categories: HR generalists, HR specialists, and HR managers.

An HR generalist is a person who handles a wide variety of duties that may range from administrative duties, recordkeeping and reporting, tracking applicants, to a wide variety of other tasks. An HR specialist is a person who has expertise in a specific area of human resources and is usually a more experienced HR professional. If you are new to the HR field, your first position will likely be as an HR generalist. Then, as you gain experience and knowledge, it is typical to eventually advance into a role as an HR specialist. The most experienced HR staff then may move into roles as HR managers or directors. In larger organizations, the most senior HR employee may be a member of the senior executive team, with titles such as VP for human resources, VP for people, or chief human resources officer (CHRO).

According to the Occupational Outlook Handbook of the Bureau of Labor Statistics, HR generalist and specialists positions are growing at 7% a year, with an average salary of $60,520 per year, with 547,800 new positions expected to be created during the ten-year period from 2016 to 2026.[33] HR manager positions are growing at 7% a year, with average salaries of $110,120, and 136,100 positions expected to be created from 2016 to 2026.[34] Figure 1.4 shows how an individual might typically advance through a career in HR.

FIGURE 1.4 Typical HR Career Path

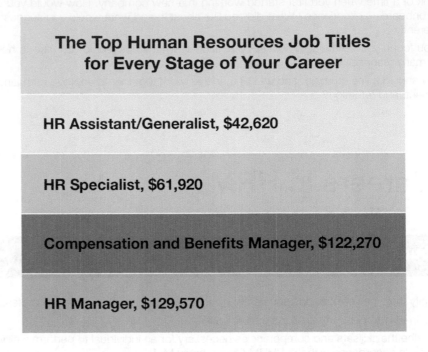

The Top Human Resources Job Titles for Every Stage of Your Career

HR Assistant/Generalist, $42,620

HR Specialist, $61,920

Compensation and Benefits Manager, $122,270

HR Manager, $129,570

The following are some of the major specialties that are available as career options in HR:

- Recruitment
- Talent Development
- Compensation
- Benefits
- Employee and Labor Relations
- Human Resources Information Systems (HRIS) Analyst

Preparing for a Career in HRM

Since you are studying HR, there is a good chance that you are wondering: How do I prepare for a career in HR? There are three general paths to an entry-level position in the HR field:[35]

- A college degree in HR.
- A college degree in a related subject, such as business administration or industrial/organizational psychology, then applying those skills to HR through experience and/or earning appropriate certification.
- Working for several years in an operational role at a company, then transitioning to HR.

However, even earning a college degree in HR is often not enough. Potential employers also look for experience, which can be obtained through an internship. Research indicates that professional experience is vital to securing employment after graduation from college, with the most valuable internships lasting at least three months.[36] Business internships are the most useful when the supervisor provides the student with direct feedback and assessment on the intern's strengths, weaknesses, and advice for professional improvement.[37] Another way to build experience is to seek an HR rotational, which is typically a full-time job lasting two to three years, in which the participant rotates through various aspects of HR within a company.

HR Talk: Cindie Melton

Division HR Director

PACCAR Corporation

PACCAR typically has several hundred internships available annually. Internships are available throughout North America in many different fields, from HR to engineering to dealer development. The opportunities are in all areas of business and we are proud to say that we frequently are able to offer full-time positions to many of our interns. Students who participate in internships gain excellent real-world experience. It provides professional experience that links their academic coursework to the disciplines that they want to pursue. Students can gain a good understanding of our industry and explore the possible long-term career fit. I think it can also give students an edge in the job market. Internship experience makes a college graduate more marketable! It gives the students a chance to learn about their strengths and weaknesses by receiving feedback from their managers, and a safe place to learn and make mistakes in a safe environment. Additionally, the professionals that interns encounter during their intern program provide a wonderful networking opportunity to learn from their future colleagues.

In the HR community, it is important to build relationships through networking. A good starting point is to attend meetings and networking events (or mixers) hosted by the local chapters of professional associations. One organization that you should consider is the Society for Human Resource Management (SHRM). SHRM is the world's largest HR professional society, representing 300,000 members in more than 165 countries.[38] They are the leading provider of resources, serving the needs of HR professionals and advancing the practice of human resource management, with more than 575 affiliated chapters within the United States and subsidiaries in China, India, and United Arab Emirates.[39] SHRM also has student chapters at many colleges and universities in the U.S. If your university has a student chapter, you should join it, and perhaps consider running for an office. If your university does not have a student chapter, then talk to a faculty member about starting one!

You may also wish to begin planning to earn an HR certification. The value of a certification is that it demonstrates to prospective employers that you have attained a specific level of knowledge and behaviors related to HR. SHRM offers several certifications: the SHRM Certified Professional (SHRM-CP) for early career professionals, and the SHRM Senior Certified Professional (SHRM-SCP) for advanced professionals. The eligibility requirements to sit for an exam are shown in Table 1.4. More than 5,000 employers are seeking SHRM credential holders every month.[40]

TABLE 1.4 SHRM Certification Eligibility Requirements
Note: Less than a bachelor's degree includes: working toward a bachelor's degree, associate's degree, some college, qualifying HR certificate program, high school diploma, or GED.

EDUCATION	WORK EXPERIENCE
HR-RELATED GRADUATE DEGREE	
SHRM-CP	In current HR role
SHRM-SCP	3 years in HR role
GRADUATE DEGREE/NON-HR	
SHRM-CP	1 year in HR role
SHRM-SCP	4 years in HR role
HR-RELATED BACHELOR'S DEGREE	
SHRM-CP	1 year in HR role
SHRM-SCP	4 years in HR role
BACHELOR'S DEGREE/NON-HR	
SHRM-CP	2 years in HR role
SHRM-SCP	5 years in HR role
LESS THAN BACHELOR'S DEGREE (HR-RELATED PROGRAM)	
SHRM-CP	3 years in HR role
SHRM-SCP	6 years in HR role
LESS THAN BACHELOR'S DEGREE (NON-HR PROGRAM)	
SHRM-CP	4 years in HR role
SHRM-SCP	7 years in HR role

Source: Based on SHRM-CP and SHRM-SCP Eligibility Chart. For more information, see: https://www.shrm.org/certification/apply/eligibility-criteria/Pages/default.aspx

Another provider of HR certification is the HR Certification Institute (HRCI). They offer widely respected certifications, with 93% of *Fortune 500* companies currently employing HRCI certification holders.[41] The most common HRCI certifications are the Professional in Human Resources (PHR), the Senior Professional in Human Resources (SPHR), and the Global Professional in Human Resources (GPHR). The HRCI eligibility requirements are shown in Table 1.5.

TABLE 1.5 HRCI Certification Eligibility Requirements

PHR®	
EDUCATION	**WORK EXPERIENCE**
Master's Degree or Higher	At least 1 year in professional-level HR position
Bachelor's Degree	At least 2 years in professional-level HR position
Less than Bachelor's Degree	At least 4 years in professional-level HR position

SPHR®	
EDUCATION	**WORK EXPERIENCE**
Master's Degree or Higher	At least 4 years in professional-level HR position
Bachelor's Degree	At least 5 years in professional-level HR position
Less than Bachelor's Degree	At least 7 years in professional-level HR position

Source: Based on HRCI, "Which Certification Is Right For You." For more information, see: https://www.hrci.org/our-programs/which-certification-is-right-for-you

HR Skillsets and Competencies

As you have seen by now, human resource management is a career with a wide variety of responsibilities. On any given day, an HR professional might engage in tasks that involve meeting with people, reviewing budgets or financial statements, handling legal issues, or a host of other types of activities. An HR career can be very exciting and challenging, as one never knows what the next day will hold. Accordingly, the skillset that HR managers need is varied and complex.

A **competency** is a cluster of observable and measurable knowledge, skills, abilities, and other characteristics (**KSAOs**) needed for effective job performance. Competencies simplify the process of tying examples of performance expectations to organizational or professional missions and goals, which increases the likelihood of a positive impact on organizational outcomes.[42]

Competencies are expressed as either technical or behavioral. A technical competency refers to the knowledge required for effective performance. In other words, they reflect what a person *knows* about a particular field. A behavioral competency refers to an observable quality or characteristic associated with effective performance and reflects what a person is able *to do*. In the HR field, an example of a technical competency is knowledge of HR-related laws and regulations, and an example of a behavioral competency is conflict resolution.

The SHRM Competency Model© is designed for all HR professionals as a resource for identifying and defining proficiency in the technical and behavioral aspects of HR.[43] It can help HR students and practitioners create a road map for achieving their professional goals by developing expertise in each competency. SHRM's Competency Model distinguishes between the technical and behavioral competencies required for four different career levels: early, mid, senior, and executive. As an undergraduate HR textbook, our focus throughout the book will be on the early career competencies.

The SHRM Competency Model©, shown here: https://www.shrm.org/learningandcareer/career/pages/shrm-competency-model.aspx and explained further in Table 1.6 consists of nine competencies: HR Expertise (a technical competency), and eight behavioral competencies organized into three clusters:

- **Leadership** (Leadership and Navigation, Ethical Practice).
- **Interpersonal** (Relationship Management, Communication, Global & Cultural Effectiveness).
- **Business** (Business Acumen, Consultation, Critical Evaluation).

competency

A cluster of observable and measurable knowledge, skills, abilities, and other characteristics (KSAOs) needed for effective job performance.

KSAOs

Knowledge, skills, abilities, and other characteristics.

Each of the eight behavioral competencies is defined in Table 1.6:

TABLE 1.6 SHRM Behavioral Competencies

SHRM Behavioral Competencies	
Leadership and Navigation	The ability to direct and contribute to initiatives and processes within the organization.
Ethical Practice	The ability to integrate core values, integrity, and accountability throughout all organizational and business practices.
Relationship Management	The ability to manage interactions, to provide service, and to support the organization.
Communication	The ability to effectively exchange information with stakeholders.
Global & Cultural Effectiveness	The ability to value and consider the perspectives and backgrounds of all parties.
Business Acumen	The ability to understand and apply information to contribute to the organization's strategic plan.
Consultation	The ability to provide guidance to organizational stakeholders.
Critical Evaluation	The ability to interpret information, to make business decisions and recommendations.

Both SHRM and HRCI have identified bodies of knowledge that outline the competencies and skills that are essential for HR professionals. This textbook is aligned with both of these sets of competencies to ensure that the reader is introduced to each of the primary areas of HR knowledge. The SHRM and HRCI bodies of knowledge are described in Table 1.7.

TABLE 1.7 SHRM and HRCI Bodies of Knowledge

SHRM BoCK™	HRBoK™
The SHRM Body of Competency and Knowledge (SHRM BoCK™) serves as the foundation for the SHRM Certification Exams and is based on the SHRM Competency Model.	HRCI's HR Body of Knowledge (HRBoK™) provides a comprehensive overview of the profession and essential HR practices. It can be used as an exam preparation tool for HRCI certification candidates, but HR professionals can also use the HRBoK™ as a reference to ensure their organizations are aligned with the HR competencies necessary to meet the ever-changing HRM profession.
The SHRM BoCK™ further outlines the HR Expertise technical competency into fifteen areas of HR knowledge, grouped into three domains: • People (HR Strategic Planning, Talent Acquisition, Employee Engagement & Retention, Learning & Development, Total Rewards). • Organization (Structure of the HR Function, Organizational Effectiveness & Development, Workforce Management, Employee & Labor Relations, Technology Management). • Workplace (HR in the Global Context, Diversity & Inclusion, Risk Management, Corporate Social Responsibility, U.S. Employment Law & Regulations).	The HRBoK™ is divided into six content areas: • Business Management Strategy. • Workforce Planning and Employment. • Human Resource Development. • Compensation and Benefits. • Employee Labor Relations. • Risk Management.
The SHRM BoCK™ can be accessed at the following link: https://www.shrm.org/certification/about/body-of-competency-and-knowledge	The HRBoK™ can be accessed at the following link: https://www.hrci.org/how-to-get-certified/preparation-overview/human-resource-body-of-knowledge

Source (left): Reprinted with permission from the Society for Human Resource Management (SHRM). © 2020. All rights reserved.

Source (right): Link used with permission from HRCI

Key Takeaways

- Human resources is one of the fastest-growing professions, and the demand for highly skilled HR professionals will continue to increase.
- There are three general paths to an entry-level position in the HR field: (1) a college degree in HR; (2) a college degree in a related subject, such as business administration or industrial/organizational psychology, then application of those skills to HR through experience and/or earning appropriate certification; or (3) working for several years in an operational role at a company, then transitioning to HR.
- The SHRM Competency Model® is designed for all HR professionals as a resource for identifying and defining proficiency in the technical and behavioral aspects of HR.
- HRCI's HR Body of Knowledge (HRBoK™) provides a comprehensive overview of the profession and essential HR practices.

What Do *You* Think?

1. Would you prefer to be an HR generalist, an HR specialist, or a solo HR practitioner?

2. What is your personal path for preparing for a career in HRM?
3. In which of the SHRM behavioral competencies are you already strongest? In which do you need to improve the most?

1.7 Conclusion

In this chapter, we reviewed the impact of human capital on the success of the organization and presented an overview of the challenges and emerging issues that managers should consider when designing the policies and practices that affect the employees in an organization. The various responsibilities of HR managers and line managers were then discussed. The chapter concluded with an overview of the various career opportunities available to those interested in HR as a career field, along with suggestions for gaining the necessary competencies and skillsets for a career in HR.

Theory-into-Practice (TIP) Exercises

1. Create a personal career development plan including the following steps:
   a. Write down your primary career interest.
   b. Identify your long-term professional goal (e.g., become an HR director).
   c. Identify the short-term goals that will contribute to reaching your long-term goal (e.g., complete a college degree in HR, spend five years as an HR generalist, etc.).
   d. List two to three activities that will help you reach each short-term goal. For each activity, write down when you will start and complete it.

   Then exchange plans with a classmate and provide each other with feedback and suggestions.

2. Contact a representative of your local or state economic development agency. Ask them about the skills shortages that exist in your area and the impact this is having on the growth of the local economy. Also inquire about what is being done to close the skills gaps.

3. Practice choosing a vendor for an HRIS system. Choose three vendors from the Best HR Software Comparison List (under Resources number 4). Go to each vendor's website and read about the features and benefits. Do a web search for each vendor and read reviews written by HR professionals. Then check with the Better Business Bureau to find out each company's rating and how many and what types of complaints have been filed. Based on your findings, which vendor would you select, and why?

Case Study: The Spec-Tacular Culture Crush at Warby Parker

Source: Dev Chatterjee / Shutterstock.com

Warby Parker is a prescription glasses and sunglasses retailer based in New York City. The name derives from an exhibition on Jack Kerouac that was being held at the New York Public Library in 2009. Co-founder Dave Gilboa stumbled upon the exhibition and took notice of two characters with unique names: Warby Pepper and Zagg Parker; thus Warby Parker emerged. Over the past nine years, Warby Parker has grown to selling their products both online and in over one hundred retail stores across the United States. Part of Warby Parker's mission is to create an environment where employees can think big, have fun, and do good.

From beginning to end, Warby Parker makes all aspects of their employees' life cycles extraordinary. Gilboa states: "You have to make people feel special and welcome from the very first moment they interact with your organization." To do this, when a new member joins the company, they receive a standard welcome packet including an office map, style guide, and a copy of Jack Kerouac's *Dharma Bums,* where the company name originates. New beginnings can be difficult, and Warby Parker helps break the ice for newcomers in some unique and quirky ways. One of these includes placing a custom helium balloon at their desk, featuring an illustrated steak wearing a pair of glasses saying, "Nice to meat you!" The balloon is a beacon, calling existing employees to introduce themselves. In addition, senior members of staff are in charge of training new employees in order to further instill their values.

Employees are required to attend weekly meetings. Although many believe such meetings are not beneficial for larger companies, Warby Parker has shown that these meetings keep their employees feeling connected, informed, and engaged. As companies get larger, communication across the organization often diminishes. In an ambitious company such as Warby Parker, communication is key. Co-founders Neil Blumenthal and David Gilboa also record The Weekly Briefing, a three-to-five-minute video highlighting the critical points of that week's meeting. Lastly, communication is presented through the *Warby Weekly,* an internal newsletter consisting of events, new launches, new features, and more.

Warby Parker places a major focus on doing good in the world. This attracts people who want to work for them simply because of their social mission. Employees who have been with the company for three years are rewarded with a trip to Guatemala to see *Buy a Pair, Give a Pair*, the company's social program, in action. There, employees are able to witness someone less fortunate receive their first pair of glasses. Being present in that specific moment is an extremely influential experience and creates a bond between the employee and the company, allowing them to become more passionate about the work they are doing.

Learning is ever present. Warby Parker has created ways for employees to continually try new things and grow their skillsets. At an annual internal conference, WarbyCon, employees are encouraged to teach a crowd of their colleagues about anything they desire. The discussions provide those who are not proficient public speakers with the freedom to hone those skills. Additionally, there is a Special Projects program, which allows employees to operate like interns within the company. Departments that need extra help on a specific project can post an application, and other employees throughout the company can apply to work with that department for an allotted amount of time.[44]

 How Warby Parker Makes Every Point in Its Employee Lifecycle Extraordinary

Warby Parker is known for being a wonderful place to work. Co-founder Dave Gilboa describes how they have constructed this culture.

View the video online at: http://www.youtube.com/embed/SrLCXrsEPZE?rel=0

Case Discussion Questions

1. Is it crucial for companies to make such an exceptional first impression when hiring new employees? Why or why not?
2. What are the benefits of having weekly meetings rather than monthly or semi-annual meetings?
3. How important is the treatment and management of employees to the success of a company?
4. Warby Parker's founders and team leaders are present in the day-to-day lives of their employees. What positive attributes can this provide for both employers and employees?
5. Does Warby Parker's Special Projects program provide their employees with a new perspective and perhaps give them a break from their usual work, to aid in their job becoming less mundane?
6. Based on the introduction of Warby Parker's employee culture, would you want to work for them? Why or why not?

Resources

1. **SHRM Certification.** Information about the SHRM Certified Professional (SHRM-CP) certification, including eligibility requirements, exam windows, and exam preparation.

   - https://www.shrm.org/certification/about/aboutshrmcertification/Pages/SHRM-CP.aspx
   - The SHRM BoCK™ can be accessed at the following link: https://www.shrm.org/certification/about/body-of-competency-and-knowledge

2. **HRCI Certification.** Information about the HRCI Professional in Human Resources certification (PHR), including eligibility requirements, exam windows, and exam preparation.

   - https://www.hrci.org/ (Link used with permission from HRCI.)
   - The HRBoK™ can be accessed at the following link: https://www.hrci.org/how-to-get-certified/preparation-overview/human-resource-body-of-knowledge (Link used with permission from HRCI.)

3. **O*Net Online.** The Occupational Information Network (O*Net) is a database containing hundreds of descriptors such as knowledge, skills, and abilities required for almost 1,000 occupations. O*Net is developed under sponsorship of the U.S. Department of Labor/Employment and Training Administration through a grant to the North Carolina Department of Commerce. O*Net Online has detailed descriptions of the world of work for use by job seekers, workforce development and HR professionals, students, and researchers.

   - https://www.onetonline.org/

4. **Best HR Software Comparison List.** A 2019 comparison of the leading providers of Human Resource Information Systems (HRIS) with descriptions, features, and links to the providers.

   - https://selecthub.com/hr-management-software/

Endnotes

1. Case written by Acerra, A. & Holt, K. (2020). Adapted from Case study: Employer branding at Google. Randstad. Retrieved February 20, 2020 from https://www.randstad.com/workforce-insights/employer-branding/case-study-employer-branding-at-google/; Google awards. Comparably. Retrieved February 20, 2020 from https://www.comparably.com/companies/google/awards; Manjoo, F. (2013). The happiness machine. Slate. Retrieved from https://slate.com/technology/2013/01/google-people-operations-the-secrets-of-the-worlds-most-scientific-human-resources-department.html; 100 best companies to work for. Fortune. Retrieved February 20, 2020 from https://fortune.com/best-companies/2017/google/

2. Pfeffer, J., Hatano, T., & Santalainen, T. (1995). Producing sustainable competitive advantage through the effective management of people. Academy of Management Executive, (9)1, 55-69.

3. The Value of People, OECD. Retrieved February 20, 2020 from https://www.oecd.org/insights/37967294.pdf

4. Grant, R.M. (1996). Toward a knowledge-based view of the firm. Strategic Management Journal (17) S2, 109-122.

5. Lepak, D., and Snell, S. (2003). Examining the human resource architecture: The relationship among human capital, employment, and human resource configurations. Journal of Management, (28) 4, 517-543.

6. Kochan, T., Finegold, D., & Osterman, P. (2012). Who can fix the "middle-skills" gap? Harvard Business Review. Retrieved from https://hbr.org/2012/12/who-can-fix-the-middle-skills-gap

7. Garmise, S. (2006). People and the Competitive Advantage of Place: Building a Workforce for the 21st Century. Armonk, NY: M.E. Sharpe.

8. Buss, D.D. (2014). Critical site selection factor #1: Availability of skilled labor an acute need. Area Development (Q4). Retrieved from https://www.areadevelopment.com/skilled-workforce-STEM/Q4-2014/skilled-labor-critical-site-selection-factors-7221554.shtml

9. Schneider, P. (2014). Workforce: The location factor companies must get right. Area Development, (Q4). Retrieved from https://www.areadevelopment.com/laborEducation/Q4-2014/creating-sustainable-flexible-evolving-workforce-29928745.shtml

10. United States Unemployment Rate. Trading Economics. Retrieved February 20, 2020 from https://tradingeconomics.com/united-states/unemployment-rate

11. Buckley, P., & Bachman, D. (2017). Meet the workforce of the future. Deloitte Review, (21), 47-61.

12. Dimock, M. (2018). Defining generations: Where millennials end and post-millennials begin. Pew Research Center. Retrieved from http://www.pewresearch.org/fact-tank/2018/03/01/defining-generations-where-millennials-end-and-post-millennials-begin/

13. Fry, R. Millennials are the largest generation in the U.S. labor force. Pew Research Center. Retrieved January 4, 2020 from http://www.pewresearch.org/fact-tank/2018/04/11/millennials-largest-generation-us-labor-force/

14. Dimock, M. (2018). Defining generations: Where millennials end and post-millennials begin. Pew Research Center. Retrieved from http://www.pewresearch.org/fact-tank/2018/03/01/defining-generations-where-millennials-end-and-post-millennials-begin/

15. Buckley, P., & Bachman, D. (2017). Meet the workforce of the future. Deloitte Review, (21), 47-61.

16. Ibid.

17. Ibid.

18. Surette, S. (2016). The status of women in leadership positions, according to an AAUW study. Huffington Post. Retrieved from https://www.huffingtonpost.com/womenas-ilab/the-status-of-women-in-le_b_10842506.html

19. Shields, J. (2018). 8 things you need to know about applicant tracking systems. Jobscan Blog. Retrieved from https://www.jobscan.co/blog/8-things-you-need-to-know-about-applicant-tracking-systems/

20. Forbes Human Resource Council. (2016). Impacting HR for the better. Retrieved from https://www.forbes.com/sites/forbeshumanresourcescouncil/2016/08/25/five-ways-technology-is-impacting-hr-for-the-better/#33efe0096f0d

21. Powell, W.W., & Snellman, K. (2004). The knowledge economy. Annual Review of Sociology, (30), 199-200. https://doi.org/10.1146/annurev.soc.29.010202.100037

22. Mohrman, S.A., & Lawler, E.E. (2012), Generating knowledge that drives change. Academy of Management Perspectives, 26(1), 41-51. Doi:10.5465/amp.2011.0141

23. Society for Human Resource Management. *SHRM's effective workplace index: Creating a workplace that works for employees and employers.* Retrieved February 21, 2020 from SHRM website: https://www.shrm.org/hr-today/trends-and-forecasting/special-reports-and-expert-views/Documents/SHRM-NSCW-Effective-Workplace-Index-Summary.pdf

24. Lifecare (2003, May 16). "LifeCare, Inc. Conference Features Xerox CEO Anne Mulcahy; Employers Challenged to Motivate and Engage Workforce." Businesswire. Retrieved from: https://www.businesswire.com/news/home/20030516005369/en/LifeCare-Inc.-Conference-Features-Xerox-CEO-Anne-Mulcahy-Employers-Challenged-to-Motivate-and-Engage-Workforce

25. World Commission on Environment and Development, GH Brundtland, chair, United Nations (1987). *Our Common Future.* Oxford: Oxford University Press..

26. Elkington, J. (1997). *Cannibals with forks: The triple bottom line of the 21st century.* London: Capstone.

27. [iii] The rise of the social enterprise: 2018 Deloitte Global Human Capital Trends. *Deloitte Insights.* Retrieved January 7, 2020 from https://www2.deloitte.com/content/dam/insights/us/articles/HCTrends2018/2018-HCtrends_Rise-of-the-social-enterprise.pdf

28. Crews, D. (2010). Strategies for implementing sustainability: Five leadership challenges. *Advanced Management Journal,* 75(2), 15-21.

29. Pandita, D., & Ray, S. (2018) Talent management and employee engagement – a meta-analysis of their impact on talent retention. *Industrial and Commercial Training,* Vol. 50 Issue: 4, pp. 185-199, https://doi-org.ezp.twu.edu/10.1108/ICT-09-2017-0073

30. Crews, D., & Bhatia, D. (2012). Supervisory practices in the transportation/logistics Industry. *Advanced Management Journal,* 77(1), 38-45.

31. Society for Human Resource Management. *Top 5 priorities for the HR department of one.* Retrieved January 18, 2020 from https://www.shrm.org/resourcesandtools/tools-and-samples/hr-qa/pages/whatisaneap.aspx

32. Heathfield, S. (2018). So you think you want a human resources career? *Thebalancecareers.* Retrieved from https://www.thebalancecareers.com/so-you-think-you-want-a-career-in-human-resources-1918365

33. Bureau of Labor Statistics. *Occupational Outlook Handbook.* Retrieved January 9, 2020 from https://www.bls.gov/ooh/business-and-financial/human-resources-specialists.htm

34. Ibid.

35. Feffer, M. (2016). How to get an entry-level job in HR. *Society for Human Resource Management.* Retrieved January 14, 2020 from https://www.shrm.org/hr-today/news/hr-news/pages/how-to-get-entry-level-hr-job.asp

36. Gault, J., Leach, E., Duey, M., & Benzing, T. (2018). Enhancing the value of professional experience in undergraduate education: Implications for academic and career counseling. *Journal of Employment Counseling, 55*(4), 144–154, https://doi-org.ezp.twu.edu/10.1002/joec.12094

37. Rothman, M. (2017) Employer assessments of business interns. *Higher Education, Skills and Work-Based Learning,* (7) 4, pp. 369-380, https://doi-org.ezp.twu.edu/10.1108/HESWBL-05-2017-0029

38. Society for Human Resource Management. *About SHRM.* Retrieved January 14, 2020 from https://shrm.org/about-shrm/Pages/default.aspx

39. Ibid.

40. Society for Human Resource Management. *Why seek SHRM certification?* Retrieved January 14, 2020 from https://www.shrm.org/certification/about/AboutSHRMCertification/Pages/keybenefits.aspx

41. HR Certification Institute. *The HRCI difference.* Retrieved January 14, 2020 from https://www.hrci.org/

42. Campion, M.A., Fink, A.A., Ruggeberg, B.J., Carr, L., Phillips, G.M., & Odman, R.B. (2011). Doing competencies well: Best practices in competency modeling. *Personnel Psychology,* 64, 225-262.

43. Society for Human Resource Management. *The SHRM Competency Model.* Retrieved January 14, 2020 from https://www.shrm.org/learningandcareer/career/pages/shrm-competency-model.aspx

44. Case written by Davenport, T. (2020). Adapted from How Warby Parker makes every point in its employee lifecycle extraordinary. *First Round.* Retrieved November 15, 2019 from https://firstround.com/review/how-warby-parker-makes-every-point-in-its-employee-lifecycle-extraordinary/

CHAPTER 2
Strategy and Workforce Planning

Learning Objectives

After reading this chapter, you should be able to do the following:

1. Describe the importance of mission, vision, values, and the four stages of strategic planning.
2. Describe how HR activities should be aligned with the overall business strategy.
3. Demonstrate methods to forecast labor demand and supply, and identify options for managing labor shortages and surpluses.
4. Recognize the appropriate use of talent analytics in workforce planning.

HR policies and practices, including talent recruitment, selection, training, and performance management, should happen in such a way that aligns with the mission of the firm, and supports the competitive advantage. HR should be a strategic business partner, not just an administrative back-office function. In today's very competitive business environment, HR departments can (and should) make a real contribution to the business by performing its business functions in ways that add value and reduce risk for the organization. Thus, it is important that HR managers understand the strategy of the organization and how workforce planning initiatives can enhance the success of the strategic initiatives.

This chapter introduces strategic concepts such as mission, vision, values, and the four stages of strategic planning. Various approaches to achieving competitive advantage are explored, along with methods that HR can align with each strategy. Workforce planning techniques such as forecasting labor demand and supply are introduced, as well as ideas for how to handle labor shortages and surpluses. The chapter concludes with an introduction to talent analytics, with an emphasis on how data is used in workforce planning.

2.1 Opening Case: LUV Is Not Blind

Southwest Airlines is the world's largest low-cost carrier.

Source: Eliyahu Yosef Parypa / Shutterstock.com

Southwest Airlines is known for low fares, few frills, and excellent customer service. Southwest does not have first class seats and practices open seating, which means that customers do not have an assigned seat, and they do not serve in-flight meals. However, Southwest is more than just a discount airline. Customers fly the airline not only for low fares, but also because they like the way they are treated by airline employees. Their success in the airline industry is unmatched, as they recently completed a forty-sixth consecutive year of profitability. A business strategy that combines cost controls, safety, and efficiency, along with a fully engaged workforce and a positive corporate culture, is the key to the Southwest success story.

Southwest's success may be due largely to its unusual focus on creating value for employees. Founders Herb Kelleher and Rollin King started the airline with one concept: If you get your passengers to their destinations when they want to get there, on time, and at the lowest possible fares, and make sure they have a good time doing it, people will fly your airline. The cornerstones of Southwest's employee-relations approach are LUV and FUN (LUV is also their stock symbol). They want the customers to love flying them, and Southwest realizes that this will not happen unless employees love to work there. Employees are encouraged to have fun on the job and to create an entertaining environment for customers. It is not unusual to hear flight attendants lead a round of "Happy Birthday" for a customer or to dress in costume for holidays.

One of the most important ingredients in creating and maintaining their company culture is hiring the right people. Southwest strives to hire individuals who will represent its branding message and exhibit a passion to help customers. Once employees are hired, the company makes significant investments in training and development, through its 382,000 square foot Training and Operational Support (TOPS) center and a 380,000 square foot Leadership Education and Development (LEAD) Center. The company has also maintained a profit-sharing program since 1973 to make sure that employees are exceptionally motivated. However, LUV is not blind. An applicant has to demonstrate potential to make a positive contribution to the company culture to get hired, and then has to deliver exceptional customer service while also meeting cost and efficiency standards.[1]

 How Southwest Airlines Built Its Culture

Southwest Airlines is consistently ranked as one of the best places to work. From recruitment to retention, co-founder Herb Kelleher shares tips for building a people-empowered culture and the secrets behind the airline's success.

View the video online at: http://www.youtube.com/embed/8_CeFiUkV7s?rel=0

Case Discussion Questions

1. How does employee satisfaction impact customer service?
2. What strategic actions could companies in other industries take to achieve the type of competitive advantage that Southwest Airlines has?
3. Would you prefer to fly an airline where the employees are having fun, and even entertaining passengers?
4. Is it important for you to have fun at work?

2.2 Strategic Planning

Learning Objectives

1. Define strategy and describe the three elements of strategy: externally oriented, forward looking, and dynamic.
2. Recognize how mission, vision, and values impact an organization's strategy.
3. Describe the four stages of the strategic planning process.

What Is Strategy?

Since this course is about human resource management, then why discuss business strategy? Isn't HR about recruitment, hiring, firing, payroll, and administering employee benefits? Yes, HR does handle all of those business functions, but as we discussed in Chapter 1, all of this should happen in a way that aligns with the mission of the firm and supports its competitive advantage. HR should be a strategic business partner, not just an administrative back-office function. The opening case demonstrates how important people are to the strategy of Southwest Airlines. In today's very competitive business environment, HR departments can (and should) make a real contribution to the business by performing its business functions in ways that add value and reduce risk for the organization.[2]

strategy

The set of managerial decisions and actions that determines the long-run performance of an organization.

Strategy is the set of managerial decisions and actions that determines the long-run performance of an organization. The word strategy comes from the Greek word *strategia*, which refers to the commander of an army. It is based on two Greek words: *stratos*, meaning a multitude or army, and *agos*, meaning a leader, or to lead.[3] In understanding strategy, it may be helpful to think in terms of what strategy is not. Strategy is often confused with tactics. They are related but different concepts. A strategy is a long-term plan for how to gain competitive advantage, while tactics are short-term actions that are taken to accomplish the overall strategy. A recruitment plan is not a strategy. An idea for how to enhance employee retention is not a strategy. A method to reduce employee health insurance costs is not a strategy. These are all tactics, but should not be confused with strategies. The distinction between the two terms is often muddled, as many people use the word strategy for things that are not really strategies. But as an old cowboy once said: "You can call your boots biscuits, and put them in the oven, but that don't make them biscuits." Just because you call something a strategy, does not make it a strategy.

In chess, each piece is strategically moved in anticipation of the competitor, and involves an analysis of the competitor's strategy. Human resources is similar in terms of strategically placing the right individual in the right place and at the right time to create a competitive advantage.

Source: © Shutterstock, Inc.

There are three characteristics of strategy that set it apart from ideas, methods, techniques, or tactics. Strategy should be externally oriented, forward looking, and dynamic.

Strategy is externally oriented because every organization is impacted by the environment in which it exists. For example, every firm has rivals, or competitors, against which it must set itself apart, in product variety, quality, customer service, cost, image, or a host of other competing factors. No organization is an island unto itself; all exist among competitors, all of whom are competing for market share. Likewise, every organization has customers, without whom it would have no reason for existing. Other external entities that impact the success or failure of a firm include government, lenders, and stockholders.

Strategy is forward looking because it deals with long-range plans. How "long-range" is defined depends on the particular industry, and it seems to be getting shorter, due to the rapid pace of technological change, consumer demand, and the nature of competition. In the 1960s and 70s, strategic plans tended to be ten years or longer. Then the '80s saw the popularity of five- to ten-year plans, which gradually became three-year plans, then one- to three-year plans. Some have even suggested that long-range strategic plans are no longer relevant in today's fast-paced business environment. However, a sustainable competitive business plan is no less necessary (perhaps even more so) in a volatile business market, as evidenced by the fact that most business disasters are caused by mistakenly pursuing short-term goals instead of long-range ones.[4]

Strategy is dynamic, as opposed to static, because it must adapt to a constantly changing environment. John F. Kennedy said, "Change is the law of life, and those who look only to the past are certain to miss the future."[5] While strategies should be long-range, they should not be fixed in stone. An organization should be agile and flexible enough to adapt the strategy quickly to changing market conditions. This concept has given rise to the notion of a strategic plan being a living document, as opposed to a book or report that never changes. New waters are continually flowing in, and each time you go to work or school, something has changed from the day before. They may be small, perhaps even imperceptible, changes. However, these incremental changes, if they continue, will eventually form a trend, which can cause significant change in the long run. Successful leaders are aware of the changing trends and are able to adapt the strategy of the organizations in response. Better yet, they create new strategies that cause the trends and are proactive in leading the marketplace, instead of simply reacting to the moves of competitors.

Mission, Vision, and Values

The starting point in a successful business strategy is to identify the mission and vision. A **mission statement** is a short statement of an organization's purpose. It might identify the customer, product, or service, and its geographic area. An easy way to remember this is that a mission statement should answer four questions:[6]

1. What do we do?
2. How do we do it?
3. Whom do we do it for?
4. What value are we bringing?

A **vision statement** identifies what a company would like to achieve or accomplish. In other words, the mission explains why the organization exists, and the vision explains what the organization wants to do. The mission and vision statements are only effective if they drive both the long-range strategy and the daily decisions that are made in the organization. For this to happen, they must be known by every employee and supplier of the organization.

A **values statement** indicates the core beliefs and values of an organization. Examples of values are responsive customer service, respect for others, excellence, accountability, ethics, and integrity. The organizational values should drive the expected conduct of all employees. To achieve this, some organizations take the values and delineate them more specifically in a **Code of Ethics and Business Conduct**, which is a set of organizational guidelines or standards regarding values, beliefs, and ethics that govern the decisions and actions of members of the organization. Table 2.1 contains examples of company missions and values. As you read them, think about the role of people and the importance of HR in the mission and values.

mission statement

A short statement of an organization's purpose that identifies the customer, product, or service, and its geographic area.

vision statement

A statement that identifies what a company would like to achieve or accomplish.

values statement

A statement that indicates the core beliefs and values of an organization.

Code of Ethics and Business Conduct

A set of organizational guidelines or standards regarding values, beliefs, and ethics that govern the decisions and actions of members of the organization.

TABLE 2.1 Company Mission and Values

Mission and Values		
Company	**Mission**	**Values**
Darden Restaurants (Olive Garden, LongHorn Steakhouse, Cheddar's Scratch Kitchen, Yard House, The Capital Grille, Seasons 52, Bahama Breeze, Eddie V's)	To be financially successful through great people consistently delivering outstanding food, drinks, and service in an inviting atmosphere, making every guest loyal.	We look to these values—Inclusion & Diversity; Respect & Caring; Always Learning, Always Teaching; Integrity & Fairness; Teamwork; Excellence; Being of Service—as we work to fulfill our mission.
Ford Motor Company	To drive human progress through freedom of movement.	We are a company driven by purpose. Whether it's our customers, employees, partners, or communities, we obsess about the wants and needs of people to drive human progress.

Mission and Values		
Glassdoor	To help people everywhere to find a job and company they love.	• We are transparent. • We are innovative. • We are good people. • We have grit.
Google	To organize the world's information and make it universally accessible and useful.	Ten things we know to be true: 1. Focus on the user and all else will follow. 2. It's best to do one thing really, really well. 3. Fast is better than slow. 4. Democracy on the web works. 5. You don't need to be at your desk to need an answer. 6. You can make money without doing evil. 7. There's always more information out there. 8. The need for information crosses all borders. 9. You can be serious without a suit. 10. Great just isn't good enough.
Cummins	Making people's lives better by powering a more prosperous world.	• Integrity: Doing what you say you will do and doing what is right. • Diversity & Inclusion: Valuing and including our differences in decision-making is our competitive advantage. • Caring: Demonstrating awareness and consideration for the well-being of others. • Excellence: Always delivering superior results. • Teamwork: Collaborating across teams, functions, businesses, and borders to deliver the best work.

Four Stages of Strategic Planning

Strategic planning has four distinct stages: environmental analysis, strategy formulation, strategy implementation, and evaluation. The first phase involves gathering information and conducting an analysis of what is happening, and the expected future trends, in the environment of the organization. In the second phase, strategies are considered, chosen, and formulated. In the third phase, the strategy is executed. Then the final stage is an evaluation of the results and, if necessary, corrective action. A useful method for remembering these four stages is Look, Think, Do, and Review. First, you look at the environment of the organization by gathering and analyzing data. Next, you think about it and formulate a plan of action. Then you do it (implement the plan), and finally, you review it to see if it is accomplishing what it was intended to.

Strategy involves analysis, planning, execution, and evaluation, but at the heart of each process is thinking. This illustrates why the development of critical thinking skills is an important aspect of education and professional development.

Source: © Shutterstock, Inc.

Environmental Analysis (Look)

During the first phase, data is gathered about the external and internal environment of the organization. One approach is to begin with the big picture of the general environment. A common practice for analyzing the general environment is to organize the data using the PESTEL (or sometimes the shortened PEST) acronym. The PESTEL analysis helps an organization identify the external forces that could impact their business, and includes the following factors:[7]

- **Political.** Government policies and actions that impact areas such as trade and taxation.
- **Economic.** Factors that impact the performance of the economy, such as interest rates, unemployment, materials cost, and foreign exchange rates.
- **Social.** Trends that impact customer demands, such as family demographics, education, attitudes, and cultural trends.
- **Technological.** Factors such as digital and mobile technology and automation, that impact production, distribution, and marketing.
- **Environmental.** Factors that impact the environment, sustainability, and social responsibility such as climate, waste, and recycling.
- **Legal.** Local, national, and international laws and regulations that govern the business, such as employment legislation, trade restrictions, and worker health and safety.

After the general environment has been scanned, attention should be turned to the industry environment. This includes data about customer trends, competitors, and suppliers, for example, which market segments are growing, and which are declining. Sometimes the data can be gathered through secondary sources, such as online searches, reports from trade associations, or data obtained from market research firms. However, the most relevant and current data comes from conducting primary research, such as surveys and focus groups.

Research should be conducted about each major competitor to better understand their business strategy, what is working for them, what is not working, and to anticipate their future strategic moves. Then attention should be given to the internal environment, i.e., the organization itself. The data gathered for the internal analysis varies by industry and organization, but might include a review of financial statements, human resource activity reports (e.g., employee turnover rates), marketing reports (e.g., market share and revenue trends), and productivity data.

Once data has been collected, then an analysis is conducted, with a focus on identifying emerging issues and future trends that demand strategic action. A useful method for conducting the analysis is the **SWOT** technique. SWOT stands for strengths, weaknesses, opportunities, and threats. The technique involves identification of the ways that strengths can be leveraged to take advantage of opportunities, and weaknesses and threats can be eliminated or minimized.

SWOT

A brainstorming technique that identifies strengths, weaknesses, opportunities, and threats.

Strategy Formulation (Think)

The purpose of the environmental analysis was to gather and understand data. The purpose of the strategy formulation stage is to act upon it. Strategy can mean different things, depending on the strategy level that is being referred to. There are three levels of strategy:

- **Corporate Level.** This strategy level answers the question: Whom will we compete against? Do we plan on growing, holding steady, or pulling back in? These are also referred to as directional strategies (growth, stabilization, and retrenchment).
- **Business Unit.** This strategy level answers the question: How are we going to compete? Companies usually compete on price, quality, selection, or service, or some combination of these. The most common business-level strategies, and how HR can align with and support them, will be explored more fully later in the chapter.
- **Functional.** This strategy level answers the question: How can the business unit align with the corporate and business-level strategies? To understand this level, think in terms of what a business function is. For example, accounting is a business function; marketing is a business function; production is a business function, and most importantly for us, HR is a business function.

Strategy Implementation (Do)

A strategy or plan is only as good as its execution. After data has been gathered and analyzed, and a strategic plan has been formulated, it is time for the hard work of implementing the plan. This is where many plans fail. According to a survey of the Conference Board, execution overall and strategy execution in particular hold the first and second positions when it comes to top issues in executives' minds.[8] Lawrence Hrebiniak of the Wharton School notes that, "Strategic success demands a simultaneous view of planning and doing. Managers must be thinking about executing even as they are formulating plans."[9]

When a business plan fails, it is often the case that the plan was not faulty, but the leaders did not get everyone on the same page in terms of executing each element of the plan. Another way of saying this is that leadership did not get all of the functional units aligned with the plan. Jim Collins and Jerry Porras, in their book *Built to Last*, said: "Building a visionary company requires one percent vision, and 99% alignment."[10]

Evaluation (Review)

Although evaluation is the last of the four stages, it should not be thought of as the end of the process. Strategic planning is an ongoing process in that the evaluation or review stage should provide feedback for future planning, as shown in Figure 2.1.

FIGURE 2.1 Four Stages of Strategic Planning

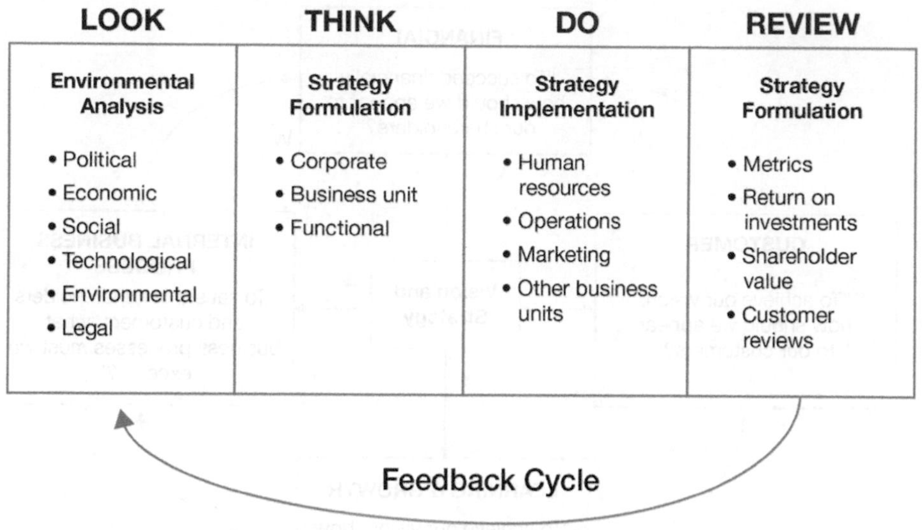

LOOK	THINK	DO	REVIEW
Environmental Analysis	**Strategy Formulation**	**Strategy Implementation**	**Strategy Formulation**
• Political • Economic • Social • Technological • Environmental • Legal	• Corporate • Business unit • Functional	• Human resources • Operations • Marketing • Other business units	• Metrics • Return on investments • Shareholder value • Customer reviews

Feedback Cycle

Evaluation involves first determining what to measure. What metrics should be used, and what is the standard for measuring whether the strategy is successful? What does success look like, and how do you measure it? Based on the performance results, one of the following approaches can be taken:

- If the strategy is working, then take steps to reinforce it and sustain the momentum.
- If the strategy seems to be the right one, but all of the metrics are not being achieved, then take corrective action.
- Sometimes it becomes apparent that a strategy is flawed. In this case, the strategy should be scrapped for a different one.

One of the most popular tools for evaluating strategies is the Balanced Scorecard (BSC). It was developed by Harvard professors Robert Kaplan and David Norton as a framework for measuring organizational performance.[11]

The BSC is a strategic planning and management system that organizations use to:

- Communicate what they are trying to accomplish.
- Align the day-to-day work that everyone is doing with strategy.
- Prioritize projects, products, and services.
- Measure and monitor progress toward strategic targets.[12]

The BSC helps to provide meaningful integration of many issues that come into play when evaluating a firm's performance. It is a set of measures that provide top managers with a fast but comprehensive view of the business. The BSC includes financial indicators, operational measures of customer satisfaction, internal processes, and the organization's innovation and improvement activities.

BSCs are used extensively in business and industry, government, and nonprofit organizations worldwide. More than half of major companies in the U.S., Europe, and Asia are using the BSC, with use growing in those areas as well as in the Middle East and Africa.[13] A recent study by Bain & Co. listed the BSC fifth on its top ten most widely used management tools around the world, with the related topic of strategic planning listed at number one.[14]

The balanced scorecard enables managers to consider their business from four key perspectives, as illustrated in Figure 2.2:

FIGURE 2.2 The Balanced Scorecard

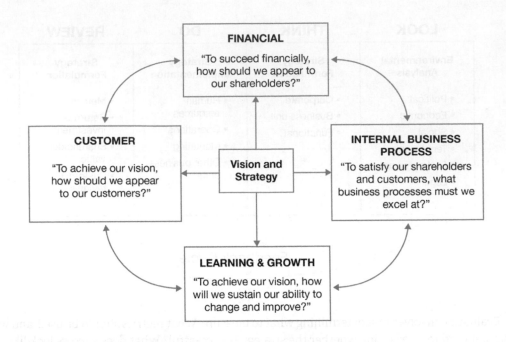

 Human Resource Strategy and Planning

The strategy an organization follows is its plan for how to compete successfully, survive, and grow. Strategic HR management refers to the appropriate use of HR management practices to gain or keep a competitive advantage.

View the video online at: http://www.youtube.com/embed/8mwCiDKgNd4?rel=0

Financial Perspective

The financial perspective views organizational performance in terms of the use of financial resources. Such measures indicate whether the company's strategy, implementation, and execution are contributing to bottom-line improvement. Typical financial goals include profitability, growth, and shareholder value. Periodic financial statements remind managers that improved quality, response time, productivity, and innovative products benefit the firm only when they result in improved service, increased market share, reduced operating expenses, or higher asset turnover. This category is often referred to as stewardship in the public sector.

Customer Perspective

This aspect views organizational performance from the perspective of the customer or other stakeholders the organization exists to serve. Managers must translate their general mission statements on customer service into specific measures that reflect the factors that really matter to customers. There are four primary categories of customer concerns: time, quality, performance and service, and cost.

Internal Business Process

This perspective views organizational performance through the lenses of product or service quality and efficiency. Customer-based measures are important. However, they must be translated into indicators of what the firm must do internally to meet customers' expectations. The internal measures should reflect business processes that have the greatest impact on customer satisfaction. This includes factors such as cycle time, quality, employee skills, and productivity.

Learning and Growth

This perspective views organizational performance in terms of how effectively the organization's capacities and resources are being utilized. The perspective includes the use of human capital, technology, infrastructure, and culture. Given the rapid rate of change in markets, technologies, and global competition, the criteria for success are constantly changing. Accordingly, a firm's ability to improve, innovate, and learn ties directly to its value. That is, only by developing new products and services, creating greater value for customers, and increasing operating efficiencies, can a company penetrate new markets, increase revenues, and grow shareholder value.

Key Takeaways

- A strategy is a long-term plan for how to gain competitive advantage, while tactics are the short-term actions that are taken to accomplish that strategy.
- A mission statement is a short statement of an organization's purpose. It might identify the customer, product or service, and its geographic area. A vision statement identifies what a company would like to achieve or accomplish.
- A values statement indicates the core beliefs and values of an organization.
- Strategic planning has four distinct stages: environmental analysis, strategy formulation, strategy implementation, and evaluation.

2.3 Aligning HR with Strategy

Learning Objectives

1. Describe how HR policies and practices can help to support the success of a low-cost business strategy.
2. Describe how HR policies and practices can help to support the success of a differentiation business strategy.
3. Describe how HR policies and practices can help to support the success of a combination business strategy.

When most people hear the term business strategy, what comes to mind is how a company competes or what gives them a competitive advantage. How do the price, quality, selection, or service differ from their competitors? This is the essence of business-level strategy. In this section, we will explore some of the major types of strategies that organizations choose and some examples of each, and then we will examine how HR functional-level strategy can support the overall business strategy. For example, we will see how the type of employees that HR managers should recruit will differ depending on the business strategy. Training, compensation, and performance management approaches may also differ. The actions of HR have a tremendous impact on the success of the strategy. For this reason, it is critical that HR managers understand the organization's strategy.[15] In short, when HR managers are making decisions about any HR activity, they should have the business strategy in mind.

HR professionals should have a thorough understanding of the how their business competes and which talent strategies are necessary to help the business succeed.

Michael Porter of Harvard University developed five generic strategies that firms can use to attain competitive advantage. The first, overall cost leadership, is based on creating a low-cost position relative to one's peers. The second, differentiation, requires that the firm create products and/or services that are unique and valued. In the third and fourth strategies, firms following a focused strategy must direct their attention toward narrow product lines, buyer groups, or geographical markets. Finally, the fifth strategy is a combination of cost leadership and differentiation.

Source: © Shutterstock, Inc.

Cost Leadership

Cost leadership requires a set of interrelated tactics such as aggressive construction of efficient-scale facilities, vigorous pursuit of cost reductions from experience, and cost and overhead control in all activities in a firm's value chain. To be successful with this strategy, a firm must be more efficient than its competitors, primarily through operating at a lower cost. Companies that implement a low-cost strategy are competing on price. They will not make very much profit on any individual unit sold, but they make it up in volume. From a marketing perspective, this is known as a market penetration strategy. HR can align with low-cost strategy by lowering the cost per hire, shortening the time to competency, and lowering employee turnover.

Differentiation

As the name implies, differentiation consists of creating differences in the firm's products or service offerings by creating something that is perceived by customers as being unique. Differentiation can take many forms such as prestige or brand image, technology, innovation, features, customer service, or dealer networks. Companies that implement a differentiation strategy are competing on uniqueness and generally charge a premium price. They will make more profit on each individual unit sold, but they will not sell as many units as a low-cost leader. From a marketing perspective, this is known as market skimming strategy. HR can support a differentiation strategy by hiring employees who are creative and customer-service oriented. The talent development aspect of HR is also crucial in supporting a differentiation strategy.

Focused Strategies

Focused strategies are based on the choice of a narrow competitive scope within an industry. A company following a focused strategy attains competitive advantages by dedicating itself to a segment of the market (also called a market niche) and tailors the product or service to the customer. There are two types of focused strategies: focused low-cost and focused differentiation. The sporting goods industry provides a good example. If you enjoy camping and are shopping for a tent, sleeping bags, and other supplies, you have many retail options. Walmart will offer a low price, in keeping with their strategy as a low-cost leader. You could also shop at Academy Sports, which usually matches Walmart on price, but has a better selection because they only carry sporting goods. Thus, Academy Sports utilizes a focused low-cost strategy. You might also go to Cabela's or Bass Pro Shops. You will pay more for the products there, partly because they tend to carry better quality products, but also because they are selling an experience (with a cafe, interactive activities, etc.) in addition to just the products. Cabela's and Bass Pro Shops are implementing focused differentiation strategies. HR can align with these strategies in similar ways as stated for the low-cost and differentiation strategies. HR can also contribute to a focused strategy by hiring employees with knowledge of the product and that the customer will relate to (for example, Bass Pro Shops could hire people with significant experience in fishing).

Combination Strategies

In the 1980s, Michael Porter originally posited four strategic possibilities: cost leadership, differentiation, focused-cost leadership, and focused-differentiation. He advised against combining the strategies because they seemed to be at odds with each other. For example, differentiating the product or service can be expensive, and if the company also tries to compete on price, then it could be difficult to be profitable. However, in the last two decades, technology advances have made it possible for some industries to differentiate (especially regarding offering customized shopping options), while still competing on price. Dell Computers was one of the first companies to prove that a combination strategy is feasible. There has been a great deal of evidence—both in observation of business practice as well as in research studies—about the strategic benefits of competitive positioning and performance implications that are inherent in combining generic strategies. Subsequently, Michael Porter has added a fifth strategy: combination (or also sometimes referred to as integration). In addition, the key benefit to be enjoyed by firms that successfully integrate cost leadership and differentiation strategies is that it is generally harder for competitors to duplicate or imitate them.

HR Talk: Bruce Waller CHR, PHR, SHRM-CP

Vice President, Corporate Relocation

Armstrong Relocation and Companies

Every organization should start with strategy. Armstrong Relocation and Companies' strategy continues to build around the vision, mission, and "DNA" principles using a "We Care" approach for alignment. This is the strategy we use to focus on performance to achieve enterprise goals. Our principles include seven DNA elements that every employee learns when entering the organization:

- Unity—We are stronger together
- Integrity—Do the right thing
- Attitude—Be positively passionate
- Value—Customers define it, we deliver it
- Relationships—We value them above all
- Communication—Listen, learn, and respond
- Generosity—Succeed and share

It's important for HR to be aligned with these elements as we use them for decision-making inside and outside of the organization every day. For example, when a move gets off track, we use integrity to do the right thing for the customer and the organization. Alignment and choices are easier for HR when the values and vision are clear. Alignment in foundational values, performance expectations, and financial rewards gives us a real advantage in our industry. Another advantage is not only in selecting the right team members, but also in selecting the right clients with which to partner.

I once heard our chairman of the board say, "If the people in the home aren't happy, then nobody is happy." There is a lot of truth to this statement. The moving experience is critical and takes a team to have success. A team of experienced professionals all moving in the same direction with a common mission "to provide the highest value to our customers and stakeholders by building an organization of passionate team members working together to deliver excellence in quality, safety, and customer satisfaction." Recruiting, retaining, and rewarding talent is more informed when there is alignment in the enterprise. If HR is not aligned, it functions as more of an adversary, which is viewed as an inhibitor to the achievement of strategic goals or, at best, a necessary evil. Alignment creates opportunity for HR to make a positive impact on our customers—both internal and external—every day.

Key Takeaways

- Cost leadership requires a set of interrelated tactics such as aggressive construction of efficient-scale facilities, vigorous pursuit of cost reductions from experience, and cost and overhead control in all activities in a firm's value chain.
- Differentiation consists of creating differences in the firm's products or service offerings by creating something that is perceived industry-wide as being unique and valued by customers.
- In general, the key benefit to be enjoyed by firms that successfully integrate cost leadership and differentiation strategies is that it is generally harder for competitors to duplicate or imitate them.

What Do *You* Think?

1. When you shop, do you prefer brands that are low-cost, differentiated, or a combination strategy?
2. Which of the strategies discussed above would be the most negatively impacted by high employee turnover?
3. If you were the HR manager for a low-cost company, what steps would you take to align the HR policies and procedures to support the business strategy?
4. What are the advantages for HR professionals being able to discuss business strategy with their colleagues?

2.4 Workforce Planning

Learning Objectives

1. Explain the benefits of workforce planning activities.
2. Compare and contrast quantitative and qualitative methods for forecasting labor demand.
3. Describe the techniques for forecasting the internal and external labor supply.
4. Discuss the options that a firm can choose from to respond to a labor shortage.
5. Discuss the options that a firm can choose from to respond to a labor surplus.

One of the most important ways in which HR can align with the organizational strategy is by ensuring that the right number of workers with the right skills are available at the right time. **Workforce planning** is the process of forecasting talent demand and supply and determining the action plans necessary to align talent availability with organizational objectives. In Chapter 1, human capital was discussed as one of the most important assets of any organization. However, despite its importance, many organizations are not aware of current or future talent gaps that will limit execution of business strategy.[16] CEOs and chief human resource officers frequently state that workforce planning and data-driven decision-making are top priorities for their organization. Despite the importance assigned to workforce planning, it is an often-overlooked aspect of HRM. This is partly because managers find it difficult to set aside time for planning because they are so busy with the day-to-day HR activities. In addition to time, another barrier to workforce planning is a lack of familiarity with the predictive analytical techniques used to prepare forecasts. Fortu-

workforce planning

The process of forecasting talent demand and supply, and determining the action plans necessary to align talent availability with organizational objectives.

nately, recent advances in talent analytics are making the forecasting process easier. An overview of a typical workforce planning process is shown in Figure 2.3.

FIGURE 2.3 The Workforce Planning Cycle

Workforce planning activities can result in the following benefits: [17]

- Aligns strategic planning with headcount and talent planning.
- Creates a clear view of talent demand and supply issues by expense area, reporting relationship, and location.
- Provides managers easy-to-use reports and tools to determine the impact of their talent decisions and prioritizes future workforce investments.
- Provides leaders the right metrics—identifying talent risk before it impacts business objectives.
- Helps control unplanned talent costs and highlights issues that limit employee productivity.
- Builds competitive advantage through planned versus reactive talent management.
- Gives business leaders consistent reporting results to quantify measurable and meaningful outcomes.

Forecasting Labor Demand

Workforce planning begins with forecasting labor demand. This should include the number of workers needed for each job position in the future. In addition to conducting an analysis by type of job, the planning process should also focus on required skillsets.

The data-gathering and analysis process can be considered as two broad categories. One approach is **qualitative analysis**. This is the use of non-numerical methods to forecast the future, based on information gathered from individuals or groups of people with knowledge of the field. Qualitative methods include surveys, interviews, and focus groups. Participants in the qualitative studies should include senior management, middle management, and front-line supervisors, in addition to industry experts. One important type of data that is gathered is revenue projections. A limitation of qualitative forecasting is that it is often inaccurate. It is important to remember that a forecast is just an educated guess about the future, and few forecasts are ever entirely accurate. According to Peter Cappelli, a researcher of workforce planning, the error rate in the U.S. on a one-year forecast of demand at the stock keeping unit (SKU) code or individual product level is over 30%.[18] This gives rise to the question: If forecasts are never accurate, then why do them at all? It may be helpful to compare this process to a weather forecast. A weather forecast is often wrong, but it is usually close. This helps people to dress accordingly and to plan events around the weather. A weather forecast helps you to plan for the contingencies that *may* happen. So, while it may not actually rain tomorrow, the fact that rain is in the forecast can help you be prepared for that contingency by taking an umbrella with you.

Another limitation of qualitative forecasting is that it is subjective, and often based on people's opinions or gut-feel. One technique for addressing this limitation is the Delphi method, a forecasting method based on the results of several rounds of questionnaires. RAND originally developed the Delphi method in the 1950s to forecast the impact of technology on warfare.[19] The method entails a group of experts who anonymously reply to questionnaires. Subsequently, each participant receives feedback in the form of statistical representation of the aggregated group response, and then the process is repeated. The method has been widely adopted in qualitative research, as it facilitates a group of experts in arriving at a consensus.[20]

During qualitative forecasting, questions should be asked of the participants that relate to the corporate- and business-level strategies and anticipated changes. For example, if a company is planning on a growth strategy, then they need to staff up. If the strategic plan calls for a retrenchment strategy, then they will need to reduce staff. If the business-level strategy requires introducing a new technology, then there may be a need to skill-up the workforce. This could be accomplished by training existing workers or by hiring new employees with the desired skillsets.

The other major type of data gathering is **quantitative analysis**. This is the use of mathematical techniques to forecast future events based on historical data. The three most common quantitative techniques of forecasting labor demand are trend analysis, ratio analysis, and regression analysis.[21]

Trend analysis is the process of projecting future demand based on historical data correlated to a specific business factor. A common factor used in HR trend analysis is to compare past revenue with the number of employees required to operate at various revenue levels.

qualitative analysis

The use of non-numerical methods to forecast the future, based on information gathered from individuals or groups of people with knowledge of the field.

quantitative analysis

The use of mathematical techniques to forecast future events based on historical data.

trend analysis

The process of projecting future demand based on historical data correlated to a specific business factor.

ratio analysis

The process of projecting future demand based on calculating the relationship between a specific business factor and the number of employees needed, and expressing the relationship as a ratio.

Ratio analysis is the process of projecting future demand based on calculating the relationship between a specific business factor and the number of employees needed and expressing the relationship as a ratio. For example, assume that in a trucking company the ratio of employees to revenue is 75,000:1. Another way of expressing this is to say that the company historically needs one employee for every $75,000 in revenue. Therefore, for every projected $75,000 increase in revenue of $75,000, the company will need to hire one new employee. A second ratio example is the relationship between truck drivers needed and tonnage hauled (or pounds of freight hauled per year). If the ratio is 8,000,000 pounds of tonnage per driver, then one driver is needed for every 8,000,000 pounds of freight. If tonnage is expected to increase by 56,000,000 pounds per year for the next three years, then the company needs to plan on hiring seven new drivers each year. This is in addition to any new hires that may be needed as the result of attrition, which is discussed in the next section of this chapter.

regression analysis

A statistical technique for estimating the relationship between a dependent variable and one or more independent variables.

Regression analysis is a statistical technique for estimating the relationship between a dependent variable and one or more independent variables. Regression analysis is conducted by statistical software, and most HRIS packages include the capability to conduct both regression analysis and ratio analysis. For regression analysis, the software first creates a scatter diagram, and then a regression line is calculated.

Talent Analytics: Workforce Forecasting

 Workforce Forecasting

Through the process of forecasting future labor requirements, we make determinations—based on both qualitative and quantitative information—of what types of jobs and how many of each type we will need to fill over a particular period of time.

View the video online at: //www.youtube.com/embed/C3ZucdY_ifl?rel=0

Forecasting Labor Supply

Estimating the demand for workers is just one side of the equation. We next turn our attention to where the workers will come from, also known as the supply of labor. The supply of labor can be divided into two aspects: internal supply and external supply. Internal supply refers to filling the need for workers through the talent that already works for the organization. Which positions might be filled from our existing talent pool by promoting or transferring from within, or through recall of laid-off workers? External supply refers to the pool of talent from which new workers can be recruited.

Employee turnover is a key metric to analyze to better predict the labor supply. While it may be difficult to predict whether any one individual will stay with an organization, aggregate data can accurately predict overall turnover, along with the reasons why people leave.

Source: © Shutterstock, Inc.

Internal Supply

The process of evaluating the internal supply of talent can be considered from a quantitative and qualitative perspective. From a quantitative perspective, talent supply is evaluated after considering **attrition**, which is the reduction in the workforce that occurs as a result of turnover, retirements, or death. **Turnover** refers to individuals who leave the company and are replaced. It includes voluntary turnover (individuals who quit their jobs) and involuntary (individuals who are fired). From a qualitative perspective, it is important to also consider the capability and performance of the talent supply.[22]

One of the most important aspects of forecasting internal supply is to understand the amount of employee turnover and the factors that cause it. Knowing which individuals are at the highest risk for turnover provides an organization the lead time to address future workforce gaps with minimal disruption to the business and enables the following outcomes:

- Creation of targeted replacement planning and knowledge transfer for critical roles.
- Understanding which talent gaps are largest, highest priority, and/or most difficult to fill internally.
- Proactive sourcing by the recruiting function based on prioritization of gaps.
- Creation of a road map of future open positions that can be filled through promotions and developmental assignments.
- Managed attrition programs for jobs that have a reduced staffing requirement in the future.[23]

Employee turnover can be expressed as a mathematical calculation called the turnover rate. This is the rate at which employees leave the company and are replaced. Turnover is usually calculated on an annual basis. "Calculating Turnover" shows the formula for calculating turnover along with an example.

attrition

The reduction in the workforce that occurs as a result of turnover, retirements, or death.

turnover

Individuals who leave the company and are replaced. It includes voluntary turnover (individuals who quit their jobs) and involuntary (individuals who are fired).

Calculating Turnover

EQUATION 2.1 Formula for Calculating Turnover

$$\frac{\text{Number of Employee Separations during a Period of Time}}{\text{Average Number of Employees during a Period of Time}} \times 100$$

Example:

Adrenaline Mountain Tours operates hiking, zip line, and rafting trips. At the beginning of the year, they employed 215 individuals, and at the end of the year, they employed 235. There were 45 employee separations during the year.

$$\frac{45}{(215 + 235/2)} = \frac{45}{225} = 20\% \text{ Annual Turnover Rate}$$

Employee turnover hit an all-time high in the United States of 19.3% in 2018.[24] This means that for every 100 employees, 19.3 of them quit and had to be replaced. The industries with the highest turnover are hospitality (31.8%), healthcare (20.4%), and manufacturing/distribution (20%).[25] In contract, the industries with the lowest turnover were banking/finance (16.7%), insurance (12.8%), and utilities (10.3%).[26] The underlying causes of employee turnover, and strategies to retain employees, are explored in depth in Chapter 11 on employee engagement.

External Supply

unemployment rate

The percentage of people who are not currently employed and are actively seeking employment.

The external supply of workers is heavily influenced by economic and demographic trends in the labor market. One of the most significant factors that impacts a firm's ability to recruit new employees is the unemployment rate. The **unemployment rate** is the percentage of people who are not currently employed and are actively seeking employment. In February of 2020, the unemployment rate in the United States was at 3.5%, one of the lowest on record.[27] For the first time in the United States, there were more jobs available than there were people seeking jobs. This created an employee's market, in which it is easier for people to change jobs. Since qualified recruits are in high demand in many industries, they have more leverage to negotiate for better job offers. Even though unemployment rates rose rapidly as a result of the COVID-19 pandemic, many economic indicators continue to point towards a long term skills shortage.

Other economic conditions, such as the rate of growth in the economy, greatly influence the external supply of workers. The supply is also impacted by demographics (such as the age of the workforce and the number of people retiring), literacy rates, educational levels, and the skills and qualifications of job seekers.

succession analysis

The process of identifying the current staffing level and projected inflows and outflows of employees during a given forecast period, which is often one year.

Two of the most important tools for forecasting the talent supply are succession analysis and Markov analysis.[28] **Succession analysis** is the process of identifying the current staffing level and projected inflows and outflows of employees during a given forecast period, which is often one year. Sources of inflows are transfers, promotions, new hires, and recalls. Sources of outflows are transfers, promotions, resignations, discharges, demotions, retirements, deaths, and layoffs.

A **Markov analysis** is also referred to as a transition matrix and is named after the Russian mathematician Andrei Andreyevich Markov. The matrix shows the probabilities of employees remaining in their jobs during the forecast period and also displays the average rate of historical movement from one job to another. Table 2.2 below shows a simple transition matrix for a line worker, a supervisor, and a manager in a manufacturing company. In this example, there is a 20% probability of a line worker leaving the company in the next year. Of the remaining 80%, there is a 5% chance of being promoted to a supervisor, and a 75% chance of remaining in the line worker job. The column labeled (4) represents separated employees.

TABLE 2.2 Markov Analysis Example
Markov Analysis for 2021

2020	2021			
	(1)	**(2)**	**(3)**	**(4)**
(1) Line Worker	.75	.05		.2
(2) Supervisor		.90	.05	.05
(3) Manager			.90	.1

A **skills inventory** is another useful tool for understanding and analyzing the labor supply. A skills inventory is a searchable list of the knowledge, skills, abilities, and qualifications of the workforce. It is used to identify suitable candidates for internal recruitment or promotion and to identify skills gaps so that proactive steps can be taken to fill these gaps before they become critical.

Few organizations today have a system in place for tracking the skills they have, and even fewer apply that knowledge to gauge what skills they lack, both now and in the future.[29] Building a skills inventory involves first identifying all of the employees by position, tenure, and employment status (full-time or part-time). Knowledge, education levels, skills, abilities, and credentials (such as industry-approved certificates) should be included. It is important to also categorize the level of each skill (beginner, intermediate, advanced, and expert). The inventory must be searchable to be useful in labor forecasting. For example, if a bank plans to expand its real estate lending division, then they could search the skills inventory to find out how many existing employees already have some background and expertise in real estate. This will identify whether a skills gap exists, so that the company can develop a plan to obtain the necessary skills, whether through internal training or external recruitment.

Markov analysis

Also referred to as a transition matrix and is named after the Russian mathematician Andrei Andreyevich Markov. The matrix shows the probabilities of employees remaining in their jobs during the forecast period and also displays the average rate of historical movement from one job to another.

skills inventory

A searchable list of the knowledge, skills, abilities, and qualifications of the workforce, used to identify suitable candidates for internal recruitment or promotion, and to identify skills gaps so that proactive steps can be taken to fill these gaps before they become critical.

Options for a Labor Shortage

After forecasting the demand and supply of workers, a company may find that they expect to have a shortage of workers. In this case, they can choose from the following approaches:

- Hire new full-time or part-time workers
- Hire temporary workers
- Offer overtime to existing workers
- Utilize independent contractors instead of hiring employees

A firm may also find that while the overall number of employees is adequate, they are facing a skills gap. In this situation, the company can consider training existing employees to fill the need or replacing current employees with more qualified individuals. They may also wish to be proactive by collaborating with other organizations, including businesses, educational institutions, and government, to develop a pipeline of future talent.

For example, demographics pose a challenge to the workforce pipeline. Businesses are facing a situation wherein older, highly skilled workers are retiring, and the pool of replacement workers is both smaller and generally less qualified.[30] For example, 5.4 million of all healthcare jobs are in middle-skill positions, and 40% of the individuals currently employed in these occupations are forty-five years or older, thus the looming retirements of baby boomers will exacerbate the worker shortage.[31] Decreased birthrates have slowed growth in the prime working-age group of twenty-five- to fifty-four-year olds, and baby boomers have begun a massive wave of retirements.[32]

In the skilled trades sector, 21% of workers are fifty-five or older, and 29% are forty-five to fifty-four.[33] Today, the average age of a welder in the United States is fifty-five, and he or she is likely to retire within ten years. Accounting for these retirements and the current talent pipeline, the American Welding Society predicts a shortage of 290,000 welding professionals.[34]

Workforce development best practices suggest that companies and regions manage their workforce pipelines like they manage their supply chains. This means investing in workforce planning and creating roadmaps for closing existing gaps. A supply chain approach to workforce development should be based on collaboration between educators, employers, economic development agencies, and workforce entities.

Options for a Labor Surplus

A labor forecast might indicate that the company has more employees on the payroll than is necessary to meet the expected volume of business. In this situation, a labor surplus exists and the company will need to reduce the size of the workforce. The following approaches can be implemented to deal with a labor surplus:

- Reduction in force or RIF (permanently eliminating positions).
- Temporary layoffs (temporarily eliminating positions but keeping the employees available for recall when business demand improves).
- Furloughs (temporarily suspending position without pay, but benefits often continue).
- Early retirement programs/buyouts (offering incentives to encourage older workers to retire early).
- Reduction in hours worked per employee (keeping the same number of employees on the payroll, but each works fewer hours per pay period).
- Wage rate reductions (keeping the number of employees and hours worked the same, but reducing overall payroll by lowering the hourly wage rate).
- Hiring freezes (reducing payroll through attrition; as employees leave the company for various reasons, they are not replaced).

It is important that HR managers be cognizant of relevant federal laws that govern reductions in force, particularly at larger facilities. For example, the Worker Adjustment and Retraining Notification Act (WARN) protects workers, their families, and communities by requiring employers with one hundred or more employees (not counting those who have worked less than six months in the last twelve months and those who work an average of fewer than twenty hours a week) to provide at least sixty calendar days advance written notice of a plant closing or mass layoffs affecting fifty or more employees at a single site of employment.[35] WARN provides for exceptions when layoffs are due to unforeseeable business circumstances, faltering companies, and natural disasters. Employees entitled to notice under WARN include hourly and salaried workers, as well as managers and supervisors. Some states also have laws that regulate plant closings and layoffs.

It is important to distinguish between layoffs and furloughs. In a layoff, employees are terminated but kept available for recall if the business needs to add positions again. The affected employees are usually not paid and do not receive any benefits. A furlough is normally for an event of short duration, in which employees are suspended without pay, but benefits such as health insurance normally continue. Furloughs are often associated with government shutdowns due to budgets, and last only days or weeks. But some businesses such as Eaton, AMP, and Honeywell used furloughs instead of layoffs during the financial crisis of 2008–2009. Many more companies implemented furloughs in 2020 due to the COVID-19 crisis.

While employees would prefer a furlough to a layoff because they maintain their benefits until recalled, the employees still have to face the financial challenge of paying their bills without a paycheck. Research indicates there are also psychological challenges such as emotional exhaustion associated with furloughs.[36] When implementing a furlough, the following steps can help to alleviate some of the employees' concerns:[37]

- Be transparent. Share data regarding how much business demand has dropped, and emphasize that the furlough is necessary for the business to survive.
- Provide clarify around benefits. Access to healthcare is especially important to employees' well-being during a global pandemic such as COVID-19.
- Do not allow furloughed employees to conduct any work, including answering work-related emails or calls during the furlough. This is required to comply with compensation laws and avoid potential claims for unpaid work.
- Communicate updates and provide mental and emotional support. Provide regular updates on the evolving business situation. Employees need to feel that they have not been forgotten and that they still are important to the organization.

HR in the Real World: Sleepless Nights

One of the most difficult situations that a manager has to face is a labor surplus, which requires difficult decisions to be made. Various events might lead to this, for example a loss of major customers, a recession, or new competitors taking market share. One of the hardest things that a manager has to do is to terminate people under any circumstances, but it is especially gut-wrenching when the employees have been performing well and are being terminated through no fault of their own. But this is sometimes a business reality.

My hardest times as a manager were the nights before I had to let someone go. I didn't sleep much those nights, and my stomach was in knots. So how do you handle these situations? The best approach is to make sure you are utilizing talent analytics to monitor the numbers of employees in each job category and compare this to revenue projections. By watching the trends, one can often identify labor surpluses early enough to be implement other actions, such as early retirements, to reduce the size of the workforce without eliminating permanent employees. But even then, occasions may arise when a reduction in force (RIF) has to be implemented immediately. When this occurs, try to make the transition as smooth as possible for the affected employees by offering severance pay, job search assistance, and access to coaching or counseling through an employee assistance program. Another option is to offer to pay for a retraining program if the employee was being replaced due to automation. Making a concerted effort to help each terminated employee to land on their feet can help you sleep better at night, and it's just the right thing to do!

Key Takeaways

- Workforce planning (or human resource planning) is the process of forecasting talent demand and supply, and determining the action plans necessary to align talent availability with organizational objectives.
- Qualitative analysis is the use of non-numerical methods to forecast the future, based on information gathered from individuals or groups of people with knowledge of the field.
- Qualitative methods include surveys, interviews, and focus groups.
- The three most common quantitative techniques of forecasting labor demand are trend analysis, ratio analysis, and regression analysis.
- Trend analysis is the process of projecting future demand based on historical data correlated to a specific business factor.

- Ratio analysis is the process of projecting future demand based on calculating the relationship between a specific business factor and the number of employees needed, and expressing the relationship as a ratio.
- Regression analysis is a statistical technique for estimating the relationship between a dependent variable and one or more independent variables.
- From a quantitative perspective, talent supply is evaluated after considering attrition, which is the reduction in the workforce that occurs as a result of turnover, retirements, or death.
- One of the most important aspects of forecasting internal supply is to understand the amount of employee turnover and the factors that cause it.
- The external supply of workers is heavily influenced by economic and demographic trends in the labor market, such as the unemployment rate.
- Succession analysis is the process of identifying the current staffing level and projected inflows and outflows of employees during a given forecast period, often one year.
- A Markov analysis (also referred to as a transition matrix) shows the probabilities of job incumbents remaining in their jobs during the forecast period, and also displays the average rate of historical movement from one job to another.
- A skills inventory is a searchable list of the knowledge, skills, abilities, and qualifications of the workforce, and is used to identify suitable candidates for internal recruitment or promotion and to identify skills gaps, so that proactive steps can be taken to fill these gaps before they become critical.
- After forecasting the demand or supply of workers, a company may find that they expect to have a shortage of workers. In this case, they can choose from the following approaches: hire new full-time or part-time workers, hire temporary workers, or utilize independent contractors instead of hiring employees.
- When a labor forecast indicates an expected surplus of workers, a company can implement downsizing, temporary layoffs/furloughs, early retirement programs/buyouts, reduction in hours worked per employee, wage rate reductions, or hiring freezes (reducing payroll through attrition).

What Do *You* Think?

1. When you make decisions, what is your natural decision-making style? Are you using analytics (gathering data and analyzing it), or do you rely more on your gut feel?
2. How important is taking statistics courses (and learning regression analysis, for example) for future HR managers?
3. Think about a company that you have worked for. When people quit working there, what were the most common reasons for leaving?
4. How can you use the networking connections you are making in college (students, faculty, organizations, and associations) to help with recruiting employees in the future?
5. How do HR managers handle the emotional aspects of having to implement a reduction in force and knowing that they are putting people out of work?

2.5 Introduction to Talent Analytics

Learning Objectives

1. Explain how metrics are used to identify the impact of HRM on the bottom line of a firm.

2. Choose appropriate HRM metrics to track using the "CARE" acronym.
3. Describe how HR dashboards and benchmarking are used to make informed and data-driven decisions about the workforce.

Financial Impacts of HRM

Does HRM impact the bottom line of a firm? The answer is of course, but a better question might be: How does HRM impact the bottom line? What is your first response to this question? You might think of the cost of recruiting and onboarding new employees, the cost of administering payroll, and the cost of employee benefits such as health insurance. But there are many other financial impacts of HRM. The role of HR professionals is drastically changing as technology automates many of the more mundane aspects of HR, such as tracking hours, computing pay, direct deposits, payroll taxes, reviewing applications, scheduling interviews, etc.

One example is how computer-based applicant tracking systems now conduct the initial applicant screening. By leveraging available technologies, HR leaders can be free to focus more of their time on strategic activities, such as being a workforce advisor, anticipating and preparing for changes in the workforce, coaching and developing employees, and analyzing how HRM can improve the bottom line. HR professionals need to have the same level of business acumen as other leaders in the organization. This means more than just knowing how to read a profit and loss statement or balance sheet. HR professionals need to understand the strategic direction of the business and the economic and social environments in which the firm operates, and align HR initiatives with organizational goals.[38]

Let's go back to the question about how HRM impacts the bottom line. One way that firms determine this is by tracking various metrics. A **metric** is a standard of measurement by which efficiency, performance, progress, or quality of a plan, product, or process can be assessed. Table 2.3 contains a list of the some of the most commonly tracked HR metrics.

metric

A standard of measurement by which efficiency, performance, progress, or quality of a plan, product, or process can be assessed.

TABLE 2.3 Most Commonly Used HR Metrics

HR Metrics	
Metric	**Definition**
Time to Hire	The number of days from the moment a vacancy opens until the new employee is hired. For revenue-generating employees, this metric should also be reported in terms of revenue lost due to vacancy days.
Cost to Hire	The total cost of hiring someone, including ad placement, sourcing costs, and time invested by HR and hiring managers.
Time to Competency	The length of time from the first day of employment until the new hire is at full productivity.
Training Spend	The number of days spent in training annually or the total annual investment in training per employee.
Exit Interviews	Standardized exit interviews that yield quantitative data (exit interviews often have open-ended questions, which yield valuable qualitative data, but these are not metrics).
Talent Distribution	Hiring, promotions, and salary by demographic variables such as age, gender, race, etc.
Employee Turnover	The percentage of employees who leave the company in a given time period.
New Hire Turnover	The percentage of new hires who do not complete their 90-day probationary period or their first year of employment.

HR Metrics	
High- and Low-Performer Turnover	The percentage of high- and low-performing individuals who leave the company.
Revenue Per Employee	Total yearly revenue divided by the average number of full-time employees.
Quality of Hire Improvement	Based on the productivity level of new hires.
Lost Time	Lost time due to sickness or injury, and reported in percent of time or dollar cost.

 HR Metrics

This video explores human resource metrics by identifying how to use metrics and then understanding what metrics to use, and how to use metrics strategically to solve organizational problems.

View the video online at: http://www.youtube.com/embed/F7t0EFXXHgE?rel=0

Competing on Talent Analytics

Now that we have looked at some of the key metrics that apply to HR activities, let's distinguish between metrics and analytics, as they are not the same thing. A metric is simply a measurement. By itself, the measurement is pretty meaningless. It only becomes useful when the number is used to inform decision-making, and that is where analytics comes into play.

It is also important to keep in mind that talent analytics is only as good as the reliability of the data upon which it is based. Other factors to consider in implementing a talent analytics system are the cost of implementation and the consistency with which it is measured. In his book *Strategic Analytics: Advancing Strategy Execution and Organizational Effectiveness*, Alec Robert Levenson summarized these criteria for choosing which metrics to track, using the acronym "CARE":

- Consistent—The data underlying the metric must be measured steadily over time.
- Accurate—Information should be precise, with few to no errors in recording it.
- Reliable—Your metrics must be a dependable proxy of what you're ultimately trying to assess.
- Efficient—The cost of collecting data must be minimal.[39]

Once metrics have been chosen and tracked over time, then the valuable work of analytics can begin. Metrics simply tell you "what" is going on using some quantifiable way to measure it. They don't tell you anything about the "why." For example, if employee turnover is on the rise, then the metric tells you that. But it does not tell you why turnover is increasing. It could be that employees are leaving for better pay or more job security, better hours, or a host of other reasons. Once you understand the why, then you are in a better position to devise a strategy for addressing the underlying problem. In this case, the employee turnover metric is not the problem. It is a symptom of a problem, and analytics should address the underlying problem, not the symptom.

Another important aspect of talent analytics is its usefulness in identifying problems early on and in predicting trends that the company should be preparing for. Metrics alone is reactive, because you are tracking historical data and examining what just happened. The real value in analytics is in using the metrics to predict what is about to happen, so that the company operations are not disrupted. Alexis Fink, director of talent intelligence analytics at Intel, puts it this way: "Most people use data the way drunks use lampposts: for support rather than illumination."[40] She adds that HR should focus less on responding to decisions that have been made and more on training executives "to come to you further upstream, to influence the decision."[41]

Many HRIS systems have built-in analytical capabilities. However, it is crucial to identify the most important metrics to track, based upon which can have the most strategic impact and help to improve organizational performance. Talent analytics technology is also changing rapidly. With smart investments in emerging technology such as artificial intelligence (AI) and predictive data, talent acquisition is poised to deliver increased value and improved organizational performance.[42]

HR Dashboards and Benchmarking

An organization can invest significant time and resources in tracking key HR and talent metrics, but if no one uses the data for decision-making, then this was a wasted effort. HR should take steps to streamline and automate the reporting processes, and this is where an HR dashboard can be helpful. An **HR dashboard** is a visual display of important HR metrics. It functions in much the same way as you would use an automobile dashboard. In your car, the dashboard shows real-time data, such as speed, engine temperature, and oil pressure. Most newer vehicles also have predictive displays, such as how many miles you can travel before you run out of gas. Thus, the vehicle dashboard helps you make informed decisions, such as when to stop for fuel. Likewise, an HR dashboard provides information for making informed decisions about the workforce.

> **HR dashboard**
>
> A visual display of important HR metrics.

An HR dashboard should provide three key benefits:

- HR monitoring. Regular reporting enables HR and managers to keep a finger on the pulse of the organization's workforce activities. New trends and opportunities can be identified early on and addressed before they become disruptive.

- Management information. The HR dashboard can help managers in doing their job better. For example, if a department is experiencing an increase in turnover and a longer time-to-hire, then managers may decide to focus on retention efforts to avoid the lost revenue that occurs due to vacancies.

- Tracking problem areas with transparency. For example, if turnover rates are shared department- and company-wide, then managers will pay closer attention to retention because their reputation, and that of their department, is on the line.[43]

HR should not expect managers outside of HR to learn to sort and analyze the information in an HR dashboard. Therefore, HR staff should repackage it for the consumption and use of management and executive teams.[44] Figure 2.4 is an example of an HR dashboard report.

FIGURE 2.4 HR Dashboard Example

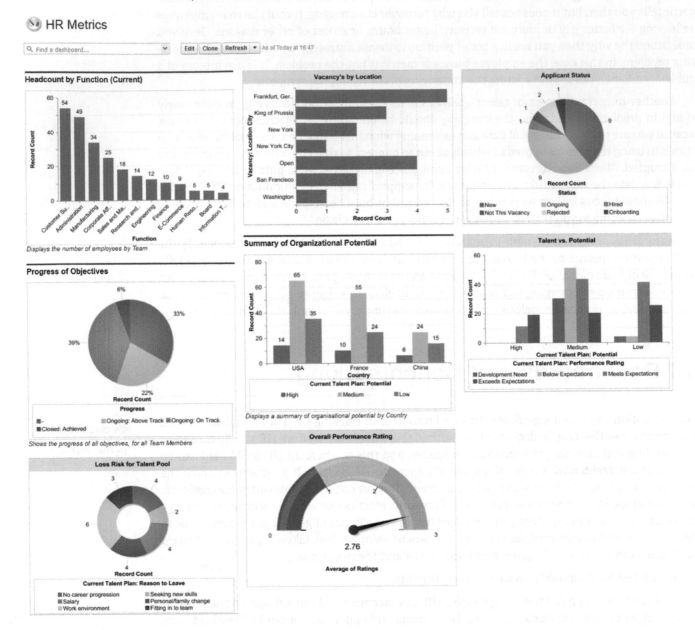

benchmarking

The process of comparing organizational performance and practices to industry averages and to best-in-class performance (industry leaders).

One final consideration in talent analytics is the role that benchmarking plays in using data. **Benchmarking** is the process of comparing organizational performance and practices to industry averages and to best-in-class performance (industry leaders). Without benchmarking, an organization has no idea of how it compares to other firms in the same or similar industries. Data should be analyzed from three perspectives:

- Trends over time. Is a particular metric improving or getting worse?
- Comparison to a baseline. This involves establishing a performance target and then measuring whether the operating results are on target.
- Comparison to industry leaders or industry averages. The approach indicates how well an organization is performing relative to its competitors.

Industry benchmark reports are available from a variety of organizations, including industry trade associations. SHRM provides a benchmarking service, reporting on almost seven hundred benchmarks in human capital, healthcare, benefits prevalence, paid leave, and talent acquisition, from a database of over ten thousand organizations.[45] The resources at the end of this chapter include a list of other popular HR benchmarking resources.

Key Takeaways

- A metric is a standard of measurement by which efficiency, performance, progress, or quality of a plan, product, or process can be assessed.
- By leveraging available technologies, HR leaders can be freed to focus more of their time on strategic activities, such as being a workforce advisor, anticipating and preparing for changes in the workforce, coaching and developing employees, and analyzing how HRM can improve the bottom line.
- HR managers should choose metrics that are consistent, accurate, reliable, and efficient (CARE).
- In talent analytics, the numbers (metrics) tell a story, and analytics is used to understand what story the numbers are telling.
- Talent analytics are useful in identifying problems early on and in predicting trends that the company should be preparing for.
- An HR dashboard is a visual display of important HR metrics and should provide three key benefits: HR monitoring, management information, and tracking problem areas with transparency.
- Benchmarking is the process of comparing organizational performance and practices to industry averages and to best-in-class performance (industry leaders).

What Do *You* Think?

1. Of all the metrics listed in Table 2.3, which do you think will be most effective in getting the attention of senior management?
2. What is the difference between an HR dashboard and a benchmark?
3. Think of a problem that you have seen happen consistently at work. Is it a true problem, or is it a symptom of an underlying problem?
4. Of the three approaches to benchmarking (trends over time, comparison to a baseline, or comparison to industry leaders or industry averages), which do you think is the most useful?
5. How can talent analytics help you be more proactive and less reactive as an HR professional?

2.6 Conclusion

This chapter introduced strategic concepts such as mission, vision, values, and the four stages of strategic planning. Various approaches to achieving competitive advantage were explored, along with methods that HR functions can align with each strategy. Workforce planning techniques such as forecasting labor demand and supply were introduced, as well as ideas for how to handle labor shortages and surpluses. The chapter concluded with an introduction to talent analytics, with an emphasis on how data is used in workforce planning.

Theory-into-Practice (TIP) Exercises

1. Make a list of five companies that you are familiar with. For each company, write down the following:

   a. What is their business-level strategy (cost leadership, focus, or differentiation)?

   b. Does the workforce provide a strategic competitive advantage for the company? Why or why not?

   c. What specific actions should HR take to support the business strategy?

2. Read the Code of Ethics and Professional Responsibility for Human Resource Management (under Resources, Number 1). Interview an HR professional and ask them if they ever feel pressured to take any actions that would violate this code. Also, ask them for advice on how to handle these types of situations when they occur.

3. If you are employed, ask your HR department what metrics they track and how they benchmark them. (If you are not employed, then partner with a classmate who is employed for this exercise.) Next, use the benchmarking reports (under Resources 4–6) to identify how the company compares to the averages.

Case Study: Alexa...Run Payroll

Source: © Shutterstock, Inc.

A recent survey of business executives reveals that HR professionals increasingly are seen as reactive more than proactive. Only 11% of the CEOs polled rate their HR professionals as "good" at using analytics in areas such as forecasting the company's employment needs and identifying talent pipelines. This is down from 20% three years ago. Executives are sometimes reluctant to include HR in decision-making in regard to future business plans because of this.

Unfortunately, in many cases, companies are short staffed, and HR spends most of its time in the trenches and dealing with day-to-day employee issues instead of using analytics to anticipate future needs and devising strategies to meet those needs. There are tools HR professionals can utilize to become more proactive, even in small or understaffed companies.

These tools include Human Resource Information Systems (HRIS) and Applicant Tracking Systems (ATS). HR departments may want to use a digital assistant to serve as a virtual coach to answer repetitive employee questions (regarding payroll, tax withholding, retirement, benefits, etc.).

Companies can also utilize analytics in all HR operations including recruiting. Walmart is one company that is using a creative way to search for data analysts. Rather than advertise through traditional channels, they set a challenge on Kaggle, a crowdsourced analytics competition platform where data scientists apply their skills to whatever analytical problems companies submit. Those who impress at Walmart's data challenge are offered jobs on the Walmart analytics team. Nissan is using a racing video game to recruit new hires to become real racing drivers.

Employee morale can also be improved by using new technology. An example of this is what talent analytics company Humanyze is doing. It offers electronic badges that capture information from employee conversations as they go about their day, including the length of the conversation, the tone of voice involved, how often people interrupt, how well they show empathy, and so on. Using this technology, a major bank noticed that its top-performing call center workers were those who took breaks together and let off steam collectively. Based on this knowledge, the bank implemented group break policies. Performance improved by 23%, and stress levels dropped by 19%. HR representatives need to take the initiative and deliver results, which in turn will cause executives to view them differently.[46]

 Using Analytics to Measure Interactions in the Workplace

Dr. Ben Waber, Co-Founder and CEO of Humanyze, discusses how his company's wearable ID badges gather data on employee interactions, which can then be used to map internal networks and predict performance.

View the video online at: http://www.youtube.com/embed/XojhyhoRl7I?rel=0

Case Discussion Questions

1. In your experience, are most HR professionals reactive or proactive?
2. What are some methods that you might use to streamline day-to-day HR duties so that you can devote more time to strategic functions?
3. How would you feel about wearing the electronic badge used by Humanyze?
4. How can you make sure that you spend sufficient time being proactive and engaging in analysis and strategic thinking?

Resources

1. **Code of Ethics.** The SHRM Code of Ethics and Professional Responsibility for Human Resource Management.

   https://www.shrm.org/about-shrm/Pages/code-of-ethics.aspx

2. **A Guide to Strategic Workforce Planning.** Resources from AIHR Analytics including processes, examples, and templates.

   https://www.analyticsinhr.com/blog/strategic-workforce-planning/

3. **Strategic Planning Basics.** Resources from The Balanced Scorecard Institute, including articles, training, certification, and software.

   https://balancedscorecard.org/strategic-planning-basics/

4. **SHRM 2017 Human Capital Benchmarking Report.** A report of key findings on turnover rates, career path ratios, succession planning, and target bonuses.

   https://www.shrm.org/hr-today/trends-and-forecasting/research-and-surveys/Documents/2017-Human-Capital-Benchmarking.pdf

5. **SHRM 2017 Talent Acquisition Benchmarking Report.** A report of key findings on recruiting expenses, time-to-hire, cost per hire, quality of hire, and time-to-separation.

   https://www.shrm.org/hr-today/trends-and-forecasting/research-and-surveys/Documents/2017-Talent-Acquisition-Benchmarking.pdf

6. **SHRM Benchmarking Service.** SHRM provides a customized benchmarking service, reporting on almost seven hundred benchmarks in human capital, healthcare, benefits prevalence, paid leave, and talent acquisition, from a database of over ten thousand organizations.

   https://www.shrm.org/resourcesandtools/business-solutions/pages/benchmarking-service.aspx

Endnotes

1. Case written by Armstead, J. (2019). Adapted from Verasai, Anna (2018). The Southwest Airlines HR success story you'll want to read today. *The HR Digest*. Retrieved from https://www.thehrdigest.com/the-southwest-airlines-hr-success-story-youll-want-to-read-today/
2. Mitsakis, F. (2014). Human Resources (HR) as a strategic business partner: Value creation and risk reduction capacity. *International Journal of Human Resource Studies, 4*(1), 154.
3. Strategy. *Online Etymology Dictionary*. Retrieved January 15, 2020 https://www.etymonline.com/word/strategy
4. Heskett, J. (2013). How relevant is long-range strategic planning? *Harvard Business School Working Knowledge*. Retrieved from https://hbswk.hbs.edu/item/how-relevant-is-long-range-strategic-planning
5. John F. Kennedy. (1963). *Address in the Assembly Hall at Paulskirche in Frankfurt, Germany*. Retrieved January 15, 2020 from https://www.goodreads.com/quotes/159557-change-is-the-law-of-life-and-those-who-look
6. Hull, P. (2013). Answer four questions to get a mission statement. *Forbes*. Retreived from https://www.forbes.com/sites/patrickhull/2013/01/10/answer-4-questions-to-get-a-great-mission-statement/#5a97f79967f5
7. What is a PESTEL analysis? *Oxford College of Marketing*. Retrieved January 15, 2020 from https://blog.oxfordcollegeofmarketing.com/2016/06/30/pestel-analysis/
8. Barrows, E. (2009). Four fatal flaws of strategic planning. *Harvard Business Review*. Retrieved January 16, 2020 from https://hbr.org/2009/03/four-fatal-flaws-of-strategic.html
9. Hrebiniak, L. (2006). Obstacles to effective strategy implementation. *Organizational Dynamics*, (35), 1, 12-31.
10. Collins, J., & Porras, J. (2002). *Built to last: Successful habits of visionary companies*. New York, NY: HarperBusiness.
11. Kaplan, R. S., & Norton, D. P. (1996). Using the balanced scorecard as a strategic management system. *Harvard Business Review, 74*(1), 75.
12. Balanced Scorecard Basics. *Balanced Scorecard Institute*. Retrieved January 16, 2020 from https://www.balancedscorecard.org/BSC-Basics/About-the-Balanced-Scorecard
13. Ibid.
14. Ibid.
15. Marler, J. (2012). Strategic human resource management in context: A historical and global perspective. *The Academy of Management Perspectives*, 26(2), 6-11.
16. Louch, P. (2014). Workforce planning is essential to high-performing organizations. *Society for Human Resource Management*. Retrieved January 17, 2020 from https://www.shrm.org/resourcesandtools/hr-topics/technology/pages/louch-workforce-planning.aspx
17. Ibid.
18. Cappelli, P. (2009). A supply chain approach to workforce planning. *Organizational Dynamics*, (38) 1, 8-15.
19. Delphi Method. *Rand Corporation*. Retrieved January 17, 2020 from https://www.rand.org/topics/delphi-method.html
20. Ibid.
21. Human Resource Information Systems. *Reference for Business*. Retrieved January 17, 2019 from https://www.referenceforbusiness.com/management/Gr-Int/Human-Resource-Information-Systems.html
22. Louch, P. (2014). Workforce planning is essential to high-performing organizations. *Society for Human Resource Management*. Retrieved January 17, 2020 from https://www.shrm.org/resourcesandtools/hr-topics/technology/pages/louch-workforce-planning.aspx
23. Ibid.
24. Employee turnover hits all-time high. (2019). *HR Specialist*, 17(1).
25. Workforce turnover rate hits all-time high. (2018). *Salary.com*. Retrieved February 11, 2019 from https://www.salary.com/news-and-events/workplace-turnover-rate-hits-all-time-high/.
26. Ibid.
27. News release. Bureau of Labor Statistics. Retrieved March 13, 2020 from https://www.bls.gov/news.release/pdf/empsit.pdf.
28. HR supply forecasting-succession analysis-Markov analysis. *WhatisHumanResource.com*. Retrieved January 18, 2020 from http://www.whatishumanresource.com/hr-supply-forecasting
29. Hesse, J. (2017). Why companies need to build a skills inventory. *Strategy+Business*. Retrieved February 11, 2020 from https://www.strategy-business.com/blog/Why-Companies-Need-to-Build-a-Skills-Inventory?gko=8b016
30. Castellano, W.G. (2013). *Practices for engaging the 21st century workforce: Challenges of talent management in a changing workplace*. Upper Saddle River, NJ: Pearson Financial Times Press.
31. Middle-skill spotlight: An analysis of four in-demand sectors with a community college focus. *EMSI*. Retrieved March 13, 2020 from https://www.smc.edu/AcademicAffairs/Workforce/Documents/EMSI_Middle_Skill_Spotlight.pdf
32. Identifying and Addressing Workforce Challenges in America's Energy Industry. (2007). *U.S. Department of Labor, Employment and Training Administration, High Growth Job Training Initiative*.
33. Middle-skill spotlight: An analysis of four in-demand sectors with a community college focus. EMSI. Retrieved March 13, 2020 from https://www.smc.edu/AcademicAffairs/Workforce/Documents/EMSI_Middle_Skill_Spotlight.pdf
34. Philips, M. (2014). Welders, America Needs You. *Bloomberg Businessweek*, 1.
35. Plant closings and layoffs. *U.S. Department of Labor*. Retrieved February 11, 2020 from https://www.dol.gov/general/topic/termination/plantclosings
36. Halbesleben, J., Wheeler, A., & Paustian-Underdahl, S. (2013). The impact of furloughs on emotional exhaustion, self-rated performance, and recovery experiences. *Journal of Applied Psychology, 98*(3), 492-503.

37. Struggling to balance the budget? Here's how to manage staff concerns the right way. *US Chamber*. Retrieved April 1, 2020 from https://www.uschamber.com/co/run/human-resources/handling-coronavirus-layoffs

38. Milligan, S. (2018). HR 2025: Reach new heights by becoming a trusted advisor. *HR Magazine*, (63)7, 30-38.

39. Levenson, A.R. (2015). *Strategic Analytics: Advancing Strategy Execution and Organizational Effectiveness*. Oakland, CA: Berret-Koehler Publishers, Inc.

40. Feffer, M. (2017). 9 tips for using HR metrics strategically. *Society for Human Resource Management*. Retrieved from https://www.shrm.org/hr-today/news/hr-magazine/1017/pages/9-tips-for-using-hr-metrics-strategically.aspx

41. Ibid.

42. Moultan, D. (2018). Prediction: Talent acquisition will use AI and predictive data to become truly embedded in the business. *Human Resources Today, Bersin, Deloitte LLP*. Retrieved February 11, 2020 from http://www.humanresourcestoday.com/analysis/metrics/talent-acquisition/?open-article-id=9353359&article-title=prediction--talent-acquisition-will-use-ai-and-predictive-data-to-become-truly-embedded-in-the-business&blog-domain=deloitte.com&blog-title=bersin-with-deloitte

43. Van Vulpen, E. What is an HR Dashboard and HR Report? Examples, visuals and a how to. *Analytics in HR Academy*. Retrieved February 11, 2020 from https://www.analyticsinhr.com/blog/hr-reporting-hr-report-hr-dashboard/

44. Dashboard: What is an HR Dashboard? *Society for Human Resource Management*. Retrieved February 11, 2020 from https://www.shrm.org/resourcesandtools/tools-and-samples/hr-qa/pages/whatisanhrdashboard.aspx

45. Benchmarking service. *Society for Human Resource Management*. Retrieved February 19, 2019 from https://www.shrm.org/resourcesandtools/business-solutions/pages/benchmarking-service.aspx

46. Case written by Crews, P. (2020). Adapted from Marr, B. (2018). Inspiring ways organizations are using HR data. *Forbes*. Retrieved from https://www.forbes.com/sites/bernardmarr/2018/05/11/5-inspiring-ways-organizations-are-using-hr-data/#29f578241872 Lee, T., & Wilkie, D. (2018). Are you practicing the HR your CEO wants? *HRMagazine*, 63(7), 41-43,46-48.

CHAPTER 3
Equal Employment Opportunity

Learning Objectives

After reading this chapter, you should be able to do the following:

1. Compare and contrast Equal Employment Opportunity (EEO), diversity, and affirmative action.
2. Explain the role of the government in regulating EEO through the Equal Employment Opportunity Program (EEOC) and the Office of Federal Contract Compliance Programs (OFCCP).
3. Identify the major federal employment laws and the key requirements of each.
4. Recognize the major types of sexual harassment and strategies that employers can utilize for prevention.

Almost every aspect of HR is impacted by legislation, case law, or regulatory agencies, at the federal, state, or local levels. HR managers need to be familiar with Equal Employment Opportunity (EEO) law, as it influences recruitment, hiring, and any of the terms and conditions of employment. If HR staff violate federal or state laws, the cost in penalties can be significant, in addition to the damage to the organization's public image.

This chapter explores the legislation related to EEO, discrimination, and affirmative action. In addition, the historical perspective is reviewed, so that students will understand the intent of the laws. The major federal employment laws are then examined. The chapter concludes with a discussion of sexual harassment, including employer liability and prevention strategies. Note that the focus of this chapter is only on EEO law. Other aspects of employment law such as compensation, employee benefits, labor law, and immigration are covered in the appropriate chapters.

3.1 Opening Case: You Didn't Catch Us in Time

Lilly Ledbetter speaks about the Paycheck Fairness Act.

Source: Julia Brownley, public domain, via Wikimedia Commons. https://upload.wikimedia.org/wikipedia/commons/b/b8/Lilly_Ledbetter_speaks_about_the_Paycheck_Fairness_Act.jpg

Lilly Ledbetter was a supervisor for Goodyear in 1979. She had worked there for two decades when she was given an anonymous note comparing her salary with her male co-workers'. She discovered that even the lowest-paid male worker made more than she. Even new hires made more money than she did. She was making up to 40% less than all of the men with equal jobs in her division.

Ms. Ledbetter decided to sue and was awarded $300,000 in back pay by the Alabama District Court. However, Goodyear appealed all the way to the Supreme Court on a 180-day technicality, and in 2007 the Court ruled in its favor. The Civil Rights Act of 1964 stated that the statute of limitations for filing a charge of discrimination begins with each paycheck affected by a discriminatory decision. Because Ms. Ledbetter did not file a complaint within the 180-day deadline, the Supreme Court reversed the earlier decision.

Senator Barbara Mikulski proposed legislation in 2009 that would allow a worker to sue whenever they became aware that they had been discriminated against. President Obama, in his first piece of legislation, signed the Lilly Ledbetter Fair Pay Act of 2009 into law. This did not help Ms. Ledbetter because she did not receive any back pay, and she knew this would be the case, but she continued the fight to help future generations.[1]

The Lily Ledbetter Fair Pay Act

Lilly Ledbetter talks about her struggle to earn equal pay as a woman for the same job done by a man.

View the video online at: http://www.youtube.com/embed/tMxsYqaFwA0?rel=0

Case Discussion Questions

1. Should a company be able to avoid prosecution on a "technicality," even when it is clearly guilty?
2. Would you have continued to fight, knowing that even if you were to change a law, it would not benefit you personally?
3. Would you be willing to be the person who informs another employee that they are being discriminated against? Would you do it anonymously? Why or why not?

3.2 Equal Employment Opportunity (EEO)

Learning Objectives

1. Understand the historical events that led to the creation of EEO laws in the U.S.
2. Define the concept of protected class in the context of EEO laws.
3. Explain the differences between diversity, EEO, and affirmative action.
4. Identify the role of the Equal Employment Opportunity Commission (EEOC) in enforcing EEO laws.
5. Identify the role of the Office of Federal Contract Compliance Programs (OFCCP) in enforcing EEO and affirmative action.

Historical Perspectives

As you will learn in this chapter, the most significant piece of federal legislation prohibiting discrimination in the workforce was the Civil Rights Act of 1964. The law prohibits discrimination not only in employment, but also in voting, public accommodations, and education. The act was forged in an atmosphere of urgency, in response to growing unrest in the U.S., emanating from the pervasive discrimination and segregation exposed during the civil rights protests of the 1950s and 1960s.[2] Racial segregation was based upon a series of unjust laws that limited African Americans' economic opportunities and required them to use separate facilities, including schools, transportation, restaurants, and bathrooms. The Civil Rights Act of 1964 was the culmination of a civil rights movement that had been gaining steam for several decades. As the opening case about Lilly Ledbetter indicates, changes in EEO laws usually came about as the result of people who were willing to make sacrifices of their time, energy, and even their privacy for the betterment of society. In the twenty-first century, it can become easy to view equal employment opportunity law as simply a set of government regulations that HR managers must comply with, and miss the overall intent of the laws. For that reason, some historical perspective is offered. The following is a timeline of some of the major events that led to the passage of the Civil Rights Act of 1964 and the creation of the Equal Employment Opportunity Commission.[3]

- In June 1941, President Franklin D. Roosevelt signs Executive Order 8802, prohibiting government contractors from engaging in employment discrimination on the basis of race, color, or national origin. This is the first action taken by a U.S. president to prevent employment discrimination by private employers holding government contracts.

- In July 1948, President Harry S. Truman signs Executive Order 9981, ordering the desegregation of the Armed Forces, and requires "equality of treatment and opportunity for all persons in the armed services, without regard to race, color, religion, or national origin."

- In May 1954, the Supreme Court decides *Brown v. Board of Education of Topeka*, striking down all local, state, and federal laws that enforce racial segregation in public education.

- In December 1955, Rosa Parks, an African American woman, refuses to give up her seat to a white man on a municipal bus in Montgomery, Alabama. Her arrest leads to a successful boycott, led by Dr. Martin Luther King, Jr.

- In September 1957, President Dwight D. Eisenhower orders federal troops to protect nine black students integrating Central High School in Little Rock, Arkansas, in response to angry white mobs protesting desegregation.

- In March 1961, President John F. Kennedy signs Executive Order 10925, prohibiting federal government contractors from discriminating on the basis of race. The order also establishes the President's Committee on Equal Employment Opportunity, and states that the order signals a "new determination to end job discrimination once and for all."

- In April 1963, Dr. Martin Luther King, Jr. selects Birmingham, Alabama as the location for continuing civil rights protests. Local law enforcement attacks the demonstrators using high-pressure water hoses and police dogs. These scenes, broadcast nightly on the national news, stir the public conscience and bring about a demand for change.

- In June 1963, Congress passes the Equal Pay Act of 1963, prohibiting discrimination on the basis of gender for men and women doing equal jobs.

On June 11, 1963, at the height of the protest and demonstrations, President John F. Kennedy went on television to address the nation, and gave the following message in response to a growing agreement among the public that discrimination has no place in American society:

"We are confronted primarily with a moral issue. It is as old as the scriptures and is as clear as the American Constitution. The heart of the question is whether all Americans are to be afforded equal rights and equal opportunities, whether we are going to treat our fellow Americans as we want to be treated. . . . One hundred years of delay have passed since President Lincoln freed the slaves, yet their heirs, their grandsons, are not fully free. They are not yet free from the bonds of injustice. . . . And this nation, for all its hopes and all it boasts, will not be fully free until all of its citizens are free. . . . Now the time has come for this nation to fulfill its promise. The events in Birmingham and elsewhere have so increased the cries for equality that no city or state or legislative body can prudently choose to ignore them. . . . We face therefore, a moral crisis as a country and as a people. It cannot be met by repressive police action. It cannot be left to increased demonstrations in the streets. It cannot be quieted by token moves or talk. It is a time to act in the Congress, in your state and local legislative body, and, above all, in all of our daily lives. . . . Next week, I will ask the Congress of the United States to act, to make a commitment it has not fully made in this century to the proposition that race has no place in American life or law."

 ## President John F. Kennedy's Civil Rights Addresss

C-SPAN provides actual footage of President Kennedy's Civil Rights Address in June 1963.

View the video online at: http://www.youtube.com/embed/7BEhKgoA86U?rel=0

The commitment to which President Kennedy referred was the Civil Rights Act of 1964. He did not get to see the legislation through to passage due to his assassination in November of 1963. However, his successor, President Lyndon B. Johnson, took up the mantle of the legislation and pressed forward until the Civil Rights Act of 1964 became law.

Four and a half decades after passage of the Civil Rights Act of 1964, social injustice and systemic racism still persists in America.

Source: Johnny Silvercloud / Shutterstock.com

Discrimination and Protected Classes

As the historical perspective illustrates, equal employment law is about prohibiting discrimination. However, when you make a hiring decision, don't you have to discriminate in some fashion? How do you decide who is more qualified for the job? The key point to remember is that the discrimination should be based on job-related factors. There are legal types of employment discrimination (job-related) and illegal types.

protected class

Any group that has legal protection from employment discrimination.

When discussing employment discrimination, we often use the term **protected class**. The EEOC defines protected class as groups protected from employment discrimination by law.[4] These groups include men and women on the basis of sex; any group which shares a common race, religion, color, or national origin; people over forty; and people with physical or mental handicaps.[5] Every U.S. citizen is a member of some protected class, and is entitled to the benefits of EEO law. However, the EEO laws were passed to correct a history of unfavorable treatment of women and minority group members.

terms and conditions of employment

A term that means that managers should be careful not to discriminate, not only in hiring decisions, but in any employment decision (including training, compensation, promotion, discharge, employee benefits, and so on).

Another concept you should be familiar with is the **terms and conditions of employment**. This is a commonly used phrase in employment discrimination legislation. When a legislative act prohibits discrimination on the basis of membership in a protected class, it normally prohibits discrimination in any of the terms and conditions of employment. This means that managers should be careful not to discriminate, not only in hiring decisions, but in any employment decision (including training, compensation, promotion, discharge, employee benefits, and so on).

EEO, Diversity, and Affirmative Action

You will want to become familiar with the differences between EEO, diversity initiatives, and affirmative action (AA). These three concepts are interrelated but different.

1. **EEO** is based on compliance with legislation that prohibits discrimination in any of the terms and conditions of employment. The basic premise is to create a level playing field by prohibiting discrimination on the basis of membership in a protected class.

2. **Diversity** is a voluntary initiative designed to recruit and retain a multicultural workforce. Managing a diverse workforce and creating a culture of inclusion is much more than just legal compliance.

3. **Affirmative action**, on the other hand, takes an entirely different approach by attempting to reverse the effects of previous discrimination. Affirmative action is a proactive process whereby individuals are hired on the basis of membership in a protected class (if the individual is qualified for the job). The goal of an AA program (AAP) is to ensure that the proportion of employees in that class is the same as the proportion in the **relevant labor market**, which is the geographic area in which employers compete for labor.

Affirmative action programs are usually implemented by employers as a condition of doing business with the federal government, but could also be implemented as a court-ordered remedy for past discrimination, or as a voluntary effort to reverse the effects of past discrimination.

Executive Order 11246, signed into law by President Lyndon B. Johnson in 1965, prohibits federal contractors and federally assisted construction contractors and subcontractors who do over $10,000 in government business in one year from discriminating in employment decisions on the basis of race, color, religion, sex, sexual orientation, gender identity, or national origin. The executive order also requires certain government contractors to take affirmative action to ensure that equal opportunity is provided in all aspects of their employment.[6]

For federal contractors and subcontractors with contracts of $50,000 or more, affirmative action must be taken to recruit and advance qualified minorities, women, persons with disabilities, and covered veterans. Affirmative actions include training programs, outreach efforts, and other positive steps.[7] These procedures should be incorporated into the company's written personnel policies. Covered employers must prepare a written program, which must be developed within 120 days from commencement of the program and must be updated annually.

AA programs require employers to:

1. Perform a workforce utilization analysis;

2. Establish goals and timetables for the employment of underutilized protected classes;

3. Develop action plans to reduce underutilization, including initiating proactive recruitment and selection methods; and

4. Monitor the progress of the program.

In addition to EO 11246, there are two other laws that require affirmative action programs. Section 503 of the Rehabilitation Act of 1973 requires contractors with fifty or more employees and contracts over $50,000 to take affirmative action with regard to qualified individuals with disabilities. The Vietnam Era Veterans' Readjustment Assistance Act of 1974 (VEVRAA), as amended by the Jobs for Veterans Act, requires contractors to take affirmative action to employ and advance in employment veterans with service-connected disabilities, recently separated veterans, and other protected veterans. VEVRAA requires that contractors with fifty or more employees and contracts of $150,000 to implement written affirmative action programs.

We should recognize that AA is a controversial issue, and there are two sides to the debate. People in favor of affirmative action believe it is a way to ensure diversity in schools and workplaces. AA is seen as a way to compensate for, and reverse the effects of, many years of oppression. Those who are against AA view it as **reverse discrimination**, which is the unfair treatment of members of majority groups resulting from employment policies that give preference to minorities. Critics of AA believe that past discrimination against certain minority groups does not justify present discrimination against non-minorities.

Consider the example of a company which requires their employees to take an aptitude test as part of the process of promoting them. Both Joshua and Marisa take the test, Josh scoring just two

equal employment opportunity (EEO)

Based on compliance with legislation that prohibits discrimination in any of the terms and conditions of employment, and is intended to create a level playing field by prohibiting discrimination on the basis of membership in a protected class.

diversity

A voluntary initiative designed to recruit and retain a multicultural workforce.

affirmative action

A proactive process whereby individuals are hired on the basis of membership in a protected class (if the individual is qualified for the job).

relevant labor market

The geographic area in which employers compete for labor.

Executive Order 11246

Prohibits federal contractors and federally assisted construction contractors and subcontractors who do over $10,000 in government business in one year from discriminating in employment decisions on the basis of race, color, religion, sex, sexual orientation, gender identity, or national origin.

reverse discrimination

The unfair treatment of members of majority groups resulting from employment policies that give preference to minorities.

points higher than Marisa. Joshua is surprised when Marisa is offered the promotion and learns that management had decided they needed to hire and promote more women and other minorities in order to be meet the goals of the company's affirmative action plan. In this example of reverse discrimination, Joshua, who is in a majority group of white males, was passed over simply because he is a man.

Equal Employment Opportunity Commission (EEOC)

The Equal Employment Opportunity Commission (EEOC) is responsible for enforcement of federal laws and regulations that prohibit discrimination against a job applicant or an employee because of the person's race, color, religion, sex (including gender and pregnancy), national origin, age (for those forty and older), disability, and genetic information. The agency was created in 1965, specifically to enforce Title VII of the Civil Rights Act of 1964. However, the role of the agency has expanded as other discrimination laws have been passed and their enforcement assigned to the EEOC.

EEOC laws generally cover employers with at least fifteen employees (twenty employees in age discrimination cases), including labor unions and employment agencies.[8] The laws apply to any of the terms and conditions of employment, including hiring, firing, promotions, harassment, training, wages, and benefits.[9]

The EEOC enforces federal laws and regulations that prohibit discrimination in employment, but they also provide guidance and training to help employers comply with the law.

Source: © Shutterstock, Inc.

The EEOC has the authority to investigate charges of discrimination against employers who are covered under the discrimination laws for which it has enforcement responsibility. The EEOC conducts investigations, and then if it finds that discrimination has occurred, it will try to settle the charge. If unable to settle, the EEOC has the authority to file a lawsuit to protect the rights of individuals and the public interest, but it only litigates a small percentage of cases. When deciding to file a lawsuit, the EEOC considers factors such as the strength of the evidence, the issues in the case, and the wider impact the lawsuit could have on the EEOC's efforts to combat workplace discrimination.[10]

The EEOC is a bipartisan commission comprised of five presidentially appointed members, including the chair, vice chair, and three commissioners.[11] The commissioners participate equally in the development and approval of commission policies, issue charges of discrimination where appropriate, and authorize the filing of lawsuits. In addition to the commissioners, the president appoints a general counsel to support the commission and provide direction, coordination, and supervision to the EEOC's litigation program.[12]

EEO laws establish a limited time period for filing a charge of discrimination. In general, a charge needs to be filed within 180 calendar days from the day the alleged discrimination occurred.[13] The filing deadline is extended to three hundred days if a state or local agency enforces a law that prohibits employment discrimination on the same basis. However, the time period for age discrimination cases is only extended to three hundred days if there is a state law prohibiting age discrimination in employment and a state agency or authority enforcing that law (the deadline is not extended if only a local law prohibits age discrimination).[14] It is also important to note that a different complaint process and timeline applies to federal employees and job applicants, and their time limit to file a claim is generally forty-five days.[15]

As one can see, the regulations can be confusing, with variations in the employers that are covered, different complaint processes, and different time limitations, depending on the type of discrimination and the type of employer (private sector or government). You may be wondering why this has not been standardized to eliminate confusion. The answer lies in the fact that the EEOC has responsibility for enforcing multiple legislative acts, each of which has its own stipulations regarding employer applicability, enforcement, time limitations, penalties, etc. The major federal acts that are under the purview of the EEOC, along with the major stipulations of each, are described later in this chapter. Figure 3.1 shows a flowchart for how a discrimination charge is typically handled by the EEOC, regardless of which act the discrimination falls under.

FIGURE 3.1 EEOC Complaint Flowchart

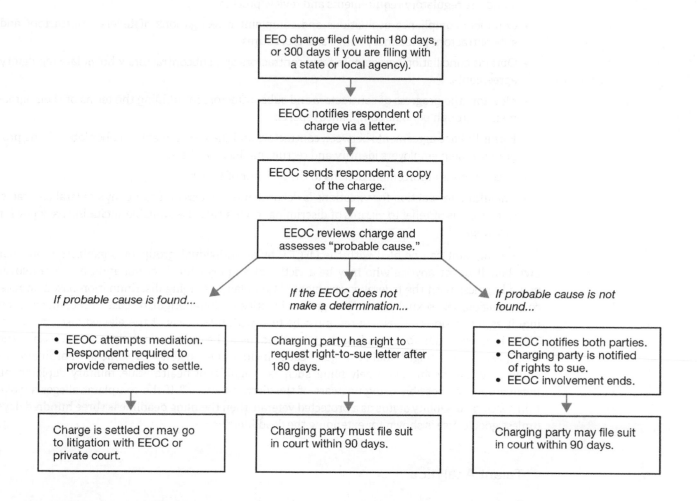

The Office of Federal Contract Compliance Programs (OFCCP)

The Office of Federal Contract Compliance Programs (OFCCP) is a U.S. government agency under the Department of Labor. The OFCCP is responsible for ensuring that those who do business with the federal government (contractors and subcontractors) comply with the legal requirement to take affirmative action and not discriminate on the basis of race, color, sex, sexual orientation, gender identity, religion, national origin, disability, or status as a protected veteran.[16] To comply with the regulations, contractors should be proactive in recruiting, hiring, training, and promoting women, minorities, people with disabilities, and veterans to ensure that all individuals have equal opportunities in employment.[17] Failure to comply can result in the loss of contracts, and therefore HR professionals and managers with federal contractors or subcontractors should be aware of their firms' obligations to comply with EEO law and to create AAPs.

The legislation and regulations that are enforced by the OFCCP include Executive Order 11246, the Americans with Disabilities Act, Section 503 of the Rehabilitation Act, the Vietnam Era Veterans' Readjustment Assistance Act, and the Indian and Native American Employment Rights Program (INAERP). In carrying out its responsibilities, the OFCCP uses the following enforcement procedures:

- Offers compliance assistance to federal contractors and subcontractors to help them understand the regulatory requirements and review process.

- Conducts compliance evaluations and complaint investigations of federal contractors' and subcontractors' personnel policies and procedures.

- Obtains conciliation agreements from contractors and subcontractors who violate regulatory agreements.

- Monitors the progress of contractors and subcontractors in fulfilling the terms of their agreements through periodic compliance reports.

- Forms linkage agreements between contractors and the Department of Labor job training programs to help employers identify and recruit qualified workers.

- Recommends enforcement actions to the Solicitor of Labor.

- The ultimate sanction for violations is debarment—the loss of a company's federal contracts. Other forms of relief to victims of discrimination may also be available, including back pay for lost wages.[18]

A complaint can be filed with the OFCCP by an individual, group, or organization on their own behalf or for anyone who may be a victim of employment discrimination by an employer doing business with the federal government.[19] Complaints alleging discrimination based on race, color, religion, sex, sexual orientation, gender identity, national origin, or based on compensation inquiries, discussions, or disclosures, must be filed within 180 days of the alleged discrimination. There is an exception for extending the filing deadline if the claimant can show good cause. Some examples of what might qualify as good cause include the existence of some extraordinary circumstance that prohibited timely filing, such as a significant health issue, military deployment, incarceration, or possibly being unaware of the discrimination.[20] If the complaint alleges a violation based on disability status as a protected veteran, then the filing deadline is three hundred days (unless good cause is shown for extending the deadline).[21]

Talent Analytics

The U.S. has always been known as a melting pot. However, when it comes to corporate America, diversity has historically been lacking. Although 92% of U.S. population growth is attributed to ethnic groups, and 36% of the workforce is comprised of people of color, only 21 minorities (that's right—21, not 21%) are *Fortune 500* CEOs. Fortunately, this norm is changing as more minorities are becoming key consumers, clients, and leaders in the workforce. Census data says that there will be no racial or ethnic majority in the United States by 2045.[22] This is already the case in several U.S. states. It's time for HR leaders to embrace the changing demographics—and thus usher in a new era of innovation. Using big data for HR (predictive analytics, talent analytics, HR analytics, and human capital analytics) may be the solution to cutting out discrimination and bias while fully embracing the demographic shift. HR analytics is not simply about raw data; it's about what insights that raw data can provide to answer questions relevant to your staff. While HR analytics may look to the past for information, its main function is to shine a light on current behavior and predict future behavior. There are four questions that HR analytics can potentially answer to improve diversity in the workplace:

1. **What variables influence our compensation structure?**

   Without in-memory technology, all HR data—turnover rates, salaries, employee demographics, lists of available positions, etc.—was stored on different places in a database. If you wanted to compare salaries to turnover rates and gender, you'd need to first locate the data, then retrieve that data before you even began analyzing; the whole process could take weeks. In-memory analytics speeds up the process with faster, cheaper, and more powerful memory chips that can be put in the server's memory rather than the database. That means complex data can be controlled and manipulated almost in real-time. For example, when deciding on performance bonuses, HR can quickly run a report detailing the twenty-year history of performance bonuses compared to years worked, department revenue, revenue by location, gender, and male-to-female ratio. Patterns of bias in the past can be easily identified, prompting bonus structures based on solid data.

2. **Who's likely to resign?**

Organizations can use predictive analytics to determine future behavior as well, such as identifying employees at risk for resigning. Recruiting diverse talent is one thing, but if your minority talent has a high voluntary turnover rate, you haven't done much to improve the diversity of your workforce. Predictive analytics can look at specific populations to determine who is likely to resign, and HR can use that information to create initiatives to improve the work experience of those populations.

3. **Will a candidate feel welcome at your company?**

Using data can also help companies identify the core values and behavioral traits of candidates—and vice versa. For example, survey company Saberr uses algorithms to compile, process and compare fundamental values, behavioral compatibility, and diversity to predict the potential strength of interpersonal relationships between certain applicants and potential employers. It does this with a survey for both the applicant and the employer that moves past skills and credentials, thereby bypassing initial bias in the hiring process.

4. **Do we really need to address this issue?**

Perhaps the most impactful use of HR analytics is presenting data visually to easily demonstrate an issue and influence decision-makers. Data can be presented in graphic and statistical reports that are easy for leaders to understand. For example, let's say 45% of your job candidates are people of color, yet only 3% of the hires are minorities. If leadership just isn't seeing the big picture when you explain it verbally, presenting the hard facts in a way that is straightforward, easy to understand, and irrefutable may be the only way to enact change.

Examples like these give us just a glimpse at the potential of big data to enhance the effectiveness of HR leaders. However, data is not the solution in and of itself—you need to ask the right questions. Minority candidates have been employed within a culture of systemic discrimination from the start, which often influences their work history. Simply taking names off of a resume and evaluating candidates by job title and education will only perpetuate the problem. HR professionals need to be careful to keep the human in human resources. If the right questions are asked, data-driven decision-making will prove to be a powerful ally to HR professionals working to reflect our country's rich cultural diversity in the workforce.[23]

Key Takeaways

- HR managers need to be familiar with Equal Employment Opportunity (EEO) law, as it influences recruitment, hiring, and any of the terms and conditions of employment.
- The most significant piece of federal legislation prohibiting discrimination in the workforce was the Civil Rights Act of 1964.
- A protected class is any group that has legal protection from employment discrimination.
- Protected classes based on federal law include minority ethnic groups, females, individuals age forty and older, individuals with a disability (or regarded as having a disability), and veterans.
- The terms and conditions of employment mean that managers should be careful not to discriminate, not only in hiring decisions, but in any employment decision (including training, compensation, promotion, discharge, employee benefits, and so on).

- The Equal Employment Opportunity Commission (EEOC) is responsible for enforcement of federal laws and regulations that prohibit discrimination against a job applicant or an employee because of the person's race, color, religion, sex (including gender and pregnancy), national origin, age (for those forty and older), disability, or genetic information.
- Diversity is a voluntary initiative designed to recruit and retain a multicultural workforce.
- EEO is based on compliance with legislation that prohibits discrimination in any of the terms and conditions of employment and is intended to create a level playing field by prohibiting discrimination on the basis of membership in a protected class.
- Affirmative action is a proactive hiring process that seeks to correct the effects of past discrimination by hiring individuals on the basis of membership in a protected class (if the individual is qualified for the job) to ensure that the proportion of employees in that class is the same as the proportion in the "relevant labor market."
- The OFCCP is responsible for ensuring that those who do business with the federal government (contractors and subcontractors) comply with the legal requirement to take affirmative action and not discriminate on the basis of race, color, sex, sexual orientation, gender identity, religion, national origin, disability, or status as a protected veteran.

What Do *You* Think?

1. Why should employers comply with EEO laws?
2. What protected class(es) do you belong to? (Most people are a member of one or more protected classes.)
3. Have you ever been discriminated against in your employment? How did you respond?
4. Can you describe, in your own words, the difference between diversity, EEO, and affirmative action?

3.3 Federal Employment Laws

Learning Objectives

1. Compare and contrast disparate treatment, disparate impact, and pattern or practice of discrimination.
2. Explain when a Bona Fide Occupational Qualification is an affirmative defense to a discrimination charge.
3. Identify the major federal EEO laws.
4. Describe the required reports and posting requirements for EEO and affirmative action.

In this section, we explore the variety of laws and regulations that apply to the terms and conditions of employment. Some of them are **statutory laws** that were legislated by Congress; these are discussed under the section titled Major Federal Laws. Some are based upon **executive orders**, which are directives issued by the president of the United States and apply to operations of the federal government. They carry the weight of law, but typically only govern federal employees (including the armed forces) and in some cases, contractors and subcontractors of the federal government. **Case law** (the law as established by rulings in previous court cases) is also important in some HR activities. Therefore, we will also look at several landmark court cases throughout this chapter.

statutory laws

Laws that are legislated by Congress.

executive orders

Directives issued by the president of the United States which apply to operations of the federal government.

case law

Laws that are established by rulings in previous court cases.

Types of Discrimination

Discrimination in employment falls under one of three categories: disparate treatment, disparate impact, and pattern or practice. Title VII of the Civil Rights Act of 1964 did not use those exact terms, but it did describe the actions involved in each of these types of discrimination.[24] Disparate treatment and disparate impact are also sometimes referred to as adverse treatment and adverse impact. Before we explore the major federal employment laws, it will be helpful to understand each of these broad categories of discriminatory acts.

Disparate Treatment

Disparate treatment, in the context of employment, occurs when a person is treated differently from others in similar situations because of that individual's membership in a protected class. The legal concept of disparate treatment also applies to other types of discrimination, for example, in housing under the Fair Housing Act of 1968. Disparate treatment is an intentional act by an employer, meaning that the employer has a discriminatory motive. The burden of proof is upon the plaintiff to establish a prima facie case of discrimination. **Prima facie** is a Latin term that means "at first appearance." The courts apply the standard set forth in *McDonnell Douglas Corp. v. Green*, 411 U.S. 792 (1973).[25] The plaintiff must establish that he or she: (1) belongs to a protected class; (2) was qualified for the job; (3) was subjected to an adverse employment action; and (4) the employer gave better treatment to a similarly situated person outside the plaintiff's protected class. The plaintiff often can meet the first two elements easily, but the other two can be difficult to establish.[26] Once the plaintiff has established a prima facie case of employment discrimination, then the burden of proof shifts to the employer to prove that the disparate action was based on a legitimate and legal reason, based on *Texas v. Burdine*, 450 U.S. 248, 254 (1981). We will look at some of those reasons in the next section of this chapter. If the employer meets the burden of proof by stating a legitimate and legal reason for its actions, then the burden of proof again shifts back to the plaintiff to show that the employer's stated reason is a pretext for discrimination, under *Cordova v. State Farm Ins. Co.* (124 F.3d 1145, 1148 (9th Cir. 1997).

disparate treatment

In the context of employment, occurs when a person is treated differently from others in similar situations, and the different treatment is because of an individual's membership in a protected class.

prima facie

A Latin term that means "at first appearance."

Disparate Impact

Disparate impact (or adverse impact) occurs when policies, practices, rules, or other systems that appear to be neutral result in a disproportionate impact on a protected group.[27] For example, an employer might administer a test as part of its applicant selection procedures. If a particular group of minority applicants scores lower on the test as a whole, then the test has a disparate impact on that protected class. The use of the test might still be legally defensible, but only if the employer can demonstrate that the test is a valid predictor of future job performance (we will explore further

disparate impact (or adverse impact)

Occurs when policies, practices, rules, or other systems that appear to be neutral result in a disproportionate impact on a protected group.

the concept of test validity in Chapter 6). Another example is height and weight requirements, which might discriminate on the basis of gender, race, or ethnicity.

Disparate impact can be unintentional. Thus, the plaintiff does not have to establish a discriminatory motive. The concept applies to a group of people who belong to a protected class, as opposed to one individual. Table 3.1 summarizes the key distinctions between disparate treatment and disparate impact.

TABLE 3.1 Comparison of Disparate Treatment and Disparate Impact

	Disparate Treatment	Disparate Impact
Intent	• Plaintiff must show intent	• Intent not necessary (can be unintentional)
Employer's Rebuttal	• State a nondiscriminatory reason or show BFOQ	• Demonstrate that the practice is job-related
Plaintiff's Response	• Prove the reason is a pretext for discrimination	• Prove the practice is not job-related
Remedies	• Consent decree • Compensatory and punitive damages	• Consent decree • Equitable relief such as back pay and legal fees

The Uniform Guidelines on Employee Selection Procedures give specific instructions for how adverse impact is determined. The guidelines set forth procedures that have been agreed upon by the EEOC, the Departments of Labor and Justice, the Office of Personnel Management, and the Department of the Treasury. We will look at these guidelines in more depth in Chapter 6. But there is one part of the guidelines that we should cover now, as it relates to the determination of adverse impact, and that is what is commonly referred to as the four-fifths rule.

The four-fifths rule is a mathematical calculation determined by following a four-step process:

1. Calculate the rate of selection for each group (divide the number of persons selected from a group by the number of applicants from that group).
2. Observe which group has the highest selection rate.
3. Calculate the impact ratios by comparing the selection rate for each group with that of the highest group (divide the selection rate for a group by the selection rate for the highest group).
4. Observe whether the selection rate for any group is substantially less (i.e., usually less than four-fifths, or 80%) than the selection rate of the highest group. If it is, adverse impact is indicated in most circumstances.[28]

The "Example of Four-Fifths Rule" shows an example of how the four-fifths rule is applied. Also, it should be noted that disparate impact is more than simple arithmetic. If the representation of a protected class falls below 80%, then discrimination has occurred. The discrimination might be illegal, or legal, based upon a number of factors, several of which are discussed next.

Example of Four-Fifths Rule

A large retail company with multiple stores across the United States hires seven hundred fifty new associates each year. The store keeps track of the race of applicants and new hires in accordance with EEOC requirements. For the most recent year, the applicants and new hires by race are shown in the table below.

Applicants	Hired	Selection Rate
2,100 White	425	425/2,100=20.2%
580 Black	113	113/580=19.48%
1,275 Hispanic	167	167/1,275=13.1%
115 Asian	45	45/115=39.1%

Impact ratios of each group with that of the highest selection group (white):

- Black: 19.48/20.2=96%
- Hispanic: 13.1/20.2=65%
- Asian: 39.1/20.2=194%

Therefore, discrimination has not occurred with blacks or Asians, since their selection rate is over 80% of the white group. However, discrimination is occurring against Hispanics, since their selection rate of 65% is less than 80% of the white group.

Pattern or Practice

A third category is a **pattern or practice** of discrimination. The courts have found pattern or practice when the evidence establishes that the discriminatory actions were the defendant's regular practice, rather than an isolated instance.[29] It does not mean that the defendant always discriminates, but that they do so on a regular basis. A pattern or practice of discrimination exists when the plaintiff can prove that the defendant regularly and repeatedly engaged in acts prohibited by statute.[30] An isolated incident does not establish a pattern or practice (although the incident might still be illegal if it constitutes disparate treatment).

pattern or practice of discrimination

Exists when the plaintiff can prove that the defendant regularly and repeatedly engaged in acts prohibited by statute.

Retaliation

Retaliation occurs when an employer punishes an employee for engaging in legally protected activity. EEO laws prohibit punishing job applicants or employees for asserting their rights to be free from employment discrimination, including harassment. For example, it is unlawful to retaliate against applicants or employees for:[31]

- filing or being a witness in an EEO charge, complaint, investigation, or lawsuit.
- communicating with a supervisor or manager about employment discrimination, including harassment.
- answering questions during an employer investigation of alleged harassment.
- refusing to follow orders that would result in discrimination.
- resisting sexual advances, or intervening to protect others.
- requesting accommodation of a **disability** or for a religious practice.
- asking managers or co-workers about salary information to uncover potentially discriminatory wages.

retaliation

Occurs when an employer punishes an employee for engaging in legally protected activity.

disability

Defined by the Americans with Disabilities Act as a physical or mental impairment that substantially limits one or more major life activities, a person who has a history or record of such an impairment, or a person who is perceived by others as having such an impairment.

The following court cases illustrate examples of retaliation. In May 2016, American Casing & Equipment, Inc., a Williston, North Dakota–based oil field service company, paid $250,000 to a Filipino worker it fired after he complained of harassment, to settle a discrimination and retaliation lawsuit filed by the EEOC. The lawsuit alleged that since November 2012, a white manager harassed the worker of Filipino heritage by directing racial slurs at him, jabbing him with a finger in the stomach and chest, and once urinating on his leg while he worked under a truck. No supervisor made any attempt to stop the abuse. The employee ultimately was fired after he complained to the company's safety manager about the harassment (*EEOC v. American Casing & Equipment, Inc.*).[32]

In February 2005, EEOC settled a retaliation case against Burger King for $65,000, on behalf of a Caucasian manager who was terminated after refusing to comply with a black customer's preference that a "white boy" not make her sandwich (*EEOC v. Star City LLC d/b/a Burger King*).

Bona Fide Occupational Qualification

bona fide occupational qualification (BFOQ)

An employment qualification that is essential for an individual to perform a job successfully.

affirmative defense

A legal term that means the defendant is admitting that the alleged action occurred but is offering a justifiable reason.

There are some limited circumstances in which an employer can legally discriminate against some protected classes. The most common such defense is the **bona fide occupational qualification (BFOQ)**. These are employment qualifications that are essential for an individual to perform a job successfully. The BFOQ is recognized as an exception and an **affirmative defense** to discrimination under Title VII of the Civil Rights Act of 1964.[33] The BFOQ rule allows for an employer to discriminate on the basis of age, religion, sex, age, or national origin. Race can never be used as a BFOQ. A job qualification must be "reasonably necessary to the normal operation of that particular business or enterprise" to be considered an exception under the BFOQ rule.[34] The courts have traditionally interpreted the BFOQ clause very narrowly, and only allow it under limited and clear circumstances.

Examples of BFOQs include the following:

- A Chinese restaurant can hire only Chinese chefs (although it would be harder to claim the BFOQ exception for wait staff or other positions).
- A church can require that its staff be of their particular religion.
- A women's sporting team can require that locker room attendants be women.
- An airline can require pilots to retire at age sixty-five because that is the maximum age for a pilot under Federal Aviation Administration regulations.
- A manufacturer of men's suits can lawfully hire only male models for advertising purposes.

Major Federal Laws

It is imperative for HR professionals to be well versed in employment law because failure to comply can result in substantial penalties and judgments from court cases that are lost. Table 3.2 shows some of the discrimination cases that have been lost by large corporations and the costs incurred. Note that this chapter only deals with federal laws. Many state laws address various aspects of the terms and conditions of employment; even some municipalities have passed EEO regulations. The scope of state and local laws is, of course, beyond what can be covered in this textbook, but the practicing HR manager should be sure to learn the applicable state and local laws that apply to their business operations.

TABLE 3.2 Top Ten Discrimination Charge Judgments

Year	Settlement	Company	Discrimination Basis
2003	$250 million	California Public Employee's Retirement System	Age
2013	$240 million	Henry's Turkey Services	Disability
2000	$192.5 million	Coca-Cola	Race
2000	$176 million	Nextel	Race, Age, Sex

Year	Settlement	Company	Discrimination Basis
2010	$175 million	Novartis	Pregnancy
1996	$172 million	Texaco	Race
2005	$132.5 million	Shoney's	Race, National Origin
1995	$81.5 million	Publix Super Markets, Inc.	Sex
2005	$80 million	Sodexho Marriott Services	Race
2001	$54 million	Morgan Stanley	Sex

The major federal laws are summarized in Table 3.3 and then discussed in the following section. The laws are covered in chronological order, based on the year the legislation was originally passed.

TABLE 3.3 Major Federal EEO Laws

Law	Description
Equal Pay Act of 1963	Prohibits discrimination on the basis of sex for equal work in the same establishment.
Title VII of the Civil Rights Act of 1964	Prohibits discrimination in employment on the basis of race, religion, sex, color, and national origin.
Age Discrimination in Employment Act of 1967 (as amended in 1986 and 1990)	Prohibits discrimination on the basis of age against individuals forty years of age or older, and restricts mandatory retirement.
Vietnam Era Veterans Readjustment Assistance Act of 1974	Prohibits employment discrimination by federal contractors and subcontractors against Vietnam veterans.
Pregnancy Discrimination Act of 1978	Prohibits discrimination against women on the basis of pregnancy, childbirth, or related medical conditions.
Americans with Disabilities Act of 1990	Prohibits discrimination in employment, public services, public accommodations and services, telecommunications, and transportation on the basis of disability.
Civil Rights Act of 1991	Codified disparate impact theory in Title VII, and provided for jury trials and compensatory and punitive damages.
Uniformed Services Employment and Reemployment Rights Act of 1994 (as amended in 1998, 2004, and 2008)	Protects civilian job rights and benefits for veterans and members of Reserves.
Genetic Information Nondiscrimination Act of 2008	Protects individuals from genetic discrimination in employment and health insurance.
Lilly Ledbetter Fair Pay Act of 2009	Amended Title VII of the Civil Rights Act of 1964 to extend the statute of limitations.

Equal Pay Act of 1963

The Equal Pay Act of 1963 was an amendment to the Fair Labor Standards Act of 1938 (FLSA). It is administered by the EEOC and prohibits sex-based discrimination between men and women in the same establishment who perform jobs that require substantially equal skill, effort, and responsibility under similar working conditions.[35]

While the Equal Pay Act requires that men and women be given equal pay for equal work, the jobs do not have to be identical. The jobs do need to be substantially equal, based on job content, not job titles. The Equal Pay Act provides that employers may not pay unequal wages to men and women who perform jobs that are substantially the same, as measured by skills, effort, and responsibility, and are performed under similar working conditions. Differences in pay are permitted when they are based on seniority, merit, quantity, or quality of production, or a job-related factor other than sex.[36] These are considered **affirmative defenses**. An affirmative defense is a legal term that means the defendant is admitting that the alleged action occurred (in this case, unequal pay), but is offering a justifiable reason.

Title VII of the Civil Rights Act of 1964

Title VII prohibits discrimination on the basis of race, religion, sex, color, and national origin. The purpose of Title VII's protections is to level the playing field by requiring employers to consider only job-related criteria in making employment decisions.[37] Title VII applies to employers in an industry affecting commerce who have fifteen or more employees for each working day for twenty or more weeks in a year and includes employment agencies and labor organizations.

The legislation outlines unlawful employment practices and specifically states that "it shall be an unlawful employment practice for an employer: (1) to fail or refuse to hire or to discharge any individual, or otherwise to discriminate against any individual with respect to his or her compensation, terms, conditions, or privileges of employment, because of such individual's race, color, religion, sex, or national origin; or (2) to limit, segregate, or classify his employees or applicants for employment in any way which would deprive or tend to deprive any individual of employment opportunities or otherwise adversely affect his status as an employee, because of such individual's race, color, religion, sex, or national origin."[38]

Title VII also established the Equal Employment Opportunity Commission and its composition and appointment of commissioners and general counsel, along with enforcement provisions. In 2019, 72,675 claims were filed with the EEOC.[39] Figure 3.2 shows the distribution of claims by protected class. During the last two decades, the annual charges filed have ranged from a low of 72,675 to a high of 99,947. The FY 2019 data shows that retaliation continued to be the most frequent charge filed with the agency, followed by disability, race, and sex.[40]

FIGURE 3.2 Distribution of 2019 EEOC Claims by Class
Note: these percentages add up to more than 100% because some charges allege multiple biases.

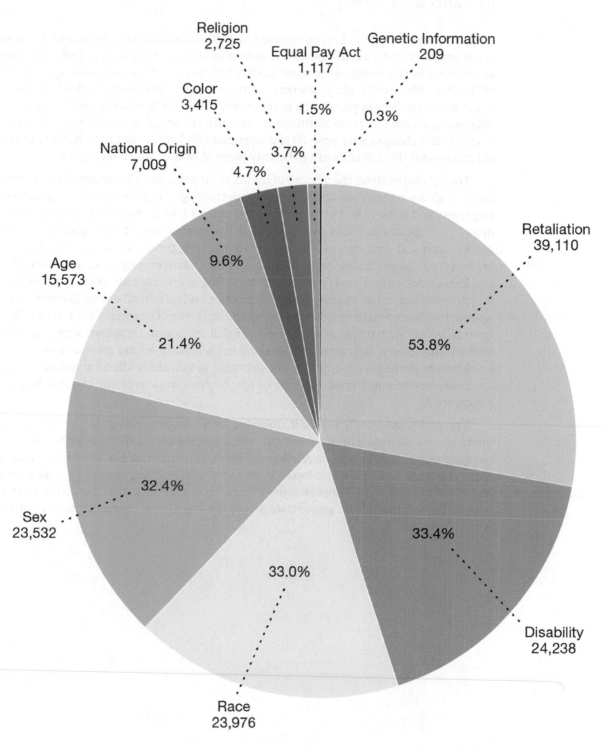

Source: EEOC

Age Discrimination in Employment Act of 1967 (as Amended in 1986 and 1990)

The Age Discrimination in Employment Act of 1967 (ADEA) originally prohibited discrimination in employment on the basis of age against individuals between the ages of forty and sixty-five. An amendment in 1986 removed the upper age limit. Then the act was amended again by the passage of the Older Workers Benefit Protection Act in 1990, which provided some flexibility for employers to use employee benefit plans (such as retirement or health insurance) that do contain age-based differences, as long as these distinctions are based on actual cost differences. For example, an employer can charge a sixty-year-old employee more for health insurance than a twenty-five-year-old employee if the cost of insuring the sixty-year-old worker is actually higher.

The legislation states the purpose of the act as "to promote employment of older persons based on their ability rather than age; to prohibit arbitrary age discrimination in employment; to help employers and workers find ways of meeting problems arising from the impact of age on employment."[41] Congress also stated their findings in the introduction to the legislation: "The Congress hereby finds and declares that—(1) in the face of rising productivity and affluence, older workers find themselves disadvantaged in their efforts to retain employment, and especially to regain employment when displaced from jobs; (2) the setting of arbitrary age limits regardless of potential for job performance has become a common practice, and certain otherwise desirable practices may work to the disadvantage of older persons; (3) the incidence of unemployment, especially long-term unemployment with resultant deterioration of skill, morale, and employer acceptability is, relative to the younger ages, high among older workers; their numbers are great and growing; and their employment problems grave; and (4) the existence in industries affecting commerce, or arbitrary discrimination in employment because of age, burdens commerce and the free flow of goods in commerce."[42]

The ADEA specifically makes it unlawful for an employer to (1) fail or refuse to hire or to discharge any individual or otherwise discriminate against any individual with respect to his compensation, terms, conditions, or privileges of employment, because of such individual's age; (2) to limit, segregate, or classify employees in any way which would deprive or tend to deprive any individual of employment opportunities or otherwise adversely affect his status as an employee, because of such individual's age; or (3) to reduce the wage rate of any employee in order to comply with this chapter.[43]

Vietnam Era Veterans Readjustment Assistance Act of 1974

The Vietnam Era Veterans Readjustment Assistance Act of 1974 (VEVRAA) was passed to provide job assistance to returning Vietnam veterans and to protect them from discrimination in employment. The VEVRAA applies to federal contractors or subcontractors with contracts worth $100,000 or more.[44] The act requires these contractors to implement affirmative action plans to employ veterans. Employers are required to:

While the Vietnam Veteran's Memorial honors those U.S. service men and women who gave their lives in the Vietnam War, the Three Soldiers Statue commemorates all who served in the war, many of whom returned home to face employment discrimination. The three soldiers represent Caucasian, African American, and Latino soldiers.

- Set a hiring benchmark using one of two methods: adopt the benchmark based on the national percentage of veterans currently in the workforce, or create an individualized benchmark based on their own interpretation of the best available data nationally and within their state/region.

- Invite voluntary self-identification by veterans seeking employment.

- Comply with OFCCP reviews by providing on-site and off-site access to documents needed for compliance and focused reviews.

- Track the effectiveness of veteran recruiting and hiring efforts.

- Provide access to job listings in a format that can be used by veterans' Employment Service Delivery Systems (ESDS).

- Communicate to subcontractors (using mandated language in federal contracts) the obligation to employ and advance protected veterans.

- Outreach and positive recruitment.[45]

Source: Pierrette Guertin / Shutterstock.com

Vietnam-era veterans are generally defined as those who served between February 28, 1961 and May 7, 1975. However, despite its name, the act is not limited to just Vietnam-era veterans. The act specifies other protected categories, which are disabled veterans, recently separated veterans, active duty wartime or campaign veterans, campaign badge veterans, and Armed Forces service medal veterans. The VEVRAA is enforced by the OFCCP.

Pregnancy Discrimination Act of 1978

The Pregnancy Discrimination Act of 1978 was passed as an amendment to Title VII of the Civil Rights Act of 1964. Essentially, the Act states that the term "sex" as a protected class includes pregnancy and childbirth. For example, refusing to hire someone because she is pregnant is a violation of Title VII because it constitutes discrimination on the basis of sex. Specifically, the act states that the terms "because of sex" or "on the basis of sex" include, but are not limited to, because or on the basis of pregnancy, childbirth, or related medical conditions; and that women affected by pregnancy, childbirth, or related medical conditions shall be treated the same for all employment-related purposes, including receipt of benefits under fringe benefit programs, as other persons not so affected but similar in their ability or inability to work. The act states that this does not require an employer to pay for health insurance benefits for abortion, except where the life of the mother would be endangered if the fetus were carried to term, or except where medical complications have arisen from an abortion.[46] The Pregnancy Discrimination Act of 1978 is enforced by the EEOC. The case study at the end of this chapter describes a recent pregnancy discrimination case.

Americans with Disabilities Act of 1990

The Americans with Disabilities Act of 1990 (ADA) is a comprehensive piece of civil rights legislation that prohibits discrimination on the basis of disability and guarantees that people with disabilities have the same opportunities as everyone else in America, in regard to employment, purchasing goods and services, public accommodations, and telecommunications.[47] The legislation applies to employers with fifteen or more employees. The ADA is comprised of five titles:

- Title I Employment
- Title II Public Services: State and Local Government
- Title III Public Accommodations and Services Operated by Private Entities
- Title IV Telecommunications
- Title V Miscellaneous Provisions

Because the ADA is so complex, there are multiple federal agencies involved with enforcement. Our focus in this textbook is Title I, which is enforced by the EEOC. The other titles are enforced by the Department of Justice, the Federal Communications Commission, the U.S. Department of Transportation, and the Federal Transit Administration.

To be protected by the ADA, one must have a disability, which is defined by the ADA as a physical or mental impairment that substantially limits one or more major life activities, a person who has a history or record of such an impairment, or a person who is perceived by others as having such an impairment.[48] How might someone be perceived as having an impairment? One example is that of a severe burn victim who suffered significant disfigurement to the face. This individual may not be impaired, but others may assume that he/she is, based solely upon appearance.

It should also be noted that the ADA was amended in 2008. In these amendments, the term "major life activities" was expanded to include "major bodily functions." The amendments include a list of major life activities and major bodily functions, which are listed in Table 3.4.[49] These lists are not exhaustive, meaning that other activities or functions might be determined by the courts to be covered, on a case-by-case basis.

TABLE 3.4 Major Life Activities and Bodily Functions under ADA

The Americans with Disabilities Act of 1990 as Amended in 2008	
Major Life Activities	**Major Bodily Functions**
Caring for oneself	Functions of the immune system
Performing manual tasks	Normal cell growth
Seeing	Digestive
Hearing	Bowel
Eating	Bladder
Sleeping	Neurological
Walking	Brain
Standing	Respiratory
Lifting	Circulatory
Bending	Endocrine
Speaking	Reproductive
Breathing	
Learning	
Reading	
Concentrating	
Thinking	
Communicating	
Working	

The ADA requires employers to provide reasonable accommodations to qualified applicants or employees. A **reasonable accommodation** is a change that accommodates employees with disabilities so they can do the job without causing the employer **undue hardship**.[50] ADA accommodations also apply to applicants for employment. There are three categories of reasonable accommodations:

- Modifications or adjustments to a job application process that enable a qualified applicant with a disability to be considered for the position such qualified applicant desires;

- Modifications or adjustment to the work environment, or to the manner of circumstances under which the position held or desired is customarily performed, that enable a qualified individual with a disability to perform the essential functions of that position; or

- Modifications or adjustments that enable a covered entity's employee with a disability to enjoy equal benefits and privileges for employment as are enjoyed by its other similarly situated employees without disabilities.[51]

Examples of specific accommodations in the EEOC's enforcement guidelines include making existing facilities accessible, job restructuring, part-time or modified work schedules, acquiring or modifying work schedules, acquiring or modifying equipment, changing tests, training materials, or policies providing qualified readers or interpreters, and reassignment to a vacant position.[52] Whether an accommodation is reasonable is dependent upon the factors in the specific situation. The accommodation must enable the individual to perform the essential functions of the job. **Essential job functions** are the basic duties of a job that a person must be able to perform. Consider the example of a greeter and loss control specialist at a retail store such as Walmart. This individual must remain near an entrance/exit, and in addition to greeting guests, must also monitor for shoplifting. The individual in this case has lower back problems and is unable to stand for an eight-hour shift. The employee requests a stool because portions of the job can be performed while seated near an entrance/exit, and sitting for fifteen minutes of each hour greatly reduces the pain and allows the individual to perform the essential job functions. This would probably be considered a reasonable accommodation. However, if this individual were a stocker (responsible for restocking shelves, lifting boxes, and operating pallet jacks), sitting for fifteen minutes each hour would probably not be a reasonable request, because it would not allow the employee to perform the essential job functions.

The ADA[53] does provide for a statutory limitation on an employer's obligation to provide a reasonable accommodation when it would impose an undue hardship on the employer. An undue hardship means the accommodation imposes a significant difficulty or expense on the employer, either due to the cost incurred, or to the unduly extensive, substantial, or disruptive nature of the accommodation that would fundamentally alter the nature or operation of the business. This is determined on a case-by-case basis and depends heavily on the financial resources of the firm. For example, if a small law office with only five employees is located on the second floor of an older building without an elevator, it might be an undue hardship for the firm to pay for the installation of an elevator to enable a disabled individual to work there. But if a firm with hundreds of employees operates on the second through fifth floors of the building, then it might be reasonable to expect a firm of this size to install an elevator.

When an individual needs an accommodation, it is up to that individual to let the employer know that they need an adjustment or change at work for a reason related to a medical condition. To request the accommodation, the individual can use plain English, meaning that they do not have to mention the phrase "reasonable accommodation" or the ADA. When a request is made, the employer is not mandated to comply with it. Think of it more in terms of a conversation between the employee and the employer. The employee must initiate the conversation. Then the employee and employer need to discuss what types of accommodation are reasonable and will enable the employee to perform the essential job functions. It is also expected that the employer should determine whether the individual's condition qualifies as a disability under the ADA definition. The employer may request documentation of the condition to

reasonable accommodation

A change that accommodates employees with disabilities so they can do the job without causing the employer undue hardship.

undue hardship

Occurs when the accommodation imposes a significant difficulty or expense on the employer, either due to the cost incurred, or the unduly extensive, substantial, or disruptive nature of the accommodation that would fundamentally alter the nature or operation of the business.

essential job functions

The basic duties of a job that a person must be able to perform.

President Franklin D. Roosevelt, who used a wheelchair later in life due to polio, as memorialized in this bronze statue in Washington, D.C., changed the perceptions of many as to what a disabled person can achieve.

Source: Nigel Jarvis / Shutterstock.com

make this determination, and also may require that the documentation comes from a qualified healthcare or rehabilitation professional.

Civil Rights Act of 1991

The Civil Rights Act of 1991 was enacted in response to the effect of at least seven decisions by the Supreme Court, which were regarded as changing the landscape of discrimination law.[54] Two of the most significant decisions that Congress addressed were *Price Waterhouse v. Hopkins* (1989) and *Wards Cove Packing Co. v. Atonio* (1989). In *Price Waterhouse*, the Court found that even where a plaintiff proves that an employer's actions were motivated by discrimination, the employer can avoid liability by proving that it would have taken the same action if it were motivated by justifiable business reasons. *Wards Cove* reinterpreted the disparate impact burden of proof and held that the burden is on the plaintiff to demonstrate that the employer lacked business justification for its actions. These and other cases tipped the balance in discrimination cases in favor of employers by making it more difficult for plaintiffs to prevail in discrimination cases.

The act added a new subsection to Title VII, which codified the disparate impact theory of discrimination. This had the effect of establishing disparate impact as a matter of legislation, instead of being subject to reinterpretation by the courts through individual case decisions. In response to the *Price Waterhouse* decision, the act provided that an employer is liable, even it proves that it would have made the same decision in the absence of a discriminatory motive.

Under the provisions of the act, parties are now able to obtain jury trials in discrimination cases and be awarded compensatory and punitive damages in Title VII and ADA lawsuits involving intentional discrimination.[55] The damages can be awarded for pecuniary damages (actual monetary losses by the plaintiff, such as lost wages), emotional pain, suffering, inconvenience, mental anguish, and loss of enjoyment of life.[56] The amount of damages is capped, depending on how many employees a firm has, as shown in Table 3.5.

TABLE 3.5 Caps on Compensatory and Punitive Damages

Caps on Compensatory and Punitive Damages under the Civil Rights Act of 1991	
Employer Size	**Maximum Amount of Damages**
15–100 employees	$50,000
101–200 employees	$100,000
201–500 employees	$200,000
501 and more employees	$300,000

Uniformed Services Employment and Reemployment Rights Act of 1994 (as Amended in 1998, 2004, and 2008)

The Uniformed Services Employment and Reemployment Rights Act of 1994 (USERRA) protects civilian job rights and benefits for veterans and members of the Reserves.[57] Unlike most civil rights laws, the act does not stipulate a minimum number of employees to be covered by the law. It applies to all employers, private and public, regardless of size.

Veterans, active duty service members, and members of Reserve components have the right to be reemployed in a civilian job if they leave that job to perform military service and meet the following criteria:

- The service member must give the employer advanced written or verbal notice of the service.
- The service member must have five years or less of cumulative service in the uniformed services while with that particular employer.

- The service member must return to work or apply for reemployment in a timely manner after the conclusion of service.
- The service member must not have been dishonorably discharged.[58]

Under the act, an employer may not deny initial employment, reemployment, retention in employment, promotion, or any benefit of employment due to uniformed service.[59] The act also guarantees employees a continuation of health benefits (at the employee's expense) for the first twenty-four months of military leave and protects pension benefits upon return from leave.[60]

Genetic Information Nondiscrimination Act of 2008

The Genetic Information Nondiscrimination Act of 2008 (GINA) protects individuals from genetic discrimination in employment and health insurance. The law was passed by Congress in response to advances in genetic testing and a long history of discrimination on the basis of genetics in the United States. You may be wondering: What is genetic testing, and what does it have to do with employment discrimination? **Genetic testing** is a type of medical test that identifies changes in chromosomes, genes, or proteins, the results of which can confirm or rule out a suspected genetic condition or help determine a person's chance of developing or passing on a genetic disorder.[61] Today, there are over one thousand types of genetic tests available.

In the introductory section of the act, Congress described their findings and said that several facts compelled them to take action, including the explosion in genetic testing and previous abuses of genetic information.[62] They cited the fact that early science of genetics became the basis of state laws that provided for the sterilization of persons presumed to have genetic defects such as mental retardation, mental disease, epilepsy, blindness, and hearing loss, among other conditions. Congress stated that many genetic conditions and disorders are associated with particular racial and ethnic groups, and therefore members of a particular group might be stigmatized or discriminated against because of genetic information.[63] One particular example given in the findings is that in the 1970s, programs were implemented to screen and identify carriers of sickle cell anemia, a disease that afflicts African Americans.[64]

Under Title II of GINA, it is illegal to discriminate against employees or applicants because of genetic information. The act prohibits the use of genetic information in making employment decisions, restricts employers from requesting or purchasing genetic information on employees (except in a few exceptions stipulated in the legislation), and imposes confidentiality requirements on employers.[65] Title II of GINA applies to all employers with fifteen or more employees and is enforced by the EEOC.

genetic testing

A type of medical test that identifies changes in chromosomes, genes, or proteins, the results of which can confirm or rule out a suspected genetic condition or help determine a person's chance of developing or passing on a genetic disorder.

Lilly Ledbetter Fair Pay Act of 2009

The Lilly Ledbetter Fair Pay Act of 2009 amended Title VII of the Civil Rights Act and overturned the Supreme Court's decision in *Ledbetter v. Goodyear Tire and Rubber Co., Inc.* (2007), which severely restricted the time period for filing complaints of discrimination in employment.[66] The act contains a retroactive provision, which provides that the statute of limitations for filing a charge of discrimination begins with each paycheck affected by a discriminatory decision. Under Title VII, the law now states that unlawful discrimination occurs when (1) a discriminatory compensation decision or other practice is adopted; (2) an individual becomes subject to a discriminatory compensation decision or other practice; or (3) an individual is affected by application of a discriminatory compensation decision or other practice, including each time wages, benefits, or other compensation is paid, resulting in whole or in part from such a decision or other practice.[67]

Lilly Ledbetter worked for the Goodyear Tire and Rubber Co. plant in Gadsden, Alabama for over two decades, and the company knowingly paid her up to 40% less than all the men with equal jobs in her division.[68] In the original court case, she won and was awarded $300,000 in back pay.

Goodyear appealed all the way to the Supreme Court, which ruled in favor of Goodyear, on the basis that the plaintiff did not file a complaint within the 180-day deadline required under the Equal Pay Act of 1963. In other words, Goodyear did not deny that discrimination occurred, but they won on a technicality. In many cases, employees are not aware of the discrimination within 180 days of when the discriminatory action happened (in this case, when Goodyear decided what they would pay Ledbetter). Under the new rules, the 180-day statute of limitations begins anew with each paycheck. The Lilly Ledbetter Fair Pay Act of 2009 was passed by Congress to ensure that companies cannot commit discriminatory acts and get away with it based on a technicality.

Reporting and Posting Requirements

Title VII of the Civil Rights Act of 1964 mandates that employers report on the racial/ethnic and gender composition of their workforce by job category. All U.S. employers with one hundred or more employees are required to file an EEO-1 form each year. Federal government contractors and first-tier subcontractors with fifty or more employees and at least $50,000 in contracts are also required to file the EEO-1.[69] The filing deadline is March 31, and the form is filed online.

There are no penalties imposed for failure to file an EEO-1 report. Under Title VII, any employer failing or refusing to file the EEO-1 can be compelled by order of a U.S. District Court to do so.[70] However, there are substantial penalties under Title VII for making willfully false statements on an EEO-1, including fines or imprisonment. Even though there are no penalties for not filing the EEO-1, it is very important to do so. If an employer is charged with discrimination, failure to file the EEO-1 report could give a jury or judge the impression that the employer does not take EEO laws seriously.

Federal contractors and subcontractors with a contract or subcontract worth $150,00 or more are required under the VEVRAA to file an annual report called the VETS-4212. The report is filed online with the Secretary of Labor between August 1 and September 30 of each year. The employer must report the number of employees in their workforces, by job category and hiring location, who are qualified covered veterans.[71] Failure to submit the report can result in the government freezing payments to the contractor and putting a hold on entering into any new contracts.

Title VII requires employers to post a notice describing the federal laws prohibiting job discrimination based on race, color, sex, national origin, religion, age, equal pay, disability, or genetic information.[72] There is no specific penalty for failure to post the notice, but in the event of a discrimination charge, it could work against the employer in terms of the perceptions of a judge or jury. Failure to post could also cause the EEOC to extend the filing deadline if the plaintiff claims that they were unaware of the filing deadline. Fortunately, the EEOC provides an "EEO is the Law" poster which summarizes all of the required information. The EEOC provides the poster free of charge, in English, Arabic, Chinese, and Spanish. The poster should be posted in a conspicuous location, such as a break room. In some situations, for example with employees who telecommute, the poster should also be posted electronically. The ADA also requires that notices be made available in a location that is accessible to applicants and employees with disabilities that limit mobility.[73]

HR in the Real World: Micro-What?

As an HR professional, I often find myself needing to explain concepts such as microaggression to employees who have never heard these terms. But educating the workforce on this topic can go a long way toward creating a culture of equal opportunity and equal treatment. How about you? Do you understand what microaggression is, and could you give an example?

Microaggression is a term used for brief and commonplace daily verbal, behavioral, or environmental indignities, whether intentional or unintentional, that communicate hostile, derogatory, or negative prejudicial slights and insults toward any group, particularly culturally marginalized groups. It is not a new term, although it is new to many in the workplace. The term was coined around the late 1960s, after the Civil Rights era, when visible and violent expressions of racism were eclipsed by subtler incarnations.

Okay then, so let's look at some examples of microagression:

- Mistaking a man for a company's CEO, when the female CEO is sitting next to him.
- Talking louder to someone because they are older.
- A white person telling a person of color that they are very articulate.
- Assuming that an Asian employee is good with math.
- Using sexist or racist language.
- Assuming that women are less logical or more emotional than men.
- Asking male employees to work late, assuming that the females need to get home to take care of children, dinner, etc. (This particular example can be referred to as benevolent sexism, in which the offending party is trying to be thoughtful, but does not realize they are marginalizing women.)
- Always asking a female to take the minutes at a meeting.
- Using ageist language, such as "okay, boomer."
- Invasion of space and inappropriate touching.

Consider this example from Ruth Terry: "White people find my halo of gravity-defying hair irresistible to the touch. I don't mind as long as they ask before they cop a feel, but they usually don't. So, after years of enduring this overfamiliarity from everyone from the stranger behind me in the checkout lane to a middle-aged male dental hygienist, I came up with a strategy. Now when that unbidden white hand starts creeping toward my head, mine starts creeping toward theirs. I go as far as they go. They usually flinch back, and then resignedly lean into my touch, laughing with recognition as their faux pas—their microaggression—sinks in. I laugh along with them—because let's keep it light, right?—and with a little thrill of victory. Teachable moment, for the win!"[74]

Key Takeaways

- Disparate treatment, in the context of employment, occurs when a person is treated differently from others in similar situations and the different treatment is because of an individual's membership in a protected class.
- Disparate impact (or adverse impact) occurs when policies, practices, rules, or other systems that appear to be neutral result in a disproportionate impact on a protected group.
- A pattern or practice of discrimination exists when the plaintiff can prove that the defendant regularly and repeatedly engaged in acts prohibited by statute.
- A bona fide occupational qualification (BFOQ) is an employment qualification that is essential for an individual to perform a job successfully.
- All U.S. employers with one hundred or more employees are required to file an EEO-1 form each year.
- Federal contractors and subcontractors with a contract or subcontract worth $150,000 or more are required under the VEVRAA to file an annual report called the VETS-4212.
- Title VII requires employers to post a notice describing the federal laws prohibiting job discrimination based on race, color, sex, national origin, religion, age, equal pay, disability, or genetic information.

What Do *You* Think?

1. What is the role of statutory law, executive orders, and case law in employment discrimination?
2. How does motive differ in cases of disparate treatment versus disparate impact?
3. In your opinion, how many instances of discrimination should occur before a pattern or practice of discrimination is established?
4. Do you or someone you work with have a disability? What are some examples of reasonable accommodations that apply in these situations?
5. Why did Congress leave the concept of "undue hardship" to be decided on a case-by-case basis, rather than defining it in the ADA?

3.4 Sexual Harassment

Learning Objectives

1. Recognize instances of sexual harassment.
2. Compare and contrast quid pro quo sexual harassment and hostile working environment.
3. Describe the situations in which employers are liable for sexual harassment.
4. Identify strategies that employers can implement to prevent sexual harassment.

What is Sexual Harassment?

sexual harassment

A form of sex discrimination that violates Title VII of the Civil Rights Act of 1964 and includes unwelcome advances, requests for sexual favors, and other verbal or physical conduct of a sexual nature, when this conduct explicitly or implicitly affects an individual's terms of employment, unreasonably interferes with an individual's work performance, or creates an intimidating, hostile, or offensive work environment.

Sexual harassment is a form of sex discrimination that violates Title VII of the Civil Rights Act of 1964.[75] Sexual harassment includes unwelcome advances, requests for sexual favors, and other verbal or physical conduct of a sexual nature, when this conduct explicitly or implicitly affects an individual's terms of employment, unreasonably interferes with an individual's work performance, or creates an intimidating, hostile, or offensive work environment. As with all of the Title VII regulations, sexual harassment law applies to employers with fifteen or more employees, employment agencies, labor organizations, and all levels of government.

A new wave of awareness exists about sexual harassment today because of the "me too" movement. Actress and activist Alyssa Milano accelerated the movement on October 15, 2017, with a tweet to her followers to reply "me too" if they had been sexually harassed or assaulted.[76] Milano was tweeting in response to the Harvey Weinstein scandal when the *New York Times* and the *New Yorker* exposed the producer's decades-long history of sexual harassment. Over the next six months, the #MeToo hashtag was used on Twitter an average of 61,911 times per day, according to a Pew analysis. In the wake of the movement, over two hundred prominent men have lost their jobs after allegations of sexual harassment, including Senator Al Franken, Fox host Bill O'Reilly, TV host Charlie Rose, TV news anchor Matt Lauer, comedian Louis C.K., and actor Kevin Spacey.[77]

Sexual harassment can occur in a variety of circumstances, including, but not limited to, the following:

- The victim as well as the harasser may be a woman or a man. The victim does not have to be of the opposite sex.

- The harasser can be the victim's supervisor, an agent of the employer, a supervisor in another area, a co-worker, or even a non-employee (e.g., a customer or supplier).

- The victim does not have to be the person harassed but could be anyone affected by the offensive conduct.

- Unlawful sexual harassment may occur with economic injury to or discharge of the victim.

- The harasser's conduct must be unwelcome. It is helpful for the victim to inform the harasser that the conduct is unwelcome, and also to report the situation through any grievance process that the employer provides.[78]

About one-third of EEOC claims are based on sex, with about 10% being specifically for sexual harassment. How can organizations create a culture that does not tolerate sexual harassment?

Source: © Shutterstock, Inc.

The Two Types of Sexual Harassment

In *Meritor Savings Bank v. Vinson* (1986), a female employee alleged that she was pressured into having sex with her superior numerous times, and she did so without reporting the matter because she was afraid of losing her job. In the decision, the court introduced the terms "quid pro quo" and "hostile working environment" to illustrate the two types of sexual harassment. **Quid pro quo** sexual harassment occurs when a job benefit is directly tied to an employee submitting to unwelcome sexual advances. The term is a Latin phrase, and literally means "this for that." It implied that if one individual gives something, then the other individual will give something in return (e.g., exchanging sexual favors for a promotion). Only an individual with authority over an employee can be guilty of quid pro quo harassment since it requires the harasser to have the authority to grant or withhold benefits.

Hostile working environment describes a workplace where unwelcome conduct of a sexual nature is pervasive or severe enough to create an environment that a reasonable person would consider intimidating, hostile, or abusive. Offensive conduct may include, but is not limited to:

- offensive jokes
- slurs
- epithets or name-calling
- physical assault or threats
- intimidation
- ridicule or mockery
- insults or put-downs

quid pro quo

Occurs when a job benefit is directly tied to an employee submitting to unwelcome sexual advances.

hostile working environment

A workplace in which unwelcome conduct of a sexual nature is pervasive or severe enough to create a work environment that a reasonable person would consider intimidating, hostile, or abusive.

- offensive objects or pictures
- interference with work performance[79]

Isolated incidents (unless extremely severe) and petty slights do not typically rise to the level of illegal harassment. A pattern or practice of discrimination has to be established for guilt to be proven of a hostile working environment. By contrast, in quid pro quo harassment, a single incident is illegal.

The courts use a reasonable person standard in determining whether a hostile work environment existed. The Supreme Court clarified this in *Harris v. Forklift Systems, Inc.* 510 U.S. 17 (1993). In Harris, the court held, that to be actionable, the work environment must be one that a reasonable person would find hostile, looking at all circumstances and that the plaintiff must have subjectively perceived the environment as hostile.[80]

Employer Liability for Sexual Harassment

In cases of hostile work environment, the plaintiff must establish a prima facie case by showing that: (1) he or she was subject to an intimidating, hostile, or offensive work environment; (2) the conduct was based on the plaintiff's protected status; (3) the conduct was sufficiently severe or pervasive to alter the terms or conditions of the plaintiff's environment for a reasonable person under similar circumstances; and (4) at the time such conduct occurred and as a result of such conduct, the plaintiff perceived his or her work environment to be abusive.[81] If the employee's supervisor was the harasser, the employer can avoid liability by proving that: (1) the employer made reasonable efforts to prevent harassment (for example by requiring all supervisors to undergo sexual harassment training), and promptly tried to correct the harassing behavior (for example by reprimanding and/or counseling the harasser), and (2) the employee failed to take advantage of opportunities for reporting or otherwise correcting the behavior that were offered by the employer. If an employer has a system in place whereby individuals can report sexual harassment, and an individual who is being harassed does not report the behavior, the employer can assert this as an affirmative defense.

The liability standard is different in cases of quid pro quo harassment. An employer is automatically liable for harassment by a supervisor that results in a negative employment action such as termination, failure to promote or hire, or loss of wages.[82]

Prevention of Sexual Harassment

The best way to minimize employer liability is to prevent sexual harassment from occurring. One approach that employers utilize is to provide mandatory sexual harassment training for all employees. Many employers also require annual refresher training to remind employees of the law and to maintain awareness of the company's policy of not tolerating sexual harassment. Equally important to training is the creation of a corporate culture that does not tolerate harassment. Employers should establish clear policies that prohibit sexual harassment not only by all employees, but also by others who interact with employees, such as customers and suppliers. Employers should also establish an effective complaint process for employees to notify the company of perceived sexual harassment. Upon receipt of a complaint, the HR department should take immediate action by conducting a thorough and neutral investigation. When an investigation finds that harassment has occurred, the employer should take corrective action, and in some cases, punitive action. Failure by the employer to respond to complaints in a timely manner and failure to take corrective or punitive action sends a message that the company does not take sexual harassment seriously and can nullify the impact of sexual harassment training. It is also unlawful for the employer to retaliate against an individual for opposing employment practices based on sex by filing a discrimination charge, testifying, or participating in an investigation or proceeding.

How to Recognize, Address, and Prevent Sexual Harassment

The EEOC provides information and training on how to prevent employment discrimination from occurring in your workplace.

View the video online at: http://www.youtube.com/embed/tVtJcVbbjcA?rel=0

HR Talk: Rodney Klein

Outreach and Education Coordinator

Equal Employment Opportunity Commission

1. **Which aspect of EEO is the most challenging for employers, and causes the most discrimination charges?**

   People tend to file charges when they feel like they have no other choice. That happens either when they feel they are being harassed or they have been discharged. In terms of compliance, the most challenging aspect of EEO law is the ADA. It is conceptually written differently than much employment law. For example, wage and hour laws give specific rules and guidelines to follow (do a, then b, then c), and employers find that fairly straightforward. But the ADA does not give specific guidelines since it is written so that it can be applied in a broad variety of situations. The ADA does not give you a lot of answers; It just tells you what questions to ask.

2. **What actions can HR professionals implement in their organizations to improve compliance with EEO regulations?**

   There are two ways to impact behavior at work: (1) the legal way, and (2) the cultural way. First, address the legal component by establishing policies and a complaint procedure. Employees should be able to file a complaint with someone other than their boss. Second, address the cultural component. Make sure people know that EEO compliance, including sexual harassment, is not just the law, but it is their company policy. The cultural should emphasize "this is who we are" along with "this is who we are not" and needs to be driven by upper management. If the company focuses just on compliance and doesn't really value inclusion, then you won't get the most out of your employees because they will not feel like their ideas are valued.

3. **What impact has the "me too" movement had on sexual harassment in the workplace?**

   It's perhaps too early to tell. But what makes this different is that it did not come from the government or from organizations, but was driven by individuals. Employees are now telling employers that what they're doing isn't working. One of the most impactful aspects of the "me too" movement is that it is taking the stigma away from coming forward with a sexual harassment claim.

Key Takeaways

- Sexual harassment is a form of sex discrimination that violates Title VII of the Civil Rights Act of 1964 and includes unwelcome advances, requests for sexual favors, and other verbal or physical conduct of a sexual nature, when this conduct explicitly or implicitly affects an individual's terms of employment, unreasonably interferes with an individual's work performance, or creates an intimidating, hostile, or offensive work environment.
- Quid pro quo sexual harassment occurs when a job benefit is directly tied to an employee submitting to unwelcome sexual advances.
- A hostile working environment is a work environment in which unwelcome conduct of a sexual nature is pervasive or severe enough to create a work environment that a reasonable person would consider intimidating, hostile, or abusive.
- In cases of hostile work environment, the plaintiff must establish a prima facie case by showing that: (1) he or she was subject to an intimidating, hostile, or offensive work environment; (2) the conduct was based on the plaintiff's protected status; (3) the conduct was sufficiently severe or pervasive to alter the terms or conditions of the plaintiff's environment for a reasonable person under similar circumstances; and (4) at the time such conduct occurred and as a result of such conduct, the plaintiff perceived his or work environment to be abusive.
- The best way to minimize employer liability is to prevent sexual harassment from occurring.
- It is also unlawful for the employer to retaliate against an individual for opposing employment practices based on sex by filing a discrimination charge, testifying, or participating in an investigation or proceeding.

What Do *You* Think?

1. Why did so many people wait (decades, in some cases) to come forward with allegations of sexual harassment in the #MeToo movement?
2. Have you ever worked in a hostile work environment? How did you respond?
3. Does sexual harassment training really work? Does it help prevent sexual harassment from occurring?
4. What steps could you take as an HR manager to discourage sexual harassment?

3.5 Conclusion

Almost every aspect of HR is impacted by legislation, case law, or regulatory agencies at the federal, state, or local levels. This chapter explored the legislation related to EEO, discrimination, and affirmative action. In addition, the historical perspective was reviewed, so that students will understand the intent of the laws and not just the letter of the law. The major federal employment laws were then examined. The chapter concluded with a discussion of sexual harassment, including employer liability and prevention strategies. It is also important to realize that there are many other aspects of employment law other than EEO. For example, there are federal laws that govern minimum wage, overtime, collective bargaining, and employee benefits. These laws will be covered in the relevant chapters.

Theory-into-Practice (TIP) Exercises

1. Assume that a friend emails you and complains that their employer is discriminating against them. Write a response in which you describe the steps of the EEOC complaint process. Also, explain how they should establish a prima facie case of discrimination.

2. Review the list of best practices for employers and human resources/EEO professionals (under Resources #2). Then write three to four recommendations for your current employer to implement that will help to improve the organizational culture and discourage discrimination and sexual harassment.

3. Complete the following table and questions using the four-fifths rule:

   a.

Applicants	Hired	Selection Rate
80 White	48	
40 Black	12	

   b. A comparison of the black selection rate of _____% with the white selection rate of _____% shows that black rate is _____% of the white rate.

   c. Is adverse impact indicated? (Hint: You will find the solution to this problem in the Uniform Guidelines on Employee Selection Procedures.)

Case Study: A Spicy Case of Pregnancy Discrimination

Source: rblfmr / Shutterstock.com

In November 2011, Doris Hernandez found out she was pregnant with her third child. She reported this to her boss, David Hahn, at Chipotle, where she was employed. Soon after, she stated, he began restricting her access to drinking water and limiting bathroom breaks. Hernandez said that when she needed a bathroom break, she was told to inform all other employees where she was going and wait for permission to leave her post. Other non-pregnant employees were not required to do this. She was scheduled for a prenatal doctor visit, which she informed Hahn of in advance. He told her that she would not be allowed the time off, and she went anyway.

She was fired the next day in front of other employees in the store. Prior to announcing her pregnancy, Hernandez had received positive performance reviews for her work at the store, where she made tortillas and salsa, rolled burritos, and prepped vegetables.

Doris Hernandez took her case to court, and in August 2016 she was awarded $550,000. After deliberating for three hours, the jury decided that she had been discriminated against and awarded her $50,000 in compensatory damages and $500,000 in punitive damages. Chipotle does not plan to appeal but denies it is guilty of the discrimination. Hernandez's troubles at Chipotle led the Washington, D.C. Council to pass the Protecting Pregnant Workers Fairness Act, which requires employers to provide pregnant workers with basic accommodations, such as access to drinking water and more frequent bathroom breaks. In February 2016, Chipotle was also ordered to pay three former general managers roughly $600,000 after a federal grand jury determined the company had discriminated against and fired the women because of their gender.[83]

 Katie Link reports for Newsy on the case of Doris Hernandez.

View the video online at: http://www.youtube.com/embed/NAGlZvkIvKU?rel=0

Case Discussion Questions

1. Do you think there was discrimination in this case? Why or why not?
2. Would you have gone to the doctor's appointment, knowing you may be fired?
3. Have you seen cases of clear discrimination on the basis of gender at your workplace or school?

Resources

1. **Title VII of the Civil Rights Act of 1964.** The full text of Title VII of the CRA of 1964.

   https://www.eeoc.gov/laws/statutes/titlevii.cfm

2. **EEOC Best Practices.** Best practices for employers and human resources/EEO professionals.

   https://www.eeoc.gov/eeoc/initiatives/e-race/bestpractices-employers.cfm

3. **Uniform Guidelines.** The full text of the Uniform Guidelines on Employee Selection procedures.

   http://www.uniformguidelines.com/uniform-guidelines.html

4. **Women's Bureau of the Department of Labor.** The Women's Bureau develops policies and standards and conducts inquiries to safeguard the interests of working women; to advocate for their equality and economic security for themselves and their families; and to promote quality work environments.

   https://www.dol.gov/wb/

Endnotes

1. Case written by Crews, P. (2020). Adapted from Dvorak, P. (2018). The equal pay fight isn't over, so Lilly Ledbetter returned to the Supreme Court steps. *Washington Post.* Retrieved from https://www.washington-post.com/local/the-equal-pay-fight-isnt-over-so-lilly-ledbetter-returned-to-the-supreme-court-steps/2018/08/30/aca360e4-ac60-11e8-a8d7-0f63ab8b1370_story.html?utm_term=.fe57e16534e4

2. Equal Employment Opportunity Commission. *Pre 1965: Events leading to the creation of EEOC.* Retrieved February 11, 2020 from https://www.eeoc.gov/eeoc/history/35th/pre1965/index.html

3. Equal Employment Opportunity Commission. *Milestones: The early years.* Retrieved February 11, 2019 from https://www.eeoc.gov/eeoc/history/35th/milestones/early.html

4. EEO terminology. *National Archives.* Retrieved March 17, 2020 from https://www.archives.gov/eeo/terminology.html

5. Ibid.

6. U.S. Department of Labor. *Executive Order 11246—Equal Employment Opportunity.* Retrieved March 23, 2019 from https://www.dol.gov/ofccp/regs/compliance/ca_11246.htm

7. U.S. Department of Labor. *Affirmative action.* Retrieved March 23, 2020 from https://www.dol.gov/general/topic/hiring/affirmativeact

8. Equal Employment Opportunity Commission. Overview. Retrieved February 12, 2020 from https://www.eeoc.gov/eeoc/index.cfm

9. Ibid.

10. Ibid.

11. Equal Employment Opportunity Commission. *The commission and the general counsel.* Retrieved February 12, 2020 from https://www.eeoc.gov/eeoc/commission.cfm

12. Ibid.

13. Equal Employment Opportunity Commission. *Time limits for filing a charge.* Retrieved February 12, 2020 from https://www.eeoc.gov/employees/time-liness.cfm

14. Ibid.

15. Ibid.

16. Department of Labor. *About OFCCP.* Retrieved February 12, 2020 from https://www.dol.gov/ofccp/aboutof.html

17. Society for Human Resource Management. (2018). *Managing federal contractor affirmative action programs.* Retrieved from https://www.shrm.org/resourcesandtools/tools-and-samples/toolkits/pages/managingaffirmativeactionprograms.aspx

18. Ibid.

19. Department of Labor. *How to file a complaint.* Retrieved February 12, 2020 from: https://www.dol.gov/ofccp/regs/compliance/pdf/pdfstart.htm

20. Ibid.

21. Ibid.

22. Frey, W.H. (2018). The U.S. will become 'minority white' in 2045, Census projects. *Brookings.* Retrieved from https://www.brookings.edu/blog/the-avenue/2018/03/14/the-us-will-become-minority-white-in-2045-census-projects/

23. Adapted from Loehr, A. (2015). 4 ways HR analytics can improve workforce diversity. Retrieved from https://www.cornerstoneondemand.com/rework/4-ways-hr-analytics-can-improve-workplace-diversity

24. Equal Employment Opportunity Commission Title VII of the Civil Rights Act of 1964. Retrieved February 14, 2019 from https://www.eeoc.gov//laws/statutes/titlevii.cfm

25. Ford, C. (2009). Gender discrimination and hostile work environment. *Employment Discrimination,* 57(2), 1-5.

26. Ibid.

27. Society for Human Resource Management. *What are disparate impact and disparate treatment?* Retrieved February 14, 2020 from https://www.shrm.org/resourcesandtools/tools-and-samples/hr-qa/pages/disparateimpactdisparatetreatment.aspx

28. Equal Employment Opportunity Commission. Adoption of questions and answers to clarify and provide a common interpretation of the Uniform Guidelines on Employee Selection Procedures. Retrieved February 14, 2020 from https://www.eeoc.gov/policy/docs/qanda_clarify_procedures.html

29. Department of Justice. *A pattern or practice of discrimination.* Retrieved February 14, 2020 from https://www.justice.gov/crt/pattern-or-practice-discrimination

30. American Bar Association. *EEOC pattern or practice litigation.* Retrieved February 14, 2020 from https://www.americanbar.org/content/dam/aba/administrative/labor_law/meetings/2010/2010_eeo_016.authcheckdam.pdf

31. U.S. Equal Employment Opportunity Commission. *Facts about retaliation.* Retrieved March 23, 2020 from https://www.eeoc.gov/laws/types/retaliation.cfm

32. U.S. Equal Employment Opportunity Commission. *Significant EEOC race/color cases.* Retrieved March 23, 2020 from https://www.eeoc.gov/eeoc/initiatives/e-race/caselist.cfm

33. *Bona fide occupational law and definition.* US Legal. Retrieved February 14, 2020 from https://definitions.uslegal.com/b/bona-fide-occupational-qualification/

34. Society for Human Resource Management. (2018). *Guidelines on Interview and employment application questions.* Retrieved from https://www.shrm.org/resourcesandtools/tools-and-samples/toolkits/pages/interviewandemploymentapplicationquestions.aspx

35. Equal Employment Opportunity Commission. *The Equal Pay Act of 1963.* Retrieved February 12, 2020 from https://www.eeoc.gov/laws/statutes/epa.cfm

36. Equal Employment Opportunity Commission. *Facts about equal pay and compensation discrimination.* Retrieved February 12, 2020 from https://www.eeoc.gov/eeoc/publications/fs-epa.cfm

37. Society for Human Resource Management. *Title VII of the Civil Rights Act of 1964.* Retrieved February 12, 2020 from https://www.shrm.org/hr-today/public-policy/hr-public-policy-issues/pages/titleviiofthecivilrights-actof1964.aspx

38. Equal Employment Opportunity Commission. *Title VII of the Civil Rights Act of 1964.* Equal Employment Opportunity Commission. Retrieved February 12, 2020 from https://www.eeoc.gov/laws/statutes/titlevii.cfm

39. Equal Employment Opportunity Commission. (2020). *EEOC releases fiscal year 2019 enforcement and litigation data.* Retrieved from https://www.eeoc.gov/eeoc/newsroom/release/1-24-20.cfm

40. Ibid.

41. Equal Employment Opportunity Commission. *The Age Discrimination in Employment Act of 1967.* Retrieved February 12, 2020 from https://www.eeoc.gov/laws/statutes/adea.cfm

42. Ibid.

43. Equal Employment Opportunity Commission. *The Age Discrimination in Employment Act of 1967.* Retrieved February 12, 2020 from https://www.eeoc.gov/laws/statutes/adea.cfm

44. Department of Labor. *Vietnam Era Veterans' Readjustment Assistance Act of 1974, as amended.* Retrieved February 13, 2020 from https://www.dol.gov/ofccp/regs/statutes/4212.htm

45. ADA Network. *Vietnam Era Veterans' Readjustment Assistance Act of 1974.* Retrieved February 13, 2019 from https://adata.org/factsheet/VEVRAA

46. Equal Employment Opportunity Commission. *The Pregnancy Discrimination Act of 1978.* Retrieved February 13, 2020 from https://www.eeoc.gov/laws/statutes/pregnancy.cfm

47. United States Department of Justice, Civil Rights Division. *Introduction to the ADA.* Retrieved February 13, 2020 from https://www.ada.gov/ada_intro.htm

48. Ibid.

49. Department of Labor. *The ADA Amendments of 2008: Frequently Asked Questions*. Retrieved February 13, 2019 from https://www.dol.gov/ofccp/regs/compliance/faqs/adafaqs.htm#Q5

50. ADA National Network. *An overview of the Americans with Disabilities Act*. Retrieved February 13, 2020 from https://adata.org/factsheet/ADA-overview

51. Equal Employment Opportunity Commission. *Enforcement guidance: Reasonable accommodation and undue hardship under the Americans with Disabilities Act*. Retrieved February 13, 2020 from https://www.eeoc.gov/policy/docs/accommodation.html#requesting

52. Ibid.

53. Ibid.

54. Equal Employment Opportunity Commission. *The Civil Rights Act of 1991*. Retrieved February 13, 2020 from https://www.eeoc.gov/eeoc/history/35th/1990s/civilrights.html

55. Ibid.

56. Equal Employment Opportunity Commission. *Damages in case of intentional discrimination*. Retrieved February 13, 2020 from https://www.eeoc.gov/laws/statutes/cra-1991.cfm

57. Department of Labor. *Vets USERRA Fact Sheet*. Retrieved February 13, 2020 from https://www.dol.gov/vets/programs/userra/userra_fs.htm

58. Department of Labor. *Know your rights*. Retrieved February 13, 2020 from https://www.dol.gov/vets/programs/userra/aboutuserra.htm#employeerights

59. Ibid.

60. American Bar Association. *A guide to leave under the Uniformed Services Employment and Reemployment Rights Act*. Retrieved February 13, 2020 from https://www.americanbar.org/content/dam/aba/events/labor_law/am/2014/2b_wood.authcheckdam.pdf

61. What is genetic testing? *Genetic Home Reference*. Retrieved February 19, 2020 from https://ghr.nlm.nih.gov/primer/testing/genetictesting

62. Equal Employment Opportunity Commission. *The Genetic Information Nondiscrimination Act of 2008*. Retrieved February 13, 2020 from https://www.eeoc.gov/laws/statutes/gina.cfm

63. Ibid.

64. Ibid.

65. Equal Employment Opportunity Commission. *Genetic Information Discrimination*. February 13, 2020 from https://www.eeoc.gov/laws/types/genetic.cfm

66. Equal Employment Opportunity Commission. *Lilly Ledbetter Fair Pay Act of 2009*. Retrieved February 14, 2019 from https://www.eeoc.gov/eeoc/publications/brochure-equal_pay_and_ledbetter_act.cfm

67. Lilly Ledbetter Fair Pay Act retroactively applied. *Labor and Employment Law Update*. Retrieved February 14, 2020 from https://laborandemploymentlawupdate.com/2011/10/21/lilly-ledbetter-fair-pay-act-retroactively-applied/

68. Dvorak, P. (2018). The equal-pay fight isn't over, so Lilly Ledbetter returned to the Supreme Court steps. *Washington Post*. Retrieved from https://www.washingtonpost.com/local/the-equal-pay-fight-isnt-over-so-lilly-ledbetter-returned-to-the-supreme-court-steps/2018/08/30/aca360e4-ac60-11e8-a8d7-0f63ab8b1370_story.html?utm_term=.0c5fa2a17398

69. Society for Human Resource Management. (2019). What are the filing requirements for the EEO-1 form? (2019). Retrieved February 14, 2020 from https://www.shrm.org/resourcesandtools/tools-and-samples/hr-qa/pages/newfilingrequirements.aspx

70. Equal Employment Opportunity Commission. *Legal basis for requirements*. Retrieved February 14, 2019 from https://www.eeoc.gov/employers/eeo1survey/legalbasis.cfm

71. Department of Labor. *Federal contractor program*. Retrieved February 14, 2020 from https://www.dol.gov/vets/contractor/main.htm#11

72. Equal Employment Opportunity Commission. "EEO is the Law" (poster). Retrieved February 14, 2020 from https://www1.eeoc.gov/employers/poster.cfm

73. Ibid.

74. Terry, R. (2019). Racial microaggressions are real: Here's how to navigate them. *yes!* Retrieved from https://www.yesmagazine.org/opinion/2019/10/23/racist-racial-microaggressions/

75. Equal Employment Opportunity Commission. *Facts about sexual harassment*. Retrieved February 15, 2020 from https://www.eeoc.gov/eeoc/publications/fs-sex.cfm

76. Piacenza, J. (2018). A year into #metoo, public worried about false allegations. https://morningconsult.com/2018/10/11/a-year-into-metoo-public-worried-about-false-allegations/

77. Ibid.

78. Ibid.

79. Equal Employment Opportunity Commission. *Harassment*. Retrieved February 15, 2020 from https://www.eeoc.gov/laws/types/harassment.cfm

80. Ford, C. (2009). Gender discrimination and hostile work environment. *Employment Discrimination*, 57(2), 1-5.

81. Ibid.

82. Equal Employment Opportunity Commission. *Harassment*. Retrieved February 15, 2020 from https://www.eeoc.gov/laws/types/harassment.cfm

83. Case written by Crews, P. (2020). Adapted from Bhattarai, A. (2016). Chipotle ordered to pay $500,000 for discriminating against pregnant worker. *The Washington Post*. Retrieved from https://www.washingtonpost.com/business/capitalbusiness/chipotle-ordered-to-pay-550000-for-discriminating-against-pregnant-worker/2016/08/09/962ac72e-5e49-11e6-8e45-477372e89d78_story.html?utm_term=.9f5e31d815a

CHAPTER 4
Job Analysis and Design

Learning Objectives

After reading this chapter, you should be able to do the following:

1. Describe the purpose of job analysis, job descriptions, and job specifications.
2. Recognize how the nature of work and jobs is changing.
3. Explain how to use psychological theories of job design to improve the motivating potential of a position.
4. Discuss the factors that influence team effectiveness and team dysfunction.

The concept of the employee life cycle (ELC) was introduced in Chapter 1. While it may seem that the first stage in recruitment and hiring a new employee would be creating a job posting or advertisement, the process of hiring an employee begins earlier, with job analysis and design. **Job analysis** is a process used to collect information about the duties, responsibilities, and required knowledge, skills, and abilities needed to perform the job successfully. It also includes the work environment and authority structure. **Job design** is the study of how jobs might be improved to increase organizational productivity and employee satisfaction. Together these concepts form the foundation for hiring the right individuals and placing them into positions designed for organizational and personal success.

    The chapter begins with an examination of job analysis methods, job descriptions, and job specifications. We will examine trends such as the gig economy that are fundamentally changing the nature of work. Theories of job design and motivation are explored, followed by several models for implementing the theories to improve satisfaction and retention. The chapter concludes with a review of work teams and how teams can be designed to improve effectiveness and reduce dysfunction.

job analysis

A process used to collect information about the duties, responsibilities, and required knowledge, skills, and abilities needed to perform the job successfully.

job design

The study of how jobs might be improved to increase organizational productivity and employee satisfaction.

4.1 Opening Case: Charming a Chatbot

Source: © Shutterstock, Inc.

Starting in the fall of 2018, thousands of job applicants seeking an entry-level position for Kraft Heinz's European division began the process by playing video games for thirty minutes. Pieter Schalkwijk, head of Kraft Heinz's talent acquisition, spends his time crunching data from the games, which are cognitive and behavioral tests. The game was developed by Pymetrics, a company that uses artificial intelligence (A.I.) to assess the personality traits of job candidates. As an example, one game evaluated a candidate's appetite for and approach to risk by inflating balloons while tapping the keyboard space bar and collecting money for each hit until they chose to cash in or the balloon burst, destroying the payoff. Other games measured memory, concentration, and how trusting or skeptical someone is. The results are measured against those of games played by other top-performing Kraft Heinz staffers. Pymetrics evaluates the data and passes it on to Schalkwijk, who then can better assess which candidates are most likely to succeed—because their traits, as represented by their gaming skills, most closely matched those of the risk-seeking, emotionally intelligent employees the company values most.

Kraft Heinz is just one of many corporations whose human resource executives are increasingly relying on artificial intelligence to assess, hire, and manage their staff. As a job candidate, you might have your application vetted by a Mya Systems chatbot at L'Oreal or Pepsico. You could respond to an A.I.-crafted job posting vetted by Textio for Expedia or ViacomCBS or record one of the automated HireVue video interviews used by Hilton and Delta Air Lines. Companies also use A.I. for setting performance targets or identifying employees for promotion opportunities, and some in-house systems might guess your plans to quit and warn managers that they should try to make you happy. One of the reasons more hiring managers are using A.I. is that it helps them save time. Others state it helps combat bias in their decision-making.

Bias in hiring employees has been, and continues to be, a problem. A.I. creators and adopters claim that A.I. can eliminate bias from the hiring process. It can create greater gender and racial diversity and give more opportunities to applicants who don't have a brand-name education. Many recruiters admit to scanning resumes to find top-tier universities, but with A.I., it doesn't matter if you're not from Yale. However, some recruiters are skeptical and say that if misused, A.I. can still lead to bias. Matissa Hollister, an assistant professor of organizational behavior at McGill University, states that a machine-learning system is only as unbiased as the information it learns from. There is a risk that the algorithm will learn that bias and perpetuate it. An example of this has happened at Amazon, which spent years building a resume-analysis-algorithm (never used) only to find that it discriminated against women. This happened because most of the previous applicants' resumes assessed were submitted by men, and the algorithm taught itself that men were always preferable hires. Another company uses A.I. to vet video interviews. The applicant uses a laptop or smartphone camera to record answers to automated questions; software analyzes factors like word choice and facial expressions. However, it was discovered that A.I. that relies on facial recognition can often misidentify or misread faces of color, especially those of darker-skinned women. Others further point out that these issues can be especially problematic when the people designing the tools are white and male.

In Amsterdam, Pieter Schalkwijk is so pleased with the results provided by Pymetrics that he is using its test in some U.S. hiring efforts. He is still proceeding with caution and states that Kraft Heinz will never make all potential hires play Pymetrics games. For one reason, there are generations of qualified applicants who did not grow up gaming, and this could lead to age discrimination.[1]

 Arnie, the HR bot

View an example of how A.I. is automating hiring at McDonald's.

View the video online at: http://www.youtube.com/embed/QrPWaj_YDAw?rel=0

Case Discussion Questions

1. What are some other ways A.I. can be used to automate HR functions?
2. What advantages for human resource managers could A.I. have? What are the potential drawbacks?
3. When developing software for A.I. hiring or promotion tools, what are some techniques or safeguards that could be put in place to either eliminate or greatly reduce bias (gender, race, age, etc.)?
4. How should HR managers assess the success of such tools?

4.2 Job Analysis

Why Is Job Analysis Useful?

Job analysis was defined in the opening paragraph of this chapter, but why is it important? In 1992, Democratic strategist James Carville coined the now infamous phrase, "It's the economy, stupid!" It was a way of summarizing the focus of the campaign in a few words. When it comes to what workers want in a job, we could say, "It's the autonomy, stupid!" So says a recent NBC News report *Research Says This is the Secret to Being Happy at Work*.[2] Only 30% of workers feel actively engaged or connected to their workplace. This can lead to low morale that can cost businesses $450 billion to $550 billion per year. Disengaged employees are more likely to be absent or late, take more sick days, and leave their job prematurely.

Employers tend to throw money at morale problems, but what workers often want is freedom from micromanagement. Employees want to be able to make decisions without always having to get approval, especially over their own responsibilities. This makes them feel more in control. Also, employees want to be able to contribute ideas and feel that their contributions are being listened to. Some employees are much happier with less supervision. Autonomy also can afford workers the ability to determine, to a certain degree, their own responsibilities. This may mean that they are able to delegate when appropriate. A recent University of Birmingham study on the effects of autonomy on employee morale found that the higher the level of autonomy that a worker had, the more they experienced job satisfaction and a general sense of well-being.[3]

While job analysis and design is about more than just autonomy, it is certainly one of the main work aspects that most people care deeply about. This gets us to the crux of why job analysis and job design are important: employees perform better and are more satisfied (and therefore stay with the company longer) when they are in a work environment that motivates them.

job specification

Refers to the qualifications that an individual should possess to adequately perform a job.

job description

A document that includes a summary of the position, the overall job duties, the essential job functions, and the job specification.

Job analysis involves collecting information about jobs, but how is this information used, and what are the benefits of spending the time and money to gather and analyze the data? Research studies indicate that the job analysis process leads to improved job performance, which is good for the organization and good for the employees.[4] In this section, we will look at the benefits for the organization and for the employees. But first, let's distinguish among four terms that will be used throughout this chapter. These four terms are job analysis, job design, job specification, and job description. We have already defined job analysis and job design. **Job specification** refers to the qualifications that an individual should possess to adequately perform a job. It may include KSAOs, education, and experience. A **job description** is a document that includes a summary of the position, the overall job duties, the essential job functions, and the job specification. It may also indicate to whom the individual reports, supervisory responsibilities, and the salary range.

From an organizational perspective, job analysis forms the basis for many HR decisions. You might think of it as serving a similar function to the foundation of a building. If the foundation is not level, then everything that follows later will not be level. This means that the walls might crack, windows and doors will not open and close properly, and cabinets and shelves will not fit properly. Just as a building rests upon a foundation, and problems with the foundation will show up as symptoms throughout the building, all HR decisions and activities rest in some way upon job analysis. A poor job analysis (or a nonexistent one) may cause issues with morale, low performance, high employee turnover, EEO legal challenges, or many other difficulties. Here are a few examples of how job analysis results are used in various aspects of HR; each is stated as a question that HR staff and organizational leaders might ask which can be answered (at least in part) by the information gathered from a job analysis:

- **Workforce planning.** What skillsets do we need? A job analysis provides useful information about the skillsets required for each position. Organizational planners can then better understand existing skills gaps and forecast projected needs.

- **Recruitment and selection.** How do we make sure that we attract a qualified pool of applicants? A job analysis allows HR to prepare a list of the education, experience, and KSAOs that are necessary for an individual to be successful in each position. The information is then used in job postings to recruit a qualified pool of applicants and to make selection decisions based upon criteria that are valid predictors of future job performance.

- **Talent development.** What skills gaps do we need to close with training and development? A job analysis identifies the gaps between KSAOs currently possessed by an employee and those that are necessary to perform well in the current job and to prepare for advancement to future positions.

- **Performance management.** What are the criteria for evaluation? The analysis process should identify the essential job functions, including the criteria for measuring job performance. Decisions based on performance (including promotions, incentive or merit pay, and disciplinary action) should always be consistent and based on data-driven methods.

- **Compensation.** What is one job worth relative to another? This depends on the KSAOs, the experience, and the education required, as well as the essential job functions. Working conditions and hours are also part of compensation decisions, since some jobs will pay a higher rate for dangerous conditions (hazard pay), or evening or weekend work (shift differentials).

- **Employee engagement.** How can jobs be structured to be more motivating and to cause employees to be more committed to their work and to the organization? This is the focus of job design, which relies on the data gathered during a job analysis.

- **EEO legal compliance.** How can we avoid discrimination? The essential job functions and the job specifications should be based upon job-related factors to ensure that hiring and all other decisions regarding the terms and conditions of employment are valid and nondiscriminatory.

- **Wage and hour laws.** When should we pay overtime? The job description should be the basis for determining which positions are exempt and which are nonexempt from wage and hour laws. If a position is exempt (or salaried), then wage and hour laws do not apply. If a position is nonexempt, the employee must be paid the federal minimum wage, and overtime must be paid for any time worked beyond forty hours in a given week.[5] Federal wage and hour laws are governed by the Department of Labor and will be explored in depth in Chapter 9.

- **ADA legal compliance.** Which reasonable accommodations should we offer to comply with ADA? The essential job functions are one determining factor, since the ADA requires employers to provide a reasonable accommodation if it will allow a qualified individual with a disability to perform the job functions and the individual requests the accommodation. So how do we know what these essential job functions are? They should be on the job description and should be based upon the results of a thorough job analysis. During a legal challenge, you can be almost certain that the job description along with any job analysis records will be subpoenaed. A **subpoena** is a legal request issued for the production of documents, or a request to testify in court or other legal proceedings. If you fail to comply with a subpoena, then you can be held in contempt of court. This also holds true for other employment law cases, including EEO and wage/hour complaints.

subpoena

A legal request issued for the production of documents, or a request to testify in court or other legal proceedings.

FIGURE 4.1 Job Analysis Foundation

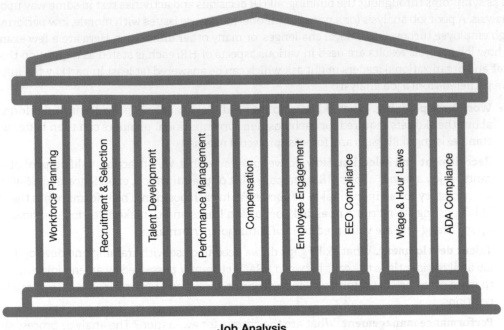

Job Analysis

HR in the Real World: Cash Is King

Note the preceding section states that decisions based on performance, including incentive pay, should be consistent and based on data-driven methods. What happens when it's not? I was the senior finance and HR executive for a warehousing company at which all full-time employees were given annual bonuses based on profits. A percentage of company earnings was set aside each year into a pool, which was then shared among employees. The bonus checks were always paid about two weeks before Christmas, and as a result the employees looked at this as a Christmas bonus in addition to a profit-sharing plan.

One year the company owner decided that cash bonuses would not be paid. Instead, each employee would receive a ham. If you have ever seen the movie "Christmas Vacation," this might remind you of Clark Griswold's employer substituting the jelly-of-the-month club for Christmas bonuses. The difference was that this was real life, not a movie, and the hams were not a gift that kept on giving. Not surprisingly, the employees were furious, especially those who had worked at the company for many years and had come to expect the bonus check to help with their Christmas shopping. At the end of the day, a group of employees decided to smash their hams in the parking lot. This got the owner's attention, and the point was made. Bonuses were then paid out, and the owner realized that when it comes to performance incentives for hourly employees, cash is king.

Job Analysis Resources and Methods

In this section, we explore various resources for collecting data to conduct a job analysis, along with several established methods to analyze the data in a consistent, valid, and reliable manner. Job analysis involves collecting information about a job that will help to differentiate it from other jobs in the same organization. The following factors help make distinctions between jobs:

- KSAOs needed

- work activities and behaviors
- interactions with others (internal and external)
- performance standards
- financial budgeting and impact
- machines and equipment used
- working conditions
- supervision provided and received[6]

There are five major sources of collecting data for a job analysis:

1. **Observation.** This can be conducted either in person or by video. It is probably the oldest of the methods of job analysis and dates back to the early days of scientific management. One might think of Frederick Taylor, the father of scientific management (introduced in Chapter 1). Taylor began working at the Midvale Steel Company in Philadelphia in the late 1870s as a machine shop laborer, and then successively became a machinist, gang boss, foreman, maintenance foreman, head of the drawing office, and chief engineer.[7] As a foreman, he began conducting time and motion studies by observing different types of workers. He would tediously observe and record every movement, and then analyze the data to determine the one best way to do the job. Taylor suggested that production efficiency in a shop or factory could be enhanced by close observation of the individual worker and elimination of wasted time through reducing motions.[8] The mental image that might come to mind is that of an engineer holding a clipboard and watch while observing and recording employees. In practice today, the process is essentially the same, except that sometimes the person conducting the job analysis will observe several employees that hold the same position and then compare the findings, and sometimes the actual observation is conducted by video and then observed and analyzed later. One drawback of observations is that it may make the employee being observed uncomfortable, even resulting in paranoia, such as fear of job loss. When conducting observations, it is helpful to first explain why the observation is occurring and how the results will be used.

Observation and analysis can make some employees uncomfortable, nervous, and perhaps even paranoid. How could you approach job analysis in a way that eases these concerns?

Source: © Shutterstock, Inc.

2. **Interviews.** The interviewer is a job analyst, and the interviewees are job incumbents and perhaps supervisors. The interview begins with a predetermined list of questions. However, one of the advantages of this method is that it allows the analyst to ask follow-up questions for clarification. It also is more personal than other methods and allows the analyst to explain the purpose of the job analysis process and put the interviewee at ease by alleviating any fears. The interview questions pertain to job duties, responsibilities, communication patterns, equipment used, hazards, etc. A list of sample interview questions is shown in Table 4.1.

3. **Questionnaires.** This method is similar to an interview, but in a written format, and more standardized than the interview method. It is a quicker and less expensive way to collect data than interviewing each individual, but it does not allow for follow-up questions.

4. **Employee diaries.** The employee keeps a log for several days or weeks and records all job duties, communications, etc. This can be a time-consuming process for the employee but is just for a short period of time and can yield valuable insights into jobs that are difficult to observe. The diary entries can be made intermittently throughout the shift, during breaks, or at the end of the shift.

5. **Subject matter experts (SMEs).** This method involves convening a group of experts in a particular line of work to develop the job analysis. They will collaborate and brainstorm together to identify the key aspects of a position and reach a consensus on the job duties, KSAOs, etc. The method is also referred to as an SME committee or focus group job analysis. Research indicates that there is general agreement on job analysis ratings made by a small committee of SMEs as compared with ratings from a larger sample of field respondents.[9]

TABLE 4.1 Sample Job Analysis Interview Questions

Sample Job Analysis Interview Questions
1. What is the overall purpose of the job?
2. Describe the location of the job.
3. What are the main duties and responsibilities of the position?
4. Describe your duties in the following categories: daily duties, periodic duties, duties performed at irregular intervals.
5. Who is your direct supervisor?
6. Do you have interactions with other managers beyond your direct supervisor?
7. Describe the interactions you have with co-workers, customers, or vendors.
8. Are you performing duties not presently in your job description?
9. What special knowledge or skills are required?
10. How long does it take a new hire to reach competency in your job?
11. Are there incentives for achieving specific performance targets?
12. Do you use special equipment or tools? If so, list the names of each major item.
13. Describe the frequency and degree with which you engage in activities such as pushing, lifting, pulling, carrying, sitting, running, kneeling, reaching, etc.
14. How do you define success in your job?
15. Are you required to adhere to specific work standards, policies, or procedures? Describe these.
16. What records or reports do you prepare/update as part of your job?
17. What is the level of authority in your position?
18. What kinds of independent actions are you allowed to take?
19. What do you need approval for?
20. What hazards are you exposed to in your work?
21. Describe your overall working conditions.

 Job Analysis

This video defines job analysis, explores the job analysis process, and highlights the most commonly used job analysis methods.

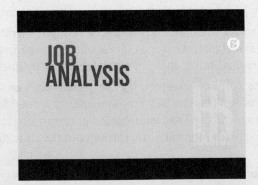

View the video online at: http://www.youtube.com/embed/NIFkJAge0EA?rel=0

Each of the above methods has advantages and disadvantages. Some are quicker and less expensive to implement, but the trade-off is that they may not yield as much insight. Regardless of which methods are used, it is important to use at least two different methods to provide validation of the data. There are also several resources available which job analysts can use to streamline the process. Two of these resources, the Position Analysis Questionnaire (PAQ) and the Occupational Information Network (O*Net) are discussed next.

The PAQ is a structured questionnaire for job analysis. It was designed by researchers to predict aptitude requirements and was based on 536 jobs across seventy organizations.[10] The questionnaire is used in combination with other job analysis methods. To complete a job analysis, the analyst might first review background information, then observe the job and conduct interviews with job incumbents. The analyst then completes the PAQ. It is generally recommended that the PAQ itself not be completed by job incumbents or supervisors.[11] This may have something to do with the fact that the PAQ is written at a reading level of college graduates.[12] The PAQ consists of 187 items related to job activities or work situations, and eight items related to compensation.[13] There are six types of rating scales used in the PAQ:

1. Extent of use
2. Importance to this job
3. Amount of time
4. Possibility of occurrence
5. Applicability
6. Item-specific scales

The PAQ is a proprietary resource, so companies must pay to use it. However, it can be useful in providing a uniform and structured method for job analysis, using a technique that is well researched with over four decades of experience.

The Occupational Information Network (O*Net) is a database containing hundreds of descriptors such as knowledge, skills, and abilities required for almost one thousand occupations. O*Net is developed under the sponsorship of the U.S. Department of Labor/Employment and Training Administration through a grant to the North Carolina Department of Commerce. This resource is free and replaced the previous Dictionary of Occupational Titles, which was a fee-based resource. It is a time-saving resource that job analysts and HR staff can use to help create job descriptions, identify training needs, redesign jobs, and set salary ranges. O*Net is also a helpful resource for individuals to conduct research on career options. Jobs can be searched by career cluster, green economy sector, industry, STEM skills, and other criteria. Job seekers can use the My Next Move link to search careers by keywords, browse careers by industry, or use the "Tell Us What You Like to Do" feature.[14]

FIGURE 4.2 O*Net Content Model

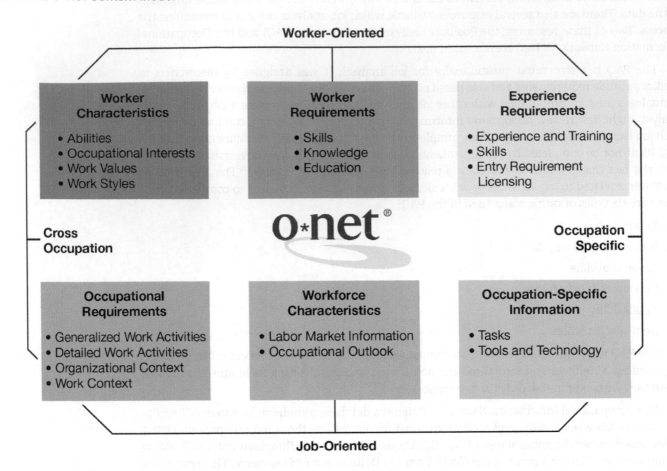

The conceptual foundation of O*Net is The Content Model, which reflects the characteristics of occupations (via job-oriented descriptors) and people (via worker-oriented descriptors).[15] These descriptors are organized into six domains, which are illustrated in Figure 4.2 and described here:

1. **Worker characteristics.** These are characteristics that may influence performance and the capacity to acquire necessary KSAOs and include preferences for work environments, natural abilities, work values, and work styles.

2. **Worker requirements.** These requirements are work-related attributes that are acquired and developed through education and experience. They include basic skills such as reading and advanced skills such as problem-solving.

3. **Experience requirements.** This domain includes previous work experience related to the type of work and can include professional or organizational certifications required for entry and advancement in an occupation, preferred training, and apprenticeships.

4. **Occupational requirements.** This domain is divided into generalized, intermediate, and detailed work activities. The generalized activities are broad and performed across most job families' industries, while the intermediate and detailed activities are increasingly more specific to a particular job family.

5. **Workforce characteristics.** This domain provides information about the broader social and economic structure and includes labor market information such as compensation/wage data and industry size, and occupational outlook. Much of this information is collected through collaborative efforts with the Bureau of Labor Statistics, the Department of Commerce, the Department of Defense, CareerOneStop, the U.S. Bureau of the Census, and the Employment and Training Administration.

6. **Occupation-specific information.**[16]

Job Descriptions

Once a thorough job analysis has been completed, then you are ready to create a job description (or revise an existing one). As we discussed earlier, job analysis has many uses, but one of the primary outcomes of a job analysis is the creation of a job description, including a job specification. A job description should include the following components:

1. Identification information (job title, hours, exempt or nonexempt status, the person the position reports to, supervisory responsibilities, location, work hours, date the job description was last updated).
2. General summary (overall description of the job).
3. Essential job functions (it is not necessary to list every possible job duty, just the essential job functions).
4. Job specifications (KSAOs, education, experience, physical requirements). It is important to distinguish between what is required and what is preferred.

A job description might seem to be a boring and mundane aspect of work. When was the last time you read through your own job description? If you supervise others, when was the last time you reviewed the job description for each of your direct reports? Even though it may seem to be a trivial HR detail, a job description can have significant legal ramifications. For example, the EEOC's ADA regulations clearly state that a written job description is evidence of the essential functions of a job.[17] One case that illustrates this is *Snead v. Florida Agricultural and Mechanical University Board of Trustees*, which involved a failure to accommodate claim. In August 2013, the new police chief at Florida A&M changed the work schedule for campus police officers from eight- to twelve-hour shifts. Stanley Snead, an officer, tried working the longer shifts but experienced medical issues related to high blood pressure, and his doctor advised him that the longer shifts were causing the medical problems. Snead requested to return to an eight-hour shift, but the university refused his request for accommodation, stating that working the twelve-hour shift was an essential job function. However, the jury found in Snead's favor and awarded him more than $250,000 because the shift length was not mentioned under the essential functions on the job description. Just as an employer can use a well-drafted job description in its favor when defending against an ADA claim, a poorly written or incomplete job description may lead to an adverse finding in a court case.[18]

Common Problems with Job Descriptions

There are several common errors with job descriptions, either with the format itself, or the way it is used (or not used) by management. They are summarized in Table 4.2.

TABLE 4.2 Common Problems with Job Descriptions

Common Problems with Job Descriptions
Provides little guidance to the job holder (too vague).
Obsolete (needs to be updated).
Job specifications not valid (not related to job success, not valid predictors of future job performance, and thus could expose the employer to discrimination charges).
Job description not given to employee (You would be surprised how often this happens.)
Job description not used by managers in making HR decisions (performance appraisals, promotions, training, etc.).

Note that one of the problems has to do with validity. Validity is a legal term related to the use of criteria for selection and performance appraisal. We will explore this term in more depth in a future chapter, but for now you should just know that validity refers to whether something is a valid predictor of future job success. A college degree is one example. If holding a bachelor's degree in the field is a valid predictor of future job success, then it can be included as a job specification. Before an employer decides on what things to include under job specifications, they should make sure that each of these criteria has been validated using a method that will stand up in court.

Figure 4.3 is a sample job description that incorporates the guidelines given in this section.

FIGURE 4.3 Sample Job Description: Retail Sales Associate

Job Title: Retail Sales Associate
Hours: Full-time, includes weekend and evening hours
FLSA Status: Non-exempt
Reports to: Department Manager
Supervisory Responsibilities: None
Location: Retail store as assigned
Date Job Description Revised: March 31, 2020

General Summary
The primary responsibilities of the retail sales associate are to facilitate sales, stock inventory, maintain merchandise displays, contribute to the appearance of the store, provide customer service, and support the store management team. Retail sales associates are the main point of contact with our customers, and thus are required to deliver the best customer experience possible, while adhering to our customer-first philosophy, company mission, and core values.

Essential Job Functions
- Ensure each customer receives outstanding service.
- Maintain awareness of all promotions and advertisements.
- Becoming knowledgeable in all areas of store merchandise.
- Answer customer questions in a friendly and helpful manner.
- Facilitate sales by becoming proficient in all cash register functions as well as special and online ordering procedures.
- Actively participate in daily huddle meetings.
- Be conscious of potential shoplifting and respond by following appropriate company procedures.
- Give appropriate directions and training to part-time sales associates.
- Maintain a safe and efficient workplace.
- Document all customer complaints, issues, or concerns for the manager.
- Assist with additional duties as manager deems necessary.

Job Specifications

Minimum Requirements
- Education: high school diploma or equivalent.
- A commitment to service excellence and customer satisfaction.
- Team player with excellent interpersonal skills.
- Effective verbal and written communication skills.
- Attention to detail and organization.
- Ability and willingness to work flexible hours including evenings, weekends, and holidays.

Preferred
- Experience working in a retail environment.
- Knowledge of retail computer systems.
- Proficient with computer word processing and spreadsheets.

Physical Requirements
- Must be able to lift, move, and handle up to 60 pounds frequently.

Key Takeaways

- The process of hiring an employee begins with job analysis and design.
- Job analysis is a process used to collect information about the duties, responsibilities, and the required knowledge, skills, and abilities needed to perform the job successfully. It also includes the work environment and authority structure.
- Job design is the study of how jobs might be improved to increase organizational productivity and employee satisfaction.
- Research studies indicate that the job analysis process leads to improved job performance, which is good for the organization and good for the employees.
- A job specification refers to the qualifications that an individual should possess to adequately perform a job. It may include KSAs, education, and experience.
- A job description is a document that includes a summary of the position, the overall job duties, the essential job functions, and the job specification. It may also indicate to whom the individual reports, supervisory responsibilities, and the salary range.
- There are five primary sources of collecting data for a job analysis: observation, interviews, questionnaires, employee diaries, and subject matter experts (SMEs).
- A job description should include the following components: identification information, general summary, essential job functions, job specifications.

What Do *You* Think?

1. Were you surprised to learn how many HR decisions are impacted by job analysis?
2. Why do you think employees might be uncomfortable with observations and keeping employee diaries? How would you feel if your supervisor were observing you?
3. How familiar are you with your own job description? Are the essential job functions current?

4.3 The Changing Nature of Work

Learning Objectives

1. Describe how the concepts of jobs and careers are changing.
2. Understand how advances in knowledge and technology affect the shelf life of expertise and the impact on job analysis and job design.
3. Identify the pros and cons of the gig economy for organizations and workers.

Jobs and Careers

Thus far in this section, we have been exploring methods of collecting data to analyze jobs within an organization. But we should recognize that what we mean by the word "job" is rapidly changing. In the twentieth century, when someone thought about a job or career, they usually had in mind a model that looks something like this: get a high school diploma, then a college degree or vocational training, land your first job, and continue working in that particular field, being promoted along the way as you gain experience until you eventually retire. However, in the twenty-first century, a different notion of what it means to have a job and a career has emerged. Today, the average person changes jobs twelve times during his or her career.[19] In January 2018, the Bureau of Labor Statistics reported the median employee tenure is 4.3 years for men and 4 years for women, noting that the median tenure increases with age (2.8 years for the twenty-five to thirty-four age group, 4.9 years for the thirty-five to forty-four age group, 7.6 years for the forty-five to fifty-four age group, and 10.1 years for the fifty-five to sixty-four group).[20]

LinkedIn co-founder Reid Hoffman believes that careers are now simply "tours of duty," and companies must now design jobs around the assumption that people will only stay a few years.[21] Thus, it is crucial that companies think about the changing nature of work when conducting job analysis and writing job descriptions. There are several specific trends that should be considered.

Advances in Knowledge and Technology

Shorter Shelf Life of Expertise

half-life of knowledge

The amount of time that has to elapse before half of the knowledge or facts in a particular field become obsolete.

Skillsets quickly become obsolete, and continuous learning and development are no longer optional for most jobs. The **half-life of knowledge** (also referred to as the half-life of facts) is the amount of time that has to elapse before half of the knowledge or facts in a particular field become obsolete. This amount of time is rapidly becoming shorter in almost every field, or as Samuel Arbesman puts it, "Everything we know has an expiration date."[22] The impact of the half-life of knowledge on knowledge and skills is shown in Figure 4.4. As skillsets and jobs change, the essential job functions on a job description quickly become out-of-date. For this reason, it is advisable to update job descriptions on a regular basis. Since job postings typically pull the job duties and functions from the existing job description, this means that many job postings are also obsolete! As a result, companies fail to attract top talent, and skills gaps are exacerbated.[23] Another strategy to offset this problem is to describe job specifications in terms of competencies rather than skills, since competencies are transferable to changing job needs.

FIGURE 4.4 Half-Life of Knowledge

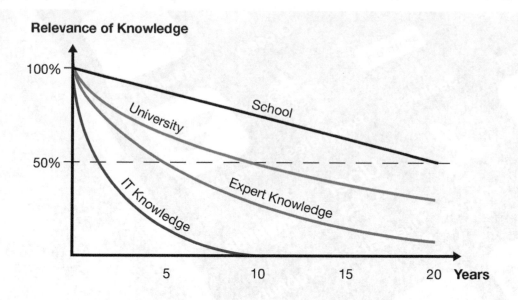

Growing Importance of Soft Skills

Skills such as math and engineering are susceptible to be being automated by technology. But a computer cannot show empathy, display emotional intelligence, or interact using social skills. This demonstrates part of the reason for the recent trend from STEM (science, technology, engineering, math) to STEAM (STEM plus the arts). Employers are increasingly seeking individuals with complex problem-solving abilities, research skills, and writing skills, along with adaptability and the ability to work with teams.[24]

The Gig Economy

The **gig economy** is a free market system in which temporary positions are common and organizations contract with independent workers for short-term engagements.[25] The term comes from the music industry, as in a musician "playing a gig." More workers are engaging in part-time work and working as independent contractors, instead of working full-time for one company. According to a 2015 survey by Kelly Services, 31% of U.S. workers considered themselves "free agents."[26] It may surprise you to learn that only 10% were forced into gig work because of economic conditions, so 90% of the free agents chose not to work for just one company, and, in essence, to be their own boss. By 2018, the Bureau of Labor Statistics reported that the number of workers in the gig economy rose to more than 35% of the U.S. workforce and was projected to be more than 40% by 2020.[27] What does this mean for you? There is almost a one-in-two chance that you will be a gig worker for at least part of your career. In the following sections, we will explore the pros and cons of the gig economy, first from the perspective of the organization, and then from that of the worker.

gig economy

A free market system in which temporary positions are common and organizations contract with independent workers for short-term engagements.

Food delivery services such as DoorDash, Grubhub, Uber Eats, Seamless, delivery.com, Postmates, and Instacart are powered by an army of gig workers.

Source: Tada Images / Shutterstock.com

Pros and Cons of the Gig Economy for Organizations

From the perspective of the employer, gig jobs save companies money by not requiring them to pay for benefits such as health insurance and retirement plans. Organizations also save on office space, equipment, and training, as gig workers often work from home and are responsible for providing their own equipment. For an example, a graphic designer might work from home (or a cafe, or wherever they want), and use their own computer. Another example is an Uber driver, who provides his or her own vehicle. Gig workers are responsible for keeping their skills updated, as opposed to having a full-time job in which the company pays for continuing education. Another advantage for organizations is they are not committed to paying for a full-time position. When there is no need for a particular type of work or skillset, the company does not incur any expenses. The gig economy enables companies to better match revenues and expenses. When the demand (and thus the revenue) is there, then they can employ workers, and when the demand is not there, they have the flexibility to reduce expenses. This is also referred to as the ability to scale up or down as business needs change.

There are disadvantages of using gig workers. These can be viewed as a trade-off to the advantages just described. When organizations use gig workers, they give up a certain amount of control over the people doing the work. With a full-time employee, companies can exert more influence to change job duties, hours, or locations. With a gig worker, an agreement has been entered into for a specified type of work, location, etc., and the gig worker is not obligated to agree to any changes in the terms or conditions of work, whereas an employee will agree to the changes to keep from getting fired. Another disadvantage is less control over the quality of work. Since gig workers are not concerned about keeping a full-time job, or promotion, or benefits, they may not be as diligent when it comes to quality or customer service.

Pros and Cons of the Gig Economy for Workers

From the perspective of the worker, gig jobs often provide numerous advantages. The individual has more flexibility to work the hours they want to work, in addition to the location, which can contribute to a better work-life balance. If someone needs to be free in the middle of the afternoon to pick up children from school, then he or she can schedule their work at other times, such as mornings or evenings. With a gig job, there is much more flexibility to choose the hours that work best for you. With collaborative internet technology such as videoconferencing and shared cloud storage, many types of jobs can be done from anywhere with an internet connection. As a result, work is increasingly becoming something that you do, as opposed to someplace that you go. Whereas previous generations said, "I have to go to work," today the phrase is often becoming, "I have to do some work."

Gig workers also are able to do the work that they feel passionate about, as opposed to a job that they are just doing to maintain full-time employment. This is not universal, of course, as gig workers still have to pay the bills, and therefore will sometimes have to take work that is not their favorite. An example of this is the writer who is passionate about writing novels but takes gigs doing the more mundane work of technical writing to pay the bills while working on a novel. Another example is a graphic artist who decides to fill the gaps in their work schedule doing other types of work, such as driving for Uber or delivering pizza. One additional advantage of gig work is increased autonomy. While their clients will have specific criteria and standards, gig workers have more independence in determining how to meet those standards than a regular worker does.

There are trade-offs to the increased flexibility and autonomy of being a gig worker. Since they do not have the benefits of a full-time employee, gig workers need to obtain their own health insurance and budget accordingly. The same is true for retirement. Gig workers do not have company-matched 401(k) plans or pensions, so they will need to plan and budget for their retirement. Another disadvantage is the lack of a steady paycheck. With this comes the uncertainty and stress of not knowing exactly how much income one will have in a particular month. People who do not handle uncertainty very well are probably not well suited for a gig job. Gig workers who are classified as independent contractors (as opposed to part-time employees) do not have any taxes withheld from their paychecks. Independent contractors should plan on setting aside 25% to 30% of their income for taxes. The IRS also requires that quarterly payments be made based on estimated taxes for the current year.

One additional drawback to gig work is that the worker is often required to supply his or her own equipment (which is the flip side to the advantage for organizations discussed in the previous section). Since gig workers have to supply the equipment and maintain it, they should be sure that their rate of pay includes enough to offset these expenses. Equipment eventually wears out or becomes obsolete and has to be replaced, and therefore the replacement cost should be included in the pay rate, and the gig worker should set these funds aside so that they have the replacement money available when the time comes. It is also very important to keep receipts on all business expenses, as these are tax-deductible. The pros and cons of gig work for organizations and for workers are summarized in Figure 4.5.

FIGURE 4.5 Pros and Cons of Gig Work

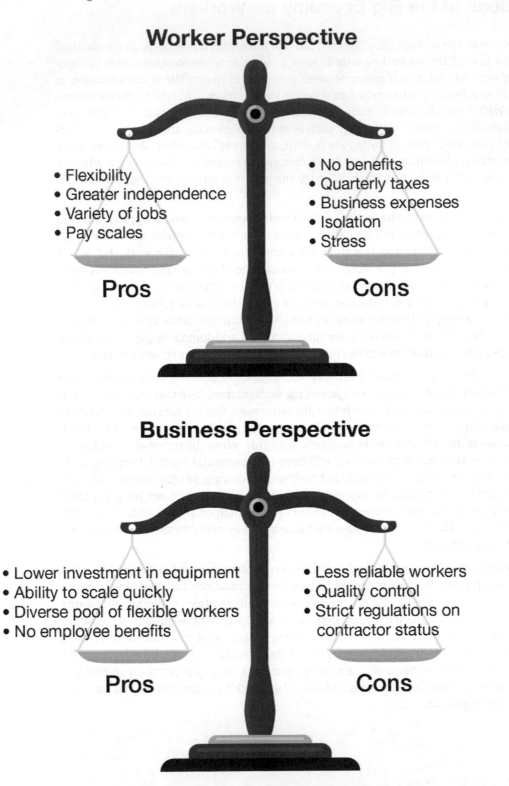

Worker Perspective

Pros
- Flexibility
- Greater independence
- Variety of jobs
- Pay scales

Cons
- No benefits
- Quarterly taxes
- Business expenses
- Isolation
- Stress

Business Perspective

Pros
- Lower investment in equipment
- Ability to scale quickly
- Diverse pool of flexible workers
- No employee benefits

Cons
- Less reliable workers
- Quality control
- Strict regulations on contractor status

Key Takeaways

- Today, the average person changes jobs twelve times during his or her career.

- Skillsets quickly become obsolete, and continuous learning and development are no longer optional for most jobs.
- The half-life of knowledge is the amount of time that has to elapse before half of the knowledge or facts in a particular field become obsolete, and is rapidly becoming shorter in almost every field.
- The number of jobs is not being reduced by automation, but employees are required to utilize more technology in their work.
- Employers are increasingly seeking individuals with complex problem-solving abilities, research skills, writing skills, along with adaptability and the ability to work with teams.
- The gig economy is a free market system in which temporary positions are common and organizations contract with independent workers for short-term engagements.
- There is almost a one-in-two chance that you will be a gig worker for at least part of your career.

What Do *You* Think?

1. What are your career and job goals? Do you think you will have multiple careers, and what might those be?
2. What is the half-life of knowledge in your occupation?
3. Do you think you would like to work in a gig economy job? What would be the advantages for you? What possible disadvantages can you identify?

4.4 Job Design

Learning Objectives

1. Describe how job design has evolved from its origins until the present day.
2. Explain how job enrichment is used to increase job satisfaction by increasing responsibility and autonomy.
3. Explain the benefits of using job enlargement to increase the variety of tasks.
4. Define job rotation and the benefits of changing the work environment.
5. Identify the key dimensions of the job characteristics model and develop a plan to increase the motivating potential of a job.
6. Consider how flexible work arrangements can be used to the advantage of an organization and its employees.

Job Design Then and Now

"It is about a search, too, for daily meaning, as well as daily bread, for recognition as well as cash, for astonishment rather than torpor; in short, for a sort of life rather than a Monday through Friday sort of dying."[28]

In the opening paragraph of this chapter, you were given the definition of job design as the study of how jobs might be improved to increase organizational productivity and employee satisfaction. Job design flows out of the job analysis process. On the one hand, job design seeks to improve the work outcomes for the organization, such as increasing efficiency and performance. But on the other hand, individuals need purpose and meaning from their work, so that it does not become drudgery, or as the oral historian Studs Terkel put it, a Monday through Friday sort of dying. Terkel interviewed everyday people about their work to collect their stories and then compiled them into *Working*, a best-selling book. A common thread from his interviews is that everyone seeks meaning in their work.

If people hate their work, then employee turnover and absenteeism will be high, and productivity will suffer. So how do we create jobs where people are engaged, motivated, and satisfied, yet at the same time are highly productive and efficient? This is the purpose of job design.

Job design has been practiced in one form or another for thousands of years. Whether it was building a pyramid or a Mayan temple, or organizing the Roman army, the practice of leaders making decisions about what work tasks each person will do, how they will do it, and the environment they will do the work in, has been happening as long as work has existed. Job design as a scientific field of study began with Adam Smith.[29] He argued in his book *The Wealth of Nations* for how the division of labor into specialized jobs would increase productivity. If jobs were specialized and simplified, then workers would become more productive by focusing on only a very few tasks.

Frederick Taylor took this concept further by applying job simplification and standardization as part of his scientific management philosophy.[30] Taylor advocated for time and motion studies to identify the best method to perform each work task and the implementation of rules to ensure that all workers follow the approved method. Under this approach, workers had little if any autonomy or discretion in how to perform their work, as decision-making was done by management. This top-down management philosophy had its drawbacks in that while it did increase productivity, it also caused a decrease in employee morale. Employees experienced mental and physical fatigue and boredom, and often engaged in counterproductive behavior, including tardiness, absenteeism, and even sabotage.[31]

A shift from this singular focus on productivity to a dual focus on productivity and employee attitudes began to occur with the Hawthorne Studies described in Chapter 1. You may recall that the Hawthorne Studies occurred during the 1920s. It was four decades before researchers and managers began to seek in earnest to understand how the employee perspective could be used to enhance job design. Today, there is a substantial body of research that establishes a relationship between good job design and positive outcomes for individuals and organizations. Despite this evidence, for the merits of well-designed work, poorly designed jobs continue to exist in many contemporary organizations.[32] In the sections that follow, we will explore the most popular job design techniques. These techniques include job enrichment, job enlargement, and job rotation. Next, a comprehensive model for job design will be introduced, and then job design will be considered in light of the most recent trends in flexible work arrangements.

Job Enrichment

job enrichment

The process of increasing job satisfaction by adding more meaningful tasks and giving employees more responsibility and autonomy.

Job enrichment is the process of increasing job satisfaction by adding more meaningful tasks and giving employees more responsibility and autonomy. The concept of job enrichment was introduced by Frederick Herzberg, who built upon the concept of employee attitudes in his Two-Factor Theory (also referred to as the Motivation-Hygiene Theory).[33] Herzberg proposed that jobs should be enriched rather than simplified in order to increase performance and job satisfaction. His research built upon Maslow's Hierarchy of Needs theory, by focusing on the relationship between the employee's growth needs and the job satisfaction that the employee experienced.[34] Herzberg divided job aspects into two categories:

1. **Hygiene factors.** Job aspects such as a decent salary, safe working conditions, and job security, which when inadequate can lead to job dissatisfaction.
2. **Motivating factors.** Job aspects such as the meaningfulness of tasks, recognition, growth and promotion opportunities, sense of achievement, and responsibility, which can lead to job satisfaction.

The basic premise of job enrichment is that job satisfaction will increase along with performance when attention is given to the motivating factors. Job enrichment can be a useful approach to job design, but it does not work in all situations. Some individuals do not want more responsibility in their work and are content in a job that has standardized work methods and procedures. The theory has also been criticized because changes have often been imposed in a top-down fashion without giving employees opportunities to make suggestions about changes in the work.[35]

Job Enlargement

Job enlargement is the process of increasing the variety of tasks in a job. This approach can relieve boredom by giving the worker an opportunity to use different skills as opposed to doing the same tasks all day, every day. The technique involves assigning additional tasks at the same skill level and thus is also referred to as **horizontal job loading**. This differs from job enrichment in which the focus is on more responsibility and autonomy (and is also referred to as **vertical job loading**). You could view this technique as the opposite of job specialization, which was an essential idea of scientific management. An important point here is that there is no one right approach to job design that works in all situations.

Even though the additional tasks are considered to be the same skill level, training might still be necessary. On the one hand, this will result in additional training expenses by the employer and downtime during the training process, but on the other hand, the employer will benefit from having more flexibility by having workers with a broader skillset. When the employees learn to complete a larger variety of tasks, then they have the ability to fill in for sick or vacationing employees and to be moved around to work in different areas as necessary to eliminate backlogs.

Volvo has successfully implemented job enlargement in its production lines. The firm moved away from the traditional assembly line model in which a worker does the same task over and over, to a team-based model in which a group of workers assembles a car from start to finish. As a result of this shift in production methods, Volvo reported sharply improved productivity, quality, and profits.[36] Maytag, IBM, and AT&T are some of the other firms that have used job enlargement to motivate their employees.[37]

job enlargement

The process of increasing the variety of tasks in a job.

horizontal job loading

A job enlargement technique that involves assigning additional tasks at the same skill level.

vertical job loading

A job enrichment technique in which the focus is on increasing responsibility and autonomy by adding additional tasks at a higher skill level.

Job Rotation

Job rotation occurs when an employee moves from one position to another in a sequence, with a set amount of time spent in each position. For example, in a retail grocery store, an employee might spend the first two hours of their shift working as a cashier, then rotate to customer service for two hours, and so on through their shift. A bank might implement job rotation by having tellers work in the drive-through for part of their shift, then move to an inside teller position for part of the day, and then help customers open new accounts.

Job rotation can be used to increase job satisfaction by providing more skill variety and giving employees the opportunity to change work settings. The technique can also be used to alleviate physical stress from repetitive motion or extreme working environments. For example, instead of a roofing worker spending all of their time on top of a roof exposed to the elements, they might spend one or two days a week making deliveries or doing warehouse work.

job rotation

Occurs when an employee moves from one position to another in a sequence, with a set amount of time spent in each position.

Job Characteristics Model

In 1976, Richard Hackman and Greg Oldham introduced a comprehensive job design model, pulling together many of the major theories. Their job characteristics model is the most widely researched approach to job design from the late 1970s until the present day.[38]

The job characteristics model proposes five core job characteristics that are expected to contribute to an employee's internal work motivation and other outcomes.[39] The five core job characteristics are:

1. **Skill variety.** The degree to which the job allows the employee to utilize a variety of knowledge, expertise, and abilities.

2. **Task identity.** The degree to which the job enables the employee to participate in a job from start to finish, and see the completed work.

3. **Task significance.** The degree to which the job makes a significant contribution to society and impacts others in a positive way.

4. **Autonomy.** The degree to which the job provides substantial freedom, independence, and discretion to the employee.

5. **Feedback.** The degree to which the job provides the employee with information about his or her performance.

Each of the core job characteristics is expected to impact one of three employee psychological states:

1. **Experienced meaningfulness of work.** Impacted by skill variety, task identity, and task significance.

2. **Experienced responsibility.** Impacted by autonomy.

3. **Knowledge of results.** Impacted by feedback.

Figure 4.6 summarizes the interrelationship between the five core job characteristics, the three employee psychological states, and the positive outcomes expected.

---

skill variety

The degree to which the job requires a variety of different activities involving the use of different skills.

task identity

The degree to which the job requires doing a whole and identifiable piece of work.

task significance

The degree to which the job has an impact on the lives of others.

autonomy

The degree to which the job provides substantial freedom, independence, and discretion to the employee.

feedback

The degree to which the job provides the employee with information about his or her performance.

experienced meaningfulness of work

An employee psychological state impacted by skill variety, task identify, and task significance.

experienced responsibility

An employee psychological state impacted by autonomy.

knowledge of results

An employee psychological state impacted by feedback.

FIGURE 4.6 Job Characteristics Model

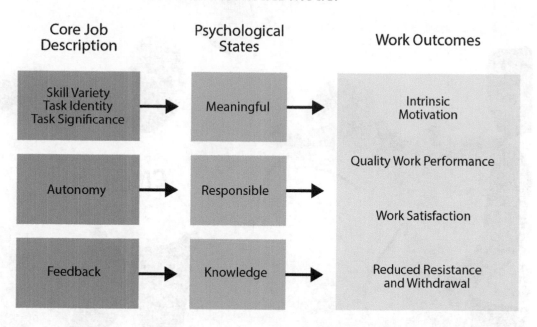

Job Characteristics Model

The Job Diagnostic Survey (JDS) was created by Hackman and Oldham to assess jobholder descriptions of the job characteristics.[40] Jobholders can take the survey, which will produce a Motivating Potential Score (MPS) for their job. Managers and HR staff can then work together to engage in job design to try to improve the MPS.

Flexible Work Arrangements

Flexible work arrangements are a job design method that gives employees greater control over when and where they do their work. According to the 2014 National Study of Employers by the Families and Work Institute, workplace flexibility is linked to greater employee productivity, higher morale and job satisfaction, decreased absenteeism, and reduced turnover.[41]

flexible work arrangements

A job design method that gives employees greater control over when and where they do their work.

Flexible work arrangements improve work-life balance, for example by allowing parents to coach their children's soccer teams.

Source: © Shutterstock, Inc.

Flextime

flextime

A system that allows employees to choose their own work hours within parameters established by the employer.

Flextime is a system that allows employees to choose their own work hours within parameters established by the employer. Flextime can be helpful in achieving work-life balance for employees, resulting in lower stress. For example, a parent of a school-age child might decide to work from 6 am to 3 pm, instead of 8 am to 5 pm, so that they can be home when their child gets out of school. Some employees who live in large urban areas with heavy traffic might opt to work a schedule that allows them to avoid commuting during rush hour. Others might want to work around their college class hours, or simply want to work the hours in which they feel the most productive. A night owl might feel most productive from 4 pm to midnight, while an early-morning person might prefer to be done by 2 pm.

Of course, business needs have to be taken into consideration, and not all jobs will work with flextime. Someone in a manufacturing environment who works in shifts will need to be at work at the same time as everyone else on their shift. But for many jobs, flextime will not inconvenience the business operations and might even offer the business the opportunity to offer expanded hours to their customers.

Compressed Workweek

compressed workweek

An employee might work longer days but fewer days per week.

In a **compressed workweek**, the employee works longer days, but fewer days per week. The most common options are four ten-hour days, three twelve-hour days, or a week of five nine-hour days followed by a week of four nine-hour days.[42] Clif Bar, for example, gives its headquarters employees the option of choosing between 9/80 (working eighty hours in nine days instead of ten) or working from home one day per week.[43] This type of arrangement offers the employee many of the same benefits of flextime, such as the ability to improve work-life balance. It can also reduce commuting expenses, such as wear and tear and gasoline for a vehicle, or public transportation costs, since the employee is working fewer shifts per week. From the employers' perspective, a compressed work-week can be a valuable recruiting and retention tool. There is a potential downside to a compressed workweek: for some individuals, the long days may lead to chronic fatigue. Also, there is less time for after-work activities or other responsibilities on workdays. For example, the three twelve-hour shift is common in healthcare. Employees have four days off a week, but on the three days they work, they have very little time to rest after factoring in commuting. Some employees might also take on additional shifts at other employers during their off days, adding to their fatigue.

Talent Analytics

Companies can track productivity for employees and can view data showing the employees' productivity by day of the week, and even the time of the day. The company can then determine the impact that compressed workweeks and flextime will have on productivity, and therefore the bottom line. But what is the optimal length of a workday?

The eight-hour workday is not based on the optimal number of hours a human can concentrate. In fact, it has little to do with the kind of work most people do now, nor the work environment. During the Industrial Revolution, ten to sixteen-hour workdays were common because companies needed to keep their factories operating. When it became clear that such long days were both brutal and unsustainable, leaders like Welsh social reformer Robert Owen (who himself owned textile manufacturing plants) advocated for shorter workdays. His slogan became: "Eight hours labour, eight hours recreation, eight hours rest."

In 1914, Henry Ford led the way in the U.S. by implementing an eight-hour workday. Today, the workday is ripe for another disruption. Research suggests that in an eight-hour day, the average worker is only productive for two hours and fifty-three minutes.[44] A study of nearly two thousand full-time office workers revealed that most people aren't working for most of the time they are at work. The most common unproductive activities were:

- **Reading online news.** One hour, five minutes.
- **Checking social media.** Forty-four minutes.
- **Discussing non-work–related things with co-workers.** Forty minutes.
- **Searching for new jobs.** Twenty-six minutes.
- **Taking smoke breaks.** Twenty-three minutes.
- **Making calls to partners or friends.** Eighteen minutes.
- **Making hot drinks.** Seventeen minutes.
- **Texting.** Fourteen minutes.

This is good news for those who work at home, which has become much more common since the COVID-19 pandemic began. It's easy to feel like you are not doing enough if you don't work at home for eight hours every day. But even if you're productive for only three hours a day, you might be matching your productivity at the office!

Telecommuting

Telecommuting is a work arrangement in which employees do not commute to a central place of business, and is also referred to as working remotely. Telecommuters often work from home, but sometimes in coffee shops or while traveling, or anywhere they want as long as there is a reliable internet connection. They "commute" electronically using telephone, email, and other internet technologies such as videoconferencing and file sharing.

Many jobs lend themselves to working remotely, including sales, insurance, customer service, IT support, software development, insurance claims, writing, online teaching or training, and many others. About 3.9 million U.S. employees, or 2.9% of the workforce, work from home at least 50% of the time.[45] Recently, even some healthcare professionals such as radiologists have begun to work at home. Some of the companies that make extensive use of telecommuting are American Express, Cigna, Cisco, Deloitte, and Intel.[46] Many more companies and their employees around the world

telecommuting

A work arrangement in which employees do not commute to a central place of business; also referred to as working remotely.

experienced telecommuting during the COVID-19 crisis of 2020. *Time* magazine referred to this period as the world's largest work-from-home experiment.[47] The work changes may have a long-term impact by increasing remote work and decreasing travel. According to a survey by 8x8, a cloud computing business, at the end of February in 2020, 44% of full-time workers had already seen COVID-19 impact the way they do business, 55% canceled travel plans, and 40% had increased their use of videoconferencing.[48]

Working remotely can save on commuting expenses and can increase productivity by lessening fatigue and stress, especially for people who commute in large urban areas with traffic problems. It can also help employees achieve a better work-life balance by eliminating the time involved with a commute. On the other hand, it does require self-discipline to focus on the work to be done, and not be distracted by things at home. For most remote workers, it is helpful to have a dedicated work area in their home, such as a home office or even just a desk. This allows the employee to flip the switch, so to speak, and enter into work mode. Working remotely can also be a solitary and lonely experience, so it may not be a good fit for the type of person who functions better when surrounded by others. From the organization's perspective, the primary benefits of telecommuting are the savings in required office space and improved productivity and morale of the employees.

Job Sharing

job sharing

A flexible work arrangement in which two or more individuals work part-time and share the same position.

In **job sharing**, two or more individuals work part-time and share the same position. Job sharing is one of the least common flexible work arrangements, but there are situations where it can benefit the employees and the employer.[49] One way that job sharing occurs is for one employee to work Monday and Tuesday, the other Thursday and Friday, and both of them working on Wednesday to coordinate on job tasks. Another approach is for one employee to work mornings, and the other employee to work afternoons, but there are many variations of job sharing. Some major employers that offer job sharing are AT&T, Aetna, United Airlines, Marriott, Qualcomm, Lockheed Martin, and the federal government.

From the perspective of the employer, job sharing can save on total costs since two (or more) part-time employees share one job, as opposed to one full-time employee with benefits. Employers should be aware that there are drawbacks to job sharing, particularly in regard to having to spend more time conducting orientation and also supervision and performance management. From the perspective of the employee, a job share provides more work flexibility for those who do want to work full-time. Some employees who share jobs do so in order to be home to care for children part of the day, because they have their own business and need supplemental income, or because they want to semi-retire.

Job sharing is not for everyone. The type of person who is a good fit for job sharing is someone who is a team player and does not mind sharing the credit when the job is done well and is willing to share the responsibility when things go wrong. Excellent communication skills are critical for job sharing to be successful, since each job partner will need to keep the other up to speed on the status of various duties. A useful communication technique for job sharing is for each employee to leave an end-of-shift status report so that their job partner can pick up where they left off.

HR Talk with Karen A. Hockins, SPHR, SHRM-SCP

Director of Human Resources and Risk Management

Fire Protection Services

We offer a variety of flexible work arrangements to our employees. Technicians can work a compressed workweek, usually 4/10s or 3/12s. This gives them more days at home, and it is productive for the company because it means less driving time, and less set-up and finish-up time at the job site. We also have employees that work remotely and some that have flextime. This allows employees to work around family needs and improves work-life balance.

Each request for a flexible work arrangement is evaluated on a case-by-case basis. We are a family-owned company, and the evaluation and decisions are made by myself and the four owners. Flexible work arrangements do not work for all types of jobs, but when it can be done, we will. This improves retention because our employees feel valued and they know that the company cares about their personal lives. After approving a flexible work arrangement, employees have to maintain their productivity, and we monitor various metrics to track this.

One of the challenges in implementing flexible work arrangements is the differences in state laws. For example, we have technicians that work in Colorado and Nevada. Under Colorado law, nonexempt employees must be paid overtime for time worked over twelve hours in a day, but under Nevada law, overtime must be paid for time worked over eight hours a day. Therefore, a 4/10 or 3/12 compressed workweek will be feasible for a technician in Colorado, but we could not approve that same type of arrangement for a technician in Nevada, because the company would have to pay the overtime cost, thus increasing our cost.

I have been able to take advantage of a flexible work arrangement myself, and I am a good example of an employee that would not have been able to stay with the company without some flexibility. I have an office at our headquarters in Ogden, Utah, but I have worked remotely from Colorado, Texas, and Kansas, due to relocations made for my spouse's job. I have been with the company for eighteen years, and this would not have been possible without being able to work remotely!

Key Takeaways

- Flexible work arrangements are a job design method that gives employees greater control over when and where they do their work.
- Flextime can help achieve work-life balance for employees, resulting in lower stress.
- In a compressed workweek, the employee works longer days, but fewer days per week. This type of arrangement offers the employee many of the same benefits of flextime, such as the ability to improve work-life balance.
- Telecommuting can save on commuting expenses, increase productivity by lessening fatigue and stress, and help employees to achieve a better work-life balance by eliminating the time involved with a commute. On the other hand, it requires self-discipline to focus on the work to be done and not be distracted by things at home.
- In job sharing, two or more individuals work part-time and share the same position. Job sharing is one of the least common flexible work arrangements, but there are situations where it can benefit the employees and the employer.

What Do *You* Think?

1. What do you want to get out of your job, besides money to pay your bills? What is important to you?
2. Think about your past and/or present jobs. To what extent did the employer implement job enrichment, job enlargement, or job rotation?
3. What can you learn from the Job Characteristics Model that you might apply as a supervisor or manager?
4. Would a flexible work arrangement appeal to you? If so, which type would you prefer?

4.5 Work Teams

Learning Objectives

1. Identify the most common types of work teams.
2. Describe the characteristics of effective work teams.
3. Recognize the signs of a dysfunctional work team.
4. Explain the role of HR in team job design.

Types of Work Teams

work team

A group of individuals who work together to accomplish a common objective, have complementary skills, and are mutually dependent upon each other for success.

The idea of using teams in the workplace is certainly nothing new. A team is much more than simply a collection of individuals; if a manager puts a group of people together in a company department, and calls them a team, that does not automatically make them a true team in practice. A **work team** is a group of individuals who work together to accomplish a common objective, have complementary skills, and are mutually dependent upon each other for success. It is implied in the definition that the team is more efficient than each of the employees working individually. Otherwise, there would not be any advantage to creating a team in the first place.

An effective team is more than a collection of individuals working in the same place. They are mutually dependent upon each other for the success of the team.

Source: © Shutterstock, Inc.

Several common types of teams occur in the workplace. These are cross-functional teams, project teams, self-managed teams, task force teams, and virtual teams. Each of these types of teams is summarized in Table 4.3.

TABLE 4.3 Types of Work Teams

Type of Team	Description
Cross-functional	A group of people with different functional expertise working toward a common goal. It may include people from finance, marketing, operations, human resource, and other departments, and typically includes employees from all levels of an organization.
Project	A group of individuals assembled to perform activities that contribute toward achieving a common task-related goal.
Self-managed	A self-organized, semiautonomous small group of employees whose members determine, plan, and manage their day-to-day activities and duties under reduced or no supervision.
Task force	A temporary group of people formed to carry out a specific mission or project or to solve a problem that requires a multidisciplinary approach.
Virtual	A virtual team usually refers to a group of individuals who work together from different geographic locations and rely on communication technology such as email, fax, and video- or voiceconferencing services to collaborate.

Characteristics of Effective Teams

The type of team that we are talking about in this chapter is a group of people working together who are performing work that meets certain standards of excellence, or what is often called a high-performing work team. Refer back to the definition of work teams in the previous section. What key aspects of an effective team do you see? There are three different characteristics that are included in the definition:

- **Sense of shared purpose.** Effective teams have common goals and a high level of commitment to achieving those goals. Every member of the team knows exactly what is expected of the team in terms of results and what their role is.

- **Complementary skills.** A successful sports team needs players with different but complementary skills to be competitive. For example, a baseball or softball team has nine players on the field at any time. A team would not function very well if all of the players were infielders. Each position on the team has a skillset unique to the position, that complement each other to form a successful team. Business teams should also be composed of a variety of skillsets that work together and support each other. Each team member can also bring a unique perspective, knowledge, ideas, and innovation in which the results of the combined team are much more effective than any one person working individually. This is the essence of the concept of **synergy**, which is the interaction of two or more individuals to produce a combined effect greater than the sum of their efforts. Thus, the result of the whole is better than the sum of its parts.

- **Mutually dependent.** When a team is mutually dependent, then the members rely on each other to get their jobs done. If you look up the term "mutually dependent" in a thesaurus, you will see words like united, integrated, fused, cohesive, blended, coherent, and the author's favorite: meshed. When a team is mutually dependent, they mesh together as one. For this to occur, the team needs open and honest communication, respect for one another, and the ability to resolve conflict in positive ways.

synergy

The interaction of two or more individuals to produce a combined effect greater than the sum of their efforts.

Team Dysfunctions

dysfunctional team

One in which excellence is not achieved because of poor communications, a lack of commitment, or inadequate leadership.

Being a part of a work team is not always a positive and productive experience. You could say the same for being part of a group of students working on a course project. If a group project team has complementary skillsets and works together well to perform at a high level, then it can be a wonderful experience. But the opposite sometimes occurs. Have you ever been part of a group project that did not communicate well, with team members who did not complete their tasks or did not complete them well, and were not held accountable? If you answered yes, then you know that being a member of a team that is not functioning well can be a miserable experience. A **dysfunctional team** is one in which excellence is not achieved because of poor communications, a lack of commitment, or inadequate leadership.

The signs of a dysfunctional team are easy to recognize: constant complaining, failure to meet deadlines and performance goals, lack of trust, inability to manage conflict, competing objectives or interests, personal agendas, relationship problems, feelings of not being appreciated, and an overall negative atmosphere. Patrick Lencioni, in his book *The Five Dysfunctions of a Team: A Leadership Fable* identifies the following five team dysfunctions: absence of trust, fear of conflict, lack of commitment, avoidance of accountability, and inattention to results. While Lencioni's book is a popular business press publication, empirical research also supports each of the characteristics put forth by Lencioni as indicators of team effectiveness.[50] Each of these five dysfunctions is described in Figure 4.7.

FIGURE 4.7 Five Dysfunctions of a Team

Lencioni's Five Dysfunctions of a Team

	Description
Inattention to Results	• The pursuit of individual goals and personal status erodes the focus on collective success.
Avoidance of Accountability	• The need to avoid interpersonal discomfort prevents team members from holding one another accountable.
Lack of Commitment	• The lack of clarity or buy-in prevents team members from making decisions they will stick to.
Fear of Conflict	• The desire to preserve artificial harmony stifles the occurrence of productive ideological conflict.
Absence of Trust	• The fear of being vulnerable with team members prevents the building of trust within the team.

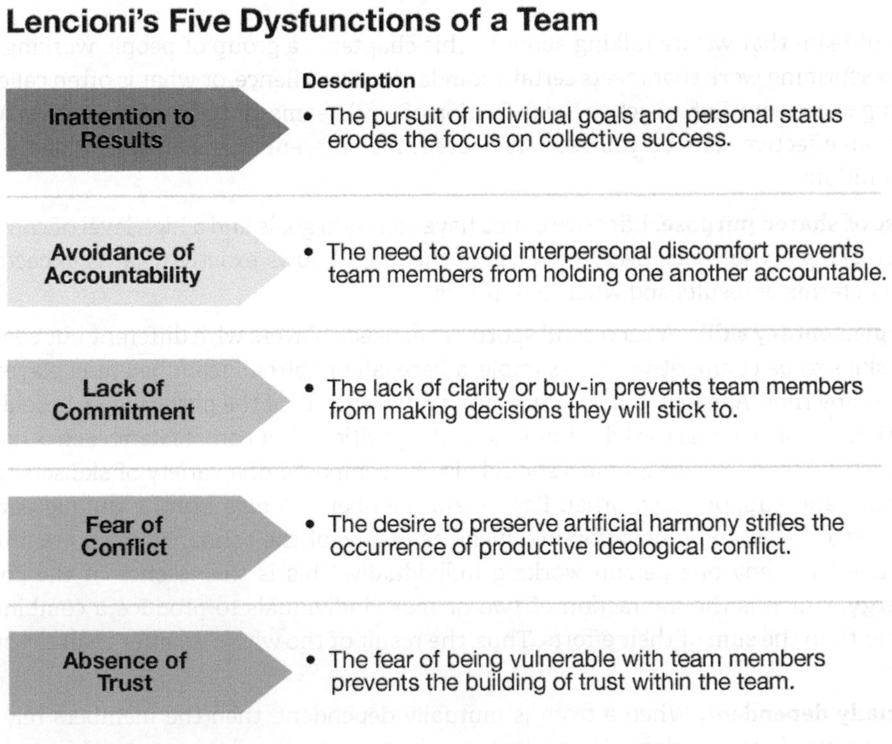

Source: Patrick Lencioni

The Role of HR in Team Job Design

HR should play a valuable role in the implementation of teams by serving in an advisory role to management regarding the design of teams, and facilitating effective team functioning. Some of the specific actions HR can take to support a team environment are:

- Recruit the right team members. Hire according to the complementary skillsets that are needed for each team (including new hires and internal employee transfers).
- Include team concepts in the new-hire orientation programs.
- Provide training and team-building activities.
- Assist with conflict resolution.
- Incorporate team incentive plans in compensation packages.
- Value diversity. HR plays a key role in making sure that teams are diverse. Research indicates a positive impact on high performance by teams with diverse ages, ethnicities, and genders.[51]
- Establish consistency across the organization in team culture and expectations.
- Provide support for virtual teams.
- Advise management on when to use teams, how to best develop teams, and how to create a high-performance team culture.

Key Takeaways

- A work team is a group of individuals who work together to accomplish a common objective, have complementary skills, and are mutually dependent upon each other for success.
- There are several common types of teams that occur in the workplace: cross-functional teams, project teams, self-managed teams, task force teams, and virtual teams.
- Effective teams have a sense of shared purpose, complementary skills, and are mutually dependent.
- Dysfunctional teams are characterized by an absence of trust, fear of conflict, lack of commitment, avoidance of accountability, and inattention to results.
- HR should play a valuable role in the implementation of teams by serving in an advisory role to management regarding the design of teams, and facilitating effective team functioning.

What Do *You* Think?

1. Do you prefer to work as part of a team, or on your own? Why do you think that is?
2. Think about a team that you were a part of that was very effective. What characteristics made the team successful?
3. Have you ever worked with a dysfunctional team? If so, which of the five dysfunctions were evident, and what could have been done differently?

4.6 Conclusion

This chapter introduced job analysis and job design. Job analysis is a process used to collect information about the duties, responsibilities, and the required knowledge, skills, and abilities needed to perform the job successfully. It also includes the work environment and authority structure. Job design is the study of how jobs might be improved to increase organizational productivity and employee satisfaction. Together these concepts form the foundation for hiring the right individuals and placing them into positions designed for organizational and personal success. The chapter began with an examination of job analysis methods, job descriptions, and job specifications. We examined trends such as the gig economy that are fundamentally changing the nature of work. Theories of job design and motivation were explored, followed by several models for implementing the theories to improve satisfaction and retention. The chapter concluded with a review of work teams, and how teams can be designed to improve effectiveness and reduce dysfunction.

Theory-into-Practice (TIP) Exercises

1. Using the Job Characteristics Model, design a plan to increase the motivational potential of a job (perhaps a current or former job of your own).

   a. On a scale of 1 to 5, rate each of the five core job characteristics, with 1 being the least motivating and 5 the highest.

   b. Then make a list of action items that could be implemented to improve any characteristic that you scored less than 5.

2. Keep a time diary of your waking hours for at least three days. This will be similar to the employee diary approach discussed in this chapter. Be sure to include your time commuting, working at a job, attending class, study time, and leisure time. Then calculate how much time you spent on each of the following activities, and answer the following questions:

   a. What are the top five activities that absorb most of your time?

   b. How much time is unaccounted for?

   c. Are you satisfied with your balance? If not, what could you do to be more efficient?

3. Update your existing job description, or create one if you do not already have one. If you are not employed, then use one of your former jobs. Begin by going to O*Net Online (see resource number three at the end of Chapter 1). You might also wish to utilize one of the free job description templates (see resource number two below).

Case Study: Independence Comes with a Price

Source: © Shutterstock, Inc.

Many companies participating in the gig economy, such as Uber and Postmates, insist that their relationship with independent contractors is key to their business model. They state that they are able to offer lower costs to consumers because it would be much more expensive to offer the contractors employee benefits and rights. In 2004 a California company, Dynamex, converted all drivers to independent contractor status, and they were sued by many of these drivers, who stated they should be employees because they only worked for Dynamex. The drivers won and California adopted a new policy, named ABC, that companies must use to determine whether or not they can classify someone as an independent contractor. There are three requirements an employer must meet to prove its workers are independent contractors: one, that the contractor provides the service free from the company's control; two, that the service provided is outside the company's core business, such as a janitor at a law firm; and three, that the contractor is an independent professional engaged in providing their service to companies other than the one in question.

Gig economy companies continue to fight for the right to use contractors. In forty states, ridesharing companies are now exempt from the ABC rule. Some are trying to create solutions. Silicon Valley assemblyman Evan Low introduced a bill that would set up shared benefits plans to which online platform companies could contribute—and in doing so, would create a new employment classification for "marketplace contractors," who would not be subject to all the laws governing regular employees. One thing is certain, the gig economy is growing, and there is a need for companies and legislative leaders to work quickly to catch up with the trend.[52]

Uber Drivers: Are They Employees or Contractors?

Ted Boutrous, a partner at Gibson, Dunn & Crutcher, and Zenefits COO David Sacks discuss the classification of Uber drivers with Bloomberg's Emily Chang.

View the video online at: http://www.youtube.com/embed/umQQ-9c5XLU?rel=0

Case Study Questions

1. Have you ever worked as an independent contractor? What do you think the advantages to the worker are? What are the disadvantages?

2. Do you think that the classification "marketplace contractors" could be the beginning of creating a solution?

3. What might be some other solutions for keeping independent contractors happy while keeping costs down for companies?

Resources

1. **U.S. Office of Personnel Management.** Free job analysis resources including presentations on how conduct a job analysis, occupational questionnaires, structured interviews, and other reference materials.

   https://www.opm.gov/policy-data-oversight/assessment-and-selection/job-analysis

2. **Free Job Description Templates.** A library of customizable job descriptions from Workable, with over 700 job titles, categorized by industry.

   https://resources.workable.com/job-descriptions/

3. **World Development Report 2019: The Changing Nature of Work.** Produced by The World Bank, this report studies how the nature of work is changing due to advances in technology.

    http://www.worldbank.org/en/publication/wdr2019k

4. **Nomad Stack.** A great resource for digital nomads, which may be the ultimate in remote work, exploring the world while working remotely. The website covers many things you need to know including work visas, taxes, and international roaming charges. The website includes jobs, conferences, blogs, podcasts, and more for the remote worker.

    https://nomadstack.com/

Endnotes

1. Aspan, M. (2020). Siri, did I ace the interview? *Fortune*, February, 86-91.
2. DeMers, J. (2017). Research says this is the secret to being happy at work. *NBC News*. Retrieved from https://www.nbcnews.com/better/careers/research-says-secret-being-happy-work-n762926
3. Ibid.
4. Safdar, R., Waheed, A., & Rafiq K.H. (2010). Impact of job analysis on job performance: Analysis of a hypothesized model. *Journal of Diversity Management, (5)*2, 17-36.
5. Exempt Employees vs. Nonexempt Employees. *Findlaw*. Retrieved March 5, 2020 from https://employment.findlaw.com/wages-and-benefits/exempt-employees-vs-nonexempt-employees.html
6. Performing a Job Analysis. *Society for Human Resource Management*. Retrieved March 11, 2020 from https://www.shrm.org/resourcesandtools/tools-and-samples/toolkits/pages/performingjobanalysis.aspx
7. Mee, J. Frederick W. Taylor, American inventor and engineer. *Encyclopaedia Brittanica*. Retrieved March 11, 2020 from https://www.britannica.com/biography/Frederick-W-Taylor
8. Ibid.
9. Maurer, T.J., & Tross, S.A. (2000). SME committee vs. field job analysis ratings: Convergence, Cautions, and a Call. *Journal of Business and Psychology, (14)*3, 489-499.
10. McCormick, E., Jeanneret, P., Mecham, R., & Feishman, E.A. (1972). A study of job characteristics and job dimensions as based on the Position Analysis Questionnaire (PAQ). *Journal of Applied Psychology, 56*(4), 347-368.
11. Position Analysis Questionnaire (PAQ). Economic Research Institute. Retrieved March 12, 2019 from https://www.erieri.com/paq
12. Ash, R., Edgell, S., & Feishman, E.A. (1975). A note on the readability on the Position Analysis Questionnaire (PAQ). *Journal of Applied Psychology, 60*(6), 765-766.
13. Position Analysis Questionnaire (PAQ). Economic Research Institute. Retrieved March 12, 2020 from https://www.erieri.com/paq
14. My next move. *O*Net*. Retrieved March 12, 2019 from https://www.mynextmove.org/
15. The Content Model. O*Net Research Center. Retrieved March 12, 2020 from https://www.onetcenter.org/content.html
16. Ibid.
17. McCoy, E. (2018). The essential role of a job description. *Jackson Lewis*. Retrieved from https://www.disabilityleavelaw.com/2018/03/articles/ada/essential-role-job-description/
18. Ibid.
19. Doyle, A. (2019). How often do people change jobs? *Thebalancecareers*. Retrieved from https://www.thebalancecareers.com/how-often-do-people-change-jobs-2060467
20. Employee Tenure Summary. (2018). *Bureau of Labor Statistics*. Retrieved March 14, 2020 from https://www.bls.gov/news.release/tenure.nr0.htm
21. Hoffman, R., Casnocha, B., & Yeh, C. (2014). *The alliance: Managing talent in the networked age*. Cambridge, Mass: Harvard Business Review Press.
22. Arbesman, S. (2013). *The half-life of facts: Why everything we know has an expiration date*. New York: Penguin Group.
23. Bates, S. (2014). Job postings remain a weak link in hiring process. *Society for Human Resource Management*. Retrieved from https://www.shrm.org/resourcesandtools/hr-topics/talent-acquisition/pages/weak-job-descriptions.aspx
24. Bersin, J. (2017). Catch the wave. *Deloitte Review, (21)*, 60-79.
25. Rouse, M. Gig economy. *WhatIs.com*. Retrieved March 20, 2020 from https://whatis.techtarget.com/definition/gig-economy
26. Sahadi, J. (2015). Gig economy: A third of U.S. workers say they're free agents. Retrieved from https://money.cnn.com/2015/09/03/pf/gig-economy-free-agents/index.html
27. Swaniker, P. (2019). What are the pros and cons of the gig economy? *Forbes*. Retrieved from https://www.forbes.com/sites/quora/2019/01/08/what-are-the-pros-and-cons-of-the-gig-economy/#2bc9928b1388
28. Terkel, S. (Ed.). (1974). *Working: People talk about what they do all day and how they feel about what they do*. New York: The New Press.
29. Smith, A. (1850). *Wealth of nations*. Edinburgh: Adam and Charles Black.
30. Taylor, F.W. (1911). *Principles of scientific management*. New York: Harper.
31. Walker, C.R., & Guest, R.H. (1952). *The man on the assembly line*. Cambridge, Mass.: Harvard University Press.
32. Parker, S.K., Andrei, D.M., & Van den Broeck, A. (2019). Poor work design begets poor work design: capacity and willingness antecedents of individual work design behavior. *Journal of Applied Psychology*, Advance online publication: http://dx.doi.org/10.1037/apl0000383
33. Herzberg, F. (1966). *Work and the nature of man*. Cleveland, Ohio: World.
34. Maslow, A.H. (1954). *Motivation and personality*. New York: Harper & Row.
35. Paul, W.J., Roberston, K.B., & Herzberg, F. (1969). Job enrichment pays off. *Harvard Business Review, 47*(2), 61-78.
36. Lohr, S. (1987). Making cars the Volvo way. *The New York Times*. Retrieved March 25, 2020 from https://www.nytimes.com/1987/06/23/business/making-cars-the-volvo-way.html
37. Ferrell, O.C., Hirt, G., & Ferrell, L. (2008). *Introduction to business*. Burr Ridge, Ill.: McGraw-Hill.
38. Ghosh, P., Rai, A., Gupta, N., and Singh, A. (2015). Exploring the moderating role of context satisfaction between job characteristics and turnover intentions of employees of Indian public sector banks. *Journal of Management Development, 34*, 1019-1030.
39. Based on Oldham, G., & Fried, Y. (2016). "Job design research and theory: Past, present, and future." Organizational Behavior and Human Decision Processes, 136, 20-35. https://doi.org/10.1016/j.obhdp.2016.05.002
40. Ibid.
41. Families and Work Institute. (2014). *National study of employers*. Retrieved March 25, 2020 from http://familiesandwork.org/downloads/2014NationalStudyOfEmployers.pdf
42. Compressed workweek. *Business Dictionary*. Retrieved March 25, 2020 from http://www.businessdictionary.com/definition/compressed-workweek.html
43. Reynolds, B. (2017). 20 companies with flexwork programs. *Flexjobs*. Retrieved from https://www.flexjobs.com/blog/post/companies-with-flexwork-programs/
44. Adapted from Curtin, M. (2016). In an 8-hour day, the average worker is productive for this many hours. *Inc*. Retrieved from https://www.inc.com/melanie-curtin/in-an-8-hour-day-the-average-worker-is-productive-for-this-many-hours.html
45. Doyle, A. (2018). What is telecommuting? *Thebalancecareers*. Retrieved from https://www.thebalancecareers.com/what-is-telecommuting-2062113
46. Brunelli, L. (2018). Top 9 telecommuting companies. *Thebalancecareers*. Retrieved from https://www.thebalancecareers.com/top-telecommuting-companies-3542783
47. Banjo, S., Yap, L., Murphy, C., & Chan, V. (2020). The Coronavirus outbreak has become the world's largest work-from-home experiment. *Time*. Retrieved from https://time.com/5776660/coronavirus-work-from-home/
48. Ibid.
49. 5 tips for a successful job share. *Work Flexibility*. Retrieved March 2, 2020 from https://www.workflexibility.org/5-tips-for-a-successful-job-share/
50. Hamlin, J., & Corkrum, R. (2008). *Team effectiveness: A validation study of Lencioni's five functions of a team*. ProQuest Dissertations Publishing.

51. Society for Human Resource Management. *Developing and sustaining high-performance teams*. Retrieved March 2, 2020 from https://www.shrm.org/resourcesandtools/tools-and-samples/toolkits/pages/developingandsustaininghigh-performanceworkteams.aspx

52. Case written by Crews, P. (2020). Adapted from DePillis, D. (2018). California ruling puts pressure on Uber, Lyft, and other gig economy workers. CNN Business. Retrieved from https://money.cnn.com/2018/05/01/news/economy/california-gig-employer-ruling/index.html

CHAPTER 5
Talent Recruitment

Unemployment rates rise and fall with economic cycles, but most researchers, economists, and HR professionals agree that employers are in a talent war, competing for the best candidates, and this is expected to continue for at least several decades. The competition for talent is fierce, and companies must be proactive in creating recruitment strategies that will attract highly qualified applicants.

This chapter introduces the recruitment process, including employer branding, public relations, and attracting diverse applicants. Internal and external recruitment methods are covered, and ideas for improving recruitment effectiveness are explored. The chapter concludes with a review of the most common techniques for evaluating the effectiveness of recruitment, including yield ratio, cost per hire, and new-hire turnover.

5.1 Opening Case: Recruiting the Best to Work for the Best

Cadence Design Systems was named one of the 2019 *Fortune* 100 Best Companies to Work For.

Source: Michael Vi / Shutterstock.com

Attracting and recruiting new hires is rapidly changing. Everything from employer branding to using more online platforms comes into play when recruiting new employees. *Fortune* magazine publishes a list of "100 Best Companies to Work For" every year. They feature one hundred companies that are highly appreciated by their workers and have some innovative ways to attract and recruit new employees.

What gets a company onto the top one hundred list? Increasingly, job candidates are interested less in higher salaries and more in the culture of their next workplace. Camden Property Trust, headquartered in Houston, has the reputation of focusing more on a prospective employee's potential for success versus prior experience. The company also spends $3.5 million a year on employee training programs, resulting in a 40% internal promotion rate. Hyatt Hotels encourages an "even playing field" culture with their "everyone's a housekeeper" mantra, which reminds employees that no job is more important than another.

Companies like Bright Horizons Family Solutions and The Cheesecake Factory offer incentives such as paying for GEDs and higher education for their employees. This results in more internal promotion as the employees become better qualified. Some companies, such as Carmax, have become very creative in attracting the best candidates by offering prizes or cash for community service. Publix supermarkets offer free English as a second language (ESL) classes for new hires.

With companies competing to hire quality employees, we will continue to see more creativity in recruiting. Prospective new hires quickly learn which companies have a good reputation for creating an enjoyable workplace and rewarding their employees in a variety of ways.[1]

The 2019 Best Companies to Work For

Fox Business's Lauren Simonetti reports on Comparably's list of the best companies to work for in 2019.

View the video online at: http://www.youtube.com/embed/KHWfkli-zaQ?rel=0

Case Discussion Questions

1. How can companies recruit applicants that have a high potential for success?
2. What are the advantages and disadvantages of recruiting internal candidates through promotions?
3. When looking for a new job, what are the three most important factors you consider?
4. What are some things you have observed at your place of employment (or another) that have attracted new hires? What has turned off possible recruits?

5.2 The Recruitment Process

Learning Objectives

1. Explain the roles of HR and hiring managers in the recruitment process.
2. Compare and contrast the reactive and proactive approaches to recruiting.
3. Describe how labor market differences impact recruitment.
4. Identify resources and methods for recruiting a diverse applicant pool.

Who Is Responsible for Recruitment?

Recruitment is the process of developing a pool of qualified applicants to fill current and future job openings. The responsibility for recruitment depends on the size of the organization. In a small business, the **hiring manager** (an owner or a manager who will oversee the employee) might handle the process by himself or herself. In a company large enough to have an HR department, recruitment is often conducted by an HR generalist or other member of the HR staff, working in collaboration with the hiring manager. In situations where a company has an HR department, the responsibilities might be divided like this:

- **HR.** Guides the overall process, serves in an advisory capacity to management, publishes job postings, and screens applicants to eliminate those who are not qualified. HR will also be responsible for ensuring that the recruitment process complies with EEO and other legal requirements.

- **Hiring Manager.** Notifies HR of openings, determines the job duties and job qualifications, consults with HR on the suitability of candidates.

Other departments and individuals in a company also may be involved in the recruiting process. The finance department may have to approve the salary and benefits, in addition to the recruiting costs before the recruitment process can begin. Diversity departments may play a role in helping to ensure that the candidate pool meets the diversity goals of the organization. Marketing even plays a significant role when it comes to employer branding, which can be impactful in getting the attention of the best candidates. Every department of an organization is responsible for some aspect of recruiting, especially when it comes to creating a reputation as a great place to work, as the opening case illustrates.

As companies grow, they may eventually have full-time recruiters. In addition to in-house staff, portions (or all) of the recruitment process are sometimes handled by third-party vendors. One type of third-party vendor is a staffing agency. A **staffing agency** finds employees for a company for a fee. The company, rather than the job seeker, is considered the client and pays the fee to the agency.[2] These are also referred to as temporary (or temp) agencies, but this can be misleading, since they also place people into permanent positions. Another variation is that they sometimes place employees into temporary positions, which are then converted into permanent positions after a probation period. Individuals are considered employees of the staffing agency, and are paid by the agency as long as they are considered temporary employees, but if they are hired permanently, then they are considered employees of the company. The largest staffing agencies in the world are Adecco, Randstad Holding, and ManpowerGroup.[3] In the U.S., the top five staffing agencies are Allegis Group, Randstad Holding, Adecco, Kelly Services, and Robert Half International.[4]

Another type of third-party vendor is used in recruitment process outsourcing (RPO). This occurs when an employer transfers all or part of its recruitment processes to an external service provider. An RPO provider may provide its own staff, or it might absorb the company's staff. In either case, an RPO differs from a staffing agency in that it assumes ownership of the design and management of the overall recruitment process and responsibility for the results.[5] RPOs can be a useful way for a company to obtain access to a broad talent pool and free up company time and resources to focus on the core business operations, and leave the recruiting to firms that specialize in it. Other types of third-party vendors include public employment agencies such as state workforce commissions, professional associations, trade communities, and labor unions.

Two Approaches to Recruitment

There are two different approaches to recruitment. One is the traditional method, which is reactive, and the other is the more modern method of proactive recruiting. Let's look first at a typical scenario in reactive recruiting. It usually happens something like this:

1. An opening occurs because an employee gives notice, is fired, is promoted, or decides to retire.
2. HR meets with the hiring manager to review the job description and job specifications.
3. The company advertises the position opening on job boards, social media, etc.
4. Wait at least several weeks.
5. Applicants are screened and interviews conducted and assessed (which can take several weeks).
6. In some cases, a second round of interviews is conducted.
7. The company makes an offer to a qualified candidate.
8. If the candidate is currently employed, then they give notice.
9. Wait several more weeks.
10. The candidate starts work.

As you can see, reactive recruiting is a lengthy process, lasting into months in many cases, and puts unnecessary pressure on HR to fill positions quickly. This kind of approach to recruitment causes the time-to-hire to increase, which also increases cost-per-hire, in addition to higher losses that stem from leaving positions vacant (lost revenue, productivity costs, temporary staffing if needed).

The proactive approach to recruitment does not wait until a hiring event occurs to start recruiting. A hiring event is any incident that creates a need to hire an additional person. It might be that someone resigned to work elsewhere, was terminated, transferred, promoted, retired, or injured. Hiring events also occur because of increases in revenue. As a company expands, more employees are needed, perhaps with different skillsets than current employees. But to a certain extent, all of these hiring events can be predicted. For example, marketing normally conducts a revenue forecast for at least the next year, if not longer. The projected revenue level can then be converted into a forecast for additional hires in various positions. For example, a customer service call center may need to hire one employee to support each $75,000 in revenue. Figure 5.1 illustrates how hiring demand for customer service representatives is correlated with revenue in this example.

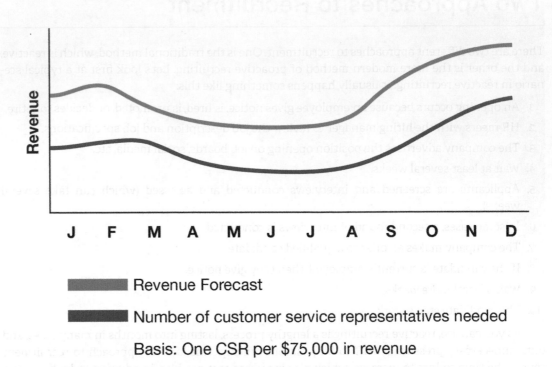

FIGURE 5.1 Hiring Demand Based Upon Revenue Projection

Revenue Forecast

Number of customer service representatives needed

Basis: One CSR per $75,000 in revenue

Proactive recruiting approaches range from simple to complex. At its simplest, proactive recruiting might be nothing more than keeping applications on file, so that when a hiring event occurs, the company has an existing talent pool to choose from.

An HRIS provides a wealth of data that can be mined to predict future hiring needs. But it is important to not rely solely on data analysis. HR staff should be in ongoing conversations with hiring managers to better understand what the HRIS is indicating. This step leads to validation of the data, but also a deeper understanding of the types of individuals who will need to be recruited.

Proactive recruiting will not eliminate all unexpected hiring events. There will be times when HR has no choice but to use the traditional reactive recruitment method. However, if properly implemented, proactive recruiting will allow companies to accelerate their time-to-hire, reduce hiring costs, and result in higher quality of hires, because recruiters will have more time to find the very best qualified candidates.

Active sourcing is another term for proactive recruiting. This can help fill openings immediately rather than waiting weeks or months.

Source: © Shutterstock, Inc.

Labor Markets

A **labor market** is the geographic area in which a company competes for labor. From a recruitment perspective, the labor market is the area in which recruiters should focus on attracting candidates. There are three factors that determine the labor market:

1. **Geography.** The supply and demand of labor differs from one area to the next as a result of the strength of the local economy. For example, in 2019, the unemployment rate in Iowa was 2.4%, but in Alaska it was 170% higher at 6.5%.[6]

2. **Occupation.** The labor market becomes larger as the job-level (education required, skillsets, salary, etc.) increases. If an insurance company is hiring staff for a customer service call center, the labor market is likely thirty miles or less, depending on how far workers on entry-level salaries are willing to commute. But if they are hiring an analyst or a manager, the labor market might be national in scope, since many applicants would be willing to relocate.

3. **Competition.** You have probably noticed that similar companies tend to locate close to each other, creating industry clusters. An **industry cluster** is a group of similar and related firms in a defined geographic area that share common resources such as suppliers and a labor force. As a result, skilled workers tend to be attracted to the area because that's where the jobs are. Figure 5.2 shows some of the major industry clusters in the United States. For example, if you are looking to hire someone with furniture-making skills, then you might focus your search in North Carolina, which is home to over three thousand furniture-related establishments, including Ashley, the largest furniture manufacturer in the world, and thirty-five thousand employees working in furniture businesses statewide.[7]

labor market

The geographic area in which a company competes for labor.

industry cluster

A group of similar and related firms in a defined geographic area that share common resources such as suppliers and a labor force.

FIGURE 5.2 Industry Clusters

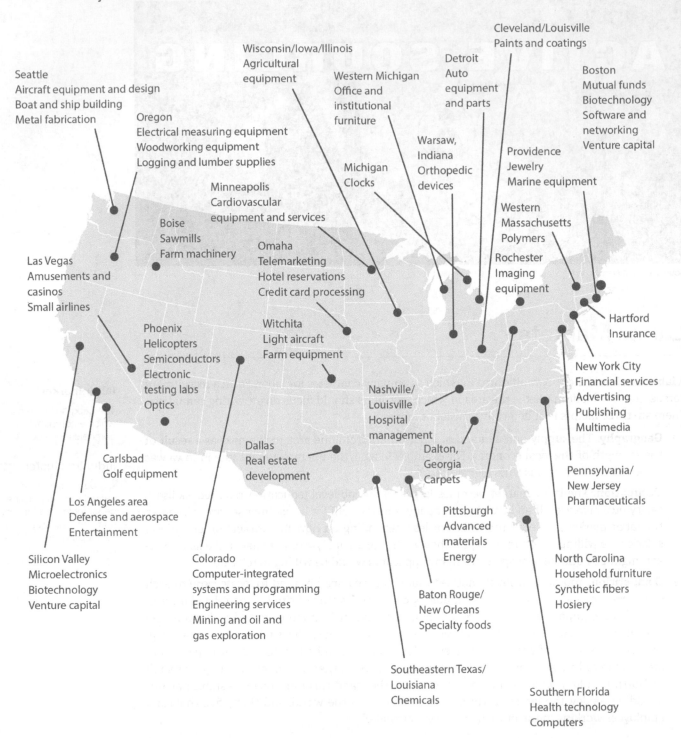

Seattle
Aircraft equipment and design
Boat and ship building
Metal fabrication

Oregon
Electrical measuring equipment
Woodworking equipment
Logging and lumber supplies

Wisconsin/Iowa/Illinois
Agricultural
equipment

Western Michigan
Office and
institutional
furniture

Detroit
Auto
equipment
and parts

Cleveland/Louisville
Paints and coatings

Boston
Mutual funds
Biotechnology
Software and
networking
Venture capital

Warsaw,
Indiana
Orthopedic
devices

Michigan
Clocks

Providence
Jewelry
Marine equipment

Minneapolis
Cardiovascular
equipment and services

Boise
Sawmills
Farm machinery

Omaha
Telemarketing
Hotel reservations
Credit card processing

Western
Massachusetts
Polymers

Las Vegas
Amusements and
casinos
Small airlines

Rochester
Imaging
equipment

Phoenix
Helicopters
Semiconductors
Electronic
testing labs
Optics

Witchita
Light aircraft
Farm equipment

Hartford
Insurance

New York City
Financial services
Advertising
Publishing
Multimedia

Nashville/
Louisville
Hospital
management

Carlsbad
Golf equipment

Dallas
Real estate
development

Dalton,
Georgia
Carpets

Pennsylvania/
New Jersey
Pharmaceuticals

Los Angeles area
Defense and aerospace
Entertainment

Pittsburgh
Advanced
materials
Energy

Silicon Valley
Microelectronics
Biotechnology
Venture capital

Colorado
Computer-integrated
systems and programming
Engineering services
Mining and oil and
gas exploration

Baton Rouge/
New Orleans
Specialty foods

North Carolina
Household furniture
Synthetic fibers
Hosiery

Southeastern Texas/
Louisiana
Chemicals

Southern Florida
Health technology
Computers

Source: U.S. Economic Development Administration

Recruiting a Diverse Talent Pool

Employers must ensure that their recruiting initiatives comply with federal discrimination laws and affirmative action programs, if one is in place. Many employers must also actively seek to increase the number of minority applicants to reach their affirmative action goals. However, even more important than legal compliance is to recognize that organizations are becoming increasingly diverse in terms of gender, race, ethnicity, and nationality.[8] This diversity brings substantial potential benefits, such as better decision-making, greater creativity and innovation, and more successful marketing to different types of customers.[9] Research indicates that a diverse workforce leads to competitive advantages.[10]

There are a number of methods for recruiting more minority applicants. There are job fairs and job banks aimed at minorities in general, and sometimes specific ethnic groups or females. Some firms recruit at predominantly minority higher-education institutions. Another method is to advertise positions in publications that are targeted to protected classes. Table 5.1 lists some of the organizations that companies use to contact and engage with minority job applicants. Other approaches to recruiting a diverse workforce are:[11]

- Target minorities based on historically black colleges and universities (HBCUs) or referrals from other women and minorities.
- Collect data on recruitment outcomes and maintain yield ratios to identify good targets.
- Use blind recruitment strategies using technology that removes identifiable information from electronic resumes in order to mitigate hiring managers' unconscious bias.
- Open training programs and internships to everyone, but target women and minorities.
- Target women and minorities in recruitment ads.
- Include images and testimonials from women and minority employees in recruitment materials.

TABLE 5.1 Minority Job Boards

Minority Job Boards
- blackjobs.com
- womensjoblist.com
- minorityjobs.net
- ihispano.com
- minoritycareers.org
- womenforhire.com
- workplacediversity.com
- naaap.org

As mentioned in Chapter 3, EEOC documentation and guidelines often refer to the relevant labor market. The relevant labor market has implications on recruiting in regard to diversity. The EEOC will look at the rate of selection for various minorities versus the proportion of the minority to the population as a whole in the relevant labor market to determine whether discrimination in hiring has occurred. For example, consider that in Mississippi, blacks are 37.6% of the population, whereas they are only 1.3% of the population in Vermont.[12] Thus, a manufacturing company in Mississippi that hires within a fifty-mile radius would be expected to hire blacks at a rate of 37.6%, whereas a similar manufacturer in Vermont would be expected to hire only at a rate of 1.3%.

HR Talk: Cara Carroll

HRIS Specialist

Gamestop

There is not just one talent recruitment method that works for all of our hiring needs. We use a variety of strategies, including social media and LinkedIn groups. We post jobs on Career Builder, Monster, and Handshake (to posting at universities). We engage in community outreach and networking and utilize our ATS and database for sourcing. One of the most effective strategies for Gamestop is employee referrals. We have higher retention with new hires that come from referrals, since employees typically only refer people that they trust and have worked with in the past. As a final resort, we will utilize agencies for harder-to-fill or niche roles.

Another innovative approach that supports our recruitment efforts is our Employee Resource Groups (ERGs). The ERGs host events and programs within these four categories: Hiring Diverse Talent; Develop & Retain; Build Relationships; and Community. Our ERG events help us to attract a diverse group of applicants, which helps Gamestop to meet its diversity goals. We have eight ERGs:

1. **Alliance**: Dedicated to education, awareness, and supporting those in the LGBTQ+ community
2. **BOLD**: Dedicated to education awareness, and supporting those of African origin
3. **NextGen**: Dedicated to supporting and developing those in the early stages of their career
4. **PAC**: Pan-Asian Council: Dedicated to education, awareness, and support of Asian cultures
5. **Unidos**: Dedicated to education, awareness, and supporting those of Hispanic origin
6. **Veteran**: Dedicated to education, awareness, and support of veterans
7. **VisAble**: Dedicated to increasing acceptance and understanding of associates with or without disabilities
8. **WLC**: Dedicated to education, awareness, and support of high potential women

Key Takeaways

- Recruitment is the process of developing a pool of qualified applicants to fill current and future job openings.
- In addition to in-house staff, portions (or all) of the recruitment process are sometimes handled by third-party vendors, including staffing agencies and recruitment process outsourcing companies.
- Reactive recruiting is a lengthy process, lasting into months in many cases, and puts unnecessary pressure on HR to fill positions quickly. This kind of approach to recruitment causes the time-to-hire to increase, which also increases cost-per-hire, in addition to higher losses that stem from leaving positions vacant (lost revenue, productivity costs, temporary staffing if needed).
- The proactive approach to recruitment does not wait until a hiring event occurs to start recruiting.
- A labor market is the geographic area in which a company competes for labor. From a recruitment perspective, the labor market is the area in which recruiters should focus on attracting candidates.
- There are three major factors that influence the labor market: geography, occupation, and competition.
- Diversity brings substantial potential benefits such as better decision-making, greater creativity and innovation, and more successful marketing to different types of customers.
- The EEOC will look at the rate of selection for various minorities versus the proportion of the minority to the population as a whole in the relevant labor market to determine whether discrimination in hiring as occurred.

5.3 The Recruitment Funnel

Learning Objectives

1. Explain how a recruiting funnel is used to narrow down a wide group of applicants.
2. Describe the concept of employer branding and why it is important in recruitment.
3. Compare and contrast sourcing and recruitment.
4. Identify methods to improve the candidate experience.

What Is a Recruitment Funnel?

The funnel concept has been in use in marketing for many years, but it is fairly new to recruitment. The **recruitment funnel** is a process for narrowing down a wide audience, and helps keep candidates engaged and eventually become employees.[13] Marketers use the funnel concept because attracting customers is expensive, and it makes sense to maximize the money spent on promotion and in trying to turn interested parties into customers. From a recruitment perspective, the purpose is similar. The basic idea is to attract interested candidates into the funnel, and then narrow the pool of candidates down, eliminating those who are either not qualified or decide the company is not the right fit for them. In the top of the funnel, you pour in applicants. Some of those are filtered out using various techniques such as reviewing resumes, administering tests, etc. The applicants who remain in the funnel are then further screened using interviews. Then the best qualified applicants emerge from the bottom as new hires.

Recruiters today realize that it is a two-way street. In developed countries, the days of placing a job posting and then being overwhelmed with qualified applicants are a thing of the past. The economy goes through ups and downs, and subsequently the unemployment rate goes through cycles. There are periods of time, usually lasting several years, in which the economy booms and unemployment is low. Jobs are harder to fill in what is sometimes called an "employee's market." Potential new hires have more job offers to choose from, and therefore more negotiating leverage, and more opportunity to be choosy. But during times of recession, the unemployment rate rises, and there are fewer available jobs. During an "employer's market," candidates are more likely to accept a job offer and have less room for negotiation.

> **recruitment funnel**
>
> A process for narrowing down a wide audience, it helps keep candidates engaged and eventually become employees.

However, regardless of economic cycles, most workforce forecasts indicate significant labor shortages for the next several decades, in what *Barron's* calls "The Great Labor Crunch."[14] The economic impact of COVID-19 certainly caused massive unemployment in 2020, but hopefully the economic impact of travel restrictions and shelter-in-place orders will be short-term. The long-term workforce forecast, based on demographic trends, still indicates a labor shortage. Recruitment is expensive, and when job openings are vacant for too long it has serious implications for lost productivity and profits. Therefore, it makes sense for HR managers to think like marketers, by being proactive in recruitment and treating potential employees the same way that marketing treats potential customers.

There are four distinct stages in the recruitment funnel: employer branding, sourcing, candidate experience, and candidate selection.[15] The employer branding stage is designed to attract the attention of highly qualified candidates. The sourcing stage engages the applicant so that they will apply for the position. The purpose of the candidate experience stage is to nurture the individual through each phase of the application process. Finally, the candidate selection stage is where applicants are converted to new hires. Each stage is further described below, and visualized in Figure 5.3.

FIGURE 5.3 The Recruitment Funnel

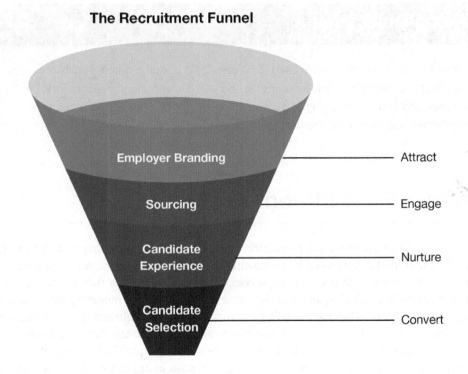

Employer Branding

The first step in attracting talented candidates is to increase awareness by building the employer brand. The **employer brand** describes an employer's reputation as a place to work. Just as a brand reputation is a potential customer's opinion about the value of the products or services of the company, the employer brand represents the opinions that potential new hires (and existing employees) have of the firm. As with all branding, crafting a strong employer brand is about good storytelling: using specific messages designed to attract the attention of the type of talent candidates you are seeking. But also, it's about living out that story you are telling. Satisfied employees are your loudest voice, particularly in an age of social media and user-generated feedback where employers aren't always completely in control of their own reputation.[16] In its Talent Trends 2014 survey, LinkedIn found that 56% of professionals cited the employer brand as the most important factor in deciding where to work.[17]

An employer's brand is its reputation as a place to work and has a direct impact on the ability to attract qualified applicants. What is your concept of an ideal place to work?

Source: © Shutterstock, Inc.

employer brand

Describes an employer's reputation as a place to work.

employer value proposition

A statement that summarizes everything that a company offers to an employee, in exchange for their time, skills, experience, and dedication.

The **employer value proposition** is a statement that summarizes everything that a company offers to an employee in exchange for their time, skills, experience, and dedication. It is a strategic statement that defines how the company wants employers to perceive them as a place to work. According to a 2017 survey by Universum (a global employer branding and market research firm based in Stockholm) and DHI Group, Inc. (a network of niche employment sites and recruiting services based in New York City), 84% of the world's top most attractive employers have crafted an employer value proposition.[18] In the survey of employers from fifty countries, they found that the following companies have created employer value propositions:

- 67% of large companies (10,000-plus employees)
- 55% of medium-sized companies (1,000–9,999 employees)
- 30% of small companies (fewer than 999 employees)[19]

According to Richard Mosley, Universum's global vice-president of strategy, "An employer value proposition provides current and future employees with clear reasons to stay with an employer. It conveys what employees can expect from an employer and what is expected of them in return."[20] Table 5.2 describes the steps in creating an employer brand and employer value proposition.

TABLE 5.2 Creating an Employer Brand

How to Create an Employer Brand	
Responsibility	Decide who is responsible for managing the employer brand. The CHRO is often ultimately responsible, but the CEO is marketing/communications play key roles.
Assess	Conduct research with existing employees to understand their perceptions of the company as a place to work. The research should include compensation, work environment, management style, benefits, work-life balance, on-the-job perks such as on-site childcare, recognition, and other aspects of the overall employee experience.
Create	Create an employer value proposition, making sure that it reflects the actual employee experience from the assessment data. If there are aspects of the experience that are not ideal, then fix those. The employer value proposition is not about presentation or spin but should be an accurate portrayal of the real employee experience.
Educate	Educate current employees about the employer value proposition and use them to spread the message. They are the company's best employer brand ambassadors.
Promote	Work with marketing and communications to promote the brand through advertising and public relations and to align it with the overall company branding.

How to Develop Your Employer Branding

A discussion of the importance of managing the employer brand and the candidate experience.

View the video online at: http://www.youtube.com/embed/I6YXUlMovJI?rel=0

HR Talk: Justin Dorsey

Senior Human Resources Manager

Ben E. Keith Company

For many years, companies with and without a formal talent acquisition department have taken a "post and pray" approached to recruiting. They will put a job ad up on a career page or job website and hope that the right person applies. During a healthy job market, employers must put the job ads in front of passive candidates who are not actively visiting job boards and career pages. Once a job is posted to our website it gets "scraped" (picked up and reposted) by the major job sites such as Indeed, Glassdoor, and LinkedIn so it is no longer as necessary to have contracts with multiple companies. The only benefit would be where the position would show up on the page or search results. Paid ads tend to show up first, and job seekers have a limited attention span, so you can increase your chances of being seen by paying to promote the ad. As a federal contractor, we also post ads to the workforce commission websites in the state where the position is located.

The most effective approaches to hiring entry- to mid-level employees tend to be referrals or posting to job sites that get the most traffic. Staffing agencies can be helpful as well if you prefer a "try before you buy" approach. For manager and executive roles, we have had success working with recruiting firms and targeted job campaigns where we proactively send the job ad to someone through LinkedIn who appears to meet the qualifications for the position. Both of these options can be quite expensive though, so you need to be able to show ROI or the support from upper management could be lost.

Employer branding has never been more important. Recruitment=Marketing! Companies tend to focus their marketing dollars on business development opportunities rather than advertising themselves as an employer of choice. However, if you Google almost any company you will see their Glassdoor score on the first page of results. Employers no longer have the luxury of neglecting their online presence. In a world of anonymous online comments, your company brand will be determined by what current and former employees are saying about you. Depending on the size of your organization, employer branding could become a full-time job. Prospective employees want to see that you are an "engaged employer" who is responding to comments and questions on their Glassdoor or Indeed company pages.

ROI can be difficult for HR to prove at times when it comes to recruiting. At a minimum, you need to understand what recruiting efforts are producing results. Include on your application a question about how someone heard about the position, ideally in a data field that can be pulled into a report or query. Time-to-fill is important, but it depends on the position and industry. Warehouse, drivers, wait staff, retail employees, etc. need to be hired quickly. It's okay to take longer on white-collar positions in order to make sure you locate the right cultural and skills fit. Turnover may not seem like a recruiting metric at first glance, but failing to vet people properly during the interview process can lead to a lot of employees not making it past their first thirty days of employment. You need to know when and why people are quitting to figure out if it can be tied back to the attraction, interview, and selection process.

Sourcing

Now that you have the attention of job candidates, the next step is to get them interested enough to apply for a position. **Sourcing** is the process of identifying qualified candidates for a job opening. At first, this may sound to you like the same thing as recruiting. The difference is that sourcing is a proactive strategy of seeking out qualified individuals for current or future openings. It is one stage of the overall recruiting process. The purpose of sourcing is to build a pipeline of talent from which to choose new hires in the future. The process should also be linked to an organization's strategic plan. For example, if a company plans to shift more of its workforce to remote work to save on office overhead, then it would make sense to source candidates who have experience working from home.

Sourcing is a proactive recruiting strategy that uses multiple channels such as networking, searching social media sites, employee referrals, and attending college recruiting events. It is the process of actively seeking out the right candidates, instead of waiting for them to come to you. For example, an accounting recruiter could place job postings on various web sites such as ZipRecruiter, Glassdoor, or Indeed. This is a reactive strategy in which the recruiter waits to be notified of an opening, then posts the job and waits for people to apply. Then the recruiter screens the resumes to determine which are the best candidates. In contrast, the recruiter could be more proactive in seeking out the best candidates and asking them to apply. One way this might occur is for the recruiter to search profiles on LinkedIn to find appropriate candidates, and then reach out to them personally.

Reactive recruiting can be an appropriate strategy for some positions, such as low-skill or entry-level jobs. For example, if a trucking company needs to hire freight handlers, or if a grocery store needs to hire stockers or cashiers, they likely will use reactive recruiting (place a job ad and wait for people to apply). They are probably not going to look for candidates on social media sites or through networking. Also, entry-level jobs tend to have higher turnover rates, and therefore it may not be worth the investment of time and other resources in active recruiting. However, active recruiting is a more strategic approach that can increase the quality of hires, especially for professional positions and in positions where employees stay with the organization long-term.

The various sources for finding candidates can be divided into two primary categories: internal and external. A section of this chapter is dedicated to each of these categories.

sourcing

The process of identifying qualified candidates for a job opening.

Candidate Experience

candidate experience

How job seekers perceive and react to an employer's recruiting process.

When a potential new hire first starts to consider working for a new employer, they have begun a journey. The **candidate experience** is how job seekers perceive and react to an employer's recruiting process. The journey includes every interaction they have with the company, from contact with recruiters, the online job posting, the application process, interviewing, assessments, hiring, and onboarding. Each interaction with a candidate is a touchpoint that can make a positive or negative impression on the applicant.

Candidates today are used to fast response times in most aspects of their lives. If they reach out to customer service via chat or phone, they expect an immediate answer. They do not want to send an email and wait for a response. If they need technical support, they want immediate help. The environment of quick responses has carried over to the job application process. Candidates today are no longer open to a lengthy, drawn-out experience. Best-in-class organizations streamline the process and use technology to deliver an immersive hiring experience that is highly targeted, personalized, and engaging.[21]

One very important aspect of the candidate experience is the length of time it takes to complete the application process. One method to track the application process is the click-to-apply ratio, which measures the percentage of job seekers who click to view a job posting and then go on to complete a job application. For example, if one hundred job seekers view a job posting, and twelve complete the application, then the click-to-apply ratio is 12%. A recent Appcast study found that the click-to-apply ratio is significantly impacted by two factors: the number of questions on the application, and the length of time it takes to complete the application.[22] On average, 10.6% of job post viewers complete an application that asks fewer than twenty-five questions. That drops by half, to 5.68%, when the application asks fifty questions or more. Perhaps even more telling is what happens to the click-to-apply ratio as the amount of time required to fill out the application increases. Application rates drop by a staggering 365% when the application takes more than fifteen minutes.[23] Figure 5.4 illustrates the impact of the number of questions on the application, and the amount of time required, on the click-to-apply ratio.

FIGURE 5.4 Click-to-Apply Ratios

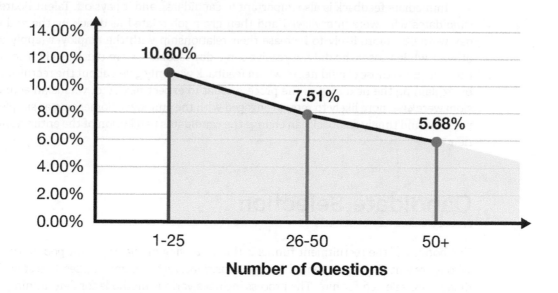

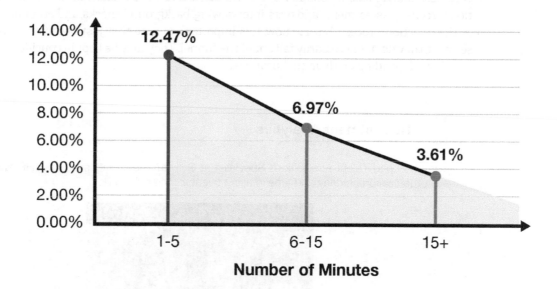

Source: Based on Forman, Chris (2015, May 7). "The Impact of Mobile Recruiting on Click-to-apply Rates." ERE. Retrieved from: https://www.ere.net/the-impact-of-mobile-recruiting-on-click-to-apply-rates/.

Another crucial aspect of the candidate experience is how the employer processes rejections. Just because an individual is not a viable candidate for a position for which they applied does not mean that they should be discarded into the scrap heap of rejected applications. He or she may be a candidate for a future opening, or perhaps even a current opening somewhere else in the organization. Every applicant, even those who are rejected, are also potential sources of referrals. Over 50% of applicants share good hiring experiences on social media, and over a third share their bad experiences.[24] Thus, every applicant can potentially have a positive or negative impact on the employer brand. The method for delivering a rejection impacts the candidate experience and can play a large role in determining whether he or she applies again or refers others. According to TalentBoard, 63% of rejections are delivered by automated email replies, 21% by personal email from the recruiter, and only 7% by personal phone calls from the recruiter or hiring manager.[25] This is significant because positive candidate ratings increase by more than 28% when they receive a personal phone call.[26] Thus, even rejected candidates can have a positive impact on the recruiting funnel if they are treated personally and with dignity and respect.

Immediate feedback is also important to candidates, and it pays off. Talent Board reports that candidates who were interviewed and then given job-related feedback by the end of that same day were 52% more likely to increase their relationship with the employer (apply again or refer others), while those who did not receive same-day feedback were twice as likely to sever the relationship. Even those candidates to whom feedback was only given about the recruiting process (e.g., by explaining the next step in the process, what to expect next, etc., versus an actual hiring decision) were 41% more likely to remain engaged with the employer. Something as simple as providing personal and timely feedback can change the candidate's perception of the entire application experience.

Candidate Selection

The bottom of the recruitment funnel is the narrowing of the applicant pool to those candidates who represent the best potential for open positions. As the name implies, this stage is where candidates are selected for hire. The process includes various methods for determining which are the very best individuals. In Chapter 6, we will discuss talent selection in detail, including application screening, assessments and tests, interviewing, background checks, and other methods utilized in the selection process. But for now, it is important to note that just because a candidate is not selected, they do not necessarily fall out of the funnel. They may be kept in consideration for future openings, depending on their qualifications.

 Recruitment Analytics

Jayla, the Lead Talent Acquisitions Specialist at Growth Tribe, discusses how HR analytics can save organizations money and time in hiring talent for the right skills.

View the video online at: http://www.youtube.com/embed/XLIaJEfbNI0?rel=0

Key Takeaways

- The recruitment funnel is a process for narrowing down a wide audience, and helps candidates stay engaged and eventually become employees.
- Recruitment is expensive, and when job openings are vacant for too long it has serious implications for lost productivity and profits. Therefore, it makes sense for HR managers to think

like marketers by being proactive in recruitment and treating potential employees the same way that marketing treats potential customers.

- There are four distinct stages in the recruitment funnel: employer branding, sourcing, candidate experience, and candidate selection.
- The employer brand describes an employer's reputation as a place to work.
- The employer value proposition is a statement that summarizes everything that a company offers to an employee, in exchange for their time, skills, experience, and dedication.
- Sourcing is the process of identifying qualified candidates for a job opening. It is also a proactive strategy to build a pipeline of talent from which to choose new hires in the future.
- The candidate experience is how job seekers perceive and react to an employer's recruiting process. The journey includes every interaction they have with the company, from contact with recruiters, the online job posting, the application process, interviewing, assessments, hiring, and onboarding. Each interaction with a candidate is a touchpoint that can make a positive or negative impression on the applicant.

What Do *You* Think?

1. Should a recruiter be someone with a degree in HR or marketing? Or is it a little of both? Should an HR student who wants to work in recruiting pursue a minor in marketing?
2. Does your current or former employer have a brand? How would you describe the employer value proposition to a job candidate?
3. What was the candidate experience like when you applied for jobs in the past? What recommendations might you offer to those organizations?

5.4 Internal Recruitment Methods

Learning Objectives

1. Understand the advantages and disadvantages of internal recruitment.
2. Explain the methods for internal job posting.
3. Recognize why using a temporary worker pool sometimes makes good business sense.
4. Identify techniques to improve succession planning as part of an internal recruitment strategy.

Companies will often look internally first to fill open positions because current employees form an existing talent pipeline of employees that already have knowledge of the company culture and are available to start work faster than candidates from external recruitment methods. There are several other advantages, and some possible disadvantages, to internal recruitment, as summarized in Table 5.3.

TABLE 5.3 Advantages and Disadvantages of Internal Recruitment

Advantages	Disadvantages
Faster time-to-hire because employees have already been recruited to the company.	Stagnant culture because employees may be used to "how things are done here."
Improved morale of existing workers due to promotion opportunities.	Some employees who are passed over for promotions may feel resentful.
Certainty of past performance and attitude of employees because their track record is easily accessible.	Need to backfill. When an employee is promoted or transferred, that creates another open position that must be filled.
Less orientation and training required, thus a faster time-to-competency.	Narrower skillset availability. There are situations in which the best applicant for a position is someone working outside the company with a different skillset, experience, and perspective.
Reduced cost-to-hire since no advertising is required (other than internal job posting).	Morale can be damaged if a hiring manager already has a candidate in mind and is just going through the motions of advertising the position internally to comply with company policy.

There are several methods to recruit employees from within an organization, including job postings, temporary worker pools, and succession planning. Each of these methods is discussed here.

Internal Job Postings

internal job posting

A notice of a job opening that is made available to all existing employees, but not the general public.

An **internal job posting** is the notice of a job opening that is made available to all existing employees, but not the general public. The methods for posting an opening vary by company, but typically might include a job-openings page on the company intranet, company publications such as newsletters, email, distribution of memos, and placement on bulletin boards in employee common areas such as break rooms or locker rooms.

Some larger companies hold internal career fairs where employees can learn about opportunities for advancement or transfers within the company. Some examples of companies that hold internal career fairs are Yelp, Allianz, KPMG, Schneider, and Sodexho. Schneider holds an annual Internal Informational Career Fair at their corporate headquarters in Green Bay, Wisconsin. The event gives Schneider associates the opportunity to network and look at different areas of the company and opportunities that are available to grow their career at Schneider.[27] The corporate recruiting team also is onsite to provide resume-writing assistance, and the employees have the opportunity to learn about networking groups available at the company, such as the Schneider Women's Network.

Temporary Worker Pools

Many companies utilize temporary workers from staffing agencies to meet peak demand periods. It is especially a useful hiring strategy for companies with seasonal or cyclical fluctuations, such as retail, tax preparation, water parks, and ski resorts. Retailers often hire additional employers during the holiday season, typically from October through December. For example, in the 2017 holiday season, Amazon hired 120,000 temporary workers, Target hired 100,000, and Macy's hired 80,000.[28] For Amazon, this is almost as much as their full-time workforce of 125,000.

Temporary workers can also be a type of internal recruitment, because companies usually have the option of converting the temp employee to a permanent one (often referred to as temp-to-hire).

When a company contracts with a staffing agency for a temporary worker, the company normally pays an hourly fee (except in the case of professional positions, in which case the fee might be weekly, monthly, or even annually). The staffing agency then pays the employee, and keeps the remainder of the fee to cover their overhead and a profit percentage. The worker is an employee of the staffing agency and is essentially on loan to the company. To convert the position to a permanent hire, there is usually a buyout fee in the contract. The staffing agency has paid the costs of recruitment, assessment, orientation, and maybe some training as well. The buyout fee makes good business sense for the staffing agency because it allows them to recoup the investment they have already made in the worker.

There are several variations for structuring the buyout fees. The buyout fee normally decreases the longer the temporary worker is placed. For example, a staffing agency may agree to waive their buyout fee if the temporary worker has been at the position for five hundred hours. This is referred to as a minimum-hours-worked structure. Another variation is a liquidate fee, which charges a fee based on how many hours the worker has completed. For example, the client might pay a buyout fee based on 15% of the worker's first year salary until the employee has worked four hundred hours. Then the fee decreases by 1% for each additional one hundred hours worked. Under this liquidation fee structure, the longer the worker remains on the staffing company payroll, the lower the fee charged.[29]

Converting temporary workers to permanent can be a useful internal recruitment strategy because the employer was able to try out the employee for as long as they wanted before committing to taking on a full-time employee. If a temporary worker is subpar in performance or attitude, then the employer does not have to terminate the employee. They simply end the contract with the staffing agency. Firing an employee is always fraught with perils, such as the possibility of a wrongful discharge, negative comments made by disgruntled ex-workers on social media, and increased payroll taxes due to more unemployment job claims made by former workers. Thus, it often makes good business sense for employees to fill permanent job openings by converting the very best of their temporary workers. In fact, in 2017, Amazon converted 10,000 of its 120,000 temporary workers into permanent hires.[30]

HR Talk: Beth Gottfried

Human Resources Group Manager

Toyota North America

One of our major challenges in recruiting is that there are more available jobs than there are skilled workers to fill those jobs. This is particularly true in skilled maintenance, tool and die, production, and warehousing. But we don't want to hire just anyone with the required skillsets. We are looking for the right types of employees. This means that they are a good fit with the culture of the company, known as The Toyota Way. The Toyota Way defines the fundamental values and business methods all our people should apply in every aspect of their day-to-day work, at every level of the company, worldwide. It is the foundation of our corporate culture. The Toyota Way is built on two pillars: Continuous Improvement and Respect for People. The second pillar embraces a collaborative and team environment, so we look for new hires that will be a good fit for this type of environment.

Employer branding is an important way of attracting the right kind of applicants. It is important in our marketing that we describe the culture of Toyota and why it is a great place to work. We engage in internal recruiting through rotation and promotion of existing employees and external recruiting through employee referrals, LinkedIn, and professional development groups.

At Toyota, we rely upon analytics to measure the success of our recruitment efforts. The metrics we trace are:

- Time-to-fill.
- Candidate surveys.
- Hiring manager surveys.

- Diversity of applicant pools.
- Interview-to-hire ratio.
- Hiring manager submission-to-interview ratio.
- Candidate correspondence time.

Succession Planning

Succession planning is a strategy to develop people to advance into new roles when an employee leaves the organization. Many CEOs express concern about the bench strength in their companies and worry about the future continuity and performance issues due to the lack of sufficient "ready now" candidates to replace losses of key leaders (planned and unplanned).[31] Despite this concern, according to recent research, two-thirds of companies have no formal succession plan in place.[32]

An effective succession plan begins with the creation of an organizational culture that values the development of employees. One research study found that managers often hire external candidates rather than promote their current employees because they have a tendency to overvalue unfamiliar candidates and undervalue known ones.[33]

From the perspective of the organization, succession planning helps to mitigate the risk of having key positions unfilled for long periods of time. For the employees, it can increase morale and retention because employees have an idea of what's next for them in their career. It can encourage employees to stay with the company long term, instead of leaving for a better opportunity. This helps reduce the chances of **brain drain**, which occurs when employees leave for better opportunities in other organizations or industries.

The following strategies and initiatives can be implemented to improve succession planning:

TABLE 5.4 Steps to Improve Succession Planning

Step 1: Leadership by Example	Senior leadership should have the overall responsibility for succession planning. This includes the CEO, CFO, and the CHRO, often referred to as the G3.
Step 2: Strategic Focus by HR	HR professionals should possess business acumen in addition to HR knowledge. The CHRO or other senior member of the HR team should have a seat at the table with other senior executives.
Step 3: Develop Talent Pipelines	Data analytics should be used to project future talent needs and develop plans to fulfill openings and prevent critical skill shortages.
Step 4: Standardize Assessment	Develop a standardized method for assessing the future potential of each employee, and create corresponding talent development initiatives.
Step 5: Use Job Design Methodology	Implement job rotation, job enlargement, and job enrichment to develop employees for future assignments.
Step 6: Use Lateral Transfers	Create a talent pool with varied skillsets and flexibility by using lateral moves for employees. This may include offering incentives for such moves and helping each employee to visualize how a lateral move can fit into their own professional development plan.

Source: Based on Walsh, J. (2019, January 14). "7 steps to successful succession planning." Forbes. Retrieved from https://www.forbes.com/sites/johnwelsheurope/2019/01/14/7-steps-to-successful-succession-planning/#5e8a4d0145fb

Key Takeaways

- Companies will often look internally first to fill open positions because current employees form an existing talent pipeline of employees who already have knowledge of the company culture, and are available to start work faster than candidates from external recruitment methods.

- An internal job posting is the notice of a job opening that is made available to all existing employees, but not the general public. The methods for posting an opening vary by company, but typically might include a job-openings page on the company intranet, company publications such as newsletters, email, distribution of memos, and placement on bulletin boards in employee common areas such as break rooms or locker rooms.

- Many companies utilize temporary workers from staffing agencies to meet peak demand periods. It is an especially useful hiring strategy for companies with seasonal or cyclical fluctuations.

- Temporary workers can also be a type of internal recruitment, because companies usually have the option of converting the employee to a permanent one (often referred to as temp-to-hire).

- Succession planning is a strategy to develop people to advance into new roles when an employee leaves the organization.

- An effective succession plan begins with the creation of an organizational culture that values the development of employees.

What Do *You* Think?

1. Have you ever worked for a company that hired an outsider for a higher-level position instead of promoting you? How did that impact your morale?

2. What might be the result if a company promotes from within, but does not post the job where everyone that is interested has the opportunity to apply?

3. Have you considered working for a temporary agency when you are between jobs?

4. Why do you think managers often have a tendency to overvalue unfamiliar candidates (external candidates) and undervalue known ones (internal candidates)?

5.5 External Recruitment Methods

Learning Objectives

1. Understand the advantages and disadvantages of external recruitment.
2. Explain the difference between active and passive candidates.
3. Recognize the methods for advertising on job boards effectively.
4. Identify the role of employee referrals for external recruitment.
5. Describe how social media can be used to reach passive candidates.
6. Explain how to conduct effective college recruitment.

We ended the previous section with step seven in a succession plan: "Don't forget to look outside." A company can be best-in-class in developing current employees and managing succession plans, but there will always be situations in which an external hire is needed. This could be because a position requires a skillset or level of experience that just does not exist in the company now. It also could be that the company needs to increase diversity. For example, women represent 58.7% of the civilian labor force in the United States.[34] Yet, women are underrepresented in management and professional positions, and are less represented the higher up they go. Based on 2017 data, in the S&P 500 companies, women represent 36.9% of first- and mid-level positions, 26.5% of executive level positions, and only 4.8% of CEOs, as shown in Figure 5.5.[35] Companies seek to fill positions with external candidates to acquire different skillsets, increase diversity, and bring fresh ideas into the organization. There are several other advantages, and some possible disadvantages to external recruitment, as summarized in Table 5.5.

FIGURE 5.5 Women in the Workforce Pyramid

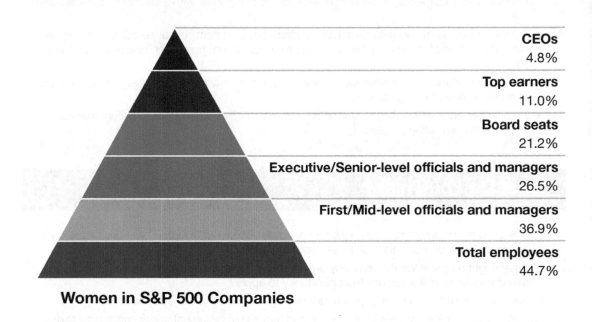

CEOs
4.8%

Top earners
11.0%

Board seats
21.2%

Executive/Senior-level officials and managers
26.5%

First/Mid-level officials and managers
36.9%

Total employees
44.7%

Women in S&P 500 Companies

Source: Catalyst, Women CEOs of the S&P 500 (2019). EY Center for Board Matters, 2016 Top Earners in S&P 500 Companies, Unpublished data. Catalyst, 2016 Catalyst Census: Women and Men Board Directors (2017). U.S. Equal Employment Opportunity Commission (EEOC), Unpublished 2015 S&P 500 EEO-1 data.

TABLE 5.5 Advantages and Disadvantages of External Recruitment

Advantages	Disadvantages
New ideas, fresh perspectives, and new sources of creativity and innovation.	Slower time-to-hire because of the time needed for recruitment and selection processes.
Not indoctrinated in existing corporate culture, and they don't know "how things have always been done here."	Some employees may be resentful that an outsider was brought in instead of promoting from within.
No need to backfill as is necessary with internal recruiting.	Risk that the employee may not work out due to poor performance, or attitude.
Able to increase diversity and minority representation.	Slower time-to-competency since the employee is new to the organization.
Opportunity to hire sources of expertise not currently available within the organization.	Increased cost-to-hire due to advertising and other recruitment expense.

The methods for recruiting new employees include advertising, employee referrals, social media, and school recruitment. Each of these methods is discussed here.

Before we begin to review these methods, let's distinguish between active and passive candidates. An **active candidate** is an individual who is actively looking for a job opportunity and is most likely to see an advertisement. This is in contrast to a **passive candidate**, who is an individual that is not actively looking for a job. Active job seekers are more likely to be searching internet advertising on job boards, while passive job seekers are more active on work-related social networking sites such as LinkedIn.[36] Why should you care about the difference between active and passive job seekers? Because passive job candidates make up 70% of the global workforce, whereas active candidates only make up 30%.[37] If you ignore passive candidates in your recruitment efforts, you are missing a large part of the potential talent pool. Also, passive candidates are content in their work. Only 52% of active candidates are satisfied with their current role, while 80% of passive candidates are satisfied.[38] Passive candidate are most likely valuable to their companies, otherwise they would be not be employed. It just makes sense to include passive candidates because if they are satisfied with the kind of work they are doing with their current employer, and they are valuable to the employer, then there is a good chance they will be successful in your organization.

Advertising

Advertising is a useful method to attract the attention of active job seekers. In the past, advertising typically referred to placing ads in the help-wanted section of newspapers or other print publications. While this is still a viable avenue for reaching some local job candidates, the vast majority of employment ads today are found on job boards or job search engines. These two terms are often used interchangeably, but they are different. A **job board** is a website that posts job notices provided by an employer, which the employer usually pays a fee for. A **job search engine** aggregates job listings from many job boards and other online sources such as employer websites.

Each job board or search engine has a unique value proposition for employers and candidates. For example, Monster is a general board with job postings across a wide variety of industries. Indeed offers more variety, such as contract positions, work-at-home opportunities, summer jobs, and volunteer work, while CareerBuilder is more focused on people with a bachelor's degree.[39] There are also industry-specific job boards. For example, Dice is a leading site for tech jobs, Career-Bank and eFinancialCareers focus on finance and banking, Variety Careers is for jobs in television, radio, and production, while TalentZoo is for advertising and marketing jobs.[40] Want to work on a cruise ship? Try allcruisejobs.com. Looking for a job in oil and gas? Try rigzone.com. The top eight job search boards for 2019 are listed in Figure 5.6.

active candidate

An individual who is actively looking for a job opportunity and is most likely to see an advertisement.

passive candidate

An individual who is not actively looking for a job.

job board

A website that posts job notices provided by an employer, which the employer usually pays a fee for.

job search engine

Aggregates job listings from many job boards and other online sources such as employer websites.

FIGURE 5.6 Top Eight Job Search Boards

1. Indeed

2. LinkedIn Job Search   Linked in

3. Glassdoor   glassdoor

4. Handshake   handshake

5. SimplyHired   SimplyHired

6. ZipRecruiter   ZipRecruiter

7. Monster   MONSTER

8. CareerBuilder Job Board   CAREER BUILDER

Regardless of which job boards you decide to use for posting jobs, the following guidelines will help you create an effective job posting:

- **Don't just post the job description.** Job descriptions tend to sound mundane and not very engaging. Think like a marketer, and write the job posting for what it is: an advertisement! Write essential job functions in an engaging way. Instead of "maintain a positive office atmosphere," perhaps use something like "create a place where everybody loves their job." Figure 5.7 highlights the differences between a job description and a job ad.

- **Tell the candidate why they should be interested in coming to work for your firm.** Recall your own mind-set when you have been looking at job postings in the past. You were probably wondering what it would be like working for this company, and your potential candidates are thinking that also. Describe how the jobholder will contribute something positive to the organization and society. Also, describe the advancement potential of the job.

- **Leverage the employer brand.** Connect the wording in the job posting to the advertising that the candidate may be familiar with. For example, if you are writing a job posting for an opening at Nike, the first line might be "Just do it: Come to work for Nike!"

- **Look at your competitor's job ads.** What do you like about them, and what would you change? How can you make your ad stand out?

- **Use interactive links such as video featuring the hiring manager.**

FIGURE 5.7 Job Ads versus Job Description

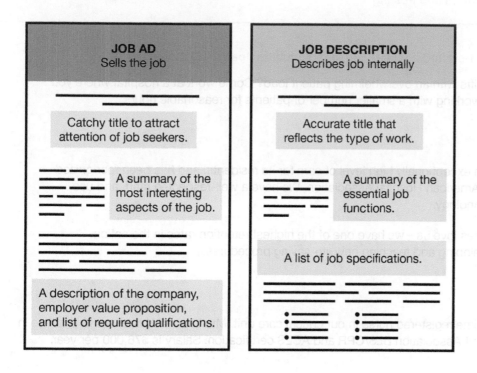

Source: Betterteam

Figure 5.8 is an example of a well-crafted job posting.

FIGURE 5.8 Example of a Well-Crafted Job Posting

Registered Nurse—Well-staffed hospital, reasonable patient loads, 15k bonus.

Tired of working long shifts with an overwhelming patient load? Come work at a hospital where you can make a difference, working with a smaller number of patients for reasonable hours.

THE COMPANY:

Betterhealth provides an exceptionally high level of care for its residents, and has been recognized numerous times by the American Hospital Association. We have a well-respected staff, and use cutting-edge health technology.

- Registered nurses love us—we have one of the highest retention rates in the nation.
- We lead in developing and teaching new life-saving procedures.

THE POSITION:

We're looking for a full-time registered nurse in our critical care unit. Must have RN licenses to practice in Michigan, American Heart Association BLS/CPR and ACLS certification. Salary is $76,000 per year.

- Very competitive benefits package.
- $15,000 commencement bonus.
- Guaranteed 8-hour shifts.

THE LOCATION:

Betterhealth is based in Ann Arbor, Michigan. We're nicknamed "tree town" because of the huge number of beautiful trees that grow in the city. We're home to the University of Michigan.

- Wide selection of top-rated schools.
- Crime rate well below national average.
- Lots to do—sporting events, concerts, museums.
- World class coffee shops.

WHY SHOULD YOU APPLY?

- Top benefits.
- Excellent growth and advancement opportunities.
- Bonus program.
- Tuition reimbursement.
- Remote working opportunities.

Source: Craigslist, Betterteam

A recent CareerXroads (a staffing strategy firm) survey reported that only 15% of job openings were filled from applicants who applied on a job board or search engine.[41] Therefore, it is crucial to use some or all of the following additional recruitment methods to reach potential qualified candidates.

HR in the Real World: The Case of the Deceptive Job Posting

I have worked for private-sector companies and also several government institutions. There is a unique aspect of recruiting in the public sector that is usually not encountered in the private sector, and that is state or federal regulations that require jobs to be externally posted before an internal candidate can be hired. Even if a government agency is filling a position and already has identified an internal candidate to fill it, they are often bound by state or federal guidelines to advertise the position. This may occur in the private sector with government contractors, or even companies that have internal policies that require jobs to be externally posted, but it is much more common in the public sector.

The intent of these laws is to ensure fair opportunities in employment. But there is a downside because when applicants find out that someone had already been identified for the position (which they often do), they will feel like it was a waste of their time. This point was brought home to me when I was interviewing a candidate for a position where an internal candidate had already been informally selected, but state law required us to post the position and conduct a search including interviews. This particular candidate had traveled to the organization from out of state for the interview and found out about the situation. The candidate asked me, "Why would you waste my time and yours? Why would you give me false hope?"

While I could not do anything about the state law and had to continue to advertise all open positions, I made a point after that to let applicants know that an internal candidate had been identified. I also told applicants that they might be considered for other positions, perhaps future ones, if they went ahead with the interview. But I never wanted to be in the position of offering false hope again.

Employee Referrals

Employee referrals are a recruiting method in which employers encourage current employees, through incentives, to refer qualified candidates for jobs in the organization. New hires who are referred by current employees tend to be better performers and have higher retention than other new hires.[42] They also have a faster time-to-hire and are less expensive than other recruitment methods.

employee referrals

A recruiting method in which employers encourage current employees, through incentives, to refer qualified candidates for jobs in the organization.

New hires from employee referrals result in faster time-to-hires, are less expensive than other recruiting methods, and have higher retention rates.

Source: © Shutterstock, Inc.

Almost 30% of new hires come from employee referrals, according to Gerry Crispin, a principal at CareerXRoads.[43] Organizations in which recruiters emphasize the employee referral program average 35% to 45% of all new hires. Some suggestions for a successful implementation of an employee referral program are:

- **Determine strategic goals and specific outcomes for the program.** These should be stated in terms of improving key metrics such as time-to-hire, retention rates, quality-of-hire, diversity goals, and employee morale.

- **Make the process quick and simple for the current employee.** Only ask for enough information to identify the referred employee, and then HR can follow up on the referral. Employees should be able to submit the referral through multiple methods: online through the company intranet, email, or paper form.

- **Design rewards that current employees value.** Cash payments are a popular incentive, but there are many other options. Consider extra vacation days, employee recognition, or experiential gifts (think cruises, weekend getaways, sporting events, concerts, wine tastings, goat yoga, cooking classes, skydiving, etc.). A Clemson study found that trips were the most popular employee incentive, followed by cash, and then merchandise.[44] Be creative and tailor the offerings to the interest of your workforce (and if you are not sure which options they are interested in, then ask them!). But note that it is important to offer employees a choice when using experiential rewards. Not everyone will want to go skydiving or participate in goat yoga, for example. A weekend getaway for two may be a great incentive for a single or married-without-children employee, but an employee with children might prefer a night-at-the-ballpark family package.

Here are just a few creative ideas that companies have implemented for their employee referral programs:

- Trustwave employees can refer their LinkedIn, Facebook, and Twitter followers for jobs.

- Salesforce hosts recruitment happy hours, where employees invite the people they want to refer and they get to meet recruiters.

- Fiverr uses gamification by offering points for sharing jobs and referring friends.

- Accenture uses emotional rewards offering a cash incentive and giving the employee the option to donate part of the cash payment to a charity of their choice. Accenture then matches the amount donated.

- Intel doubles its referral bonus when employees successfully refer women and minorities.

- InMobi offered their employees in India a choice of a Royal Enfield motorcycle (sort of the Harley Davidson of India) and U.S. employees a Vespa or a trip to Bali to watch the sunrise over a volcano. The bikes were parked right at the front entrances of the offices to give employees a daily reminder of the referral program.[45]

Another specific type of employee referral is nomination by managers. This method involves asking managers to nominate high-performing employees for promotion. This tends to be a system driven by the knowledge that direct supervisors have regarding the career potential of their direct reports and in some firms is also driven by data analysis of previous performance appraisals of the employees. There is a substantial downside to consider with this approach, and that is the potential for accusations (perceived or real) of favoritism or unlawful discrimination.[46]

Social Media

Social media is an excellent avenue to reach passive job candidates. These individuals are not actively looking for work, so they will not find out about your job opportunities through a job posting. For decades, research has indicated that 60% to 70% of jobs are filled through networking. But a recent study found that this number might be has high as 85%.[47] And this is exactly what professional social media is . . . networking.

The following tips will help you to reach out more effectively to locate potential new hires:

- **Don't overlook the niche sites.** Of course, when we talk about using social media to reach job candidates, we are talking primarily about LinkedIn, Twitter, Instagram, and Facebook. But don't overlook the niche sites. You might find software developer candidates on GitHub or Stack Overflow, or a digital marketer on Warrior Forum. If you are hiring for Petco, then try Dogster or Catster. If you are looking for more minority candidates, try blackplanet.com. If you are a movie cinema looking for new hires, try Flixster.

- **Participate in groups that are focused on the industry or occupation that are related to the job opening.** LinkedIn alone has over one million groups to choose from.

- **Use hashtags to get your job openings in front of the right candidates.** If you are hiring for an HR position in Cleveland, try #Clevelandjobs, or #HRinCleveland (or maybe #HRRocksCleveland).

- **Fully complete your company page if the site offers that feature.** A completed company page on LinkedIn is more likely to show up in search results.

- **Use filters to find the right candidates.** Many social media sites have advanced search options where you can filter by occupation, experience, job title, years of experience, current and former company, and other factors.

- **Reach out personally.** Don't copy and paste the same message to each candidate you reach out to. Look at their profile and find something you can use to personalize your message. Compliment them by mentioning what it was about the candidate that grabbed your attention.

College and School Recruitment

Recruiting from colleges and universities is a valuable source of candidates who are about to enter a profession that requires a degree. Secondary schools are a valuable recruiting source for positions that do not require post-secondary education. Most higher education institutions and high schools have a career services office that provides career coaching to students (e.g., resumé advice, training on interviewing skills, etc.). Many also host career fairs, which gives employers the opportunity to come on campus to recruit potential employees. Many also engage on a regular basis with employers looking for job candidates. Some schools have their own job boards, and there is even a social media site (Handshake) dedicated to making connections between college students and recent grads and potential employers.

It is helpful to keep in mind what students are looking for in a potential employer (and yes, if you are reading this book, you are probably a college student, but perhaps not in the traditional eighteen-to-twenty-two-year-old age group; the median age for a college student in the U.S. is now twenty-seven). See if you relate to what the research indicates that college students are looking for in a job[48]:

- **Meaningful work.** Students are searching for an opportunity to do more than just exchange their hours for a paycheck. They want to do work that is meaningful and makes a contribution to society.

- **Health benefits.** Benefits are now on the student priority short list. According to Sean M. Schofield, assistant director of internships at Cohen Career Center at William & Mary, a recent survey of students found that benefits made the number-two spot for job search priorities for students (after meaningful work).

- **Learning about the work they will be doing.** In the job search process, students want to know what the job actually entails, and are not interested in busy work.

- **Professional development.** Graduates know that skillsets change rapidly, and they want to work for a company that will provide training and development to keep them up to speed.

- **A clear career path.** They want to know about the pathway for future career development and advancement.

- **Flexible work arrangements.** Students are interested in maintaining work-life balance, and therefore flexible work arrangements such as remote work and compressed workweeks are valuable to them.

- **A supportive workplace culture.** Students want to work somewhere they are valued and supported. Mentorship programs, employee discounts, and recognition programs will attract student interest.

Talent Analytics

Talent analytics can provide useful insights into questions that HR managers should be asking, and that senior managers almost certainly want to know. Some of these questions are:

- How long does it take us to fill an open position?
- How many applicants do we attract for each opening? Is it the right amount, or too many, so that we waste too much time filtering through unqualified candidates?
- What does it cost the company to have vacant positions?
- What is the quality of our new hires? Could it be improved? Are we finding the right candidates? Are line managers happy with the quality of our recruits?
- How long do new hires stay with the company? How is our retention compared to the competition?

The answers to these (and many other) questions can be determined through talent analytics. This gets to the heart of talent analytics. Data can be used to give managers valuable insights into how to improve the effectiveness of the company's recruiting efforts and to identify areas that need work. Recruitment analytics specifically has made tremendous advances in recent years due to the large amounts of data that are available from social media platforms such as LinkedIn and from applicant tracking systems and the ability of HRIS systems to automate much of the data analysis process.

One critical method to improve recruitment effectiveness is to develop an accurate predictive profile of the ideal candidate. Aditya Narayan Mishra, CEO, CIEL HR Services, shares his thoughts on this:

> *Organizations have a huge amount of data about their employees: their personal details, education, family background, and so on. They also have data about employees' performance and behaviors. Hence, they can correlate all these dimensions to determine the typical profile of an employee who is likely to be successful with them. That's the power of predictive analytics![49]*

Some of the key metrics to track are yield ratio, cost per hire, time-to-fill, new hire turnover, and quality of hire.

Yield Ratio:

A **yield ratio** indicates how many applicants a company needs for each new hire. For example, if a company needs to receive ten applications to have enough qualified applicants to fill two positions that are open, the yield ratio of applications to new hires is 20% (2/10 = .20). If the company needs to fill ten positions, then they know that they need to collect fity (10/.20 = 50) applications.

Cost Per Hire:

Cost per hire is the average amount of money spent per person hired. This is an important figure to know because it is a data-driven method for determining an overall recruitment budget. For example, if the cost per hire is $2,500, and the company needs to hire 150 new employees in the next fiscal year, then the recruiting budget should be $2,550 x 150=$375,000.

Cost per hire can be calculated based on this formula:[50]

$$ \text{CPH} = \frac{\text{Internal Recruiting Cost} + \text{External Recruiting Cost}}{\text{Total Number of Hires}} $$

Internal recruitment costs should include all organizational overhead including recruiters' salaries, money spent on employee referral programs, campus recruiting, career fairs, interviewing costs, and the ATS.

External recruitment talent costs include all money spent outside the organization such as the cost of job board postings, agency costs, candidate travel costs, relocation costs, and selection costs such as assessments and background checks.

---

yield ratio

Indicates how many applicants a company needs for each new hire.

cost per hire

The average amount of money spent per person hired.

time-to-fill

The amount of time that elapsed between a position becoming open and a candidate accepting the position.

new hire turnover

Refers to the number of new employees who leave an organization, voluntarily or through terminations, within a specified time period.

quality of hire

The value a new hire adds to the organization.

Time-to-Fill:

The **time-to-fill** metric is pretty straightforward and self-explanatory. It is the amount of time that elapses between a position becoming open and a candidate accepting the position. It is usually expressed in days, weeks, or months. Time-to-fill has been increasing throughout the past decade. A recent study conducted by Bersin by Deloitte found that in 2011, companies filled vacant positions in forty-eight days, but now take an average of fifty-two days to fill an opening.[51]

New Hire Turnover:

New hire turnover refers to the number of new employees that leave an organization, voluntarily or through terminations, within a specified time period. The time period used varies by company and industry, but some common calculations are the turnover rates during the first thirty days, forty-five days, and one year. On average, new hire turnover averages 20% in the first forty-five days.[52]

Quality of Hire:

Quality of hire is the value a new hire adds to the organization. According to a LinkedIn survey, 40% of talent acquisition leaders cite quality of hire as their top recruitment priority.[53] Despite its importance, it is one of the most difficult metrics to quantify and track, because there is not a standard accepted formula.

Some common factors that companies include in their quality-of-hire ratings are:

- Hiring satisfaction by managers.
- Job performance data or supervisory performance appraisals.
- Employee engagement based on self-ratings.
- New hire turnover (an unusually high turnover rate could be a sign of poor quality of hire).

Key Takeaways

- The methods for recruiting new employees include advertising, employee referrals, social media, and college/school recruitment.
- An active candidate is an individual who is actively looking for a job opportunity and is most likely to see an advertisement. This is in contrast to a passive candidate, who is an individual that is not actively looking for a job.
- A job board is a website that posts job notices provided by an employer, which the employer usually pays a fee for. A job search engine aggregates job listings from many job boards and other online sources, such as employer websites.
- Employee referrals are a recruiting method in which employers encourage current employees, through incentives, to refer qualified candidates for jobs in the organization.
- Social media is an excellent avenue to reach passive job candidates. These individuals are not actively looking for work, so they will find not out about your job opportunities through a job posting.
- Recruiting from colleges and universities is a valuable source of candidates who are about to enter a profession that requires a degree, and recruiting from high schools is an effective method to recruit applicants for positions that do not require post-secondary education.

What Do *You* Think?

1. One of the advantages of external hiring is that new hires bring in different ideas, fresh perspectives, and new sources of creativity and innovation. But why might some current employees respond negatively? How can this be overcome?
2. Do you have a favorite job board? If so, what do you like about it?

3. Which type of employee referral incentive would you prefer?
4. Are you currently connected to any groups on your professional social media? If not, then should you be?
5. How can you maximize your own future job opportunities with your college's career office?

5.6 Conclusion

Competition for talent is fierce, and companies must be proactive in creating recruitment strategies that will attract highly qualified applicants. This chapter introduced the recruitment process, including employer branding, public relations, and attracting diverse applicants. Internal and external recruitment methods were covered, and ideas for improving recruitment effectiveness were explored. The chapter concluded with a review of the most common techniques for evaluating the effectiveness of recruitment, including yield ratio, costs per hire, and new hire turnover.

Theory-into-Practice (TIP) Exercises

1. Using the guidelines in this chapter, write a job posting for a position you are familiar with (such as a current or former job). Then ask a classmate or friend to read it, and rate it on a scale of 1–10 for how engaging it is. Ask for suggestions on how to make it more engaging and interesting to job candidates.

2. Interview a recruiter and ask them the following questions:

   a. What is the most challenging aspect of your role?

   b. Which recruiting methods are effective in finding the very best qualified candidates?

   c. What advice do you have for new recruiters?

   d. What advice do you have for candidates who have been contacted by a recruiter?

3. Obtain a real job application form (perhaps from your employer, a friend who works in HR, or even just download one from the internet). Review each item on the application and answer the following questions:

   a. How is the item job related?

   b. Could it lead to illegal discrimination?

Then prepare a list of recommendations for how to improve the application.

Case Study: Trouble in Paradise

Source: © Shutterstock, Inc.

Most of us would jump at the chance to win a free trip to Hawaii, but few people are as eager to live and work there. Being 2,500 miles away from the nearest talent hub, having a higher cost of living, and having a 2% unemployment rate can result in difficulty when searching to fill new positions. The government of Hawaii experienced these hiring challenges for decades. On average, their job postings would get only five or six applications, and it would take up to two years to fill a role.

This changed with the hiring of Todd Nacapuy as the state's chief information officer in 2015. He convinced the government to fund a major overhaul of the state's recruitment process. He started by changing his department's culture and invested in recruitment marketing and smart candidate targeting. Hawaii reduced its time-to-fill rate to six months and hired sixty new employees in just a few years.

Nacapuy developed several methods to attract new talent. Because working for the government does not appeal to many people, he worked on transforming the employee value proposition (EVP). Working alongside his HR partner and recruiter-in-chief, Jennifer Pegarido, they took that insight and packaged it into a message that if you work for the state of Hawaii, you will make an important impact on others as well as develop a career, not just a job. Nacapuy has also spent more on recruitment, used platforms such as LinkedIn, and created videos that show the company culture rather than just talk about it (see Figure 5.8"How the Government of Hawaii Transformed its Recruiting Process").[54]

How the Government of Hawaii Transformed its Recruiting Process

Governor David Ige and CIO Todd Nacapuy of the state of Hawaii, along with others, discuss how the state was able to overcome some of their recruiting roadblocks and reach a broader pool of talent.

View the video online at: http://www.youtube.com/embed/yHrf6LcXRGw?rel=0

Case Study Discussion Questions

1. Using platforms such as LinkedIn and creating videos to attract talent are just two ways that use technology to attract new hires. What are some others?
2. What are some other creative ways to attract qualified applicants in a market where positions are hard to fill?
3. How can analytics be used to assess the effectiveness of recruitment initiatives?

Resources

1. **Resources from Talent Board.** A nonprofit organization focused on the elevation and promotion of the candidate experience, including webinars, articles, and white papers.

   https://www.thetalentboard.org/resources/

2. **Bringing Your Employer Brand to Life.** A free ebook from Symphony Talent.

   https://bit.ly/2TpMU12

3. **DiversityJobs.** A job board search engine for employers dedicated to diversity hiring, including job postings, job fair listings, and blogs.

   https://diversityjobs.com/c/

4. **LinkedIn Talent Solutions.** Free recruiting resources from LinkedIn including webinars, articles, blogs, case studies, templates, and more.

   https://business.linkedin.com/talent-solutions/recruiting-resources-tips#alltopics/allaudiences/allproducts

Endnotes

1. Case written by Crews, P. (2020). Adapted from Bush, M.C., & Tkaczyk, C. (2019). 100 best companies to work for. *Fortune, 179*(3), 57.

2. Doyle, A. (2019). How to get a job through a staffing agency. *thebalancecareers*. Retrieved from https://www.thebalancecareers.com/getting-a-job-through-a-staffing-agency-2063929

3. World-SIA list ranks largest global staffing firms for 2017. (2017). *SIA*. Retrieved from https://www2.staffingindustry.com/eng/Editorial/Daily-News/World-SIA-list-ranks-largest-global-staffing-firms-for-2017-Adecco-remains-largest-43656

4. 2018 list of largest US staffing firms. (2018). *SIA*. Retrieved from https://www2.staffingindustry.com/site/Editorial/Daily-News/2018-list-of-largest-US-staffing-firms-143-with-revenue-of-over-100-million-46896

5. What is RPO? *Recruitment Process Outsourcing Association*. Retrieved March 15, 2020 from https://www.rpoassociation.org

6. Bureau of Labor Statistics. *Labor area unemployment statistics*. Retrieved March 15, 2020 from https://www.bls.gov/web/laus/laumstrk.htm

7. Furniture. *EPDNC*. Retrieved March 15, 2020 from https://edpnc.com/industries/furniture/

8. Cox, T. (1991). The multicultural organization. *Academy of Management Perspectives, 5*(2), 34-47.

9. Ibid.

10. Cox, T., & Blake, S. (1991). Managing cultural diversity: Implications for organizational competitiveness. *Academy of Management Perspectives, 5*(3), 45-56.

11. Lambert, J. (2020). personal communication.

12. Black population by state 2017. *World Population Review*. Retrieved March 15, 2020 from http://worldpopulationreview.com/states/black-population/

13. The recruiting funnel: What it is & how to use it. (2018). *Symphony Talent*. Retrieved March 15, 2020 from https://resources.symphonytalent.com/blog/the-recruiting-funnel-what-it-is-and-how-to-use-it

14. Salzman, A. (2018). The great labor crunch. *Barron's*. Retrieved from https://www.barrons.com/articles/the-great-labor-crunch-1520655014

15. The recruiting funnel deconstructed. *Jobvite*. Retrieved March 10, 2020 from https://www.jobvite.com/the-recruiting-funnel-deconstructed/

16. Lybrand, S. (2018). What is employer branding and how can it grow your business? *LinkedIn*. Retrieved from https://business.linkedin.com/talent-solutions/blog/employer-brand/2018/employer-branding

17. Ignatova, M. (2014). 56% of professionals rank talent brand as top factor when picking a job. *LinkedIn*. Retrieved from https://business.linkedin.com/talent-solutions/blog/2014/04/employer-brand-stats

18. Maurer, R. (2017). Employer value propositions are brand building blocks. *Society for Human Resource Management*. Retrieved March 10, 2020 from https://www.shrm.org/resourcesandtools/hr-topics/talent-acquisition/pages/employer-value-propositions-are-brand-building-blocks.aspx

19. Ibid.

20. Ibid.

21. The recruiting funnel: What it is & how to use it. (2018). *Symphony Talent*. Retrieved March 10, 2020 from https://resources.symphonytalent.com/blog/the-recruiting-funnel-what-it-is-and-how-to-use-it

22. Forman, C. (2015). The impact of mobile recruiting on click-to-apply rates. *ERE Recruiting Intelligence*. Retrieved March 10, 2020 from https://www.ere.net/the-impact-of-mobile-recruiting-on-click-to-apply-rates/

23. Ibid.

24. The recruiting funnel: What it is & how to use it. (2018). *Symphony Talent*. Retrieved April 4, 2019 from https://resources.symphonytalent.com/blog/the-recruiting-funnel-what-it-is-and-how-to-use-it

25. The 2018 TalentBoard North American candidate experience benchmark research report now available. *TalentBoard*. Retrieved March 10, 2020 from https://www.thetalentboard.org/press-releases/the-2018-talentboard-north-american-candidate-experience-benchmark-research-report-now-available/

26. Ibid.

27. Campillo, S. (2016). Choosing a career path: Internal fair empowers associates to customize careers. *Schneider*. Retrieved March 10, 2020 from https://schneiderjobs.com/blog/culture/choosing-career-path-internal-fair-empowers-custom-careers

28. Bomey, N. (2017). Amazon to add 120,000 temporary workers for holidays. *USA Today*. Retrieved from https://www.usatoday.com/story/money/2017/10/12/amazon-holiday-jobs/756914001/

29. Phillips, J. (2018). 6 steps to make your temporary jobs permanent. *Adecco*. Retrieved from http://blog.adeccousa.com/make-temporary-job-permanent/

30. Ibid.

31. Goldsmith, M. (2009). 4 tips for efficient succession planning. *Harvard Business Review*. Retrieved from https://hbr.org/2009/05/change-succession-planning-to

32. Charan, R., Barton, D., & Carey, D. (2018). *Talent wins: The new playbook for putting people first*. Boston, Mass.: Harvard Business Review Press.

33. How to implement an effective process for a new HR management system. (2005). *HR Focus*, 3.

34. United States Census Bureau. Quick facts: United States. Retrieved March 12, 2020 from https://www.census.gov/quickfacts/fact/table/US/LFE046217

35. Quick take: Women in the workforce—United States. (2018). *Catalyst*. Retrieved from https://www.catalyst.org/research/women-in-the-workforce-united-states/#footnote19_wbhwnwd

36. Nikolaou, I. (2014). Social networking web sites in job search and employee recruitment. *International Journal of Selection and Assessment 22*(2), 179-189.

37. Kappel, M. (2018). For hard-to-fill positions, try passive candidates. *Forbes*. Retrieved from https://www.forbes.com/sites/mikekappel/2018/10/04/for-hard-to-fill-positions-try-finding-passive-candidates/#572eb40c1a82

38. Passive is positive. (2014). *Jobvite*. Retrieved from https://www.jobvite.com/sourcing-and-nurturing/passive-positive/

39. Doyle, A. (2019). Difference between a job board and a job search engine. *thebalancecareers*. Retrieved from https://www.thebalancecareers.com/difference-between-a-job-board-and-a-job-search-engine-2061865

40. Ibid.

41. Morgan, H. (2014). Don't believe these 8 job search myths. *U.S. News & World Report*. Retrieved from https://money.usnews.com/money/blogs/outside-voices-careers/2014/09/17/dont-believe-these-8-job-search-myths

42. iCIMS. (2015). The impact of successful employee referral programs. Retrieved April 1, 2020 from https://www.icims.com/hiring-insights/for-employers/ebook-the-impact-of-successful-employee-referral-programs

43. Zielinski, D. (2013). HR technology referral booster: Social media platforms are expanding employers' recruiting reach. *HR Magazine*, (58)3. Retrieved from https://www.shrm.org/hr-today/news/hr-magazine/pages/0313-social-sourcing.aspx

44. Poe, A. Boost employee loyalty with vacation days. *allBusiness*. Retrieved March 31, 2020 from https://www.allbusiness.com/boost-employee-loyalty-with-extra-vacation-days-16681000-1.html

45. Verlinden, N. 7 brilliant employee referral programs examples. *Digital HR Tech*. Retrieved from https://www.digitalhrtech.com/employee-referral-programs-examples/

46. Recruiting internally and externally. (2018). *Society for Human Resource Management*. Retrieved from https://www.shrm.org/resourcesandtools/tools-and-samples/toolkits/pages/recruitinginternallyandexternally.aspx

47. Adler, L. (2016). New survey reveals 85% of all jobs filled via networking. *LinkedIn*. Retrieved from https://www.linkedin.com/pulse/new-survey-reveals-85-all-jobs-filled-via-networking-lou-adler/

48. Fall 2017 college recruitment: Emerging trends and challenges [White paper]. *NAS Recruitment Innovation*. Retrieved April 1, 2020 from https://www.collegerecruiter.com/blog/2017/07/27/fall-2017-college-recruitment-emerging-trends-and-challenges/

49. Basumallick, C. (2018). 3 ways predictive analytics is changing recruitment practices. *HR Technologist*. Retrieved from https://www.hrtechnologist.com/articles/recruitment-onboarding/3-ways-predictive-analytics-is-changing-recruitment-practices/

50. Bika, N. Recruiting costs FAQ: Budget and cost per hire. *Workable*. Retrieved from https://resources.workable.com/tutorial/faq-recruitment-budget-metrics

51. James, D. (2018). How long does talent acquisition take to fill a position? *FirstPerson*. Retrieved from https://www.furstperson.com/blog/how-long-does-talent-acquisition-take-to-fill-a-position

52. Pavlou, C. New hire turnover rate. *Workable*. Retrieved from https://resources.workable.com/tutorial/new-hire-turnover-rate

53. A how-to-guide for improving your quality of hire. *Ideal*. Retrieved April 1, 2020 from https://ideal.com/quality-of-hire/

54. Case written by Crews, P. (2020). Adapted from Ignatova, M. (2018). 4 ways the government of Hawaii modernized its hiring process to attract tech talent. *LinkedIn Talent Blog*. Retrieved from https://business.linkedin.com/talent-solutions/blog/recruiting-strategy/2018/4-ways-the-government-of-hawaii-modernized-its-hiring-process-to-attract-tech-talent

CHAPTER 6
Talent Selection

Learning Objectives

After reading this chapter, you should be able to do the following:

1. Explain the selection process and the laws and regulations that apply.
2. Describe the methods for conducting the initial screening of applicants.
3. Identify assessment tools that are useful in selection and the importance of reliability and validity.
4. Demonstrate various interviewing techniques and consider the legality of interview questions.

A successful and productive workforce is dependent on hiring the right people. Individuals with the appropriate knowledge, skills, and abilities will achieve competency in their jobs quicker and will outperform lesser-qualified candidates in the long run.

This chapter introduces the selection process, including the roles of HR and the hiring manager, screening methods, selection bias, and various approaches to making a selection decision. Various methods for performing initial applicant screening are introduced, followed by a review of assessment methods and interviewing skills. The chapter concludes with a section on the process of negotiating an offer and completing the hiring process.

6.1 Opening Case: When Hiring Goes Wrong

Source: © Shutterstock, Inc.

Can a company be held liable due to negligence for the murder of one of its employees? According to a recent court case, *Anicich v. Home Depot USA Inc., et al.*, a company can be held responsible for the murder of an employee by a supervisor due to negligent hiring practices. Home Depot argued that the murder of Alisha Bromfield and her unborn daughter was committed off company premises and without the use of company property. Therefore, under Illinois law, the company could not be held liable for negligence. A U.S. District Court dismissed the lawsuit, and it was later brought before the Seventh Circuit Court, which overturned the previous ruling and held that Home Depot allowed the murderer to have supervision over the employee even after they knew he had a history of harassing female subordinates.

Brian Cooper, the perpetrator, had a history of harassing female employees. After being hired by Home Depot, he continued his trend of sexual harassment through the intimidation and verbal abuse of Alisha Bromfield. He threw things at her, controlled and monitored her both during and outside work hours, and required her to come with him on business trips. He was ordered to take anger management classes by the company but never attended them, and the company never followed up to see if he attended. This treatment continued for five years, after which he used his supervisory authority to require Alisha to come on a personal trip with him—an out-of-state family wedding—by threatening to fire her or cut her hours if she refused. After the wedding, he killed and then raped her. Cooper was sentenced to two life terms without the possibility of parole. Alisha's mother, acting as administrator of the estate, then sued Home Depot.

When considering the hiring process, there is a potential liability as it relates to routine background checks for those applying for supervisory roles. The courts will consider the facts on a case-by-case basis, but if a background check indicates someone has a history of violent tendencies or other risk factors, an employer could be held liable for the negligent conduct of that employee if a court determines it was reasonably foreseeable that individual could harm another employee and the employer did nothing to intervene.[1]

 Pregnant 21-year Old Alisha Bromfield Dies at Hands of Boss

"Crime Watch Daily"'s Nerissa Knight reports on the case.

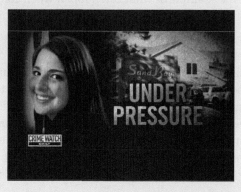

View the video online at: http://www.youtube.com/embed/LL2QK-xd7Iw?rel=0

Case Study Discussion Questions

1. Do you think the company should have been held liable for negligence leading to the murder of Alisha Bromfield? Why or why not?
2. Besides a background check, what other methods can a company use to prevent potential bad hires?
3. Despite conducting due diligence in the selection process, a company can find itself with an employee who is potentially violent. What actions should the company take in those circumstances?

6.2 The Selection Process

Learning Objectives

1. Understand the impact that talent selection has on organizations.
2. Identify the steps in the selection process.
3. Distinguish between hiring for competence, character, and cultural contribution.

Importance of Talent Selection

Talent selection is the process of evaluating candidates for a specific job and selecting individuals for employment, based on valid and reliable job-related criteria. Our focus in the previous chapter was on the importance of finding qualified applicants, and the value that the right person can add to the organization. But what is the result of hiring the wrong person? The opening case about Home Depot gives one extreme example of what can happen when companies do not screen applicants thoroughly. Consider these additional impacts of making a bad hire:

- **Lower morale.** A new hire who does not get along well with others or has a poor work ethic damages morale. If an employee is abrasive or disagreeable, is not open to learning new things, makes derogatory or discriminatory statements, says or does inappropriate things, or otherwise engages in antisocial behaviors, this can quickly create a toxic culture. The best-case scenario when a company has made this type of hire is to take decisive action to remedy the situation quickly. However, if the company ignores the situation, the impact can be much worse because other employees might quit (no one wants to come to work in a toxic environment). Further, negative behaviors can be contagious. If a new employee is allowed to get by with bad behaviors or poor performance, then the company may start to see the same behavior in others.

- **Damaged customer or vendor relations.** A bad hire can offend customers or suppliers either through inappropriate behaviors, or just plain poor performance such as missing deadlines, providing inaccurate information, or not following through on work tasks.

- **Lower productivity.** Bad hires can make mistakes that cause the company to lose money. This could happen by poor product quality or service, or by working too slowly. As opposed to the scenario of lower morale, this can happen even with an otherwise good hire. A new hire might be a pleasant person who gets along well with others but just is not able to perform at the pace required.

- **Overall financial costs to the organization.** Just as a good hire should help the organization to be more profitable, a bad hire directly impacts the bottom line. A CareerBuilder study cites the following financial costs for bad hires: an average of $7,000 to $10,000 for entry- or mid-level positions and more than $40,000 for management positions.[2] The U.S. Department of Labor puts the cost of a bad hire at a minimum of 30% of the employee's first-year earnings.[3]

If the cost of a bad hire is so significant, then why do companies find themselves making bad hires? There are at least four common reasons:

1. **Many HR staff and managers do not fully comprehend the cost of a bad hire.** Some may have the attitude that since we have a ninety-day probationary period, we can move quickly with hiring new employees, and if they don't work out, then we have an "out" with the ninety-day probation.

2. **Sometimes HR is just in a hurry to fill a position.** Even though they do not have a qualified applicant, they go ahead and hire a less-qualified person just to fill the job. HR is often under pressure from managers to fill positions quickly because of the impact of having vacant positions. The pressure can also come from employees who are having to take up the slack for a vacant position until the new hire comes on board.

3. **Poor information.** The people making the hiring decision sometimes have poor information. This could be because they do not have enough information (for example, during the reference checks, the previous employers would only confirm the hire dates, but would not release any information regarding performance, attendance, attitude, or disciplinary actions), or because of misrepresentation (the applicant lied about education, experience, skills, etc.).

4. **Lack of knowledge about effective selection procedures.** Even many experienced HR staff are not properly trained in the use of selection procedures that can be implemented to avoid bad hires. (But after completing this chapter, that won't be you!)

Steps in the Selection Process

Figure 6.1 shows the steps in the selection process. All of the steps do not occur in every instance, and not always in the same order. There will be variations by industry and company, and even differences in various jobs within the same organization. For example, a manufacturing company might not require a physical exam for accounting staff, but they probably would for plant employees who need to be able to lift heavy objects regularly. There are also variations between exactly what is required in each step. Background checks are a good example: a bank would probably not include an applicant's driving record in the background check for teller positions, but they certainly would for couriers who transport documents between branches. Thus, the selection process is variable. The primary consideration is whether a particular selection procedure is job-related and a good predictor of future job performance. Another important point to make here is that very little in the selection process is mandatory. Most selection devices discussed in this chapter are discretionary. Organizations do not have to conduct interviews, reference checks, background checks, or any type of pre-employment testing. It is up to the HR staff, working in collaboration with hiring managers, to determine which are the most appropriate selection procedures for a given job.

FIGURE 6.1 Steps in the Selection Process

Candidate Submits Application/Resume

Preliminary Screening
(May include a quick-look background check for sensitive positions)

Pre-Employment Testing

Background Investigation and Reference Checks

Interviews

Conditional Job Offers

Medical and Drug Screening

Hiring Offer

negligent hiring

A claim made by an injured party against an employer based on the theory that the employer knew or should have known about the employee's background, which, if known, indicates a dangerous or untrustworthy character.

One other aspect to consider is that negligent hiring is a legal concept and can result in a company being sued. **Negligent hiring** is a claim made by an injured party against an employer based on the theory that the employer knew or should have known about the employee's background, which, if known, indicates a dangerous or untrustworthy character.[4] This is based on state law, and roughly half of the states in the U.S. legally recognize that an employer is responsible for, and can be held accountable for checking backgrounds and references of job candidates before placing them in a position where they can be harmful.[5] Background checks, drug testing, and reference checks are some of the ways negligent hiring claims can be avoided.

Assisting in the selection of the best individuals to hire is arguably one of the most impactful things that an HR professional will ever do for their organization.

Hiring for Success

Throughout this chapter, you will learn about a variety of selection tools and methods to help determine who are the best hires and to identify bad hires. But before we look at each method, you may find it helpful to see how all of the tools come together in making a hiring decision. When you hire someone, you are looking for the person who has the highest potential for success. One way to approach this is to look for the Three Cs:

Competence

Does the applicant have the required KSAOs to perform the job? This is typically the easiest part of the selection process. Determining whether someone is competent is a matter of good screening and conducting proper testing. If you refer back to Figure 6.1, you will see that the Three Cs are in the same chronological order as the steps in the selection process. In other words, an efficient approach to selection is to first eliminate candidates who are not competent and do not possess the required KSAOs to do the job well. If they are not competent, then why go any further and waste company time and other resources on further selection processes? Likewise, why waste the applicants' time if they are not qualified?

Character

This is a little more difficult to determine than competence. But it can be done, and very effectively, as you will see in the HR Talk feature on background checks. You want to find out about the applicant's work ethic, values, and moral compass. Background and reference checks are some of the selection tools that help determine an applicant's character. The interviewing process can be helpful in this regard also, particularly the use of behavioral interview questions, which we will discuss later in the chapter.

Screening applicants for character can help reduce instances of employee theft, which can range from simple office supplies, to embezzlement or theft of confidential company data such as customer lists or trade secrets.

Source: © Shutterstock, Inc.

Cultural Contribution

Even if an applicant is competent and of strong character, the individual may still not possess a high potential for success in the position and organization. For example, a company or industry that has an environment of constant change may be difficult for someone who likes routine. A company that requires a more formal dress code (e.g., banking, some accounting firms, or many government agencies) may not be engaging for someone who likes to wear t-shirts and jeans to work. Cultural contribution can also be considered at the job level. Even if a person appears to possess the potential for success in a particular organization, he or she may not be suited for a particular position. For example, someone who does not focus well on the same types of tasks day-in and day-out may not be a good candidate for an analyst position, which typically requires working with data most of the time (think sitting at a desk and working on a computer for long periods of time).

In determining cultural contribution, the goal is to predict an applicant's ability to contribute in a positive way to organizational results. This does not necessarily mean hiring candidates who are similar to existing employees. To the contrary, it can be beneficial to ask the following questions: Does this person offer a dimension that our culture may be missing? In what ways might this person challenge our thinking and processes in a positive manner?

A **realistic job preview** (RJP) is a hiring tool used to communicate the important aspects of a job prior to making an employment offer to a candidate. The purpose is to give the candidate an idea of what the job actually entails on a day-to-day basis, including positive as well as any challenging or negative aspects of the job. One popular method for providing RJPs is by creating a video that includes one or more testimonials from current employees. TimkenSteel has created an excellent RJP video, which can be found here: http://www.selectinternational.com/realistic-job-preview.

For some positions, companies might even have candidates spend a day shadowing a current employee. This is a larger time investment for the candidate and the company, but it may pay dividends if a candidate learns that the job is not what they were looking for and pulls out of the hiring process, thereby saving the cost of having employee turnover down the road.

realistic job preview

A hiring tool used to communicate the important aspects of a job prior to making an employment offer to a candidate.

Key Takeaways

- Talent selection is the process of evaluating candidates for a specific job and selecting individuals for employment based on valid and reliable job-related criteria.
- The steps in the selection process are:
  - Candidate submits application/resume
  - Preliminary screening
  - Pre-employment testing
  - Background investigation and reference checks
  - Interviews
  - Conditional job offers
  - Medical and drug screening
  - Hiring offer
- Negligent hiring is a claim made by an injured party against an employer based on the theory that the employer knew or should have known about an employee's background which, if known, indicates a dangerous or untrustworthy character.
- The Three Cs of selection are competence, character, and cultural contribution.

What Do *You* Think?

1. Have you worked anywhere that the company made what you considered to be a bad hire? What were the negative consequences? Could the company have avoided making a bad hire by doing due diligence?
2. None of the steps in the selection process are mandatory, but what might be the result if a company skips a step?
3. How would you describe the company culture where you could make a positive contribution?
4. Which type of selection bias do you think might tend to engage in as a recruiter or hiring manager?

6.3 Initial Screening Methods

Learning Objectives

1. Identify the criteria used to screen resumes and cover letters.
2. Explain how to create a streamlined application process and what questions to avoid asking for legal reasons.
3. Recognize what types of background checks are available for employers to use to screen employees and the legal restrictions on credit checks.
4. Understand how to conduct reference checks on applicants.

Resumes and Cover Letters

Reviewing resumes and cover letters is normally the first step in the screening process. For many years, this screening method has been used to eliminate unqualified or undesirable candidates from the applicant pool, and it continues to be the most common method for initial screening. Fifty-two percent of talent acquisition leaders say that resume screening from a large candidate pool is the hardest part of recruitment.[6] This is not because it is especially difficult, but because it is time-consuming. On average, twenty-three hours are spent on resume screening just for one hire.[7]

Technology has recently been introduced into the process, as we will discuss in this section, but the criteria for review are still consistent. Criteria should first be based on the job specifications for the position. Recall that job specifications are the qualifications that an individual should possess to adequately perform a job. These are most often expressed in terms of education, experience, KSAOs, and physical capabilities. Figure 6.2 shows an example of the job specifications for a director of human resources position.

FIGURE 6.2 Job Specifications for a Director of Human Resources

Experience

- 5+ years of progressively responsible positions in human resources.
- Experience in managing a multi-state human resources department.
- Experience in recruiting and managing a professional staff.
- Experience in managing global operations is preferred.

Education

- Bachelor's degree in human resources or bachelor's degree in business with a minor in human resources.
- Master's degree in business administration or human resources management preferred.
- HR certification (SHRM or HRCI) is preferred but not required.

Knowledge, Skills, Abilities, and Other Characteristics (KSAOs)

- Knowledge of employment law including EEO, labor relations, compensation, and employee benefits.
- Effective leadership skills.
- Ability to communicate effectively at all levels of an organization.
- Demonstrated ability to attain results with a high functioning team.
- Experiencing recruiting and managing a team of diverse HR professionals.
- Demonstrated commitment to lifelong learning for self, team, and all members of the organization.
- A commitment to continuous improvement.
- Experience in leading change efforts.
- Familiarity with current HR technology including HRIS, ATS, and talent analytics.

Source: thebalancecareers

There is no standard resume format, and therefore screening resumes can be a subjective process. By relying on the job specifications as part of the screening criteria, HR staff can help to ensure a fair and unbiased review. The criteria can then be used to create an applicant score chart by assigning a point value to each of the criteria. When multiple people are involved in the hiring process, then the chart can be completed by each member of the hiring team, and the scores can be averaged. Then a cutoff is established, i.e., applicants below the cutoff are eliminated, and applicants at or above the cutoff move to the next phase of screening.

There are two approaches to the screening process: manual screening (meaning a real person reviews each resume/cover letter) and automated screening through an **applicant tracking system** (ATS). An ATS is a software program that manages the recruitment and hiring process, including job postings and applications. This automated process saves labor time, but the downside is that qualified applicants could potentially be eliminated because the ATS was unable to locate the relevant information in the resume. Some candidates also try to stack their resumes with keywords from the job description to "work the system." There is even an online service through Jobscan to help applicants develop ATS-compliant resumes, thus increasing their odds of getting to the interview stage.[8]

> **applicant tracking system**
>
> A software program that manages the recruitment and hiring process, including job postings and applications.

There are other criteria besides the job specifications that can be used in screening resumes/cover letters, and some of these are better suited to human evaluation rather than automated screening:

- **Layout.** The resume should be organized, easy-to-follow, and job/industry appropriate. For example, someone applying for a graphics design position might be expected to demonstrate their use of visual layout in the design of their resume. For a marketing position, a candidate might be expected to use persuasive and engaging language. If they are not able to market themselves, then why should a company hire them to market their product or service?

- **Cover letter.** This should be personalized to the position. Consider eliminating candidates who appear to be using boilerplate language that has been cut and pasted. Ideal candidates have taken the time to research the organization and the position and tailor their cover letters.

- **Errors.** Typos, grammatical mistakes, and other types of errors can indicate inattention to detail and quality of work.

- **Embellishments and lies.** In HireRight's 2018 Employment Screening Benchmark Report, 84% of respondents (talent acquisition professionals) have found a lie or misrepresentation on a resume or application, often centered around educational claims. Interestingly, this has increased from 66% five years ago.[9] Many applicants do not include an outright fabrication on their resume, but rather misrepresent or embellish the facts. For example, candidates do not normally say they have a bachelor's degree from a school they never attended. But it is not uncommon for an applicant to say they have a degree from a school that they only attended but never graduated from. Figure 6.3 gives some actual examples of resume misrepresentation.

FIGURE 6.3 Liar, Liar, Applicant on Fire

1. A University of Notre Dame head football coach had to resign after admitting to falsely claiming had played football at New Hampshire and had a master's degree from New York University.

2. A newly hired high school principal resigned after the school's journalism students found she'd claimed two degrees from a university that closed years before she supposedly graduated.

3. The head of a city housing authority was terminated after the agency's board realized he couldn't keep his story straight when discussing degrees he allegedly earned.

4. A government appointee withdrew his nomination after allegations of resume padding; the nominee blamed the discrepancies on a tornado that hit his prior employer.

5. A state agency hired a new spokesperson despite knowing he'd fabricated information on his resume – a fact that thrust the agency into an uncomfortable spotlight once the media learned of the situation.

6. A celebrity chef was fired from his own show on the Food Network when it was uncovered that he didn't actually design the wedding cake for Prince Charles and Princess Diana, but that he only attended the school where it was made and contributed by picking fruit for the cake.

7. An MIT dean never received any college degrees despite claiming to have bachelor's and master's degrees.

8. The president of a subsidiary of IBM lied about his academic and military background. He said he was a pilot when he was actually an air traffic controller and a captain when was actually a first lieutenant in the Marines. He also said he got his PhD from Pepperdine, but actually got it from an unaccredited corre-spondence school.

9. The CEO of a major software firm lied about getting an MBA from Stanford, and the company's stock dove when the truth surfaced.

One final aspect of screening resumes/cover letters that you should consider is the potential for biases and discrimination. For example, one research study found that qualified applicants with stereotypically black-sounding names had to send out fifteen resumes to get an interview, whereas candidates with stereotypically white-sounding names only had to send in ten.[10] Workplace diversity literature demonstrates that racial minorities encounter barriers to employment at a greater rate than whites.[11] Despite companies increasingly recognizing diversity as a competitive advantage and revamping their hiring practices to promote equal treatment, discrimination against racial minorities persists.[12]

Applications for Employment

Most companies require job candidates to complete an application (online or paper form). Let's assume that you are a talent acquisition specialist for Target, and all of your applicants are armed with resumes. Why should you have applicants take time to complete the Target application online when the information is probably already included in their resume? There are several reasons:

- Requiring that all candidates complete the organization's application ensures that you gather consistent information from all candidates.

- A standardized form makes it easier for a screener (whether a person or an ATS) to accurately score all candidates and eliminate those who are unqualified.

- When an applicant is asked to sign a statement that all information on the application is true, and acknowledges that they are subject to termination for submitting false information, it discourages applicants from misrepresentation. For those who do lie, it is easier to catch them. For example, on a resume, a screener or even an ATS might not catch missing dates or overlapping dates. Discrepancies in employment are easier to identify when applicants submit the same type of data in a standardized format.

In the previous chapter, we discussed the importance of having a streamlined application process so that qualified applicants do not abandon the process of applying. Here are a few more tips for creating and implementing an application process:

- Use qualifying questions, but keep them to a minimum. Qualifying questions can be used to screen candidates at the beginning of the application process. For example, assume that a retailer is hiring a supervisor, and requires a minimum of five years of retail experience. The qualifying question is: "Do you have a minimum of five years of experience in retail?" This would be a yes/no question, and an online application system could immediately inform the candidate that they are not qualified and they should not proceed further.

- Test your organization's online application from mobile devices, since many candidates now apply using such devices.

- Ask the applicant to sign a statement indicating that all of the information submitted is true and accurate.

- HR managers and hiring managers should try completing an online application themselves to help identify glitches and possible areas of confusion and frustration for applicants.

Are there questions that are illegal to ask on an application? For the most part, there are no illegal questions per se. But employers should not ask applicants any questions that would cause the applicant to share with them information that could potentially be used to discriminate. From the employer's perspective, if an applicant charges that he or she was discriminated based on race, and the application asked them to identify their race, then this information could go in favor of the applicant and be used as evidence that the employer intended to discriminate. There are a few states that have prohibited specific questions, but mostly it is up to employers to decide what questions to ask and not ask. With that in mind, here are general guidelines for questions to avoid:[13]

- **Birth dates.** Making inquiries about an applicant's birth date can give the perception that the employer is using age as a deciding factor. If the federal or state government mandates a minimum age for a specific occupation, then the employer can ask applicants if they are at least the minimum age.

- **Graduation dates.** Making inquiries of an applicant's school graduation dates can reveal an applicant's age. Education questions should be restricted to the name of the school and degree or diploma.

- **Military discharge information.** Military discharge questions could result in obtaining information about an applicant's medical disability, which is protected by the ADA. It is acceptable to ask whether an applicant is a veteran to determine the veteran's preference for reporting purposes, but employers should refrain from asking for specifics about the discharge or asking for copies of discharge papers (DD-214).

- **Previous sick days used in employment.** Both the Family and Medical Leave Act (FMLA) and the ADA prohibit discrimination, including retaliation against applicants who have exercised their rights under those acts.

- **Race, color, religion, national origin.** An employer should never ask for an applicant's race, color, religion, or national origin since these are protected classes (along with age) under Title VII of the Civil Rights Act of 1964. The exception is that the employer can ask questions about color, religion, or national origin if it is a BFOQ (recall from Chapter 3 that race cannot be a BFOQ).

- **Citizenship.** Inquiries about citizenship or country of birth are inappropriate because they can be perceived as discrimination based on national origin. Employers can (and should) ask candidates if they are legally eligible to work in the United States and can require proof as a condition of hire.

- **Name prefixes such Mrs., Miss, Ms., or maiden names.** Many states prohibit discrimination on the basis of marital status, thus any questions that might reveal the marital status could be evidence of discrimination.

- **Salary history.** Some states prohibit an employer from requesting salary history information from candidates. These laws are designed to promote greater pay equality by forcing employees to develop salary offers based on job requirements and pay levels.

- **Criminal history.** Many state and local laws require employers to remove criminal-history questions to protect applicants convicted of a crime from automatic disqualification. A criminal background check can still be conducted later in the process.

Background Checks

background check

A review of a person's employment, criminal, and sometimes financial history.

Employers use a variety of background checks including investigations and reports provided by third-party vendors, such as Imperative, as noted in the HR Talk feature on background screening. A **background check** is a review of a person's employment, criminal, and sometimes financial history. Some form of background investigation is used by 95% of all employers.[14] Employers find background checks helpful for several reasons. First, it confirms that the candidate is really who they say they are. Do they really have the degrees, credentials, and experience that they claim on their resume? Background investigations can also provide insight into their character and behavior. As Mike Coffey states in the HR Talk feature, "The employment application is the least expensive integrity test you will ever give." If an employee lied or embellished on their application or resume, this will usually be uncovered in a thorough background investigation. Second, a background investigation can help protect the employer from negligent hiring lawsuits. Criminal background checks can keep a company from hiring dangerous people who might bring harm to other employees, customers, patients, students, or other constituents. Some states have laws that require criminal background checks on specific occupations, such as educators.

Some people find themselves with poor credit ratings due to circumstances beyond their control. Do you agree with employers using credit reports as part of applicant background checks?

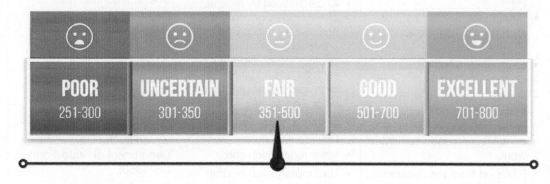

POOR	UNCERTAIN	FAIR	GOOD	EXCELLENT
251-300	301-350	351-500	501-700	701-800

Source: © Shutterstock, Inc.

Background checks may include employment records, criminal history, driving record, credit history, identity verification, medical examinations, and drug testing. The latter two categories should only be done as part of a conditional job offer according to ADA law, which is an offer of employment subject to the candidate meeting certain conditions and passing specific tests. For example, if a candidate is unable to pass a medical exam, fails a drug test, or is unable to produce proof of employment eligibility, then the offer can be rescinded.

Identification verification can be done through verifying employment eligibility. Employers are required to complete an I-9 form on every applicant. Those who fail to do so are subject to substantial fines ranging from $375 to $16,000 per violation.[15] Within three business days of the date employment begins, the employee must present to you an original document or documents that show their identity and employment authorization. For example, if an employee begins employment on Monday, you must review the employee's documentation and complete Section 2 on or before Thursday of that week. However, if you hire an individual for less than three business days, you must complete Section 2 no later than the first day of employment. The employee must be allowed to choose which document(s) they will present from the Form I-9 Lists of Acceptable Documents. You cannot specify which document(s) an employee will present from the list.[16]

TABLE 6.1 Form I-9 Lists A, B, and C

List A	List B	List C
• U.S. passport or passport card. • Permanent resident card or alien registration receipt card (Form I-551). • Employment Authorization Document Card (Form I-766). • Foreign passport with Form I-94 or Form I-94A with arrival departure record, and containing an endorsement to work. • Passport from the Federated States of Micronesia (FSM) or the Republic of the Marshall Islands (RMI) with Form I-94A. • Foreign passport containing a Form I-551 stamp or Form I-551 printed rotations.	• Driver's license. • ID card issued by federal, state, or local government agencies or entities, provided it contains a photograph or information such as name, date of birth, gender, height, eye color, and address. • School ID card with photograph. • Voter registration card. • U.S. military card or draft record. • Military dependent's ID card. • U.S. Coast Guard Merchant Mariner Document (MMD) card. • Native American tribal document. • Driver's license issued by a Canadian government authority.	• U.S. Social Security card that does not contain work restrictions. • Consular Report of Birth Abroad (Form FS-240). • Certification of Birth Abroad issued by the U.S. Department of State (Form FS-545). • Certification of Report of Birth issued by the U.S. Department of State (Form DS-1350). • Original or certified copy of a birth certificate issued by a state, county, municipal authority, or outlying territory of the United States bearing an official seal. • Native American tribal document. • U.S. citizen ID card (Form I-197). • Identification Card for Use of Resident Citizen in the United States (Form I-179). • Employment authorization document issued by the Department of Homeland Security (DHS).

Source: U.S. Citizenship and Immigration Services

Physically examine each original document the employee presents to determine if the document reasonably appears to be genuine and relates to the person presenting it. Make sure the person who examines the documents is the same person who attests and signs Section 2. The employee must be physically present with the document examiner. Examine one selection from List A or a combination of one selection from List B and one selection from List C. If an employee presents a List A document, do not ask or require the employee to present List B or List C documents. If an employee presents List B and List C documents, do not ask or require the employee to present a List A document.[17] Table 6.1 displays the types of acceptable documents for each list. Figure 6.4 and Figure 6.5 show an I-9 form.

FIGURE 6.4 I-9 Form Section 1 (Employee Portion)

Employment Eligibility Verification
Department of Homeland Security
U.S. Citizenship and Immigration Services

USCIS
Form I-9
OMB No. 1615-0047
Expires 10/31/2022

▶START HERE: Read instructions carefully before completing this form. The instructions must be available, either in paper or electronically, during completion of this form. Employers are liable for errors in the completion of this form.

ANTI-DISCRIMINATION NOTICE: It is illegal to discriminate against work-authorized individuals. Employers **CANNOT** specify which document(s) an employee may present to establish employment authorization and identity. The refusal to hire or continue to employ an individual because the documentation presented has a future expiration date may also constitute illegal discrimination.

Section 1. Employee Information and Attestation *(Employees must complete and sign Section 1 of Form I-9 no later than the **first day of employment**, but not before accepting a job offer.)*

Last Name *(Family Name)*	First Name *(Given Name)*	Middle Initial	Other Last Names Used *(if any)*

Address *(Street Number and Name)*	Apt. Number	City or Town	State	ZIP Code

Date of Birth *(mm/dd/yyyy)*	U.S. Social Security Number	Employee's E-mail Address	Employee's Telephone Number
	☐☐☐ - ☐☐ - ☐☐☐☐		

I am aware that federal law provides for imprisonment and/or fines for false statements or use of false documents in connection with the completion of this form.

I attest, under penalty of perjury, that I am (check one of the following boxes):

☐ 1. A citizen of the United States

☐ 2. A noncitizen national of the United States *(See instructions)*

☐ 3. A lawful permanent resident   (Alien Registration Number/USCIS Number): _____

☐ 4. An alien authorized to work   until (expiration date, if applicable, mm/dd/yyyy): _____
      Some aliens may write "N/A" in the expiration date field. *(See instructions)*

Aliens authorized to work must provide only one of the following document numbers to complete Form I-9:
An Alien Registration Number/USCIS Number OR Form I-94 Admission Number OR Foreign Passport Number.

1. Alien Registration Number/USCIS Number: _____
      OR
2. Form I-94 Admission Number: _____
      OR
3. Foreign Passport Number: _____
      Country of Issuance: _____

QR Code - Section 1
Do Not Write In This Space

Signature of Employee	Today's Date *(mm/dd/yyyy)*

Preparer and/or Translator Certification (check one):
☐ I did not use a preparer or translator.   ☐ A preparer(s) and/or translator(s) assisted the employee in completing Section 1.
(Fields below must be completed and signed when preparers and/or translators assist an employee in completing Section 1.)

I attest, under penalty of perjury, that I have assisted in the completion of Section 1 of this form and that to the best of my knowledge the information is true and correct.

Signature of Preparer or Translator	Today's Date *(mm/dd/yyyy)*

Last Name *(Family Name)*	First Name *(Given Name)*

Address *(Street Number and Name)*	City or Town	State	ZIP Code

🛑 *Employer Completes Next Page* 🛑

Form I-9 10/21/2019

Page 1 of 3

Source: https://www.uscis.gov/i-9

FIGURE 6.5 I-9 Form Section 2 (Employer Portion)

Employment Eligibility Verification
Department of Homeland Security
U.S. Citizenship and Immigration Services

USCIS
Form I-9
OMB No. 1615-0047
Expires 10/31/2022

Section 2. Employer or Authorized Representative Review and Verification

(Employers or their authorized representative must complete and sign Section 2 within 3 business days of the employee's first day of employment. You must physically examine one document from List A OR a combination of one document from List B and one document from List C as listed on the "Lists of Acceptable Documents.")

Employee Info from Section 1	Last Name *(Family Name)*	First Name *(Given Name)*	M.I.	Citizenship/Immigration Status

List A — Identity and Employment Authorization	OR	List B — Identity	AND	List C — Employment Authorization
Document Title		Document Title		Document Title
Issuing Authority		Issuing Authority		Issuing Authority
Document Number		Document Number		Document Number
Expiration Date *(if any) (mm/dd/yyyy)*		Expiration Date *(if any) (mm/dd/yyyy)*		Expiration Date *(if any) (mm/dd/yyyy)*
Document Title		Additional Information		QR Code - Sections 2 & 3 — Do Not Write In This Space
Issuing Authority				
Document Number				
Expiration Date *(if any) (mm/dd/yyyy)*				
Document Title				
Issuing Authority				
Document Number				
Expiration Date *(if any) (mm/dd/yyyy)*				

Certification: I attest, under penalty of perjury, that (1) I have examined the document(s) presented by the above-named employee, (2) the above-listed document(s) appear to be genuine and to relate to the employee named, and (3) to the best of my knowledge the employee is authorized to work in the United States.

The employee's first day of employment *(mm/dd/yyyy)*: _____ *(See instructions for exemptions)*

Signature of Employer or Authorized Representative	Today's Date *(mm/dd/yyyy)*	Title of Employer or Authorized Representative
Last Name of Employer or Authorized Representative	First Name of Employer or Authorized Representative	Employer's Business or Organization Name
Employer's Business or Organization Address *(Street Number and Name)*	City or Town	State / ZIP Code

Section 3. Reverification and Rehires *(To be completed and signed by employer or authorized representative.)*

A. New Name *(if applicable)*			B. Date of Rehire *(if applicable)*
Last Name *(Family Name)*	First Name *(Given Name)*	Middle Initial	Date *(mm/dd/yyyy)*

C. If the employee's previous grant of employment authorization has expired, provide the information for the document or receipt that establishes continuing employment authorization in the space provided below.

Document Title	Document Number	Expiration Date *(if any) (mm/dd/yyyy)*

I attest, under penalty of perjury, that to the best of my knowledge, this employee is authorized to work in the United States, and if the employee presented document(s), the document(s) I have examined appear to be genuine and to relate to the individual.

Signature of Employer or Authorized Representative	Today's Date *(mm/dd/yyyy)*	Name of Employer or Authorized Representative

Form I-9 10/21/2019   Page 2 of 3

Form I-9 verification can be submitted to the federal government using E-Verify. It is a web-based system that allows enrolled employers to confirm eligibility of their employees to work in the United States.[18] E-Verify employers verify the identity and employment eligibility of newly hired employees by matching information provided by employees on the Form I-9 against records available to the Social Security Administration (SSA) and the Department of Homeland Security (DHS). E-Verify is a voluntary program, however employers with federal contracts or subcontracts may be required to participate. Employers may also be required to participate if their states have legislation mandating the use of E-Verify, such as a condition of business licensing.

Credit checks are used by 47% of employers for some or all job applicants.[19] A credit check can provide insights into a candidate's ability to make good decisions, to manage budgets, and to meet obligations. However, this area of background checking has several federal and state legal requirements.

Under the Fair Credit Reporting Act (FCRA), employers are allowed to use credit checks (along with other types of background checks which the act collectively refers to as consumer reports) for employment decisions including hiring, promotion, reassignment, and retention. Under the FCRA, employers must take the following steps before obtaining a consumer report:

- Tell the applicant or employee that you might use information in their consumer report for decisions related to their employment. This notice must be in writing and a stand-alone format. The notice cannot be in an employment application.

- Get written permission from the applicant or employee. This can be part of the document you use to notify the person that you will get a consumer report.

- Certify compliance with the company from which you are getting the applicant's or employee's information. You must certify that you:

  - Notified the applicant or employee and got their permission to get a consumer report;

  - Complied with all of the FCRA requirements; and

  - Will not discriminate against the applicant or employee or otherwise misuse the information, as provided by any applicable federal or state equal opportunity laws or regulations.[20]

There are also FCRA requirements that employers must comply with before and after taking adverse action, as summarized in Table 6.2.

TABLE 6.2 FCRA Requirements

FCRA Employer Requirements Before and After Taking Adverse Action	
Before Taking Adverse Action	**After Taking Adverse Action**
Must give the applicant or employee the following: • A notice that includes a copy of the consumer report the employer relied upon to make the decision. • Must give the applicant or employee a copy of *A Summary of Your Rights Under the Fair Credit Reporting Act*.	Must give the applicant a notice that includes: • Name, address, and phone number of the consumer reporting company that provided the report. • A statement that the company that supplied the report did not make the decision to take the unfavorable action and can't give specific reasons for it; and • A notice of the person's right to dispute the accuracy or completeness of any information the consumer reporting company furnished, and to get an additional free report from the company if the person asks for it within sixty days.

After the employer is finished using a consumer report, the FCRA requires that it be securely disposed of by either burning or shredding of paper documents, or disposing of electronic information so that it cannot be read or reconstructed.

After the 2008 financial crisis and the subsequent recession, several states passed laws restricting an employer from considering credit history when making employment decisions. The rationale for these laws is that it is unfair to punish someone for past financial difficulties, and if someone is denied employment due to debt problems, it can make it even harder for them to recover financially. The state laws are not usually complete prohibitions. For example, they often allow employers to conduct credit checks on sensitive positions that might have access to cash or are responsible for financial recordkeeping. The lesson here is that credit checks can be used, but be sure to become familiar with any state laws that apply and to comply with the FCRA.

 Employment Background Checks

Dustin Paschal of Simon/Paschal PLLC discusses important things to know if you are an employer and you perform background checks on applicants and employees.

View the video online at: http://www.youtube.com/embed/wF8jwnw7Jr8?rel=0

HR Talk: Mike Coffey, SPHR

President, Imperative

Bulletproof Background Screening

The biggest mistake that most employers make is focusing exclusively on competency instead of behaviors. You can train a competent person to do just about anything, but it is difficult to change behavior. Some need more direction than others, some are not compliant with instructions, policies, or procedures, and some have criminal tendencies. These bad behaviors can result in poor performance and damaged customer relationships.

How should employers use background screening to avoid bad hires? First, the application is the least expensive integrity test you will ever give. Many people lie on their applications, and what they lie about most often is their educational background. So take the time to verify educational credentials. Reference checks and criminal background checks also tell you much about a person's past behavior, and the best predictor of future behavior is past behavior. Ask specific questions during the reference check. For example, if you are hiring a driver, then you might ask the following: Did they ever act in a threatening manner? Did they have any accidents? Did they ever fail a drug test? One other tool that we use, and one that is often overlooked, is civil litigation searches. For example, if a person has ever had a restraining order placed on them, then the employer should be aware of that, and learn more about the situation. I advise my clients to consider the totality of evidence on any new hire. One negative reference check, or restraining order, for example, should not necessarily preclude a person being hired. But look at their background screen in total to make a reasonable decision whether this is a candidate that you should hire.

HR in the Real World: The Case of the Missing Air Jordans

One of our customers was Foot Locker, and we handled warehousing and distribution for them. Shoes were typically packed eight pairs to a case. Air Jordans by Nike were one of their most popular shoes, selling from $90 to $300. Applying an average price of $150, a case of Air Jordans is worth $1,200. After a rash of missing shoes, we decided to install cameras inside each overhead door of the warehouse. We already had cameras in the parking lot that filmed outside of the doors, but not inside the warehouse. It did not take long to discover what was happening. A dock employee was loading cases of shoes onto a truck and would nonchalantly kick a case over the dock when he thought no one was watching. The case would then fall into a dumpster in the parking lot beside the door. The employee would then come back after hours and retrieve the stolen shoes from the dumpster and sell them on the street. Instead of confronting the employee directly, we hired an off-duty police officer to surveil the parking lot. The employee was arrested when he retrieved the next box of stolen shoes. This is the kind of bad hire that could have been avoided by conducting criminal background checks. We previously had a practice of conducting these checks for drivers but not dock employees, but this practice was subsequently expanded to include all employees.

Reference Checks

Reference checks are a specific type of background check in which the prospective employer contacts individuals whom the candidate has worked for or with to ask questions about the candidate's work history. A reference check allows you to verify the facts given by the candidate on their resume. But it also allows the employer to obtain more in-depth information and to learn about how the candidate performs and works with others, and their overall work behaviors and habits. Reference checks include contacting references that the candidate has given. Of course, the candidate is only going to put down people who will give them a positive reference (although sometimes candidates can be surprised when they put down a reference who they think will say positive things about them, only to be caught off guard when the referrer says negative things about them). So, as a side-note: Before you add people to your list of references, be sure to contact them and ask their permission, and politely ask if they would be willing to give you a positive reference. But in addition to the references that the candidate gives, employers should at least contact the last employer and preferably talk to the employee's direct supervisor.

One problem that employers encounter in checking references is that some previous employers are hesitant to give any information beyond just confirming dates of employment and job title, for fear of being sued for defamation of character. To protect employers from these types of lawsuits, some states give employers immunity when giving reference information.[21] This means that the former employee cannot sue the employer for giving out the information as long as the employer acted in good faith. State laws also vary regarding other aspects of employment references. For example, some states require the written consent of the applicant prior to contacting references. For a multistate employer, it is a good practice to ask for written consent as a standard company policy, even if all states do not require it.

References can be conducted by email or by asking for a reference form to be completed. These can be useful in regard to providing documentation that HR can keep on file for future reference if needed. But a best practice is to also conduct a telephone reference, thus follow-up questions can be asked if needed. Table 6.3 gives some sample reference check questions.[22]

reference checks

A specific type of background check, in which the prospective employer contacts individuals whom the candidate has worked for or with to ask questions about the candidate's work history.

TABLE 6.3 Sample Questions for Reference Checks

Sample Questions for Reference Checks
1. Please verify the individual's position, dates of employment, and compensation.
2. Why did the individual leave the position?
3. Please describe the individual's job responsibilities.
4. How long have you known the individual and in what capacity?
5. Do you think this individual will make a positive cultural contribution to our company?
6. Was this individual an effective team member?
7. What are the strengths and weaknesses of this individual?
8. Would you rehire this individual? Why or why not?
9. Who else might I speak with about this individual that might provide helpful information?
10. Is there any other useful information you can provide?

Key Takeaways

- Reviewing resumes and cover letters is normally the first step in the screening process. For many years, this step method has been used to eliminate unqualified or undesirable candidates from the applicant pool, and it continues to be the most common method for initial screening.

- By relying on the job specifications as part of the screening criteria, HR staff can help to ensure a fair and unbiased review. The criteria can then be used to create an applicant score chart, by assigning a point value to each of the criteria.

- There are two approaches to the screening process: manual screening (meaning a real person reviews each resume/cover letter), and automated screening through an ATS.

- Requiring that all candidates complete the organization's application ensures that you gather consistent information from all candidates.

- A standardized form makes it easier for a screener (whether a person or an ATS) to accurately score all candidates, and eliminate those who are unqualified.

- A background check is a review of a person's employment, criminal, and sometimes financial history. Some form of background investigation is used by 95% of all employers.

- Background checks may include employment records, criminal history, driving record, credit history, identity verification, medical examinations, and drug testing. The latter two categories should only be done as part of a conditional job offer according to ADA law, which is an offer of employment subject to the candidate meeting certain conditions and passing specific tests.

- Under the Fair Credit Reporting Act (FCRA), employers are allowed to use credit checks (along with other types of background checks which the act collectively refers to as consumer reports) for employment decisions including hiring, promotion, reassignment, and retention, but there are specific guidelines the employer must follow.

- Reference checks are a specific type of background check in which the prospective employer contacts individuals whom the candidate has worked for or with to ask questions about the candidate's work history.

What Do *You* Think?

1. Is there anything wrong with stacking a resume with keywords from a job posting to make it ATS compliant?

2. What should you do if you are completing an application for employment and it is asking for information that you know is discriminatory, such as race or age?

3. How do you feel about the use of credit checks for employment screening?

4. If you are making a reference check on an applicant, and the reference does not want to provide any information other than confirm employment dates, how might you respond?

6.4 Pre-Employment Testing

Learning Objectives

1. Define reliability and explain how it is measured.
2. Define validity and understand the three major types: content, criterion-related, and construct.
3. Identify the most common types of pre-employment tests.

Reliability and Validity

A **pre-employment test** is an objective and standardized device designed to measure a person's knowledge, skills, abilities, personality, or other characteristics. They usually result in a score or category that can be compared to data about individuals who have been successful in the position for which the person is applying. This refers to the job-relatedness of an employment test and it is important that this is determined. Failing to adhere to this basic job-relatedness principle can result in the employer losing legal challenges regarding discrimination.

According to the Uniform Guidelines on Employee Selection Procedures established by the EEOC (see Chapter 3), any employment requirement set by an employer is considered to be a test.[23] The Uniform Guidelines apply to all selection procedures used to make employment decisions, including written tests, interviews, review of experience or education from application forms, resumes, work samples, physical requirements, and evaluations of performance.[24] As we explore the concepts of reliability and validity, keep in mind that they apply not only to the pre-employment tests described later in this section but also to all selection procedures.

Let's first define what we mean by reliability and validity. **Reliability** is the degree to which a test is consistent and stable in measuring what it is intended to measure.

Reliability is usually expressed by the **reliability coefficient**, which is a quantified measure of consistency, and is denoted by the letter "r." Reliability coefficients range from 0.00 (no reliability) to 1.00 (perfect reliability).[25] You should not expect to find a pre-employment test with perfect reliability, but an acceptable range for most assessments is .80 or higher.[26] Table 6.4 shows some general guidelines for interpreting reliability coefficients.[27]

TABLE 6.4 Interpreting Test Reliability

Reliability Coefficient Range	Interpretation
.90 and up	Excellent
.80–.89	Good
.70–.79	Adequate
Below .70	Poor

pre-employment test

An objective and standardized device designed to measure a person's knowledge, skills, abilities, personality, or other characteristics.

reliability

The degree to which a test is consistent and stable in measuring what it is intended to measure.

reliability coefficient

A quantified measure of consistency, denoted by the letter "r," with a range from 0.00 (no reliability) to 1.00 (perfect reliability).

test-retest reliability

A measure of the consistency of a test given over time.

inter-rater reliability

Indicates how consistent test scores are likely to be if the test is scored by two or more raters.

validity

The degree to which a test measures what it claims to measure.

content validity

Occurs when the content of a test represents important job-related behaviors.

criterion-related validity

Refers to the test's ability to predict how well a person will perform on the job.

concurrent validity

Occurs when an employer tests employees and compares scores with job performance ratings so that the test scores and performance are measured at the same time.

predictive validity

Occurs when an employer compares the applicant's test results with their subsequent job performance.

construct validity

Refers to the degree to which a selection device measures a particular characteristic (or construct) that is important to successful performance of the job.

If you take a test on your Excel skills today, and then take the same test next week, the test should yield consistent scores if it is reliable (assuming that you have not studied or practiced Excel in the interim). This is known as **test-retest reliability**. On some tests, two or more individuals evaluate test responses or work samples and then score them. **Inter-rater reliability** indicates how consistent test scores are likely to be if the test is scored by two or more raters. A high inter-rater reliability coefficient indicates that the judgment process is stable and the resulting scores are reliable.[28] There are additional advanced measures of reliability, but these are beyond the scope of our discussion here.

Validity is the degree to which a test measures what it claims to measure. For pre-employment tests, this means that a test is a valid predictor of future job performance. You might find a simple word association to help remember these concepts: associate the word "consistency" with reliability, and the word "predictor" with validity. By establishing reliability, you know that a test or other selection tool will give consistent results each time it is administered. By establishing validity, you are establishing that the selection tool is job-related, and not discriminatory. Note that a selection tool can cause an adverse impact, and be legally defensible, as long as it has been established to be valid (in other words, job-related).

The Uniform Guidelines on Employee Selection Procedures establish three main methods for determining test validity:

1. **Content validity.** This means the content of a test represents important job-related behaviors. Some examples are a mathematics test, typing test, or computer skills test.

2. **Criterion-related validity.** This refers to the test's ability to predict how well a person will perform on the job. It requires demonstrating a correlation between test performance and on-the-job performance. There are two different approaches to measuring criterion-related validity. In an assessment of **concurrent validity**, an employer tests employees and compares scores with job performance ratings so that the test scores and performance are measured at the same time.[29] In an assessment of **predictive validity**, the employer compares the applicant's test results with their subsequent job performance.[30]

3. **Construct validity.** This refers to the degree to which a selection device measures a particular characteristic (or construct) that is important to successful performance of the job. Examples are intelligence tests, personality tests, mechanical aptitude tests, and commercial driving road tests.

Establishing reliability and validity is time-consuming and requires a degree of knowledge about statistical methods. Most employers do not have the resources and skills to adequately determine reliability and validity on their own in-house created tests. It makes good business sense for companies to only use tests from reputable vendors. When selecting a test, inquire with the test vendor about their reliability and validity studies and ask to see research reports that establish job-relatedness. Conducting due diligence and keeping these records on file will help with a legal defense if a test is ever challenged in court as being discriminatory.

Types of Pre-Employment Tests

Personality Tests

Personality tests measure psychological characteristics such as personality, emotional adjustment, and interpersonal relationship skills. Some of the more common ones are the Big Five personality test, the Myers-Briggs Type Indicator® (MBTI®), and Birkman. The Big Five is the most widely used and has been the focus of many empirical research studies. The Big Five personality factors are:

1. **Extroversion.** The degree to which someone is talkative, sociable, active, aggressive, and excitable.

2. **Agreeableness.** The degree to which someone is trusting, amiable, generous, tolerant, honest, cooperative, and flexible.

3. **Conscientiousness.** The degree to which someone is dependable and organized and perseveres in tasks.

4. **Neuroticism.** The degree to which someone is secure, calm, independent, and autonomous.

5. **Openness to experience.** The degree to which someone is intellectual, philosophical, insightful, creative, artistic, and curious.[31]

An example of how a personality test might be job-related is that an extroverted personality might be more successful in a sales position, while a conscientious person might be more successful in an accounting or finance position.

A potential concern with personality tests is the reliability and validity of self-reported questionnaires. Do you think it is possible to "game" a personality test and make the results come out in a way that makes an applicant look more favorable to an employer for a specific position?

> **personality tests**
>
> Measurements of psychological characteristics such as personality, emotional adjustment, and interpersonal relationship skills.

Source: © Shutterstock, Inc.

Cognitive Ability Tests

cognitive ability tests

Measurements of a candidate's general mental capacity or an aptitude that is specific to a particular job.

Cognitive ability tests measure a candidate's general mental capacity or an aptitude that is specific to a particular job. Some common types are IQ tests, verbal and math skills, spatial perception, or inductive and deductive reasoning. A word of caution is warranted here, as cognitive tests are vulnerable to racial and ethnic differences and may pose a risk of disparate impact. *Griggs v. Duke Power Company* is a landmark case concerning the illegality of using intelligence tests in employment decisions when they are not job-related (see the case study at the end of the chapter).

Polygraph Tests

polygraph tests

Involve the use of a polygraph machine that attempts to detect dishonesty by measuring and recording several physiological indicators such as blood pressure, pulse, respiration, and skin conductivity while a person is asked and answers a series of questions.

Polygraph tests, also called lie detector tests, involve the use of a polygraph machine that attempts to detect dishonesty by measuring and recording several physiological indicators such as blood pressure, pulse, respiration, and skin conductivity while a person is asked and answers a series of questions. The Employee Polygraph Protection Act (EPPA) prohibits most employers from using polygraph tests, either for pre-employment screening or during employment.[32] The only employers that can administer polygraphs under the EPPA are security service firms (armored car, alarm, and guard) and pharmaceutical manufacturers, distributors, and dispensers.

Honesty and Integrity Tests

honesty and integrity tests

Measurements of an individual's propensity toward undesirable behaviors such as stealing, lying, or misrepresentation.

Honesty and integrity tests measure an individual's propensity toward undesirable behaviors such as stealing, lying, or misrepresentation. Integrity testing began as an attempt to detect dishonesty in applicants without using polygraph tests.[33] Critics have said these tools are an invasion of privacy and that people try to manipulate the tests (liars lie on the test, trying to alter the outcome). However, they are generally found to be accurate predictors of counterproductive work behaviors.[34]

Physical Ability Tests

physical ability tests

Measures of specific physical tasks that a job involves and usually involve strength, endurance, or muscular coordination.

Physical ability tests measure specific physical tasks that a job involves and usually involve strength, endurance, or muscular coordination. They are common for firefighters, law enforcement officers, military, and medical personnel. For example, a paramedic would need to be able to lift a patient onto a stretcher, and thus a physical test simulating this activity would be a valid predictor of future job performance. However, height and weight requirements should be avoided unless based on actual job requirements. Height and weight requirements tend to disproportionately limit the employment opportunities of some protected groups, and unless the employer can demonstrate how the need is related to the job, they may be viewed as illegal under federal law.[35]

Key Takeaways

- A pre-employment test is an objective and standardized device designed to measure a persons' knowledge, skills, abilities, personality, or other characteristics. They usually result in a score or category that can be compared to data about individuals who have been successful in the position for which the person is applying.
- Reliability is the degree to which a test is consistent and stable in measuring what it is intended to measure. Reliability is usually expressed by the reliability coefficient, which is the

quantified measure of consistency, and is denoted by the letter "r." Reliability coefficients range from 0.00 (no reliability) to 1.00 (perfect reliability).

- If you take a test on your Excel skills today, and then take the same test next week, then the test should yield consistent scores if it is reliable (assuming that you have not studied or practiced Excel in the interim). This is known as test-retest reliability.
- Inter-rater reliability indicates how consistent test scores are likely to be if the test is scored by two or more raters.
- Content validity means the content of a test represents important job-related behaviors.
- Criterion-related validity refers to the test's ability to predict how well a person will perform on the job. In an assessment of concurrent validity, an employer tests employees and compares scores with job performance ratings so that the test scores and performance are measured at the same time. In an assessment of predictive validity, the employer compares the applicant's test results with their subsequent job performance.
- Construct validity refers to the degree to which a selection device measures a particular characteristic (or construct) that is important to successful performance of the job.
- Common pre-employment tests include personality, cognitive ability, honesty, and physical ability. Polygraph tests are not legal for pre-employment except for certain job applicants of security service firms (armored car, alarm, and guard) and pharmaceutical manufacturers, distributors, and dispensers.

What Do *You* Think?

1. What pre-employment tests have you taken in the past? Do you think they were valid predictors of future job performance?
2. If you were trying to establish criterion-related validity, what factors might influence your decision on whether to use concurrent or predictive validity?
3. How do you feel about the use of personality testing for screening applicants?

6.5 Interviewing

Learning Objectives

1. Identify the major types of interviewing methods.
2. Recognize how interview questions can explore an applicant's competence, character, and cultural contribution.
3. Explain how to prepare for and conduct an interview.
4. Distinguish between legal and illegal interview questions.
5. Explain the most common types of selection bias.

Types of Interviews

There are several types of interview methods, as described in Table 6.5.

TABLE 6.5 Interviewing Methods

Interviewing Methods	
Unstructured	Uses broad, general questions, for more freedom for the applicant to talk. Usually, this type of interview is lower in reliability and validity and does not yield comparative data for the applicants, since each interview is structured differently.
Structured	Requires strict adherence to a standardized set of questions, high in reliability and validity, and provides comparable data for all applicants.
Situational or Behavioral	The applicant is asked to give a response to a specific situation or scenario.
Panel Interview	A committee of individuals interviews the applicants.
Simulations	It allows the applicant to actually perform some of the job requirements in a simulated work setting.

Interviewing Questions and Techniques

Sometimes a quirky question is asked during an interview, such as: If you could be a superhero, what would your superpowers be? What do you think is the purpose of these types of questions?

Source: © Shutterstock, Inc.

Asking appropriate questions of applicants is the best method for gathering information about the "Three Cs" described earlier in the chapter. Be specific in your questions. Ask the applicant to explain, quantify, specify, and describe. In other words, the applicant should do more talking than the interviewer. Ask questions that require the applicant to elaborate. Here are a few examples:

To explore character issues: Ask the applicant to tell you the three characteristics that describe them the most. After the applicant identifies their three characteristics, ask them to pick the top two. Observe how the applicant handles the situation. Is there frustration? Irritation? Or is the applicant engaged in and energized by this situational dilemma? Then ask the applicant to pick the one characteristic that describes them the most. Then ask the applicant to tell of a situation or event where the characteristic was challenged to the point of being compromised. What did they learn from the situation? If the person draws a blank, the characteristic may not be a primary one, or the person has very little self-knowledge.

Ask the applicant what other colleagues say about them. Typically, positive statements are given. Then ask, if those same people were here, what would they say your deficit areas are?

To explore cultural contribution: Solicit information about what this person considers an ideal work situation. Is structure important or not? Does the applicant prefer to work alone or with others? Does he or she prefer to be given a task and left to complete it, or are check-in points desired? How does the person handle conflict? What is their communication style? The responses will give you a feel for the applicant's potential to contribute in your organization. Behavioral interviews are an excellent method to explore a candidate's potential cultural contribution (see Table 6.6 for sample questions).

TABLE 6.6 Sample Behavioral Interview Questions

Sample Behavioral Interview Questions	
Adaptability	Tell me about a time when you had to adjust to a colleague's working style in order to complete a project or achieve your objectives.
Analytical Skills/ Problem Solving	Tell me about a situation where you had to solve a difficult problem. What did you do? What was your thought process? What was the outcome? What do you wish you had done differently?

Sample Behavioral Interview Questions	
Communication	What is your typical way of dealing with conflict? Give me an example.
Presentation Skills	Tell me about a time when you had to use your presentation skills to influence someone's opinion.
Creativity	Tell me about a problem that you've solved in a unique or unusual way. What was the outcome? Were you happy or satisfied with it?
Decision-Making	Tell me about a difficult decision you've made in the last year. Tell me about a time when you had to make a decision without all the information you needed. How did you handle it? Why? Were you happy with the outcome?
Goal Setting	Give me an example of a time when you set a goal and were able to meet or achieve it.
Leadership	Give me an example of a time when you motivated others. Tell me about a time when you delegated a project effectively.
Planning and Organization/Time Management	How do you determine priorities in scheduling your time? Give examples. Tell me about a time when you had too many things to do and you were required to prioritize your tasks. How do you manage projects to ensure completion on time and on budget? Give me some examples.
Teamwork	Tell me about a time you were able to successfully deal with another person even when that individual may not have personally liked you (or vice versa). Tell me about a recent situation in which you had to deal with a very upset customer or co-worker. Describe a situation where you have had to work as part of a team to achieve a result. What was your role in this? Describe a situation where others you were working with on a project disagreed with your ideas. What did you do?

Preparing for and Conducting the Interview

The secret to conducting a successful interview is to prepare. Before conducting an interview, the following steps will help you approach it with confidence:

- **Review the job description and job specifications.** Most HR staff and line managers conduct interviews for a variety of positions, and it can become confusing. You should be able to discuss the position during the interview without having to read from the job description during the interview.

- **Decide where the interview will occur.** Will it be in your office, a conference room, or a common area? Will it involve a tour? For candidates who will be doing testing during the visit, or interviewing with more than one person, then prepare a schedule. Many companies are using video interviews to save on travel expenses. Video interviews can also be used as part of a business continuity plan during a pandemic such as COVID-19.

- **Send the candidate the interview schedule, directions, and clarify the date and time.** For candidates coming from other states or doing video interviews, be sure to note the time zone.

- **Develop a list of questions that you will ask each candidate.** Make sure that each question is job-related to avoid asking for potentially discriminatory information. It is acceptable to ask follow-up questions as long they are job-related.

Then, on the day of the interview, these guidelines may help the interview go more smoothly:

- **Greet the candidate, and ask if they would like water, coffee, etc., if the interview is in person.** Put the candidate at ease and be warm and personable. Remember how stressful an interview can be when you are in the hot seat!

- **Exchange pleasantries, but don't draw it out too long.** Ask them how their day is going, or how the trip to the interview location went. Then move on to the interview.

- **Prepare to give the candidate a realistic and clear understanding of the job.** What are the expectations? What is the work environment like? Tell the candidate what people in the job now like and don't like about it. Be upfront to avoid any surprises later.
- **Ask your questions, but try not to be robotic.** You want it to be conversational, and encourage the candidate to elaborate by asking open-ended questions.
- **Give the candidate an opportunity to ask any questions that he or she may have.**
- **Conclude the interview by thanking the candidate for their time, and then explain the next steps in the selection process.**

What About Illegal Questions?

You should avoid questions that could be used to discriminate on the basis of any of the protected classes discussed in Chapter 3. This means that you should not ask questions related to race, religion, sex, color, national origin, age, disability, pregnancy, physical health, marital status, or sexual orientation. On the other hand, there are times when you need to know that the applicant can perform the essential job functions. So how do you ask what you need to know for job-related reasons but without asking an illegal question? Table 6.7 gives you some examples of illegal and legal questions that may help to clarify this dilemma.

TABLE 6.7 Illegal and Legal Questions

Illegal	Legal
How old are you? When did you graduate? What year were you born?	Are you over the minimum age for the hours or working conditions?
Do you have any disabilities? What is your medical history?	Can you perform the job duties?
How many children do you have?	Is there any reason you would not be able to work the required hours? Can you work overtime?
Are you married? What is your maiden name? Will your spouse mind you traveling? With whom do you reside?	Whether the applicant has worked for another employer under any other name, and if so, what name.
Are you a U.S. citizen? Where were you born?	Do you have the legal right to remain permanently in the U.S.? Are you able to provide proof of employment eligibility upon hire?
What is your race? You look biracial, is that right?	None.
Where do you go to church? What is your religious affiliation?	Can you work on Saturdays? Can you work on Sundays?
Do you own your home or rent? With whom do you live?	Are you able to get to work regularly and on time?
Are you pregnant? Do you plan on having any more children?	None.
What's the origin of your last name?	None (unless the national origin is a BFOQ).

Making a Selection Decision

How do you actually make a selection decision after you have gathered all of your data and input using the various selection tools and methods? Should you weigh some criteria more than others? The reason that the textbook does not go deeply into this topic is mainly that there is really no set standard for this step in the process. There are two basic approaches: judgment or intuition, and using a scoring system. Sometimes the decision is made by one individual, but often it is a team approach, comparing evaluations of applicants. Scoring systems vary by company and by the job, and most are developed in-house to fit the specific needs of the company. One concept that always applies, regardless of the selection method, is that the selection decision should be made using criteria that are job-related, reliable, and valid.

Selection Bias

HR professionals should be aware of biases that can occur at any phase of the selection process, but most often in the screening of resumes and applications, and during interviews. The most common types of talent selection bias are summarized in Table 6.8.

TABLE 6.8 Selection Bias

Talent Selection Bias	
First Impression Error	Making a decision too early in the selection process.
Halo Effect	Rating an applicant too high overall because of a positive rating on one criterion.
Horns Effect	Rating an applicant too low overall because of a negative rating on one criterion (opposite of the halo effect).
Similar to Me Error	Rating an applicant too high because he or she is similar to the interviewer (e.g., in terms of gender, age, race, interests, education, lifestyle, etc.).
Different from Me Error	Rating an applicant too low overall because he or she is different from the interviewer (opposite of the similar to me error).
Contrast Error	This occurs when the person making a hiring decision is unduly influenced by the characteristics of other candidates.

Talent Analytics

As shown in the movie *Moneyball*, Billy Beane reinvented the Oakland A's and outsmarted the richer baseball teams to turn a losing team into a competitor. How did he do it? Using talent analytics, he identified the key talent metrics that make a baseball team successful and chose players based on that data. Thanks to advances in HRIS and ATS data, businesses now have a wealth of data to mine to inform their selection decisions and help them choose the best talent.

Before you can use data to select employees, you first have to know who you're looking for. What does your ideal employee look like? What qualifications and characteristics do they have? A hiring template allows HR to make decisions that are based on sound data instead of guesswork or intuition. A template shows what a model employee should possess before he or she is hired, along with what skills and qualifications are needed. This makes evaluating candidates for new positions more efficient, and more effective.

In other words, talent analytics takes much of the guesswork out of hiring. The chart below reflects the findings of a statistical analysis of sales productivity and turnover conducted by a large financial services company. According to Bersin by Deloitte, the analysis looked at sales performance over the first two years of a new employee and correlated total performance and retention rates against a variety of demographic factors.[36]

What is remarkable is the fact that the heretofore tried-and-true beliefs that education and references had a direct impact were proven to be completely untrue. Moreover, when this same company instituted a new screening process for employees based on these results, their revenues increased by $4 million!

Selecting the Best Sales Professionals
Data Showed Six Things Matter:

What is Highly Correlated with Success:

1. No typos, errors, grammatical mistakes on resume.
2. Did not quit school before obtaining *some degree*
3. Had experience selling real-estate or autos
4. Demonstrated success in prior jobs
5. Ability to succeed with vague instruction
6. Experience planning time and managing lots of tasks

What Did NOT Matter:

- Where they went to school
- What grades they had
- The quality of their references

The Traditional Belief System Was Wrong

Within six months of implementing a new screening process *revenues increased by $4 million*

Source: Forbes

 ### A Sample Behavioral Interview Question: "Tell Me About a Time You Failed"

Hira with Careerly tackles a common behavioral interview question.

View the video online at: http://www.youtube.com/embed/TGuUo0a99fw?rel=0

Key Takeaways

- Interviewing methods include unstructured, structured, situational or behavioral, panel, and simulations.
- Asking appropriate questions of applicants is the best method for gathering information about character, competency, and cultural contribution.
- You should avoid questions that could be used to discriminate on the basis of any of the protected classes discussed in Chapter 3. This means that you should not ask questions related to race, religion, sex, color, national origin, age, disability, pregnancy, physical health, marital status, or sexual orientation.
- There are two basic approaches to making a selection decision: judgment or intuition, and using a scoring system.
- The most common types of selection bias are first impression error, halo effect, horns effect, similar to me error, different from me error, and contrast error.

What Do *You* Think?

1. What types of interviewing method were used when you applied for jobs in the past? Were they effective, or could the interviewer(s) have chosen better methods?
2. Have you ever been asked an illegal question in an interview? How did you respond? How should you respond?
3. How would you prefer to make selection decisions? Would you rely more on judgment and intuition or a scoring system?

6.6 Conclusion

This chapter introduced the selection process, including the roles of HR and the hiring manager, screening methods, selection bias, and various approaches to making a selection decision. Various methods for performing initial applicant screening were introduced, followed by a review of assessment methods and interviewing skills.

Theory-into-Practice (TIP) Exercises

1. Make a list of which selection biases you think you might be susceptible to. Then take the Project Implicit test (see resource number one below) and compare your conscious and unconscious bias results to your previous list.
2. In groups of three, conduct a mock behavioral interview.

    Each member of the group will take turns being the "applicant." For each round of interviews, complete the following steps:

    a. Applicant: Tell the interview panel the name of the organization and the position for which you are interviewing.

b. Interview panel: Ask three questions of the candidate. You can select from the list of questions provided in Table 6.6, or create your own questions. It is acceptable to ask a follow-up question for clarification or to get the applicant to elaborate on their answer.

c. Feedback: After the interview, the interview panel should give constructive feedback to the candidate.

   i. Tell the applicant what they did well.

   ii. Give the applicant some tips on what they could improve on.

3. Download one of the free applicant tracking systems (see resource number four below). Then ask several classmates to submit their resumes to the system so that you can practice screening them.

Case Study: Not a Power-Ful Test

Source: © Shutterstock, Inc.

Before the passage of the Civil Rights Act of 1964, Duke Power (like many other corporations) discriminated against African Americans in hiring and promotion, restricting them to the company's labor department. Duke Power later required those applying for any job, besides those in the labor department, to have a high school diploma. Later, after the Civil Rights Act of 1964 passed, they began allowing non–high school graduates from the labor department to transfer to other departments if they could earn sufficient scores on a general mental ability test and another test that was intended to predict job performance in mechanical fields. Duke Power required a median score that was the same as those for high school graduates. All involved, including Duke Power, agreed that whites fared better than African Americans on these tests. This put African Americans at a disadvantage in Duke's hiring and advancement.

These actions led to a lawsuit, *Griggs v. Duke Power Co.* brought by Willie Griggs and twelve other African Americans. They contended that Title VII of the Civil Rights Act of 1964 forbade race-based discrimination in employment and prohibited tests that would likely exclude African Americans from being hired or receiving promotions. A federal District Court ruled in favor of Duke Power. Next, the Fourth Circuit Court of Appeals ruled that the tests administered by Duke Power were not discriminatory. In 1970, the U.S. Supreme Court finally heard the case and overturned the lower courts' rulings. It ruled that intelligence test scores and diplomas are not, in themselves, illegal under Title VII. However, if they limit ethnic minority hiring and do not pertain to job skills or performance, they are illegal.

None of the three federal courts thought that Duke Power had any discriminatory intent. One of the main issues was that Duke Power made no serious effort to determine or demonstrate the legitimacy of diploma and intelligence tests as predictors of job performance. According to his testimony, the vice-president stated that executives at Duke Power simply believed that these requirements would result in the hiring of better workers.[37]

 Disparate Impact

Discrimination does not have to be intentional. As in the *Griggs v. Duke Power Co.* case, discrimination can take a more subtle and usually unintentional form, known as disparate impact, or adverse impact.

View the video online at: http://www.youtube.com/embed/bE1M3qZw1Y8?rel=0

Case Discussion Questions

1. Have you ever had to take a test when applying for a job? Do you think it was a valid predictor of future job performance?

2. Do you think the Supreme Court's ruling was the right one? Why or why not? Now that you have read the chapter, what are some of the things the executives at Duke Power could have done to avoid this lawsuit?

3. As a current or future professional in HR or management, what are the lessons that you can apply from this case in regard to validity of employment tests?

Resources

1. **Project Implicit.** A free survey of your conscious and unconscious preferences, which may give you some insight into your possible selection biases. Project Implicit is a nonprofit organization and international collaboration between researchers who are interested in implicit social cognition—thoughts and feelings—outside of conscious awareness and control.

   https://implicit.harvard.edu/implicit/research/

2. **Behavioral Interviewing Resources.** Examples of behavioral questions to ask a candidate during an interview and other resources.

   https://cardinalatwork.stanford.edu/manager-toolkit/resources/behavioral-interviewing-resources

3. **Best Background Check Companies of 2019.** From Business News Daily.
   https://www.businessnewsdaily.com/7638-best-background-check-services.html

4. **The Top 8 Free/Open-Source Applicant Tracking Software Solutions.**
   https://blog.capterra.com/top-8-freeopen-source-applicant-tracking-software-solutions/

Endnotes

1. Case written by Crews, P. (2020). Adapted from Kirila, J.S. (2017). The Home Depot murder case teaches that the employer may be held liable. *Lexology*. Retrieved from https://www.lexology.com/library/detail.aspx?g=5a3ba1f2-2e66-473f-88ec-c321c9771689

2. McIntyre, B. (2018). How much does a bad hire really cost? *Business2community*. Retrieved April 13, 2018 from https://www.business2community.com/human-resources/how-much-does-a-bad-hire-really-cost-02108605

3. Fatemi, F. (2016). The true cost of a bad hire: It's more than you think. *Forbes*. Retrieved from https://www.forbes.com/sites/falonfatemi/2016/09/28/the-true-cost-of-a-bad-hire-its-more-than-you-think/#3515f8514aa4

4. Negligent hiring law and legal definition. *USLegal*. Retrieved April 1, 2020 from https://definitions.uslegal.com/n/negligent-hiring/

5. Ibid.

6. Resume Screening. *Ideal*. Retrieved April 13, 2019 from https://ideal.com/resume-screening/

7. Ibid.

8. Increase your interview chances. *Jobscan*. Retrieved April 1, 2020 from https://www.jobscan.co/#

9. 2018 Employment Screening Benchmark Report. *HireRight*. Retrieved April 2, 2020 from https://www.hireright.com/resources/view/2018-employment-screening-benchmark-report

10. Luo, M. (2009). Whitening the resume. *The New York Times*. Retrieved from https://www.nytimes.com/2009/12/06/weekinreview/06Luo.html

11. Pager, D., Western, B., & Bonikowski, B. (2009). Discrimination in a low-wage labor market: A field experiment. *American Sociological Review*, 74: 777–799.

12. Quilian, L., Pager, D., Hexel, O., & Midtboen, A.H. (2017). A meta-analysis of field experiments shows no change in racial discrimination in hiring over time. *Proceedings National Academy of Science*, 114 (41), 10870-10875.

13. Society for Human Resource Management. What commonly asked questions should not be on an employment application? Retrieved April 2, 2020 from https://www.shrm.org/resourcesandtools/tools-and-samples/hr-qa/pages/applicationslegalissueswhatcommonlyaskedquestionsshouldnotbeonanemploymentapplication.aspx

14. National Association of Professional Background Screeners. How human resource professionals view the use and effectiveness of background screening methods. Retrieved from https://pubs.napbs.com/pub.cfm?id=9E5ED85F-C257-C289-9E8E-A7C7A8C58D00

15. U.S. Immigration and Customs Enforcement. Form I-9 Inspection Overview. Retrieved April 17, 2019 from https://www.ice.gov/factsheets/i9-inspection

16. U.S. Citizenship and Immigration Services. Completing section 2 of Form I-9. Retrieved April 2, 2020 from https://www.uscis.gov/i-9-central/40-completing-section-2-form-i-9

17. Ibid.

18. U.S. Department of Homeland Security. About E-Verify. Retrieved April 2, 2020 from https://www.e-verify.gov/

19. Greene, L. (2018). Are credit checks essential to hiring good employees? Yes—Here's Why. *Glassdoor*. Retrieved from https://www.glassdoor.com/employers/blog/are-credit-checks-essential-to-hiring-good-employees-yes-heres-why/

20. Federal Trade Commission. Using consumer reports: What employers need to know. Retrieved April 2, 2020 from https://www.ftc.gov/tips-advice/business-center/guidance/using-consumer-reports-what-employers-need-know

21. Repa, B.K. State laws on references and statements by former employers. *NOLO*. Retrieved April 13, 2019 from https://www.nolo.com/legal-encyclopedia/free-books/employee-rights-book/chapter9-6.html

22. Lennon, D. The 10 best questions to ask when checking references. *WorkBright*. Retrieved April 13, 2019 from https://workbright.com/blog/the-10-best-questions-to-ask-when-checking-references/

23. Uniform Guidelines on Employee Selection Procedures of 1978. *Code of Federal Regulations*. Retrieved April 13, 2019 from https://www.govinfo.gov/content/pkg/CFR-2014-title29-vol4/xml/CFR-2014-title29-vol4-part1607.xml

24. U.S. Office of Personnel Management. Assessment policy. Retrieved March 16, 2020 from https://www.opm.gov/FAQs/QA.aspx?fid=a6da6c2e-e1cb-4841-b72d-53eb4adf1ab1&pid=402c2b0c-bb5c-44e9-acbc-39cc6149ad36

25. Bardhoshi, G., & Erford, B.T. (2017). Processes and Procedures for Estimating Score Reliability and Precision. *Measurement & Evaluation in Counseling & Development, 50*(4), 256–263.

26. Ibid.

27. Adapted from Chapter 3: Understanding test quality—Concepts of reliability and validity. *HR-Guide*. Retrieved April 13, 2019 from https://www.hr-guide.com/Testing_and_Assessment/Reliability_and_Validity.htm

28. Chapter 3: Understanding test quality—Concepts of reliability and validity. *HR-Guide*. Retrieved April 13, 2019 from https://www.hr-guide.com/Testing_and_Assessment/Reliability_and_Validity.htm

29. Society for Human Resource Management. (2018). Screening by means of pre-employment testing. Retrieved from https://www.shrm.org/resourcesandtools/tools-and-samples/toolkits/pages/screeningbymeansofpreemploymenttesting.aspx

30. Ibid.

31. Judge, T., Higgins, C., Thoresen, C., & Barrick, M. (1999). The big five personality traits, general mental ability, and career success across the life span. *Personnel Psychology, 52*(3), 621-652.

32. United States Department of Labor. Employee Polygraph Protection Act. Retrieved April 2, 2020 from https://www.dol.gov/whd/polygraph/

33. Berry, C.M., Sackett, P.R., & Wiemann, S. (2007). A Review of Recent Developments in Integrity Test Research. *Personnel Psychology, 60*(2), 271–301.

34. Ibid.

35. U.S. Equal Employment Opportunity Commission. Pre-employment inquiries and height & weight. Retrieved April 2, 2020 from https://www.eeoc.gov/laws/practices/inquiries_height_weight.cfm

36. Olenski, S. (2016). Using talent analytics when hiring for your brand. *Forbes*. Retrieved from https://www.forbes.com/sites/steveolenski/2016/10/05/using-talent-analytics-when-hiring-for-your-brand/#7655d2491f97

37. Case written by Crews, P. (2020). Adapted from *Griggs v. Duke Power, North Carolina History Project*. Retrieved March 15, 2020 from https://northcarolinahistory.org/encyclopedia/griggs-v-duke-power/

CHAPTER 7
Talent Development

Learning Objectives

After reading this chapter, you should be able to do the following:

1. Identify the processes used to collect and analyze data as part of a needs assessment.
2. Choose the appropriate training method considering the characteristics of the learner, the instructional objectives, and resource constraints.
3. Evaluate the effectiveness and efficiency of training and development programs.
4. Explain the role of assessment, education, job experiences, and coaching in employee development.

Talent development plays a major role in the competitiveness of individuals, organizations, regions, and societies. The availability of skilled talent is a major factor in attracting and growing industries in a region and is now cited by economic developers as the major factor in site selection decisions.[1] Individual organizations strive to align talent development with their strategic goals to gain a competitive advantage in their industry, whether for-profit or nonprofit. Organizations in the United States spend an average of $1,299 per employee on employee learning, and employees spend an average of over thirty-four hours per year on formal learning programs.[2] Talent development represents a major investment in human capital and should be managed in a manner that maximizes the return on this investment.

This chapter begins with a discussion of the importance of needs assessment and various methods for identifying training and development needs. Traditional and e-learning approaches to training are explored, as well as the evaluation of training initiatives. The chapter closes with a review of employee development methods, including a few specific applications such as assessment, job experiences, and coaching.

7.1 Opening Case: Level Up in Spark City

Source: play.google.com

Walmart is requiring its employees to play video games while getting paid, and they are hoping for better employees because of it! In January 2019, Walmart introduced gaming into some of its employee training programs. Spark City is a virtual reality video game by which department managers and other employees interested in becoming department managers can be educated on daily responsibilities.

The employee creates an avatar and starts the game as a manager of a Walmart dry grocery department. One exercise they can perform is changing prices: increasing and decreasing prices based on different factors. They receive performance scores based on inventory, customer satisfaction, and sales. The game's creator, Daniel Shepherd, states, "It is a simulation-based game that puts the player in the shoes of the department manager. We use Spark City to reinforce and connect a lot of different things into one long routine. It's an environment they can make mistakes in."[3]

Spark City

DJ's Gamebox offers a glimpse of game play on Spark City.

View the video online at: http://www.youtube.com/embed/yD8p9mzn9Fg?rel=0

Case Study Discussion Questions

1. Do you think that video games can be beneficial in employee training?
2. Suppose you have an older employee who does not want to participate in playing a video game as part of their training. How would you handle the situation?
3. How would you measure whether this training technique is successful?

7.2 Needs Assessment

Learning Objectives

1. Recognize why a needs assessment is necessary before designing a talent development initiative.
2. Identify the steps in the needs assessment process.
3. Distinguish between organizational and individual barriers to learning.

Why Is Needs Assessment Important?

needs assessment

The process of determining what training is designed to accomplish, helps to ensure that it will be well received by employees, that transfer of training will take place, and that it will produce positive organizational outcomes.

Training programs today do not have to be boring lectures or death by PowerPoint. Thanks to technology, training can actually be fun, as the opening case about training gamification at Walmart illustrates. But it does little good to implement a training program without first determining the need for it among the target population. There needs to be an alignment with the organization's mission and vision concerning the talent development strategy. Many organizations have wasted both money and the time of their employees, conducting training programs just because a senior member of management believed that it would help organizational performance or a trainer made a convincing case. A **needs assessment** is the process of determining what training is designed to accomplish and helps to ensure that it will be well received by employees, that transfer of training will take place, and that it will produce positive organizational outcomes.

The most important question to answer during a needs assessment is the question: "Is this a training problem?" A talent development professional might work full-time for an organization and is routinely approached by managers asking for training for a particular group of employees. Others are independent consultants who work to provide training and development for many different clients. But regardless of whether the client is internal or external, a similar process should occur. This process is a conversation that the trainer should have with the client, to determine whether they are dealing with a training problem. In other words, will training solve the problem?

For example, assume that you are the director of talent development for a large hospital, and the chief nursing officer (CNO) asks you to conduct a training program for all employees on how to use the new medical records system. When you inquire further, you find that the problem the CNO is trying to solve is high employee turnover. The CNO has heard several nurses complaining about the new medical records system, even saying that it makes them want to quit, and has made the conclusion, based on anecdotal evidence, that this is the cause of the employee turnover. But after completing a thorough needs assessment, you might find that the most common reason employees give for quitting is that they do not have a good relationship with their supervisor (and in fact, research studies indicate that 80% of employee turnover is due to supervision, which has given rise to the saying that "People don't quit their jobs, they quit their bosses.") In this case, there is indeed a training problem, but the training that will have the most impact on employee turnover is supervisory skills training for the charge nurses, not medical records training for all nurses.

The main point here is that a needs assessment should begin with a conversation about pain. If you go to a doctor, then he or she might begin by saying, "Tell me about your pain." When a training client asks for a specific type of training, you might start with a conversation about the problem they are trying to solve. Figure 7.1 gives ten questions to ask your training client during this conversation.

FIGURE 7.1 10 Questions to Ask Your Training Client

10 Questions to Ask Your Training Client

☐ 1. Tell me about your pain. What problem are you trying to solve?

☐ 2. How long has this been a problem?

☐ 3. When and how frequently does it occur?

☐ 4. What would indicate to you that the problem has been solved?

☐ 5. What other training initiatives or interventions have you tried?

☐ 6. What type of knowledge, skills, or abilities do you think the employees/
team members/associates need in order to solve the problem?

☐ 7. What is the estimated number of trainees?

☐ 8. Do you have a time frame in mind for the training?

☐ 9. What is the budget you have allocated to solve this problem?

☐ 10. Who is involved in the decision to implement a training initiative?

One of the principal paradoxes of training is whether or not deficiencies in workplace training are resolved by more training. This can suggest a counterintuitive answer when looked at more strategically. The bigger issue in true performance management is whether the performance deficit is a "can't" issue or a "won't" issue. The former partially suggests a training intervention, but can also be analyzed through the lens of organizational systems, procedures, and flows. It is not inconceivable that the performance deficit is the result of unclear goals, poor workflow analysis, or any number of other organizational or cultural issues not related to individual competencies.

Performance deficiencies might also be the result of motivation issues. An under-motivated team member can receive a great amount of additional training and still choose not to perform at his or her maximum. The strategies for such performance deficits have little to do with training.

With so many possible variables affecting performance, it is critical to assess whether training really will result in improved performance. This is the role of the needs assessment.

The Needs Assessment Process

An effective needs assessment looks at all three levels of need: organizational, task, and person analyses. Training may appear to be needed, when in fact there are other organizational issues or person capabilities that demand addressing before (or instead of) training. In other words, what type of problem needs to be solved, and is it a training problem?

There are three levels of needs analysis:

1. **Organizational.** Involves determining the appropriateness of training, given the organization's strategy, resources, and leadership support for the training.

2. **Task.** Involves identifying the tasks to be performed, as well as the knowledge, skills, abilities, and other characteristics (KSAOs) that are required to perform those tasks.

3. **Person.** Involves determining:

   a. Whether performance deficiencies are due to a lack of knowledge, skills, or abilities, or problems with work design, lack of resources needed, or motivation.

   b. Identification of who needs training.

   c. Employee readiness for training.

The collection of data for the needs assessment is a crucial step in the process of determining skill gaps. However, there is an even more crucial decision that must be made first, and that is what type of data will help us to understand the training problem, and how can that data be obtained? Data may come in many forms, including existing company reports, customer reviews, surveys, and skill and aptitude assessments. In addition, interviews can be conducted with various employees to gain a perspective on the situation. Keep in mind that data is needed for all three levels (organizational, task, and person) to assess the situation accurately. It is also very important that management makes a commitment to follow through with a program to close skills gaps and solve training problems. If employees are asked to participate in assessments and surveys, but then nothing is done about the problems, they will eventually become jaded and will stop taking needs assessments seriously.

In addition to helping understand the training problem, data also helps to establish a **baseline**. A baseline is a starting point used for comparison. Data can then be collected again after a training initiative, and the progress can be measured. In other words, we can then determine if we have closed the gap, and by how much, and how far we have to go.

organizational analysis

Involves determining the appropriateness of training, given the organization's strategy, resources, and leadership support for the training.

task analysis

Involves identifying the tasks to be performed, as well as the knowledge, skills, abilities, and other characteristics (KSAOs) that are required to perform those tasks.

person analysis

Involves determining whether performance deficiencies are due to a lack of knowledge, skills, or abilities, or problems with work design, lack of resources needed, or motivation; identification of who needs training; and employee readiness for training.

baseline

A starting point used for comparison when collecting and analyzing data.

The job of a package delivery driver is complex. They must possess many KSAOs to succeed in their work, including operational safety, appropriate decision-making, positive customer interaction, and physical stamina.

Source: MikeDotta / Shutterstock.com

Talent Analytics

Talent analytics is designed to solve business issues, not HR issues. The real value in talent analytics is that when used properly, they help HR to focus on solving problems.

There are four different types of analytics:

1. **Descriptive.** What's happened in the past.
2. **Diagnostic.** Why it happened.
3. **Predictive.** What might happen in the future.
4. **Prescriptive.** How can we make it happen?

Prescriptive analytics uses multivariate modeling to propose data-based options that can be weighed against each other to choose the optimal solution. Most companies (86%) are using descriptive analytics now. But only 10% are using predictive analytics. This percentage is expected to grow rapidly as more leaders are beginning to understand how prescriptive analytics can be used in decision-making and to identify which talent development solutions are most likely to yield the desired results.

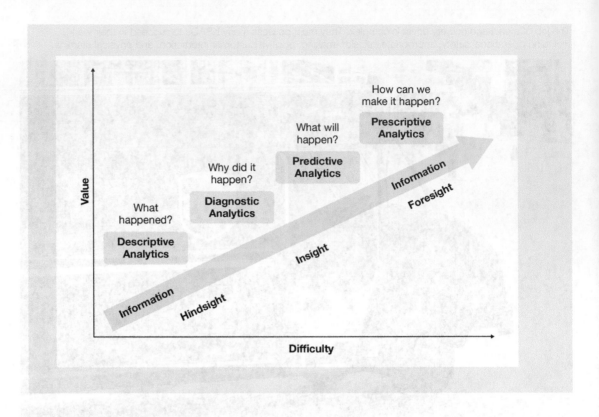

Barriers to Learning

Before we begin to consider various approaches to design a learning experience, there is one additional aspect of needs assessment that we need to consider, and that is the obstacles or barriers to learning. These barriers can be either organizational or individual. In this section, we will briefly look at three barriers: cost, resistance to change, and lack of readiness to learn.

Cost

return-on-investment (ROI)

A performance measure used to express the financial return from an investment made in learning and development.

At the organizational level, one barrier is cost. Training is expensive and time-consuming, and managers might be tempted to focus on the cost of downtime during training rather than the long-term benefits of the training. One method for expressing the cost of training and the benefits is the **return-on-investment (ROI)**. ROI is used for any type of investment made by an organization, including real estate, equipment, and others. Within the context of this chapter, ROI is a performance measure used to express the financial return from an investment made in learning and development. Later in this chapter, you will learn how to calculate the ROI of a training program.

HR professionals should prepare ROI projections on learning and development initiatives to convince upper management to make the necessary investment in human capital. However, there is a caveat that should be considered. What if the ROI is negative? In fact, many learning and development programs have negative ROIs.[4] Why then should management invest in a training program with a projected negative return? One answer is that the training might prepare employees to use new technology, and it is necessary just to keep up with what competitors are doing.[5] Another example is the types of training that mitigates risk. Sexual harassment training, for example, should reduce the chances of the company facing a lawsuit and the cost of punitive damages. Safety training reduces the risk of workplace accidents, which can be very expensive in terms of actual damages and workers' compensation costs. These types of benefits are intangible because they are unknown and therefore are not reflected in an ROI calculation. Nevertheless, the cost of not doing the training can be an important reason to invest.

Resistance to Change

Change management is the subject of many entire books, and there are undergraduate and graduate courses on the topic. Therefore, we will not discuss the topic in-depth in this course. We will simply explore why people tend to resist change, and then introduce a model to help you understand the stages of resistance that people go through when experiencing a change (and all training programs essentially involve asking people to change something about the way they do their jobs, or a change in their workplace attitude).

Change is often uncomfortable and results in active resistance.

PARDON MY
KICKING
AND SCREAMING

(I'm in the midst of change)

Source: © Shutterstock, Inc.

Why do people resist training? First, let's try a brainstorming exercise. Stop reading and make a list of what you think are the common reasons that people resist. See if you can think of at least five. You don't have to stop there; keep listing as many as you can think of, but try to list at least five before reading further.

Okay, let's see how you did. Table 7.1 displays ten reasons why people resist training.

TABLE 7.1 Why People Resist Training

Why People Resist Training
• The purpose of the training is not clear.
• It takes time away from doing their work, and they are already swamped.
• Employees don't know what to do differently after the training.
• Inconvenience: they are being asked to step out of their comfort zone.
• Fear of loss (particularly when it comes to the loss of their job, power, or position).
• Those affected by the training are not involved in planning the change.
• Fear of failure (such as mastering new skills).
• Satisfaction with the status quo.
• Experienced employees may think they will not learn anything new.
• Failure to see the relevance to their job.

Change Curve

A model for understanding how people react to significant change.

You may notice two themes running throughout the previous list. One theme is fear and then the other theme is lack of communication. To help you better understand the stages of resistance to change we are going to explore a model called the **Change Curve**. The Change Curve is a model for understanding how people react to significant change and can be used to predict people's reactions to change and help them adapt to it more quickly and successfully. The Change Curve is attributed to the psychiatrist Dr. Elisabeth Kübler-Ross, and it resulted from her work on personal transitions that people go through during the stages of grief and bereavement. It has been adapted appropriately to the stages that people go through in adapting to change. It helps you predict how people will react to change so that you can help them make their own personal transitions and make sure that they have the help and support that they need. The Change Curve model describes the four stages most people go through as they adjust to change, and is shown in Figure 7.2.

FIGURE 7.2 The Change Curve

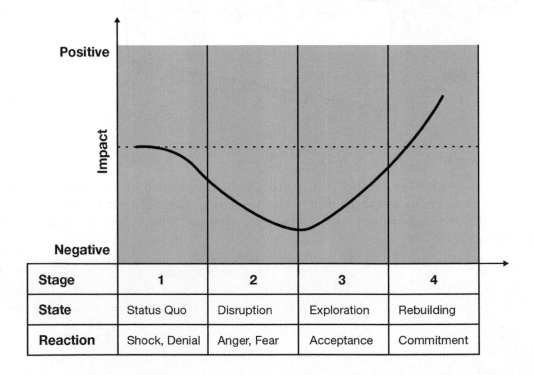

Stage	1	2	3	4
State	Status Quo	Disruption	Exploration	Rebuilding
Reaction	Shock, Denial	Anger, Fear	Acceptance	Commitment

When a change is first introduced, people's initial reaction may be shock or denial as they react to the challenge to the status quo: the equilibrium has been changed. This is Stage One of the Change Curve. Once the reality of the change starts to hit, people tend to react negatively and move to Stage Two of the Change Curve. They may fear the impact, they may feel angry, or they may actively resist and push back and protest against the changes. Some will wrongly fear the negative consequences of the change, while others will correctly identify real threats to their position or their well-being. As a result, the organization experiences disruption, which, if not carefully managed, can quickly spiral into chaos.

As long as people resist the change and remain at Stage Two, the change will be unsuccessful, at least for those who are reacting in this way. This can be a very stressful and unpleasant stage for everyone involved. It is much healthier to move on to Stage Three of the Change Curve, where pessimism and resistance begin to give way to some optimism and acceptance as people start to explore new ways of dealing with the change. At Stage Three, people stop focusing on what they have lost, they start to let go, they start to accept the changes, and they begin exploring and testing ideas about what these changes mean. Moving on to Stage Four, they not only accept the changes, but they start to embrace them. They begin to rebuild their concept of how things are done in this organization and begin to accept what the future looks like. Only when people get to this stage can the organization start to reap the benefit of the change.

If you like emojis, here is a different visual of the Kübler-Ross Change Curve (see Figure 7.3).

FIGURE 7.3 Emoji Change Curve

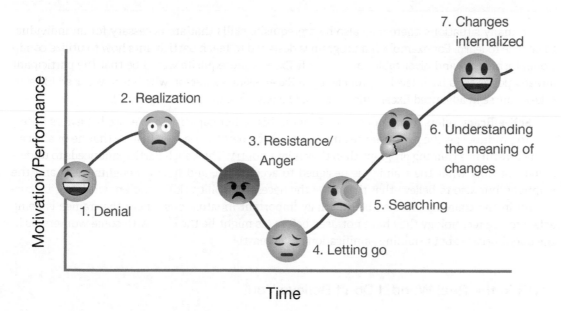

Source: © Shutterstock, Inc.

 Change Happens!

The author conducts a mini-lecture on the nature of change.

View the video online at: http://player.vimeo.com/video/146426113

Readiness to Learn

readiness to learn

The ability and motivation of a person to learn.

Another way of explaining how the Change Curve relates to the success of a training program is to examine the employee's **readiness to learn**. If an employee is ready to learn, then they have the ability and motivation to learn.[6] The ability to learn includes having basic learning skills such as reading, writing, and math. There are additional skills beyond literacy, which are necessary for workplace success. These basic employability skills are listed in Table 7.2.[7]

TABLE 7.2 Basic Employability Skills

Basic Employability Skills
• Basic literacy and numeracy skills.
• Critical thinking skills.
• Management skills.
• Leadership skills.
• Interpersonal skills.
• Information technology skills.
• Systems thinking skills.
• Work ethic disposition.

In many situations, there may also be prerequisite skills that are necessary for an individual to be able to learn. For example, if a program is designed to teach participants how to utilize conditional formatting and pivot tables in Microsoft Excel, a prerequisite would be that the participant already possesses a basic level of proficiency in Excel. Asking a person who has never used Excel to take a course in advanced Excel functions would likely be setting them up to fail.

self-efficacy

Refers to an individual's belief in his or her capacity to execute behaviors necessary to produce specific performance attainments.

Self-efficacy refers to an individual's belief in his or her capacity to execute behaviors necessary to produce specific performance attainments.[8] If a person does not believe that he or she can be successful in a training program, then they might not try. Thus, each participant needs to understand not only what the training is designed to accomplish, and how it benefits them and the company, but also to believe that they have the necessary ability, skills, and knowledge to be successful in the training. This can be especially important in situations where the trainee is being asked to use technology they have not used before (as might be the case with some workers, as in the opening case about training gamification at Walmart).

HR in the Real World: I Don't Believe You!

Think of data as more than numbers or survey answers. Data tells a story. In the needs assessment phase, data tells a story about the training problem, and it establishes a measurable baseline as the starting point. Data can also tell the instructional designer and management whether they properly understand the nature of the problem. In one case, I was conducting a needs assessment with a client, and this included one-on-one interviews with approximately 140 employees in three locations. Management knew they had an organizational culture problem, and employees were dissatisfied, resulting in high turnover. Management initially believed the training problem was related to inadequate policies, procedures, and employee training for job skills. However, the overwhelming consensus of the employee interviews was they felt micromanaged, and that the CEO did not listen to their input. This was not what the CEO wanted to hear, and she rejected the survey results. Management thought they needed to exert more control through policies and procedures, but the autocratic style of management was what was causing the turnover in the first place. In this situation, management was the training problem! The lesson here is that before conducting a needs assessment, prepare management to be open to hearing and acting upon the assessment results, even if it means changing their management style.

Key Takeaways

- The use of proper training and development needs assessment methodology helps to ensure that training will be well received by employees, that transfer of training will take place, and that it will produce positive organizational outcomes.
- The most important question to answer during a needs assessment is the question, "Is this a training problem?"
- The three levels of a needs analysis are organizational, task, and person.
- In addition to helping understand the training problem, data also helps to establish a baseline.
- Training is expensive and time-consuming, and managers might be tempted to focus on the cost of downtime during training, rather than the long-term benefits of the training.
- The Change Curve is a model for understanding how people react to significant change, and can be used to predict people's reactions to change and help them adapt to it more quickly and successfully.
- If an employee is ready to learn, then they have the ability and motivation to learn.
- Data tells a story about the training problem and it establishes a measurable starting point with which to measure progress.
- Prepare management to be open to hearing and acting upon the assessment results.

What Do *You* Think?

1. Have you ever been asked by your employer to complete a survey regarding your perspective on job-related issues? Was there any follow-up?
2. When advised of upcoming mandatory training, what is your initial reaction? If you have a negative reaction, what could the organization do to make your feel more positive about the training?
3. What could a trainer do to reduce resistance to training and help move participants along the change curve?

7.3 Training Methods

Learning Objectives

1. Distinguish between the ADDIE and SAM instructional design models.
2. Identify when classroom instruction is an appropriate methodology, and compare various classroom layouts.
3. Recognize when synchronous distance learning is the appropriate methodology, and identify the responsibilities of the facilitator.
4. Recognize the advantages of asynchronous learning, and explain the role of a learning management system.
5. Describe how on-the-job training is used to develop talent.
6. Explain how simulations, gamification, and virtual reality are used to teach job skills and practice various scenarios.

modality

The form of delivering training, such as live instructor-led, online self-paced, or on-the-job training.

An important decision that is made during the design phase is to choose the training **modality**. A modality is a form of delivering training, such as live instructor-led, online self-paced, or on-the-job training. In this section, we will examine some of the more common training modalities.

Instructional Design Models

ADDIE

The mainstream instructional design model since the 1970s, following the linear steps of analysis, design, development, implementation, and evaluation.

Before choosing a delivery modality, it is helpful to first have an instructional design model to guide the assessment, development, and implementation of a learning initiative. **ADDIE** (which stands for analysis, design, development, implementation, and evaluation) has been the mainstream instructional design model since the 1970s. It is a linear model that provides designers with a roadmap for creating training. It can be described as a series of ordered steps, which creates standardization but also can lead to prolonged development cycles, cumbersome processes, and communication challenges between designers and users.

The steps in the ADDIE model are:

1. **Analyze.** Identify the problem or opportunity and the target audience, define the learning objectives, choose delivery modality, determine scope of the project, budget, and timeline.
2. **Design.** Outline the content into modules and lessons using flowcharts and storyboards, sequence content, select or design assessment instruments, choose multimedia elements.
3. **Develop.** Create curriculum prototype, then Beta and pilot test.
4. **Implement.** Facilitator training occurs, then final product is made available to learners. Assessment is performed and feedback obtained from learners and trainers.
5. **Evaluate.** Identify successes and lessons learned. Review learning objectives to ensure needs were met. Revise curriculum accordingly.

Successive Approximation Model (SAM)

An agile development model with multiple steps happening at the same time.

The **Successive Approximation Model (SAM)** was developed as a response to some of the problems with ADDIE and has seen increased traction in the industry since Michael W. Allen outlined the SAM model in his book *Leaving ADDIE for SAM: An Agile Model for Developing the Best Learning Experiences*.[9] SAM is an agile development model with multiple steps happening at the same time. The SAM process is nonlinear and iterative, allowing for evaluation and changes to the project as needed (as opposed to evaluation happening at the end of the project in the ADDIE approach). SAM also encourages ongoing collaboration between the instructional designers and customers at every stage of the development process.[10] There are two versions of SAM, referred to as SAM 1 and SAM 2. SAM 1 is for simpler projects that do not require as much collaboration. For comparative purposes, we are only discussing SAM 2. The steps in SAM 2 are:

1. **Preparation Phase.** Collect background information on the problem to be solved, and the characteristics of learners such as prior knowledge, and establish overall goals of the project. This phase concludes with the Savvy Start, which brings all stakeholders together to brainstorm the design of training and potential delivery modalities.
2. **Iterative Design Phase.** The team generally becomes smaller and is narrowed down to subject matter experts and instructional designers. This phase includes setting project timelines and budgets, and the assigning of task to be completed. For any one content area, the design team should strive to create three potential designs, to spur creativity and think beyond the obvious solutions.
3. **Iterative Development Phase.** Once a design has been agreed upon, the project moves into a loop of developing, implementing, and feedback/evaluation. The Alpha stage is the first complete version of the project (similar to a pilot in ADDIE). The Beta stage is a final opportunity to review and revise the project before the Gold version (or final version) is rolled out.

Figure 7.4 compares the steps in the ADDIE and SAM models.

FIGURE 7.4 Comparison of ADDIE and SAM

ADDIE

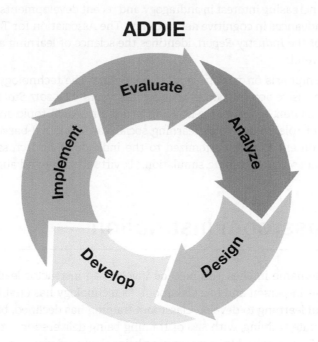

SAM

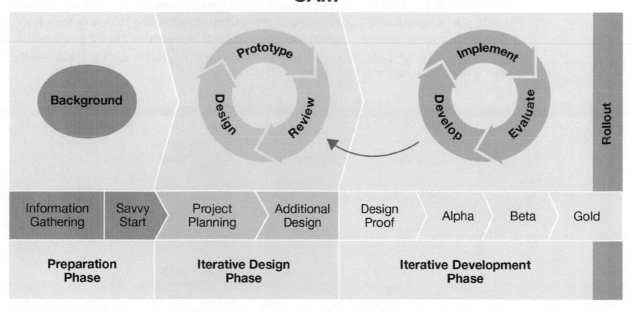

In addition to changes in instructional design, there are two other major trends in the field of talent development that will impact any needs assessment:

1. Increasing interest in andragogy and recent developments in the science of learning, including advances in cognitive neuroscience. The Association for Talent Development, in the *2017 State of the Industry Report*, identifies the science of learning as one of its top research topics and trends.

2. Emphasis on next generation e-learning: The technology of talent development has seen a massive acceleration in the past few years. The *2017 State of the Industry Report* also identifies next-generation e-learning as a top research topic and trend. Areas of emphasis include microlearning, mobile learning, social learning, cloud-based content, personalized learning (i.e., content that is customized to the individual), and cross-platform content, which includes video, audio, gaming, simulation, 3D, virtual reality, and augmented reality.

Classroom Instruction

As the name implies, this method involves an instructor leading a group of students through a course, in-person and in a classroom. As technology has enabled different methods of online and virtual learning to develop, classroom training has declined, but it still represents the majority of corporate training, with 51% of training being delivered in a classroom.[11] However, the impact of COVID-19 may lead to more training being delivered virtually in the future. Classroom instruction provides the opportunity for more efficient interaction between the instructor and students. For example, when you take an online class, and you have a question for your instructor, then you might post a question in a Q&A forum, or email the instructor, and then wait for a response. In a classroom, you can ask the question and get an immediate response. Then if you need clarification or have a follow-up question, you can ask it immediately. All of the other participants in the class also benefit from hearing the questions and answers.

Classroom instruction should be much more than lecture and should include interaction and skills practice to engage trainees.

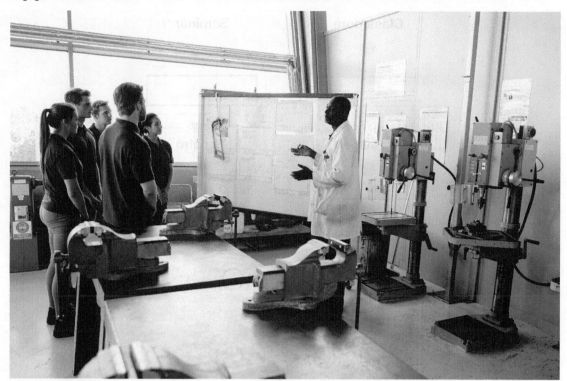

Source: © Shutterstock, Inc.

Classroom instruction can also provide opportunities for more interaction between the participants, for example in class discussions and group activities. Classroom layouts can be designed to help facilitate the type of interaction that is desired. Figure 7.5 shows the most common classroom layouts. As you review these layouts, consider the lines of sight between the instructor and the participants and between participants. For example, the traditional classroom layout is useful for a course that involves disseminating knowledge from the instructor (lecture/presentation). There is a good line of sight between the instructor and the participants. But if more group interaction is desired, then one of the other layouts should be used, which allow the participants to see each other better.

FIGURE 7.5 Classroom Layouts

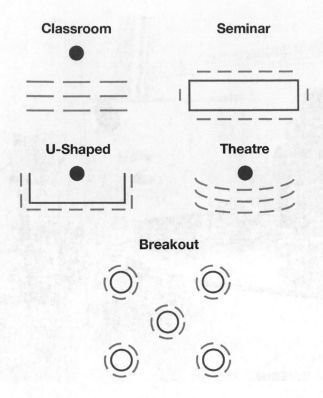

Consider how this has worked in your own experience. When you walk into a classroom, and it is set up in a traditional classroom style, the participants go into a passive mode. They sit down and prepare to be lectured to. You have a good line of sight to the instructor, but when it comes to the other students in the class, you are looking at the backs of their heads. If however, you walk into a classroom, and it is set up in a U-shape layout, you know you can see the instructor and the other students, which will put everyone in a more active mind-set and lead to more engaging discussions and interactions.

Classroom instruction is especially effective for teaching skills that require skills demonstration and practice, such as giving presentations, using equipment, or following specific procedures. For example, large pest control companies have to train many field technicians. Classroom training can be used to teach knowledge about various chemicals and insecticides, and the equipment that is used to apply them, including safety procedures. As part of the training, technicians can be required to demonstrate the proper way to handle chemicals and use equipment.

Virtual Instructor-Led

Virtual instructor-led training involves an instructor leading a group of students through a course using virtual technology such as distance learning, remote classrooms via satellite, and webinars. The primary advantage of virtual instructor-led training is that it provides immediate interaction between the instructor and student, but it saves on travel costs and time. This is particularly advantageous for companies with many employees located in many geographic areas. About 10% of all training is delivered using virtual instructor-led methods.[12] This type of training is considered **synchronous distance learning** because all participants and the instructor are signed into the training at the same time.

Whether classroom-based or virtual, one thing that instructor-led training methods have in common is rather obvious: there is an instructor who guides the learning experience. In the corporate training environment, this person is often referred to as a facilitator. The word facilitator comes from the Latin word facile, which means "to make easy." An effective facilitator is someone who is an expert in the subject matter being taught but also has skills in instructional techniques, communications, and problem-solving, to create an environment conducive to learning.

virtual instructor-led training

Involves an instructor leading a group of students through a course using virtual technology such as distance learning, remote classrooms via satellite, and webinars.

synchronous distance learning

Online learning in which all participants and the instructor are signed into the training at the same time.

Self-Paced E-Learning

In self-paced e-learning, participants complete the learning experience on their own schedule. This category includes online courses, podcasts, mobile learning, and virtual reality. This type of training is considered **asynchronous distance learning** because participants do not all have to be signed in at the same time. The primary advantage is that participants have the flexibility to complete the training whenever and wherever works best for them. While it does save on travel costs, companies need to consider the up-front development time and associated cost.

One of the decisions that needs to be made before deciding whether to choose e-learning as the delivery modality is how many hours of development time will be required. So how long does it take to develop e-learning? The answer is that it depends on many factors, such as the types of media used and the complexity of the content. Videos, for example, will take more time to create than digital interactives, such as drag-and-drop exercises. Advanced courses take more time to develop than basic courses. For budgeting and planning purposes, instructional designers need to be able to at least estimate the number of hours required. A good rule of thumb is that it takes two and a half to three hours to develop one minute of e-learning for a basic course.[13] Thus, a one-hour course may take 160 hours to develop. Advanced content can take five to six hours to develop one minute of content, or over three hundred hours!

Another important consideration in e-learning is how to track participants' enrollment, progress, and completion. A **learning management system (LMS)** is a software application for the administration, documentation, tracking, reporting, and delivery of learning and development programs. Employers can also assess the skills of employees before and after training using an LMS. An LMS has two components:

- A server that performs the core functions (e.g., storing and delivering course content, authenticating users, grading assessments, issuing completing certificates, sending user notifications, etc.).

- A user interface that runs inside a browser (similar to how Blackboard or Canvas work for online courses) that is used by staff, instructors, and students.

An LMS makes it easy and efficient to create and store content, organize it into courses, deliver the content, enroll participants, and monitor and assess course progress.

asynchronous distance learning

Online learning in which participants and the instructor do not have to be all signed in at the same time.

learning management system (LMS)

A software application for the administration, documentation, tracking, reporting, and delivery of learning and development programs.

On-the-Job Training

On-the-job training (OJT) is a method by which employees learn by doing the actual job. The employee is instructed by a supervisor or an experienced employee. OJT is viewed by some to be potentially the most effective means of facilitating learning in the workplace. [14]

OJT has many advantages. The employee can immediately transfer the training to the job and can be given immediate feedback regarding job performance. The learning is less abstract than knowledge gained in a classroom because the employee can apply it right away. An effective trainer monitors the progress of the trainee, notes the areas where he or she needs to improve, and provides additional training in response. Thus, OJT is highly personalized to the needs of each trainee.

On the other hand, OJT can be an expensive method to train, since it is essentially a one-to-one approach, in contrast to one instructor training a large group of people at one time in a classroom. Another potential drawback to OJT is that when the employee makes a mistake, it can impact productivity or customer service. For example, OJT is used widely in the restaurant industry. You have probably experienced this yourself as a restaurant customer, and your waiter was a trainee. If a waiter makes a mistake on an order, then that inconveniences the customer. Another example is a cashier. If a cashier in training makes a mistake and gives too much change to a customer, that causes a loss of real dollars to the company, as opposed to hypothetical dollars if the same mistake is made in a classroom training activity. Table 7.3 summarizes the advantages and disadvantages of OJT.

TABLE 7.3 Summary of Advantages and Disadvantages of OJT

Advantages	Disadvantages
Many people learn best by actually performing a task.	If the trainee makes a mistake, it is a real problem that has to be corrected.
The trainer can give immediate feedback to the trainee.	Some trainers are better than others, so the training can be inconsistent.
Trainers are usually highly competent and experienced with the job tasks.	The training can disrupt the work environment.
The training is immediately transferable to the job.	Customers can be annoyed if their service takes longer than usual.
The training can be customized to the specific areas that the trainee needs assistance with.	If the work environment is hazardous, injuries could occur due to inexperience.

If OJT programs are implemented without significant planning, they may not achieve the desired results. An effective OJT program should follow the four-step process described here.

1. **Create the learning objectives and a task list.** This will help to standardize the OJT training so that each trainee learns the same knowledge and gains the same skillset. If this step is overlooked, then trainees may not learn critical job functions and might even put themselves, co-workers, or customers at risk. The learning objectives and task list should be reviewed with the trainee so he or she understands what is expected.

2. **The trainer demonstrates each task.** Trainees should not be thrown into doing the job until they have the opportunity to observe an experienced person conducting the tasks. This can also be a form of **job-shadowing**, in which a trainee follows a trainer and observes them for a set period of time, whether a few hours, a day, a week, or even longer.

3. **The trainee performs the task.** Next, the trainee performs each task on the job, under the supervision of the trainer.

4. **Assess, remediate, and coach.** The trainer should rate the trainee's performance on each task. This is more than just checking off the item on a task list. After rating the performance, the

trainer should provide coaching and require additional practice to remediate any performance issues.

Simulations

A **simulation** is the use of the actual equipment used in a job, along with a computer-based model, to create real-world types of environments. Some simulations that you may be aware of are flight simulators and driving simulators that are used in driver education programs (including first-time drivers and commercial truck drivers). Other types of simulations include firefighting, ship navigation, and air traffic control. Healthcare simulations use dummy models to teach CPR and other techniques. The military makes extensive use of simulations to practice various scenarios and to teach skills on specific equipment such as tanks.

simulation

The use of the actual equipment used in a job, along with a computer-based model, to create real-world types of environments.

 Firefighter Simulation Training

This video shows an example of firefighter simulation training.

View the video online at: http://www.youtube.com/embed/1WtstbO212A?rel=0

Simulations are used instead of OJT when putting a trainee in charge of equipment in an actual situation could result in harmful events such as the loss of life or equipment. For example, a driver could crash a truck in a simulator without harming anyone or causing equipment or property damage. The driver then learns from his or her mistakes without causing harm. Another benefit of a simulation is that it allows individuals to learn how to handle drastic situations that one hopes never actually occurs. For example, an airline pilot might train on a flight simulator for what happens if a bird flies into an engine or there is a sudden loss of hydraulic pressure, causing the landing gear to malfunction.

Gamification and Virtual Reality

gamification

The application of typical elements of game playing (e.g., point scoring, competition with others, rules of play) to other areas of activity such as training.

Gamification is the application of typical elements of game playing (e.g., point scoring, competition with others, rules of play) to other areas of activity such as training. Many companies have developed training programs that are built on video gaming platforms such as Spark City, described in the opening case. GameStop created the LevelUp training platform, which uses classic gaming strategies to make it compelling and engaging for employees. Trainees receive points and badges for everything they do, such as logging on and taking a quiz or finishing a learning mission. They also get bonus points for perfect scores on quizzes. As they receive points, their progress bar fills. Once it is full, they move on to the next level. They also can see where they stand on the leader board as individuals and as a store.[15]

virtual reality

The computer-generated simulation of a three-dimensional image or environment that can be interacted with in a seemingly real or physical way by a person using electronic equipment.

Virtual reality (VR) is the computer-generated simulation of a three-dimensional image or environment that can be interacted with in a seemingly real or physical way by a person using electronic equipment such as VR goggles and gloves fitted with sensors. Three-hundred-sixty-degree VR allows the user to look around them in all directions, just as they can in real life. British Petroleum (BP) uses VR to train their employees in start-up and emergency exit procedures at its refinery in Hull, England. Employees are able to learn from mistakes made in the virtual world and thus reduce the probability of making the same error in the real world. Kentucky Fried Chicken (KFC) developed a virtual employee training escape room designed to teach them how to prepare chicken properly. At United Parcel Service (UPS), student delivery drivers practice in a 360-degree VR world that includes pedestrians, parked cars, and oncoming traffic.

 UPS is Training Drivers with Virtual Reality

Before hitting the streets in 10,000 lb delivery trucks, new UPS drivers are testing out their skills in VR.

View the video online at: http://www.youtube.com/embed/tPaMIguKjvw?rel=0

Key Takeaways

- The steps in the ADDIE model are: analysis, design, development, implementation, and evaluation.
- SAM is an agile development model with multiple steps happening at the same time. The SAM process is nonlinear and iterative, allowing for evaluation and changes to the project as needed (as opposed to evaluation happening at the end of the project in the ADDIE

approach). SAM also encourages ongoing collaboration between the instructional designers and customers at every stage of the development process.

- Classroom instruction provides the opportunity for more-efficient interaction between the instructor and students.
- The primary advantage of virtual instructor-led training is that it provides immediate interaction between the instructor and student, but it saves on travel costs and time and is advantageous for companies with many employees located in many geographic areas.
- In synchronous distance learning, all participants and the instructor are signed into the training at the same time. In asynchronous distance learning, participants have the flexibility to complete the training whenever and wherever works best for them.
- In self-paced e-learning (including online courses, podcasts, mobile learning, and virtual reality), participants complete the learning experience on their own schedule.
- A learning management system (LMS) is a software application for the administration, documentation, tracking, reporting, and delivery of learning and development programs.
- On-the-job training (OJT) is a method by which employees learn by doing the actual job.
- A simulation is the use of the actual equipment used in a job, along with a computer-based model, to create real-world types of environments.

What Do *You* Think?

1. Which method of training do you prefer: classroom instruction, virtual instructor-led, or self-paced e-learning? Why do you prefer that method?
2. Think of a recent classroom instruction that you were in (either as part of a college class or corporate training). How did the classroom layout impact participation and interaction?
3. Have you ever been thrown into a job without any on-the-job training? What was the result?
4. Can you think of a situation where a simulation might have been helpful in learning a job skill for a job you have held?

7.4 Evaluating Learning Impact

Learning Objectives

1. Describe how formative evaluation is used during the development of a talent development initiative to improve quality.
2. Explain how summative evaluation is used to judge the worth of a program upon completion.
3. Identify the role of beta and pilot testing in program development.
4. Recognize the four levels of Kirkpatrick's evaluation model.
5. Discuss how the transfer of training improves talent development results.
6. Calculate the return on investment for a talent development initiative.

Evaluation is the process of examining a program or process to determine what's working, what's not, and why. The overall goal is to determine student success in learning and to create a blueprint for ongoing course improvement. But will the evaluation results be used primarily for improving how the course is taught, or for measuring the effectiveness of the course? These are both necessary and valuable uses of evaluation data, and they complement each other. We refer to these complementary approaches as formative evaluation and summative evaluation.

Formative Evaluation

Even the most conscientious course designer is not likely to develop a perfect lesson or course the first time through. **Formative evaluation** is a method for judging the worth of a program while the program activities are forming (in progress). It can be conducted during any phase of the ADDIE process. This part of the evaluation focuses on the process. Its function is to inform the instructor or design team how well the instructional program is serving the objectives as it progresses.

Formative evaluation allows the design team to discover and correct deficiencies as the course is being developed. It is primarily a building process that accumulates a series of components of new materials, skills, and problems into an ultimate meaningful whole.

Test results, reactions from learners, observations of learners, reviews by subject matter experts, and suggestions from colleagues may indicate deficiencies in the learning sequence, procedures, or material.

Kemp, Morrison, and Ross, in their book *Designing Effective Instruction*, suggest the following questions that might be used to gather data during formative evaluation:[16]

1. Given the objectives for the unit or lesson, is the level of learning acceptable? What weaknesses are noted?

2. Are learners able to use the knowledge or perform the skills at an acceptable level? Are any weaknesses indicated?

3. How much time did the instruction and learning require? Is this acceptable?

4. Did the activities seem appropriate and manageable to the instructor and learners?

5. Were the materials convenient and easy to locate, use, and file?

6. What were the learners' reactions to the methods of study, activities, materials, and evaluation methods?

7. Do the unit tests and other outcome measures satisfactorily assess the instructional objectives?

8. What revisions in the program seem necessary (content, format, etc.)?

9. Is the instructional context appropriate?

Summative Evaluation

Summative evaluation is directed toward measuring the degree to which the major outcomes are attained at the end of the course. A summative evaluation is a method of judging the worth of a program at the end of the program activities (summation). The focus is on the outcome.

The various instruments used to collect the data are questionnaires, surveys, interviews, observations, and testing. The model or methodology used to gather the data should be a specified step-by-step procedure. It should be carefully designed and executed to ensure the data is valid and reliable (see the discussion of validity and reliability in Chapter 6).

Questionnaires are the least-expensive procedure for external evaluations and can be used to collect large samples of information from completers. The questionnaires should be trialed before using to ensure the recipients understand their operation the way the designer intended.

In addition to measuring the effectiveness of participant learning, summative evaluations also frequently include:

- Efficiency of learning (material mastered/time to mastery).
- Cost of program development.

- Ongoing instructional costs.
- Participant reactions to the course.
- Long-term benefits of the course.
- Functionality of technology.
- Usefulness and appropriateness of delivery modality.

Beta and Pilot Testing

Instructional designers normally carry out several tests of their content and courses before full rollout. The most common types are **beta testing** and **pilot testing**, and they are considered part of the formative evaluation. A beta test occurs before the course content is finalized. This involves a full walk-through of the content and all of its elements. For an online course, this includes testing the navigation, branching, menus, and links to ensure that everything is functional. A beta test will often take longer than the actual training because pauses may occur for discussion or revision of the content.

A pilot differs from a beta test in that it mimics the exact parameters of the course. All course content must be finalized before a pilot test is conducted. In a beta test, some of the content might be considered tentative, pending the results of the test.

beta test

Occurs before the course content is finalized and involves a full walk-through of the content and all of its elements.

pilot test

Mimics the exact parameters of the course; all course content must be finalized before being conducted.

Kirkpatrick's Four-Level Evaluation Model

Perhaps the best-known evaluation methodology for judging learning processes is Donald **Kirkpatrick's Four-Level Evaluation Model**, which was first published in a series of articles in 1959 in the *Journal of American Society of Training Directors* (now known as *TD Magazine*). However, it was not until his 1994 book was published, *Evaluating Training Programs*, that the four levels became popular.[17] His four levels remain a cornerstone of evaluation in the learning industry today.

The four steps of evaluation consist of:

Level One: Reaction. How well did the learners like the learning process? (These are sometimes referred to as "smile sheets.")

Level Two: Learning. What knowledge and skills did they learn? (This level used to be called knowledge, but many sources use the term learning now.)

Level Three: Behavior. What changes in job performance resulted from the learning process? (This level evaluates learners' capability to perform the newly learned skills while on the job.)

Kirkpatrick's Four-Level Evaluation Model

A model for determining the effectiveness of training, developed by Donald Kirkpatrick and based upon four levels of evaluation: reaction, learning, behavior, and results.

reaction level

Refers to how well the learners liked a learning process.

learning level

Refers to the knowledge and skills that were learned in a learning process.

behavior level

Refers to the changes in job performance resulting from a learning process.

254	Mastering Human Resource Management

results level

Refers to the tangible results of a learning process in terms of reduced cost, improved quality, increased production, efficiency, etc.

Level Four: Results. What are the tangible results of the learning process in terms of reduced cost, improved quality, increased production, efficiency, etc.?

Survey tools such as SurveyMonkey are making data collection easier for levels one and two. Levels three and four have traditionally been more challenging to assess. However, artificial intelligence and machine learning are now being used to analyze courses completed, along with data on the career progression to make recommendations for further training.[18]

Transfer of Training

transfer of training

Means that learners can transfer the knowledge and skills gained in a training session to their jobs.

We can design an effective and engaging training experience, but if the effects wear off within a short period after the training event is over, then it was of little long-term value. **Transfer of training** means that learners can transfer the knowledge and skills gained in a training session to their jobs. This concept refers to the trainees' ability to continually apply what they learned in training, resulting in positive performance outcomes, and is often referred to in the industry as "making training stick." Learned skills and behaviors cannot yield long-term results until they become a habit, and this occurs through use, encouragement, and measurable progress.[19]

In 2017, *Training Magazine* estimated that U.S. organizations spent about $161.5 billion on training each year, and globally the expenditure is $362.3 billion.[20] Also, recall that the chapter introduction stated that organizations in the United States spend an average of $1,299 per employee on employee learning, and employees spend an average of over thirty-four hours per year on formal learning programs.[21] Yet, research indicates that even some of the most successful training programs fail to transfer knowledge and new skills to learners.[22] Many talent development professionals believe that only 10% to 20% of training is actually transferred to the work environment in the long term.[23]

Given the significant expenditure that organizations are making in talent development, and the fact that only 10% to 20% of this investment results in improved workplace behaviors and performance, transfer of training is one of the most important aspects of any program design. There are three theories for how the transfer of training occurs: the theory of identical elements, stimulus generalization, and the cognitive theory of transfer.[24] Each theory is based on a different approach to learning.

Theory of Identical Elements

The **theory of identical elements** proposes that transfer occurs when what is being learned in the training session is identical to what the trainee has to perform on the job. According to this theory, transfer will more likely occur when the tasks, materials, and equipment are similar to those used in the actual work environment. The transfer is more challenging when the learning material is similar, but not identical to the work environment. Therefore, a distinction is made between **near transfer** and **far transfer**. Near transfer refers to the trainee's ability to apply new knowledge and skills directly to a specific work situation. Far transfer refers to the trainee's ability to adapt new knowledge and skills to work situations that are dissimilar from the training environment.[25]

The degree of flexibility and autonomy in the skills and variability that the learner needs for successful performance is important to consider in determining the extent to which the learning environment and conditions should match the job.[26] When programs need to be designed with near transfer in mind, they should follow standardized procedures, processes, and checklists that are used in the actual position.[27]

A distinction is also made between open and closed skills. **Closed skills** refer to training objectives that are linked to specific skills that the learner is expected to produce identically on the job. **Open skills** are linked to more general learning principles and are more challenging for training transfer because they require the trainee to not only acquire specific skills but also to adapt them to a wider range of circumstances.

The identical elements approach has also been used to develop instruments that are designed to measure the similarity of jobs.[28] Measure of job similarity can be used to determine the extent to which the training (and subsequent knowledge, skills, and abilities acquired) for one job prepares the individual to perform well in a different job.

Stimulus Generalization

The **stimulus generalization approach** emphasizes general learning principles that can be adapted to a wide variety of work situations. It is appropriate when the work situation cannot be replicated identically, and thus the theory is focused on far transfer. Based on social learning theory, this approach utilizes modeling, practice, feedback, and reinforcement.

Cognitive Theory of Transfer

The **cognitive theory of transfer** proposes that successful training transfer occurs when the learner can retrieve and apply relevant prior learning. This approach is based on the information processing theory of learning. A major advantage of the theory is its high level of applicability to all types of training programs.

This theory also places importance on providing the learner with cognitive strategies for coding and retrieving information, such as mental models and mnemonics. Thus, the instructional designer should create training that includes materials that will trigger prior learning and experience and help the learner to associate the new knowledge and skills with what has been learned previously and to see how the new learning integrates and builds upon prior learning.

A popular method for the use of cognitive approach in training programs is action learning. This method requires trainees to identify a real work problem or situation and use the learning experience to design an action to solve the problem.

theory of identical elements
Proposes that transfer occurs when what is being learned in the training session is identical to what the trainee has to perform on the job.

near transfer
Refers to the trainee's ability to apply new knowledge and skills directly to a specific work situation.

far transfer
Refers to the trainee's ability to adapt new knowledge and skills to work situations that are dissimilar from the training environment.

closed skills
Refers to training objectives that are linked to specific skills that the learner is expected to produce identically on the job.

open skills
Are linked to more general learning principles, and are more challenging for training transfer because they require the trainee to not only acquire specific skills but also to adapt them to a wider range of circumstances.

stimulus generalization approach
Emphasizes general learning principles that can be adapted to a wide variety of work situations.

cognitive theory of transfer
Proposes that successful training transfer occurs when the learner can retrieve and apply relevant prior learning.

Transfer of Training Matrix

Mary Broad and John Newstrom researched how transfer occurs, and developed the Transfer of Training Matrix.[29] In their book, *Transfer of Training*, they show why the full transfer of learned skills to the workplace is critical for an organization's growth and survival. They break down the time periods (before, during, and after training) when learning transfer can be influenced. They also identify the three main roles, which are manager, participant, and trainer. They then combine the time dimensions with the roles to produce a 3x3 transfer matrix of nine cells, shown in Table 7.4.

TABLE 7.4 Transfer of Training Matrix

	Before	During	After
Manager	1	8	3
Participant	6	5	7
Trainer	2	4	9

The numbers 1–9 represent the importance of each role in achieving transfer of training, with 1 being the most important. Note that two of the top three combinations involve the manager (manager before and manager after). This reveals how important the learner's manager is to ensuring that the training transfers to improved job skills and behaviors. Note also that the second-most important role is that of the trainer before the learning event. Manager support is one of the key determining factors for the transfer of training.[30] Research indicates that feedback from managers after a training program is directly related to the degree that the skills taught are transferred to the job.[31]

The main goal for instructional designers should be to foster the trainees' motivation to use new skills on the job.[32] Research also indicates that peer support is significantly influential on transfer of training.[33] Peer collaboration, networking, and the sharing of ideas relating to the content can act as support for skill transfer in trainees.[34] Some aspects of the organization culture can also influence transfer. Whether the organization values learning can have a direct impact on employee performance.[35] Although it is the supervisor who is generally thought of as a coach to help recently trained employees transfer skills to their job, experienced peers can also take on this role.[36]

Return on Investment

We defined return on investment (ROI) earlier in this chapter. While the talent development professional may be concerned primarily with the quality and effectiveness of training and development efforts, managers outside of HR are primarily concerned with the bottom line. When presented with a request to fund a training program, there are primarily two questions that they want answers to: How much will it cost, and what are the financial benefits? ROI calculations are important because they provide the answer to both of these questions. ROI can also be very beneficial for talent development staff because it forces them to identify the impact of training in terms of results. It also can be used to enhance employee engagement and lessen resistance to the training by explaining the bottom-line impact of the training to the participants before the program begins.

Don't think of ROI as just something that is done after a training or development program is completed. Ideally, ROI should be estimated before the training is begun, and it can play a major role in whether the expenditure is approved. Then ROI should be tracked during and after completion of the training, and comparisons of the actual results to the estimates should then be made. If the results are lower than anticipated, then the reasons should be identified, and the training modified as necessary.

ROI is calculated using the following formula and is expressed in terms of a percentage:

$$(MB - TC)/TC \times 100$$

MB represents monetary benefit and TC represents total costs. For example, if a training program for sales representatives is estimated to generate additional sales of $75,000 annually, and the total cost of the program is $21,000, then the ROI would be:

$$(75,000 - 21,000)/21,000 \times 100 = 257\% \text{ ROI}$$

In this example, the ROI is 257%. Another way of stating this is that for every $1 invested in the training, the company receives a benefit of $2.57. The following "Example 1" and "Example 2" show several additional examples of ROI calculations.

Example 1

A manufacturing company implemented quality control training for 75 line employees which results in an annual reduction in scrap costs of $85,000, due to fewer units not meeting quality standards. The cost of the training was:

- Instructor: $15,000
- Materials: $125 per trainee
- Trainee Time: Salaries and benefits of $18 per hour for 75 employees participating in 8 hours of training

What is the ROI of training?

Solution:

The total monetary benefit of the training is:

- Annual reduction in scrap costs of $85,000.

The total cost of training is:

$$\text{Instructor: } \$15,000$$
$$+ \text{ Materials: } \$9,375$$
$$+ \text{ Trainee Time: } \$10,800$$
$$= \$35,175$$

The ROI calculation is:

$$(85,000 - 35,175)/35,175 \times 100 = 142\% \text{ ROI}$$

Example 2

A financial services company with 160 employees implemented supervisory training for 15 supervisors, with the intention of lowering employee turnover. The average employee earnings was $48,000, and the cost of employee turnover was calculated to be 50% of the employee's annual salary. Before the training, the annual turnover was 12 employees. After the training, the turnover was 4 employees. The training was delivered online. The cost of the training was:

- Online Facilitator: $4,500
- Course Management System (CMS): $200 per trainee
- Curriculum Development: $12,000
- Trainee Time: Salaries and benefits of $40 per hour for 15 supervisors participating in 24 hours of training

What is the ROI of training?

Solution:

The total monetary benefit of the training is:

- Reduction of turnover by 8 employees, valued at $24,000 per employee = $192,000.

The total cost of training is:

$$\text{Facilitator: } \$4,500$$
$$+ \text{ CMS: } \$2,400$$
$$+ \text{ Curriculum Development: } \$12,000$$
$$+ \text{ Trainee Time: } \$14,400$$
$$= \$33,300$$

The ROI calculation is:

$$(192,000 - 33,300)/33,300 = 476.5\% \text{ ROI}$$

Identification of the training cost is usually fairly straightforward. The costs might include:

- Curriculum design and development.
- Salary of the instructor or fee if outsourced.
- Training materials.
- Travel expenses for instructor and participants when applicable.
- LMS cost for e-learning.
- Room rental.
- Refreshments and/or meals.

For most people, the more difficult aspect of an ROI calculation is in identifying the monetary benefit. Training programs often have learning objectives that are intangible and hard to quantify. Nevertheless, it is important to put forth the effort to monetize the benefits. Examples of monetary benefits are:

- Increased revenue generated.
- Increased productivity.
- Decreased cost of production or operations.
- Increased quality.
- Lower employee turnover.
- Fewer workplace accidents.
- Decreased likelihood of discrimination complaints/lawsuits.

Sometimes it is possible to come up with an indirect way to calculate ROI. For example, a customer service program might be expected to increase customer satisfaction by a specified percentage. How do you monetize this? The marketing department probably already knows the value of a customer in terms of annual revenue, the cost of attracting a new customer, and the cost of customer attrition. So in this case, increased customer satisfaction might be correlated to one of these other customer value calculations to come up with a monetary benefit for the ROI calculation. Another example is team building. How do you assign a monetary benefit to a team-building event? HR may already know the cost of employee turnover and absenteeism or the cost of mediating employee disputes. Since a team-building event leads to a more cohesive team and more engaged employees, it could be correlated to one of these other costs to estimate the ROI.

Key Takeaways

- Evaluation is the process of examining a program or process to determine what's working, what's not, and why.

- Formative evaluation is a method for judging the worth of a program while the program activities are forming (in progress).

- Summative evaluation is directed toward measuring the degree to which the major outcomes are attained at the end of the course.

- A beta test occurs before the course content is finalized. This involves a full walk-through of the content and all of its elements.

- A pilot differs from a beta test in that it mimics the exact parameters of the course. All course content must be finalized before a pilot test is conducted.

- The four steps of Kirkpatrick's evaluation model are reaction, learning, behavior, and results.

- Transfer of training means that learners can transfer the knowledge and skills gained in a training session to their jobs.

- The theory of identical elements proposes that transfer occurs when what is being learned in the training session is identical to what the trainee has to perform on the job.

- Near transfer refers to the trainee's ability to apply new knowledge and skills directly to a specific work situation. Far transfer refers to the trainee's ability to adapt new knowledge and skills to work situations that are dissimilar from the training environment.

- Closed skills refer to training objectives that are linked to specific skills that the learner is expected to produce identically on the job. Open skills are linked to more general learning principles and are more challenging for training transfer because they require the trainee to not only acquire specific skills but also to adapt them to a wider range of circumstances.

- The stimulus generalization approach emphasizes general learning principles that can be adapted to a wide variety of work situations.

- The cognitive theory of transfer proposes that successful training transfer occurs when the learner can retrieve and apply relevant prior learning.

- Return on investment (ROI) is a performance measure used to express the financial return from an investment made in learning and development.

What Do *You* Think?

1. Think of a class or a corporate training session that you took more than a year ago. How much of the content can you recall? How much of it do you use?

2. Give an example of a training class that is designed based upon the theory of identical elements.

3. Have you ever asked a manager to send you some type of training? What steps did the manager take before and after the training to help ensure transfer of training? What would you do differently if you were the manager?

4. How would you increase peer support in a training program to positively affect transfer of training?

7.5 Employee Development

Career Development

Talent development professionals can help employees to identify career goals and the steps they can take to achieve those goals.

Source: © Shutterstock, Inc.

employee development

Refers to learning and development experiences designed to prepare employees for different and expanded roles in the organization.

Throughout this chapter, we have been exploring various methods for training employees. What is the difference between training and development? When we use the word training, we are referring to the learning methods to ensure that employees have the knowledge, skills, and abilities to perform their current job well. We now turn our attention to **employee development**, which refers to learning and development experiences designed to prepare employees for different and expanded roles in the organization. Put more simply, training deals with the present, whereas development is future-oriented.

First, let's define what we mean by a **career**. A career is an occupation undertaken for a significant period of a person's life, and usually has opportunities for progress. In contrast, a job is any task undertaken for payment. But we should recognize that what we mean by the word job or career is rapidly changing. In the twentieth century, when someone thought about a job or career, they usually had in mind a model that looks something like this: get a high school diploma, then a college degree or vocational training, land your first job, and continue working in that particular field, being promoted along the way as you gain experience until you eventually retire. However, in the twenty-first century, a different notion of what it means to have a job and a career has emerged. Today, the average person changes jobs an average of twelve times during his or her life.[37] In January 2018, the Bureau of Labor Statistics reported the median employee tenure is 4.3 years for men and 4 years for women, noting that the median tenure increases with age (2.8 years for the twenty-five to thirty-four age group, 4.9 years for the thirty-five to forty-four age group, 7.6 years for the forty-five to fifty-four age group, and 10.1 years for the fifty-five to sixty-four group).[38] Thus, it is crucial that companies think about the changing nature of work when conducting job analysis and writing job descriptions. Several specific trends should be considered:

Shorter Shelf-Life of Expertise

Skillsets quickly become obsolete, and continuous learning and development are no longer optional for most jobs. The **half-life of knowledge** was introduced in Chapter 4. This amount of time is rapidly becoming shorter in almost every field, or as Samuel Arbesman puts it, "Everything we know has an expiration date."[39] As skillsets and jobs change, the essential job functions on a job description quickly become out of date. For this reason, it is advisable to update job descriptions on a regular basis. Since job postings typically pull the job duties and functions from the existing job description, this means that many job postings are also obsolete. As a result, companies fail to attract top talent, and skills gaps are exacerbated.[40] Another strategy to offset this problem is to describe job specifications in terms of competencies rather than skills, since competencies are transferable to changing job needs.

Technological Advances

Fears that robots will take jobs away from people have been a popular discussion topic lately, but the 2019 World Development Report, *The Changing Nature of Work*, finds that this appears to be unfounded.[41] The number of jobs is not being reduced by automation, but employees are required to utilize more technology in their work. Nowhere is this more evident than with the demand for data analysts, a field which Burning Glass calls a "new genome" for jobs.[42] Continuous connectivity through mobile devices is also changing how work is done, as the line between work and personal life has become blurred. In a world where we are "always on," employees may feel that they are expected to respond to emails around the clock. This can lead to increased stress and burnout and reduce employee engagement.

Growing Importance of Soft Skills

Skills such as math and engineering are susceptible to be being automated by technology. But a computer cannot show empathy, display emotional intelligence, or interact using social skills. This demonstrates part of the reason for the recent trend from STEM (science, technology, engineering, math) to STEAM (STEM plus the arts). Employers are increasingly seeking individuals with complex problem-solving abilities, research skills, writing skills, along with the ability to work with teams, and with adaptability.[43]

career

An occupation undertaken for a significant period of a person's life; usually has opportunities for progress.

half-life of knowledge

The amount of time that has to elapse before half of the knowledge or facts in a particular field becomes obsolete.

career plateau

Occurs when an employee reaches the point in his or her career where there are no further advancement opportunities.

Career development can be considered in terms of where an individual is in the employee life cycle (ELC). New employees begin with onboarding, which is explored further in Chapter 11. Once a person has established competency in their position, then they may be preparing for an advancement up the career ladder. Career development can help to motivate employees that might be experiencing a **career plateau**. This occurs when an employee reaches the point in his or her career where there are no further advancement opportunities. This could be because they have been promoted into the most senior level in their profession, but it also could happen to employees at lower levels, when advancement is difficult for a variety of reasons.

For example, an HR specialist might be ready to advance into a director of HR position, but that position is currently occupied by someone who may be many years away from retirement. The HR specialist might be considering moving to a different company instead of remaining in the same company for many years and possibly becoming stagnant. In this situation, career development could help provide a way for the HR specialist to find new challenges through a lateral move into a different specialist position, or by providing the opportunity to learn new skills for a special project.

Assessment

Assessments can be used to identify work skills an employee might develop to become more effective and prepare to assume new responsibilities. The most common types of assessments are psychological, social/communication style, emotional intelligence, strengths-based, and performance appraisals. We will explore performance appraisals in detail in Chapter 8, so let's review the other four categories now:

- **Psychological.** Assessments in this category focus on personality types and how individuals act, react, communicate, make decisions, and solve problems. Some of the most popular psychological assessments are the Myers-Briggs Type Indicator® (MBTI®) and the Birkman Method. The MBTI® is a personality inventory; the essence of the theory is that much seemingly random behavior is quite orderly and consistent, being due to basic differences in the ways individuals prefer to use their perception and judgment and whether they are introverts or extroverts.[44] The Birkman Method is a suite of self-assessment tools designed to interpret and apply data that can be used for team building, talent development, hiring and selection, executive coaching, high potential and leadership development, stress management, career exploration, conflict resolution, and motivation/feedback.[45]

- **Social/communication style.** Assessments in this category focus on how individuals socialize or communicate with others. Popular assessments in this category are those that use the DISC method. This is an assessment that identifies a person's behavior in terms of four approaches: dominance, influence, steadiness, and conscientiousness. Some trainers and coaches prefer to use social style assessments rather than personality assessments. People may tend to be defensive if you suggest that there is something about their personality that is ineffective in the workplace. It sounds as if you are saying they need to change their personality, and that there is something wrong with them as a person. However, people can learn to adapt their behavior, such as the way they communicate with others, and this can make them more effective in negotiations, conflict resolution, sales, and many other instances in which socialization and communication are involved at work. Extended DISC® reveals not only a person's DISC style but their natural style and their adapted style. The natural style is how a person naturally communicates, and the adapted style reflects how they are adapting their natural style within their current work setting. Extended DISC® assessments are used in leadership development, sales training, team building, communication skills training, customer service training, executive coaching, career development, stress and time management, and self-awareness development.[46] Figure 7.6 shows an example of an Extended DISC® assessment.

FIGURE 7.6 Extended DISC

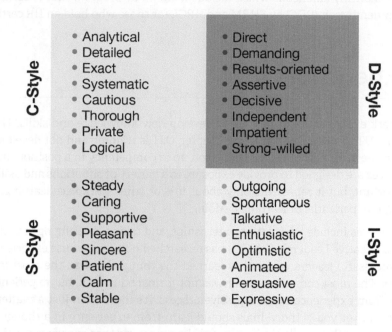

- Emotional intelligence. This is a recent type of assessment that was popularized by Daniel Goleman in his 1995 book *Emotional Intelligence*.[47] **Emotional intelligence** is the capacity to be aware of, control, and express one's emotions, and to handle interpersonal relationships judiciously and empathetically. Emotional intelligence assessments yield an Emotional Quotient (EQ). There are four domains of emotional intelligence: self-awareness, self-management, social awareness, and relationship management. The Mayer-Salovey-Caruso Emotional Intelligence Test (MSCEIT) is one of the more popular assessments of emotional intelligence. Some researchers question the validity and reliability of these types of assessments. However, there is some evidence in the business arena that high levels of emotional intelligence provide employees with a greater chance of success as they move up in the organization.[48] You can probably think of people who are brilliant but have not had much success because they lack people skills. And, vice versa: you can probably think of people who are very successful but are not considered highly intelligent in the traditional IQ sense. They are successful because they understand how to relate to people. That's emotional intelligence. As President George W. Bush once said in a commencement address: *"To those of you who received honors, awards, and distinctions, I say well done. And to the C students, I say you, too, can be president of the United States."*[49]

- Strengths-based. The strengths-based approach focuses on the talents of a person, rather than the weaknesses. The approach has been used in coaching, education, social work, pediatrics, and other areas. Research also indicates that strength-based coaching may be effective in leadership development.[50] The HR Talk with Brent O'Bannon explains how this approach is used by professional coaches to help their clients improve performance.

emotional intelligence

The capacity to be aware of, control, and express one's emotions and to handle interpersonal relationships judiciously and empathetically.

Formal Education

Formal education includes any type of organized program designed to improve knowledge and skills. While college certificates and degrees are included in this category, it is much broader and includes short courses and seminars that are offered by colleges, private training companies such as SkillPath and CareerTrack, and professional associations. For example, most SHRM affiliate chapters offer monthly luncheons which include a one-hour program that is certified for professional development credit (PDC) by SHRM and HRCI, for those who hold an HR certification.

Job Experience

On-the-job work experiences can be used to develop new knowledge and skills. This is not to be confused with OJT, discussed earlier in the chapter. OJT is training and not development because the focus is on the skills needed to bring a person up to competency in a position. In development, work experiences are designed to provide exposure to a variety of situations and skills. Formal education is important, but it represents only about 10% of adult workplace learning. About 70% of adult learning is experiential or learning by doing.[51]

Job experiences include job rotation, internships, and taking challenging stretch assignments. The Center for Creative Leadership® (CCL®) has researched how leaders use experiences to develop. They asked successful leaders where they learned the things that had the most impact on their future success. The most common answer was not formal education, but experiences. CCL notes that learning from experience is not a passive process. It's more than just a matter of letting life experience wash over you.[52] Individuals should learn from experience in a thoughtful, reflective, and strategic manner. You no doubt have heard the old saying that experience is the best teacher. The suggestion here is to take a different perspective on the old saying and replace that with another version: *Properly evaluated* experience is the best teacher. One role of HR is to ensure that job experiences involve reflection and evaluation by the participant.

Mentoring and Coaching

mentoring

A professional relationship in which an experienced colleague (the mentor) assists another (the mentee) in developing skills and knowledge. Mentoring is done by a business colleague with more experience than the mentee.

coaching

Conducted by a professional coach who offers advice on issues such as time management, effectiveness, communication skills, organizational politics, and many other areas.

Two powerful employee development methods are related to interpersonal relationships in the workplace. These methods are mentoring and coaching. **Mentoring** is a professional relationship in which an experienced colleague (the mentor) assists another (the mentee) in developing skills and knowledge. The colleague may be someone within the same organization, but might also be external. **Coaching** is normally conducted by a professional coach, who offers advice on issues such as time management, effectiveness, communication skills, organizational politics, and many other areas.

HR Talk: Brent O'Bannon

CEO/Principal

Strengths Finder Coaching

Professional coaching is about helping people to be more successful. The purpose of coaching should never be considered as remediation, therapy, or identifying what someone is doing wrong. Rather, it is about finding, maximizing, mobilizing, and monetizing talent.

The most effective approach to coaching, based on my experience and reinforced by empirical research, is strengths-based. It is important for my coaching clients to understand that I am not the expert that is going to come on the scene and tell them how to do their jobs better. They are the expert on themselves, their job, and their industry. My role is to provide expertise in a process of appreciative inquiry to help them improve their performance.

I begin the coaching process with a research-based assessment of client strengths. The assessment that I use the most often is CliftonStrengths®. This assessment by Gallup measures thirty-four specific areas of talent. The process identifies an individual's most- and least-natural categories of talents, which are recurring and consistent patterns of thought, feeling, or behavior. I then engage the client in coaching sessions (usually virtual) to help the client identify their strengths or talents, to spot patterns of previous success, and then apply that knowledge to their current challenges and goals. I tell my clients that we are going to focus on what they're strong at, not what they're wrong at.

Formal mentoring programs can reduce turnover, enhance recruitment, and improve performance, especially for women and people of color.[53] Effective mentoring programs do the following:

- Match mentors and mentees based on skills and development needs.
- Outline and track goals.
- Designate minimum time commitments.
- Monitor the mentoring relationship.
- Hold both parties accountable.
- Link mentoring to talent management and business strategy goals.[54]

HR Talk: Mark Hacker

Leadership Development Advisor and Senior Faculty
Human Capital Institute

Employee development is a shared responsibility between HR, managers, and employees. For example, if HR creates a generic leadership development program and requires all supervisors to go through the program, then it becomes something that HR does "to the employee" instead of "with the employee."

Organizations should begin by building a profile of what a successful manager looks like in their organization. This establishes a baseline for individual employee assessment. We recommend they then use The Birkman Method and PDI Profiler to assess employees and identify gaps that can be addressed through employee development. We suggest these assessment tools as opposed to personality-based assessments because we find them to be more valid and better predictors of which development initiatives will lead to better management effectiveness.

At the Human Capital Institute, we use analytics to establish a baseline for individuals in three areas of focus, which we refer to as the "Three Es": Experience, exposure, and education. In working with our clients, some of the most effective development programs have been mentoring/coaching and stretch assignments. Without stretch assignments, twenty years of experience might be the same experience repeated twenty times.

Key Takeaways

- Employee development refers to learning and development experiences designed to prepare employees for different and expanded roles in the organization.
- Assessments can be used to identify work skills an employee might develop to become more effective and prepare to assume new responsibilities. The most common types of assessments are psychological, social/communication style, emotional intelligence, strength-based, and performance appraisals.
- Formal education includes any type of organized program designed to improve knowledge and skills and includes college certificates and degrees, and short courses and seminars that are offered by colleges, private training companies, and professional associations.

- On-the-job work experiences can be used to develop new knowledge and skills and include job rotation, internships, and taking challenging stretch assignments.
- Mentoring normally is done by a business colleague with more experience than the mentee. Coaching is normally conducted by a professional coach, who offers advice on issues such as time management, effectiveness, communication skills, organizational politics, and many other areas.

What Do *You* Think?

1. How do you plan to replace job knowledge that becomes obsolete after you graduate?
2. Have you ever taken a personality assessment? How did you feel about the results?
3. What types of job experiences could you plan in the immediate future?
4. Can you think of a few individuals who would make good mentors for you? (Be realistic; try to think of people who could actually mentor you. The answer is probably not Bill Gates).

7.6 Conclusion

This chapter began with a discussion of the importance of needs assessment and various methods for identifying training and development needs. Traditional and e-learning approaches to training were explored as well as the evaluation of training initiatives. The chapter closed with a review of employee development methods, including a few specific applications such as assessment, job experiences, and coaching.

Theory-into-Practice (TIP) Exercises

1. Calculate the return-on-investment for this scenario. A large automobile dealership decides to provide a one-day onsite training for its sales associates to help them be effective in explaining the features and benefits of extended warranties. The dealership sells 3,500 automobiles a year. Before the training, only 25% of customers purchased an extended warranty. After the training, 30% of customers are purchasing the extended warranty. Extended warranties sell for $200. The costs of the training are:

   - Trainer: $2,500
   - Travel expenses for trainer: $1,200
   - Curriculum: $500
   - Refreshments and lunch: $350

2. A national retail pet supply store has three hundred stores. In addition to pet supplies, they also provide dog grooming services. For each of the training situations below, identify the most appropriate training method: Classroom instruction, job rotation, role-play , OJT, e-learning.

   _____ A retail store manager needs the associates to be able to do each others' jobs when they take vacations.

   _____ A customer service manager has asked HR for training to become more effective in coaching.

   _____ The vice-president for sales wants all three hundred store managers trained on new cybersecurity procedures for the online sales portal.

_____ Newly hired grooming staff need to be trained in the proper methods for washing and grooming dogs.

_____ Each store must have a half-day of training once a year for all of the store employees to update them on new types of animal foods, including ingredients, health benefits, etc. The corporate office has a trainer who visits each store once a year to conduct the training.

3. Using the links under the Resources section, download a group activity (icebreaker, trust-building, etc.) and try it with your class. Then conduct a summative evaluation by asking the class what worked well and what could be improved.

Case Study: Maybe Your Ducks Should Not All Be in a Row

Source: © Shutterstock, Inc.

Steelcase is a furniture company out of Grand Rapids, Michigan, that was founded in 1912. They were originally named Metal Office Furniture Co., and their first patent was for a metal wastebasket. In 1915 their product line increased to safe deposit vault equipment, lockers, strong boxes, steel shelving, and finally desks. By 1951, Steelcase Foundation was created, and throughout the years they adjusted and modified their equipment to be attainable for all customers. Steelcase now focuses on making furniture suitable for any learning experience and training site so that the trainees can get the most out of learning. They focus on innovation and push limits to help transform schools and offices into effective learning sites. They helped refurbish the Grand Valley State University library to make it relevant for the twenty-first-century learning centers. They have twenty-nine different types of seating within the library, along with a variety of different workspaces for students to use to work on individual or group assignments.

They lead the furniture market in creating great experiences with architecture, furniture, and technology within their products. Steelcase focuses on being environmentally sustainable as well as economical in the changes they have made within the company. Their research shows that, on average, only 54% of office space is used throughout the day and over 37% of employees are not engaged at work, which is why Steelcase designed a way for people to work in different settings.

In their headquarters building in Michigan, they have several different types of areas to allow for different interactions of employees. There are spaces for people to work alone in private individual rooms, in group areas, or in open individual areas.

When considering a site design, Steelcase focuses on noise, color, room structure, lighting, furniture, outlets, acoustics, and technology. They conducted a survey on classroom designs for active learning by both students and instructors. Steelcase Education researchers wanted to understand more about how to create engagement from students and teachers within the classroom, so they developed a survey called the Active Learning Post Occupancy Evaluation (AL-POE) tool. This was a way to measure the impact of learning based on the training site's effectiveness. The design and layout of a room can make or break the learning and transfer of training.

The AL-POE showed that classrooms intentionally designed to support active learning increase student engagement on multiple measures as compared to a traditional classroom setting. Class-rooms at four U.S. universities were designed with Steelcase furniture to test the active learning setting. The research was designed to analyze student engagement by asking participants to compare their experiences in a traditional classroom ("pre/old") setting with row-by-row seating with a classroom designed for active learning ("post/new") where physical space supports a focus on engaging experiences for students and faculty. They asked questions six to eight weeks into the evaluation about "pre/old" and "post/new" settings for each aspect of the room design and the practices and solutions that were conducted in it. Students and faculty both saw improve-ments in the engagement of students and the amount of information that was retained, versus a traditional classroom layout where all the students are seated in rows.

Many companies strive to have a strong and effective training program and site to facilitate effec-tive learning for their employees. With the AL-POE, other companies are now able to learn from them and collaborate with them to create the most engaging learning site they can. Steelcase now has furnished several universities across the country and is leading in the furniture industry. With their new way of providing spaces that improve students' engagement and concentration, learning is improving on college campuses and in corporate training environments.[55]

 ### Collaborative Spaces: Design Story

Hear the design thinking behind the development of c:scape and media:scape, part of a new services of collaborative space solutions by Steelcase, designed to create landscapes that help people connect and collaborate.

View the video online at: http://www.youtube.com/embed/sU-jrv3UXi0?rel=0

Case Discussion Questions

1. Why do you think changing the layout or furniture in a room can increase learner engagement?

2. What are other ways the company could have evaluated to see if changing the room setting was helping the learners to engage and learn more?

3. Do you think all educational institutions/companies should change from traditional training sites to advanced learning rooms? Why or why not?

4. What are the advantages and disadvantages of conducting only a post-test evaluation?

Resources

1. **Facilitator's Tool Box.** A collection of five facilitator toolboxes, including online portals and libraries of workshop activities, group facilitation techniques, icebreakers, trust-building exercises, brainstorming techniques, and more.

   https://www.sessionlab.com/blog/facilitation-technique-toolkits/

2. **Trainer Resources.** Over seventy resources for trainers, including professional associations, conferences, publications, blogs, forums, podcasts, and apps.

   https://elearningindustry.com/training-resources-for-modern-trainers-2018-beyond-70-counting

3. **The Training and Development World.** Free resources for trainers, facilitators, and organizational development practitioners, including articles, FAQs, training activities, and icebreakers.

   http://thetrainingworld.com/

4. **Library of Professional Coaching (LPC).** Free access to curated resources associated with the field of professional coaching. Includes research, case studies, tools, and applications.

   https://libraryofprofessionalcoaching.com/about-us/

Endnotes

1. Schneider, P. (2014). Workforce: The location factor companies must get right. *Area Development*, (Q4). Retrieved from https://www.areadevelopment.com/laborEducation/Q4-2014/creating-sustainable-flexible-evolving-workforce-29928745.shtml

2. ATD Research. (2019). *2019 State of the industry: Talent development benchmarks and trends.* Retrieved from https://www.td.org/research-reports/2019-state-of-the-industry

3. Case written by Crews, P. (2020). Adapted from Hroncich, C. (2019). Walmart bets on simulation video game for employee training. *EBN*. Retrieved from https://www.benefitnews.com/news/walmart-bets-on-simulation-video-game-for-employee-training

4. Percival, J.C., Cozzarin, B.P., & Formaneck, S.D. (2013). Return on investment for workplace training: the Canadian experience. *International Journal of Training & Development*, 17(1), 20–32. https://doi-org.ezp.twu.edu/10.1111/ijtd.12002

5. Ibid.

6. Cox, C., & Beier, B. (2014). Too old to train or reprimand: The role of intergroup attribution bias in evaluating older workers. *Journal of Business and Psychology*, 29(1), 61-70.

7. Rosenberg, S., Heimler, R., & Morote, E. (2012). Basic employability skills: A triangular design approach. *Education Training*, 54(1), 7-20.

8. Bandura, A. (1997). *Self-efficacy: The exercise of control.* New York: W. H. Freeman.

9. Allen, M. (2012). *Leaving ADDIE for SAM: An agile model for developing the best learning experiences.* Alexandria, Va.: The American Society for Training & Development.

10. Ibid.

11. Association for Talent Development (2017). *2017 State of the Industry Report.* Alexandria, Va.

12. Ibid.

13. Ferriman, J. (2015). estimating e-learning development time. Retrieved from https://www.learndash.com/estimating-elearning-development-time/

14. Salas, E., & Cannon-Bowers, J.A. (2001). The science of training: A decade of progress. *Annual Review of Psychology*, 52(1), 471. https://doi-org.ezp.twu.edu/10.1146/annurev.psych.52.1.471

15. Gale, S.F. (2016). GameStop takes training to the next level. *Chief Learning Officer*. Retrieved from https://www.chieflearningofficer.com/2016/04/11/gamestop-takes-training-to-the-next-level/

16. Kemp, J., Morrison, G.R., & Ross, S.M. (1998). *Designing effective instruction* (2nd ed.). Upper Saddle River, N.J.: Merrill.

17. Kirkpatrick, D.L. (1994). *Evaluating training programs: The four levels.* San Francisco, Calif.: Berrett-Koehler.

18. Vance, D. (2020). Measure, analytics, and reporting. *Chief Learning Officer*, 19(3), 40-65.

19. Wurth, A., & Wurth, K. (2018). *Training reinforcement: The 7 principles to create behavior change and make learning stick.* Hoboken, N.J.: Wiley.

20. Freifeld, L. (2012). Transfer of training: moving beyond the barriers. *Training Magazine*, https://trainingmag.com/content/transfer-training-moving-beyond-barriers/

21. ATD Research. (2019). *2019 State of the industry: Talent development benchmarks and trends.* Retrieved from https://www.td.org/research-reports/2019-state-of-the-industry

22. Change, E., & Hampson, I. (2008). Transfer and training: A review and new insights. *International Journal of Management Reviews*, 10(4), 327-341.

23. Freifeld, L. (2012). Transfer of training: moving beyond the barriers. *Training Magazine*, https://trainingmag.com/content/transfer-training-moving-beyond-barriers/

24. Royer, J.M. (1979). Theories of the transfer of learning. *Educational Psychologist, 14*, 53-69.

25. Thorndike, E.L, & Woodworth, R.S. (1901). The influence of improvement of one mental function upon the efficiency of other functions. *Psychological Review 8*(4), 384-395.

26. Yelon, S.L., & Ford, J.K. (1999). Pursuing a multidimensional view of transfer. *Performance Improvement Quarterly, 12*, 58-78.

27. Kim, J., & Lee, C. (2001). Implications of near and far transfer of training on structured on-the-job training. *Advances in Developing Human Resources, 3*(4), 442-451.

28. Sparrow, J.A. (1989). The measurement of job profile similarity for the prediction of transfer or learning. *Journal of Occupational Psychology, 62*(4), 337-341.

29. Broad, M.L., & Newstrom, J.W. (1992). *Transfer of training: Action-packed strategies to high payoff from training investment*. New York: Perseus Publishing.

30. Cromwell, J., & Kolb J. (2004). An examination of work environment support factors affecting the transfer of supervisory skills to the workplace. *Human Resource Development Quarterly, 15*(4), 449-471.

31. Diamantidis, A.D., & Chatzoglou, P.D. (2014). Employee post-training behavior and performance: Evaluating the results of the training process. *International Journal of Training and Development, 18*(3), 149-170.

32. Liebermann, S., & Hoffmann, S. (2008). The impact of practical relevance on training transfer: Evidence from a service quality training program for German bank clerks. *International Journal of Training and Development, 12*(2), 74-76.

33. Burke, L.A., & Hutchins, H.M. (2008). A study of best practices in training transfer and proposed model for transfer. *Human Resource Development Quarterly, 19*(2), 107-28.

34. Hawley, J.D., & Barnard, J.K. (2005). Work environment characteristics and implications for training transfer: A case study of the nuclear power industry. *Human Resource Development International, 8*(1), 65–80.

35. Alvarez, K., Salas, E., & Garofano, C.M. (2004). An integrated model of training evaluation and effectiveness. *Human Resource Development Review, 3*(4), 385–416.

36. Bergman, T. (1993). Job performance learning: A comprehensive approach to high-performance training design. *Employee Relations Today, 20*(4), 399-409.

37. Doyle, A. (2019). How often do people change jobs? *Thebalancecareers*. Retrieved from https://www.thebalancecareers.com/how-often-do-people-change-jobs-2060467

38. Bureau of Labor Statistics. (2018). *Employee Tenure Summary*. Retrieved March 14, 2020 from https://www.bls.gov/news.release/tenure.nr0.htm

39. Arbesman, S. (2013). *The half-life of facts: Why everything we know has an expiration date*. New York: Penguin Group.

40. Bates, S. (2014). Job postings remain a weak link in the hiring process. *Society for Human Resource Management*. Retrieved from https://www.shrm.org/resourcesandtools/hr-topics/talent-acquisition/pages/weak-job-descriptions.aspx

41. The World Bank. *World Development Report 2019: The Changing Nature of Work*. Retrieved from http://www.worldbank.org/en/publication/wdr2019

42. Ibid.

43. Bersin, J. (2017). Catch the wave. *Deloitte Review (21)*, 60-79.

44. The Myers-Briggs Foundation. MBTI Basics. Retrieved June 29, 2019 from https://www.myersbriggs.org/my-mbti-personality-type/mbti-basics/home.htm?bhcp=1

45. Birkman. The Birkman Method: One assessment. Retrieved April 3, 2020 from https://birkman.com/the-birkman-method/

46. Extended DISC assessment. Extended DISC. Retrieved April 3, 2020 from https://www.extendeddisc.org/disc-assessments/

47. Goleman, D. (1995). *Emotional intelligence*. New York: Bantam Books.

48. Maul, A. (2012). The validity of the Mayer–Salovey–Caruso Emotional Intelligence Test (MSCEIT) as a measure of emotional intelligence. *Emotion Review, 4*(4), 394-402.

49. George W. Bush Quotes. *BrainyQuote*. Retrieved March 15, 2020 from https://www.brainyquote.com/quotes/george_w_bush_135842

50. MacKie, D. (2014). The effectiveness of strength-based executive coaching in enhancing full range leadership development: A controlled study. *Consulting Psychology Journal: Practice and Research, 66*(2), 118-137.

51. Skill development: Developmental experiences. *Berkeley Human Resources*. Retrieved March 20, 2020 from https://hr.berkeley.edu/development/career-development/skill-development/developmental-experiences

52. Center for Creative Leadership. How to use experience to fuel leadership development. Retrieved March 30, 2020 from https://www.ccl.org/blog/use-experience-fuel-leadership-development/

53. Society for Human Resource Management. Developing Employees. Retrieved April 2, 2020 from https://www.shrm.org/resourcesandtools/tools-and-samples/toolkits/pages/developingemployees.aspx

54. Ibid.

55. Case written by Hutchins, D. (2019). Adapted from: How classroom design affects student engagement. *Steelcase*. Retrieved from https://www.steelcase.com/research/articles/topics/active-learning/how-classroom-design-affects-student-engagement/

Performance Management and Appraisal

Performance appraisal is commonly conducted by direct supervisors, and many of them find this to be one of their least favorite aspects of being in a management role. Employees often enjoy the process about as much as a trip to the dentist. However, HR staff should serve in a consulting and support role, helping to design performance management systems that result in positive organizational outcomes while also enhancing employee engagement. If performance management and appraisal are approached correctly, they can be less burdensome on the supervisor and positive experiences for the employee.

This chapter distinguishes between performance management and performance appraisal and describes the process for each. We explore assessor variations such as supervisor, subordinate, peer, and 360-degree evaluations. Some of the common problems with traditional performance appraisals are discussed, including rater errors and biases. Methods of assessing performance are reviewed, including management by objectives, rating scales, the critical incidents method, and informal appraisal processes. Then we will examine how and why many organizations are reinventing their approach to performance management.

8.1 Opening Case: A Performance Bucket List

Source: © Shutterstock, Inc.

In February 2016, a former employee sued Yahoo, claiming that a manipulated employee-rating system and gender bias led to his termination. Gregory Anderson was an editorial director in charge of autos, homes, travel, shopping, and small business sites for the tech company in Sunnyvale. Before being fired, he stated that he was praised for his performance, promoted, and given a salary increase; but, shortly thereafter was told he was in the bottom 5% of Yahoo's employees after going through his quarterly performance review. He learned of his termination while doing a fellowship at the University of Michigan (which he states his superiors had approved). He was one of six hundred employees terminated after quarterly performance reviews were conducted.

Tamara Devitt, a labor and employment attorney, admits that it is not uncommon for people to claim they were wrongfully terminated due to performance reviews. However, Anderson's case is unusual because he claims that the system was manipulated to result in his termination. "He is really taking on the whole industry of employment performance reviews and how people do them," Devitt said.

Quarterly performance reviews (QPR) were conducted by managers, who rated employees on a scale from 1 to 5 by comparing their performance with peers. After being rated, each employee was put in one of the five categories or buckets. There had to be a certain percentage of employees in each bucket, even if there were more employees who actually performed higher or lower. Then, upper-level management gave input on each employee, regardless of whether they had any contact with them. Employees were never advised of their numeric score or how it was determined. They were only informed of their rank and termination. "This manipulation of the QPR process permitted employment decisions, including terminations, to be made based on personal biases and stereotyping," stated Devitt.

Anderson also says he may have been terminated because he reported that an employee tried to bribe him to reduce a co-worker's performance score. The lawsuit says that the employee had a personal relationship with Anderson's manager, who later gave Anderson a low score. He further stated that the company was much more favorable to women employees.[1]

Abolish Performance Reviews? The Great Debate

Dave Vagnoni and Andy Cohen square off in a lively debate over this question: Should companies get rid of annual employee performance reviews? Dave thinks so, but Andy disagrees.

View the video online at: http://www.youtube.com/embed/J9HYzCyLysI?rel=0

Case Study Discussion Questions

1. How would you describe the problems with the performance review process at Yahoo?
2. Can you think of any ideas for how these types of situations could be avoided?
3. What might be the impact of the bucket system on employee morale and motivation?

8.2 The Performance Appraisal Process

Learning Objectives

1. Distinguish between performance management and performance appraisal.
2. Identify the various assessors that participate in performance appraisals.
3. Explain the most common types of rater bias that influence the validity of performance appraisals.

Performance Management versus Appraisal

If you have ever had a job, then you have probably had a performance evaluation. It may have been a formal process whereby your supervisor assigned ratings to you, then reviewed your performance and discussed steps that you might take going forward to maintain and perhaps improve your performance. Or, the appraisal process might have been less formal and consisted of regular feedback and coaching. There are many different approaches to conducting performance appraisals, and we will explore those in this chapter. But one thing they all have in common is that typically people do not look forward to them, and supervisors hate to do them. You may find this surprising because as we have discussed throughout the text, people are the greatest asset to any organization. Employees often feel the process is unfair, like Gregory Anderson in the opening case.

Much of the focus of HR is on attracting, developing, and keeping high-performing individuals. With the productivity and performance of a company depending so much on the talent, doesn't it make sense to evaluate how each person is performing and identify opportunities for improvement? However, managers and employees are equally skeptical that performance management adds value, and it is often seen as a waste of time and resources.[2] Fortunately, research indicates that there are processes and procedures that companies can implement in their performance management methodology that will foster perceptions of justice among employees.[3]

You most likely intuitively understand the value of performance management. If we invest money in an asset, we expect that asset to perform up to its potential. If it doesn't, then we are probably going to take some actions to either improve the performance or replace the asset. For example, when you buy a car, you have certain performance expectations. You might have bought the car because it is economical to drive, perhaps getting twenty-eight miles per gallon. After driving the car for a while, if you realize you are getting only eighteen miles per gallon, you most likely are going to try to rectify the situation. You might try to improve performance by getting the car tuned up. Or you might try to alter the way you drive, maybe by not accelerating so fast. Or you might try a fuel additive to increase mpg. If all of your attempts to improve the fuel economy fail, you may realize that the car just does not perform as you expected, and eventually decide that you need a different car.

Managing people as assets follows much of the same line of thinking. When a company invests in a person, there should be specific performance expectations. Sometimes the expectations are not made clear to the employee, and sometimes they have not even been clearly identified by the organization. This raises the question: how can someone perform at or above expectations if those expectations do not exist? But let's assume that clear performance criteria have been identified and the employee is aware of them. If the individual does not perform at these levels, then actions should be taken to improve performance. If all attempts at performance improvement fail, then an organization may eventually decide that this individual is not able to perform at the required level and will look for a replacement. As you will learn in this chapter, effective performance management and appraisal depend on having clear expectations; then data must be gathered to monitor performance, followed by giving feedback to the employees.

performance management

Refers to the activities, policies, and interventions designed to improve the performance of human resources.

Let's begin with distinguishing between performance management and appraisal. **Performance management** refers to the activities, policies, and interventions designed to improve the performance of human resources. In a knowledge economy, performance management at the individual employee level is essential, thus the business case for implementing a system to measure and improve employee performance is strong.[4]

performance appraisal

Refers to a periodic process by which employees are evaluated relative to the requirements of the job, for the purpose of indicating where improvements are needed.

Performance appraisal refers to a periodic process by which employees are evaluated relative to the requirements of the job, for the purpose of indicating where improvements are needed. Many organizational decisions are made based on performance appraisals, including training or development, promotion, incentive pay, disciplinary action, and termination. You might think of performance appraisal as one part of the performance management process. Just as you cannot assess the fuel economy of your car unless you monitor data (miles per gallon), employees must be assessed to determine whether they are achieving their full potential.

Data needs to be gathered regarding employee performance to conduct accurate appraisals. Soft skills are often considered the most difficult to assess. How might soft skills be measured in objective ways that are not subject to supervisor bias?

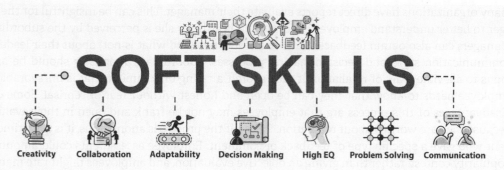

Source: © Shutterstock, Inc.

Performance appraisals have traditionally been conducted annually or semi-annually. Recently, many companies are transitioning to ongoing feedback and coaching, either in addition to periodic appraisals, or in lieu of them. This is because employees need regular feedback on their performance.[5] Employees also benefit from candid assessments of their performance. Committing management time and effort to monitoring performance also decreases turnover rates.[6] Employees and their managers often see appraisal as a chore and something they have to do because HR requires it. The process will be more effective and seen as productive and useful if the employees and managers keep their purpose in mind. The primary purpose of performance appraisal should be to help employees to continuously improve their performance.[7]

In the last few years, there have been calls for reinventing performance management systems, and some companies such as Netflix, Deloitte, and Adobe, have abandoned them altogether.[8] [9] We will delve into the reasons why some companies are moving away from performance appraisal later in the chapter. But for now, let's just note that these companies are not doing away with performance management, but are changing their approach to how it is implemented.

Variations of Assessors

What many people picture when they think of a performance appraisal is a supervisor evaluating the performance of a direct report. This is the most common type of performance appraisal, but there are other variations. Appraisals are sometimes conducted by supervisors, subordinates, peers, customers, and even oneself. There also is a comprehensive approach that includes input from a variety of assessors, known as a 360-degree evaluation. Each of these variations has advantages and disadvantages, and each can be useful when implemented correctly and in the right set of circumstances.

Supervisors

This is the traditional approach to conducting a performance appraisal, and for good reason. In many situations, the supervisor is the person who is best capable of assessing whether a person performs the job task at or above performance standards. But supervisors sometimes have so many direct reports that they do not have time to adequately observe the performance of each individual. The **span of control**, or the number of people for whom a supervisor is responsible, has been steadily increasing in the U.S., and it is not uncommon for a supervisor to oversee as many as twenty-five employees, compared to five or six direct reports in the past. Another potential problem occurs with knowledge workers, who have areas of expertise that their supervisor is not completely familiar with.

span of control

The number of people for whom a supervisor is responsible.

Subordinates

Many organizations have direct reports evaluate their manager. This can be insightful for the manager to better understand employee concerns and how he or she is perceived by the subordinates. Managers can also obtain feedback into what is effective (and what is not) about their leadership, communication style, and decision-making processes. Subordinate appraisals should be anonymous to alleviate fears of retaliation if they submit a rating or comment that is unfavorable. The employee needs to know that they can be open and honest without fear of reprisal. Some of the disadvantages of this process are that employees may not be frank and open in their evaluation because they are worried about retaliation.[10] Even if the process is anonymous, it is sometimes evident who gave a specific type of feedback or comment. Employee assessments could amount to a popularity contest, rather than giving an objective evaluation, and employees might rate managers higher who give them preferential treatment. Just as supervisors might be guilty of favoritism and giving high appraisal marks to employees they like, subordinates also can be biased and give higher marks to a supervisor that they like or are personal friends with.

Peers

Peer evaluations are conducted by individuals the employee works with on a regular basis (co-workers, team members, professional colleagues). Peers can provide insights that a supervisor may not be aware of because the person being appraised might interact differently with the supervisor than with peers. In other words, most people are going to be on their best behavior with their boss, because they know that he or she will eventually be evaluating them, and it could impact their raises, promotions, or even whether they have a long-term position at the company. If people know that their peers are going to be evaluating them, then they will tend to also put forth their best efforts when working as part of a team, and to establish better working relationships with their colleagues. Peer evaluations can provide information that a supervisor might not ever otherwise know. For example, a supervisor might find that one particular employee shows more leadership skills than they realize, even though the job description doesn't require them to.[11] One possible disadvantage is that the feedback could be subjective and vulnerable to bias. Some employees may get along well and give each other better assessments, while others may not fit in as well and receive lower scores.[12] Another potential disadvantage is that employees may not have a good understanding of the requirements of their co-workers' jobs. For this reason, it is important to ask questions related to areas that they have knowledge about, such as communication skills, interpersonal relational aspects, leadership, and whether the individual contributes to a positive team environment.

Customers

Some companies include customer feedback in the appraisal process. This can encourage the employee to be more customer-centric, since they will not want negative customer comments as part of their appraisal. There is a potential downside in that customers may not have a full understanding of the employee's role, and might use the feedback process as an opportunity to vent about issues that the employee has no control over (e.g., price increases, warranty problems, or product quality).

Self-Appraisal

Self-evaluation can be an enlightening process of reflection. Most people are so busy during the workday that they just don't have the opportunity to stop and reflect on what they are doing that is effective and what is ineffective. Writing a self-assessment usually occurs prior to an appraisal meeting with the manager. It is an opportunity for the employee to document their value to the company and their accomplishments during the evaluation period, and also to identify areas of focus for professional development and improvement. It is important to ensure that employees know that their self-appraisal becomes part of their permanent employee record, which will encourage them to make sure the appraisal reflects their best effort at self-analysis. It may also be helpful to offer templates or even examples of self-appraisals to the employees (see "Self-Appraisal Example from ClearCompany").

Self-Appraisal Example from ClearCompany

Self-Assessment Example, Sales Representative

In my first three months as a sales representative for Acme Rocket Company, I have met and exceeded new hire expectations for sales performance. While I was informed during the hiring process that it usually takes up to three months for new hires to start achieving their monthly revenue targets, I was able to meet and exceed my personal revenue targets in all of my first three months, selling 109% of my target in March, 111% in April, and 105% of my sales target in May. The biggest factor in my success has been my attention to detail and responsiveness throughout the sales process. Between April and May, I responded to 92% of inquiries from prospective customers inside my territory within 24 hours, regardless of when or how the inquiry was received. The remaining 8% were responded to within 48 hours. My timely responses and attention to detail have resulted in a 78% closing rate for new customer inquiries and enabled me to exceed my sales targets in each month.

Source: ClearCompany

360-Degree

The 360-degree method gathers and appraises performance data from a wide variety of sources.

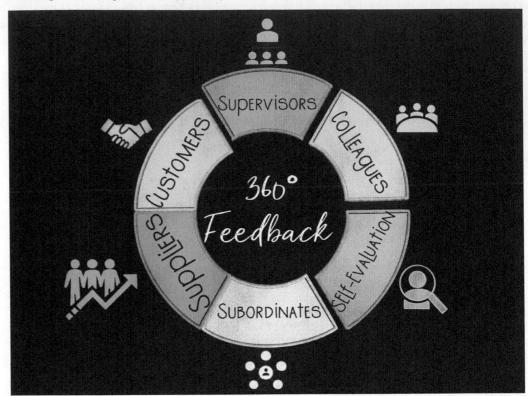

Source: © Shutterstock, Inc.

360-degree performance appraisal

A comprehensive review that collects feedback from a wide span of the employee's touchpoints, and normally includes supervisors, co-workers, subordinates, and sometimes customers.

A **360-degree performance appraisal** is a comprehensive review that collects feedback from a wide span of the employee's touchpoints. This normally includes supervisors, co-workers, subordinates, and sometimes customers. One advantage of this method is that the results are not dependent on just one person's viewpoint of the employee. It can be helpful when the supervisor works in a different location (perhaps even a different state or country) and does not have many opportunities to directly observe the employee's behavior. In these types of situations, it can be helpful to get perspectives from subordinates, peers, or customers. Negative comments or ratings by one individual may be offset by positive comments from others. The process takes into account that everyone has strengths and weaknesses and performs better in some aspects of their job than others. Critics of the process argue the process is often abused. If the feedback is used for development and coaching purposes, then it can be beneficial. But if it is used to make decisions about promotions, compensation, or employee discipline, then it can be fraught with problems. Co-workers or subordinates might use the opportunity to strike out at the person being evaluated. The fact that 360s are conducted on an anonymous basis leads to an environment in which there is no accountability for the feedback that is given. Figure 8.1 illustrates a typical 360-degree performance appraisal process.

FIGURE 8.1 360-Degree Performance Appraisal Process

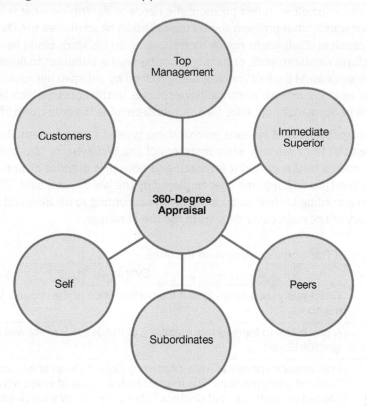

Common Problems

There is a basic human tendency to make judgments about those with whom one is working.[13] But because humans are involved, there is the potential for unfairness, misunderstandings, and lack of consistency. Employees sometimes push back against performance appraisals because they don't think they are a fair representation of their effort. There are several problems that lead to this perception, but they all have one word in common and that word is bias. **Bias** is the prejudice in favor of or against one thing, person, or group compared with another, usually in a manner considered to be unfair. There are two major types of bias that are common in performance appraisal processes:

1. Attribution error.
2. Rater error.

Attribution error is a theory of social psychology that describes the inclination to overemphasize the influence of a person's dispositional factors while ignoring the influence of situational factors on a person's behavior. Imagine that someone cuts you off in traffic, causing you to slam on your brakes. You might be upset, honk your horn, and shake your fist at them (or you might have some other gestures, but we won't mention those here). Most people will assume that the other driver is a jerk and just plain inconsiderate. These are based on assumptions that we make about a person's disposition. But what if the other driver is a man rushing his wife to the hospital because she is in labor? Now, there are situational factors that explain the behavior, rather than the driver's disposition. In this example, we might be tempted to attribute the driver's behavior to being a jerk (disposition) when the real cause was that his wife was in labor (situational).

Now let's apply this concept to workplace performance management. Consider the situation of Zach, a garage door installer for a large overhead door company. In his most recent performance review, his supervisor, Julie, noted that the frequency of callbacks on his installations is 20% higher than average. A callback occurs whenever a customer has a problem with a new installation. Each

bias

The prejudice in favor of or against one thing, person, or group compared with another, usually in a manner considered to be unfair.

attribution error

A theory of social psychology that describes the inclination to overemphasize the influence of a person's dispositional factors while ignoring the influence of situational factors on a person's behavior.

callback is conducted free of charge to the customer, thus the company incurs only an expense for a callback. Now put yourself in Julie's position: she needs to determine what is the cause of the callbacks. In other words, what problem should the callbacks be attributed to? The problem might be a disposition problem (Zach might not be concentrating on his work, could be distracted or not motivated to perform excellent work, or he might not be paying attention to detail). But the problem could also be situational (lack of training, being rushed by a dispatcher to move more quickly and get on to the next job, or even electrical power surges in the area in which he works). Before completing Zach's performance appraisal, Julie should determine the true cause of the callbacks.

Most performance appraisal systems involve some type of rating system. Ratings have been used since at least the third century, when members of the Wei dynasty (221 to 265 AD) rated the official family members. You may find it interesting to note that outcries of unfairness and rater bias have been around just as long! One rater employed by the Wei dynasty said, "The Imperial rater seldom rates men according to their metrics, but always according to his likes and dislikes."[14] Table 8.1 gives a summary of the main developments in the use of ratings.

TABLE 8.1 History of Performance Appraisal Systems

Dates	Events
221–265	Wei dynasty uses raters to rate the performance of the imperial family members.
1540–1560	A procedure to formally rate members of the Jesuit Society was established by Ignatius Loyola.
1800–1817	Performance appraisals were initiated by Robert Owen at his cotton mills in Scotland using monitors. The monitors were cubes of wood with different colors painted on each side and displayed above the workstation of each employee. The color of the visible side of the cube was associated with a rating to indicate performance (see "Figure 8.1, 360 Degree Performance Appraisal Process").
1850–1914	Industrial Revolution in America; workers were evaluated and paid primarily on the basis of quantity produced.
1870–1915	Frederick Taylor stressed the importance of scientific management, time and motion studies, and the individual worker by advocating the payment of individually based financial incentives (piecework).
1918–1955	Widespread use of performance appraisal techniques with blue-collar employees began after World War I. Appraisal systems for managerial and professional employees became common after 1955.
1957	Emergence of performance appraisals based on management by objectives.
1964–1990	Passage of EEO laws, beginning with Title VII of the Civil Rights Act of 1964, created the need for improvement in appraisal practices to help eliminate discrimination and bias.

FIGURE 8.2 Silent Monitor at Owen Mills

Robert Owen, a textile mill owner in Scotland in the early nineteenth century, was opposed to the use of corporal punishment which was used to discipline employees in other mills. He devised a unique system to keep discipline at the New Lanark Mills.

This four-sided wooden block was known as a "silent monitor" and hung next to each worker in the mill, with each side displaying a different color.

Bad behavior was represented by the color black; indifferent was represented by blue; good by yellow; and excellent by white.

New Lanark Mill,
a World Heritage Site

The superintendent was responsible for turning the monitors every day, according to how well or badly the worker behaved.

Source: © Shutterstock, Inc.

Psychologists began studying rater error in earnest in the 1920s. Research has provided evidence of so much bias that some researchers believe that performance ratings may reveal more about the rater than the ratee.[15] This body of research traces its beginning to Thorndike's classic article "A Constant Error in Psychological Ratings."[16] He identified what later became known as the halo effect. This and other common types of rater bias established by research studies are summarized here:

halo effect

Occurs when the evaluator forms an overall positive general impression and then extends that positive impression to all aspects of the rating.

horns effect

The opposite of the halo effect, occurs when the evaluator forms an overall negative impression and then extends that negative impression to all aspects of the rating.

distribution errors

Occur when an evaluator has the tendency to rate everyone the same way.

strictness error

Occurs when the evaluator rates everyone low, regardless of actual performance.

leniency error

Occurs when the evaluator rates everyone high, regardless of actual performance.

central tendency error

Occurs when the evaluator rates everyone as average.

recency effect

Happens when the evaluator puts too much emphasis on the most recent part of the time period under evaluation.

contrast error

Occurs when an individual's performance is compared to a co-worker, rather than to a job standard.

similar-to-me error

Occurs when an evaluator rates an individual high because they have something in common.

idiosyncratic rater effect

- **Halo effect.** Occurs when the evaluator forms an overall positive general impression and then extends that positive impression to all aspects of the rating.
- **Horns effect.** This is the opposite of the halo effect and occurs when the evaluator forms an overall negative impression and then extends that negative impression to all aspects of the rating.
- **Distribution errors.** These occur when an evaluator has the tendency to rate everyone the same way; distribution errors fall into three categories:
  - **Strictness.** Occurs when the evaluator rates everyone low, regardless of actual performance.
  - **Leniency.** Occurs when the evaluator rates everyone high, regardless of actual performance.
  - **Central tendency.** Occurs when the evaluator rates everyone as average.
- **Recency effect.** This happens when the evaluator puts too much emphasis on the most recent part of the time period under evaluation. For example, if a payroll analyst is being evaluated for a one-year period and had good performance overall but made a significant payroll error one week before the appraisal, then a supervisor who rated the employee low based on this one recent event has committed a recency error.
- **Contrast error.** This occurs when an individual's performance is compared to a co-worker, rather than to a job standard. If the employee works in a department with one or more poor performers, then the appraiser may have a tendency to rate this individual higher than would be justified by comparison to the job standard. The converse is also true: if the employee works in a department with outstanding performers, then their performance might seem inferior by comparison.
- **Similar-to-me error.** When an evaluator rates an individual high because they have something in common, then the similar-to-me error has occurred. For example, if the evaluator and the individual being evaluated both attended the same school, then there might be a tendency to rate the individual higher than normal. Or perhaps they engage in similar after-work activities, follow the same sports teams, or live in the same neighborhood. The similar-to-me error can also occur due to similarities based on race, religion, gender, national origin, age, and other aspects of a protected class, which can lead to charges of discrimination. This type of error can also give rise to perceptions of favoritism.
- **Idiosyncratic rater effect.** This refers to the tendency of humans to view things differently and subjectively through their own biases. When two or more people see the same situation, they have a tendency to describe it differently. Three different studies have confirmed this effect, as published in a 1998 article in *Personnel Psychology*, a 2000 paper in the *Journal of Applied Psychology*, and a 2010 article, again in *Personnel Psychology*. Each study found that the idiosyncrasies of the person doing the rating accounted for 71%, 58%, and 55% of variation, respectively.[17] [18] [19] Thus, in each study, over half of the variation in ratings was attributed to the rater, not the person being rated, which indicates that ratings say more about the rater than the ratee.

Companies have tried several approaches to reduce rater error, with mixed results. One approach is **forced ranking**, which requires managers to rate employees into three to five categories, such as excellent, good, and poor, as was illustrated in the chapter opening case. The ratings have to follow a bell curve, or a normal distribution, thus forcing managers to rate a percentage of the employees in every category. The most famous proponent of this method was Jack Welch, who required GE managers to identify and terminate the bottom 10% of performers every year, giving rise to the derisive name of "rank and yank" to this approach.[20] At one time during the 2000s, some experts estimated that at least 20% of *Fortune* 1,000 companies were using forced rankings.[21] Figure 8.3 gives an example of a forced ranking.

> The tendency of humans to view things differently and subjectively through their own biases.
>
> **forced ranking**
>
> Requires managers to rate employees into three to five categories, such as excellent, good, and poor.

FIGURE 8.3 Normal Distribution Curve

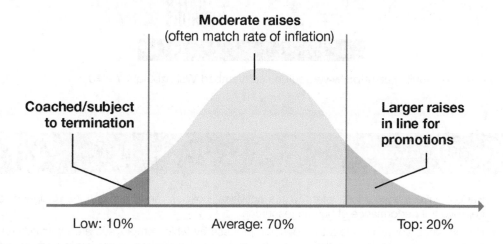

Typical Bell Curve Distribution for Forced Ranking

Moderate raises (often match rate of inflation)

Coached/subject to termination

Larger raises in line for promotions

Low: 10%   Average: 70%   Top: 20%

Forced ranking is a controversial process because it forces managers to evaluate employees against each other, instead of comparing to an objective performance standard, giving rise to dysfunctional competition and allegations of favoritism. Consider what your response might be if a professor graded on a forced ranking along with a normal distribution. This would mean that some individuals in the class would fail, even if they made good grades on all assignments, and vice versa, some students would receive As, even if they never earned an A on an exam.

Another approach to reducing rater bias is **calibration**, which refers to a process in which a group of managers comes together to discuss the performance of employees and achieve agreement on previously assigned appraisal ratings. This group of managers (or calibration committee) reviews the distribution of ratings and makes adjustments before the ratings are conveyed to the employees. You might be thinking: how is this any different than a forced ranking? And that is a good question. In essence, this is a type of forced ranking by a committee. The difference is that the rankings do not necessarily have to follow a normal distribution. Calibration is a relatively new development in performance appraisal, and very little research has been conducted. What research has been done reveals mixed results. According to one study, calibration was effective in reducing excessive leniency, which often happens because supervisors are afraid of assigning unfavorable ratings.[22] The calibration committee reduced the mean of the overall rating distribution. However, from the perspective of an employee, it may not seem fair that their supervisor assigned one rating, only to be overruled by a committee. The employee may feel (and rightly so) that the supervisor is the individual most familiar with their work and best able to assign an appropriate rating.

> **calibration**
>
> A process in which a group of managers comes together to discuss the performance of employees and achieve agreement on previously assigned appraisal ratings.

Research also indicates that calibration results in a tendency to increase central tendencies.[23] Although the overall mean tends to be lower, the distribution is narrower. In other words, everyone's rating went down, but they were closer together.

Performance Appraisal Rater Errors

There are many possible sources of error in the performance appraisal process. One of the major sources is the rater. Although completely eliminating errors is impossible, making raters aware of potential errors and biases helps to reduce them.

View the video online at: http://www.youtube.com/embed/WsFhzb3lqVo?rel=0

Key Takeaways

- Performance management refers to the activities, policies, and interventions designed to improve the performance of human resources.
- Performance appraisal refers to a periodic process by which employees are evaluated relative to the requirements of the job, for the purpose of indicating where improvements are needed.
- In many situations, the supervisor is the person who is best capable of assessing whether a person performs the job task at or above performance standards.
- Subordinates can provide managers with feedback regarding what is effective (and what is not) about their leadership, communication style, and decision-making processes.
- Peers can provide insights that a supervisor may not be aware of because the person being appraised might interact differently with the supervisor than with peers.
- Customer feedback in the appraisal process can encourage the employee to be more customer-centric since they will not want negative customer comments as part of their appraisal.
- A self-evaluation can be an enlightening process of reflection.
- A 360-degree performance appraisal is a comprehensive review that collects feedback from a wide span of the employee's touchpoints and normally includes supervisors, co-workers, subordinates, and sometimes customers.
- Attribution error is a theory of social psychology that describes the inclination to overemphasize the influence of a person's dispositional factors while ignoring the influence of situational factors on a person's behavior.
- The most common types of rater bias are halo effect, horns effect, distribution errors, recency, contrast, similar-to-me, and the idiosyncratic rater effect.
- Forced ranking is a controversial process because it forces managers to evaluate employees against each other instead of an objective performance standard, giving rise to dysfunctional competition and allegations of favoritism.
- One approach to reducing rater bias is calibration, which refers to a process in which a group of managers comes together to discuss the performance of employees and achieve agreement on previously assigned appraisal ratings.

8.3 Performance Appraisal Methods

Learning Objectives

1. Describe the management by objectives appraisal method.
2. Explain the advantages and disadvantages of rating scales.
3. Recognize how the critical incidents method is used to improve performance appraisals.
4. Identify the methods used in informal performance appraisal.

Management by Objectives (MBO)

Management by objectives (MBO) is a results-oriented performance management method that strives to increase organizational achievement through mutual agreement of goals between employee and manager. MBO was first widely used in the 1950s, in part because of the writings of management theorist Peter Drucker. MBO is results-oriented and seeks to measure individual performance by examining the extent to which predetermined work objectives were met.

The steps in the MBO process are:

1. Define organizational goals and metrics.
2. Cascade to departmental goals and metrics.
3. Supervisors and employees achieve mutual agreement on individual goals and metrics.
4. Implementation.
5. Performance evaluation.
6. Feedback.

One of the strengths of the MBO approach is that it aligns individual goals with organizational goals. Also, the emphasis on results can minimize bias because the evaluation of goal attainment of established metrics is more objective than many performance appraisal methods. However, MBO can lead to unrealistic expectations, and if the goals are too aggressive, then the method can set employees up to fail. Therefore, it is crucial for supervisors to help each individual set goals that are challenging, but not overly optimistic.

management by objectives (MBO)

A results-oriented performance management method that strives to increase organizational achievement through mutual agreement of goals between employee and manager.

Rating Scales

rating scales

A performance appraisal method whereby each employee is rated according to specific characteristics.

Rating scales are a performance appraisal method whereby each employee is rated according to specific characteristics. Rating scales can be numeric (e.g., 1,2,3...) or alphabetic (e.g., a, b, c...) with each number or letter corresponding to a level of performance, such as "5 = excellent" or "2 = needs improvement." Rating scales typically have from three to five options for rating each characteristic. A simple three-level rating is easier to administer, but the five-level rating provides more differentiation between performance levels. Some rating scales also have space for the rater to write comments such as examples of positive or negative work behaviors to support the rating.

Regardless of whether numbers or letters are used, it is important that raters be provided with training on how to complete the scale and examples of specific behaviors, skills, and other data that will help them choose the appropriate rating levels.

behaviorally anchored rating scale (BARS)

A performance appraisal method designed to bring the benefits of both qualitative and quantitative data to the appraisal process by using behavioral statements as anchors for each rating level.

One variation of this method is the **behaviorally anchored rating scale (BARS)**. The BARS method is designed to bring the benefits of both qualitative and quantitative data to the appraisal process by using behavioral statements as anchors for each rating level. An example of a BARS is shown in Table 8.2. BARS are time-consuming to develop but may provide improved accuracy of the ratings. They are normally developed by a committee of supervisors and subordinates. The group establishes anchor statements, and then a larger group reviews the proposed scale. Then, only anchor statements with which at least 70% indicate agreement are retained on the scale. BARS tend to be very job-specific because of the behavioral descriptions, and therefore a separate BARS may need to be developed for each job.

TABLE 8.2 BARS Example

Performance	Points	Behavior
Extremely good	7	Can expect trainee to make valuable suggestions for increased sales and to have positive relationships with customers all over the country.
Good	6	Can expect to initiate creative ideas for improved sales.
Above average	5	Can expect to keep in touch with the customers throughout the year.
Average	4	Can manage, with difficulty, to deliver the goods in time.
Below average	3	Can expect to unload the trucks when asked by the supervisor.
Poor	2	Can expect to inform only a part of the customers.
Extremely poor	1	Can expect to take extended coffee breaks and roam around purposelessly.

Critical Incidents

critical incidents method

A performance appraisal technique in which a manager keeps a log of positive and negative work behaviors of subordinates.

The **critical incidents method** is a performance appraisal technique in which a manager keeps a log of positive and negative work behaviors of subordinates. A critical incident occurs when employee behavior results in an unusual success or unusual failure to perform on the job. Managers then keep a record of these situations in which something went well or something went wrong.

The critical incidents method is based on a description of the event and does not use rankings. It can be a very useful method because it allows managers to be able to discuss specific work incidents as examples of either positive or negative performance.

It is important for managers to record incidents as soon as possible after they occur, ideally the same day, while it is fresh in their mind. Then, when it is time to conduct a performance appraisal, the manager can review the log and be reminded of specific work behaviors that occurred throughout the evaluation period (typically a year). Otherwise, managers will go from memory, which in most cases will be limited to events that occurred recently. Thus, the critical incidents method is an ideal way to reduce the probability of the recency error and can also be combined with any of the other performance appraisal methods.

Informal Appraisal Processes

Informal appraisal systems usually involve much more frequent feedback. For example, a supervisor might provide feedback upon completion of a project, or perhaps even weekly. Appraisals might be unscheduled and impromptu, occurring whenever a manager sees an opportunity to provide feedback or suggestions, or just to inquire with an employee as to how a project is going. Another variation is that they might be regularly scheduled, such as weekly or monthly. But we still categorize them as informal because they do not involve a formal rating process. These regular meetings are sometimes referred to as "one-on-ones" or "check-ins." Proponents of this approach claim that it engenders more of a coaching or mentoring management style, as opposed to an authoritative one.

One method for informal appraisal is based on the book *The One Minute Manager*, which was developed and written ahead of its time in 1982, by Ken Blanchard and Spencer Johnson. This method emphasizes using one minute of praise and one minute of reprimand. The message is that managers should take every opportunity to praise employees and also provide quick and concise feedback when a mistake has been made.

Some companies use appraisal cards. These cards are given to managers and have a list of key criteria for employee work, such as customer service, efficiency, reliability, etc. When a manager witnesses an employee excelling in something, the manager can praise them, or if an employee is making a mistake, they can be given quick feedback.

Companies can also use informal recognition programs. This can include informal employee meetings where they are praised or given gift certificates or other incentives. These are all part of the trend to move away from the formal workplace evaluation process and provide a more effective way to give feedback to employees.[24]

 Dilbert Gets a Performance Review

The Boss informs Dilbert that he needs to improve on anticipating problems.

View the video online at: http://www.youtube.com/embed/XqfwYkpOLg4?rel=0

HR in the Real World: Supervising Daily

I have supervised employees at many levels, including entry-level workers, maintenance technicians and mechanics, and professional staff such as accountants, marketing staff, faculty and trainers, middle management, and executive staff. I have never really counted how many performance appraisals I have conducted in the past forty years, but it is certainly over one thousand. I cannot recall a single occasion where an employee protested an appraisal or filed any type of complaint regarding unfairness. I attribute this to a technique which I refer to as supervising daily. Early in my career, I was assigned to read *The One Minute Manager* in a college business course, and it changed the way that I managed performance.

Supervising daily means giving immediate feedback and coaching. If I see someone excel in their performance, I stop and have a conversation with them. I also try to be specific about their performance and the behavior or action that is commendable. If I see someone make a mistake, or their performance is sub-par, I stop and have a conversation with them. Again, I try to be specific about their performance, and the behavior or action that needs to change. Then as soon as I can, I note the conversation in a critical incidents log that I keep for each of my direct reports. As a result, when the time comes to do a periodic formal performance appraisal, there are no surprises. If the employee's performance was sub-par, they already knew about it, because we had been having conversations about it. If there are surprises during a formal performance appraisal, then it may be time to rethink your daily supervision style.

Key Takeaways

- Management by objectives (MBO) is a results-oriented performance management method that strives to increase organizational achievement through mutual agreement of goals between employee and manager.
- Rating scales are a performance appraisal method whereby each employee is rated according to specific characteristics.
- The behaviorally anchored rating scale (BARS) method is designed to bring the benefits of both qualitative and quantitative data to the appraisal process by using behavioral statements as anchors for each rating level.
- The critical incidents method is a performance appraisal technique where a manager keeps a log of positive and negative work behaviors of subordinates.
- Informal appraisal systems usually involve much more frequent feedback. These regular meetings are sometimes referred to as "one-on-ones" or "check-ins." Proponents of this approach claim that it engenders more of a coaching or mentoring management style, as opposed to an authoritative one.

What Do *You* Think?

1. If your manager asked you to set goals for the upcoming year for an MBO plan, how would you ensure that the goals are challenging, but not overly optimistic?
2. Do you think rating scales are a fair basis to use for promotion decisions? Should the individuals with the best ratings always be promoted over those with lower ratings?
3. As a manager, what would be the most efficient way for you to keep a critical incidents log for each of your direct reports?

8.4 Reinventing Performance Management

Learning Objectives

1. Recognize why many organizations have eliminated performance appraisals.
2. Explain how companies are using ongoing and faster feedback to improve employee engagement.
3. Identify the emerging trends in performance management.

Up to this point in the chapter, our focus has been on how performance management has been done in the past. That's important for you to know because many companies still use some variation of the methods that you have learned about thus far. But over the past few years, there has been an abundance of research that tells us performance processes are overengineered and time-consuming and tend to demotivate employees while hindering candid and honest conversations.[25] In addition, as was mentioned at the beginning of the chapter, they are typically deplored by employees and their managers. Amber Lloyd of HCM Strategy puts it this way: "Times have changed, and so should our notions about employee performance. After all, an annual performance discussion is kind of like waiting a year to tell your spouse what you appreciate about him or her or waiting until the start of the next school year to offer suggestions to your teenagers on study techniques that could help them be more effective. It just doesn't work in a fast-paced environment where agility, retention, and engagement are key to a competitive advantage."[26]

There are hundreds, if not thousands of resources (books, websites, checklists, sample feedback phrases, etc.) to assist managers in doing performance reviews. But the question that is often being asked now is: why do them at all? In the age of knowledge workers, do performance review methods that were developed during the Industrial Revolution make any sense? Fred Nickols, senior consultant with the Distance Learning Company, says, "The blunt truth is that, if they have any objectives at all, most people set their own."[27] Many supervisors of knowledge workers just do not have the expertise of their employees and are not in a position to set work objectives, to monitor accomplishments, or to supervise their efforts.

There is a growing movement among some companies to reinvent performance management. More than fifty large firms have transformed their performance appraisal systems and moved away from traditional rating systems.[28] Bersin by Deloitte reports that around 70% of companies are reconsidering their performance management strategy. These trends are so new that there is little research or theory to cite here. Instead, let's take a look at some of these companies, why they have changed the process of performance appraisals (and in some cases done away with them altogether), and what is taking their place.

Netflix

Netflix was one of the first companies to eliminate formal performance reviews. People tend to look seriously at how Netflix approaches talent management because they have been tremendously successful. They are dominating the streaming industry with a subscriber base of almost 150 million, and a year-over-year increase of 16.6% in the first quarter of 2019.[29] By some estimates, up to a third of peak residential internet traffic in the U.S. comes from customers streaming Netflix movies.[30] Netflix founder and CEO Reed Hastings describes the five tenets of their approach to managing talent:

1. **Hire, reward, and tolerate only fully formed adults.**

If you're careful to hire people who will put the company's interests first, who understand and support the desire for a high-performance workplace, 97% of your employees will do the right thing. Most companies spend endless time and money writing and enforcing HR policies to deal with problems the other 3% might cause. Instead, we tried really hard to not hire those people, and we let them go if it turned out we'd made a hiring mistake.

2. **Tell the truth about performance.**

Many years ago, we eliminated formal reviews . . . we asked managers and employees to have conversations about performance as an organic part of their work.

3. **Managers own the job of creating a great team.**

I ask managers to imagine a documentary about what their team is accomplishing six months from now. . . . I ask them to think about the skills needed to make the images in the movie a reality.

4. **Leaders own the job of creating culture.**

It's a waste of time to articulate ideas about values and culture if you don't model and reward behavior that aligns with those goals.

5. **Good talent managers think like businesspeople and innovators first, and like HR people last.**

During 30 years in business, I've never seen an HR initiative that improved morale. . . . Instead of cheerleading, people in my profession should think of themselves as business-people. What's good for the company? How do we communicate that to employees?[31]

The overall Netflix approach seems to be that of demanding performance, but creating an environment of freedom in how individuals and teams decide to achieve their performance. For example, the Netflix jobs website describes the company culture and states that their policy for travel, entertainment, gifts, and other expenses is five words long: "Act in Netflix's best interest." They do not have compliance departments and procedures that most companies have to enforce their policies.[32] Their vacation policy is: "Take vacation." There are no rules about how many days to take or when. The website states: "You might think that such freedom would lead to chaos. But we also don't have a clothing policy, yet no one has come to work naked. The lesson is you don't need policies for everything. Most people understand the benefits of wearing clothes at work."

Adobe

Adobe moved away from traditional performance appraisals because of the number of hours and the cost involved in the process. They discovered that the annual performance appraisal process required eighty thousand hours of time from its two thousand managers, the equivalent of forty full-time employees.[33] Their internal surveys also suggested that the workforce felt less motivated and inspired after each appraisal. In 2012, Adobe's then senior vice-president of people resources, Donna Morris, was feeling frustrated with annual performance reviews. The process was complex, bureaucratic, and paperwork-heavy. It also created barriers to teamwork and innovation, since the experience of being rated and stack-ranked for compensation left many employees feeling under-valued and uninspired.[34]

Hear Donna Tell the Check-in Story

In lieu of annual appraisals, Adobe implemented a frequent "Check-In" process. As part of this process, managers provide coaching and advice on a regular basis, as opposed to once a year. The process facilitates an ongoing two-way dialogue between managers and employees. The objectives of the Check-In are to help employees gain clarity about what is expected of them, guide them through performance improvement, and assist in their professional growth and development. Table 8.3 summarizes the differences between the old performance appraisal system and the new Check-In process.[35]

Source: https://www.adobe.com/check-in.html

TABLE 8.3 Adobe Performance Management: Then and Now

	Before: The Annual Performance Review	After: Check-In
Setting Priorities	Employee priorities set at the start of the year and often not revisited.	Priorities discussed and adjusted with the manager regularly.
Feedback Process	Long process of submitting accomplishments, soliciting feedback, and writing reviews.	Ongoing process of feedback and dialogue with no formal written review or documentation.
Compensation Decisions	Onerous process of rating and ranking each employee to determine salary increase and equity.	No formal rating or ranking; manager determines salary and equity annually based on performance.
Cadence of Meetings	Feedback sessions inconsistent and not monitored. Spike in employee productivity at the end of the year, timed with performance review discussions.	Feedback conversations expected quarterly, with ongoing feedback becoming the norm. Consistent employee productivity based on ongoing discussions and feedback throughout the year.

	Before: The Annual Performance Review	After: Check-In
HR Team Role	HR team managed paperwork and processes to ensure all steps were completed.	HR team equips employees and managers to have constructive conversations.
Training and Resources	Manager coaching and resources came from HR partners who couldn't always reach everyone.	A centralized Employee Resource Center provides help and answers whenever needed.

Deloitte

Deloitte redesigned their performance management system after realizing that the old process for evaluating people, and then training, promoting, and paying them accordingly, was out of step with their objectives, and very costly.[36] Deloitte tallied the number of hours the organization was spending on performance management and found that completing the forms, holding the meetings, and creating the ratings consumed close to two million hours a year! They wanted something more nimble, real-time, individualized, and focused on fueling performance in the future rather than assessing it in the past.

The new system that Deloitte created had no cascading objectives, no annual reviews, and no 360-degree feedback tools. The hallmarks of the new system are speed, agility, one-size-fits-one, and constant learning, and it is underpinned by a new way of collecting reliable performance data.[37] The central component of Deloitte's redesigned performance management system is the performance snapshot. This allows leaders to see performance quickly and across the organization, freeing them to spend more time engaging with people. Deloitte created the performance snapshot by focusing on:

1. **The criteria.** Each part of the snapshot had to contain a single, easily understood concept. They chose four questions: one each about pay, teamwork, poor performance, and promotion.

2. **The rater.** They were looking for someone with a vivid experience of the individual's performance and whose subjective judgment was important. They chose team leaders because they are the closest to the actual performance of the ratees.

3. **Testing.** Validity testing was conducted by analyzing the mean responses and range of responses. They knew that if there was a tight cluster of responses, the snapshot would not yield the differentiation they were looking for.

4. **Frequency.** Since Deloitte works mostly in a project structure, they chose to produce a performance snapshot at the end of each project. For longer-term projects, they chose to evaluate quarterly.

IBM

IBM recently transformed its ten-year-old annual performance review system, with the new program aimed at spreading employee goals throughout the year and including more frequent feedback.[38] Under the previous system, employees set their annual goals in January, had a mid-year review with their manager, and would receive an evaluation and a final score at the end of the year, which represented their overall performance for the year. The difficulty with the old system was that goals set early in the year often changed and the actual work assigned to employees was realigned in response.

Many HR departments would bring in a consultant or a few performance management companies to analyze the situation and suggest solutions. IBM HR did not just request proposals, analyze them, and pick one. It turned to its 380,000 employees in one hundred seventy countries to crowdsource the process. Diane Gherson, IBM's chief human resource officer, posted a message on "Connections," IBM's internal social media platform, asking employees to share ideas for a new performance management system.[39] Her post received seventy-five thousand views and two thousand comments from employees. The company then organized the comments into themes. The new performance management system that resulted from the process is an app-based performance review system called Checkpoint. You can view the IBM Checkpoint app interface here: https://young-mavericks.com/portfolio-item/ibm-checkpoint-app/.

Using Checkpoint, IBM employees set shorter-term goals, and managers provide feedback on their progress at least every quarter. At the end of the year, employees are judged across five criteria—business results, impact on client success, innovation, personal responsibility to others, and skills. Managers assess whether employees have exceeded or achieved expectations for their role in each of those five dimensions or if there's a need for improvement.[40]

There is no single measure of an employee's performance like before. In the old system, there was one score, and Gherson said that people tended to be obsessed with that. The new system leads to richer feedback and more meaningful discussions between the employee and the manager.

GE

Even GE, whose "rank and yank" forced ranking system became legendary, has transformed its performance management system. Annual performance appraisals and forced rankings have long been associated with GE and their former CEO, Jack Welch. The fact that the company which business people most associate with annual performance ratings has abandoned the practice may signal that the annual performance review is an endangered species.

GE has transitioned to a new performance management app, "PD@GE," an acronym for "performance development at GE." Sonia Boyle, GE Canada's vice-president of human resources, said that the business exists in an environment of rapid change that does not follow a prescriptive annual performance cycle.[41]

GE sought input from thirty thousand employees around the world, representing about 10% of its workforce. The feedback indicated a desire for a system that would focus on work that matters and be available in real time. One aim of the PD@GE is to foster productive conversations.[42] Employees set priorities in the app and can ask for insights from anyone else. They can also provide feedback to others; thus the dialogue is much broader than simply manager to employee.

Talent Analytics

It is difficult to analyze data with traditional paper-based performance appraisal processes. Some companies will manually enter the scores in a spreadsheet and then use the software to perform statistical analysis. However, this process is labor intensive and prone to errors. Automating the process can give you a wealth of data with which to perform real-time performance analytics. Web- or cloud-based solutions to performance analytics can provide the following benefits:[43]

- Identify and address calibration problems.
- Identify organizational strengths and weaknesses.
- Identify high-potential employees for leadership development and succession planning.

- Identify low-performing areas for coaching.
- Identify areas of low bench strength that need to be deepened.
- Identify and consolidate training needs.
- Identify areas for reward and recognition.

Note that each of these benefits begins with the word "identify," but this is just one step in talent analytics. The real benefit is in what comes next. Once a problem, need, or opportunity has been identified, then a strategy should be developed and implemented in response.

 HR Workforce Analytics

In a workplace where advanced analytics tools are readily available, HR must evolve from focusing on policy and compliance to making better analytics-based decisions. KPMG looks at the future of the HR practice and how workforce analytics will continue to evolve.

Mike DiClaudio
Principal
People & Change
KPMG

View the video online at: http://www.youtube.com/embed/DTnbXsotH0s?rel=0

The Road Forward

Many other organizations, in addition to those described above, have transitioned to performance management systems that provide more frequent and often project-based feedback. This reinvention of performance management has spread across a wide variety of industries, including retail (Gap), pharmaceuticals (Pfizer), insurance (Cigna), investing (Oppenheimer Funds), and accounting (all Big Four firms).[44] Many of the companies that have reinvented their performance management systems have done so in response not only to a vast base of empirical research that glaringly showed the flaws and bias in performance ratings, but also because of the feedback they received from their own employees through surveys, focus groups, and crowdsourcing.

As we consider the road forward, and what the future of performance management will look like, several trends emerge:

- People want feedback more frequently, and this could be at the end of a project, or even in real time. Faster feedback also allows for course corrections to be made as soon as a problem is identified, instead of waiting until the end of the year.
- The idea of setting annual goals has become obsolete in many work settings. Due to the rapid pace of change and customer demands, goals are constantly morphing, and the accompanying work tasks have to be realigned.

- Performance management systems should provide input on future direction, rather than being focused on past performance. Instead of giving feedback, consider giving feedforward, a term coined by Marshall Goldsmith.[45] Feedforward focuses on providing input for future development. There is a place for feedback, such as when poor performance warrants a post mortem. People do need to learn from their mistakes, but the overall emphasis should be on the future.

- Conversations are important. Employees and managers want to engage in meaningful dialogue about how to maximize performance. Employees also want to engage their peers across the organization.

- Employees want transparency. When their performance is being discussed, employees deserve to have all of the facts and to understand how decisions are being made.

- Performance evaluation discussions (such as calibration meetings) should not be done behind closed doors where the employee is not present.

- One size does not fit all. Salaried workers should be managed differently than hourly workers. Professional workers are in a better position to manage their own projects and work tasks than industrial workers.

There are two notes of caution that should be considered in regard to the emerging performance management approaches. First, we don't really know if they work or not. The approaches described above are so new that very little empirical research has been conducted into their effectiveness. It appears that these approaches are effective, or at least that employees like them better. But whether they actually improve performance—the jury is still out on that. Second, companies moved away from the traditional performance rating because of the rater bias. But many of the new systems still involve some type of performance evaluation and therefore bias is inherent. In fact, it may be that bias will be harder to discover without the ability to analyze ratings by protected class (race, gender, age, etc.).

HR Talk: Drew Dunsmuir

People Services Manager
DaVita Kidney Care

I prefer regularly scheduled conversations to discuss goals and progress over a formal annual process. I also prefer clearly defined performance metrics that tie back to measurable items that have an impact on the business. The best systems I have seen have clearly defined outcomes that indicate what a person has to achieve to get a 1 to 5 rating. It is also nice to have a more subjective behavioral component to balance out the metrics to help drive the right behaviors consistent with the culture of the organization. Lastly, I've seen systems that track progress toward goals evaluated in real time throughout the year, and I like that approach. A balance of clearly defined metrics, a behavioral component, and progress toward goals is best with regular conversations as close to real time as possible.

In the absence of clearly defined metrics, I have seen subjective measures translate into what can feel like a popularity contest. If the interval between reviews is longer than two to three months, recency bias can be a problem. If the review process is too labor-intensive, managers tend not to invest the time in doing it properly, and it can demotivate rather than motivate employees. If managers do not receive sufficient training, they can create legal risk by artificially inflating or deflating scores and/or capturing inappropriate comments in a permanent record.

My company is going to move away from the old review process and toward a lighter, forward-looking performance development approach. I believe it is the future of performance management. I like the fact that most of these systems create a focus on improving the quality of the conversation. This creates more focus on driving employee engagement and a motivational environment conducive to a growth mind-set and performance development.

Key Takeaways

- Over the past few years, there has been an abundance of research that tells us performance processes are overengineered and time-consuming, and they tend to demotivate employees while hindering candid and honest conversations.
- There is a growing movement among some companies to reinvent performance management. Bersin by Deloitte reports that around 70% of companies are reconsidering their performance management strategy.
- People want feedback more frequently, and this could be at the end of a project, or even in real time. Faster feedback also allows for course corrections to be made as soon as a problem is identified, instead of waiting until the end of the year.
- Performance management systems should provide input on future direction, rather than being focused on past performance.
- When their performance is being discussed, employees deserve to have all of the facts and to understand how decisions are being made.
- One size does not fit all. Salaried workers should be managed differently than hourly workers. Professional workers are in a better position to manage their own projects and work tasks than industrial workers.

What Do *You* Think?

1. What is your perception of performance appraisals? Are they effective overall, or should they be done away with?
2. Of the companies described in this section, which do you think is using the best method to motivate employees to achieve high levels of performance?
3. What do you think about the feedforward method? What might be the disadvantages of this method?

8.5 Conclusion

This chapter distinguished the difference between performance management and performance appraisal and described the process for each. We explored assessor variations such as supervisor, subordinate, peer, and 360-degree evaluations. Some of the common problems with traditional performance appraisals were discussed, including rater errors and biases. Methods of assessing performance were reviewed, including management by objectives, rating scales, the critical incidents method, and informal appraisal processes. Then we examined how and why many organizations are reinventing their approach to performance management.

Theory-into-Practice (TIP) Exercises

1. Interview three individuals who are employed full-time and have been evaluated through an appraisal process. Ask them what they liked about the process, and what they didn't like. Then write down a few recommendations for how you might reinvent the performance management process for that company if you were a consultant.

2. With a classmate, practice giving feedback to each other in regard to your performance in the class (or practice this exercise with a co-worker at your job). Use resource number one to help you identify phrases to use in giving feedback.

3. Write a self-appraisal of your performance as a college student. Next, ask a peer (or another student who knows you well) to appraise your performance, and then ask a faculty member to do the same. You now have the essential ingredients for a simple 360-degree performance appraisal. In reviewing all of the input, write down three action items that you could do to improve your performance.

Case Study: Misbehaving . . . Off the Clock

Source: © Shutterstock, Inc.

Ben Taub Hospital is part of Harris County Health Systems. It is renowned for its top Level 1 trauma center for the southeast region of Texas. It has a hospital bed capacity of 586 and over 100,000 emergency room encounters per year. Its emergency department also houses a twenty-four-hour emergency psychiatric center. Medical faculty and students belong to the prominent Baylor University Medical Center.

In late December 2012, ten employees from Ben Taub decided to go out to celebrate the holidays. They all met at the hospital, where they parked their cars and then boarded a party bus that took them to various bars in downtown Houston. When the night ended, the party bus returned to the hospital and dropped the partygoers near the ambulance dock off from the emergency care center entrance.

Some of the partiers decided to go into the hospital to use the restroom. They were dressed in their civilian clothing, without badges, but they began saluting and cheering on their on-duty co-workers. After some time, they departed and continued their path to their parked cars.

The next morning, all ten employees were suspended, and after a week-long investigation, they were terminated. A hospital representative claimed "the group acted inappropriately during an early morning visit to a restricted area and were laughing and shouting near a bereavement room."[46] However, cameras did reveal that not all ten employees were in designated staff-only areas.

A grievance was filed on the behalf of all ten employees by a union representative through the American Federation of State, County, and Municipal Employees. A representative from the AFSCME named this an "unorthodox" termination. This was based on factors such as: No alcohol test was performed on the employees, the ER is already a loud and convoluted environment, the employees had on civilian clothes and were not wearing badges, and the party bus was parked off of hospital property.[47]

 ## Should Off-the-Clock Behavior be Grounds for Termination?

Rebel News reporter Emily Pratt asks people on the street whether off-the-clock behavior should be grounds for termination.

View the video online at: http://www.youtube.com/embed/FhVb4Bd-35o?rel=0

Case Discussion Questions

1. Do you think there is enough to justify the terminations of these employees based on "inappropriate behavior?" Would coaching and a write-up in the employees' files be sufficient?

2. If one the employees decided to go solo and not as a union member to file a grievance, do you believe he or she would have a better opportunity of being reinstated?

3. Should all ten employees receive the same level of punishment?

4. Knowing that these employees worked in a high-stress environment, what are some recommendations you could provide to Ben Taub's organizational development team regarding stress relievers and teamwork?

5. In your opinion, should the hospital supervisor intervene when the actions were occurring, or should he wait until the next day to file a report and review the evidence (camera footage) with human resource representatives?

Resources

1. **2000+ Performance Review Phrases: The Complete List.** A compilation of over two thousand different phrases that can be used on writing a performance appraisal, divided into categories.

   https://status.net/articles/performance-review-phrases-examples/

2. **70+ Free Employee Performance Review Templates.** Free templates in Word, PDF, & Excel formats.

    https://uptickapp.com/blog/free-performance-review-templates/

3. **Free Employee Performance Review Templates.** Free templates in Excel format for employee performance reviews.

    https://www.smartsheet.com/free-employee-performance-review-templates

4. **Performance Appraisal Software.** A review of over one hundred seventy performance appraisal software programs.

    https://www.capterra.com/performance-appraisal-software/

Endnotes

1. Case written by Crews, P. (2020). Adapted from Masunagam S., & Lien, T. (2016). Yahoo ex-employee sues, alleging manipulation of performance reviews and gender bias. *Los Angeles Times*. Retrieved from https://www.latimes.com/business/technology/la-fi-tn-yahoo-lawsuit-20160202-story.html

2. Aguinis, J., & Gottfredson. (2011). Why we hate performance management—And why we should love it. *Business Horizons, 54*(6), 503-507.

3. Thurston, P., & McNall, L. (2010). Justice perceptions of performance appraisal practices. *Journal of Managerial Psychology, 25*(3), 201-228.

4. Barends, E., & Briner, R. (2014). Teaching evidence-based practice: lessons from the pioneers: An interview with Amanda Burls and Gordon Guyatt. *Academy of Management Learning & Education, 13*(3), 476-483.

5. Johnson, S., Garrison, L., Hernez-Broome, G., Fleenor, J., & Steed, J. (2012). Go for the goal(s): Relationship between goal setting and transfer of training following leadership development. *Academy of Management Learning & Education, 11*(4), 555-569.

6. Allen, D.G., Bryant, P.C., & Vardaman, J.M. (2010). Retaining talent: Replacing misconceptions with evidence-based strategies. *Academy of Management Perspectives, 24*(2), 48–64. https://doi-org.ezp.twu.edu/10.5465/AMP.2010.51827775

7. Duffy, M., Scott, K., Shaw, J., Tepper, B., & Aquino, K. (2012). A social context model of envy and social undermining. *The Academy of Management Journal, 55*(3), 643-666.

8. McCord, P. (2014). How Netflix reinvented HR. *Harvard Business Review.* Retrieved from https://hbr.org/2014/01/how-netflix-reinvented-hr

9. Buckingham, M., & Goodall, A. (2015). Reinventing performance management. *Harvard Business Review.* Retrieved from https://hbr.org/2015/04/reinventing-performance-management

10. Thompson, S. The advantages and disadvantages of comprehensive performance evaluations by subordinates. *Small Business Chronicle.* Retrieved March 10, 2020 from https://smallbusiness.chron.com/advantages-disadvantages-comprehensive-performance-evaluations-subordinates-65528.html

11. Rehn, K. (2014). The pros and cons of peer assessments in performance reviews. *HH Staffing*. Retrieved from https://hhstaffingservices.com/pros-cons-peer-assessments-performance-reviews/

12. Ibid.

13. Dulewicz, V. (1989). *Performance appraisal and counseling,* in Herriot, P., *Assessment and selection in organizations: methods and practices for recruitment and appraisal.* New York: John Wiley & Sons. 645-649.

14. Thompson, D. (2014). The case against performance reviews. The Atlantic. Retrieved from https://www.theatlantic.com/business/archive/2014/01/the-case-against-performance-reviews/283402/

15. Schleicher, D., Baumann, H., Sullivan, D., Levy, P., Hargrove, D., & Barros-Rivera, B. (2018). Putting the system into performance management systems: A review and agenda for performance management research. *Journal of Management, 44*(6), 2209-2245.

16. Thorndike, E. (1920). A constant error in psychological ratings. *Journal of Applied Psychology, 4*(1), 25-29.

17. Mount, M.K., Judge, T.A., Scullen, S.E., Sytsma, M.R., & Hezlett, S.A. (1998). Trait, rater and level effects in 360-degree performance ratings. *Personnel Psychology, 51*(3), 557–576. https://doi-org.ezp.twu.edu/10.1111/j.1744-6570.1998.tb00251.x

18. Scullen, S., Mount, M., & Goff, M. (2000). Understanding the latent structure of job performance ratings. *Journal of Applied Psychology, 85*(6), 956-970.

19. Hoffman, B., Lance, C., Bynum, B., & Gentry, W. (2010). Rater source effects are alive and well after all. *Personnel Psychology, 63*(1), 119-151.

20. Bates, S. (2003). Forced ranking. *Society for Human Resource Management*. Retrieved from https://www.shrm.org/hr-today/news/hr-magazine/pages/0603bates.aspx

21. Ibid.

22. Doris, A. (2018). Performance ratings: Is calibration the answer? *Emory Business.* Retrieved from https://www.emorybusiness.com/2018/05/01/performance-ratings-is-calibration-the-answer/

23. Ibid.

24. Case written by Crews, P. (2019). Adapted from Kokemuller, N. *Chron.* Retrieved August 15, 2019 from https://work.chron.com/methods-informal-appraisals-workplace.html

25. Lloyd, A. (2017). Viewpoint: A new way of looking at performance management. *Society for Human Resource Management.* Retrieved from https://www.shrm.org/resourcesandtools/hr-topics/employee-relations/pages/viewpoint-a-new-way-of-looking-at-performance-management.aspx

26. Ibid.

27. Heathfield, S. (2018). Are annual performance reviews enough to ensure employee success? *Thebalancecareers.* Retrieved from https://www.thebalancecareers.com/performance-management-is-not-an-annual-appraisal-1918847

28. Milam, C. Why are companies ditching performance appraisals? *Expedite.* Retrieved August 28, 2019 from https://expedite-consulting.com/companies-ditching-performance-appraisals/

29. Nahata, S. (2019). Can Netflix double its subscriber base by 2024? *MarketRealist.* Retrieved from https://marketrealist.com/2019/06/can-netflix-double-its-subscriber-base-by-2024/

30. McCord, P. (2014). How Netflix reinvented HR. *Harvard Business Review.* Retrieved from https://hbr.org/2014/01/how-netflix-reinvented-hr

31. Ibid.

32. Netflix jobs. *Netflix.* Retrieved February 17, 2020 from https://jobs.netflix.com/culture

33. Milam, C. Why are companies ditching performance appraisals? *Expedite.* Retrieved August 28, 2019 from https://expedite-consulting.com/companies-ditching-performance-appraisals/

34. The story of Check-in. *Adobe.* Retrieved February 17, 2020 from https://www.adobe.com/check-in.html

35. Ibid.

36. Buckingham, M., & Goodall, A. (2015). Reinventing performance management. *Harvard Business Review.* Retrieved from https://hbr.org/2015/04/reinventing-performance-management

37. Ibid.

38. Milam, C. Why are companies ditching performance appraisals? *Expedite.* Retrieved August 28, 2019 from https://expedite-consulting.com/companies-ditching-performance-appraisals/

39. Ibid.

40. Zillman, C. (2016). IBM is blowing up its annual performance review. *Fortune.* Retrieved from https://fortune.com/2016/02/01/ibm-employee-performance-reviews/

41. Birt, M. (2017). Why General Electric moved away from traditional HR review practices. *Financial Post.* Retrieved from https://business.financialpost.com/executive/why-general-electric-moved-away-from-traditional-hr-review-practices

42. Ibid.

43. Adapted from Getting useful workforce analytics data from your performance management process. *Saba.* Retrieved April 6, 2020 from https://www.saba.com/products/performance-management

44. Capelli, P., & Tavis, A. (2018). HR goes agile. *Harvard Business Review.* Retrieved from https://hbr.org/2018/03/the-new-rules-of-talent-management

45. Goldsmith, M. (2015). Try feedforward instead of feedback. *Marshall Gold-smith*. Retrieved from https://www.marshallgoldsmith.com/articles/try-feedforward-instead-feedback/

46. Case written by Narvaez, A. (2020). Adapted from: Nurses, technicians fired from Ben Taub after off-duty holiday party. KHOU. Retrieved February 28, 2020 from https://www.khou.com/article/news/nurses-technicians-fired-from-ben-taub-after-off-duty-holiday-party/285-32106066

47. Case written by Narvaez, A. (2020). Adapted from: Nurses, technicians fired from Ben Taub after off-duty holiday party. KHOU. Retrieved February 28, 2020 from https://www.khou.com/article/news/nurses-technicians-fired-from-ben-taub-after-off-duty-holiday-party/285-321060662

CHAPTER 9
Managing Compensation

Learning Objectives

Learning Objectives

After reading this chapter, you should be able to do the following:

1. Design an effective compensation plan, considering strategic goals along with internal and external determinants of pay structure.
2. Describe the major theories of compensation.
3. Explain the job-ranking, point-factor, factor comparison, and job classification methods of job evaluation.
4. Identify the federal legislation and regulations that govern compensation.
5. Recognize the characteristics of individual, group, and enterprise incentive plans.

Compensation plays a crucial role in ensuring that a workforce is productive and motivated. It includes direct compensation (cash or cash equivalents) and indirect compensation such as paid time off, health insurance, and retirement programs. This chapter covers direct compensation, and Chapter 10 addresses indirect compensation (benefits). An effective compensation strategy should also improve employee retention by establishing a culture of competitive and fair compensation.

This chapter begins with a discussion of the strategic aspects of compensation and the determinants of pay structure. Compensation theories and issues such as equity, comparable worth, and pay compression are explored. Specific job evaluation methods are introduced, and the federal laws and regulations that govern compensation are reviewed. Incentive plans are then covered, and the chapter closes with a look at the current controversy around executive compensation.

9.1 Opening Case: Work Hard, Have Fun, Make History

Source: © Shutterstock, Inc.

Many employers offer their associates not only base pay for their employment but also indirect compensation such as benefits, bonus pay, and vacation time. But should employers be increasing the base pay? Amazon uses "work hard, have fun, make history" as a recruiting slogan. It appears that they could now add "earn more." In 2019, Amazon decided to raise its minimum wage for all of its workers to $15 an hour. Higher pay and better benefits incentivize an employee to stay with a company long-term. It can be an ethical conversation, but it is also a profit conversation. Higher pay means introducing better candidates and better retention. Also, better benefits will cause employees to think twice before leaving their job.

Amazon has faced constant criticism throughout the years regarding the treatment of their employees, specifically the warehouse workers. From the extended hours to limited pay, many consider Amazon to have unethical labor practices. The decision to raise their minimum wage did not come because Amazon believes those are the wages their employees deserve; the decision came from high turnover and bad consumer reception. It did not help that the CEO of Amazon, Jeff Bezos, is one of the richest men in the world.

Through exit interviews, stay interviews, recruiter feedback, and engagement events, there should be a point where a company can accurately see what is causing its turnover. Many times, companies believe it is the mass-hiring industry they're in; there are more floor workers than supervisors can handle and provide with actual work and career guidance.

People want to be paid well and have access to benefits such as health insurance. It is a matter of a company deciding if their turnover costs could actually be lowered by making some changes. Workers will always want more money, but an employee is more likely to stay if they know that their rent is going to be paid.

Turnover costs include many things: recruiting, onboarding, training, and opening the job requisition when the associate leaves. For a simple job that requires minimal effort and workers that can be easily replaced for minimal cost, a company might benefit and experience a better profit by minimizing benefits and wages. A compensation and turnover analysis should be done to better grasp what solution is better for each company.

No employer wants its profits to go down. But floor and factory workers are the people who actually provide the service that the company is selling. Many companies will invest whatever money is necessary on the right machines and equipment—are human workers any different? Are they worth the investment? When you look at your product and service, the quality will only be as good as what you invested in it. So where is the profit? The profit is within the employees.[1]

 ### Amazon Associates React to $15 Minimum Wage Announcement

Amazon announces it is increasing its minimum wage to $15 for all full-time, part-time, temporary, and seasonal employees across the U.S.

View the video online at: http://www.youtube.com/embed/td_ZxRLXJDQ?rel=0

Case Study Discussion Questions

1. How would you combat high turnover rates?
2. Do you think Amazon's $15 minimum wage will be effective? Does it need to be higher?
3. Does higher pay really assist with turnover? If so, in what way?
4. Do materials and employees deserve the same level of investment?

9.2 Compensation Theories and Issues

Learning Objectives

1. Design an equitable compensation plan in alignment with organizational strategy.

2. Describe expectancy theory and how it relates to compensation.
3. Explain comparable worth theory and how it differs from equal pay.
4. Recognize when and why pay compression occurs.
5. Understand the implications of pay secrecy policies.

Strategic Aspects of Compensation

The saying that "time is money" takes on new meaning in regard to external equity. If employees do not perceive that their compensation is worth their time, then they may look for a job elsewhere.

Source: © Shutterstock, Inc.

compensation philosophy

A statement that describes the organization's compensation goals.

compensation plan

A set of policies and procedures to determine base pay, incentive pay, and employee benefits to align with the compensation philosophy.

external equity

The employees' perception of the conditions and rewards of their employment, compared with those of the employees of other firms.

When you are looking for a job and are reviewing job postings online, what is one of the first things you want to know? If you said money, then you are not alone. Survey after survey indicates that the number one most important thing to employees is salary.[2] And that just makes sense, right? We all want to be paid what we are worth in the marketplace. After all, we are there to earn a living, not to volunteer our time. But you might also say that there are other things you would like from your employer, such as health insurance, time off, or work-life balance. As the opening case illustrates, organizations need to balance their efforts to attract and retain employees through competitive wages with the bottom line. In this chapter, we explore compensation, beginning with how companies design a strategy for paying their talent. Then in the following chapter, we will look more in-depth at employee benefits.

You may recall that throughout this book, we have emphasized how HR policies and procedures should be aligned with the strategic objectives of the organization. This is also true of compensation. Specifically, there are two steps to developing a compensation strategy:

1. **Develop a compensation philosophy.** This is a statement that describes the organization's compensation goals. It might look something like this: "When employees are fully proficient in their position and are meeting or exceeding expectations, their compensation should be consistent with the seventy-fifth percentile of the competitive market." In this example, the organization has decided that its employees will make more than 75% of those in the same or similar positions at competitors. If a company wants to be right in the middle of the market, then they would choose the fiftieth percentile. Of course, this implies that the starting point is to conduct research to determine what the average wages are for each job within the company and across the industry. Then an organization should determine whether it will lead, match, or lag the market rates.

2. **Design a compensation plan.** With the philosophy as a guide, the organization then needs to determine base pay, incentive pay, and employee benefits (including paid time off, health insurance, and others).

Why is it important to know what other companies are paying, and then decide what percentile you choose for your compensation strategy? If you and a friend both have the same type of job at two different companies, and you find out that your friend makes $17 per hour, compared to your $14 an hour, how might you react? You may decide that the situation is neither fair nor equitable. People tend to compare how they are paid with others. **External equity** is the employees' perception of the conditions and rewards of their employment, compared with those of the employees of other firms. If an employee perceives their situation is not equitable, then they may feel taken advantage of and look for work at another employer who pays more. Thus, external equity has an impact on employee retention and turnover.

People also tend to compare their salary with other employees in their company. **Internal equity** is the employees' perception of the conditions and rewards of their employment, compared with those of employees in similar positions within their organization. If an employee perceives inequity, the result might be that the employee first asks for a raise. If he or she is not given the raise, then they might begin looking for work elsewhere. Thus, internal equity also impacts retention and turnover. Even if an employee chooses to stay in a position where they do feel treated unfairly, morale and productivity will likely suffer. Internal equity comparisons should also be done proactively by the company to ensure that discrimination is not taking place (comparing salaries by gender, race, age, etc.).

internal equity

The employees' perception of the conditions and rewards of their employment, compared with those of employees in similar positions within their organization.

HR Talk: Ashlie Bagley

Director of Human Resources, EWIS Americas Division

Safran Electrical & Power

One of the most critical factors to consider in establishing a pay structure is compensation philosophy. How does the organization view compensation, and how do they want to place themselves in the market in comparison with competitors and other industries? Very closely aligned is the consideration of culture. Some inherent values and behaviors are uniquely assumed within every organization, and those cultural components can have close ties and an impact on the compensation structure. Largely tied to culture is the consideration of historical aspects of compensation structure. It is important to understand how the compensation structure was established previously and why it was important to have that structure in the context of the business.

Scope is another key component with the consideration of countries, geographic regions, and positions that will be included in the structure. In addition, the presence of bargaining units and the particular regulatory aspects based on the scope must be reflected appropriately in the structure. Finally, consideration of the support available in building the structure is critical. A sole HR practitioner developing a compensation structure might take a very simplistic approach as compared to an international organization utilizing the support of a global consulting firm.

Operating in an international organization has unique implications on the compensation structure. The structure must be considerate to the international scope and system, but it must also have adaptability for local application. For example, some countries have much more robust social benefits plans, which are a large cost for employers. Often, salaries and bonuses are not as large in these sites because the social programs consume so much of total compensation. In the United States, we have moderate social benefit plans combined with moderate salary and bonus structures. Therefore, an organization may need to be able to align to a global grading structure in terms of level and scope of position while having a unique country-specific compensation range and bonus eligibility attached to the compensation structure.

In addition, the HR practitioner must develop a base understanding of international differences. To effectively communicate on compensation topics across countries or in consideration of international mobility packages, it is important to understand how other countries' total compensation packages are comprised and the values placed on different aspects of the system. Finally, international operations can also affect the approval process for compensation matters. Context can include new hire packages, promotions, and annual merit and bonus processes. It is key to understand who should be involved at what level to provide strong communications and education on local compensation practices. Oftentimes, this may include providing a more robust explanation of reasoning or comparisons than what may typically be required for local compensation approvals.

Expectancy Theory

expectancy theory

A theory of motivation which predicts that one's level of motivation depends on the attractiveness of the rewards sought and the probability of obtaining those rewards.

The **expectancy theory** of motivation predicts that one's level of motivation depends on the attractiveness of the rewards sought and the probability of obtaining those rewards.[3] The theory is based on Victor Vroom's formula, shown in Figure 9.1.

FIGURE 9.1 Expectancy Theory Formula

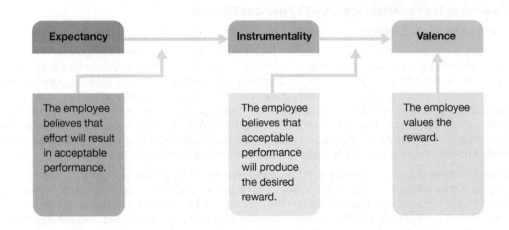

(Motivation = Expectancy × Instrumentality × Valence)

Expectancy	Instrumentality	Valence
The employee believes that effort will result in acceptable performance.	The employee believes that acceptable performance will produce the desired reward.	The employee values the reward.

expectancy

A person's perception of their ability to accomplish or probability of accomplishing an objective.

instrumentality

The perception that a particular level of performance is likely to result in a reward.

valence

The value a person places on an outcome or reward.

Expectancy is the person's perception of their ability to accomplish or the probability of accomplishing an objective. **Instrumentality** is the perception that a particular level of performance is likely to result in a reward. **Valence** refers to the value a person places on the outcome or reward. Not all people desire the same rewards from their work. One individual might want a cash bonus, while another employee might prefer to have some extra time off.

Note that expectancy and instrumentality are based on a person's perception, which may or may not be based in fact. Expectancy is based on the individual's belief that they will be able to perform the job. This belief is influenced by factors including possession of the appropriate knowledge and skills, availability of the required resources, support, and guidance when needed, and adequate time to complete the job. Instrumentality is based on the individual's belief that if they perform the task, they will be rewarded for it.

Another important aspect is that the expectancy model is multiplicative, not additive. To calculate motivating potential, one does not add the values of expectancy, instrumentality, and valence. They are multiplied, so if one of the three is at or near zero, the motivating potential is also zero, indicating the individual is not motivated to perform.[4]

Comparable Worth

In a free market economy, wages are typically determined by forces of supply and demand. For example, if there are fewer nurses, then nurses are likely to be paid more. The concept of **comparable worth** is the idea that men and women should receive equal pay when they perform work that involves comparable skills and responsibility, or that is of comparable worth to the employer. Comparable worth suggests that the free market theory is not applicable when comparing female-dominated occupations with male-dominated occupations, and that the pay differences between the two are due to systematic discrimination against women rather than market forces.[5]

Comparable worth is sometimes confused with the concept of **gender equity**. They are related concepts, but gender equity is more comprehensive and includes issues beyond pay. Gender equity means fairness of treatment for women and men, according to their respective needs. This may include equal treatment or treatment that is different but is considered equivalent in terms of rights, benefits, obligations, and opportunities.

> **comparable worth**
>
> The idea that men and women should receive equal pay when they perform work that involves comparable skills and responsibility or that is of comparable worth to the employer.
>
> **gender equity**
>
> Fairness of treatment for women and men, according to their respective needs.

Women are striving for gender equality around the world, as evidenced in this 2019 Women's Day March in Peru.

Source: Myriam B / Shutterstock.com

Comparable worth should also not be confused with equal pay. As discussed in Chapter 3, the Equal Pay Act of 1963 was an amendment to the Fair Labor Standards Act of 1938 (FLSA). It is administered by the EEOC and prohibits sex-based discrimination between men and women in the same establishment who perform jobs that require substantially equal skill, effort, and responsibility under similar working conditions.[6] While the Equal Pay Act requires that men and women be given equal pay for equal work, the jobs do not have to be identical. The jobs do need to be substantially equal, based on job content, not job titles.

Comparable worth is also not legislated as equal pay is. Rather, it is a concept or strategy to put women on a level playing field with men. In practice, comparable worth consists of raising wages for traditionally female-dominated jobs to the level of those for comparable male-dominated jobs.[7] Proponents of comparable worth argue that gender discrimination in wages has been built into society, and that women have been historically devalued in the workplace.[8] Thus, comparable worth intends to right the effects of past wrongs, in much the same way as affirmative action plans.

The intent of comparable worth is to close the gender gap. So, is it working? The answer is yes and no. The gap has closed somewhat, but it is persistent. In 1980, women earned 64% of that of their male counterparts. The gender gap has narrowed since then, with women earning 82% of what men earned in 2017. Based on this estimate, it would take an extra forty-seven days of work for women to earn what men did in 2017.[9] However, that gap has remained relatively stable for the past fifteen years, except for young workers, as shown in Figure 9.2.

FIGURE 9.2 Gender Pay Gap

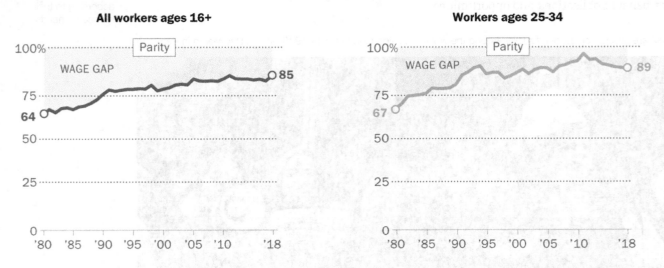

The gender pay gap is narrower among young adults than among workers overall

Median hourly earnings of U.S. women as percentage of men's median among ...

Note: Estimates are for civilian, non-institutionalized, full- or part-time employed workers with positive earnings. Self-employed workers are excluded.
Source: Pew Research Center analysis of Current Population Survey data.

PEW RESEARCH CENTER

Source: Pew Research Center

Pay Compression

pay compression

Occurs when there is a small difference in pay between employees regardless of their skills or experience.

Pay compression occurs when there is a small difference in pay between employees regardless of their skills or experience. Consider the following example: Jason is hired as a customer service representative for the call center of a credit card company. He was hired in 2014 at a salary of $25,000. Jason has a stellar job record, consistently receives excellent feedback from customer surveys, and has been given an average salary increase of 3% each year. In 2019, he now earns a salary of $28,981 per year, and he feels rewarded for his five years of experience with the company and his efforts to be a high performer. Then in 2019, the company expands and hires a new customer service representative to work alongside Jason. During a lunch break, Jason learns that the new hire was started at a salary of $28,455, only $526 a year less than him. How would you feel if you were Jason? You most likely would feel that the new hire should not be paid almost as much as you, given that you have been loyal to the company for five years, have proven yourself, and are more qualified by virtue of your experience with the company and its processes and procedures.

A related concept is **pay inversion**, which occurs when new hires are paid more than incumbent employees with similar qualifications, tasks, and responsibilities. Both pay compression and pay inversion lead to internal inequity and will cause the employees who have been with the company longer to become dissatisfied with their pay. At best, the company will have unhappy employees, and at worst a high rate of turnover.

So why does pay compression or pay inversion happen? This situation sometimes occurs because the market rate for a given job outpaces the regular pay increases given to job incumbents. Therefore, new employees can only be recruited by offering them as much or more than senior employees. A second reason is that pay increases have not kept pace with inflation. While an employee may be receiving annual increases, if the increase does not exceed the rate of inflation, then the employee is not being compensated for seniority or job performance but is merely keeping pace with the cost of living. The inflation rate in the U.S., as measured by the Consumer Price Index (CPI) was 2.4% in 2020.[10] In the example of Jason, he has been receiving 3% raises each year for five years. Assuming a constant inflation rate over five years, then his real increase, adjusted for inflation, has only been 0.6% a year. Thus, the inflation rate explains some, but not all of the reasons why a new hire was offered almost as much as Jason earns. The remaining difference might be explained by labor market conditions. For example, the unemployment rate might be lower, making jobs harder to fill, causing employers to make higher initial job offers to attract qualified candidates.

Pay compression and inversion can be avoided by regularly conducting compression studies to ensure that employees are paid at the market rate. Organizations should examine salary structure at least every three to five years, although some HR professionals recommend every eighteen months to catch problems early on.[11] The analysis should include the calculation of compa-ratios. A **compa-ratio** (short for comparison ratio) is a compensation metric that compares the salary an employee is paid to the midpoint of the salary range for their position or similar positions at other organizations.[12] A compa-ratio reveals how far an employee's pay is from the market midpoint. If an employee has a compa-ratio of 100%, then he or she is being paid at market, while a ratio of 80% would mean that he or she is paid 20% below market, and a ratio of 105% would mean he or she is being paid 5% over market. Figure 9.3 below gives an example of a compa-ratio chart.

pay inversion

Occurs when new hires are paid more than incumbent employees with similar qualifications, tasks, and responsibilities.

compa-ratio

A compensation metric that compares the salary an employee is paid to the midpoint of the salary range for their position or similar positions at other organizations.

FIGURE 9.3 Compa-Ratio

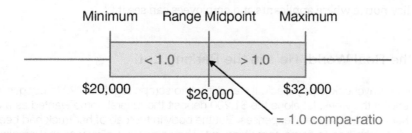

| Minimum | Range Midpoint | Maximum |

$20,000 $26,000 $32,000

= 1.0 compa-ratio

Compa-Ratio

A quick number to identify employee's pay relative to the midpoint of the range. Calculated by:

= Employee Pay / Midpoint

Compa-Ratio < 1.0
EE Pay is below proficiency point

Compa-Ratio = 1.0
EE Pay is at the proficiency point

Compa-Ratio > 1.0
EE Pay is above the proficiency point

Pay Secrecy

Employers sometimes have overt or implicit prohibitions on employees sharing pay information, and some even put these policies in writing.[13] A survey of U.S. employees found that 19% of employees say they work in a place where discussions of pay are formally prohibited and employees caught discussing wages are punished. Thirty-one percent of employees said that pay discussions were discouraged. Thus, over half of the employees work in an environment where pay discussions are either discouraged or outright prohibited. Only 16% said that pay could be discussed among employees.[14]

On the other hand, there is a trend among some companies toward more transparency, not only in pay matters but in company workforce practices in general. For example, Namasté Solar in Colorado decided to practice complete salary transparency.[15]

Besides eliminating time-wasting salary speculation among the team, transparency can narrow the gender pay gap. The Lilly Ledbetter case discussed in Chapter 3 is an example of how pay secrecy can contribute to gender bias in pay.

Transparency will require more time on the part of managers in explaining to some employees why they are paid less than others. But this process will be smoother if the managers are trained on how to handle these conversations and if the salaries are set according to a rational, consistent, and fair compensation plan. If the company tries to hide what employees make, it tends to create an environment of mistrust. Most of the time, people are going to talk anyway, and salary information eventually gets out. If employees understand salary differences, then this will help to create a culture of internal equity.

There also is a legal aspect to consider. There are no federal regulations that apply to all employers. However, Executive Order 13665, the Non-retaliation for Disclosure of Compensation Information (less formally referred to as the Pay Transparency Rule) took effect in 2016. The order prohibits a federal contractor or subcontractor from retaliating against employees who discuss pay information, and states "the contractor will not discharge or in any other manner discriminate against any employee or applicant for employment because such employee or applicant has inquired about, discussed, or disclosed the compensation of the employee or applicant or another employee or applicant."[16] The regulations also require that contractors post a mandatory pay transparency policy notice where applicants and employees can see it.[17]

HR in the Real World: He's in the Parking Lot!

Frances lived paycheck to paycheck. It was difficult to scrape together $20 to put gas in her truck near the end of the week, let alone the $1,200 deposit the funeral home wanted as a down payment on her husband's funeral expenses. But the body in the cab of her truck had been dead for three days, so she had to figure something out. The company policy was that employees could get an advance on a paycheck up to $500, and she needed more than twice that amount. So, she mustered the courage to go see HR.

She explained what had happened to the HR director. She and her husband were not living together but were still legally married. He lived alone in an apartment in a neighboring town. He apparently had a heart attack while sitting in his pickup truck in the parking lot of the apartment complex. No one noticed him for two days because he had slumped over. Finally, an apartment resident parked next to his truck and saw him and called the apartment manager. The manager then called Frances since she was listed as the emergency contact.

It was 11 pm when Frances arrived at the apartment complex. She didn't know what to do, so she loaded her husband's body in the cab of her truck and went back home. She called a funeral home the next morning and discovered that they wanted the $1,200. Not having the money, she decided she better go to work and ask for a payroll advance. After she explained the situation, the HR director asked, "Frances. . . where is your husband's body now?" Frances replied, "He's in the parking lot!" Frances got the $1,200 advance.

Key Takeaways

- There are two steps to developing a compensation strategy: developing a compensation philosophy and designing a compensation plan.
- External equity is the employees' perception of the conditions and rewards of their employment compared with those of the employees of other firms.
- Internal equity is the employees' perception of the conditions and rewards of their employment compared with those of employees in similar positions within their organization.
- The expectancy theory of motivation predicts that one's level of motivation depends on the attractiveness of the rewards sought and the probability of obtaining those rewards.
- Expectancy is the person's perception of their ability to accomplish or the probability of accomplishing an objective. Instrumentality is the perception that a particular level of performance is likely to result in a reward. Valence refers to the value a person places on the outcome or reward.
- Comparable worth is the idea that men and women should receive equal pay when they perform work that involves comparable skills and responsibility, or that is of comparable worth to the employer.
- Gender equity means fairness of treatment for women and men, according to their respective needs.
- Pay compression occurs when there is a small difference in pay between employees regardless of their skills or experience.
- Pay inversion occurs when new hires are paid more than incumbent employees with similar qualifications, tasks, and responsibilities.
- A compa-ratio (short for comparison ratio) is a compensation metric that compares the salary an employee is paid to the midpoint of the salary range for their position or similar positions at other organizations.

What Do *You* Think?

1. What is the compensation philosophy of your employer? Do they have one?
2. What is the difference between comparable worth and gender equity?
3. If you found out that you were a victim of pay compression or pay inversion, would you bring it to the attention of your employer? How would you present your argument for a pay raise?
4. Have you ever worked for an organization where you were told not to discuss wages? Why do you think that was?

9.3 Job Evaluation Methods

Learning Objectives

1. Describe the advantages and disadvantages of the job-ranking method of job evaluation.
2. Describe the advantages and disadvantages of the point-factor method of job evaluation.
3. Describe the advantages and disadvantages of the factor-comparison method of job evaluation.
4. Describe the advantages and disadvantages of the job classification system method of job evaluation.

job evaluation

The process of determining the worth of each position in an organization relative to other positions within the same organization.

Deciding how much to pay an employee for a particular position is an important decision that impacts the labor expense of the organization (and therefore the bottom line), and also is a major factor in employee retention. As we discussed in the opening section, there are external and internal issues to consider. One of the primary methods for gathering information about the internal aspect of compensation is to conduct a job evaluation. **Job evaluation** is the process of determining the worth of each position in an organization relative to other positions within the same organization. The most common job evaluation methods are job-ranking, point-factor, factor-comparison, and job classification systems. Before introducing each of these methods, let's consider where job evaluation fits within the three steps of establishing salary ranges. The three steps are:

1. Determine the organization's overall compensation strategy.
2. Conduct job analyses.
3. Conduct job evaluation.

Thus, there are three important factors to consider before evaluating jobs using any of the following methods. First, job evaluation should be conducted with a strategic compensation approach in mind (lead, match, or lag the market). Second, job evaluation should be based on up-to-date job analyses. This is critical, especially in an environment of rapid change, where job duties are constantly evolving. Third, keep in mind that you are evaluating jobs, not the people who hold those jobs. Job evaluation should be based on the job content to determine the worth of jobs relative to others in the organization and the level of responsibility and authority of each job.

Job-Ranking Method

job-ranking method

The process of placing jobs from lowest to highest, or vice versa, based on their relative worth to the organization.

The **job-ranking method** is the process of placing jobs from lowest to highest, or vice versa, based on their relative worth to the organization. It is the simplest of the job evaluation methods and can be done quickly and easily. One approach is to write each job on a card or Post-it, along with a summary of the job duties, responsibilities, and qualifications. A single manager or a committee can then place them in rank order.

The job-ranking method, although simple and inexpensive, has several disadvantages. First, it is a subjective method and is not based on any quantitative data, as are some of the more advanced methods. Since it is subjective, the ranking process can be biased. This is even more true when only one person does the ranking. Another disadvantage is the process yields a rank order but does not identify the degree of difference between each position. Nevertheless, the method can be appropriate for small organizations (twenty-five or fewer employees) in which managers have a high degree of knowledge of the relative worth of each job.

Point-Factor Method

The **point-factor method** determines the relative worth of a job based on the degree to which a compensable factor is present or required. A **compensable factor** is a job characteristic that an organization values and chooses to pay for. The point-factor method originated in the scientific management movement, and the basic steps have changed little since the early twentieth century.[18] The point-factor method has several advantages. Because it is quantitative in nature, it is less subjective than the job-ranking method. It also provides the ability to differentiate jobs on multiple factors, which helps to specify the degree of difference between jobs. Each factor is assigned a number of points, to the degree that it is present or required in each job. The points are totaled, and the more points assigned to a job, the more worth that job has to the organization.

The Korn Ferry Hay Group method (commonly referred to as the Hay point method) is the most accepted point-factor method and is used by over half the world's largest employers.[19] The Hay method is based on three compensable factors, each of which includes two to three subfactors. The three factors are accountability, know-how, and problem-solving. Table 9.1 summarizes the subfactors of each category.[20]

point-factor method

Determines the relative worth of a job based on the degree to which a compensable factor is present or required.

compensable factor

A job characteristic that an organization values and chooses to pay for.

TABLE 9.1 Hay Method Factors and Subfactors

Factor	Subfactors
Accountability. Measures the type and level of value a job adds to an organization.	1. Freedom to act. The degree of organizational empowerment to take action and the guidance provided to focus on decision-making. 2. Nature of impact. The scope and influence on organizational results, whether the impact is primary, contributory, or shared. 3. Magnitude. The business measure(s) the job is designed to positively impact.
Know-how. The sum total of every capability or skill, however acquired, needed for fully competent performance.	1. Practical/technical knowledge. Depth and breadth of technical or specialized knowledge and skills. 2. Planning, organizing, and integrating. The requirement to undertake managerial functions, such as planning, organizing, staffing, directing, and leading.
Problem-solving. Refers to the use of know-how to identify, delineate, and resolve problems.	1. Thinking environment. The freedom to think; the degree to which problems and solutions are organizationally guided and defined through strategy, policy, precedents, procedures, and rules. 2. Thinking challenge. The nature of addressable problems and the degree to which thinking is required to arrive at solutions that add value.

Table 9.2 shows a comparison of several positions in a retail organization, based upon ten compensable factors.

TABLE 9.2 Point-Factor Method Example for Two Positions in a Retail Company

Compensable Factor	Degree 1 (1–20)	Degree 2 (21–40)	Degree 3 (41-60)	Degree 4 (61-80)	Degree 5 (81-100)
Experience	10		45		
Education		25		68	
Customer Service Skills			55	75	
Responsibility for Work of Others	5				
Freedom to Act		35		67	
Planning and Organizing		22			81
Communicating and Influencing				75	90
Technical Knowledge		38 33			
Physical Effort	18		43		
Initiative and Originality		24			85

Total Points:

Marketing Manager (numbers in pink above) = 547 points

Retail Associate (numbers in blue above) = 347 points

Descriptions for each degree should be provided to the rater. For example, the degrees for education might be:

Degree 1: GED or high school diploma.

Degree 2: Some post-secondary education/training required but less than a two-year degree.

Degree 3: Requires an Associate Degree.

Degree 4: Requires a Bachelor's Degree.

Degree 5: Requires a graduate degree.

Variations within each degree category allow for assigning of points relative to individual positions such as difficulty of degree or specialized knowledge.

 Point Method of Job Evaluation

The information derived from a job analysis is vital for establishing the relative worth of the jobs within the company through a systematic process called job evaluation.

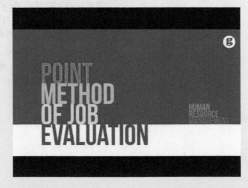

View the video online at: http://www.youtube.com/embed/L07rWAQJAoY?rel=0

Factor Comparison Method

The **factor comparison method** combines the point-factor and ranking methods. Using this method, a group of jobs is identified to be benchmark jobs. The jobs chosen as benchmarks are typically positions that would be found in similar organizations, such as Accountant I, Accountant II, Recruiter, Senior Recruiter, etc. Points are assigned to each benchmark job as with the point-factor method based on compensable factors. The benchmark jobs are then rank-ordered, and finally, all other jobs in the organization are compared to the benchmark jobs to determine each job's placement in the ranking. The factor comparison method uses both objective (compensable factors) and subjective (ranking) approaches.

factor comparison method

Combines the point-factor and ranking methods, using a group of jobs as benchmarks.

Job Classification Systems

The U.S. National Park Service is one of many employers that use the General Schedule (GS) system of the U.S. federal government.

Source: christianthiel.net / Shutterstock.com

The **job classification systems method** is an approach that classifies all jobs within a company according to a standardized scale, based on the overall tasks, responsibilities, and duties associated with each job. A description is first written for each job, and then jobs are grouped into categories referred to as grades based on the required tasks, duties, and skills required. Managers then evaluate each job in the organization by comparing the job description to the grade description and placing the job into the grade category that is the closest match. It is not as precise as the point-factor method because the approach is based on a manager's subjective option about the job as a whole, as opposed to multiple compensable job factors. However, it is a useful method for categorizing a wide variety of jobs in a relatively simple manner, and pay differences are easily explained to employees. One of the most familiar job classification systems to most people is the General Schedule (GS) system of the U.S. federal government, an example of which is shown in Table 9.3.

job classification systems method

An approach that classifies all jobs within a company according to a standardized scale, based on the overall tasks, responsibilities, and duties associated with each job.

TABLE 9.3 GS Pay Scale Example

Grade	Step 1	Step 2	Step 3	Step 4	Step 5	Step 6	Step 7	Step 8	Step 9	Step 10
1	9.36	9.68	9.99	10.30	10.61	10.79	11.10	11.41	11.42	11.71
2	10.53	10.78	11.13	11.42	11.55	11.89	12.23	12.57	12.91	13.25
3	11.49	11.87	12.25	12.64	13.02	13.40	13.79	14.17	14.55	14.93
4	12.90	13.33	13.76	14.19	14,62	15.05	15.48	15.91	16.33	16.76
5	14.43	14.91	15.39	15.87	16.35	16.83	17.32	17.80	18.28	18.76
6	16.08	16.62	17.16	17.69	18.23	18.76	19.30	19.84	20.37	20.91
7	17.87	18.47	19.06	19.66	20.26	20.85	21.45	22.04	22.64	23.23
8	19.79	20.45	21.11	21.77	22.43	23.09	23.75	24.21	25.07	25.73
9	21.86	22.59	23.32	24.05	24.78	25.51	26.24	29.96	27.69	28.42
10	24.08	24.88	25.68	26.48	27.29	28.09	28.89	29.69	30.50	31.30
11	26.45	27.33	28.21	29.10	29.98	30.86	31.74	32.62	33.50	34.39
12	31.70	32.76	33.82	34.88	35.93	36.99	38.05	39.10	40.16	41.22
13	37.70	38.96	40.21	41.47	42.73	43.98	45.24	46.50	47.76	49.01
14	44.55	46.04	47.52	49.01	50.49	51.98	53.46	54.94	56.43	57.91
15	52.40	54.15	55.90	57.64	59.39	61.14	62.89	64.63	66.38	68.13

Source: Based on data from https://www.opm.gov/policy-data-oversight/pay-leave/salaries-wages/salary-tables/20Tables/html/GS_h.aspx

Talent Analytics

Using Talent Analytics at Safran Electrical & Power

Ashlie Bagley, Director of Human Resources, EWIS Americas Division

Job grading has been an effective job evaluation method I have used most frequently in my career. It allows flexibility in establishing mid-point progression and range spread based on the complexities and considerations of the individual organization. Generally, you begin with a review and potential consolidation of job descriptions across the scope. Next, a market analysis is performed on a minimum of 50% of the positions to ensure strong consideration of market factors. Once the market data is finalized, you create the appropriate number of grades, considering the factors of mid-point progression and grade range. The positions with benchmark data are placed appropriately into the grading structure with review and approval by the HR organization. Finally, those positions not benchmarked to market data are slotted accordingly into the structure by considering similar internal equity, comparable job progression, standard qualifications, and general leveling across the organization. Grading offers flexibility to consider future market shifts in specific positions because a single position can move grades without actually touching the value of the grade itself, allowing for adjustment of market competitiveness in a particular job.

Analytics are an important consideration in the effectiveness of compensation programs. It is important to understand the market data in the geographic regions where a business operates to ensure a competitive compensation program. This can come both from formal benchmarking surveys and from market details acquired during recruitment exercises interacting with external applicants. It is also key to perform an incumbent analysis of the pay structure. Some variables to consider in such an analysis could be time in job and performance history. Based on this calculation, evaluate if the incumbent is placed well in the range. Exit interviews can be a good data point to understand if the total compensation package is competitive to the market. In addition, this data can indicate if compensation is a major contributor to attrition levels. Compensation analytics are useful in consideration of special talent pools, such as high potentials and designated experts. The comparison of pay from these talent pools with the overall population is of interest, and retention of these pools is especially important to the long-term talent management strategies. Finally, analytics are important to mitigate regulatory matters related to compensation.

Key Takeaways

- Job evaluation is the process of determining the worth of each position in an organization relative to other positions within the same organization.
- The three steps in determining salary ranges are determining the organization's overall compensation strategy, conducting job analyses, and conducting job evaluations.
- The job-ranking method is the process of placing jobs from lowest to highest, or vice versa, based on their relative worth to the organization.
- The point-factor method determines the relative worth of a job based on the degree to which a compensable factor is present or required.
- A compensable factor is a job characteristic that an organization values and chooses to pay for.
- The factor comparison method combines the point-factor and ranking methods. Using this method, a group of jobs is identified to be benchmark jobs.
- The job classification systems method is an approach that classifies all jobs within a company according to a standardized scale, based on the overall tasks, responsibilities, and duties associated with each job.

What Do *You* Think?

1. From the perspective of an HR manager, which of the job evaluation methods would you prefer, and why?
2. From the perspective of an employee, which of the job evaluation methods would you prefer, and why?
3. What do you think about the job-ranking method? Does it cause competition among employees, and is that a good thing or a bad thing?

9.4 Legal Aspects of Compensation

Learning Objectives

1. Determine whether a worker should be classified as an employee or an independent contractor.
2. Explain the impact of the Fair Labor Standards Act of 1938 (as amended) on compensation plans.
3. Distinguish between exempt and nonexempt employees.
4. Explain the requirements of the Davis-Bacon Act of 1931 with regard to wages.
5. Explain the requirements of the Walsh-Healey Act of 1936 with regard to wages.

Employee versus Independent Contractor Status

When a company uses independent contractors, it does not have to pay Social Security and Medicare taxes, withhold income taxes, or pay unemployment tax on wages. It is crucial to correctly classify independent contractors in compliance with IRS regulations, as substantial penalties may be assessed for paying someone as an independent contractor when they should be classified as an employee.

In determining whether the person providing service is an employee or an independent contractor, the main criteria are the degree of control the company exerts over the individual and the degree of independence the individual has.[21] HR managers should examine the facts that determine the degree of control and independence and keep documentation on file in the case of an IRS audit. These facts fall into three categories:

1. **Behavioral.** Does the company control or have the right to control what the worker does and how the worker does his or her job?

2. **Financial.** Are the business aspects of the worker's job controlled by the payer? These include things like how the worker is paid, whether expenses are reimbursed, who provides tools and supplies, etc.

3. **Type of relationship.** Are there written contracts or employee-type benefits (i.e., retirement plan, insurance, vacation pay, etc.)? Will the relationship continue and is the work performed a key aspect of the business?

Fair Labor Standards Act of 1938 (as Amended)

While President Franklin Roosevelt was in Bedford, Massachusetts, campaigning for re-election, a young girl tried to pass him an envelope. But a policeman threw her back into the crowd. Roosevelt told an aide, "Get the note from the girl." Her note read:

> *I wish you could do something to help us girls...We have been working in a sewing factory, and up to a few months ago, we were getting our minimum pay of $11 a week. Today the 200 of us girls have been cut down to $4 and $5 and $6 a week.*

To a reporter's question, the president replied, "Something has to be done about the elimination of child labor and long hours and starvation wages."[22] As part of the New Deal, President Roosevelt signed the Fair Labor Standards Act of 1938 (FLSA). The act has been amended over twenty times, most of which served to increase the minimum wage. The FLSA protects workers through its requirements that employees be paid a minimum wage for all hours worked, and overtime premium pay for hours worked in excess of forty hours in a workweek. The initial minimum wage was $0.25 per hour, and the normal workweek was forty-four hours. The minimum wage is increased periodically as an amendment to the act, and the workweek has been reduced to forty hours. The act also banned businesses from employing workers younger than fourteen, with some exceptions which will be described below. At the time the FLSA was enacted, it was a radical change for the government to establish pay standards for private industry.[23]

The FLSA establishes minimum wage, overtime pay, child labor standards, and recordkeeping requirements, affecting employees in the private sector and federal, state, and local governments.[24]

Minimum Wage

The federal minimum wage is $7.25 per hour effective July 24, 2009. Many states also have minimum wage laws. In cases where an employee is subject to both state and federal minimum wage laws, the employee is entitled to the higher minimum wage.

Overtime Pay

A **nonexempt employee** must receive overtime pay for hours worked over forty per workweek. A workweek is defined by the Department of Labor as a fixed and regularly recurring period of one hundred sixty-eight hours—seven consecutive twenty-four-hour periods.[25] It does not have to coincide with a calendar week but may begin on any day and at any hour of the day. Different work-weeks may be established for different groups of employees.

An **exempt employee** is not entitled to overtime pay. Some jobs are classified by definition under the FLSA as exempt. For example, outside sales employees are exempt (although inside sales employees are not).[26] But for most employees, whether they are exempt or nonexempt depends on how much they are paid, how they are paid, and the type of work they do. These are referred to as three tests: the salary level test, the salary basis test, and the duties test.

- **Salary level test.** Employees who are paid less than $35,568 per year ($684 per week) are automatically nonexempt. Another way of stating this is that to qualify as an exempt employee, the individual must be paid more than $35,568 per year.

- **Salary basis test.** Exempt employees must be paid a predetermined, fixed salary. This does not include bonuses, merit pay, stock options, etc., but refers to a minimum guaranteed salary, or base salary. The base salary may not be reduced based on the quality or quantity of their work.

- **Duties test.** The FLSA provides an exemption for a bonafide executive, administrative, professional, computer, and outside sales employees. To qualify for the exemption, employees must perform certain job functions. A summary of the duties is shown in Table 9.4. Note that the job title assigned to an employee is not a factor in determining exempt status. For example, if an office manager does not primarily perform exempt administrative functions as listed in the table below, then he or she would be classified as a nonexempt employee, despite the fact that the word "manager" appears in the job title.

nonexempt employee

An employee who is paid hourly and must receive overtime pay for hours worked over forty per workweek.

exempt employee

A salaried employee who is not entitled to overtime pay.

TABLE 9.4 Exempt Job Duties

Exempt Job Duties Under the FLSA

Executive Exemption

- The employee's primary duty must be managing the enterprise or managing a customarily recognized department or subdivision of the enterprise.
- The employee must customarily and regularly direct the work of at least two or more other full-time employees or their equivalent.
- The employee must have the authority to hire or fire other employees, or the employee's suggestions and recommendations as to the hiring, firing, advancement, promotion, or any other change of status of other employees must be given weight.

Administrative Exemption

- The employee's primary duty must be the performance of office or nonmanual work directly related to the management or general business operations of the employer or the employer's customers; and
- The employee's primary duty includes the exercise of discretion and independent judgment with respect to matters of significance.

Professional Exemption

- The employee's primary duty must be the performance of work requiring advanced knowledge, defined as work which is predominantly intellectual in character and includes work requiring the consistent exercise of discretion and judgment.
- The advanced knowledge must be in a field of science or learning; and
- The advanced knowledge must be customarily acquired by a prolonged course of specialized intellectual instruction.
- To qualify for the creative professional exemption, the employee's primary duty must be the performance of work requiring invention, imagination, originality, or talent in a recognized field of artistic or creative endeavor.

Computer Employee Exemption

- The employee must be employed as a computer systems analyst, computer programmer, software engineer, or another similarly skilled worker in the computer field performing the duties described below.
- The employee's primary duty must consist of:
  1. The application of systems analysis techniques and procedures, including consulting with users, to determine hardware, software, or system functional specifications;
  2. The design, development, documentation, analysis, creation, testing, or modification of computer systems or programs, including prototypes, based on and related to user or system design specifications;
  3. The design, documentation, testing, creation, or modification of computer programs related to machine operating systems; or
  4. A combination of the aforementioned duties, the performance of which requires the same level of skills.

Outside Sales Exemption

- The employee's primary duty must be making sales or obtaining orders or contracts for services or for the use of facilities for which a consideration will be paid by the client or customer; and
- The employee must be customarily and regularly engaged away from the employer's place or places of business.

Source: U.S. Department of Labor. September 2019. *Fact sheet #17A: Exemption for executive, administrative, professional, computer, and outside sales employees under the Fair Labor Standards Act (FLSA).* Retrieved August 31, 2019 from https://www.dol.gov/whd/overtime/fs17a_overview.htm

Child Labor Provisions

The FLSA child labor provisions are designed to protect the educational opportunities of youth and prohibit their employment in jobs under certain conditions detrimental to their health or safety.[27]

A child under the age of fourteen is only allowed to:

- Deliver newspapers to customers;
- Babysit on a casual basis;
- Work as an actor or performer in movies, TV, radio, or theater;
- Work as a homeworker gathering evergreens and evergreen wreaths; and
- Work for a business owned entirely by his or her parents as long as it is not in mining, manufacturing, or any of the seventeen hazardous occupations.

The FLSA child labor provisions prevent the use of children in hazardous occupations such as this group working at a Pennsylvania coal mine in 1911.

Source: © Shutterstock, Inc.

A child aged fourteen or fifteen is restricted in the hours they can work, and the type of work they can do. All work must be performed outside school hours and they may not work:

- more than three hours on a school day, including Friday;
- more than eighteen hours per week when school is in session;
- more than eight hours per day when school is not in session;
- more than forty hours per week when school is not in session; and
- before 7 a.m. or after 7 p.m. on any day, except June 1st through Labor Day, when nighttime work hours are extended to 9 p.m.

They may work the following jobs (if a job is not on the list of those permitted under the FLSA, then it is prohibited):

- retail occupations;
- intellectual or creative work such as computer programming, teaching, tutoring, singing, acting, or playing an instrument;
- errands or delivery work by foot, bicycle, and public transportation;
- clean-up and yard work which does not include using power-driven mowers, cutters, trimmers, edgers, or similar equipment;
- work in connection with cars and trucks such as dispensing gasoline or oil and washing or hand polishing;
- some kitchen and food service work including reheating food, washing dishes, cleaning equipment, and limited cooking;
- cleaning vegetables and fruits, wrapping, sealing, and labeling, weighing, pricing, and stocking of items when performed in areas separate from a freezer or meat cooler;
- loading or unloading objects for use at a worksite including rakes, handheld clippers, and shovels;
- fourteen and fifteen-year-olds who meet certain requirements can perform limited tasks in sawmills and woodshops; and
- fifteen-year-olds who meet certain requirements can perform lifeguard duties at traditional swimming pools and water amusement parks.

A child who is sixteen or seventeen has no restrictions on the hours he or she can work and can perform any job that has not been declared hazardous by the Secretary of Labor.

Chipotle Fined for Child Labor Law Violations

Many states have child labor laws that are stricter than federal laws. Chipotle was fined $1.4 million in 2020 for violating Massachusetts child labor laws, by letting teenagers work too many hours per week and too late on school nights.

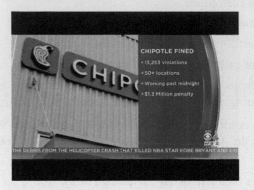

View the video online at: http://www.youtube.com/embed/pSwlzu0mAgA?rel=0

Recordkeeping

Employers must display an official poster outlining the requirements of FLSA (see Figure 9.4). Employers must also keep employee time and pay records for at least three years. Table 9.5 is a list of the specific records the employer must maintain for each nonexempt employee.[28]

FIGURE 9.4 FLSA Poster

EMPLOYEE RIGHTS
UNDER THE FAIR LABOR STANDARDS ACT

FEDERAL MINIMUM WAGE
$7.25 PER HOUR
BEGINNING JULY 24, 2009

The law requires employers to display this poster where employees can readily see it.

OVERTIME PAY   At least 1½ times the regular rate of pay for all hours worked over 40 in a workweek.

CHILD LABOR   An employee must be at least 16 years old to work in most non-farm jobs and at least 18 to work in non-farm jobs declared hazardous by the Secretary of Labor. Youths 14 and 15 years old may work outside school hours in various non-manufacturing, non-mining, non-hazardous jobs with certain work hours restrictions. Different rules apply in agricultural employment.

TIP CREDIT   Employers of "tipped employees" who meet certain conditions may claim a partial wage credit based on tips received by their employees. Employers must pay tipped employees a cash wage of at least $2.13 per hour if they claim a tip credit against their minimum wage obligation. If an employee's tips combined with the employer's cash wage of at least $2.13 per hour do not equal the minimum hourly wage, the employer must make up the difference.

NURSING MOTHERS   The FLSA requires employers to provide reasonable break time for a nursing mother employee who is subject to the FLSA's overtime requirements in order for the employee to express breast milk for her nursing child for one year after the child's birth each time such employee has a need to express breast milk. Employers are also required to provide a place, other than a bathroom, that is shielded from view and free from intrusion from coworkers and the public, which may be used by the employee to express breast milk.

ENFORCEMENT   The Department has authority to recover back wages and an equal amount in liquidated damages in instances of minimum wage, overtime, and other violations. The Department may litigate and/or recommend criminal prosecution. Employers may be assessed civil money penalties for each willful or repeated violation of the minimum wage or overtime pay provisions of the law. Civil money penalties may also be assessed for violations of the FLSA's child labor provisions. Heightened civil money penalties may be assessed for each child labor violation that results in the death or serious injury of any minor employee, and such assessments may be doubled when the violations are determined to be willful or repeated. The law also prohibits retaliating against or discharging workers who file a complaint or participate in any proceeding under the FLSA.

ADDITIONAL INFORMATION
- Certain occupations and establishments are exempt from the minimum wage, and/or overtime pay provisions.
- Special provisions apply to workers in American Samoa, the Commonwealth of the Northern Mariana Islands, and the Commonwealth of Puerto Rico.
- Some state laws provide greater employee protections; employers must comply with both.
- Some employers incorrectly classify workers as "independent contractors" when they are actually employees under the FLSA. It is important to know the difference between the two because employees (unless exempt) are entitled to the FLSA's minimum wage and overtime pay protections and correctly classified independent contractors are not.
- Certain full-time students, student learners, apprentices, and workers with disabilities may be paid less than the minimum wage under special certificates issued by the Department of Labor.

 **≡WHD** WAGE AND HOUR DIVISION
UNITED STATES DEPARTMENT OF LABOR

1-866-487-9243
TTY: 1-877-889-5627
www.dol.gov/whd

WH1088   REV 07/16

Source: FLSA, https://www.dol.gov/agencies/whd/posters/flsa.

TABLE 9.5 Recordkeeping Requirements Under the FLSA

Recordkeeping Requirements Under the FLSA
1. Employee's full name and Social Security number.
2. Address, including zip code.
3. Birthdate, if younger than nineteen.
4. Sex and occupation.
5. Time and day of the week when employee's workweek begins.
6. Hours worked each day.
7. Total hours worked each workweek.
8. Basis on which employee's wages are paid (e.g., "$9 per hour," "$440 a week," "piecework.")
9. Regular hourly pay rate.
10. Total daily or weekly straight-time earnings.
11. Total overtime earnings for the workweek.
12. All additions to or deductions from the employee's wages.
13. Total wages paid each pay period.
14. Date of payment and the pay period covered by the payment.

Davis-Bacon Act of 1931

The Davis-Bacon Act of 1931 was the first federal law passed that regulates wages. The law applies to contractors and subcontractors performing on federally funded or assisted contracts in excess of $2,000 for the construction, alteration, or repair of public buildings or public works.[29] Employers subject to the Act must pay their laborers and mechanics, employed under the contract, no less than the locally prevailing wages and fringe benefits for corresponding work on similar projects in the area. The Davis-Bacon Act has generated controversy since it became law. Critics argue that it raises wage levels, artificially boosting the cost of federal construction projects, and discriminates against nonunion and minority workers.[30] But recent research suggests that prevailing wage laws do not affect construction cost, promote worker safety and training, and do not have a racially discriminatory impact.[31]

Walsh-Healey Act of 1936

The Walsh-Healey Public Contracts Act (PCA), as amended, establishes minimum wage, maximum hours, and safety and health standards for work on contracts in excess of $15,000 for the manufacturing or furnishing of materials, supplies, articles, or equipment to the U.S. government or the District of Columbia.[32] Covered workers must be paid not less than the FLSA federal minimum wage and overtime pay of at least one and one-half times the worker's regular rate of pay for all hours worked in excess of eight hours per day or forty hours per workweek.

The PCA also sets standards for child and convict labor, as well as job sanitation and safety standards. All provisions of the PCA are administered by the Wage and Hour Division except for the safety and health requirements, which are administered by the Occupational Safety and Health Administration (OSHA).

Key Takeaways

- The FLSA protects workers through its requirements that employees be paid a minimum wage for all hours worked, and overtime premium pay for hours worked in excess of forty hours in a workweek.
- A nonexempt employee must receive overtime pay for hours worked over forty per workweek.
- An exempt employee is not entitled to overtime pay.
- Exemption is based on three tests: the salary level test, the salary basis test, and the duties test.
- The FLSA child labor provisions are designed to protect the educational opportunities of youth and prohibit their employment in jobs under certain conditions detrimental to their health or safety.
- Employers must display an official poster outlining the requirements of FLSA. Employers must also keep employee time and pay records for at least three years.
- The Davis-Bacon Act of 1931 applies to contractors and subcontractors performing on federally funded or assisted contracts in excess of $2,000 for the construction, alteration, or repair of public buildings or public works.
- Employers subject to the act must pay their laborers and mechanics, employed under the contract, no less than the locally prevailing wages and fringe benefits for corresponding work on similar projects in the area.
- The Walsh-Healey Public Contracts Act (PCA), as amended, establishes minimum wage, maximum hours, and safety and health standards for work on contracts in excess of $15,000 for the manufacturing or furnishing of materials, supplies, articles, or equipment to the U.S. government or the District of Columbia. Covered workers must be paid not less than the FLSA federal minimum wage, and overtime pay of at least one and one-half times the worker's regular rate of pay for all hours worked in excess of eight hours per day or forty in a workweek.

What Do *You* Think?

1. The current minimum wage is $7.25. Do you think it should be raised? If so, what would you say to the small business owners who oppose raising it because they fear it could put them out of business?
2. If you became aware that your salaried position does not comply with the exemption tests under the FLSA, and you were entitled to retroactive compensation, how would you go about bringing this situation to the attention of your employer?
3. What do you think about the current child labor restrictions? Are they appropriate? Are they too strict, or not strict enough?

9.5 Pay for Performance

Learning Objectives

1. Explain how individual incentive programs can be used to encourage higher levels of productivity and performance.

2. Describe enterprise incentive plans that are based on the overall success of an organization.

3. Recognize the trends and issues with regard to executive compensation plans.

Individual Incentive Plans

Incentive programs can be used to encourage higher levels of productivity and performance and can play a role in talent acquisition and employer branding. The better an employee performs, the more they tend to expect incentive rewards based on performance.[33] Incentive pay is also an effective approach to using compensation as a recruitment strategy, as it helps to attract high-performing individuals.[34] In a 2015 WorldatWork survey, 94% of respondents said that their organizations offered employees some form of short-term incentives, and 53% offered long-term incentives beyond regular pay.

But do incentives work? A recent Talent Management and Rewards Pulse Survey of HR executives at large and midsize U.S. and Canadian employers found that:

- Only 32% said their merit pay program is effective at differentiating pay based on individual performance.

- Only 20% found merit pay to be effective at driving higher levels of individual performance at their organization.

- Just over half, 51%, reported using consistent performance measures across the organization to determine the award funding pool and individual incentive pay amounts.[35]

What this indicates is that while individual merit pay programs are popular and successful in attracting applicants, they are not necessarily viewed as effective by those already working in the organization. This may be due in part to perceived inequity in how merit awards are determined. It also suggests the need for further research regarding the correlation between merit pay and performance.

There are seven common approaches to individual incentive pay:

1. **Sales commissions.** Incentive payments are based on a percentage of sales. There are two variations: straight commission and base plus commission. In a **straight commission** plan, 100% of the employee's salary is from commissions earned. In a **base plus commission** plan, the employee earns a guaranteed base salary and then is paid a commission on sales beyond a specified amount.

2. **Piecework.** Employees are paid a specific amount for each unit produced. As with sales commissions, this approach is sometimes combined with a base guaranteed salary.

3. **Annual incentive plans.** Incentive awards are tied to specific results during a year.

4. **Recognition awards.** These incentives recognize special contributions as they occur.

5. **Retention bonuses.** Payments that are given to key individuals as an incentive to remain with the company.

6. **Project bonuses.** Payments for successfully completing a project on time and/or on budget.

Group and Enterprise Incentive Plans

Incentive plans are often based on group accomplishment of objectives. A group could be a department, team, or the entire organization (enterprise). An **enterprise incentive plan** refers to any incentive that is based on the success of the entire organization. There are four major types of group/enterprise incentive plans:

---

sales commissions

Incentive payments that are based on a percentage of sales.

straight commission

A type of incentive pay in which 100% of the employee's salary is from commissions earned.

base plus commission

A type of incentive pay in which the employee earns a guaranteed base salary and then is paid a commission on sales beyond a specified amount.

piecework

A type of incentive pay in which employees are paid a specific amount for each unit produced.

annual incentive plans

Incentive awards that are tied to specific results during a year.

recognition awards

Incentives awards that recognize special contributions as they occur.

retention bonuses

Payments that are given as an incentive to retain a key individual.

project bonuses

Payments for successfully completing a project on time and/or on budget.

enterprise incentive plan

Any incentive that is based on the success of the entire organization.

profit sharing

A plan through which the employees share in the organization's profits.

stock purchase plan

An incentive plan that offers employees the right to buy a specific number of shares of company stock, at a specified price, within a specific number of years.

employee stock ownership plan (ESOP)

A stock incentive plan which qualifies as an ERISA tax-deferred retirement plan.

gainsharing plan

An incentive program that rewards employees for exceeding performance or productivity goals during a set period of time.

discretionary bonus plan

An approach in which management determines the size of the bonus pool and the amounts to be allocated to each employee, typically at the end of a fiscal year.

1. **Profit sharing.** A plan through which the employees share in the organization's profits. The plan normally is based upon a predetermined percentage of the profits that is set aside for distribution to employees.

2. **Stock purchase plan.** A stock purchase plan offers employees the right to buy a specific number of shares of company stock, at a specified price, within a specific number of years. If the market value of the stock is greater than the option price at the time the option is exercised, then the employee has a gain. Stock options typically have a vesting date and an expiration date. Employees cannot exercise their options before the vesting date or after the expiration date. For example, a company might allow employees to purchase one hundred shares of stock for $75 per share at any time within the next five years. If the stock is trading at a price higher than $75, the employee receives compensation in the form of increased stock value. This is different than an **employee stock ownership plan (ESOP)**, which qualifies as an Employee Retirement Income Security Act (ERISA) tax-deferred retirement plan, similar to a 401(k). In an ESOP, the company contributes to the retirement plan with shares of stock. Setting up and maintaining an ESOP requires significant legal and tax expertise, but there are tax advantages, as the contributions are tax deductible for the company and the money is tax deferred for the employee until retirement. Similar to other tax-deferred retirement plans, ESOP participants do not have access to their balances until they retire or leave the company. In contrast, with a stock purchase plan, employees can sell their shares of tax at any time, but will pay tax on any gain when they sell.

3. **Gainsharing plans.** A gainsharing plan is any incentive program that rewards employees for exceeding performance or productivity goals during a set period of time. Gainsharing plans have been in use for about fifty years. They are typically based on a formula that compares a baseline of performance with actual productivity during a given period.[36] When the actual productivity is greater than the baseline, then a percentage of the savings (gain) is shared with the employees.

4. **Discretionary bonus plan.** An approach in which management determines the size of the bonus pool and the amounts to be allocated to each employee, typically at the end of a fiscal year.

Executive Compensation

An executive's compensation differs from that of other employees in many organizations. A typical compensation package for an executive is oriented more toward actual results. If a company meets or exceeds its annual objectives (most often based on earnings or stock price), then the executives receive the bonus. The advantage of executive compensation plans is that they help companies attract and retain executive talent.

Executive compensation plans are often criticized because they have been growing at such a rapid rate compared to the wages of other employees. Management theorist Peter Drucker believed the proper ratio between a chief executive's pay and that of the average worker should be around 20-to-1, as it was in 1965.[37] Figure 9.5 compares the ratio of CEO to average worker pay in various countries. The Economic Policy Institute reports that CEO pay has risen by 807% or 937% (depending on how it is measured—using stock options granted or realized) from 1978 to 2016. At 937%, that rise is more than 70% faster than the rise in the stock market. A typical worker's compensation over the same period rose at a rate of 11.2%.

FIGURE 9.5 Growth of CEO Pay versus Average Worker

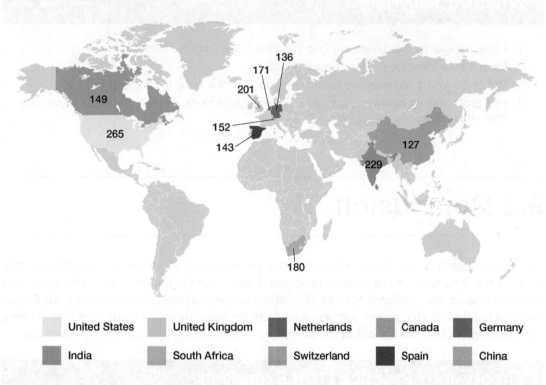

Source: Data from Statista, https://www.statista.com/statistics/424159/pay-gap-between-ceos-and-average-workers-in-world-by-country/

One of the outcomes of excessive executive pay was the Dodd-Frank Wall Street Reform and Consumer Protection Act (Dodd-Frank Act) of 2010. The Dodd-Frank Act placed some significant limits on executive pay in public corporations and also added some new requirements for both reporting of compensation and shareholder involvement with executive compensation.[38]

Key Takeaways

- Incentive programs can be used to encourage higher levels of productivity and performance and can play a role in talent acquisition and employer branding.
- There are six common approaches to individual incentive pay: sales commissions, piece-work, annual incentive plans, recognition awards, retention bonuses, and project bonuses.
- An enterprise incentive plan refers to any incentive that is based on the success of the entire organization.
- There are four major types of group/enterprise incentive plans: profit sharing, stock options, gainsharing, and discretionary bonus plans.
- A typical compensation package for an executive is oriented more toward actual results.
- Executive compensation plans are often criticized because they have been growing at such a rapid rate, compared to the wages of other employees.
- The Dodd-Frank Act placed some significant limits on executive pay in public corporations and also added some new requirements for both reporting of compensation and shareholder involvement with executive compensation.

What Do *You* Think?

1. Have you ever received merit pay? Do you think it was awarded fairly?
2. Do you think incentive pay increases productivity?
3. Out of the four group incentive plans, which do you think is the most effective?
4. In a profit-sharing incentive plan, what percentage of profit should companies share with their employees?

9.6 Conclusion

The chapter began with a discussion of the strategic aspects of compensation and the determinants of pay structure. Compensation theories and issues such as equity, comparable worth, and pay compression were explored. Specific job evaluation methods were introduced, and the federal laws and regulations that govern compensation were reviewed. Incentive plans were then covered, and the chapter closed with a look at the current controversy around executive compensation.

Theory-into-Practice (TIP) Exercises

1. Explore the Career Center at WorldatWork Total Rewards Association (see the link under resource number one). Click on some of the job postings and read the job descriptions. Would you be interested in a position as a compensation specialist?
2. According to Glassdoor, the average salary of a retail sales associate in the United States is $32,175. Based on this average, calculate the compa-ratio for each of the following positions:

    a. A retail sales associate at a grocery store earning $22,450.

    b. A retail sales associate at a jewelry store earning $37,825.

    c. A retail sales associate at a pet store earning $33,850.

    d. A retail sales associate at a discount department store earning $28,125.

    e. A retail sales associate at an apparel store earning $24,500.

    If you were the HR director for one of these companies, how could this information be used in establishing a compensation philosophy and plan?

3. Salary caps are used in business and sports. Read the following background about salary caps:

    https://www.sports-management-degrees.com/faq/what-is-a-salary-cap/

    Then use the following link to see a real-time salary cap tracker for NFL teams. If you have a favorite team, determine how much space they have in their salary cap, as compared to other teams in their division. Feel free to alter this exercise for your favorite sport!

    https://www.spotrac.com/nfl/cap/

Case Study: The Stagecoach Scandal

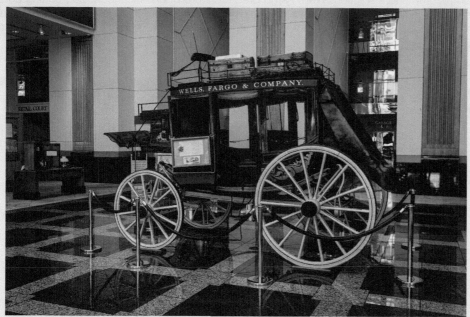

Source: Chris Allan / Shutterstock.com

Henry Wells and William G. Fargo structured a joint-stock company, Wells, Fargo & Company, on March 18, 1852, to provide express banking services to California during the California Gold Rush. They offered banking and express delivery of gold and anything else valuable. In 1858, the company expanded its services into overland mail and was awarded a government contract to carry mail from the southeast to California for the U.S. Post Office in their famous six-horse stage-coach. Over time, Wells Fargo developed new banking concepts and changed the way people banked. In the 1980s Wells Fargo became the seventh-largest bank in the nation and launched its online service.

Wells Fargo began cross-selling all services including credit cards, mortgages, and treasury management. They persuaded each retail customer to buy an average of six products, roughly twice the level of the previous decade. It was an aggressive sales culture with daily mandatory quotas, and employees began reporting that sales goals were unrealistic and unobtainable. A former New Jersey employee called an ethics hotline and sent an email to human resources in 2013, flagging unethical sales activities he was being instructed to do, and was subsequently terminated. There were deficiencies with a decentralized organization resulting in constrained corporate control. The local business units would address any issues only locally. For instance, if something was wrong, the chief risk officer in the retail bank would report it to the head of the retail bank only and they would handle the issue. It would never reach the corporate level.

In 2016, the Wells Fargo account fraud scandal came to light, and they announced that a $185 million fine would be paid to federal regulators and the city of Los Angeles to settle allegations that their employees had created millions of fake financial accounts for customers in order to get bonuses. Over five thousand employees were dismissed due to their conduct over a span of five years that lead to the $185 million payout. The conduct dated back to at least 2011 and involved more than 1.5 million checking and savings accounts and about 500,000 credit card accounts, with many customers getting hit with unexpected fees, according to federal officials. The year before the scandal came to light, the company made $20 billion.

Wells Fargo reconfigured incentives at the branch level to emphasize customer service instead of cross-selling metrics, and product sales goals were eliminated. The company also developed new procedures for verifying account openings and introduced additional training and control mechanisms to prevent violations. They also now spend more money on compliance. A third party helped them design a short survey for employees to determine needs and address issues. Senior leadership now visits local branches to interact with team members and address any needs. Now, if something happens at the local branch level, the chief risk officer reports to the corporate chief risk officer as well.

Appropriate training of relevant individuals can help them to identify what is causing lower sales and then recommend a solution. Wells Fargo bred a culture of unethical behavior, setting unrealistic sales goals for its employees and encouraging them to game the system in order to keep their jobs. That is why training, compensation management, and career development are all important in preventing these types of situations.[39]

 Wells Fargo Scandal Explained

Financial Times correspondent Alistair Gray reports on the fallout of the Wells Fargo scandal.

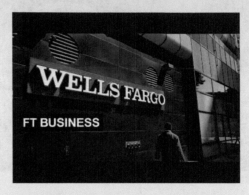

View the video online at: http://www.youtube.com/embed/9zeH-S3A6pg?rel=0

Case Discussion Questions

1. Were managers to blame more than the low-level employees?
2. Was a small percentage of employees the problem at Wells Fargo or was it a company culture issue?
3. How would you measure the culture within the company post-cultural change?
4. What part should have human resources played in preventing the scandal?

Resources

1. **WorldatWork Total Rewards Association.** Compensation management resources including research, surveys, white papers, discussions, an HR vendor director, and a career center.

   https://bit.ly/34y4KFv

2. **Compensation case studies.** Four real-world compensation case studies from Management Compensation Resources.

   http://www.mgmtcomp.com/

3. **Compensation management software reviews.** Reviews of thirty-eight compensation management software systems.

   https://www.softwareadvice.com/hr/compensation-management-comparison/

Endnotes

1. Case written by Aguayo, T. (2019). Adapted from: Salinas, Sara C. (2018). Amazon raises minimum wage to $15 for all US employees. *CNBC*. Retrieved from https://www.cnbc.com/2018/10/02/amazon-raises-minimum-wage-to-15-for-all-us-employees.html; Matsakis, L. (2018). Why Amazon really raised its minimum age to $15. *Wired*. Retrieved from https://www.wired.com/story/why-amazon-really-raised-minimum-wage/

2. Stahl, A. (2016). Employers, take note: Here's what employees really want. *Forbes*. Retrieved from https://www.forbes.com/sites/ashleystahl/2016/10/12/employers-take-note-heres-what-employees-really-want/#18b171bd1c83

3. Vroom, V. (1964). *Work and motivation*. New York: Wiley.

4. Renko, M., Kroeck, K., & Bullough, G. (2012). Expectancy theory and nascent entrepreneurship. *Small Business Economics, 39*(3), 667-684.

5. What is comparable worth? *HR Zone*. Retrieved April 6, 2020 from https://www.hrzone.com/hr-glossary/what-is-comparable-worth

6. Equal Employment Opportunity Commission. *The Equal Pay Act of 1963*. Retrieved February 12, 2019 from https://www.eeoc.gov/laws/statutes/epa.cfm

7. Comparable worth. *Legal Dictionary*. Retrieved April 5, 2020 from https://legal-dictionary.thefreedictionary.com/Comparable+Worth

8. Ibid.

9. Graf, N., Brown, A., & Patten, E. (2018). The narrowing, but persistent gender gap. *Pew Research Center*. Retrieved from http://leametz.pbworks.com/f/Gender pay gap has narrowed, but changed little in past decade.pdf

10. Bureau of Labor Statistics. *Consumer Price Index*. Retrieved March 21, 2020 from https://www.bls.gov/cpi/

11. How pay compression can kill employee engagement and why it matters. (2017). *Custominsight*. Retrieved March 17, 2020 from https://www.custominsight.com/blog/7-tips-to-battle-or-prevent-salary-compression-employee-engagement.asp

12. Compa-ratio. (2019). *Paycor*. Retrieved from https://www.paycor.com/hcm-basics/compa-ratio

13. Supreme decision touches on employees sharing pay data. *HR Focus* (84)10, 12.

14. Pay secrecy and paycheck fairness: New data shows pay transparency needed. (2010). *Institute for Women's Policy Research*. Retrieved from https://iwpr.org/pay-secrecy-and-paycheck-fairness-new-data-shows-pay-transparency-needed/

15. Lehoczky, E. (2016). Clearing the air: How to do salary transparency right. *Inc., 38*(4), 20.

16. Government Publishing Office. *Executive Order 13665*. Retrieved April 3, 2020 from https://www.govinfo.gov/content/pkg/DCPD-201400250/pdf/DCPD-201400250.pdf

17. Obama-era blacklisting rules meet their official demise. (2017). *Balanceview*. Retrieved from https://www.berkshireassociates.com/balanceview/obama-era-blacklisting-rules-meet-their-official-demise

18. Kilgour, J.G. (2008). Job Evaluation Revisited: The Point Factor Method: The point factor method of job evaluation consists of a large number of discretionary decisions that result in something that appears to be entirely objective and, even, scientific. *Compensation & Benefits Review, 40*(4), 37–46. https://doi.org/10.1177/0886368708320563

19. Korn Ferry Hay Group. Job evaluation: Foundations and applications. Retrieved September 1, 2019 from https://dsqapj1lakrkc.cloudfront.net/media/sidebar_downloads/Job-Evaluation.pdf

20. Ibid.

21. Internal Revenue Service. *Independent contractor (self-employed) or employee?* Retrieved April 6, 2020 from https://www.irs.gov/businesses/small-businesses-self-employed/independent-contractor-self-employed-or-employee

22. Roosevelt, F.D. (1936). *Public papers and addresses, Vol. V*. New York: Random House.

23. Nagele-Piazza, L. (2018). The FLSA after 80 years: How has it changed, and what lies ahead? *Society for Human Resource Management*. Retrieved from https://www.shrm.org/resourcesandtools/legal-and-compliance/employment-law/pages/flsa-after-80-years.aspx

24. U.S. Department of Labor. *Compliance assistance—Wages and the Fair Labor Standards Act (FLSA)*. Retrieved from https://www.dol.gov/whd/flsa/

25. U.S. Department of Labor. *Overtime pay*. Retrieved April 2, 2020 from https://www.dol.gov/whd/overtime_pay.htm

26. FLSA coverage. *Chamberlin, Kaufmann, and Jones*. Retrieved April 2, 2020 from https://www.flsa.com/coverage.html

27. U.S. Department of Labor. *Fair Labor Standards Act advisor*. Retrieved April 2, 2020 from https://webapps.dol.gov/elaws/whd/flsa/screen5.asp

28. U.S. Department of Labor. *Fact sheet #21: Recordkeeping requirements under the Fair Labor Standards Act (FLSA)*. Retrieved from https://www.dol.gov/whd/regs/compliance/whdfs21.pdf

29. U.S. Department of Labor. *Davis-Bacon and related acts*. Retrieved April 2, 2020 from https://www.dol.gov/whd/govcontracts/dbra.htm

30. The Heritage Foundation. *Trimming the cost of Davis-Bacon*. Retrieved April 2, 2020 from https://www.heritage.org/jobs-and-labor/report/trimming-the-huge-cost-davis-bacon

31. Duncan, K., & Ormiston, R. (2019). What does the research tell us about prevailing wage laws? *Labor Studies Journal, 44*(2), 139-160.

32. U.S. Department of Labor. *Compliance assistance—Walsh-Healey Public Contracts Act (PCA)*. Retrieved April 2, 2020 from https://www.dol.gov/whd/govcontracts/pca.htm

33. Nyberg, A. (2010). Retaining your high performers: Moderators of the performance–job satisfaction–voluntary turnover relationship. *Journal of Applied Psychology, 95*(3), 440-453.

34. Ibid.

35. Miller, S. (2016). Employers seek better approaches to pay for performance. *Society for Human Resource Management*. Retrieved from https://www.shrm.org/resourcesandtools/hr-topics/compensation/pages/better-pay-for-performance.aspx

36. Is gainsharing for you? *Quality Digest*. Retrieved April 3, 2020 from https://www.qualitydigest.com/jul/gainshre.html

37. Karabell, S. (2018). Executive compensation is out of control. What now? *Forbes*. Retrieved from https://www.forbes.com/sites/shelliekarabell/2018/02/14/executive-compensation-is-out-of-control-what-now/#387e7672431f

38. U.S. Commodity Futures Trading Commission. Dodd-Frank Act. Retrieved April 3, 2020 from https://www.cftc.gov/LawRegulation/DoddFrankAct/index.htm

39. Case written by P. Crews (2019). Adapted from: Egan, M. (2016). I called the Wells Fargo ethics line and was fired. *CNN Business*. Retrieved from https://money.cnn.com/2016/09/21/investing/wells-fargo-fired-workers-retaliation-fake-accounts/index.html

CHAPTER 10
Managing Benefits

Learning Objectives

After reading this chapter, you should be able to do the following:

1. Design a benefit package, taking into consideration the overall compensation strategy and industry benchmarks.
2. Identify the federal statutory benefits that apply to various types of employers.
3. Identify major categories of voluntary employee benefits and the characteristics of each.

Employee benefits include any type of compensation that is not in the form of cash (wages or bonuses). They include mandatory benefits (those that are required by law) and voluntary benefits, such as health insurance, retirement programs, and paid time off. In the U.S., employee benefits represent almost a third of total compensation.[1] Therefore, it is imperative that companies efficiently manage benefits to control cost, while also using benefits packages to attract and retain qualified talent.

The chapter begins with a discussion of benefits as part of an overall compensation strategy and industry benchmarking. Mandatory benefits are examined, including Social Security, Medicare, unemployment insurance, federal legislation, and workers' compensation. Then voluntary benefits are explored, with a focus on retirement plans, time off, other types of insurance, and employee wellness and assistance programs.

10.1 Opening Case: Raising the Clif Bar

Source: ZikG / Shutterstock.com

When searching for the best job, people are not only looking for the highest pay but are thoroughly researching company benefits such as healthcare and vacation days. However, more and more companies are going a step forward with added benefits. They are attracting more qualified employees with a wider variety of free and discounted services. Here are some examples:

- Two of the leaders in this new trend are Salesforce and Google. Salesforce, a California-based company, offers reimbursements for commuting costs, $100 per month for massage therapy or yoga classes, and tuition/book reimbursement. It also encourages donations to charities by matching the employees' donations (up to $5,000). Google also has become very creative when designing it benefits package. There are on-site medical care and childcare, massages, and physical therapy. They provide extra cash and vacation time to new mothers and also pay for college courses (related to the employee's job).

- Southwest Airlines and Clif Bar are two other leaders in providing exceptional benefits to employees. Southwest allows free airline travel for employees and their families and discounts on hotels, car rentals, and other airlines. They give employees a 10% discount on stocks and allow them to participate in profit-sharing plans and 401Ks. Clif Bar offers many benefits that encourage a healthy lifestyle, such as paying workers to spend up to one hundred fifty minutes per week in the company health club. They reimburse up to $350 for employees' entrance fees to athletic competitions such as marathons and 5Ks and offer free nutritionist consultations.

These amazing benefits packages greatly improve many workers' lives. They also enhance productivity, cut medical expenses, and help companies retain staff members. The bottom line is that such programs are mutually beneficial in numerous ways.[2]

Onsite Childcare: It's Paying Off at Clif Bar

Kate Torgerson, an 18-year employee, explains how bringing her three children to the company's "Base Camp" childcare center has benefited her as a working mother.

View the video online at: http://www.youtube.com/embed/XDhc05HVTYM?rel=0

Case Discussion Questions

1. Do you think the cost of providing such tremendous benefits is worth it?
2. How would you go about finding out whether the added costs are improving the company's bottom line?
3. Would these types of benefits cause you to more seriously consider a potential employer? Would you be more likely to stay with a company with such benefits?

10.2 Benefits Design

Learning Objectives

1. Explain how employee benefits are part of the talent acquisition and retention strategy of an organization.
2. Identify sources for obtaining industry benchmarking data.
3. Describe the key trends in employee benefits.

Benefits as Part of the Overall Compensation Strategy

benefit

Any type of compensation paid by an employer to an employee that is not in the form of cash.

direct compensation

Wages and salaries paid to an employee.

indirect compensation

Noncash benefits that are part of an employee's compensation.

total rewards

Refers to an entire compensation package, including direct and indirect compensation.

Employee benefits are a very important recruitment and retention strategy, and also a key factor in employer branding. As the opening case illustrates, many companies are raising the bar with regard to employee benefits. An employee **benefit** is any type of compensation paid by an employer to an employee that is not in the form of cash. Wages and salaries are sometimes referred to as **direct compensation**, and employee benefits are referred to as **indirect compensation**. Another term that is sometimes used is fringe benefits. HR professionals now commonly use the term **total rewards** in reference to a total compensation package.[3]

The concept of providing employee benefits is relatively recent when you consider the history of work. In 1910, Montgomery Ward & Company became the first private employer to offer health insurance to its employees. They were having difficulty finding workers in the mail-order industry and used the health insurance plan as a strategy to compete for workers against competitors like Sears Roebuck, and Company.[4] Benefits became more commonplace during the 1950s, and have consistently become a greater portion of total rewards. Figure 10.1 illustrates a breakdown of a typical dollar of compensation.

FIGURE 10.1 Where a Dollar of Compensation Goes

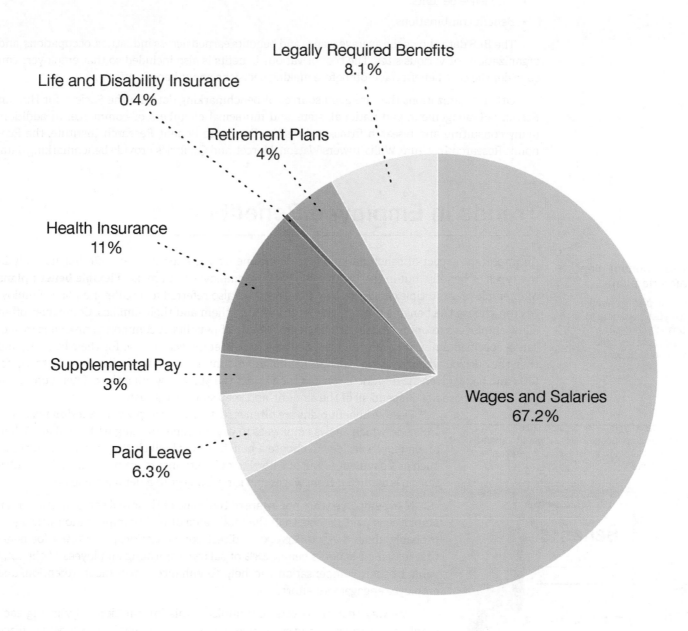

Industry Benchmarking

As discussed in Chapter 5, employer branding is an essential aspect of recruitment, and the benefits offered are a significant part of the brand or the employer value proposition. Employers need up-to-date information about what other organizations are offering in the way of benefits to be competitive in attracting and retaining employees. One excellent source is the Bureau of Labor Statistics (BLS). The BLS publishes a National Compensation Survey—Benefits that includes comprehensive data on the incidence (the percentage of workers with access to and participation in employer-provided benefit plans) and provisions of selected employee benefit plans.[5] The survey includes data with the following benefits data tables:

- Retirement benefits.
- Healthcare benefits.

- Life, short-term disability, and long-term disability insurance benefits.
- Paid leave benefits.
- Benefit combinations.

The BLS data shows the average wages and benefits earned across industries, occupations, and organizations of various sizes. The cost of various benefits is also included so that employers can consider the cost-benefit trade-off before making decisions about benefit offerings.

Other organizations that are good sources of benchmarking data are the Society for Human Resource Management, and national, state, and municipal chambers of commerce. In addition, many consulting and research firms, such as the Employee Benefit Research Institute, the Economic Research Institute, Willis Towers Watson, Mercer, and Qualtrics provide benchmarking data.

Trends in Employee Benefits

flexible benefit plan (cafeteria plan)

A benefit plan that offers employees the ability to choose the benefits that are the most useful to them and their families.

An important aspect of benchmarking is to determine what competitors are offering, not only in the types of benefits but in the various choices that employees can make. **Flexible benefit plans** offer employees multiple choices of benefits. These are also referred to as cafeteria plans. Employees can choose the benefits that are the most useful to them and their families. Companies often allow employees to opt for extra cash payments in lieu of benefits. A common approach is to allocate a specified amount (or percentage of salary) for the employees to use for their benefits, and then they decide what they want within that dollar amount. It would be similar to going to a cafeteria and being given $12 for lunch. You can then spend the $12 on anything the cafeteria offers. Or you could choose not to spend all of the amount, and keep some extra cash.

Flexible benefit plans (or cafeteria plans) allow employees to choose how they want to spend their benefit dollars. What are your personal top three benefits?

Flexible benefit plans are often structured to comply with **Section 125** of the IRS code, which allows employees to pay for benefits using pretax dollars. When an employee decides to choose a benefit toward which they have to contribute, such as a payment for all or a portion of health insurance premiums, that contribution is deducted from wages and is not subject to federal income tax.

Source: © Shutterstock, Inc.

Many employees are not aware of the value of their real compensation. If an employee is paid $35,000, then the total value of their compensation package is probably about $46,500 ($35,000 in direct compensation plus $11,480 for benefits—based on benefits being 32.8% of salary). Informing employees of the total value of their compensation can help to enhance recruitment, retention, and employee engagement efforts.

Section 125

The section of the IRS code which allows employees to pay for benefits using pretax dollars.

One way that employers communicate this information is by giving each employee a **total rewards statement** statement annually. This is a personalized statement for each employee that lists the financial value of every benefit the company offers. These types of statements have been in use for about twenty years and have been called "employee benefits statements" or "total compensation statements." More than half of top-performing companies provide a total rewards statement to employees, as compared to 38% of all companies.[6]

total rewards statement

A personalized statement for each employee that lists the financial value of every benefit the company offers.

Best practices in issuing total rewards statements can be found here: https://www.paycor.com/resource-center/how-to-drive-employee-engagement-with-total-compensation-statements.

FIGURE 10.2 Total Rewards Statement

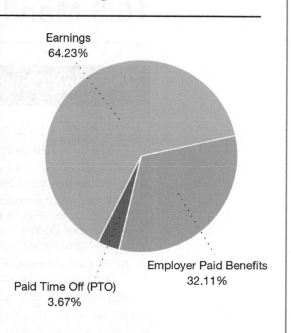

Confidential Information Enclosed

Company Name
Dallas, Texas

John Smith
123 Main St.
Dallas, Texas 12345

We are pleased to provide you with this personalized statement of your total rewards for 2021. It is our sincere desire that the protection and security of these benefits will make life better for you today as well as provide a more secure future for you and your dependents. We appreciate your continued service and dedication to the company.

Your 2021 Total Compensation Package

Earnings:	
Current Annual Earnings	$40,155.23
Paid Time Off (PTO)	2,335.88
2020 Bonus	800.00
Your 2021 Total Earnings	**$43,291.11**

Benefits	
Employer Provided Health Insurance	$12,550.75
Employer FICA Contributions	3,133.08
Employer 401(k) Match	3,276.42
Life Insurance	750.00
Unemployment Insurance	245.73
On-site Child Care	440.00
Employee Assistance Program	45.00
Employee Wellness Program	36.00
Total Benefits	**$20,476.98**
Your Total Compensation	**$63,768.09**

Earnings 64.23%

Employer Paid Benefits 32.11%

Paid Time Off (PTO) 3.67%

Key Takeaways

- An employee benefit is any type of compensation paid by an employer to an employee that is not in the form of cash. Wages and salaries are sometimes referred to as direct compensation, and employee benefits are referred to as indirect compensation.
- Total rewards refers to an entire compensation package, including direct and indirect compensation.
- Employers need up-to-date information about what other organizations are offering in the way of benefits to be competitive in attracting and retaining employees.

- Flexible benefit plans (cafeteria plans) offer employees the ability to choose the benefits that are the most useful to them and their families.
- Flexible benefit plans are often structured to comply with Section 125 of the IRS code, which allows employees to pay for benefits using pretax dollars.
- A total rewards statement is a personalized statement for each employee that lists the financial value of every benefit the company offers.

What Do *You* Think?

1. Have you ever been employed at an organization that offered a flexible benefit plan? Which benefits are the most important to you? How might that differ as your life situation changes in the future?
2. Have you ever received a total rewards (or employee benefits) statement? Were you surprised at the value of your total compensation?
3. Why might charts and graphs be a better way to present the value of employee benefits than numbers?

10.3 Mandatory Employee Benefits

Learning Objectives

1. Explain how Social Security and Medicare taxes are assessed to employees and employers.
2. Identify the different parts of Medicare and the benefit that each provides.
3. Describe the employer requirements for federal unemployment taxes and the eligibility requirements and benefits for individuals.
4. Recognize the employer compliance provisions of the Family and Medical Leave Act of 1993 (FMLA), the Patient Protection and Affordable Care Act of 2010 (ACA), the Consolidated Omnibus Budget Reconciliation Act of 1985 (COBRA), and the Uniformed Services Employment and Reemployment Rights Act of 1994 (USERRA).
5. Explain how workers' compensation insurance programs provide benefits to employees who are injured on the job or who suffer from a work-related illness.
6. Describe the cost containment strategies that employers use for health insurance.

Employee benefits can be divided into two categories: mandatory benefits that the employer is required to offer by federal or state law, and voluntary benefits that employers can choose whether to offer and at what level. Mandatory benefits are also referred to as statutory benefits because they are legislated by statute. The mandatory benefits that all U.S. employers are required to offer or participate in are Social Security, Medicare, unemployment insurance, family and medical leave, provisions governing insurance and time off under the Family and Medical Leave Act of 1993 (FMLA), the Patient Protection and Affordable Care Act (ACA), the Consolidated Omnibus Budget Reconciliation Act of 1985 (COBRA), the Uniformed Services Employment and Reemployment Rights Act of 1994 (USERRA), and workers' compensation insurance.

Social Security

Throughout human history, people of all cultures have faced the problem of providing for the economic and healthcare needs of the elderly and the disabled. In the U.S., the primary government program that addresses these needs is the Old Age, Survivors and Disability Insurance Program, or OASDI, which is the official name of the program that we normally refer to as **Social Security**. This is a federal program that provides benefits to retirees and disabled people and their spouses, children, and survivors.

One of the first Americans to propose a scheme for retirement security in the U.S. was the writer and revolutionary Thomas Paine, author of *Common Sense*.[7] In 1797, he published the pamphlet *Agrarian Justice* calling for the establishment of a public system of economic security. Paine called for the creation of a system whereby those inheriting property would pay a 10% inheritance tax to create a special fund out of which a one-time stipend of fifteen pounds sterling would be paid to each citizen upon reaching the age of twenty-one, to give them a good start in life, and annual benefits of ten pounds sterling would be paid to every person fifty and older to guard against poverty in old age.[8] You probably do not think of fifty as old age, but in the 1700s in the U.S., the life expectancy was in the late thirties, and during the 1800s it was in the mid-forties.[9] Today, the U.S. life expectancy is 78.6.[10] Thomas Paine was about one hundred forty years ahead of his time, as the U.S. would eventually create a tax-based program for providing for retirees, their dependents, and the disabled, but this would not happen until 1935.

Before passage of FICA in 1935, there were no federal programs to provide assistance for the elderly or disabled.

Source: © Shutterstock, Inc.

Because of the impacts of the Depression during the early 1930s, with an unemployment rate of 25% and increasing poverty, Congress passed the Federal Insurance Contributions Act (FICA), creating the Social Security program in 1935. Social Security and Medicare are funded by payroll taxes that are shared equally between the employer and employee. Employees may not think of Social Security and Medicare as benefits. They may instead think of them as something they earned and paid for. Many employees are not aware of the employer's contribution, which is one reason why the annual statement of benefits is important, because it reminds the employee of what their true compensation is, beyond just wages earned.

For the year 2020, the employee's portion of the FICA tax is 7.65% (6.2% for Social Security and 1.45% for Medicare).[11] The Social Security tax is only paid on the first $137,700 of income (referred to as the **wage base limit**). There is no wage base limit for Medicare. In addition, there is an additional Medicare tax of 0.9% for highly compensated individuals, on wages paid in excess of $200,000 per year. The employer matches the employee's portion of FICA taxes. Therefore, for an employee earning up to $137,700 annually, the total tax paid is 15.3% (7.65% employee's portion plus 7.65% employer's portion). The following are several examples of how Social Security and Medicare taxes are assessed. Someone self-employed must pay the combined employee and employer amount, which is a 12.4% Social Security tax on the first $137,700 of earnings, plus a 2.9% Medicare tax on all earnings.

Example 1:

Joshua is a Talent Acquisition Specialist earning $62,500 annually. His FICA deduction will be:

  Social Security: $62,500 x 6.2% = $3,875.00

  Medicare: $62,500 x 1.45% = $906.25

  Total FICA Tax Deduction: $4,781.25

Example 2:

Tanesha is a Biomedical Engineer earning $165,000 annually. Her FICA deduction will be:

Social Security: $137,700 (Wage Base Limit) x 6.2% = $8,537.40

Medicare: $165,000 x 1.45% = $2,392.50

Total FICA Tax Deduction: $10,929.90

* Note that the Social Security wage base limit is normally adjusted upward each year.

Example 3:

Lorenzo is a Chief Operating Officer earning $225,750 annually. His FICA deduction will be:

Social Security: $137,700 (Wage Base Limit) x 6.2% = $8,537.40

Medicare: $225,750 x 1.45% = $3,273.38

Additional Medicare Tax for Highly Compensated: $25,750 x 0.9% = 231.75

Total FICA Tax Deduction: $12,042.53

* Note that the Social Security wage base limit is normally adjusted upward each year.

For anyone born after 1959, the retirement age is sixty-seven; however, individuals can take early retirement with a reduced monthly benefit as long as they are at least sixty-two. Individuals can also delay starting their Social Security benefit up to age seventy, with an increased monthly benefit. Income during retirement is even more important today, given that many of us will live beyond the average life expectancy. More than one in three sixty-five-year-olds today will live to age ninety, and more than one in seven will live to age ninety-five. Since Social Security benefits last as long as you live, they protect against outliving savings and other sources of retirement income.[12]

Individuals must work a specified period of time and earn at least a minimum amount during those periods to be eligible for Social Security benefits. The Social Security Administration bases eligibility on a system of credits, and for most people, the minimum number needed is forty.[13] The way a credit is earned has changed over the years, but currently, individuals can earn up to four credits a year, and most people need forty credits, earned over their lifetime, to receive retirement benefits. The amount of earnings it took to earn a credit in 2020 was $1,410, so earnings of $5,640 in the year earned a maximum of four credits.[14]

Once eligible, the actual monthly benefit that retirees receive is based on their actual earnings and FICA contributions. The benefit is also increased for cost-of-living adjustments, based on the Consumer Price Index (CPI). In 2020, the average monthly benefit was $1,503, and the maximum was $3,011.[15]

We the Voters: How Will Millennials Benefit from Social Security?

Social Security is a system that is supposed to benefit everyone. CBS reports on whether millennials will benefit.

View the video online at: http://www.youtube.com/embed/JJSlePKbnPw?rel=0

Medicare

Thirty years after the creation of Social Security, the Medicare bill was passed. **Medicare** is a federal health insurance program that pays for some healthcare expenses for individuals sixty-five and older and some adults under sixty-five with approved medical conditions or qualifying permanent disabilities.[16] It is administered by the Centers for Medicare & Medicaid Services (CMS). The comments from President Lyndon Johnson at the time capture the purpose of the Medicare program:[17]

> *Thirty years ago, the American people made a basic decision that the later years of life should not be years of despondency and drift. The result was an enactment of our Social Security program. Since World War II, there has been increasing awareness of the fact that the full value of Social Security would not be realized unless provision was made to deal with the problem of costs of illnesses among our older citizens. Compassion and reason dictate that this logical extension of our proven Social Security system will supply the prudent, feasible, and dignified way to free the aged from the fear of financial hardship in the event of illness.*

Medicare has different parts, each of which covers specific services:[18]

- **Medicare Part A (hospital insurance).** Covers inpatient hospital stays, care in a skilled nursing facility, hospice care, and some home healthcare.
- **Medicare Part B (medical insurance).** Covers certain doctors' services, outpatient care, medical supplies, and preventive services.
- **Medicare Part D (prescription drug coverage).** Covers prescription drugs including vaccines.

There is also a Medicare Part C, which is a bundled plan which includes Parts A and B, and usually Part D. Medicare Part A is free for most people, as long as they are eligible for Social Security. There is a premium for Parts B and D, along with deductibles and copayments.[19]

Medicare

A federal health insurance program that pays for some healthcare expenses for individuals sixty-five and older and some adults under sixty-five with approved medical conditions or qualifying permanent disabilities.

Unemployment Insurance

unemployment insurance

A joint federal-state insurance program funded through a payroll tax paid by employers, intended to safeguard individuals against financial distress for a short period of time after they become unemployed.

Unemployment insurance is a method of safeguarding individuals against financial distress for a short period of time after they become unemployed. It is designed to compensate only employable persons who are able and willing to work and are unemployed through no fault of their own. Unemployment is a joint federal-state insurance program and is funded through a payroll tax paid by employers. The federal program was created by the Federal Unemployment Tax Act of 1939 and is often referred to as FUTA. State unemployment insurance programs are referred to as SUTA.

The Federal Unemployment Tax Act of 1939 was passed in response to massive unemployment during the Depression of the 1930s. This art installation at the Franklin D. Roosevelt Memorial in Washington, D.C., shows a bread line of five men to commemorate the Great Depression.

Source: Matt Ragen / Shutterstock.com

FUTA was passed in response to the high unemployment rate during the Great Depression, which reached 25% of the U.S. workforce in 1932. The sentiment was captured by Stanley King, in the *American Labor Legislative Review* in 1933:

> *The fundamental case for unemployment protection lies in the fact that under a democratic form of society, we are forced to prevent any large-scale starvation. Funds must be provided somehow...it is practical sense to build a system which will gather funds in good times and disburse them in bad times.*[20]

What King was describing was an insurance plan. Insurance plans gather premiums from a large group in good times, and then disburse to those with a qualifying event during bad times, with the qualifying event, in this case, being unemployed, arising through no fault of their own. The resulting FUTA is, in fact, a plan to insure against becoming unemployed, with the premium being paid by employers, and claims being paid to the unemployed.

Employers are required to pay federal unemployment tax if they:

- Paid wages of $1,500 or more to employees in any calendar quarter.
- Had one or more employees for at least some part of a day in any twenty or more different weeks during the tax year.[21]

Employers must file Form 940 annually with the IRS. Form 940 is the Employer's Annual Federal Unemployment (FUTA) tax return. The FUTA tax rate as of 2020 was 6% and applies to the first $7,000 in wages paid each employee during the year.[22] The $7,000 is referred to as the FUTA wage base. The maximum FUTA tax per employee, then, is $420 annually ($7,000 x .06). If employers also paid state unemployment taxes, they can receive a credit against the FUTA tax of up to 5.4%. If an employer is entitled to the maximum 5.4% credit, the FUTA tax rate after the credit is 0.6%.

Eligibility criteria and benefits are determined by each state, although the state's program must be within guidelines established by federal law. For example, in Texas, the unemployment benefit is a percentage of earnings, up to a maximum of $521 per week for twenty-six weeks.[23] To maintain eligibility for employment, the individual must be able to work, able to accept a job, and actively looking for work.

Unemployment insurance benefits are often extended during periods of recession. Critics of long-term unemployment insurance programs cite research that indicates the extension of benefits makes unemployment persist, rather than supporting a recovery.[24] Research indicates that the long-term extension of benefits has a negative effect on job search intensity.[25] Under normal times, an individual has, on average, six months of unemployment insurance. Each person receiving unemployment benefits must be actively looking for work to qualify. But they may tend to get more serious about looking for a new job as they get closer to the time when their benefits will run out.

One example of the expansion of benefits occurred during the COVID-19 crisis. The Coronavirus Aid, Relief, and Economic Security Act (CARES) was passed in response to the impacts of the COVID-19 crisis in 2020. The CARES act greatly expanded unemployment insurance to include individuals not normally covered, including part-time workers, self-employed, and freelance or gig workers. There are three aspects of the act that expanded unemployment compensation:

- **Pandemic Unemployment Compensation (PUC).** Paid an additional $600 in weekly compensation in addition to the normal state unemployment insurance payment.
- **Pandemic Unemployment Assistance (PUA).** Provided an additional $600 in weekly compensation to those who do not normally qualify for state unemployment insurance benefits and were out of work as a direct result of COVID-19.
- **Pandemic Emergency Unemployment Compensation (PEUC).** Extended state unemployment insurance benefits an additional thirteen weeks after the state benefit ends. Most states provide twenty-six weeks of unemployment benefits, so this granted workers a total of thirty-nine weeks.

Family and Medical Leave Act of 1993 (FMLA)

The FMLA provides for parents to take unpaid, job-protected leave upon the birth of a child or to provide care for a newborn within one year of birth.

Source: © Shutterstock, Inc.

The Family and Medical Leave Act of 1993 (FMLA) is designed to provide employees temporary job security when faced with the need to take time off from work because of health-related care responsibilities. The act was passed to promote work-life balance and to support the principle that no worker should have to choose between the job they need and the family they love.[26] Since its enactment, the FMLA has been used more than one hundred million times to help workers balance the demands of the workplace with the needs of their families.[27]

The FMLA applies to employers with fifty or more employees. For an employee to be eligible, they must have worked at least twelve months for the employer (does not have to be consecutive) and worked at least 1,250 hours for the employer during the twelve months prior to the FMLA leave.[28]

The FMLA entitles eligible employees of covered employers to take unpaid, job-protected leave for specified family and medical reasons with continuation of group health insurance coverage under the same terms and conditions as if the employee had not taken leave.[29] Specifically, employees are entitled to twelve workweeks of unpaid leave in a twelve-month period for:

- The birth of a child and to care for the newborn child within one year of birth.
- The placement with the employee of a child for adoption or foster care and to care for the newly placed child within one year of placement.
- To care for the employee's spouse, child, or parent who has a serious health condition.
- A serious health condition that makes the employee unable to perform the essential functions of his or her job.
- Any qualifying exigency arising out of the fact that the employee's spouse, son, daughter, or parent is a covered military member on covered active duty.

An amendment to the FMLA provides Military Caregiver Leave for twenty-six workweeks of leave during a single twelve-month period to care for a covered service member with a serious injury or illness if the eligible employee is the service member's spouse, son, daughter, parent, or next of kin.

Patient Protection and Affordable Care Act of 2010 (ACA)

The Patient Protection and Affordable Care Act of 2010 (ACA) was passed to provide numerous rights and protections intended to make healthcare more fair and easy to understand and to make it more affordable. The act is also referred to as Obamacare or PPACA. This textbook will refer to the act as the ACA. The ACA was intended to expand access to insurance, increase consumer protections, emphasize prevention and wellness, improve quality and system performance, expand the health workforce, and curb rising healthcare costs.[30] The act was over nine hundred pages in length and therefore is very complex. A summary of the basic provisions of the ACA is listed in the following tables.[31]

TABLE 10.1 ACA Provisions to Expand Access to Insurance Coverage

ACA Provisions to Expand Access to Insurance Coverage
Required employees to cover their workers, or pay penalties, with some exceptions for small employers.
Provided tax credits to certain small businesses that cover specified costs of health insurance for their employees.
Required individuals to have health insurance, with some exceptions, such as financial hardship or religious belief.
Required creation of state-based (or multistate) insurance exchanges to help individuals and small businesses purchase insurance.
Expanded Medicaid to cover people with incomes below 133% of federal poverty guidelines.
Required creation of temporary high-risk pools for those who cannot purchase insurance on the private market due to preexisting conditions.
Required insurance plans to cover young adults on parents' policies until they turn twenty-six.
Established a national, voluntary long-term care insurance program for community living assistance services and supports (CLASS).
Required health plans to provide minimum essential coverage (MEC) to avoid paying a penalty.

TABLE 10.2 ACA Provisions to Emphasize Prevention and Wellness

ACA Provisions to Emphasize Prevention and Wellness
Established a Prevention and Public Health Fund to provide grants to states for prevention activities such as disease screening and immunizations.
Created the National Prevention, Health Promotion, and Public Health Council to coordinate federal prevention efforts, including those to address tobacco use, physical inactivity, and poor nutrition.
Required insurance plans to cover certain preventive care without cost-sharing, such as immunizations, preventive care for children, and specified screenings for adults, such as high blood pressure, high cholesterol, diabetes, and cancer.
Established a federal home-visiting initiative to help states foster health and well-being for children who live in at-risk communities.
Required restaurant chains with twenty or more locations to label menus with calorie information and to provide other information, upon request, such as fat and sodium content.
Required Medicaid programs to cover tobacco cessation services for pregnant enrollees.
Required a federal public education campaign about oral health.

The ACA has some provisions that apply only to large employers. These are referred to as applicable large employers (ALEs) and include employers with 50 or more full-time employees. The most important provision is the annual reporting responsibilities. ALEs must annually file Form 1094-C (Transmittal of Employer-Provided Health Insurance Offer and Coverage Information Returns), and Form 1095-C (Employer-Provided Health Insurance Offer and Coverage). The Form 1094-C is an information return filed with the IRS, and Form 1095-C is sent to each employee, similar to a W-2 form. Figure 10.3 is an example of a Form 1095-C.

FIGURE 10.3 Form 1095-C

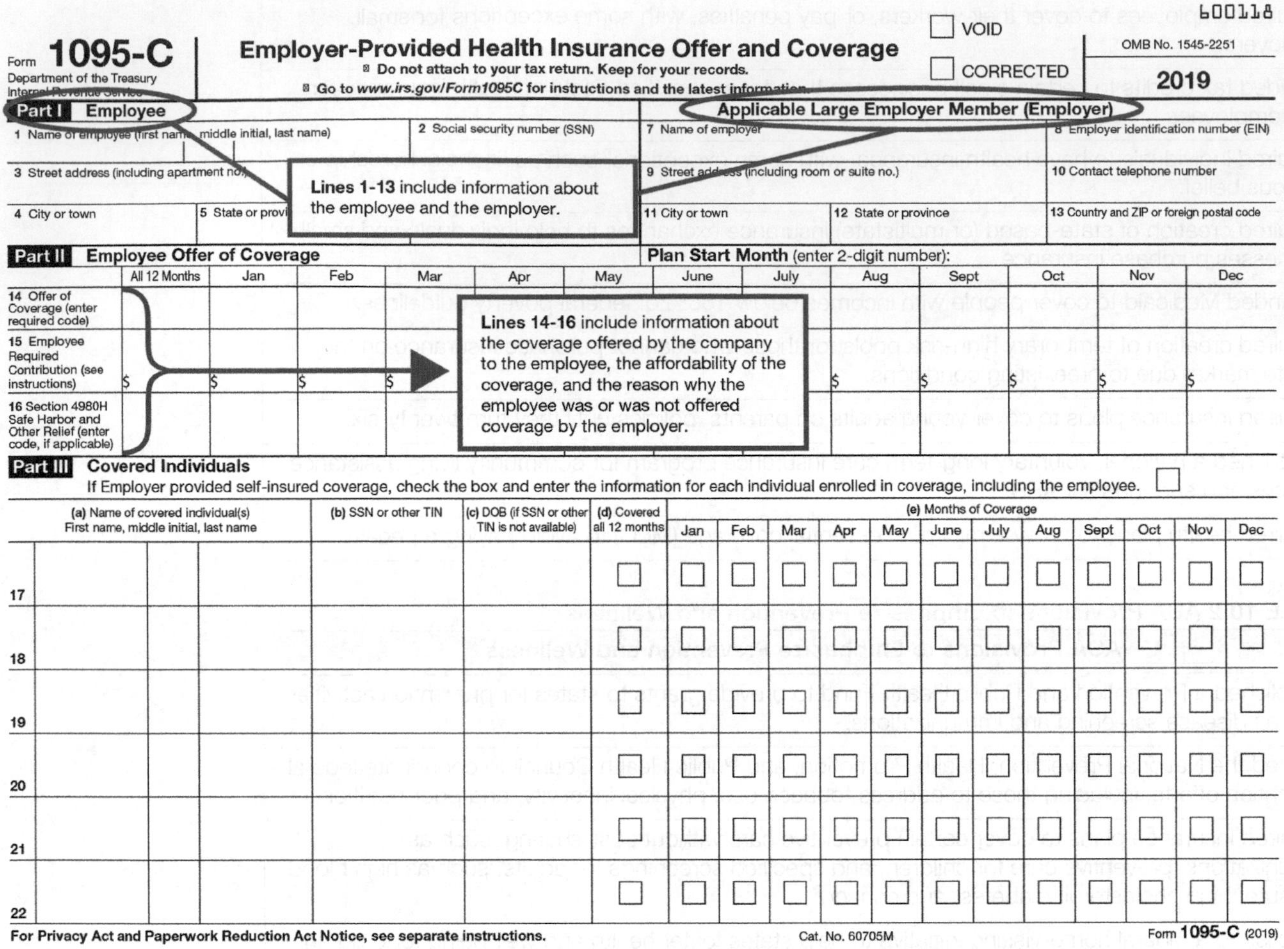

600118

Form **1095-C** Department of the Treasury Internal Revenue Service

Employer-Provided Health Insurance Offer and Coverage

Do not attach to your tax return. Keep for your records.

Go to www.irs.gov/Form1095C for instructions and the latest information.

VOID

CORRECTED

OMB No. 1545-2251

2019

Part I Employee

Applicable Large Employer Member (Employer)

1 Name of employee (first name, middle initial, last name)

2 Social security number (SSN)

7 Name of employer

8 Employer identification number (EIN)

3 Street address (including apartment no.)

9 Street address (including room or suite no.)

10 Contact telephone number

4 City or town

5 State or province

11 City or town

12 State or province

13 Country and ZIP or foreign postal code

Lines 1-13 include information about the employee and the employer.

Part II Employee Offer of Coverage

Plan Start Month (enter 2-digit number):

	All 12 Months	Jan	Feb	Mar	Apr	May	June	July	Aug	Sept	Oct	Nov	Dec
14 Offer of Coverage (enter required code)													
15 Employee Required Contribution (see instructions)	$	$	$	$					$	$	$	$	$
16 Section 4980H Safe Harbor and Other Relief (enter code, if applicable)													

Lines 14-16 include information about the coverage offered by the company to the employee, the affordability of the coverage, and the reason why the employee was or was not offered coverage by the employer.

Part III Covered Individuals

If Employer provided self-insured coverage, check the box and enter the information for each individual enrolled in coverage, including the employee.

	(a) Name of covered individual(s) First name, middle initial, last name	(b) SSN or other TIN	(c) DOB (if SSN or other TIN is not available)	(d) Covered all 12 months	(e) Months of Coverage Jan	Feb	Mar	Apr	May	June	July	Aug	Sept	Oct	Nov	Dec
17				☐	☐	☐	☐	☐	☐	☐	☐	☐	☐	☐	☐	☐
18				☐	☐	☐	☐	☐	☐	☐	☐	☐	☐	☐	☐	☐
19				☐	☐	☐	☐	☐	☐	☐	☐	☐	☐	☐	☐	☐
20				☐	☐	☐	☐	☐	☐	☐	☐	☐	☐	☐	☐	☐
21				☐	☐	☐	☐	☐	☐	☐	☐	☐	☐	☐	☐	☐
22				☐	☐	☐	☐	☐	☐	☐	☐	☐	☐	☐	☐	☐

For Privacy Act and Paperwork Reduction Act Notice, see separate instructions. Cat. No. 60705M Form **1095-C** (2019)

Consolidated Omnibus Budget Reconciliation Act of 1985 (COBRA)

The Consolidated Omnibus Budget Reconciliation Act of 1985 (COBRA) gives workers and their families who lose their health benefits the right to choose to continue group health benefits provided by their group health plan for limited periods of time under specific circumstances. Qualified individuals may be required to pay the entire premium plus an additional 2% for administrative fees (102% of the actual premium).[32]

COBRA applies to employers with twenty or more employees. If a covered employee offers a group health plan, the COBRA benefits must be offered to all qualified beneficiaries. A qualified beneficiary includes:[33]

- Employees, including part-time employees.
- Their spouses.
- Their dependents.
- Retirees (unless they are eligible for Medicare).
- Partners in a partnership.

Employers do not have to offer COBRA coverage to an employee who is not yet eligible for the group health plan (such as an employee who only worked for sixty days with a company that has a ninety-day waiting period for health insurance), an eligible employee who declined to participate in the group health plan, or any individual who is enrolled for benefits under Medicare.

COBRA applies when a qualifying event occurs. These are also sometimes referred to as trigger events. The following events qualify as COBRA triggers:[34]

- An employee's voluntary or involuntary termination, except for gross misconduct.
- An employee's reduction in hours of employment (e.g., from full-time to part-time, and thus no longer eligible for a group health plan).
- A covered spouse's divorce or legal separation from an employee.
- An employee's death.
- An employee's entitlement to Medicare.
- A covered dependent's change in status (for example, turning twenty-six, thus no longer being eligible under a parent's plan).
- Active military duty when healthcare coverage is not maintained.
- Failure to return to work at the end of FMLA leave, where coverage was in effect at the beginning of the leave but was lost during the leave.
- Bankruptcy of the employer.

COBRA benefits must be extended for eighteen months when the qualifying event is the termination of employment or reduction in hours, and thirty-six months for other qualifying events. COBRA law sets forth specific communication duties on the part of the employer and the insurer. These communication requirements are summarized in Figure 10.4.

FIGURE 10.4 COBRA Communication Requirements

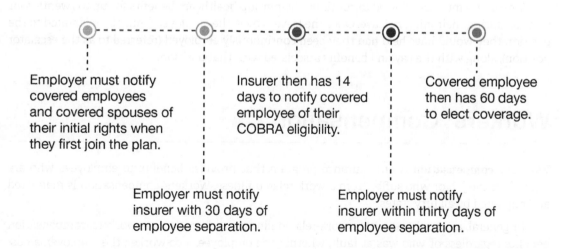

HR in the Real World: Oops . . . Here's $5,000

Javier was the general manager of a store for a national pet retailer and worked there for almost a decade. He is married with two children, and the family was covered under the company's health insurance plan. Javier decided to pursue a management opportunity with a well-known pest control company. He and his family were covered under his new employer's health plan. However, after eight months, Javier left the pest control company and went back to work for his previous employer. An HR representative at the pet retailer told him that since he left and was returning within the same year, there would be no waiting period for health insurance, and his family would be covered immediately. Three weeks after going back to work for the pet supply company, Javier's seven-year-old son became very ill and was diagnosed with Henoch-Schonlein purpura (HSP), a rare disorder affecting children. His son was being treated at a children's hospital, and the hospital informed him that the health insurance company said that he did not currently have coverage.

When Javier contacted HR about the issue, he was told that the HR representative was incorrect, and he would not have insurance until ninety days after his reemployment date. But then later that day, HR contacted him to tell him that he had been approved for a $5,000 sign-on bonus. Fortunately, he was well within the time frame to activate COBRA coverage with his previous employer and use the $5,000 signing bonus to pay for the coverage until his ninety-day waiting period was over (which is probably what HR intended but was not going to say so and admit their error).

Uniformed Services Employment and Reemployment Rights Act of 1994 (USERRA)

Employers are required to grant leave for military service under federal law and some state laws. The Uniformed Services Employment and Reemployment Rights Act of 1994 (USERRA) protects civilian job rights and benefits for veterans and members of the reserves.

The USERRA establishes the cumulative length of time that an individual may be absent from work for military duty and reemployment rights as five years.[35] There are exceptions to the five-year limit, including initial enlistments lasting more than five years, periodic National Guard and reserve training duty, and involuntary active duty extensions and recalls, especially during a time of national emergency.

Employees must be allowed to continue their group healthcare benefits for up to twenty-four months during their military leave. Once the leave is over, the employees must be reinstated to the position they would have held had they been continuously employed (referred to as the escalator position), along with the pay and benefits associated with that position.

Workers' Compensation

workers' compensation

An insurance program that provides benefits to employees who are injured on the job or who suffer from a work-related illness.

Workers' compensation is an insurance program that provides benefits to employees who are injured on the job or who suffer from a work-related illness. Workers' compensation is mandated and regulated by all fifty states.

In general, an employee with a work-related illness or injury can get workers' compensation benefits regardless of who was at fault, whether the employee, a co-worker, the employer, a customer, a supplier, or another third party.[36] In most states, coverage can be denied in the following situations:

- Injuries suffered while the employee was not on the job.
- Injuries suffered while engaged in conduct that violated company policy.
- Injuries suffered while the employee was in the act of committing a crime.
- Injuries that are self-inflicted.

Workers' compensation benefits in most states pay for hospital and medical expenses and disability payments (usually two-thirds of the employee's regular salary, rehabilitation, and in some cases retraining).

Injured employees are not required to accept workers' compensation benefits. This is important because, in most states, workers' compensation is an **exclusive remedy**. This is a provision that prohibits injured employees from suing their employers if they are receiving workers' compensation benefits. Simply put, if an employee is injured on the job, and accepts workers' compensation, then he or she loses the right to sue their employer.

There are some federal workers' compensation regulations, but they only apply to federal employees. The Office of Workers' Compensation Programs (OWCP) is an agency of the U.S. Department of Labor and administers disability compensation programs that apply to federal workers who are injured at work or acquire an occupational disease.[37] These benefits include wage replacement, medical treatment, and vocational rehabilitation. Other specific groups are covered by the following agencies under federal statutes or regulations:

- Federal Employees' Compensation Program.
- Longshore and Harbor Workers' Compensation Program.
- Federal Black Lung Program.
- Energy Employees Occupational Illness Compensation Program.
- Protecting Our Workers and Ensuring Reemployment (POWER) Initiative.

> **exclusive remedy**
>
> A provision that prohibits injured employees from suing their employer if they are receiving workers' compensation benefits.

According to the National Safety Council, the most common workplace injury is overexertion, for example by lifting a heavy box.

Source: © Shutterstock, Inc.

Cost Containment Strategies

Healthcare costs continue to increase each year. Large companies estimated their healthcare coverage expense per employee to reach an average of $15,375 in 2020, up from $14,642 in 2019, a 5% increase.[38] Employers are paying about 70% of the cost, while the employee shoulders 30%. As healthcare costs increase, employers sometimes shift the price increases to the employee.[39] This occurs through increasing deductibles, copayments, coinsurance percentages, and out-of-pocket costs. Each of these terms is defined below.

deductible

The amount a covered individual pays for services before the insurance plan pays for anything.

copayments

A flat amount a covered individual pays for a doctor or hospital visit.

coinsurance

A percentage of the costs that an individual pays for a doctor or hospital visit.

out-of-pocket costs

The maximum amount of healthcare cost that a covered individual will have to pay in a year. Most plans have a maximum total out-of-pocket for an individual and a separate amount for a family. For example, a covered family of four might have an annual out-of-pocket maximum of $2,500 for each individual, but a total of $4,000 for the entire family.

primary care physician (PCP)

A general healthcare physician who is considered the patient's main doctor and is responsible for most healthcare issues, in addition to referring the patient to specialists as needed.

managed care

A system of healthcare in which patients agree to visit only certain doctors and hospitals and in which the cost of the treatment is monitored.

- **Deductible.** The amount a covered individual pays for services before the insurance plan pays for anything. Deductibles are typically on an annual basis.
- **Copayments.** A flat amount a covered individual pays for a doctor or hospital visit.
- **Coinsurance.** A percentage of the costs that an individual pays for a doctor or hospital visit.
- **Out-of-pocket costs.** The maximum amount of healthcare cost that a covered individual will have to pay in a year. Most plans have a maximum total out-of-pocket for an individual and a separate amount for a family. For example, a covered family of four might have an annual out-of-pocket maximum of $2,500 for each individual, but a total of $4,000 the entire family.

Consider how this might work for Alayna, who has a health insurance plan through her employer. She has a $500 deductible, a $25 copay for her **PCP**, a $40 copay for specialists, and a $150 copay for emergency room (ER) visits. There is also a 20% coinsurance for all services other than office visits, and an out-of-pocket individual maximum of $2,500. If Alayna visits her PCP for the flu, and she has already met her annual $500 deductible, she will pay a flat fee of $25. If she visits the ER, is treated and then released, she will pay a flat fee of $150 for the copay. If she has other services such as respiratory therapy, she will pay 20% of those costs. If she incurs $2,500 in healthcare expenses in a year (including deductible, copays, coinsurance, and other expenses), then the insurance company will pay 100% of her healthcare costs for the remainder of the year.

Managed care is a system of healthcare in which patients agree to visit only certain doctors and hospitals and in which the cost of the treatment is monitored. These are in contrast to traditional indemnity insurance plans where coverage is provided regardless of provider or hospital used. There are a variety of managed care plan options:

- **Health maintenance organization (HMO).** A healthcare plan that provides comprehensive healthcare in a geographic area by member physicians with limited referral to outside specialists. It has deductibles and fixed copays for doctor visits. HMOs require covered individuals to select a PCP whom they will see for regular checkups and referrals to specialists. Medical care given by a provider that is outside of the network is not covered, except in an emergency.

- **Exclusive provider organization (EPO).** A healthcare plan that offers a network of doctors and hospitals to choose from. Services are not covered outside of the network, except in an emergency. They may or may not require referrals from a PCP to visit a specialist. The networks are typically larger than HMOs, and therefore might be preferred over an HMO for someone who travels often. Premiums are higher than HMOs but lower than PPOs.

- **Preferred provider organization (PPO).** A healthcare plan that gives economic incentives to patronize certain physicians, laboratories, and hospitals that agree to supervision and reduced fees. The providers are referred to as in-network. When a covered individual uses a provider that is out-of-network, then the insurance pays less of the medical costs and the insured pays more. PPO premiums are more expensive than HMOs but they provide more flexibility in choosing healthcare providers.

- **Point of service (POS).** A healthcare plan that is a hybrid of both HMO and PPO plans. Similar to an HMO, participants designate an in-network PCP. But like a PPO, the plan covers out-of-network healthcare services.

Table 10.3 highlights the differences between each of the managed care plans.

TABLE 10.3 Managed Care Plans

	HMO	PPO	EPO	POS
PCP Required	Yes	No	Often, not always	Yes
Out-of-Network Coverage	No, except for medical emergencies	Yes	No, except for medical emergencies	Yes
Referrals Needed	Yes	No	No	Yes

Key Takeaways

- Employee benefits can be divided into two categories: mandatory benefits that the employer is required to offer by federal or state law, and voluntary benefits that employers can choose whether to offer and at what level.

- In the U.S., the primary government program that addresses these needs is the Old Age, Survivors, and Disability Insurance Program, or OASDI, which is the official name of the program that we normally refer to as Social Security. Congress passed the Federal Insurance Contributions Act (FICA), creating the Social Security program in 1935.

- Social Security and Medicare are funded by payroll taxes that are shared equally between the employer and employee.

- Medicare is a federal health insurance program that pays for some healthcare expenses for individuals sixty-five and older and some adults under sixty-five with approved medical conditions or qualifying permanent disabilities.

- Unemployment insurance is a method of safeguarding individuals against financial distress for a short period of time after they become unemployed. It is designed to compensate only employable persons who are able and willing to work and are unemployed through no fault of their own.

- Unemployment is a joint federal-state insurance program and is funded through a payroll tax paid by employers.

- The Family and Medical Leave Act of 1993 (FMLA) is designed to provide employees temporary job security when faced with the need to take time off from work because of

health maintenance organization (HMO)

A healthcare plan that provides comprehensive healthcare in a geographic area by member physicians with limited referral to outside specialists.

exclusive provider organization (EPO)

A healthcare plan that offers a large network of doctors and hospitals to choose from.

preferred provider organization (PPO)

A healthcare plan that gives economic incentives to patronize certain physicians, laboratories, and hospitals that agree to supervision and reduced fees.

point of service (POS)

A healthcare plan that is a hybrid of both HMO and PPO plans.

health-related care responsibilities. Employees are entitled to twelve workweeks of unpaid leave in a twelve-month period when a qualifying event occurs.

- The Patient Protection and Affordable Care Act of 2010 (ACA) was passed to provide numerous rights and protections intended to make healthcare more fair and easy to understand and to make it more affordable.

- The Consolidated Omnibus Budget Reconciliation Act of 1985 (COBRA) gives workers and their families who lose their health benefits the right to choose to continue group health benefits provided by their group health plan for limited periods of time under specific circumstances.

- The Uniformed Services Employment and Reemployment Rights Act of 1994 (USERRA) protects civilian job rights and benefits for veterans and members of reserves.

- Workers' compensation is an insurance program that provides benefits to employees who are injured on the job or who suffer from a work-related illness. Workers' compensation is mandated and regulated by all fifty states.

- One approach that employers have taken to control the cost of healthcare insurance is to transfer more costs to the employee. This occurs through increasing deductibles, copayments, coinsurance percentages, and out-of-pocket costs.

- Managed care is a system of healthcare in which patients agree to visit only certain doctors and hospitals and in which the cost of the treatment is monitored.

What Do *You* Think?

1. After reading about how FICA taxes are assessed (fifty-fifty split between employer and employee), do you think the amount paid by the employer is fair? Should the employer pay more or less?

2. Do you think that the extension of unemployment insurance discourages individuals from seeking employment?

3. Do you think a company should pay a penalty for not providing health insurance to its employees?

4. How much of total healthcare costs should a company shift to its employees?

10.4 Voluntary Employee Benefits

Learning Objectives

1. Distinguish between defined benefit plans and defined contribution plans.
2. Describe the types of paid-time-off benefits that employers provide.
3. Identify the types of insurance programs that employers can voluntarily provide.
4. Explain the major components of employee wellness and employee assistance programs.

All other types of employee benefits not mentioned in the previous section are voluntary. These include retirement plans, paid time off, other types of insurance (life insurance, dental, vision, short-term and long-term disability, and employee assistance programs). Employer-sponsored health insurance can also be considered a voluntary benefit, but only for small organizations, since employers with fifteen or more employees are required to offer at least a minimum level of health insurance under the ACA. These voluntary benefit programs are often offered as part of the organizational strategy to attract and retain quality employees.

Employers also increasingly view voluntary benefits as an important piece of their employee engagement efforts.[40] In a 2018 Willis Towers Watson survey, 95% of clients said voluntary benefits would play an important role in their total rewards strategy, versus 59% only five years earlier.[41]

Employers cite the following top five reasons for offering voluntary benefits:[42]

- To enrich existing core benefits by offering more personalized options.
- To appeal to a multigenerational workforce.
- To support employee financial well-being.
- To attract new employees.
- To support employee retention.

Retirement Benefits

There are two categories of employer-sponsored retirement plans: **defined benefit plans**, and **defined contribution plans**. A defined benefit plan provides a fixed, pre-established benefit for employees at retirement. These plans are paid by the employer, and the benefit is normally based upon the length of service and the salary earned at retirement. Some plans use an average of the last few years of service to determine the benefit. This is a very costly type of plan and is becoming increasingly rare. Defined benefit plans are protected, with some limitations, by the Pension Benefit Guaranty Corporation (PBGC), which is a U.S. government agency designed to protect retirement assets. Defined benefit plans (often referred to as pensions) typically require the employee to work a set number of years, commonly five or seven, before they are **vested**. Once an employee is vested, then they have earned the right to receive pension benefits. If an employee terminates employment before becoming vested, he or she receives no retirement benefit.

Defined benefit plans also have rules that stipulate when an employee can retire. One such rule that is common is known as the **Rule of 80**. This means that an employee can retire when their age plus years of service equals eighty. Using this rule, an employee who is fifty-five and has twenty-five years of service could retire, as could an employee who is fifty with thirty years of service. But someone with only fifteen years of service could not retire until age sixty-five.

A defined contribution plan is a tax-deferred retirement plan, in which employees contribute a fixed amount or percentage of each paycheck to a retirement savings account. Many companies also contribute to the plan by matching a portion of the employee contributions as a benefit. One advantage of a defined contribution plan is that the employee is vested immediately with regard to their contributions (although they may have to work for a set number of years to become vested with regard to the employer contributions). Table 10.4 displays the most common types of employer-sponsored defined contribution plans, each of which is named after the IRS code with which it is associated. Contributions are tax-deferred, meaning the employer only portion is not taxed until the funds are withdrawn. If individuals withdraw funds before the age of fifty-nine and a half, then the IRS assesses a 10% early withdrawal penalty.

defined benefit plan

An employer-sponsored retirement plan provides a fixed, pre-established benefit for employees at retirement.

defined contribution plan

An employer-sponsored retirement plan that is tax-deferred, in which employees contribute a fixed amount or percentage of each paycheck to a retirement savings account.

vested

Having earned the right to receive pension benefits after having been employed at an organization for a certain length of time.

Rule of 80

A retirement eligibility rule that an employee can retire when their age plus years of service equals 80.

TABLE 10.4 Defined Contribution Plans

	Types of Defined Contribution Plans
401(k)	Offered by for-profit organizations. Employee is often able to direct how the funds are invested. Contributions are capped each year, with the total employee contribution limited to $19,000 in 2019, with an additional $6,000 per year catch-up contribution for individuals fifty and older.
Roth 401(k)	Offered by for-profit organizations. Allows employees to withdraw earnings on their retirement accounts tax-free.
403(b)	Offered by nonprofit organizations. Contribution limits are the same as 401(k).
457	Offered by state and local governments. Contribution limits are the same as 401(k).

A potential downside to employer-sponsored retirement savings programs is that some employees withdraw funds or take loans against them or cash them out when they change employers. A 2016 survey of more than four thousand workers conducted by Transamerica found that 25% of workers in small companies and 28% in large companies have taken some form of loan, early withdrawal, or hardship withdrawal from a 401(k) plan, suggesting they lacked a family budget or were unable to keep expenses within their budget.[43] Table 10.5 gives an example of the negative impact of withdrawals on accumulated retirement savings.

TABLE 10.5 Impact of Withdrawals on Accumulated Retirement Savings
(Based upon 6% annual investment return)

Investor's Current Age	Years to Retirement	Value of $10,000 at Retirement (Investment loss if withdrawn)	Value of $20,000 at Retirement (Investment loss if withdrawn)	Value of $30,000 at Retirement (Investment loss if withdrawn)
57	10	$17,908	$35,817	$53,725
47	20	$32,071	$64,143	$96,214
37	30	$57,435	$114,870	$172,305
27	40	$102,857	$205,714	$308,572

There are several steps that employers can take to encourage employees not to draw down their retirement savings:[44]

- Change plan design to eliminate or reduce situations where participants can take out plan loans or take hardship withdrawals.
- Educate employees about the impact a loan or withdrawal could have on their retirement savings.
- Provide financial education to employees to help them manage their money better and avoid the need to tap retirement assets.
- Offer emergency loans that can be repaid with a payroll deduction.
- Provide for payroll deductions into an emergency savings fund.
- Educate departing employees about the need to roll over retirement assets into an IRA or their new employer's retirement plan.
- Implement an automatic rollover program so that employee's retirement plan assets end up in an IRA rather than being cashed out.

The **Employee Retirement Income Security Act (ERISA)** is a federal law that sets minimum standards for most voluntarily established retirement and health plans in private industry to provide protection for individuals in these plans. ERISA requires plan providers to provide participants with information about the plan, provides fiduciary responsibilities for those who manage and control plan assets, requires plans to establish a grievance and appeals process for participants to get benefits from their plans, and gives participants the right to sue for benefits and breaches of fiduciary duty.[45]

The purpose of ERISA is to assure that employees who rely on a retirement plan will receive the money when they retire, and to protect the funds from mismanagement, misappropriation, and embezzlement. Companies are not required to offer retirement or health insurance plans, but if they do, they must comply with ERISA requirements. Companies that do not adhere to ERISA are subject to substantial penalties.

> **Employee Retirement Income Security Act (ERISA)**
>
> A federal law that sets minimum standards for most voluntarily established retirement and health plans in private industry to provide protection for individuals in these plans.

Paid Time Off (PTO)

Paid time off (PTO) refers to a company policy that combines sick time, vacation, and personal leave into a single bank of days that employees can take off. Employees typically can use these days at their discretion and do not need to explain to their supervisor why the day is needed. No federal laws govern PTO, with the exception of the Families First Coronavirus Response Act (FFCRA), which will be discussed later in this section, but there are state regulations. As of 2019, eleven states plus Washington, D.C., and thirty municipalities required employers to offer sick leave.[46]

Organizations should have a written policy that states how much PTO is accumulated, how much notice should be given before taking PTO, and whether accumulated PTO can be carried over at the end of a year. Unused PTO may have to be paid to employees upon separation from the organization, and therefore many employers require employers to "use it or lose it," or perhaps allow a limited amount of PTO to be carried over. This prevents the company from having the financial burden of paying out large amounts of PTO when long-term employees separate.

Some employers give employees the opportunity to engage in community volunteer activities as part of their PTO programs.

Source: Kathy Hutchins / Shutterstock.com

> **paid time off (PTO)**
>
> A company policy that combines sick time, vacation, and personal leave into a single bank of days that employees can take off.

PTO policies provide many advantages for employees and the employer:[47]

- PTO treats employees as adults who are entitled to use PTO at their discretion without oversight. Managers are not put in the position of having to monitor and report employees' use of sick, vacation, and personal leave.

- Employees value the flexibility that PTO provides. It gives them the option of using the time for whatever they need: whether to care for a sick child, take a pet to the vet, take the family to an amusement park, or just take a mental health day.

- PTO eliminates friction and conflict between employees and supervisors and allows the employee to maintain their privacy since they do not need to explain their reason for taking time off or ask permission (although employers can stipulate how much advance notice needs to be given, except for sick days; employers can also limit when PTO can be taken based on scheduling needs, such as major shopping days for retailers).

- PTO simplifies recordkeeping for companies, as opposed to having separate banks for each category of time off (sick, vacation, and personal days).

There are also some potential disadvantages to be aware of:[48]

- Some research shows that employers who adopt PTO may give employees fewer overall days than they had previously.

- Employees tend to use all of their time off under a PTO policy, where in the past they may not have used all of their sick days.

- Some employees view their PTO as vacation time and will come to work even when sick to preserve their PTO for vacation.

These potential problems with PTO can be addressed through the PTO policies, modeling appropriate behavior, and coaching employees when needed.

An additional type of leave that employers will encounter is jury duty. Most states have laws prohibiting employees from discharging employees for responding to a jury summons or serving on a jury.[49] Eight states also require employers to pay employees while serving on a jury: Alabama, Colorado, Connecticut, Louisiana, Massachusetts, Nebraska, New York, and Tennessee.

Congress enforced paid leave requirements on private employers for the first time in 2020. The Families First Coronavirus Response Act (FFCRA) required certain public employers and private employers with fewer than five hundred employees to provide paid sick leave or expanded family and medical leave for specified reasons related to COVID-19. The additional expense to the employer was offset by federal tax credits. The act provided that employees of covered employees were eligible for:[50]

- Two weeks (up to eighty hours) of paid sick leave at the employee's regular rate of pay where the employee was unable to work because the employee is quarantined (pursuant to federal, state, or local government order or advice of a healthcare provider), and/or experiencing COVID-19 symptoms and seeking a medical diagnosis.

- Two weeks (up to eighty hours) of paid sick leave at two-thirds the employee's regular rate of pay because the employee was unable to work because of a bona fide need to care for an individual subject to quarantine.

- Up to an additional ten weeks of paid expanded family and medical leave at two-thirds the employee's regular rate of pay where an employee, who had been employed for at least thirty calendar days, was unable to work due to a bona fide need for leave to care for a child whose school or childcare provider was closed for reasons related to COVID-19.

Other Insurance

Employers often will provide employees with optional insurance coverage, either paid for by the company or by the employee through payroll deduction. These plans provide a benefit to the employee because the insurance rates for a group plan are usually lower than if the employee bought an individual policy. Another benefit is that medical exams are sometimes waived for life insurance. (The ACA made it illegal to exclude individuals from coverage based on preexisting conditions, but life insurance is not regulated by the ACA.) The most common types of optional insurance are life, dental, vision, and disability (short-term and long-term).

Employers need to decide whether to offer the insurance benefit to all employees or just a specific group. If an employer wants to offer a benefit only to a few key employees, then they will not be able to deduct the premiums for federal tax purposes unless they meet certain nondiscrimination requirements.[51] The IRS defines key employees as officers of the company with gross compensation in excess of $180,000, or employees who own 5% or more of the company or own 1% of the company and whose gross compensation is more than $150,000. In the case of group term life insurance, the nondiscrimination rules are:[52]

- The plan must benefit at least 70% of the company's employees.

- At least 85% of all employees who participate in the plan must not be highly-compensated or key employees.

- The plan must benefit employees who qualify under a classification that is set up by the employer and found by the IRS not to discriminate in favor of key employees.

HR Talk: Marisa Gonzalez

Benefits Specialist

SRS Distribution, Inc.

Many of our decisions, whether for benefits or business operations, stem from employee feedback. We obtain feedback in various forms whether directly through in-person discussions or through anonymous surveys administered by Culture IQ.

We also utilize our insurance broker, Lockton, to detail employer costs and statistical data that would be useful in choosing our plans for our employee population. We are continually adjusting our voluntary benefits to assist the needs of our employees based on an accumulation of these practices. Recent changes include FSA employer contribution, HSA employer contribution, employer-paid Short Term Disability, removing a mid-tier PPO plan, and offering the choice of either a Premium PPO plan or a HDHP (High Deductible) plan. Finally, as the majority of our employees work in a labor intensive environment, we have also included in 2021 voluntary accident insurance, hospital indemnity, and critical illness. While the cost of healthcare is continually on the rise and rates for our employees continue to increase, we hope to subsidize some of that burden by offering employer contributions to a few of our voluntary benefits.

Our voluntary benefits must be able to not only address the needs of our employees, but can also be easily implemented and accessible to anyone across the country, since we have 480 branches across the United States (including Hawaii) employing over 5,000 people.

Our voluntary benefits must also be competitive and portable as we are committed to acquiring 10 businesses annually. In an effort to make a seamless transition during acquisition, we research what competitors may offer and ensure that we have benefits in place that will be comparable, if not better, than the previous company's benefits.

The greatest challenge in managing our benefits program is educating our employees in choosing the best plans for themselves and their dependents. We find that a large portion of our employees in the field have never had exposure to the fundamentals of benefits. Understanding deductibles, co-pays, out-of-pocket maximums, etc. is foreign to many. This is of course no fault of their own; the subject matter is vast and dense. I do believe, though, that some people would rather opt out of coverage because they are uncomfortable with choosing benefits. Not understanding the terminology and services provided can be very intimidating for some, and they would rather not enroll at all as a result.

We take field calls with questions concerning our plans and create informative videos and documents to educate our employees about healthcare, but it's a challenge to get the information to those who need it most.

I see dependent care as a trending benefit whether it includes company subsidies for dependent care, on-site daycare, or FSA employer contributions. Dependent care, along with implementing parental leave, have been repeated requests in our field, and we are thrilled to be offering both in 2021. Trending as well are requests for well-being programs that provide opportunities to improve physical, mental, and emotional health. We have seen numerous requests for stress reduction programs, smoking cessation programs, and other incentives for making healthy choices. I believe employers are revamping their benefit plans to include total rewards packages that focus on holistic well-being.

Employee Programs

In the ideal world, everyone would come to work ready to focus and be productive and not have any distractions from personal problems. But every employee is unique and faces various issues that can cause emotional or physical distress and can adversely affect an employee's job performance. There are two common types of programs that organizations offer at no cost to employees to promote health lifestyles. First, **employee wellness programs (EWPs)** are resources designed to maintain or improve the health of employees. They typically include medical screenings, incentives, fitness programs, education, and sometimes behavioral change interventions, such as smoking cessation. One of the most significant substance abuse issues is the opioid epidemic. Opioids (including prescription opioids, heroin, and fentanyl) caused the death of over 47,000 people in 2017, more than any year on record.[53] The Bureau of Labor Statistics reported that overdose deaths at work from nonmedical use of drugs or alcohol rose by at least 25% annually between 2013 and 2017.[54] Workplace consequences of alcohol and drug abuse include poor performance, fighting, insubordination, and occupational injuries.[55] Employees with a substance abuse disorder miss an average of 14.8 days per year, while those with a pain medication disorder miss 29 days a year, as compared to an average for all employees of 10.5 days.[56] Employers can use the following five strategies to address substance abuse by employees:[57]

1. **Assess the workplace.** Start with a needs assessment to determine the impact of substance abuse in the workplace. Is the organization prepared if a substance abuse issue happens?

2. **Develop substance-free policies.** Polices should address risk management and provide guidance to employees and managers.

3. **Educate employees.** Prevention of substance abuse at work should include a focus on safety, health, personal life, and work performance.

4. **Train leaders.** Supervisors should be trained on policies and be capable of explaining the policy to employees, and to understand legal implications regarding confidentiality and union contracts. They also should be trained in recognizing the symptoms of a substance abuse problem.

5. **Provide support.** Encourage early treatment and provide referrals to appropriate professional services such as addiction treatment programs.

Employee assistance programs (EAPs) are voluntary intervention programs designed to assist employees in resolving personal problems that may have adverse impacts on work performance. They often provide help with issues including substance abuse, financial or legal problems, parenting or elder care, and relationship challenges. Services can be provided by telephone hotlines, online chat, email, video counseling, or they can be face-to-face. In addition, EAP services are normally available not only to the employee, but also to the employee's spouse, nonmarital partner, and children living in the same household. EAPs can include assessments, counseling, referrals, and follow-up services for issues including financial, emotional, or substance abuse. EAPs are paid for by the employer and are usually operated through an agreement with a third-party administrator.[58] This provides confidentiality for the employee, since the EAP does not share any personal information with the employer.

EAPs sometimes offer medical advice through nurse hotlines or provide information about mental health counseling or health services. They are not insurance plans, but if they offer access to medical-related support, including mental health counseling or treatment for substance abuse, then the EAP is subject to ERISA and COBRA guidelines.

Because EAPs are a fairly new approach to employee health, the research into the impacts is limited. However, they have been shown to reduce workplace injury.[59] EAPs have also been shown to reduce absenteeism due to employees taking fewer sick days.[60]

In addition to the benefits described in this chapter, some employers are getting creative and offering innovative benefits to attract and retain employees. In the opening case, you read about some of creative approaches taken by Salesforce, Google, Southwest Airlines, and Clif Bar. Some employers also offer legal service plans, identity theft protection plans, student loan assistance programs, long-term care insurance, on-site daycare, on-site cafeterias, and even pet insurance. Some employers offer student loan forgiveness. PricewaterhouseCoopers offers employees up to $1,200 a year in student loan repayment assistance with a $10,000 lifetime benefit. Peloton, Penguin Random House, Staples, Honeywell, Estee Lauder, and Carvana each offers its employees repayment assistance from $100 to $150 a month.

Some companies try to create a work environment where employees can take a break from work. These include quiet spaces, nap pods, and fun spaces with features such as foosball and pool. Companies are having bring-your-child-to work and bring-your-pet-to-work days to promote a sense of family. There is no limit to the innovative ideas you can implement to create a work culture that helps to create an attractive employer brand.

 Extraordinary Employee Wellness Programs

The Institute for Health and Productivity Studies at Johns Hopkins University examines three extraordinary employee well programs.

View the video online at: http://www.youtube.com/embed/s-QbV_OstxQ?rel=0

Talent Analytics

What is the ROI of an EWP or EAP? A recent survey of over three hundred leading medical insurers by Willis Towers Watson shows that increases in healthcare costs continue to escalate, with an increase in the U.S. of 7.6% in 2019, compared to 7.1% in 2018 and 6.7% in 2017.[61] Thus, healthcare cost increases are about three times the overall rate of inflation, as measured by the Consumer Price Index.

The top three conditions that cause the highest number of claims are cardiovascular (54%), musculoskeletal (49%), and cancer (42%).[62] However, the prevalence of other conditions such as diabetes and mental health issues is increasing rapidly.

The more risk the employee holds by maintaining an unhealthy lifestyle, the more the company has to pay for comprehensive health insurance. For example, insurers can charge tobacco users up to 50% more than those who do not use tobacco.[63] Healthy workers are also more productive and contribute positively to the bottom line.[64]

It is difficult for any organization to avoid these risks. All of a business's collective employees would have to be drastically different than the country's average demographics. The Centers for Disease Control and Prevention estimates that 75% of U.S. healthcare spending is on people with chronic conditions which cause death, lifelong disability, and compromised quality of life, and that many of these can be prevented.[65] The facts are arresting:[66]

- Seven out of ten deaths among Americans each year are from chronic diseases.
- About one-fourth of people with chronic conditions have one or more daily activity limitations.
- Health disparities in chronic disease incidence and mortality are widespread among members of racial and ethnic minority populations. For example, heart disease death rates are higher among African Americans than whites, and diabetes rates are substantially higher among American Indians and Alaska Natives than whites.
- Mental illnesses and chronic diseases are closely related. Chronic diseases can exacerbate symptoms of depression, and depressive disorders can themselves lead to chronic diseases.

Wellness and employee assistance programs aren't just beneficial in helping to ward off things people know they're at risk for but also promote practicing strong preventative health. The bottom is that healthy people are less expensive for employers to insure.[67] EWP and EAP programs contribute directly to the bottom line by not only improving physical and mental health, but also by mitigating risk, which together can lower insurance cost and improve productivity. Thus, the ROI is impacted in two ways: by saving the company money through lower health insurance premiums and by improving profits through productivity increases.

Key Takeaways

- There are two categories of employer-sponsored retirement plans: defined benefit plans and defined contribution plans.
- A defined benefit plan provides a fixed, pre-established benefit for employees at retirement.
- A defined contribution plan is a tax-deferred retirement plan, in which employees contribute a fixed amount or percentage of each paycheck to a retirement savings account.
- Paid time off (PTO) refers to a company policy that combines sick time, vacation, and personal leave into a single bank of days that employees that can take off.
- Most states have laws prohibiting employees from discharging employees for responding to a jury summons or serving on a jury.
- Employers often will provide employees with optional insurance coverage, either paid for by the company, or by the employee through payroll deduction.
- The most common types of optional insurance are life, dental, vision, and disability (short-term and long-term).
- Employee wellness programs (EWPs) are resources designed to maintain or improve the health of employees. They typically include medical screenings, incentives, fitness programs, education, and sometimes behavioral change interventions, such as smoking cessation.
- Employee assistance programs (EAPs) are voluntary intervention programs designed to assist employees in resolving personal problems that may adversely affect their work performance. They often provide help with issues including substance abuse, financial or legal problems, parenting or elder care, and relationship challenges.

What Do *You* Think?

1. When searching for a job, how important are retirement benefits to you?
2. Assume that you have worked someplace for five years and have $25,000 in a 401(k) plan. What would you do with that money if you left to accept a position with another employer?
3. Would you rather be offered a set number of sick days and vacation days or a PTO bank that you could use for any reason?

10.5 Conclusion

The chapter began with a discussion of benefits as part of an overall compensation strategy and industry benchmarking. Mandatory benefits were examined, including Social Security, Medicare, unemployment insurance, federal legislation, and workers' compensation. Then voluntary benefits were explored, with a focus on retirement plans, time off, other types of insurance, and employee wellness and assistance programs.

Theory-into-Practice (TIP) Exercises

1. Rank order the following voluntary benefits, with 1 being the most important to you, and 14 being the least important. Then compare your results with a classmate.

    Retirement plan

    Life insurance

    Dental insurance

    Vision insurance

    Pet insurance

    Short-term disability

    Long-term disability

    Employee assistance program

    Long-term care insurance

    Onsite daycare

    Onsite cafeteria

    Student loan assistance

    Legal services plan

    Identity theft protection

2. Research the workers' compensation regulations in your state. Then make a list of the action items that an employer must do to comply with the regulations.

3. Using the benchmarking reports listed under number one and number two of the Resources section, analyze the employee benefits plan at your employer to see how they compare. Do they offer more benefits, about average, or fewer benefits than similar companies? (If you are not currently employed, then use the employer of a classmate, friend, or relative for the comparison.)

Case Study: Cigna Insures Growth Opportunities

Source: Piotr Swat / Shutterstock.com

Cigna is a global health service company that offers a variety of services to over 168.2 million customers and employs more than 40,000 employees. The vast services Cigna offers its customers include Medicare and Medicaid products, and health, life, and accident insurance for both individuals and families. Cigna's roots trace back to more than 225 years ago when a group of citizens in Philadelphia formed the Insurance Company of North America (INA). Later, in 1865, the governor of Connecticut signed into law the Connecticut General Life Insurance Company (CG). In 1982 INA and CG merged into one entity, and the new name became Cigna as we know it today.

Financially, Cigna seems to be doing well. Widespread political debate about changes in healthcare coverage has many in the field unsure about the future of healthcare services providers. While others in the managed healthcare industry are experiencing falling share prices, Cigna has issued a statement saying they are confident to maintain their forecasted share prices for 2021. In 2019, Cigna reported its customer base rose exponentially to 168.2 million as compared to 97.2 million from the previous year.

Along with the demand to cater to its growing customer base, Cigna is focusing on strengthening and retaining its employee population. Their website says Cigna acknowledges that the success of the company is in direct correlation to the employees' feeling of satisfaction in the workplace. Cigna is redesigning its approach to employee development opportunities. In 2018, they unveiled an improved Human Capital Management System intended to give employees greater access to advanced mentoring opportunities and career planning pathway resources. One of these strategies is Cigna University. The university uses social technology to connect people. Classes include the following focus areas: employee wellness, human rights, nondiscrimination, and safety. The expansive topics range from meditation and eating healthy to preventing workplace harassment and violence prevention. Cigna University courses are available to all employees and their family members 24/7. All full-time and salaried employees also participate in the Connect for Growth program, an online platform encouraging collaboration across online groups and over sixty online communities.

Cigna is now making headlines for its approach to redefining its Educational Reimbursement Program (ERP). In many organizations, tuition reimbursement has mainly been viewed as a benefit or perk to employees; however, Cigna has new insight into this process. Cigna shared its data on the expense and impact of its tuition assistance program with the Lumina Foundation and Accenture study groups. The study period (2012 to 2014), reported 2,200 of the 31,000 employees sought assistance through tuition reimbursement. The findings reveal Cigna experienced a surprising 129% ROI for tuition reimbursement costs between 2012 and 2014. In other words, for every dollar invested in tuition, Cigna got that dollar back while also saving $1.29 on talent management costs. Savings were inclusive of employee promotions, retention of employees, and transfers within the organization. Reimbursement participants are also 8% more likely to remain at Cigna.[68]

 ## Meet Annie | Cigna Employee

Hear Cigna employee Annie talk about her experience with the company's technology early career development program.

View the video online at: http://www.youtube.com/embed/ZU6LntTzqyg?rel=0

Case Discussion Questions

1. Do you think a company can sustain continued investments in education as the program gains popularity and the costs continue to increase?

2. Do you think customers find value in knowing Cigna is investing in their employees?

3. Will applicants consider Cigna a better employment option if they know the company is willing to invest in furthering their education?

4. What happens to employee morale when they have made an investment to further their education but have not experienced the professional advancement or salary increase within the time frame they expected?

5. How can Cigna improve employee career satisfaction for those employees who have no desire to commit to long-term education pathways?

Resources

1. **Employee Benefits Benchmarking Study.** Based on responses from 8,072 employers sponsoring 14,131 health plans covering over one million employees nationwide.

   https://www.griffinbenefits.com/employeebenefitsblog/employee-benefits-2018-benchmarking-study

2. **National Compensation Survey.** Published by the Bureau of Labor Statistics—includes comprehensive data on the incidence (the percentage of workers with access to and participation in employer-provided benefit plans) and provisions of selected employee benefit plans.

    https://www.bls.gov/ncs/

3. **Employee Benefits News.** A website that provides information and updates on retirement plans, employee wellness, voluntary benefits, employer strategies, and more.

    https://www.benefitnews.com/

Endnotes

1. Bureau of Labor Statistics. (2000). *Employer costs for employee compensation summary*. Retrieved from https://www.bls.gov/news.release/ecec.nr0.htm

2. Case written by Crews, P. (2020). Adapted from: 5 companies with the best benefits. *Human Resources MBA*. Retrieved from https://www.humanresourcesmba.net/lists/5-companies-with-the-best-benefits/

3. What is total rewards. *WorldatWork*. Retrieved January 10, 2020 from https://www.worldatwork.org/total-rewards-model/

4. How did we get here? A history of benefits. (2018). *Evive*. Retrieved from https://goevive.com/latest/thinking/history-of-benefits/

5. Bureau of Labor Statistics. *Employee Benefits Survey*. Retrieved January 15, 2020 from https://www.bls.gov/ncs/ebs/

6. How to drive employee engagement with total compensation statements. (2018). *Paycor*. Retrieved from https://www.paycor.com/resource-center/how-to-drive-employee-engagement-with-total-compensation-statements

7. Social Security Administration. *Historical Background and Development of Social Security*. Retrieved January 5, 2020 from https://www.ssa.gov/history/briefhistory3.html

8. Ibid.

9. Hacker, J. (2011). Decennial life tables. *National Institutes of Health*. Retrieved from https://www.ncbi.nlm.nih.gov/pmc/articles/PMC2885717/

10. How does U.S. life expectancy compare to other countries? (2019). *Peterson-Kaiser*. Retrieved from https://www.healthsystemtracker.org/chart-collection/u-s-life-expectancy-compare-countries/

11. Internal Revenue Service. *Topic No. 751: Social Security and Medicare Withholding Rates*. Retrieved September 4, 2019 from https://www.irs.gov/taxtopics/tc751

12. Social Security Administration. *Retirement Benefits*. Retrieved April 8, 2020 from https://www.ssa.gov/benefits/retirement/

13. Ibid.

14. Social Security Administration. *Social Security Credits*. Retrieved April 7, 2020 from https://www.ssa.gov/planners/credits.html

15. Social Security Administration. (2020). Fact Sheet: 2020 Social Security Changes. Retrieved from https://www.ssa.gov/news/press/factsheets/colafacts2020.pdf

16. Facts about Medicare. *eHealthMedicine*. Retrieved April 7, 2020 from https://www.ehealthmedicare.com/about-medicare-articles/facts-about-medicare/

17. Historical background and development of Social Security. Social Security Administration. Retrieved December 2, 2020 from https://www.ssa.gov/history/briefhistory3.html

18. Medicare. *What's Medicare?* Retrieved April 5, 2020 from https://www.medicare.gov/what-medicare-covers/your-medicare-coverage-choices/whats-medicare

19. Medicare. *Your Medicare Costs*. Retrieved April 5, 2020 from https://www.medicare.gov/your-medicare-costs

20. Social Security: Unemployment Insurance. *The Social Welfare History Project*. Retrieved April 5, 2020 from https://socialwelfare.library.vcu.edu/social-security/social-security-unemployment-insurance/

21. Internal Revenue Service. *Topic No. 759 Form 940—Employer's Annual Federal Unemployment (FUTA) Tax Return—Filing and Deposit Requirements*. Retrieved April 5, 2020 from https://www.irs.gov/taxtopics/tc759

22. Internal Revenue Service. *Topic No. 759 Form 940—Employer's Annual Federal Unemployment (FUTA) Tax Return—Filing and Deposit Requirements*. Retrieved April 5, 2020 from https://www.irs.gov/taxtopics/tc759

23. Texas Workforce Commission. Eligibility and benefit amounts. Retrieved April 7, 2020 from https://www.twc.texas.gov/jobseekers/eligibility-benefit-amounts

24. The wages of unemployment: A new study shows how jobless insurance increased joblessness. (2013). *Wall Street Journal*. Retrieved from https://www.wsj.com/articles/the-wages-of-unemployment-1382050539

25. Schwartz, J. (2013). Unemployment insurance and the business cycle: What adjustments are needed? *Southern Economic Journal, 79*(3), 680-702.

26. U.S. Department of Labor. *Family and Medical Leave Act*. Retrieved April 5, 2020.

27. Ibid.

28. Family and Medical Leave Act (FMLA). *Employment Law Handbook*. Retrieved April 5, 2020 from https://www.employmentlawhandbook.com/federal-employment-and-labor-laws/fmla/

29. U.S. Department of Labor. *Family and Medical Leave Act*. Retrieved April 5, 2020 from https://www.dol.gov/whd/fmla/

30. The Affordable Care Act: A brief summary. *National Council of State Legislatures*. Retrieved April 5, 2020 from http://www.ncsl.org/portals/1/documents/health/HRACA.pdf

31. The Affordable Care Act: A brief summary. *National Council of State Legislatures*. Retrieved April 5, 2020 from http://www.ncsl.org/portals/1/documents/health/HRACA.pdf

32. U.S. Department of Labor. *Health Plans & Benefits: Continuation of Health Coverage—COBRA*. Retrieved March 20, 2020 from https://www.dol.gov/general/topic/health-plans/cobra

33. What is COBRA? What employers need to know. *Wolters Kluwer*. Retrieved March 20, 2020 from https://www.bizfilings.com/toolkit/research-topics/office-hr/what-is-cobra-what-employers-need-to-know

34. Ibid.

35. Veterans' Employment & Training Service. *VETS USERRA Fact Sheet 3*. Retrieved March 20, 2020 from https://www.dol.gov/agencies/vets/programs/userra/userra_fs

36. Workers' compensation benefits FAQ. *Nolo*. Retrieved March 20, 2020 from https://www.nolo.com/legal-encyclopedia/workers-compensation-benefits-faq.html

37. U.S. Department of Labor. *Workers' Compensation*. Retrieved March 20, 2020 from https://www.dol.gov/general/topic/workcomp

38. Mercado, D. (2019). Your health insurance costs are about to up in 2020. *CNBC*. Retrieved from https://www.cnbc.com/2019/09/26/your-health-insurance-costs-are-about-to-go-up-in-2020.html

39. Roehr, B. (2010). US workers bear cost increase in employer based health insurance. *BMJ: British Medical Journal, 341*(7772), 526-527.

40. Wisenberg Brin, D. (2019). Using voluntary benefits to support workforce strategy. *Society for Human Resource Management*. Retrieved from https://www.shrm.org/resourcesandtools/hr-topics/benefits/pages/voluntary-benefits-support-workforce-strategy.aspx

41. Ibid.

42. Ibid.

43. 17th annual Transamerica retirement survey. (2016). *Transamerica Center for Retirement Studies*. Retrieved from https://www.transamericacenter.org/docs/default-source/retirement-survey-of-workers/tcrs2016_sr_retirement_survey_of_workers_compendium.pdf

44. Sammer. J. (2017). Retirement plans are leaking money. Here's why employers should care. *Society for Human Resource Management*. Retrieved from https://www.shrm.org/resourcesandtools/hr-topics/benefits/pages/401k-leakage.aspx

45. U.S. Department of Labor. *ERISA*. Retrieved April 8, 2020 from https://www.dol.gov/general/topic/health-plans/erisa

46. A list of states and cities with paid sick leave laws. (2019). *Zenefits*. Retrieved from https://www.zenefits.com/workest/the-definitive-list-of-states-and-cities-with-paid-sick-leave-laws/

47. Heathfield, S.M. (2019). Paid time off (PTO) policy: Pros and cons. *thebalancecareers*. Retrieved from https://www.thebalancecareers.com/paid-time-off-policy-pto-1918232

48. Ibid.

49. Jury duty laws. *Employment Law Handbook*. Retrieved from Most states do require employers to grant time off for jury duty without pay.

50. U.S. Department of Labor. *Families First Coronavirus Response Act: Employee Paid Rights*. Retrieved April 8, 2020 https://www.dol.gov/agencies/whd/pandemic/ffcra-employee-paid-leave

51. Offering life insurance as an employee benefit. *Bizfilings*. Retrieved March 25, 2020 from https://www.bizfilings.com/toolkit/research-topics/office-hr/offering-life-insurance-as-an-employee-benefit

52. What are the non-discrimination requirements for life insurance? (2018). *Zenefits*. Retrieved from https://help.zenefits.com/Life_Insurance/Learn_About_Life_Insurance_for_Employers/04_Non-Discrimination_Requirements_for_Life_Insurance/

53. Centers for Disease Control and Prevention. *Opioids in the workplace*. Retrieved March 27, 2020 from https://www.cdc.gov/niosh/topics/opioids/data.html

54. Ibid.

55. Spicer, R., & Miller, S. (2016). The evaluation of a workplace program to prevent substance abuse: challenges and findings. *The Journal of Primary Prevention, 37*(4), 329-343.

56. Centers for Disease Control and Prevention. *Opioids in the workplace*. Retrieved March 27, 2020 from https://www.cdc.gov/niosh/topics/opioids/data.html

57. Adapted from Greco-Sanchez, A. (2018). Substance abuse in the workplace: Six steps employers can take to support their employees stay at work and return to work, while mitigating risk. *The Official Publication of the Ontario Occupational Health Nurses Association, 37*(2), 7-9.

58. Taylor, T. (2018). Employee assistance programs (EAP). *thebalancecareers*. Retrieved from https://www.thebalancecareers.com/about-employee-assistance-programs-eap-1177842

59. Waehrer, G., Miller, T., Hendrie, D., & Galvin, D. (2016). Employee assistance programs, drug testing, and workplace injury. *Journal of Safety Research, 57*, 53.

60. Nunes, A., Richmond, P., Pampel, M., & Wood, K. (2018). The effect of employee assistance services on reductions in employee absenteeism. *Journal of Business and Psychology, 33*(6), 699-709.

61. Global heathcare benefit costs expected to increase 7.6% in 2019. *Willis Towers Watson*. Retrieved April 7, 2020 from https://www.willistowerswatson.com/en-US/News/2018/11/global-health-care-benefit-costs-expected-to-increase-7-6-percent-in-2019

62. Ibid.

63. U.S. Centers for Medicare and Medicaid Services. *How insurance companies set health premiums*. Retrieved April 7, 2020 from https://www.healthcare.gov/how-plans-set-your-premiums/

64. Workforce Health and Productivity. (2017). *Health Affairs, 36*(2), 200-201.

65. Centers for Disease Control and Prevention. *The power of prevention: Chronic disease . . . the public health challenge of the 21st century*. Retrieved April 7, 2020 from https://www.cdc.gov/chronicdisease/pdf/2009-power-of-prevention.pdf

66. Ibid.

67. Adapted from: Baughman, D. 5 perks for businesses that offer wellness programs. *Insurance Quotes*. Retrieved September 9, 2019 from http://www.insurancequotes.org/business/5-perks-for-businesses-to-offer-wellness-programs/

68. Case written by John, E. (2020). Adapted from Cappelli, P., Tavis A. (2018). HR goes agile. *Harvard Business Review*. Retrieved from https://hbr.org/2018/03/the-new-rules-of-talent-management; Cohen,S. (2017). Driving robust social learning at Cigna. Retrieved from https://www.td.org/insights/driving-robust-social-learning-at-cigna; Mathews, A.W., Chin K. (2019). Cigna posts strong results for first full quarter after Express Scripts deal. *Wall Street Journal*. Retrieved from https://www.wsj.com/articles/cigna-profit-rises-led-by-strength-in-health-services-medical-units-11556793223; McCann, D. (2016). Cigna gets 129% ROI on tuition reimbursement costs. Retrieved from https://www.cfo.com/training/2016/04/cigna-gets-129-roi-tuition-reimbursement-costs/; Lumina Foundation. (2016). Talent investments pay off. Retrieved from https://www.luminafoundation.org/files/resources/talent-investments-pay-off-cigna-full.pdf

CHAPTER 11

Employee Engagement

Learning Objectives

After reading this chapter, you should be able to do the following:

1. Define employee engagement and explain its relationship to organizational goals.
2. Identify the metrics used to measure employee engagement.
3. Describe the organizational, management, and HR drivers of employee engagement.
4. Design an appropriate employee initiative to create a culture of engagement.

Employee engagement is the extent to which employees feel positive about their jobs, are committed to the organization's goals and values, and are motivated to contribute beyond the minimum required. HR is in a unique position to create the conditions in which employee engagement thrives, by building a culture based on trust, communications, and integrity.

The chapter begins with an introduction of the importance of employee engagement to organizational goals, and an exploration of individual needs and team orientation. Several methods for measuring engagement are then examined. The organizational, management, and HR-related driving factors of employee engagement are discussed. The influence of organizational culture is reviewed, followed by methods and techniques for designing employee engagement initiatives.

11.1 Opening Case: Getting Employee Best Buy-In

Source: Sean Pavone / Shutterstock.com

In 2012, employee engagement at Best Buy was in shambles. The company, a big-box retailer out of Minnesota, was losing sales to Amazon, and the CEO had just resigned due to an inappropriate relationship with an employee. In addition, employee engagement was at an all-time low, and Best Buy was rated as having one of the highest employee turnover rates and low work satisfaction. But new CEO Hubert Joly refocused on employee engagement, which resulted in reduced turnover rates and gave Best Buy the boost it needed to stay in the retail race.

When Joly took over, he made employees his number-one focus by going into the stores to gain insight directly from employees. He actually worked in a store for one week and implemented one-on-one employee interviews to find out what employees needed and valued. He learned that employees really liked the former employee discount program and needed regular training. He also learned that employees were struggling with the internal search engine that was used to locate products in stock. Ultimately, he restored the employee discount program. Under Joly, Best Buy has reduced its employee turnover to 32% in an industry where average turnover is 60%.

Best Buy saw a 17% share surge in February 2019, after coming off a better than expected quarter. Joly stated the company saw increased interaction with their customers and in turn, customers noted an improved experience within the stores. An improved customer experience is directly related to improved employee engagement. If employees are happy, so are customers. Investing in employees helps fight turnover, and Best Buy has shown that it actually works.[1]

Leading with Purpose and Humanity: A Conversation with Hubert Joly

Hubert Joly reflects on a business's reason for being by defining it around purpose and humanity.

View the video online at: http://www.youtube.com/embed/kvDZmFq6s5U?rel=0

Case Discussion Questions

1. What do you think the employees thought about the one-on-one interviews conducted by Joly and his team?
2. What advantages does Best Buy have over other retail companies that are predominantly online?
3. Why do you think retail is one of the industries with the highest turnover?

11.2 The Nature of Employee Engagement

Learning Objectives

1. Define employee engagement and explain its relationship to organizational goals.
2. Describe how employee engagement is motivated by individual needs.
3. Recognize the ways in which team orientation leads to employee engagement.

Importance of Employee Engagement to Organizational Goals

Many factors can impact employee engagement. Which of these aspects of a work environment can be influenced by HR or line managers?

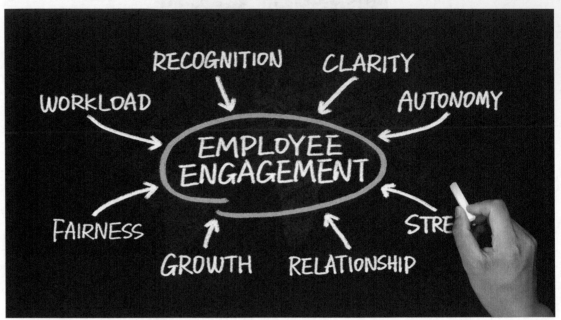

Source: © Shutterstock, Inc.

employee engagement

The emotional and attitudinal commitment an employee has to the organization and its goals, which influences his or her behaviors and level of effort in work activities.

What is employee engagement, and why does it matter to HR professionals and organizational managers? **Employee engagement** is the emotional and attitudinal commitment an employee has to the organization and its goals, which influences his or her behaviors and level of effort in work activities. Employee engagement matters because of the impact on employee turnover and business results, as was the experience of Best Buy described in the opening case study. In 2018, the rate of employee turnover in the U.S. reached an all-time high of 19.3%, rising almost a full percentage point from 2017, and more than 3.5% since 2014.[2] Figure 11.1 illustrates turnover by industry.

FIGURE 11.1 Employee Turnover by Industry

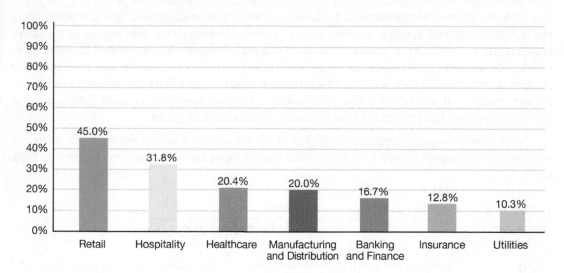

Industries with the Highest Turnover

Higher turnover means increased recruitment and training costs and a negative impact on pro-ductivity and profits due to vacant positions. But there are other reasons to be concerned about employee engagement. Organizations that are the best in engaging their employees achieve earn-ings-per-share growth that is more than four times that of their competitors.[3] According to a recent Gallup meta-analysis, business units in the top quartile of employee engagement are 17% more productive, suffer 70% fewer safety incidents, experience 41% less absenteeism, have 10% bet-ter customer service ratings, and are 21% more profitable compared with business units in the bottom quartile.[4]

Only about a third of Americans are engaged in their jobs in any given year, and this finding has remained consistent since 2000, when Gallup began measuring and reporting on employee engagement in the American workplace.[5] Managers and executives tend to be the most engaged, while manufacturing workers are the least.[6] Table 11.1 shows employee engagement by occupa-tion.[7]

TABLE 11.1 Employee Engagement by Occupation

Occupation	Engagement %
Managers and executives	38
Professional workers	34
Construction or mining workers	34
Clerical or office workers	33
Sales workers	33
Farming, fishing, or forestry workers	33
Installation or repair workers	32
Service workers	31
Transportation workers	30
Manufacturing workers	25

Employee engagement can be considered as two components: attitudinal and behavioral. As an attitude, engagement represents an employee's focus, effort, motivation, and passion for the job. It also includes emotional commitment to the organization and its objectives. But it is when these positive attitudes and feelings transfer into workplace behaviors that the results of employee engagement are reflected in business results. Engaged employees are motivated to exert more effort to do whatever it takes to achieve high levels of performance, not just because they should or are told to, but because they want to. **Discretionary effort** is the difference between the level of activity one is capable of bringing to a work task, and the minimum level required. Simply put, it is that activity above and beyond the bare minimum required to just get by.

What does an engaged employee look like? There are various levels of engagement, as we will explore in this chapter. It may help to consider the four employee engagement profiles in Table 11.2.[8]

TABLE 11.2 Four Profiles of Engaged Employees

Engagement Category	Attitudes and Behaviors
Highly Engaged	Employees feel a strong personal alignment to the mission, vision, and objectives of the organization. With this emotional connection comes behavior—namely, active pursuit of opportunities to improve operations and/or the general work environment.
Moderately Engaged	Employees possess positive attitudes toward work and may engage in productive behaviors, but they are not fully invested in terms of commitment and significant discretionary behavior.
Passive	Employees simply come to work and go through the motions without any particular interest in work. While not as problematic as the actively disengaged, passive employees do not create a positive environment for innovation and progress.
Actively Disengaged	Employees feel disconnected from their jobs and tend to be unsatisfied at work. Their poor attitudes and emotions spread through the organization, which can result in their own poor performance and poor performance of others.

Individual Needs

Before we can begin to measure engagement and design initiatives to improve it, we need to have a better understanding of the conditions that create an environment in which engagement flourishes. Engagement is good for both organizations and individuals because it generally promotes positive performance and the broadening of employee resources such as creativity and innovation.[9] Employee engagement is the result of individual needs being met by either being part of an organization or a team within the organization, or the work itself. Several scholars have suggested engagement is a positive psychological state, rather than a trait.[10] Engagement has also been described as a specific behavioral outcome.[11]

Is engagement, then, a psychological state or a behavioral outcome? The answer is, it's a little of both. Rich et al. proposed a three-dimensional model of engagement based upon cognitive, emotional, and behavioral factors.[12]

The **cognitive dimension** refers to how an employee perceives their work and the context in which the work is occurring. As the name implies, it is a rational process of thinking about one's work and the work environment. Cognitively engaged employees share a common purpose with their organization, understand that purpose, and are willing to consider making a personal investment of the resources they have influence over.[13]

Emotional engagement is an affective process whereby the employee identifies with the organizational purpose and has positive feelings about their work, such as pride, excitement, a sense of accomplishment, or an emotional response to the significance of the work. Emotionally engaged employees tend to commit their knowledge, skills, abilities, and effort to accomplishment of the organization's objectives. They also tend to go about their work with a sense of urgency, focus, and intensity.[14]

The **behavioral dimension** is what many people think of when they try to visualize or describe employee engagement. This is because the behavioral aspect of engagement is the only dimension that can be externally observed. It is the tangible result (i.e., performance outcomes) when an employee commits their resources with determination, passion, focus, and intensity. However, the premise of this three-dimensional model is that the first two states (cognitive and emotional) must precede behavior. Using this conceptual model, employee engagement is (1) something that involves thinking (that's cognitive), (2) something that is felt (that's emotional), and (3) something that is done (that's behavioral). Engagement is highest when all three dimensions are optimized in a holistic manner.

Team Orientation

Now that we have a common framework for understanding how to describe individual employee engagement, let's turn our attention to the context in which it occurs. External forces such as interpersonal, intergroup, and organizational factors also affect the personal engagement of employees.[15] One important influence is whether a team orientation exists within the organization. A **team orientation** is the degree to which organizational members stress collaboration and cooperation in performing work activities and in making decisions. Organizations which emphasize team orientations have higher levels of employee performance.[16] Recent research also indicates that a strong team orientation in an organization leads to higher levels of employee engagement.[17]

Another important influence on engagement is the design of the job itself. This refers to the assignment of work tasks, level of autonomy, feedback, and other aspects of job design which were discussed in Chapter 4. Studies have also shown training and development, leadership style, trust, and communication to be correlated with employee engagement. As we explore these various influences on engagement through this chapter, consider how they can be aligned to create a holistic approach to employee engagement, as illustrated in Figure 11.2.

---

emotional engagement

An affective process whereby the employee identifies with the organizational purpose and has positive feelings about their work, such as pride, excitement, a sense of accomplishment, or an emotional response to the significance of the work.

behavioral dimension

The tangible results (i.e., performance outcomes) when an employee commits their resources with determination, passion, focus, and intensity.

team orientation

The degree to which organizational members stress collaboration and cooperation in performing work activities and in making decisions.

FIGURE 11.2 Alignment of Influences on Employee Engagement

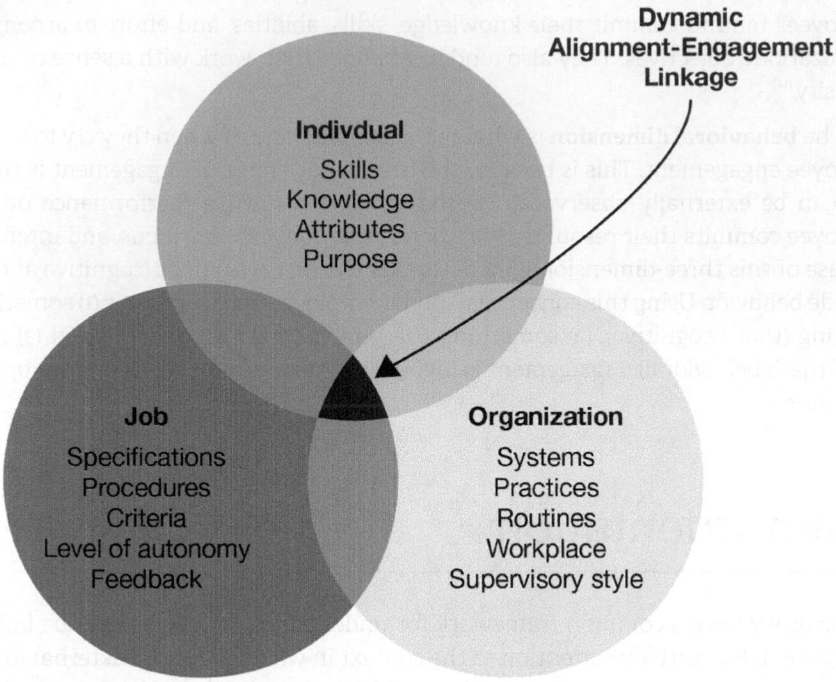

Dynamic Alignment-Engagement Linkage

Indivdual
Skills
Knowledge
Attributes
Purpose

Job
Specifications
Procedures
Criteria
Level of autonomy
Feedback

Organization
Systems
Practices
Routines
Workplace
Supervisory style

Later in this chapter, we will take a closer look at how managers and HR policies and practices influence employee engagement. But first, we will turn our attention to how employee engagement is measured.

Key Takeaways

- Employee engagement is the emotional and attitudinal commitment an employee has to the organization and its goals, which influences his or her behaviors and level of effort in work activities.

- According to a recent Gallup meta-analysis, business units in the top quartile of employee engagement are 17% more productive, suffer 70% fewer safety incidents, experience 41% lower absenteeism, have 10% better customer service ratings, and are 21% more profitable compared with business units in the bottom quartile.

- Employee engagement can be considered as two components: attitudinal and behavioral.

- Discretionary effort is the difference between the level of activity one is capable of bringing to a work task, and the minimum level required.

- Employee engagement is the result of individual needs being met by either being part of an organization or a team within the organization, or the work itself.

- The cognitive dimension refers to how an employee perceives their work and the context in which the work is occurring.

- Emotional engagement is an affective process whereby the employee identifies with the organizational purpose and has positive feelings about their work, such as pride, excitement, a sense of accomplishment, or an emotional response to the significance of the work.

- The behavioral dimension is what many people think of when they try to visualize or describe employee engagement.

- A team orientation is the degree to which organizational members stress collaboration and cooperation in performing work activities and in making decisions.

11.3 Measuring Employee Engagement

Learning Objectives

1. Identify the major trends in employee engagement.
2. Describe the various survey approaches to measure employee engagement.
3. Recognize the features of the most common third-party engagement surveys.

Trends in Measuring Engagement

The first step in improving employee engagement is to measure it, so that a baseline can be established against which future engagement initiatives can be compared. Since employee engagement is closely related to productivity, profitability, and other aspects of organizational performance, it follows that measuring it and planning ways to improve it should be a priority. Large organizations (with one thousand or more employees) are more likely to measure engagement, with 72% indicating they measure it, according to a recent study.[18] But only 54% of all organizations measure it. If employee engagement has such an impact on organizational performance, then why don't more organizations measure it? It may be that leaders in small or medium-size companies feel that they already understand their employees' needs and do not need formal surveys or other measurements to tell them what they already know.

The most common method for measuring engagement is employee surveys. But 83% of organizations that measure engagement do so using multiple methods. Figure 11.3 illustrates the most commonly used engagement measures.

FIGURE 11.3 Most Commonly Used Engagement Measures

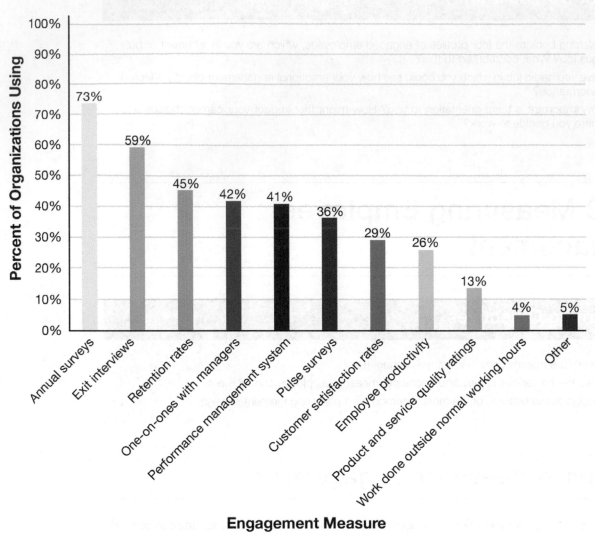

Surveys

There are various approaches to implementing surveys, including annual surveys and exit interviews. Traditional survey approaches have several drawbacks. They can be time-consuming to develop and implement, and employees might resist taking surveys that take too much of their time to complete. A comprehensive survey can take months to analyze and disseminate the findings, and by the time action is taken to improve engagement based on the survey data, employee attitudes might have changed. For this reason, many organizations are administering shorter and more frequent surveys. Surveys can also be subject to some types of rater bias, which were discussed in Chapter 8. For example, employees may tend to think only of recent events (the recency error) when answering survey questions. If an employee had a conflict with a supervisor right before completing an engagement survey, then they may not be "feeling" very engaged that day. But their answers on a similar survey a month from now may be quite different.

Surveys typically ask employees to rate their own level of engagement. Self-reported data is useful in that it provides insight into how employees are perceiving their level of commitment to the organization. However, it does not provide objective data on how engaged they actually are, as measured by discretionary effort and performance results. Stated another way: surveys indicate how engaged employees perceive themselves to be, while other measurements can provide data on how engaged they really are. For this reason, organizations should not rely on surveys as the sole measure of engagement.

With those caveats on the use of surveys, let's explore some best practices in using employee engagement surveys. When an employee can make the following statements (see Table 11.3) with confidence, they are more likely to be engaged:[19]

TABLE 11.3 Employee Engagement Statements

Employee Engagement Statements	
Individual Needs	• I have a clear understanding of the performance expectations for my job. • My manager seems to genuinely care about me. • I am recognized for my contributions. • I have received the necessary training to do my job well. • I have the resources need to perform my job well.
Team Orientation	• I have a clear understanding of my organization's mission and purpose, and my role in achieving the mission. • My team has a sense of shared purpose. • My coworkers are engaged and care about the quality of their work. • My team exhibits a high level of trust and respect for each other. • There is clear communication among my coworkers and conflicts are normally resolved in a positive manner.
Professional Growth	• My manager has conversations with me about my professional growth. • I receive constructive feedback and guidance on a regular basis. • I have a clear understanding of what I must achieve for to be eligible for upward mobility. • My organization offers me opportunities to learn and grow. • I am frequently given stretch assignments.

The following guidelines should be considered when developing employee engagement surveys:[20]

- Include questions that could be asked every year or more frequently. This will provide a baseline for management of employee engagement.

- Keep language neutral or positive. For example, ask, "Is our line-to-staff ratio correct for a company our size?" instead of, "Are there too many staff for a company our size?" Avoid negatively worded items.

- Focus on behaviors. Good questions probe supervisors' and employees' everyday behaviors.

- Beware of loaded questions. For example, questions such as "Do you look forward to work on Mondays?" might elicit a negative response, even from engaged employees.

- Keep the survey length reasonable. Long surveys reduce participation rates and may result in skewed responses because the respondents may start just choosing answers to finish the survey quickly, without really putting thought into it.
- If you work with a vendor who has a list of standard questions, consider tailoring questions to reflect specific organizational needs.

Third-Party Surveys

Utrecht Work Engagement Scale (UWES)

An employee engagement survey developed by Wilmar Schaufeli and Arnold Bakker at Utrecht University.

If you choose to use an established survey, then be sure the reliability and validity of the survey have been established through empirical research. One of the most researched surveys is the **Utrecht Work Engagement Scale (UWES)**, an employee engagement survey developed by Wilmar Schaufeli and Arnold Bakker at Utrecht University. They state that:[21]

> *Work engagement is the assumed opposite of burnout. Contrary to those who suffer from burnout, engaged employees have a sense of energetic and effective connection with their work activities, and they see themselves as able to deal well with the demands of their job.*

Schaufeli et al. proposed that engagement is a multidimensional construct consisting of three dimensions:[22]

vigor

Characterized by high levels of energy, effort, and resilience, persistency, and motivation to invest in the work.

1. **Vigor.** Characterized by high levels of energy, effort, and resilience, persistency, and motivation to invest in the work.

dedication

Characterized by involvement in work, enthusiasm, and a sense of pride and inspiration.

2. **Dedication.** Characterized by involvement in work, enthusiasm, and a sense of pride and inspiration.

absorption

Characterized by immersion in one's work and the sense of time passing quickly.

3. **Absorption.** Characterized by immersion in one's work and the sense of time passing quickly.

Items under each of the three dimensions are presented as statements to which people respond on a seven-point scale, with anchors 0 (Never) to 6 (Always or Every Day). Reliability ratings have been found to be acceptable, generally ranging from .80 to .90.[23] The UWES has also proven to have strong validity as a measure of employee engagement and future job performance.[24] The UWES is the most widely used engagement questionnaire.[25]

Gallup Q12 Employee Engagement Survey

An employee engagement survey developed by the Gallup corporation which identified twelve core elements that are correlated to business outcomes.

Another popular standardized survey is the **Gallup Q12 Employee Engagement Survey**, which was developed by the Gallup corporation and has been administered to over thirty-five million employees worldwide.[26] Based on behavioral economic research, Gallup identified twelve core elements that are correlated to business outcomes. Gallup provides an online dashboard to set up the survey and view results, along with a unique survey hyperlink to send directly to employees. Table 11.4 shows the twelve questions that make up the Gallup Q12.[27]

TABLE 11.4 The Gallup Q12

The Gallup Q12
1. I know what is expected of me at work.
2. I have the materials and equipment I need to do my work right.
3. At work I have the opportunity to do what I do best every day.
4. In the past seven days, I have received recognition or praise for doing good work.
5. My supervisor, or someone at work, seems to care about me as a person.
6. There is someone at work who encourages my development.

The Gallup Q12
7. At work, my opinions seem to count.
8. The mission or purpose of my company makes me feel my job is important.
9. My associates or fellow employees are committed to doing quality work.
10. I have a best friend at work.
11. In the last six months, someone at work has talked to me about my progress.
12. This last year, I have had opportunities at work to learn and grow.

Because of the desire to obtain more timely feedback from employees, a recent trend is to use a pulse survey. A **pulse survey** is a short list of engagement questions which is administered frequently and provides quick feedback to managers. You might think of this as taking a quick pulse to determine the health and well-being of a patient, with the patient in this case being the employees of an organization. About 74% of companies still use traditional annual surveys, but this number is trending downward quickly, down from 89% since 2015.[28]

The marketplace for pulse surveys is growing rapidly, with most of the platforms being mobile friendly and many app-based. Some are always-on pulse systems where employees can give their feedback anytime they think of it (or are prompted to), as opposed to a regularly scheduled survey. They are becoming popular, in part because of the plethora of vendors that specialize in pulse surveys. FICO, an analytics survey company well known for its credit-scoring business, implemented pulse surveys using the Glint platform, collecting new data each quarter from their 3,300 employees. Managers immediately saw results on a dashboard, which enabled them to determine priorities and how to best communicate with employees. The dashboard identified each team's high and low engagement scores, and the managers could then click through to recommended focus areas and develop action plans for improvement. Within two years of implementation, FICO experienced an 11% rise in employee engagement, and also improved its internal communications rating, the perception of its reward package, and its employees' work-life balance.[29]

But they are not without their detractors. Pulse surveys have been criticized because firms might take a flawed survey that used to be administered annually, and deploy baby versions of it more frequently.[30] Effective pulsing requires the right metrics strategy, by asking questions that will yield useful insights and not start unnecessary conversations. Without the right metrics, pulse surveys can become a complaint forum. Questions such as "What do you think about ... " may start a work-based conversation that is not helpful or productive.[31]

Employee engagement can also be measured through exit interviews, individual conversations between employees and managers, or through tracking related metrics such as productivity, customer satisfaction, or quality. However engagement is measured, it is important to link it to business metrics and be transparent about how the data is used. Kelly Heard, vice-president of HR for Symantec, an information management company with 17,500 employees, puts it this way, *"If you are not going to use the data to effect change, don't take employees' time to do surveys. Be realistic about how long it takes to effect change. How can you possibly have an engaged workforce if you ask for feedback and then don't acknowledge it or don't do anything about it?"*[32]

pulse survey

A short list of engagement questions which is administered frequently and provides quick feedback to managers.

What Makes Gallup's Q12 Survey the Best Way to Measure Employee Engagement?

Jim Harter, Ph.D., Gallup's Chief Scientist of Workplace Management and Well-being, provides an overview of Gallup's Q12 survey of employee engagement.

View the video online at: http://www.youtube.com/embed/cX2f0LEGZn8?rel=0

Talent Analytics

Employee engagement surveys provide employee answers to questions, usually based on a scale from rarely to always, or disagree to agree. The results can be useful just by looking at the mean or median for each question. But do HR data analysts use more advanced statistical techniques to glean more meaningful information from the data? Absolutely! For example:

- If HR has a hunch that there are many subgroups of employees within the organization (i.e., different scoring patterns), then an analyst might use discriminant analysis.

- If HR wants to know the engagement survey factors that correlate with each other and perhaps even with a second or third factor (such as productivity or turnover), then an analyst might use factor analysis.

- If HR needs to check variability and reliability of factors in order to determine their relevance or compare the same surveys conducted at different times, then the analyst might use analysis of variance (ANOVA) and/or t-tests.

- Based on findings, HR might want to field-test new ideas/experiments in employee engagement and predict their impact. In this case, an HR data analyst might use factorial design of experiments (DOE).[33]

Yes, you really will use these methods that you learn in business statistics courses . . . even in HR. Perhaps especially in HR.

Key Takeaways

- The first step in improving employee engagement is to measure it, so that a baseline can be established against which future engagement initiatives can be compared.

- The most common method for measuring engagement is employee surveys.

- If you choose to use an established survey, then be sure the reliability and validity of the survey have been established through empirical research.

- Vigor is characterized by high levels of energy, effort, resilience, persistency, and motivation to invest in the work.

- Dedication is characterized by involvement in work, enthusiasm, and a sense of pride and inspiration.
- Absorption is characterized by immersion in one's work and the sense of time passing quickly.
- A pulse survey is a short list of engagement questions which is administered frequently and provides quick feedback to managers.

What Do *You* Think?

1. Have you ever worked for an organization that measured employee engagement? What method was used, and was it effective?
2. How effective do you think surveys are? Are employee self-reports of engagement an accurate method for measuring engagement?
3. Do you think pulse surveys are a better approach? Why or why not?
4. How should management share the results on engagement measures?

11.4 Drivers of Employee Engagement

Learning Objectives

1. Identify the organizational factors that drive employee engagement.
2. Describe how management style influences employee engagement.
3. Explain how HR can implement policies and procedures that promote engagement.

Organizational Factors

Now that we have described employee engagement and examined various methods for measuring it, let's explore the factors that drive it. These factors fall into three categories: organizational, management influences, and HR policies and practices.

About 80% of respondents in a recent engagement survey believe that engagement is highly linked to trust in leadership and the relationship with the immediate supervisor.[34] Although these are the most significant, there are other factors that impact engagement, including a sense of purpose, organizational culture, and career growth. Figure 11.4 shows the factors most highly related to employee engagement.

FIGURE 11.4 Factors that Drive Engagement

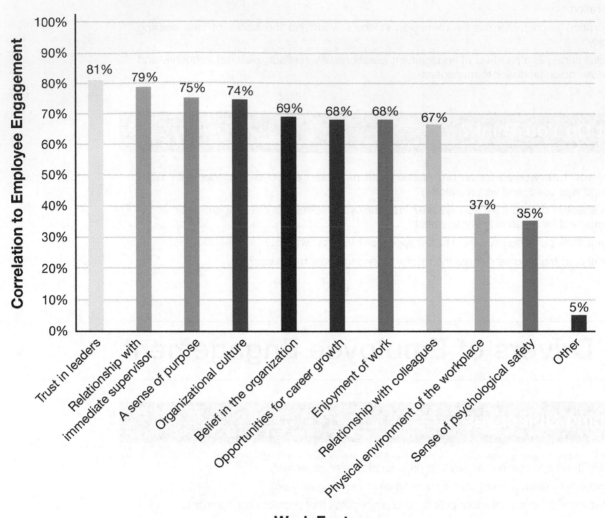

Work Factors

Quantum Workplace (the research firm behind the "Best Places to Work" program) has identified six drivers of employee engagement that have the greatest impact:[35]

1. The leaders of the organization are committed to making it a great place to work.
2. Trust in the leaders of the organization to set the right course.
3. Belief that the organization will be successful in the future.
4. Understanding of how I fit into the organization's future plans.
5. The leaders of the organization value people as their most important resource.
6. The organization makes investments to make employees more successful.

As you read the above list, you may be thinking that some of these drivers sound like organizational factors, but others appear to be related to management influences. If you thought this, then you are on the right track, because the two aspects are related. After all, an organization is really the sum of the impact of many management decisions. When an employee is asked how they like working for an organization, they are probably answering in terms of how they like working for one specific person (their supervisor) or a leadership group as a whole.

Management Influences

Research indicates managers account for as much as 70% of variance in engagement scores.[36] Given that only about a third of employees are engaged, we can logically conclude that about two thirds of managers need to do something different. When an employee is not engaged, it is often because their manager has not created an environment where they feel motivated and inspired. The same is true for voluntary separations: when an employee quits a job, they often are really quitting their supervisor and going somewhere else where they hope to feel more valued. A Gallup survey found that one in two U.S. adults had left a job just to get away from their manager.[37]

Employee recognition programs can be formal, such as an "Employee-of-the-month" program or informal. Something as simple as an occasional Post-it note can impact employee engagement.

Source: © Shutterstock, Inc.

What specifically, then, is it about management style that causes employees to be disengaged? Communications and decision-making are at the heart of the matter. People want to feel like they have a voice at work, and that they have a role in decision-making. At this point, you might be recalling Chapter 4 Section 4 and the importance of autonomy and feedback as two of the core job characteristics that lead to motivation. In fact, one study found that autonomy accounted for 35% of employee engagement.[38] The lack of autonomy also leads to higher employee turnover. (Research indicates that an authoritarian culture causes employees to start a job search to find someplace else to work.)[39]

Supervisor behaviors that have been correlated with high levels of employee engagement are:

1. Supervisors developing a positive relationship with their employees and communicating with them personally.

2. Giving recognition and letting the employee know they are cared about.

3. Giving employees the necessary equipment and training to do their job well.

4. Allowing employees the authority necessary to do their jobs, make improvements, and solve problems.

5. Building trust between the supervisor and employee.

HR Policies and Practices

From one perspective, HR is part of management, and many of the same influences that we just described for managers apply also to the HR team. But HR is in a unique position to impact employee engagement through HR policies and practices. For example, job descriptions, training, employee development, compensation plans, benefits, and many more very personal aspects of the job fall under HR. When organizations place an emphasis on providing employees with internal career opportunities (instead of hiring externally), training programs, job security, clear job descriptions, and participative decision-making, employees engage more in their jobs.[40] To foster a culture of engagement, HR should lead the way in identifying engagement metrics, administering regular measurement, and then designing and implementing policies and practices that lead to higher levels of engagement.

The following HR policies and practices can impact employee engagement:

- **Job design.** The extent to which variety, meaning, autonomy, and feedback are present in a job.

- **Recruitment and selection.** Making employee engagement part of the employer value proposition. Targeting applicants who are likely to view the type of work and the organizational culture as interesting and engaging.

- **Training and development.** Providing effective onboarding programs to help employees understand how their role contributes to the success of the organization. Also, providing regular opportunities to enhance skillsets and development for career progression. Accenture, for example, has put its own twist on the concept of upskilling via its internal New Skilling program. The program targets displaced employees, such as those who have found their jobs made redundant by technology—by helping them to learn new skills that will allow them to stay with the firm.[41] American Express has made upskilling a priority through its Colleague Value Proposition initiative, which is built on the idea of helping employees succeed at their jobs.[42]
- **Compensation planning and performance management.** Strategically utilizing incentive programs to enhance engagement. Rewarding high performers and disincentivizing low performers.

Key Takeaways

- The factors that drive engagement fall into three categories: organizational, management influences, and HR policies and practices.
- About 80% of respondents in a recent engagement survey believe that engagement is highly linked to trust in leadership and the relationship with the immediate supervisor.
- Other factors that impact engagement are having a sense of purpose, organizational culture, and career growth.
- Research indicates that managers account for as much as 70% of variance in engagement scores.
- Communications, involvement in decision-making, and autonomy are highly correlated with employee engagement.
- To foster a culture of engagement, HR should lead the way in identifying engagement metrics, administering regular measurement, and then designing and implementing policies and practices that lead to a higher level of engagement.

What Do *You* Think?

1. How important is trust in leadership to you at your work? Do you trust your leaders? Why or why not?
2. Have you ever quit a supervisor? If so, what were the main factors behind your decision?
3. If you loved every other aspect of your job, but had issues with your supervisor, how would you handle it? Would you try to talk to the supervisor about it or just leave for another job?

11.5 Designing Employee Engagement Initiatives

Learning Objectives

1. Describe the actions that managers and HR leaders can take to create a culture of engagement.

2. Distinguish between employee orientation and onboarding.

3. Explain how an effective onboarding experience influences engagement.

Creating a Culture of Engagement

What actions can managers and HR leaders take to improve employee engagement? With our understanding of the drivers of engagement, we can design initiatives to improve it.

Research indicates that frequent, open, and honest communication between management and employees is crucial in building trust and high performance.[43] Organizations that receive "Best Places to Work" awards have senior leaders who engage their employees through personal connections and communications.[44] We are not talking about all-employee emails, newsletters, blogs, vlogs, or Monday morning memos. These can cause information overload to employees who are already overwhelmed with information, and they are impersonal. Mass communications do not engage employees on a personal level.

What we are referring to here is one-on-one communications between leaders and employees. The most important of these is between employees and their direct supervisor, but employees also should feel like upper management knows them, their contribution to the organization, and cares about them personally. A simple short conversation in a hallway or elevator in which a leader shows that they know the employee by name, what their role is, and perhaps something about their family, will go a long way. Creating a culture of engagement happens one conversation at a time. There are no shortcuts.

HR in the Real World: You Can't Manage from Behind a Desk

My first job as a supervisor was director of administration for a mid-size transportation company. I had over twenty direct reports, employees in billing, payroll, accounting, tax, and reception. I was an analyst by nature and needed to improve my interpersonal relationship skills. I had a tendency to sit behind my desk all day and manage by reviewing reports and analyzing data. My boss, the president of the company, gave me some advice on several occasions, "You can't manage from behind a desk." But I guess it didn't really sink in at that time. I eventually lost that job and was told by the CEO that I didn't have the respect of the employees. I was shocked and angry, but I learned from the experience. In my next management job, I was determined to get out of my office and spent at least half of my time where my direct reports were working. This gave me opportunities to communicate with my staff every day and also build trust. I never needed to look at reports after that, because I already knew where we stood on workflow. If payroll was running behind, I already knew it. If there was a performance problem, I already knew about it and addressed it, usually through coaching. Some might call this "management by walking around." But getting out from behind the desk (or getting away from the computer...or off your phone) can make all the difference in creating a culture of trust, respect, and engagement.

Gallup reports that engagement is highest among employees who have some form (face-to-face, phone, or digital) of daily communication with their managers. Further, when employees attempt to contact their manager, engaged employees report their manager returns their calls or messages within twenty-four hours.[45]

In one case, a company changed its focus to begin to engage employees on an individual basis, working in the language of the business through conversations and without any additional training.[46] Based on their knowledge of their own work tasks, employees identified over one hundred things to improve. Many of these changes were implemented quickly, and employee engagement was ignited. Profits improved 30% within six months, and within one year, the company was able to pursue and achieve its first contract with Toyota.

Another aspect of engaging employees is to create a work environment where every employee feels accepted, valued, and treated equally and with respect. Trust and respect are reciprocal, and once respect is lost, it is difficult to regain.[47] Research also indicates that diversity practices are associated with a trusting climate that, in turn, is positively related to employee engagement.[48] Table 11.5 gives additional specific actions in regard to work-life balance, career development, and inclusion, that organizations can implement to create a culture of engagement.[49]

TABLE 11.5 Action Items to Create a Culture of Engagement

Action Items	
Encourage Work/Life Balance:	• Provide flextime opportunities. • Encourage employees to take their vacation time. • Eliminate expectations of working long hours. • Match employee charitable contributions. • Offer employees PTO to volunteer their time for non-profit activities.
Enhance Career Development Opportunities:	• Have regular conversations with employees to discuss their career development. • Offer opportunities for job rotation and stretch assignments. • Give regular constructive feedback regarding performance. • Create formal employee recognition programs. • Provide tuition assistance programs for employees to further their education.
Create an Inclusive Work Environment:	• Implement Employee Resource Groups. • Create a zero-tolerance culture regarding discrimination. • Provide diversity and inclusion training for all employees. • Provide mentoring programs targeted towards women and minority groups. • Increase the representation of women and minorities in senior leadership positions.

Onboarding

The most effective time to engage employees is when they first start to work for an organization. Onboarding programs not only increase performance by up to 11%, but 66% of organizations with onboarding programs claim a higher rate of successful assimilation of new hires into the organizational culture, 62% had higher time-to-productivity ratios, and 54% reported higher engagement.[50]

But let's start by distinguishing onboarding from orientation. An **employee orientation** is the process of introducing new hires to their jobs, co-workers, responsibilities, and workplace policies and procedures. New hire paperwork (such as I-9 forms, W-4s, and benefits enrollment) is also completed. Orientation is a one-time event, and often does not last more than one day.

Onboarding is a series of events (including orientation) which helps prepare the employee to be successful in their job and engaged with the organization. Onboarding programs can last from several days to a full year.

One-third of employees in a recent survey by BambooHR indicated they had quit a job within six months of starting it.[51] Around 17% left within the first ninety days. This means that organizations are losing one of every six new hires in the first three months. What caused them to quit? About 23% said that "receiving clear guidelines as to what my responsibilities were" would have caused them to be more likely to stay. Another 21% said they wanted "more effective training." Interestingly, 17% percent said "a friendly smile or helpful co-worker would have made all the difference." This helps to explain why one of the Gallup Q12 questions is "I have a best friend at work," in case you were wondering about that! Another 17% said they wanted to be "recognized for their unique contributions," and 9% said they wanted more attention from the "manager and co-workers."

Companies can get very innovative and creative with onboarding, which helps to engage the employee right away. Figure 11.5 shows an example of how the Texas Rangers engage their new employees and make them feel like a part of the family. Each new hire receives their own baseball card, complete with resume and walk-up song.

employee orientation

The process of introducing new hires to their jobs, co-workers, responsibilities, and workplace policies and procedures.

onboarding

A series of events (including orientation) which helps prepare the employee to be successful in their job and engaged with the organization.

A crucial goal of onboarding is to help new employees become comfortable in their new environment.

Source: © Shutterstock, Inc.

FIGURE 11.5 Baseball Card

Source: Provided by Eri Cuevas

French postal service Formaposte has been using gamification to address one of its most pressing challenges—retention in the first weeks of joining. They were losing one of every four recruits. Their gamification platform Jeu Facteur Academy walks candidates through a routine day as a postal carrier. From waking up early, to learning about the job procedures, to familiarizing themselves with job ethics, candidates get a real feel of the job before they even start work. Formaposte saw dropout rates fall from 25% to 8% using gamification. This approach also can be described as a realistic job preview and demonstrates how onboarding can in some cases be part of the employee selection process. Gamification can also be used to facilitate virtual onboarding for remote workers.

Gamification of onboarding is a good fit for automation and artificial intelligence for routine tasks, freeing up HR and line managers to focus on the human elements of onboarding. Jen Stroud, HR transformation leader at ServiceNow, a company that provides an onboarding platform, says, "If you can use automation to take care of much of the administrative work, it frees you to focus on creating people connections and relationships that strengthen the bonds for new hires and improve retention."[52]

You may find it helpful to think of onboarding activities in terms of first day, first month, ninety days, and first year. Table 11.6 offers suggested activities at each checkpoint.

TABLE 11.6 Suggested Onboarding Activities

Suggested Onboarding Activities	
First Day	Set expectations. Social interaction with co-workers. Host a lunch. Orient to workspaces. Assign an existing employee as an orientation buddy.
First Month	Ask employee for feedback on their comfort level with the job. Assign a mentor for ongoing development. Clarify expectations and assess performance.
Ninety Days	Conduct a check-in with employee. Again clarify expectations and assess performance. Set long-term goals and expectations.
One Year	Celebrate and recognize one-year anniversary. Ask employee for feedback on the onboarding process. Transition from job training to continuous development. Assign as an orientation buddy to new hires.

There you have it: employees want clear guidelines, effective training, friends, recognition, and personal attention. All of these factors of engagement can be impacted during onboarding (and even before they start their first day on the job). But if they are not engaged in the first ninety days, then you will lose one-sixth of them.

Dilbert: Employee Orientation

Catbert, the Evil Director of Human Resources, Squashes Wally's Hope

View the video online at: http://www.youtube.com/embed/XppuRfHy3TU?rel=0

HR Talk: Qiara Suggs

Director, HR Business Partners

Not-for-Profit Health System

Human resources should be the lead in creating and developing people strategies in organizations. In fact, it's extremely critical that employee engagement aligns with all organizational goals and outcomes. Workforce members essentially drive organizational goals. As an example, in healthcare, employees must feel empowered to deliver exceptional care for every patient, in all interactions. An employee's effort often starts with an employee's perception of their work environment and their perception of interactions with leadership and peers. All of these aspects are critical elements to employee engagement. Leaders help to create an environment in which employees feel connected and valued. HR's role is often to ensure that leaders are equipped with tools and are empowered and effective in doing so.

Some of the methods that I have found to be effective include implementing strategies that engage employees prior to joining the organizations. This includes expressing expectations and a realistic job preview to ensure that leaders are hiring staff that align with their organization's values and goals. Once hired, the appropriate onboarding process should take place, which includes openly defining departmental and job-specific goals to clarify focus for an employee. After onboarding, ongoing discussions should take place to ensure that employees understand where they stand from a performance standpoint. This includes leaders rewarding and recognizing where appropriate and managing performance as necessary. Most importantly, pulsing engagement through formal and informal methods is necessary. Focus groups, department meetings, pit stop conversations, and intentional one-on-ones are some great methods that prove to be effective in managing engagement.

Culture is the driver of an organization's success. An organization's engagement with workforce members should help to support and mold the culture. Clearly defined goals and behaviors should support an organization's existence. As a leader of an organization that has achieved the National Malcolm Baldrige award, I can say that the true value and outcomes of an organization are contingent upon the level of engagement with staff. Engagement is a feeling that cannot be forced, yet employees contribute to and nurture an environment where people choose to stay. When workforce members feel safe, excited, and valued, they often perform at their highest levels. They generate the same energy with their peers and often become more active than just doing their day-to-day jobs.

Key Takeaways

- Frequent, open, and honest communication between management and employees is crucial in building trust and high performance.
- Engagement is highest among employees who have some form (face-to-face, phone, or digital) of daily communication with their managers.
- Another aspect of engaging employees is to create a work environment where every employee feels accepted, valued, and treated equally and with respect.
- An employee orientation is the process of introducing new hires to their jobs, co-workers, responsibilities, and workplace policies and procedures.
- Onboarding is a series of events (including orientation) which helps prepare the employee to be successful in their job and engaged with the organization.

What Do *You* Think?

1. Have you worked for, or heard about, an organization that excels in creating a culture of engagement? What are some of the specific things they do to create this culture?
2. How important do you think it is for an organization to implement thorough onboarding programs? Why?
3. Do you have friends at your current or former job? How did that impact your job satisfaction and engagement?

11.6 Conclusion

The chapter began with an introduction of the importance of employee engagement to organizational goals and an exploration of individual needs and team orientation. Several methods for measuring engagement were then examined. The organizational, management, and HR-related driving factors of employee engagement were discussed. The influence of organizational culture was reviewed, followed by methods and techniques for designing employee engagement initiatives.

Theory-into-Practice (TIP) Exercises

1. Create a short (three-question) pulse survey for employee engagement, and then have some of your co-workers complete the survey. Then analyze the results and prepare a one-paragraph summary of the state of employee engagement. If you are not currently working, then adapt the survey to take the pulse of student engagement in your class.

2. From the perspective of your current or former job, answer the Gallup Q12 questions on a scale of 1 to 5, with:

   1 = Never

   2 = Rarely

   3 = Some days

   4 = Most days

   5 = Always

   Then add your responses and compare to the following scale:

   <12 Completely disengaged

   13–41 Somewhat disengaged and needs improvement

   42–53 Somewhat engaged but still room for improvement

   54–60 Highly engaged

   Then answer the following questions:

   a) Were you surprised at all by the result?

   b) If you are not fully engaged, what are the main causes?

   c) What specific actions could be taken that would result in you being more engaged?

3. Interview five people who work for different organizations about the onboarding process when they started. Then rank the five organizations from least effective to most effective onboarding. Then make a list of what the most effective onboarding programs do differently (better) than the least effective.

Case Study: A Working Vacation

Source: BigTunaOnline / Shutterstock.com

The mission statement of Airbnb states it wants "to create a world where you can belong anywhere." Airbnb is a platform that was created in 2008 by two roommates, Brian Chesky and Joe Gebbia, who had moved from San Francisco to New York, and needed income to help sustain their living situation. They bought a few airbeds and put up a website called Air Bed and Breakfast. It worked out well, and more opportunities arose to host strangers in their home. As innovators, they seized the opportunity to begin something that changed the outlook on the perfect "getaway" as we know it.

Employee experience is the key component in employee retention and satisfaction. Building "a world where anyone belongs" is the company identity. In 2016, Airbnb was voted by Glassdoor as the best company to work for, based on anonymous surveys. Ninety percent of employees said they would recommend working at Airbnb to others. LinkedIn also put Airbnb on its list of the *Top Companies Where the US Wants to Work Now*. The Airbnb office culture highlights climate, persona, and vibes of the workplace. It is managed by Mark Levy, global head of employee experience and backed by his team, Ground Control. Levy was the force behind reinventing the human resources and recruitment department. Levy and the owners incorporated a unique culture through workspace environment, internal communications, events, celebrations, and recognition programs. Airbnb executives referred to this reinvention as the EX (employee experience) team.

Employee experience is the driver of retention at Airbnb. Levy describes his employee experience model as the glue that holds everything together with a seamless service delivery model and support for employees. Employee experience focuses on work facilities, amenities, and employee development through rewards.

The average tenure for an employee is 2.6 years. An employee travel coupon is used as a reward and can be used on travel expenses through Airbnb, meals, and fitness classes. Conference rooms in offices are designed to mimic popular listings around the world, ranging from an apartment to a tree house. The layout is very unconventional, minimalistic, and millennial. There are no desktop computers or corded phones, so no one is chained to a desk. Employees can work in any area of the office they see fit, which also leaves room for environment changes within the office.

Facility perks include an on-site chef for lunchtime who rings the bell to announce that it's time for lunch. A large array of competitive health benefits and retirement plans are available to employees. 401Ks, stock options, performance bonuses, charity gift matching, childcare, adoption assistance, fertility assistance, and the employee travel credit have non-Airbnb employees jealous. Each employee is given a quarterly $500 travel stipend to travel anywhere in the world and stay in an Airbnb, and the allowance can roll over from year to year.

There are Airbnb recruiters on LinkedIn, but this company does not rely much on head-hunting and seeking talent. The company has a reputation that lures in candidates. In 2016, they received 180,000 resumes for nine hundred open positions.[53]

 ### Airbnb: Spearheading the Employee Experience

Mark Levy was hired by Airbnb in 2013 as Head of Employee Experience. In three years, he helped the company to reach the number-one spot on Glassdoor's Best Places to Work ranking.

View the video online at: http://www.youtube.com/embed/nlkBm-4FEl0?rel=0

Case Discussion Questions

1. What lessons can other organizations learn from Airbnb about how to create a welcoming culture for employees?
2. Why do you think Airbnb supports employees in need of adoption and fertility?
3. In 2016, Airbnb had 180,000 applicants for only nine hundred positions, which is two hundred for each opening. Is that too many?

Resources

1. **Employee Engagement Pulse Survey Tools.** A review of the top twenty employee engagement software programs and survey tools. The site also includes employee engagement strategy ideas.

   https://learn.g2.com/employee-engagement

2. **The HR and Employee Engagement Community.** An online employee engagement library with white papers, e-books, infographics, and other resources.

   https://gethppy.com/resources

3. **Onboarding software.** A review of the top software programs for employee onboarding.

   https://www.capterra.com/sem-compare/onboarding-software?gclid=CjwKCAjw0vTtBRBREiwA3URt7hZa-cZqvj6p8SoywILJzDapmkRnFPKd8KLao3cj-0q8tha-0Yja9xoC5IQQAvD_BwE

4. **Employee onboarding.** A resource website for employee onboarding, with templates, checklists, and strategies.

   https://www.officevibe.com/employee-engagement-solution/employee-onboarding

Endnotes

1. Case written by Norbert-Harrell, J. (2019). Adapted from Abbema, Alex (2018). How Best Buy cut its staff turnover more than 30 percent in four years. *Minneapolis/St. Paul Business Journal*. Retrieved from https://www.bizjournals.com/twincities/news/2018/12/06/how-best-buy-cut-its-staff-turnover-more-than-30.html

2. Patton, C. (2018). Are your employees leaving? Here's how to stop them. *Human Resource Executive*. Retrieved from https://hrexecutive.com/heres-how-to-stop-employees-from-leaving/

3. Harter, J. (2018). Employee engagement on the rise in the U.S. *Gallup*. Retrieved from https://news.gallup.com/poll/241649/employee-engagement-rise.aspx

4. Rigoni, B., & Nelson, B. (2016). Few millennials are engaged at work. *Gallup*. Retrieved from https://news.gallup.com/businessjournal/195209/few-millennials-engaged-work.aspx

5. Harter, J., & Adkins, A. (2015). What great managers do to engage employees. *Harvard Business Review*. Retrieved from https://hbr.org/2015/04/what-great-managers-do-to-engage-employees

6. State of the American workplace. (2017). *Gallup*. Retrieved from https://www.gallup.com/workplace/238085/state-american-workplace-report-2017.aspx

7. Ibid.

8. Rubin, D.P., Oehler, K., & Adair, C. (2013). Managing employee engagement during times of change. *AON*. Retrieved from https://www.aon.com/attachments/human-capital-consulting/2013_Managing_Engagement_During_Times_of_Change_White_Paper.pdf

9. Song, et al. (2012). Role of transformational leadership in effective organizational knowledge creation practices: Mediating effects of employees' work engagement. *Human Resource Development Quarterly, 23*(1), 65-101.

10. Macey, W.H., & Schneider, B. (2008). The meaning of employee engagement. *Organizational Psychology, 1*, 3-30; see also Parker, S.K., & Griffin, M.A. (2011). Understanding active psychological states: Embedding engagement in a wider nomological net and closer attention to performance. *European Journal of Work & Organizational Psychology, 20*, 60-67.

11. Parker, S.K., & Griffin, M.A. (2011). Understanding active psychological states: Embedding engagement in a wider nomological net and closer attention to performance. *European Journal of Work &. Organizational Psychology, 20*, 60-67; see also Shuck, B., & Reio, T. (2013). Employee engagement and wellbeing: A moderation model and implications for practice. *Journal of Leadership Studies & Organizational Studies, 21*(1), 43-58.

12. Rich, B.L., Lepine, J.A., & Crawford, E.A. (2010). Job engagement: Antecedents and effects on job performance. *The Academy of Management Journal, 53*(3), 617-635.

13. Alagaraja, M., & Shuck, B. (2015). Exploring organizational alignment-employee engagement linkages and impact on individual performance: A conceptual model. *Human Resource Development Review, 14*(1), 17-37.

14. Ibid.

15. Heyns, M., & Rothmann, S. (2018). Volitional trust, autonomy satisfaction, and engagement at work. *Psychological Reports, 121*(1), 112-134.

16. Cohen, S., & Bailey, D. (1997). What makes teams work: Group effectiveness research from the shop floor to the executive suite. *Journal of Management, 23*(3), 239-290.

17. Rahman, U., Rehman, C., Imran, M., & Aslam, U. (2017). Does team orientation matter? Linking work engagement and relational psychological contract with performance. *Journal of Management Development, 36*(9), 1102-1113.

18. HR Research Insitute. (2019). *The state of employee engagement in 2019* [White paper]. Retrieved from https://www.glintinc.com/resource/the-state-of-employee-engagement/

19. Gleeson, B. (2018). 3 simple elements for measuring employee engagement. *Forbes*. Retrieved from https://www.forbes.com/sites/brentgleeson/2018/03/20/3-simple-elements-for-measuring-employee-engagement/#61b8e8455100

20. Adapted from Society for Human Resource Management. *Developing and sustaining employee engagement*. Retrieved April 7, 2019 from https://www.shrm.org/resourcesandtools/tools-and-samples/toolkits/pages/sustainingemployeeengagement.aspx

21. Schaufeli, W., & Bakker, A. (2004). Utrecht Work Engagement Scale. *Utrecht University*. Retrieved from https://www.wilmarschaufeli.nl/publications/Schaufeli/Test Manuals/Test_manual_UWES_English.pdf

22. Schaufeli, W., Salanova, B., González-romá, M., & Bakker, V. (2002). The measurement of engagement and burnout: A two sample confirmatory factor analytic approach. *Journal of Happiness Studies, 3*(1), 71-92.

23. Mills, M., Culbertson, S., & Fullagar, S. (2012). Conceptualizing and measuring engagement: An analysis of the Utrecht Work Engagement Scale. *Journal of Happiness Studies, 13*(3), 519-545.

24. Martin, P. (2017). Job performance and employee engagement – The validity of Utrecht Work Engagement Scale (UWES-9). *Journal of Social and Psychological Sciences, 10*(2), 56.

25. Schneider, B., Yost, A., Kropp, A., Kind, C., & Lam, H. (2018). Workforce engagement: What it is, what drives it, and why it matters for organizational performance. *Journal of Organizational Behavior, 39*(4), 462-480.

26. Gallup Q12 Employee Engagement Survey. *Gallup*. Retrieved April 10, 2020 from https://q12.gallup.com/public/en-us/Features.

27. Stoyanova, T., & Iliev, I. (2017). Employee engagement factor for organizational excellence. *International Journal of Business and Economic Sciences Applied Research, 10*(1), 23-29.

28. BasuMallick, C. (2019). Pulse surveys vs. annual surveys: Which is a better measure of employee engagement? *HR Technologist*. Retrieved from https://www.hrtechnologist.com/articles/employee-engagement/pulse-surveys-vs-annual-surveys-which-is-a-better-measure-of-employee-engagement/

29. Bell, J. (2017). Take my pulse. *Talent Development, 71*(10), 96.

30. Welbourne, T. (2016). The potential of pulse surveys: Transforming surveys into leadership tools. *Employment Relations Today, 43*(1), 33-39.

31. Ibid.

32. Tyler, K. (2011). Prepare for impact: Linking employee engagement to crucial business metrics shows leaders how to improve the bottom line. *HRMagazine, 56*(3), 53.

33. Adapted from Employee engagement analytics: How to do it and add value. *AIRH Analytics*. Retrieved April 10, 2020 from https://www.analyticsinhr.com/blog/employee-engagement-analytics/

34. Ibid.

35. Society for Human Resource Management. *Developing and sustaining employee engagement*. Retrieved April 9, 2020 from https://www.shrm.org/resourcesandtools/tools-and-samples/toolkits/pages/sustainingemployeeengagement.aspx

36. Harter, J., & Adkins, A. (2015). What great managers do to engage employees. *Harvard Business Review*. Retrieved from https://hbr.org/2015/04/what-great-managers-do-to-engage-employees

37. Ibid.

38. Heyns, M., & Rothmann, S. (2018). Volitional trust, autonomy satisfaction, and engagement at work. *Psychological Reports, 121*(1), 112-134.

39. Kim, S., Tam, L., Kim, J., & Rhee, Y. (2017). Determinants of employee turnover intention. *Corporate Communications: An International Journal, 22*(3), 308-328.

40. Pradhan, R., Dash, S., & Jena, L. (2019). Do HR practices influence job satisfaction? Examining the mediating role of employee engagement in Indian public sector undertakings. *Global Business Review, 20*(1), 119-132.

41. *Fortune* 100 best companies to work for 2020. *Fortune, 181*(3), 115-120.

42. Ibid.

43. Marrelli, A. (2011). Employee engagement and performance management in the federal sector. *Performance Improvement, 50*(5), 5-13.

44. Ibid.

45. Harter, J., & Adkins, A. (2015). What great managers do to engage employees. *Harvard Business Review*. Retrieved from https://hbr.org/2015/04/what-great-managers-do-to-engage-employees

46. Vragel, P. (2013). Creating an employee engagement culture: Employee engagement begins with individual activity. *Ceramic Industry, 163*(10), 27-28.

47. Mcmanus, J., & Mosca, J. (2015). Strategies to build trust and improve employee engagement. *International Journal of Management & Information Systems (IJMIS), 19*(1), 37-42.

48. Downey, S., Werff, L., Thomas, K., & Plaut, V. (2015). The role of diversity practices and inclusion in promoting trust and employee engagement. *Journal of Applied Social Psychology, 45*(1), 35-44.

49. Adapted from Lockwood, N.R. (2007). Leveraging employee engagement for competitive advantage: HR's strategic role. (2007 SHRM[R] Research Quarterly). *HRMagazine, 52*(3), S1-S11.

50. Maurer, R. (2015). Onboarding key to retaining, engaging talent. *Society for Human Resource Management*. Retrieved from https://www.shrm.org/ResourcesAndTools/hr-topics/talent-acquisition/Pages/Onboarding-Key-Retaining-Engaging-Talent.aspx

51. Ibid.

52. Zielinski, D. (2019). Optimizing onboarding. *HR Magazine, 64*(2). 96-98.

53. Case written by Granger, A. (2019). Adapted from Bovim, R.D. (2016). How Airbnb became the world's best place to work. *Linkedin*. Retrieved from https://www.linkedin.com/pulse/how-airbnb-became-worlds-best-place-work-roar-v-bovim; Fagan, K. (2018). Silicon Valley techies get free food and dazzling offices, but they're not very loyal—here's how long the average employee stays at the biggest tech companies. Retrieved from https://www.google.com/amp/s/amp.businessinsider.com/average-employee-tenure-retention-at-top-tech-companies-2018-4; Top companies 2019: Where the U.S. wants to work now. *Linkedin*. Retrieved July 3, 2019 from https://www.linkedin.com/pulse/top-companies-2019-where-us-wants-work-now-daniel-roth; R., H. (2018). The importance of company culture at Airbnb. Retrieved July 4, 2019, from https://inside.6q.io/the-importance-of-company-culture-at-airbnb/; Stinson, L. (2013). Airbnb's kooky new HQ Is the envy of Silicon Valley. Retrieved July 4, 2019, from https://www.google.com/amp/s/www.wired.com/2013/12/airbnb-gets-stylish-new-headquarters/amp; Yohn, D. (2018). What happened when Airbnb blew up its HR department to focus on "employee experience." Retrieved July 4, 2019, from https://www.linkedin.com/pulse/what-happened-when-airbnb-blew-up-its-hr-department-focus-denise-yohn

CHAPTER 12
Labor Relations and Employee Rights

Learning Objectives

After reading this chapter, you should be able to do the following:

1. Explain why employees unionize, the historical perspective of union membership, and the emerging trends.
2. Identify the federal legislation and regulations that govern labor relations.
3. Describe the labor relations process, including union elections, collective bargaining, and grievance procedures.
4. Recognize the rights that employees are legally entitled to in regard to job protection, privacy, and due process.

In a broad sense, labor relations is the study of the relationship between an organization and its workers. In practice, the term usually refers to a work setting in which the employees are represented by a union and have a collective bargaining agreement. Employee rights refers to the various rights that have been established over time that employees are legally entitled to. However, not all employees have the same rights. For example, collective bargaining agreements establish specific rights only for those employees covered under the agreement, and government employees are covered under specific laws that do not apply to private-sector employees.

This chapter begins with an overview of labor relations: why employees unionize, some historical perspectives, and current trends in unionization. The federal laws governing labor relations are introduced, and the labor relations processes for elections, bargaining, and resolving grievances are examined. The legal rights of employees are then discussed, including job protection and privacy. The chapter concludes with an overview of due process and disciplinary procedures.

12.1 Opening Case: A Crude Case of Worker Demands

Source: © Shutterstock, Inc.

On February 1, 2015, the United Steelworkers (USW) union went on strike, in what was the largest oil refinery strike in thirty-five years. The strike included twelve refineries, responsible for 20% of the U.S. crude processing capability. Their main goal was to improve the safety of working conditions for union members. The union felt that the cost-cutting measures that companies were taking to increase profits were creating an unhealthy environment for workers and the community because working with oil and petroleum during the refinery process is highly risky.

Members felt that their safety was being jeopardized by the oil companies taking cost-cutting measures after oil prices dropped in the 2014 fourth quarter. These cost-cutting measures included twelve-hour work shifts, forced overtime on top of the twelve-hour shifts, the use of under-skilled nonunion contract workers, and the understaffing of employees. The USW said that overtime, fatigue, and hiring of nonunion workers without training were exacerbating risks of mistakes, which could lead to deadly accidents affecting workers and the communities around the refineries.

On February 18, 2015, a large explosion and fire occurred at the ExxonMobil Torrance Refinery. This situation brought a heightened awareness of the safety issues. Harnessing their power, the USW decided to speak up and hold oil refineries responsible for providing a safe work environment. Some of the demands included annual wage increases and medical insurance, but the main dispute was the continuing practice by oil companies of reducing the number of men and women working at their refineries. There was a great desire to slow down the growth of contractual nonunion member employees. Providing a resolution to the increasing number of nonunion workers had to be carefully reviewed as to not infringe upon right-to-work laws, which allow employees the right to work for an employer without being required to join a union.

Was this strike a success? The USW says yes. It may have taken six weeks of negotiating, but the union was able to deliver to its members a contract that addressed cost-of-living increases for the next four years, use of under-skilled contract workers, under-staffing, and worker fatigue. The twelve oil refinery companies agreed to the inclusion of union personnel during the assessment of work assignments, routine plant upkeep, and staffing. Also, in order to appease union concerns over untrained and nonunion workers taking union jobs, the employers agreed to develop hiring plans in conjunction with recruitment and training programs.[1]

 California Oil Refiner Blast Sends Flames Shooting Into the Sky

Peter Daut reports for CBS on a powerful blast at an ExxonMobil oil refinery that rocked Torrance, California.

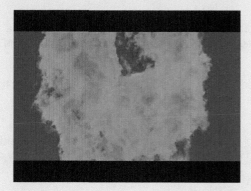

View the video online at: http://www.youtube.com/embed/ioXAhpGRk7c?rel=0

Case Discussion Questions

1. Would the employees have been able to demand a safer work environment and get the results if they were not in a union?
2. What are some other changes the oil refineries could have proposed to deal with the under-training of nonunion contract workers?
3. Reflecting on the industry you work in, does your industry have a union that fully aligns with your concerns? If you are not part of a union, what working conditions would lead you to join a union?
4. Do you feel unions are still needed for employees to receive/demand fair labor practices?

12.2 An Overview of Labor Relations

Learning Objectives

1. Explain why employees elect to join a labor union.
2. Describe the major historical events that led to the formation of labor unions.
3. Identify the trends for union representation in the U.S.

Let's start out with a little quiz to test your labor relations knowledge:

Test Your Labor Relations Know-How

1. An auto mechanic applied for a job with an automotive dealership. He was denied employment because of his union membership. Was the employer's action lawful?

   Yes _____   No _____

2. During a labor organizing drive, supervisors questioned individual employees about their union beliefs. Was this questioning permissible?

   Yes _____   No _____

3. When members of a union began wearing union buttons at work, management ordered the buttons to be removed. Was management within its rights?

   Yes _____   No _____

4. While an organizing drive was under way, an employer agreed, as a social gesture, to furnish refreshments at a holiday party. Was the employer acting within the law?

   Yes _____   No _____

5. A company distributed to other antiunion employers in the area a list of job applicants known to be union supporters. Was the distribution unlawful?

   Yes _____   No _____

6. During a union organizing drive, the owner of Servo Pipe promised her employees a wage increase if they would vote against the union. Can the owner legally make this promise to her employees?

   Yes _____   No _____

7. Employees have the right to file unfair labor practice charges against their union.

   Yes _____   No _____

8. An employee who is a union member has been scheduled for a disciplinary hearing. The employee requests that the union steward attend the meeting, but the request is denied. Can management legally deny this request?

   Yes _____   No _____

9. John Green, a maintenance engineer, has a poor work record. Management wishes to terminate his employment. However, Green is a union steward, and he is highly critical of the company. Can management legally discharge this employee?

   Yes _____   No _____

10. During an organizing drive, an office manager expressed strong antiunion beliefs and called union officials "racketeers," "big stinkers," and a "bunch of radicals." He told the employees who joined the union that they "ought to have their heads examined." Were the manager's comments legal?

    Yes _____   No _____

(Answers found after chapter conclusion here: "Answers to Test Your Labor Relations Know-How".)

Why Employees Unionize

labor union

An organized association of workers, often in a trade or profession, formed to protect and further their rights and interests.

A **labor union** is an organized association of workers, often in a trade or profession, formed to protect and further their rights and interests. What comes to mind when you think of labor unions? Perhaps you would say higher wages, better benefits, better working conditions, or more protection from job loss. If you answered along these lines, you probably have a somewhat "pro-union" attitude. Or perhaps you would say other things come to mind: high union dues, corruption, organized crime, violence associated with strikes, wages so high that companies cannot be competitive globally and therefore lose market share, etc. If you answered along these lines, then you probably have a somewhat "antiunion" attitude. How did you answer the questions in the opening case regarding the United Steelworkers union? My point is this: most people lean one way or the other. They are either pro-union or antiunion. People usually have some preconceived notions about unions that are based upon factors such as where they have lived, what their parents do for a living, etc. Often these preconceived notions are not well informed. One purpose of this chapter is for you to see both sides of the issue: the positive impact and the negative impact of the union movement. Then you will be able to objectively make informed decisions regarding labor relations issues.

So why do employees vote to form a union? The simplest answer is that they are not satisfied with their current salary, benefits, working conditions, or other terms and conditions of employment. Employees who are more dissatisfied with various aspects of their jobs are more likely to demand union representation.[2] Furthermore, economic or extrinsic satisfaction appears to be more important than noneconomic or intrinsic satisfaction in determining the desire for unionization among blue workers.[3] There is a significant body of research that demonstrates that labor unions are associated with better pay and benefits.[4] In other words, the primary reason for unionizing is for more money. But there is also evidence that union members are more satisfied with their overall quality of life than nonmembers, and this appears to be consistent across demographic groups, regardless of whether someone is rich or poor, male or female, young or old.[5] In this chapter, we will study **labor relations**, which is the relationship between the management of an organization and its workforce.

> **labor relations**
>
> The relationship between the management of an organization and its workforce.

Historical Perspectives

Let's begin with a little history. The forerunners to modern unions were the craft guilds of the middle ages. These organizations were first formed to regulate entrance into a craft, thus regulating the supply of labor, and therefore keeping prices higher. The first unions in the U.S. were also craft unions. During the industrial era (beginning around the 1870s to the 1880s), large organizations began to emerge. For the first time, individuals found themselves working for companies with hundreds or sometimes thousands of employees, as opposed to being self-employed or working for a very small local firm. Concurrent with the growth of large organizations was the movement toward scientific management, and the focus on productivity and efficiency. Companies sometimes abused their employees by requiring them to work unreasonable hours, often in poor working conditions for little pay. Until the 1930s, the government normally supported businesses during any labor disputes. The government did not recognize the right to strike, and often the local police, sheriff, or National Guard were utilized to break up groups of striking and/or picketing workers. It was not unusual for striking employees to be arrested and given jail terms. The passage of the National Labor Relations Act in 1935 gave employees the right to organize and join a union and required the employers to bargain collectively once a union had been selected through an employee vote. Figure 12.1 describes a historic massacre that occurred in 1914 which helped spur the U.S. government to pass labor relations legislation.

Mary G. Harris Jones (shown here with President Calvin Coolidge), known as Mother Jones from 1897 onwards, was an Irish-born American schoolteacher and dressmaker who became a prominent union organizer, community organizer, and activist. She helped coordinate major strikes and co-founded the Industrial Workers of the World.

Source: © Shutterstock, Inc.

FIGURE 12.1 The Ludlow Massacre

About 10,000 miners had been on strike in 1913 in the coalfields of Colorado. Miners demanded better wages, an eight-hour work day, a safe workplace, less company control over their lives, and the right to organize. After the United Mine Workers of America (UMWA) called a strike in September, 1913, the coal companies evicted thousands of miners and their families from their homes and company towns. The UMWA leased land, provided tents, and even issued a small allowance. Ludlow was the largest tent colony, with about 200 tents and 1,200 people.

A culturally diverse group maintained solidarity during the strike. Local Hispanic people and European immigrants provided the majority of the labor force. People spoke at least twenty-four distinct languages. These different groups pulled together to form a community with a common goal.

Violence on both sides plagued the strike. Governor Elias Ammons called out the Colorado National Guard to help keep the peace. By April, 1914, membership in the local militia units consisted mostly of company employees, who sided against the miners. On April 20, 1914, hostilities came to a head, which resulted in the Ludlow massacre. Throughout the day, the militia and miners exchanged gunfire. Lives were lost on both sides. Under suspicious circumstances, the tent colony burned. Two women and eleven children suffocated in a cellar dug beneath their tent. While accounts differ, around twenty-one people died.

The events of the Ludlow Massacre shocked the nation and embarrassed John D. Rockefeller, Jr., the majority owner of the Colorado Fuel and Iron Company, the largest coal company operating in the area. This event initiated many of the labor reforms that workers now take for granted.

Source: Shutterstock.com (left) and Grossinger / Shutterstock.com (right)

Union membership grew rapidly, peaking at 34.8% of the U.S. workforce in 1954.[6] Workers were more successful in forming unions in some industries than others. The most successful organizing attempts occurred in settings where the workers had greater disruptive capacities due to the high cost of being replaced during work stoppages.[7] The highest replacement costs were associated with three conditions: scarcity of skilled labor, geographically isolated worksites that raised the cost of importing strikebreakers, and time-sensitive tasks that rendered replacement workers economically impractical.[8] Union membership declined throughout the 1970s and 1980s to about 12.4% of the U.S. workforce today. Why the decline? This is a very complicated question, but there are a couple of major factors. The poor reputation that many unions received because of involvement in organized crime and corruption probably has something to do with it. Another major factor is that much of what unions bargained for during the 1940s and 1950s is either guaranteed to us by employment legislation that has been passed since 1964 or is offered by companies just to attract and retain good employees (health benefits, retirement plans, etc.). Some experts predicted that union membership would continue to fall to about 5% to 8% of the workforce. But this has not happened. In fact, the decline leveled off, and there has been some slight growth in union membership during the last decade. Table 12.1 gives an overview of some significant events in the history of U.S. labor relations.

TABLE 12.1 United States Labor Relations Timeline

United States Labor Relations Timeline	
1619	The first labor strike in North America was organized and staged by Polish workers and artisans in Jamestown.
1677	First recorded prosecution against strikers in New York City.
1791	First strike for a ten-hour workday by carpenters in Philadelphia.
1847	New Hampshire enacts first state ten-hour workday law.
1885	Successful strikes by Knights of Labor on the Southwest System; the Missouri Pacific; the Missouri, Kansas, and Texas; and the Wabash railroads.
1886	General strike at Haymarket Square turns into a riot resulting in at least eight deaths.
1890	United Brotherhood of Carpenters and Joiners of America successfully strike for an eight-hour workday.
1903	Mother Jones organizes a children's march from Philadelphia to New York to improve enforcement of child labor laws.
1914	Ludlow massacre of thirteen women and children and several men in Colorado coal miners' strike.
1919	One of every five workers walks out in wave of nationwide strikes.
1926	Railway Labor Act establishes procedures for settling railway labor disputes and forbids discrimination against union members.
1932	Norris-LaGuardia Act prohibits injunctions in most major disputes.
1935	National Labor Relations Act passed, to protect the rights of employees and employers, to encourage collective bargaining, and to curtail certain private-sector labor and management practices, which can harm the general welfare of workers, businesses, and the U.S. economy.
1947	Taft-Hartley Act (also known as the Labor Management Relations Act) passed, to restrict the power and activities of labor unions.
1959	Landrum-Griffin Act (also known as the Labor Management Reporting and Disclosure Act) passed, to regulate labor unions' internal affairs and their officials' relationships with employers.

The Matewan Massacre of 1920

An overview of one of the most significant events of the West Virginia coal wars.

View the video online at: http://www.youtube.com/embed/dURTV6hm1Uo?rel=0

Trends in Unionization

A majority of Americans (55%) hold a favorable view of unions versus 33% who hold an unfavorable view.[9] Despite the favorable views, union membership has been on a slow downward trend since 1954. The union membership rate in the U.S. was 10.5% in 2018, down 0.2% from 2017, according to the Bureau of Labor Statistics.[10] Figure 12.2 shows union membership since 1983 (the first year the BLS started tracking union data).

FIGURE 12.2 U.S. Union Membership from 1983 to 2019

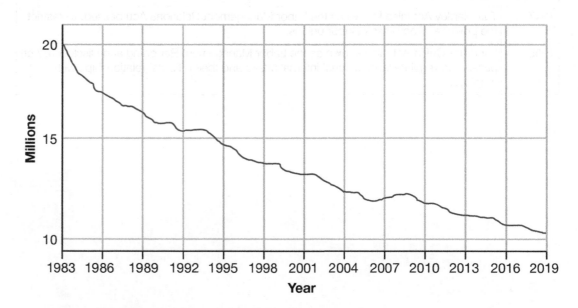

*This chart begins in 1983 because that is the first year in
which comparable data was tracked by the Bureau of Labor Statistics.

Source: Based on data from https://www.bls.gov/news.release/pdf/union2.pdf.

The union membership rate of public-sector workers (33.9%) is more than five times higher than the private sector (6.4%).[11] The highest unionization rates are among workers in protective services (e.g., law enforcement and firefighters) at 33.9%, and in education/training/library occupations at 33.8%. Among the states, Hawaii and New York have the highest union membership rates (23.1% and 22.3% respectively), while North Carolina and South Carolina have the lowest (2.7% each). Figure 12.3 shows union membership by state.

FIGURE 12.3 U.S. Union Membership by State

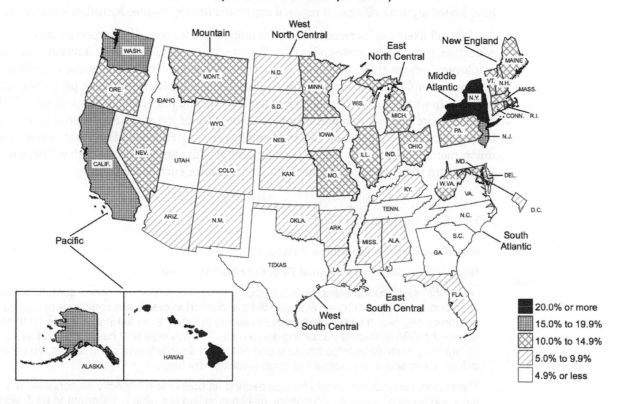

Chart 1. Union membership rates by state, 2019 annual averages

(U.S. rate = 10.3 percent)

Legend:
- 20.0% or more
- 15.0% to 19.9%
- 10.0% to 14.9%
- 5.0% to 9.9%
- 4.9% or less

Source: https://www.bls.gov/news.release/pdf/union2.pdf

When you consider that labor relations laws were passed from 1926 to 1959, it can give one the idea that labor law and the NLRB are relics of the past. But the federal government is still very active in regulating the manager-employee relationship. In 2019, electric-car maker Tesla was charged with violating federal labor law after CEO Elon Musk suggested in a tweet that employees who joined a union would have to give up their stock options.[12] Musk tweeted that nothing was stopping Tesla employees from voting for a union, "but why pay union dues and give up stock options for nothing?" Administrative Law Judge Amita Baman Tracy ruled that "Musk's tweet can only be read by a reasonable employee to indicate that if the employees vote to unionize then they would give up stock options," and that he threatened to take away a benefit enjoyed by the employees as a consequence for voting to unionize, which violates federal labor law. The judge further ordered the company to reinstate a fired union supporter, to revoke a warning to another worker, and to hold a meeting at its Fremont, California, plant to inform employees that the company violated the National Labor Relations Act.

In March 2019, University of Illinois at Chicago student workers went on strike to demand that the university recognize the union and begin collective bargaining negotiations.[13] In June 2019, University of Chicago graduate student workers also went on strike with them for the same demands. Student workers at other universities, including Boston College, Columbia, and Yale are also asking for union recognition and the right to bargain. However, the NLRB issued a proposed rule in October 2019 stating college or university students working in jobs connected to their studies are not employees covered by the National Labor Relations Act.[14] In a reversal of its previous ruling in 2016, the board concluded that payments to the students are provided to help pay the cost of students' education and are better viewed as financial aid than as consideration for work.

Since the 1980s, the NLRB has even ventured into labor relations aspects of professional sports. The board brought an end to a 1995 baseball strike by issuing an injunction against team owners when they unilaterally imposed changes to negotiated wages.[15] In 1994, the board secured a $30 million back pay settlement for the National Football League Players Association when teams refused to allow 1,300 returning striking players to participate in games after the strike ended, and they have issued injunctions against regional soccer and hockey leagues for unfair labor practices.[16]

We will likely see increased interest in union representation in the service sector (healthcare, education, etc.) and in white-collar jobs. The unions are targeting these industries and classes of employees because they traditionally have not had high representation levels, so there is potential for union membership to grow. Many workers in these fields currently are paid low wages, partly because they have not had strong union membership and leadership in the past. We will also probably see more interest in union membership because of job security concerns (due to corporate layoffs, subcontracting, use of part-time employees, etc.). For the industries that have had strong union membership for decades, the wages and benefits are very competitive. These unions will instead turn their attention to other issues in the future, such as job security.

HR Talk with Steve Larsen

Vice-President for Workforce Relations

North Texas Society for Human Resource Management

Unfortunately, the union-management relationship has developed into one of conflict, not cooperation and trust. All too frequently, supervisors and union stewards are constantly at odds where a portion of the union members feel the supervisor is being unfair or asking people to do things outside of the CBA (collective bargaining agreement). Top management has not helped the situation by granting themselves large bonuses and not being flexible. Layoffs and strikes are particularly difficult times and make recovery of good relations very hard.

The negotiation process should be approached as openly and honestly as possible. This is not easy and takes a lot of pre-negotiations meetings to find out what is important to each side. Find out what management wants that can be "traded" for items that the union wants. This will cover most things, but there are always the "sore" topics that are going to cause a problem. These items need to be thoroughly understood so they can be presented and defended.

I don't see a lot of changes in the immediate future in labor relations. Too many factors continue to be relevant: management bonuses, sending jobs overseas for cheaper labor costs, reduction of manufacturing jobs, progress in automation, etc., are all areas of irritation that are not going to change. On the union side, their unwillingness to use automation and the lack of efficiency caused by such items at union judication, causes businesses to be less profitable. I see the unions changing to represent more of the service and information jobs. Manufacturing jobs will continue to decline, and automations will continue to take a toll on the jobs available. I believe the percentage of American workers that are unionized will remain about the same. It is just the jobs represented that will change.

Politically, every time there is a change of party in the White House, the Labor Relations Board changes and then overturns some of the prior administration's decisions. This constant redirection makes it difficult to make lasting decisions and agreements.

Are unions good or bad? The answer is—yes. The history of unions is one of controlling power. As the power balance tends to shift back and forth between unions and management, the one in power tends to abuse that power and fall into disfavor. I have never seen an industry or company become unionized that did not deserve it. I have also seen companies that have been unionized for a while that would be better without a union. But we need unions to balance the power when management abuses their power.

Key Takeaways

- The forerunners to modern unions were the craft guilds of the middle ages. These organizations were first formed to regulate entrance into a craft, thus regulating the supply of labor and therefore keeping prices higher.
- Until the 1930s, the government normally supported businesses during any labor disputes. The government did not recognize the right to strike, and often the local police, sheriff, or National Guard were utilized to break up groups of striking and/or picketing workers.
- The passage of the National Labor Relations Act in 1935 gave employees the right to organize and join a union and required the employers to bargain collectively once a union had been selected through an employee vote.
- Union membership grew rapidly, peaking at about one-third of the U.S. workforce in the 1950s.
- Despite the favorable views, union membership has been on a slow downward trend since 1954. The union membership rate in the U.S. was 10.5% in 2018.

What Do *You* Think?

1. Is your attitude toward unions positive or negative? What has influenced your opinion?
2. Have you or anyone you know belonged to a union? What were the benefits? Were there any negative aspects?
3. What do you think will be the future trends in unionization in the U.S.?

12.3 Government Regulation of Labor Relations

Learning Objectives

1. Identify the requirements of the Railway Labor Act of 1926.
2. Describe how the Norris-LaGuardia Act of 1932 limited the ability of companies to use injunctions to stop labor organizing activities.
3. Explain how the National Labor Relations Act of 1935 provides the structure for union organizing campaigns, the collective bargaining process, and the creation of the National Labor Relations Board.

4. Recognize how the Labor Management Relations Act (LMRA) helped restore the balance of power between companies and unions by applying unfair labor practices to unions, and not just companies.

5. Discuss how the Labor Management Reporting and Disclosure Act (LMRDA) provided safeguards to union member rights by preventing racketeering and other unscrupulous practices by employers and union officers.

There are five major pieces of federal legislation that govern labor relations. They are the Railway Labor Act of 1926, the Norris-LaGuardia Act of 1932, the National Labor Relations Act of 1935, the Labor Management Relations Act of 1947, and the Labor Management Reporting and Disclosure Act of 1959.

Although the major U.S. labor laws were passed in the 1930s through the 1950s, they continue to provide important protection for worker rights today. In 2020, employees across various industries, including food service, meat processing, retail, manufacturing, transportation, and healthcare, protested working conditions and lack of safety protections during the COVID-19 pandemic.

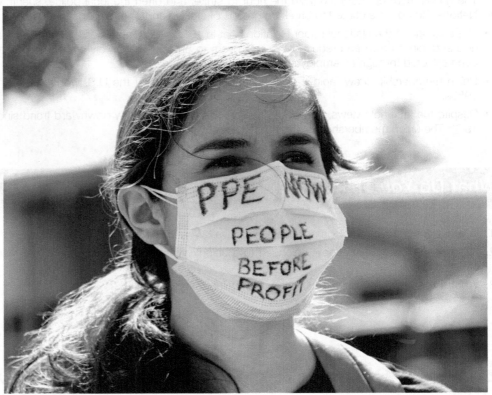

Source: Sheila Fitzgerald / Shutterstock.com

Railway Labor Act of 1926

Railway Labor Act (RLA)

An act passed by Congress in 1926 in an attempt to avoid work stoppages that threatened to substantially interrupt interstate commerce.

In 1926, Congress passed the **Railway Labor Act (RLA)** in an attempt to avoid work stoppages that threatened to substantially interrupt interstate commerce. Decades of railroad labor unrest had led to widespread and often violent strikes. In 1924, President Calvin Coolidge asked railroads and unions to recommend legislation to reduce the threat of railroad shutdowns.[17] The railroad companies and unions jointly drafted the legislation which became the Railway Labor Act when President Coolidge signed the legislation in 1926.

The act was the first major federal labor legislation, and it was a precursor to future legislation in that it paved the way for collective bargaining. The RLA covers freight, commuter railroads, and airlines (which were added in a 1936 amendment), but also applies to companies directly or indirectly controlled by railroads or airlines and that perform services related to transportation of freight or passengers.

Some question whether the RLA still meets the transportation industry's needs while adequately protecting the interests of organized labor.[18] Changes in the airline industry due to deregulation have created a more competitive environment, putting pressure on airlines to lower costs. As a result, the airlines have been increasingly seeking concessions from labor to achieve profitability, often resulting in strikes. One particular issue is the use of intermittent strikes by airline employees. An **intermittent strike** is a concerted activity which involves work stoppages that are of limited duration but periodically repeated. They are also referred to as CHAOS™ tactics, because of the disruption they cause to company operations. However, whether intermittent strikes are protected activity or illegal is often disputed and is unclear under the RLA.

intermittent strike
A concerted activity which involves work stoppages that are of limited duration but periodically repeated.

Norris-LaGuardia Act of 1932

The Great Depression of 1929–1939 changed attitudes toward labor relations and spurred Congress to begin considering new approaches to economic policy, wages, and job security. Congress passed the **Norris-LaGuardia Act (NLGA)** in 1932, which severely restricted the ability of employers to obtain an injunction forbidding a union from engaging in peaceful picketing, boycotts, or various striking activities. Previously, federal court injunctions had been an effective antiunion weapon because they forced unions to either cease such activities or suffer the penalty of being in contempt of court.

Congress passed the NLGA to remedy a long history of management hostility and employee abuse in federal court, specifically the judiciary's liberal grants of injunctive relief in favor of management in labor disputes to halt worker strikes.[19] The NLGA continues to play an integral role in modern labor conflicts. For example, in 2011 the National Football League's (NFL) lockout of its players reached a legal resolution after attorneys argued competing interpretations of the NLGA before the Eighth Circuit Court in *Brady v. NFL*, with the court ruling in favor of the NFL owners, and stating that the NLGA did not extend to employee lockouts in this case.

Norris-LaGuardia Act (NLGA)
An act passed by Congress in 1932 which severely restricted the ability of employers to obtain an injunction forbidding a union from engaging in peaceful picketing, boycotts, or various striking activities.

National Labor Relations Act of 1935

Also referred to as the Wagner Act, the **National Labor Relations Act (NLRA)** was passed in 1935. The purpose of the act was to serve the public interest by reducing interruptions in commerce caused by industrial strife.[20] The act created the National Labor Relations Board (NLRB) to govern labor relations in the United States (including overseeing union elections and enforcing and interpreting labor law). The NLRB is a five-member board nominated by the president and confirmed by the Senate. It also employs forty administrative law judges who help decide cases.

The act guarantees the right of private-sector workers to organize and bargain collectively. Section 7 of the act describes employee rights as follows: "Employees shall have the right to self-organization, to form, join, or assist labor organizations to bargain collectively through representatives of their own choosing, and to engage in concerted activities, for the purpose of collective bargaining or other mutual aid or protection, and shall also have the right to refrain from any or all of such activities except to the extent that such rights may be affected by an agreement requiring membership in a labor organization as a condition of employment."

National Labor Relations Act (NLRA)
An act passed by Congress in 1935 to serve the public interest by reducing interruptions in commerce caused by industrial strife.

unfair labor practice

An action taken by an employer or union that violates the provisions of federal labor laws.

The act also created the National Labor Relations Board as an independent federal agency. Employers and employees alike are protected from **unfair labor practices** and have an impartial forum in the NLRB for the resolution of disputes. An unfair labor practice is an action taken by an employer or union that violates the provisions of federal labor laws. Some of these provisions apply to the interactions between the employer and the union, but individual workers are also protected from unfair treatment by an employer or union. The NLRB has two major functions:[21]

1. To determine and implement, through secret-ballot elections, the free democratic choice by employees as to whether they desire union representation in dealing with their employers, and if so, by which union.

2. To prevent and remedy unlawful acts (unfair labor practices), by either employers or unions or both.

Excluded from coverage under the act are public-sector employees (employees of state, federal, and local governments and their subdivisions), agricultural and domestic workers, independent contractors, workers employed by a parent or spouse, employees of air and rail carriers covered under the Railway Labor Act, and supervisors.[22]

Labor Management Relations Act of 1947

Labor Management Relations Act (LMRA)

An act passed by Congress in 1947 to help restore the balance of power between companies and unions by applying unfair labor regulations to unions and not just companies.

Also referred to as the Taft-Hartley Act, the **Labor Management Relations Act (LMRA)** was passed in 1947. From the time the Wagner Act became law, there were many bills, resolutions, and riders introduced each year in Congress.[23] By 1947, there were about one hundred fifty such attempts to alter the act. The campaign to amend the Wagner Act was led by Senator Robert A. Taft of Ohio, chairman of the Senate Labor Committee, and Representative Fred A. Hartley, Jr., of New Jersey, chairman of the House Education and Labor Committee. Under the Wagner Act, only employers were subject to the NLRB's unfair labor practice prohibitions. The LMRA made unions subject to the NLRB's unfair labor practice mandates as well.

Because the bargaining power of unions increased significantly after the passage of the Wagner Act, certain restraints on unions were considered necessary. For example, the collective bargaining process was being corrupted by use of bribery and extortion. As the Supreme Court explained in *Arroyo v. United States*, Congress enacted the LMRA in order to curb those practices "which Congress considered inimical to the integrity of the collective bargaining process."[24] In short, Congress balanced the rights and duties of labor and management with the act. The act gave employees the right to engage in antiunion speech. The act also defined the following as unfair labor practices:

- Restraint or coercion of employees in the exercise of their rights.
- Restraint or coercion of employers in the selection of the parties to bargain on their behalf.
- Persuasion of employers to discriminate against any of their employees.
- Refusal to bargain collectively with an employer.
- Participation in secondary boycotts.
- Attempt to force recognition from an employer when another union is already the certified representative.
- Charge of excessive initiation fees and dues.
- Featherbedding practices that require payment of wages for services not performed.

Labor-Management Reporting and Disclosure Act of 1959

Also called the Landrum-Griffin Act, the **Labor Management Reporting and Disclosure Act (LMRDA)** was passed in 1959. The LMRDA was enacted to safeguard union member rights and prevent racketeering and other unscrupulous practices by employers and union officers. Provisions include nomination and election of union officers, secret-ballot voting process, the right of union members to participate in union meetings, and holding union officials accountable for union funds.

From 1957 to 1959, the U.S. Senate's Select Committee on Improper Activities in the Labor or Management Field (better known as the McClellan Committee) held hearings on the problem of labor corruption.[25] The work of the committee drew widespread media attention, particularly with news stories about union corruption. James Hoffa's leadership of the Teamsters offered perhaps the most well known and egregious example of union misrule and the dangers that it presented for the economy as a whole.

Other problematic practices by unions were **secondary boycotts** and **hot cargo agreements**. The LMRDA amended Taft-Hartley in several major respects, as listed in Table 12.2. A secondary boycott is an attempt to stop others from purchasing products from, performing services for, or otherwise doing business with a company that does business with another company that is involved in a labor dispute. For example, in 2008 the Unite Here Local 1 union was engaged in a long-running strike against the Congress Plaza Hotel in Chicago. As a pressure tactic to induce the hotel to meet its demands, the union began targeting trade associations that had no role in the labor dispute but made arrangements to reserve large blocks of rooms, and urging them to cancel their plans (i.e., boycott the hotel).[26] A hot cargo agreement involves employers committing themselves in advance to boycott any other employer involved in a dispute with the union.

Labor Management Reporting and Disclosure Act (LMRDA)

An act passed by Congress in 1959 to provide safeguards to union member rights by preventing racketeering and other unscrupulous practices by employers and union officers.

secondary boycott

An attempt to stop others from purchasing products from, performing services for, or otherwise doing business with a company that does business with another company that is involved in a labor dispute.

hot cargo agreement

Involves employers committing themselves in advance to boycott any other employer involved in a dispute with the union.

TABLE 12.2 Provisions of the Landrum-Griffin Act

Provisions of the Landrum-Griffin Act
• State courts and labor relations boards were given jurisdiction over cases declined by the NLRB.
• Secondary boycott prohibitions were tightened and hot cargo agreements were outlawed.
• A new unfair labor practice made it unlawful for a union to picket for recognition or organizational purposes in certain circumstances.
• Pre-hire and seven-day union shop contracts were legalized for the construction industry.
• Permanently replaced economic strikers were given the right to vote in representation elections within one year of the beginning of the strike.
• The NLRB was authorized to delegate most of its authority to define bargaining units and to direct elections to its regional directors, subject to discretionary review.
• Established a code of conduct for unions, guaranteeing certain rights to union members within their union, and imposing certain reporting requirements on unions, union officers, employers, and consultants, which the law assigned for administration to the Department of Labor.

Key Takeaways

- In 1926, Congress passed the Railway Labor Act (RLA) in an attempt to avoid work stoppages that threatened to substantially interrupt interstate commerce.
- An intermittent strike is a concerted activity which involves work stoppages that are of limited duration but periodically repeated.

- Congress passed the Norris-LaGuardia Act (NLGA) in 1932, which severely restricted the ability of employers to obtain an injunction forbidding a union from engaging in peaceful picketing, boycotts, or various striking activities.
- The National Labor Relations Act (NLRA) was passed in 1935 to serve the public interest by reducing interruptions in commerce caused by industrial strife.
- The NLRA created the National Labor Relations Board (NLRB) to govern labor relations in the United States (including overseeing union elections, and enforcing and interpreting labor law). The NLRB is a five-member board nominated by the president and confirmed by the Senate. It also employs forty administrative law judges who help decide cases.
- An unfair labor practice is an action taken by an employer or union that violates the provisions of federal labor laws.
- The Labor Management Relations Act (LMRA) was passed in 1947 to help restore the balance of power between companies and unions by applying unfair labor practices to unions, and not just companies.
- The Labor Management Reporting and Disclosure Act (LMRDA) of 1959 provided safeguards to union member rights by preventing racketeering and other unscrupulous practices by employers and union officers.
- A secondary boycott is an attempt to stop others from purchasing products from, performing services for, or otherwise doing business with a company that does business with another company that is involved in a labor dispute.
- A hot cargo agreement involves employers committing themselves in advance to boycott any other employer involved in a dispute with the union.

What Do *You* Think?

1. Do you think that federal labor law needs to be updated to reflect modern workforce issues?
2. Have you experienced a secondary boycott? Did you feel it was fair to the company being boycotted?
3. Is the structure of the National Labor Relations Board too political? Should board members be elected rather than appointed by the president?

12.4 The Labor Relations Process

Learning Objectives

1. Explain the steps in an organizing campaign.
2. Distinguish between the three categories of bargaining topics in a collective bargaining agreement, as defined by the NLRB.
3. Identify the main types of unfair labor practices by employers and unions.
4. Describe a typical grievance procedure.

Organizing Campaigns

The first step in an organizing campaign is to determine the **bargaining unit**. A bargaining unit is a group of employees represented or seeking representation by a union. A bargaining unit is generally determined on the basis of a "community of interest" of the employees.[27] Employees who have the same or similar interests with respect to wages, hours, and other working conditions may be grouped together into a bargaining unit. A union and the employer may agree on the appropriate bargaining unit. If they cannot agree, then a determination is made by the NLRB.

Unions will sometimes seek smaller bargaining units because it betters the chance of union representation being approved in a vote. The International Association of Machinists and Aerospace Workers (IAM) had failed to unionize about 2,700 workers at a Boeing plant in South Carolina. In 2019, the IAM attempted to represent a smaller group, and the NLRB's regional director approved a bargaining unit made up of about 178 flight readiness technicians and inspectors.[28] But Boeing argued that the mechanics should be included in the larger community of workers and asked the board to review the decision. The board ruled in favor of Boeing and ruled that the two job classifications were too disparate and did not meet the standard of "community of interest."

Having too many small bargaining units can be problematic for employers, unions, and employees. Employers can lose operational flexibility since workers in one department might not be able to pick up shifts in others if different unions represent the departments.[29] Employees might lose opportunities for cross-training, promotion, and transfer as they can be hindered when one department is unionized and the other is not, or when they are both unionized but represented by different unions.

The NLRB monitors the process of organizing a union. The following steps must be followed:

1. Establish appropriate bargaining unit.
2. Obtain signatures of employees on authorization cards (minimum 30%).
3. If over 50% of signatures are obtained, the union may request the employer to consent to union recognition without an election.
4. If more than 30%, but less than 50% of employees sign an authorization card, or if the employer refuses to consent, then the election is contested by the employer.
5. The union and the employer both conduct a campaign, trying to persuade employees to vote a certain way.
6. Secret-ballot election is held (supervised by NLRB).
7. If a majority of the employees elect the union, then the union is recognized as the official bargaining agent of the employees and the employer must engage in collective bargaining with the union.
8. If a majority of the employees reject the union, then the issue cannot be voted on again for at least twelve months.

bargaining unit

A group of employees represented or seeking representation by a union.

The Collective Bargaining Process

Once a union has been recognized (elected by a majority of the employees in the bargaining unit), then the union and the company begin to negotiate. The negotiations result in a **collective bargaining agreement (CBA)**, which sets forth the terms and conditions of employment, including provisions in regard to rates of pay, hours of work, promotion, grievance procedures, and other terms of employment.

There are three main categories of bargaining topics, as defined by the NLRB. The first is mandatory items, sometimes referred to as compulsory subjects. These are categories that one side must discuss, or put on the bargaining table, if the other side requests it. For example, wages, hours, and other conditions of employment are all compulsory subjects. If the union wants to negotiate wages, the employer has to discuss it. The second category is permissive items. These topics are those that one side does not have to discuss or put on the bargaining table. For example, the location of plants, plant closings, and company reorganizations are all permissive subjects. If the union wants to discuss plant closings, the employer can negotiate this topic if they so desire, but they are not required to under law. The final category is illegal subjects, which neither the union nor the employer may negotiate. Mandatory retirement is an example of an illegal subject. It may not be negotiated, because to do so would violate federal law, in this case the Age Discrimination in Employment Act.

Unfair Labor Practices

Unfair labor practices are defined by the NLRA and subsequent amendments as part of the LMRA and the LMRDA. Table 12.3 summarizes the unfair labor practices by employers and unions.

TABLE 12.3 Unfair Labor Practices

By Employers	By Unions
Cannot interfere with, restrain, or coerce employees in their right to form or join a union.	Cannot restrain or coerce employees to join or not join a union.
Cannot threaten employees with the loss of their jobs and benefits if they vote to form or join a union.	Cannot threaten employees with the loss of their jobs if they do not support unionization.
Cannot threaten to close a plant should employees choose to be represented by a union.	Cannot cause an employer to discriminate against employees with respect to the conditions of employment.
Cannot raise wages to discourage workers from joining or forming a union.	Cannot boycott or strike an employer that is a customer or supplier to an employer that the union is trying to organize (secondary boycott).
Cannot discriminate against employees with respect to the conditions of employment (e.g., fire, demote, or give unfavorable work assignments) because of union activities.	Must bargain in good faith with respect to wages, hours, and other working conditions.
Must bargain in good faith with respect to wages, hours, and other working conditions.	

An unfair labor practice may be filed by an employee, employer, labor union, or other person (such as a company impacted by a secondary boycott). After a charge is filed, the regional staff of the NLRB will investigate to determine whether an unfair labor practice has occurred. If a charge has merit, the regional director will first attempt a voluntary settlement. If this effort fails, then the case will be decided by an NLRB administrative law judge, and this decision can be appealed to the five-member NLRB.

In 2019, 20,000 members of the Communications Workers of America (CWA) in nine southern states went on strike against AT&T over alleged unfair labor practices committed by AT&T management during contract negotiations.

Source: Christopher V Jones / Shutterstock.com

Grievance Procedures

Union election campaigns and the process of negotiating collective bargaining agreements are the aspects of labor relations that most people are familiar with. This is primarily due to media coverage of strikes and also to popular movies. But the routine administration of labor agreements is where managers and union representatives actually spend most of their time. A **grievance** refers to a claim by an employee or the union that the employer is not complying with the terms of the CBA. The grievance procedure is considered by some to be the heart of the bargaining agreement or the safety valve that gives flexibility to the whole system of collective bargaining.[30]

CBAs normally include a grievance procedure, which outlines the steps by which a dispute is presented and settled. A typical grievance procedure is:

grievance

A claim by an employee or the union that the employer is not complying with the terms of the CBA.

union steward

An employee of a company and a union official who represents and defends the interest of fellow employees.

arbitration

The hearing and determining of a dispute or the settling of differences between parties by a person or persons chosen or agreed to by them.

- The employee makes their complaint to a union representative, normally the **union steward**, who represents and defends the interest of fellow employees.
- The union steward submits the grievance to the union for review.
- If the grievance is not settled at lower levels, then the union files it with the company.
- Arbitration is often then used to settle the dispute. **Arbitration** is the hearing and determining of a dispute or the settling of differences between parties by a person or persons chosen or agreed to by them.

Talent Analytics

Did you know that labor relations analytics is now an HR specialist position? The job description found here (https://lensa.com/labor-relations-analytics-intern-spring-2020-jobs/dallas/jd/2a6ee35f1d7b9ed22fea586507a2d268) is for an internship in labor relations analytics posted in 2019 by Southwest Airlines. Is this a career option that interests you?[31]

Key Takeaways

- A bargaining unit is a group of employees represented or seeking representation by a union. A bargaining unit is generally determined on the basis of a "community of interest" of the employees.
- Once a union has been recognized (elected by a majority of the employees in the bargaining unit), then the union and the company begin to negotiate. The negotiations result in a collective bargaining agreement (CBA) which sets forth the terms and conditions of employment, including provisions in regard to rates of pay, hours of work, promotion, grievance procedures, and other terms of employment.
- An unfair labor practice may be filed by an employee, employer, labor union, or other person (such as a company impacted by a secondary boycott).
- After a charge is filed, the regional staff of the NLRB will investigate to determine whether an unfair labor practice has occurred. If a charge has merit, the regional director will first attempt a voluntary settlement. If this effort fails, then the case will be decided by an NLRB administrative law judge, and this decision can be appealed to the five-member NLRB.
- A grievance refers to a claim by an employee or the union that the employer is not complying with the terms of the CBA.
- Arbitration is the hearing and determining of a dispute or the settling of differences between parties by a person or persons chosen or agreed to by them.

What Do *You* Think?

1. Have you or has anyone you know ever been on strike? What was the experience like, and how was it resolved?
2. If you entered into a collective bargaining agreement with your employer, what would your demands be?
3. If you witnessed an employer trying to coerce your co-worker to vote against a union, would you report it?

12.5 Employee Rights

Learning Objectives

1. Recognize basic employee rights and the psychological contract.
2. Distinguish between right-to-work and employment-at-will doctrines.
3. Explain under what conditions an employee has a right to privacy.
4. Identify the elements of due process.

Psychological Contract

In addition to the right to join a union and engage in collective bargaining, there are other rights that apply to employees. **Employee rights** are guarantees of fair treatment that are granted to employees by legislation, judicial decisions, or employers. We have discussed some employee rights previously in the textbook, such as the right to freedom from discrimination and harassment, equal opportunity in the terms and conditions of employment, freedom from retaliation for filing a complaint against an employer, and compliance with wage and hour law provisions. In Chapter 13, we will also explore the right to a safe workplace free of unnecessary hazards such as dangerous working conditions or exposure to toxic substances. In this section, we will look at a few other aspects of employee rights including job protection, privacy, and due process.

When you accept a job, you probably have certain expectations about the relationship between you and your employer. This is sometimes referred to as the **psychological contract**. It is the set of promises or expectations that are exchanged between an employer and employee. For example, you might agree to give forty hours per week of your time, knowledge, skills, and abilities to an organization in exchange for a compensation package. But the psychological contract goes further than this. You also most likely want to be treated with dignity and respect and to not be demoted or fired without good cause.

The psychological contract is not legally mandated, but it has led to specific legislation and case law that governs job protection. The primary concepts in this regard are right-to-work, employment at will, privacy, free speech, wrongful discharge, and due process.

Right-to-Work

The **right-to-work** guarantees that no person can be compelled, as a condition of employment, to join or not to join, nor to pay dues to a labor union. Employees who join a union can cancel their membership at any time without being afraid of losing their jobs. There are no federal right-to-work laws. Section 14(b) of the Taft-Hartley act affirms the rights of states to enact right-to-work laws. In 2020, twenty-seven states had right-to-work laws, as shown in Figure 12.4.

employee rights

Guarantees of fair treatment that are granted to employees by legislation, judicial decisions, or employers.

psychological contract

The set of promises or expectations that are exchanged between an employer and employee.

right-to-work

A legal doctrine that means employees are entitled to work in unionized workplaces without actually joining the union or paying union dues.

FIGURE 12.4 Right-to-Work Laws by State

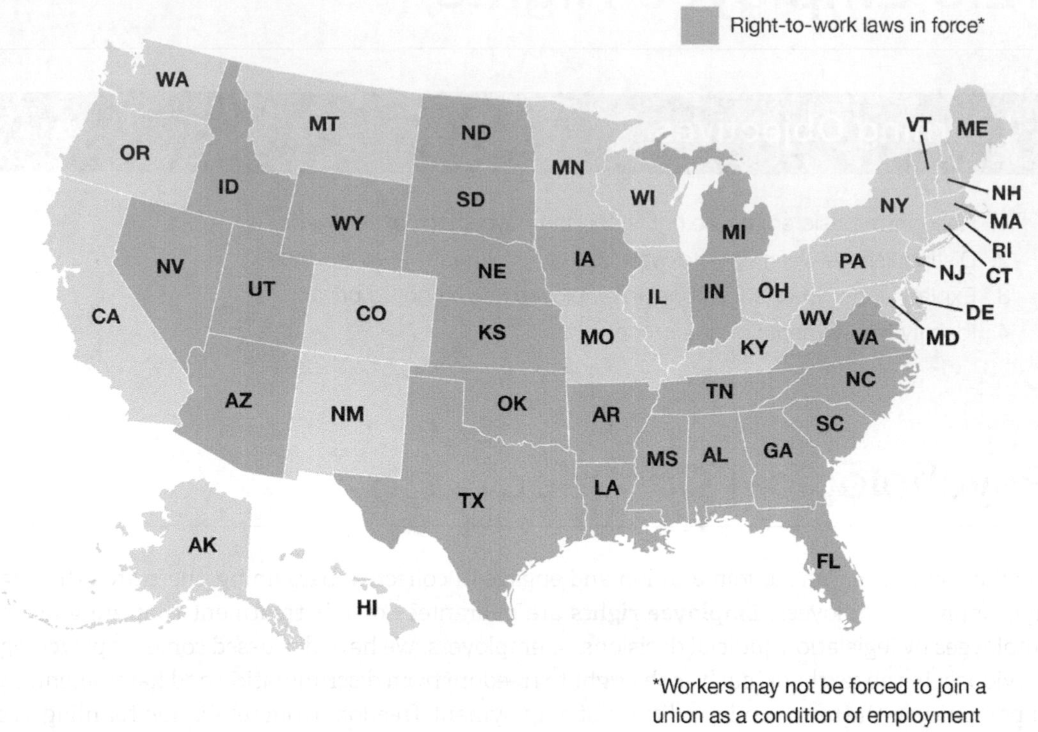

Right-to-work laws in force*

*Workers may not be forced to join a
union as a condition of employment

Source: Based on data from Economist.com

open shop

A unionized workplace in
which union membership
is optional.

closed shop

A unionized workplace in
which employees can be
required to join the union
and pay dues in order to
work there.

employment at will

A legal doctrine that states
the right of an employer to
fire an employee or the
right of an employee to
quit at any time, without
giving a reason.

wrongful discharge

The illegal termination of
an employee.

In a right-to-work state, a union workplace is considered an **open shop**, meaning union membership is optional. By contrast, a union workplace in a non-right-to-work state is a **closed shop**, meaning that in order to work in a union workplace, employees can be required to join the union and pay dues. Note that in an open shop, nonunion (or right-to-work) employees are still covered by the union, even though they are not members and are not paying dues.

Right-to-work is a controversial issue. Right-to-work proponents argue that it expands workers' rights, specifically to make their own decision whether to join a union.[32] On the other hand, opponents argue that right-to-work encourages freeloading because an employee can enjoy the advantages of union representation without paying dues.

The employment relationship has historically adhered to the common-law doctrine of **employment at will**. This is the right of an employer to fire an employee or the right of an employee to quit at any time, without giving a reason. In 1908 the Supreme Court upheld this doctrine in *Adair v. United States*, and this continues to be the standard in employment relationships, unless a contract exists that states otherwise. In addition to the existence of an employment contract, there are three main exceptions to this principle. If an employer violates one of these principles, then a **wrongful discharge** has occurred. A wrongful discharge is the illegal termination of an employee. Wrongful discharge can also occur when an employee is terminated for discriminatory reasons in violation of EEO laws or for engaging in union activity.

1. **Public policy exception.** This occurs when an employee is terminated for refusing to commit a crime, for reporting criminal activity to government authorities, or for disclosing unethical or unsafe employer practices.

2. **Implied contract.** This occurs when the employer has implied either in writing or orally, that an employee has a guarantee of employment for a specific period of time, and the employee relies on this as a term and condition of employment.

3. **Implied covenant.** This occurs when the employer has acted without good faith and fair dealing. Examples of this are when an employer terminates an employee to avoid paying commissions on sales or takes actions intended to make an employee quit.

Privacy

In most states, employees have certain privacy rights in the workplace. This applies to personal possessions, including handbags, backpacks, briefcases, storage lockers accessible only by the employee, and private mail addressed only to the employee.[33] Employees may also have a right to privacy in their telephone conversations, voicemail, email, or messages while using their personal phone, computer, or mobile device. However, employees generally do not have a right to privacy when using the employer's phones or computers.

Employees are considered to have a reasonable expectation of privacy. What is considered reasonable can vary significantly from one person to another, and for this reason employers may want to develop a clear policy addressing workplace privacy issues and communicate this policy to employees.[34] There is also one federal law that applies to privacy and monitoring. The **Electronic Communications Privacy Act of 1986 (ECPA)** was passed as an amendment to the federal Wiretap Act. The act prohibits interception of electronic and wire communications, which include "any aural transfer made in whole or in part through the use of facilities for the transmission of communications by the aid of wire, cable, or other like connection" and "any oral communication uttered by a person exhibiting an expectation that such communication is not subject to interception under circumstances justifying such expectation."[35] This includes any conversation where there is the expectation that no third party is listening.

However, the ECPA contains several exceptions to intercepting and monitoring employees' oral, wire, and electronic communications. The first is known as the **business purpose exception**, which permits employers to monitor oral and electronic employee communications when there is a legitimate business purpose. The second is the **consent exception**, which occurs when the employee gives the organization permission to monitor their communications.

Why might an employer want to monitor company email, computer usage, or phone calls, or use video surveillance of the workplace? The answer has to do with issues related to workplace violence, property theft, and on-the-job accidents and injuries. Employers have a duty of care to provide a safe workplace, and a legitimate business purpose to reduce its risk of loss from theft (either of property or trade secrets such as customer lists, patents, etc.). While guarding against these risks, and performing its duty of care, an organization needs to balance its business reasons with the reasonable expectation of privacy by its employees.

HR should ensure that all employee monitoring is narrowly tailored and supported by a legitimate business justification.[36] Advising employees that they will be monitored removes employees' reasonable expectation of privacy, which is the element that most often forms the basis of invasion-of-privacy lawsuits.

Electronic Communications Privacy Act of 1986 (ECPA)

An act passed by Congress in 1986 which prohibits interception of electronic and wire communications.

business purpose exception

An exception to the ECPA that permits employers to monitor oral and electronic employee communications when there is a legitimate business purpose.

consent exception

An exception to the ECPA that occurs when the employee gives the organization permission to monitor their communications.

Due Process

No matter how careful and diligent you are in recruiting and selecting qualified employees, there are occasions when an employee has to be disciplined or even fired. Figure 12.5 lists some of the most common behavior problems that lead to disciplinary actions. Fortunately, these are exceptions to the rule. There are legal principles that HR managers should be familiar with that impact all decisions to discipline or discharge an employee. **Discipline**, as the term is used in HR, refers to methods used to correct the behavior of employees to help them perform better. The word discipline has negative connotations to most people, and many think of it as a form of punishment for doing something wrong. But in management and HR, it should primarily be used as a technique to bring about positive changes in an employee's performance. For this reason, it is sometimes referred to as positive discipline.

discipline

Refers to methods used to correct the behavior of employees to help them perform better.

FIGURE 12.5 Common Employee Behavior Problems

Attendance Issues	Inappropriate Behaviors	Performance Problems
• Chronic absenteeism • Unexcused absences • Chronic tardiness • Leaving early without permission • Not returning on time from lunch or other breaks	• Sexual harassment • Bullying • Insubordination • Horseplay • Fighting • Smoking in unauthorized areas • Illegal substance abuse • Intoxication • Verbal abuse of co-workers • Failure to use PPE • Threats or intimidation • Unauthorized possession of weapons • Theft	• Poor quality • Slow pace • Forgetfulness • Missing deadlines

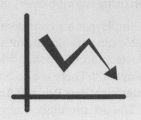

HR in the Real World: The Case of the Missing Batteries

We wondered why deliveries of batteries for one of our largest customers kept coming up short. These were consumer batteries (sizes AAA, AA, C, and D) and were shipped on pallets with shrink wrap around them. Therefore, stealing a box of batteries would be difficult to do without getting caught. We also had an alarm system after hours, so the theft had to be happening during the day (or so we thought). But it was not boxes of batteries that were turning up missing; it was entire pallets. We put our warehouse manager in charge of the investigation, and for a while there were no missing pallets, but also no leads in the investigation. After a few months, pallets started to go missing again. One day the FBI showed up and wanted to interview our warehouse manager in the conference room. He was interviewed for about an hour, and then was escorted out in handcuffs.

The warehouse manager had confessed to the FBI. He had been coming in at night, turning off the alarm system, loading a pallet of batteries into a delivery truck, and then dropping them off in his garage. He would then sell the batteries to salvage companies. The moral of this real HR story: when employee theft becomes a problem, never rule out the person who is conducting the investigation, especially if they have keys to the facility and the alarm code!

due process

A legal doctrine that states that employees have the right to be informed of unsatisfactory performance and have a right to defend themselves and improve before an adverse employment action is taken.

In any disciplinary action, employees have a right to **due process**, which means recognizing the employee's right to be informed of unsatisfactory performance, and their right to defend themselves and improve before an adverse employment action is taken. You might be thinking: Wait . . . I thought that employers have the right to terminate employment at any time, under the employment-at-will doctrine. And that is true. These are two competing legal doctrines (employment at will versus due process). On the one hand, employers have the right to adjust the size and skillsets of their workforce according to business necessity. But this does not mean that employers can terminate an employee for cause without providing the employee due process. The elements of due process are:

1. The employee must understand the job expectations, performance standards, and work rules.
2. The employee must understand the consequences of failing to meet performance standards or violating a work rule. The employer should be consistent in application of its standards and rules.
3. The discipline should be appropriate for the offense. Occasional minor problems should not warrant termination.
4. The employee should be given the opportunity to respond and give his or her side of the issue.
5. The employee should be given a reasonable period of time to improve performance (except for severe violations, which might result in immediate termination). Some organizations will place an employee on a **performance improvement plan (PIP)** which outlines the performance problem, the improvement necessary, and the time frame within which the employee must correct their performance or be terminated.

One common approach to employee performance or behavior problems is **progressive discipline**. This is the process of applying corrective measures in varying degrees in which each step is more severe. For example, if an employee in manufacturing is performing work that is substandard in quality, a progressive process might look like this:

- **First infraction.** Oral warning from supervisor.
- **Second infraction.** Written reprimand from supervisor.
- **Third infraction.** Placed on ninety-day PIP.
- **Fourth infraction.** Termination.

One final perspective should be considered, and that involves very egregious actions by an employee. Due process applies to many performance issues, but the law and the courts recognize that there are severe actions that employees can take that should result in immediate termination, including theft of company property, fighting, threatening other employees, customers, or vendors, or incarceration causing them to be unable to attend work.

---

performance improvement plan (PIP)

A document which outlines a performance problem, the improvement necessary, and the time frame within which the employee must correct their performance or be terminated.

progressive discipline

The process of applying corrective measures in varying degrees in which each step is more severe.

Key Takeaways

- Employee rights are guarantees of fair treatment that are granted to employees by legislation, judicial decisions, or employers.
- A psychological contract is the set of promises or expectations that are exchanged between an employer and employee.
- The right-to-work means that employees are entitled to work in unionized workplaces without actually joining the union or paying union dues.
- In a right-to-work state, a union workplace is considered an open shop, meaning union membership is optional. By contrast, a union workplace in a non-right-to-work state is a closed shop, meaning that in order to work in a union workplace, employees can be required to join the union and pay dues.
- Employment at will is the right of an employer to fire an employee or the right of an employee to quit at any time, without giving a reason.
- The Electronic Communications Privacy Act of 1986 (ECPA) was passed as an amendment to the federal Wiretap Act. The act prohibits interception of electronic and wire communications.
- The business purpose exception permits employers to monitor oral and electronic employee communications when there is a legitimate business purpose, and the consent exception occurs when the employee gives the organization permission to monitor their communications.
- Discipline, as the term is used in HR, refers to methods used to correct the behavior of employees to help them perform better.

- In any disciplinary action, employees have a right to due process, which means recognizing the employee's right to be informed of unsatisfactory performance and have a right to defend themselves and improve before an adverse employment action is taken.
- Progressive discipline is the process of applying corrective measures to varying degrees in which each step is more severe.

What Do *You* Think?

1. How would you describe the psychological contract for your current or former job?
2. Do you think that right-to-work laws are a good idea? Why or why not?
3. Have you ever worked in an environment where you were being monitored? Did it ever bother you, or did it feel like an invasion of privacy? Or was it for a legitimate business purpose?

12.6 Conclusion

This chapter began with an overview of labor relations: why employees unionize, some historical perspectives, and current trends in unionization. The federal laws governing labor relations were introduced, and the labor relations processes for elections, bargaining, and resolving grievances were examined. The legal rights of employees were then discussed, including job protection and privacy. The chapter concluded with an overview of due process and disciplinary procedures.

Answers to Test Your Labor Relations Know-How

1. No. Applicants are considered as employees and, as such, are protected under the law.
2. No. Individual questioning of employees about their union membership or activities is unlawful.
3. No. Except in specific situations (for example, to promote safety), employees have the right to wear union insignia.
4. Yes.
5. Yes. Blacklisting of job applicants or employees is against labor law.
6. No. During an organizing drive, an employer cannot promise improvements in wages or benefits as a means of defeating the union.
7. Yes. Both employers and unions are subject to unfair labor practice charges.
8. No. Employees are allowed union representation during disciplinary hearings.
9. Yes. Employees can be disciplined or discharged for work-related misconduct but not solely because of their union affiliations or union sentiments.
10. Yes. Antiunion remarks are not unlawful, provided they are not coercive.

Theory-into-Practice (TIP) Exercises

1. Using any of the links under the Resources section, find two or three labor relations cases that have been filed with the NLRB. What could the company or the union have done to avoid this charge being filed?

2. With a classmate, have a debate on labor relations, with one of you representing labor (a union) and the other representing management (a company).

3. Working individually or in teams, select three different unions to research, and then report on the following:

   a. History of the union.

   b. Memberships (types of employees represented and how many).

   c. The union leadership structure.

   d. National officers.

   e. List of the employers with whom they have a CBA.

   f. Benefits the union provides to employees.

   g. Union dues.

Case Study: Don't Drop into my Dropbox

Source: Koshiro K / Shutterstock.com

Many employers maintain policies that limit employee rights to privacy on company-owned devices, but due to a recent court decision, these may not always protect employers from invasion of privacy claims. On March 19, 2019, Judge Kim R. Gibson partially denied a public employer's motion to dismiss, permitting the plaintiff Elizabeth Frankhouser's claim for Fourth Amendment violations as well as her state law claim for invasion of privacy.

The plaintiff was an executive director for an educational facility (the defendant) in Pennsylvania. Her job required extensive work on her work-issued computer, and she used Dropbox often to store files. Dropbox is an application that allows people to store files on the cloud using a username and password. In the plaintiff's case, her Dropbox account was personal, but her employer allowed her to store work-related files on it. Thus, her Dropbox account contained both personal and private files.

The plaintiff's employer's IT administrator, Tim Walk, used Ms. Frankhouser's username and password to access her Dropbox (he knew she kept this information on a spreadsheet). He discovered some private photographs of the plaintiff's boyfriend which could be deemed explicit, and also of the plaintiff at parties. The superintendent of the facility was made aware of the photos, and Ms. Frankhouser was forced to resign, and subsequently filed the lawsuit.

Ultimately, the court determined that Ms. Frankhouser did, in fact, have a reasonable expectation of privacy with respect to her personal Dropbox material for the following reasons: (1) it was her own private account, (2) it was password-protected, and (3) plaintiff never accessed or downloaded the photographs while on the employer's system. As such, the court declined to dismiss the Fourth Amendment and invasion of privacy claims.[37]

 Privacy Rights versus Employee Tracking

Employment law attorney Dan Eaton discusses the circumstances under which employers in California can legally monitor employees.

View the video online at: http://www.youtube.com/embed/U-mqdz-20Xs?rel=0

Case Discussion Questions

1. Do you agree with the court's decision? Why or why not?
2. Have you ever been reprimanded or fired because of something your employer discovered in your private life? Was it fair?
3. In light of this case, as an HR manager, how would you structure employee privacy policies?

Resources

1. **National Labor Relations Board.** The official website of the NLRB, including many helpful resources such as cases, publications, e-filing for charges and petitions, and guidance documents.

   https://www.nlrb.gov/

2. **Labor Relations Today.** Publishes legal updates on NLRB cases and other labor issues.

   https://www.laborrelationstoday.com/

3. **Labor Relations Institute.** Resources for companies with a current union contract or undergoing a union campaign, including tips for creating a positive work culture to avoid unionization attempts.

   https://lrionline.com/

Endnotes

1. Case written by Carter, A. (2019). Adapted from Oil refinery strike widens to largest U.S. plant. *Huffpost*. Retrieved from https://www.huffpost.com/entry/us-refinery-strike-wide_n_6727736

2. Friedman, B., Abraham, S., & Thomas, R. (2006). Factors related to employees' desire to join and leave unions. *Industrial Relations: A Journal of Economy and Society, 45*(1), 102-110.

3. Ibid.

4. Goldfield, M., & Bromsen, A. (2013). The changing landscape of US unions in historical and theoretical perspective. *Annual Review of Political Science, 16*, 231-257. See also Blanchflower, D., & Bryson, G. (2004). What effect do unions have on wages now and would Freeman and Medoff be surprised? *Journal of Labor Research, 25*(3), 383-414. See also Card, D. (1996). The effect of unions on the structure of wages: A longitudinal analysis. *Econometrica, 64*(4), 957-979.

5. Flavin, P., & Shufeldt, G. (2016). Labor union membership and life satisfaction in the united states. *Labor Studies Journal, 41*(2), 171-184.

6. DeSilver, D. (2014). American unions membership declines as public support fluctuates. *Pew Research Center*. Retrieved from https://www.pewresearch.org/fact-tank/2014/02/20/for-american-unions-membership-trails-far-behind-public-support/

7. Kimeldorf, H. (2013). Worker replacement costs and unionization: Origins of the U.S. labor movement. *American Sociological Review, 78*(6), 1033-1062.

8. Ibid.

9. DeSilver, D. (2014). American unions membership declines as public support fluctuates. *Pew Research Center*. Retrieved from https://www.pewresearch.org/fact-tank/2014/02/20/for-american-unions-membership-trails-far-behind-public-support/

10. Bureau of Labor Statistics. *Union members—2018*. Retrieved December 20, 2019 from https://www.bls.gov/news.release/pdf/union2.pdf

11. Ibid.

12. Nagele-Piazza, L. (2019). Judge says Tesla CEO's tweet violated federal labor law. *Society for Human Resource Management*. Retrieved from https://www.shrm.org/resourcesandtools/legal-and-compliance/employment-law/pages/judge-says-tesla-ceo-tweet-violated-federal-labor-law.aspx

13. Rhodes, D. (2019). We wanted a union then, and we deserved a union then: University of Chicago grad student workers go on strike. *Chicago Tribune*. Retrieved from https://www.chicagotribune.com/news/breaking/ct-met-university-of-chicago-graduate-student-strike-20190604-story.html

14. Smith, A. (2019). NLRB proposed that college student workers can't organize unions. *Society for Human Resource Management*. Retrieved from https://www.shrm.org/resourcesandtools/legal-and-compliance/employment-law/pages/nlrb-proposed-rule-student-workers.aspx

15. National Labor Relations Board. *Impact of the NLRB on professional sports*. Retrieved October 25, 2019 from https://www.nlrb.gov/about-nlrb/who-we-are/our-history/impact-nlrb-professional-sports

16. Ibid.

17. Pennsylvania Federation. *The Railway Labor Act simplified*. Retrieved April 10, 2020 from http://www.pennfedbmwe.org/Docs/reference/RLA_Simplified.html

18. Tulk, L.C. (2004). The 1926 Railway Labor Act and the modern American airline industry: Changes and chaos outline the need for revised legislation. *Journal of Air Law and Commerce, 69*(3), 8. Retrieved from https://scholar.smu.edu/cgi/viewcontent.cgi?article=1709&context=jalc

19. Belke, D. (2013). Blitzing Brady: Should section 4(A) of the Norris-LaGuardia act shield management from injunctions in labor disputes? *Columbia Law Review, 113*(1), 53-96.

20. National Labor Relations Board. (2015). *80 years of protecting employee rights*. Retrieved October 26, 2019 from https://www.nlrb.gov/sites/default/files/attachments/basic-page/node-1536/NLRB 80th Anniversary.pdf

21. National Labor Relations Board. (2015). *80 years of protecting employee rights*. Retrieved October 26, 2019 from https://www.nlrb.gov/sites/default/files/attachments/basic-page/node-1536/NLRB 80th Anniversary.pdf

22. National Labor Relations Board. *Are you covered?* Retrieved April 10, 2020 from https://www.nlrb.gov/rights-we-protect/whats-law/employees/i-am-represented-union/are-you-covered

23. National Labor Relations Board. (2015). 80 years of protecting employee rights. Retrieved October 26, 2019 from https://www.nlrb.gov/sites/default/files/attachments/basic-page/node-1536/NLRB 80th Anniversary.pdf

24. Lavin, H.S., and DiMichele, E.E. (2013). Can something intangible be a "thing of value"? The permissibility of neutrality agreements under the Labor Management Relations Act. *Employee Relations Law Journal, (39)*1, 88-71.

25. Witwer, D. (2002). The Landrum-Griffin Act: A case study in the possibilities and problems in anti-union corruption law. *Criminal Justice Review, 27*(2), 301-320.

26. Court draws line against union hotel boycotts: National Labor Relations Act bans "secondary boycotts." (2014). *Holland and Knight*. Retrieved from https://www.jdsupra.com/legalnews/court-draws-line-against-union-hotel-boy-92594/

27. National Labor Relations Act: The right to join a union and bargain collectively. (2015). *Congressional Digest, 94*(6), 2-2.

28. Nagele-Piazza, L. (2019). Labor board rejects Boeing workers' micro-bargaining unit. *Society for Human Resource Management*. Retrieved from https://www.shrm.org/resourcesandtools/legal-and-compliance/employment-law/pages/labor-board-rejects-micro-bargaining-unit-at-boeing.aspx

29. Ibid.

30. LaRocco, J.B. (2004). Ambiguities in labor contracts: Where do they come from? *Dispute Resolution Journal, 59*(1), 38-41.

31. Labor Relations Analytics Intern. (2019). *Lensa*. Retrieved from https://lensa.com/labor-relations-analytics-intern-spring-2020-jobs/dallas/jd/2a6ee35f1d7b9ed22fea586507a2d268

32. Niznik, J.S. (2019). Learn about right-to-work laws. *The Balance Careers*. Retrieved from https://www.thebalancecareers.com/right-to-work-2071691

33. Employee rights 101. *Findlaw*. Retrieved April 10, 2020 from https://employment.findlaw.com/employment-discrimination/employees-rights-101.html

34. Bruce, S. (2013). 11 common workplace privacy issues. *HR Daily Advisor*. Retrieved from https://hrdailyadvisor.blr.com/2013/12/11/11-common-workplace-privacy-issues-and-4-common-law-claims-2/

35. Electronic Privacy Information Center. *Electronic Communications Privacy Act (ECPA)*. Retrieved April 10, 2020 from https://epic.org/privacy/ecpa/

36. Society for Human Resource Management (2019). *Managing workplace monitoring and surveillance*. Retrieved from https://www.shrm.org/resourcesandtools/tools-and-samples/toolkits/pages/workplaceprivacy.aspx

37. Case written by Crews, P. (2020). Adapted from Shea, R. (2019). When monitoring employees' computer activity, don't overreach. *Lexology*. Retrieved from https://www.lexology.com/library/detail.aspx?g=0f1f5a9f-a0dd-4258-bc16-07e83631fda8

CHAPTER 13
Workplace Health, Safety, and Security

Learning Objectives

After reading this chapter, you should be able to do the following:

1. Identify the federal legislation and regulations that govern workplace safety and health.
2. Recognize the major occupational risks to employee health and design strategies to mitigate these risks.
3. Develop a workplace security plan, addressing awareness, preparedness, and emergency procedures.

Workplace health and safety is an area that is subject to numerous federal laws and regulations that HR managers should be familiar with. Beyond the legal requirements, managers have a moral and ethical responsibility to ensure a healthy and safe work environment. It also makes good business sense. Effective health and safety programs can reduce workplace injuries and illnesses, saving lost work time, medical expenses, and legal costs. Workplace security plans are important in protecting employees, customers, and others that might be onsite.

The chapter begins by reviewing federal legislation and regulations governing workplace health and safety, including guidelines for compliance. Strategies for creating a culture of safety also will be explored. Then employee health issues such as cumulative trauma disorders and exposure to toxic chemicals are examined. The chapter closes with a discussion of emergency preparedness including pandemics and workplace security awareness.

13.1 Opening Case: The Best Laid Plans . . .

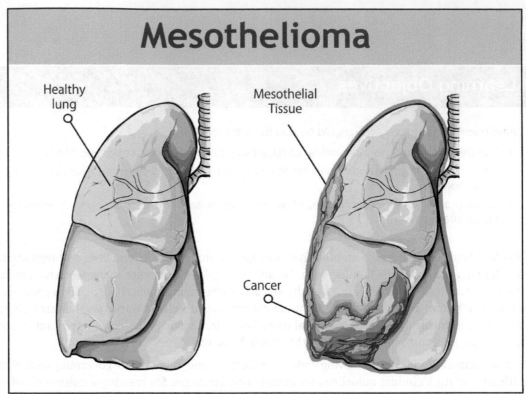

Source: © Shutterstock, Inc.

Pleural mesothelioma is a cancer of the protective lining of the lung, known as the pleura. It is caused by inhaling asbestos fibers into the lungs. Most pleural mesothelioma cases have been attributed to on-the-job exposure to asbestos. Occupational exposure has been most common in construction, shipyard, and mining workers. According to World Health Organization estimates, 125 million people have been exposed in the workplace to asbestos, and there are more than 100 million reported occupational deaths from diseases such as lung cancer, mesothelioma, and asbestosis.

When workers are exposed to asbestos without taking proper safety measures, the microscopic fibers circulate in the air and are inhaled into the lungs. Unlike other particles, these fibers are not easily expelled from the lungs. The inhaled asbestos becomes trapped and accumulates in the lungs over time. The fibers penetrate the lung tissue and enter the pleura, the protective layers of tissue that protect the lungs. This scarring worsens and impairs the lungs over time and can cause cancer.

Starting in the late 1800s, when Canadian companies began mining asbestos, many industries embraced the fibrous mineral for its resistance to heat, flame, and electrical and chemical damage. These qualities and affordability motivated many companies to incorporate asbestos into thousands of consumer and industrial products such as textiles, building materials, and insulation. Until the 1960s, the public knew little or nothing about the lethal consequences of working with asbestos. By the 1970s, about 200,000 Americans made their living manufacturing asbestos products. Many of these workers handled the material on a daily basis, in poorly ventilated areas, with no safety equipment. Many buildings, including schools, were constructed with materials made of asbestos, such as ceiling and floor tiles and drywall. The intent was good, because the belief was that the fire-retardant asbestos would protect schoolchildren, teachers, and staff in the event of a fire. But instead, hundreds of thousands of students and faculty were exposed to asbestos.

There has been a dramatic reduction in the use of asbestos products in industrial settings, but workers are still being exposed by demolishing asbestos-contaminated buildings and repairing automotive parts that also contain the substance. It is imperative for workers in the construction and automotive repair industries, as well as some others, to make sure that employers are actively promoting safety measures to avoid or limit exposure of asbestos to their employees.[1]

Mesothelioma: Causes, Signs and Symptoms, Diagnosis and Treatment

Mesothelioma is a type of cancer that develops from the thin layer of tissue that covers many of the internal organs (known as the mesothelium). More than 80% of mesothelioma cases are caused by exposure to asbestos.

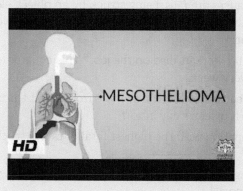

View the video online at: http://www.youtube.com/embed/18Db8qZYosl?rel=0

Case Discussion Questions

1. Have you or anyone you know been exposed to asbestos or other dangerous products in the workplace? Were proper safety measures in place?
2. There are occupations that require employees to work with toxic chemicals. What would be the first steps you would take to assure them that your company is taking their safety seriously?
3. There have been hundreds of thousands of lawsuits regarding mesothelioma or asbestos-related illnesses in the workplace. How can companies protect themselves from lawsuits for occupational illnesses?

13.2 Workplace Safety

Learning Objectives

1. Explain the major employer requirements of the Occupational Safety and Health Act (OSH).

2. Describe the research and resources provided by the National Institute for Occupational Safety and Health.
3. Identify the leadership strategies that can create a culture of safety.

Occupational Safety and Health Act (OSH)

The construction industry accounts for one in five worker deaths, with falls being the most common cause of injury.

Source: © Shutterstock, Inc.

Consider the following facts about workplace safety in the U.S.:

- Every seven seconds, a worker is injured on the job.[2]
- Construction accounts for a little over 20%, or one in five, worker deaths. The leading causes are falls, being struck by an object, electrocution, and caught-in/between incidents. Eliminating these "Fatal Four" would save 582 workers' lives every year.[3]
- In 2017, 5,147 workers died on the job.[4] This equates to about ninety-nine worker deaths every week.
- Worker deaths are down on average, from about thirty-eight worker deaths a day in 1970 to fourteen a day in 2017.[5]
- The occupation with the highest fatality rate is trucking, with 918 driver deaths in 2016.[6]
- Overexertion (including lifting, lowering, and repetitive motion) was the most common cause of workplace injury in 2017.[7]

These facts contain some tragic and perhaps frightening information. The opening case illustrates the potential chronic and even terminal illness that can occur from exposure to toxic substances. But there also is good news in that fatal workplace injuries are down 68% from 1970, which happens to be the year that the Occupational Safety and Health Act was passed.

Occupational Safety and Health Act (OSH)

An act passed by Congress in 1970 to assure safe and healthful working conditions for working men and women and to authorize enforcement of the standards developed under the act.

The **Occupational Safety and Health Act (OSH)** was passed by Congress in 1970. As stated in the preamble of the act, the purpose of the legislation is:[8]

To assure safe and healthful working conditions for working men and women; by authorizing enforcement of the standards developed under the Act; by assisting and encouraging the States in their efforts to assure safe and healthful working conditions; by providing for research, information, education, and training in the field of occupational safety and health; and for other purposes.

Occupational Safety and Health Administration (OSHA)

A federal agency that is part of the Department of Labor and enforces the provisions of the OSH.

The act also created the **Occupational Safety and Health Administration (OSHA)**. OSHA is part of the Department of Labor.[9] OSHA covers most private-sector employers and their workers, in addition to some public-sector employers, in the fifty states and some other federal jurisdictions. These other jurisdictions include the District of Columbia, Puerto Rico, the Virgin Islands, American Samoa, Guam, Northern Mariana Islands, Wake Island, Johnson Island, and the Outer Continental Shelf Lands.[10]

Table 13.1 summarizes employer responsibilities, and Table 13.2 summarizes employee rights under the OSH.[11]

TABLE 13.1 Employer OSHA Responsibilities

Employer OSHA Responsibilities
• Follow all relevant OSHA safety and health standards.
• Find and correct safety and health hazards.
• Inform employees about chemical hazards through training, labels, alarms, color-coded systems, chemical information sheets, and other methods.
• Notify OSHA within eight hours of a workplace fatality or within twenty-four hours of any work-related inpatient hospitalization, amputation, or loss of an eye (1-800-321-OSHA[6742], or https://www.osha.gov/report).
• Provide required personal protective equipment at no cost to workers.
• Keep accurate records of work-related injuries and illnesses.
• Post OSHA citations, injuries, and illness summary data, and the *OSHA Job Safety and Health—It's the Law* poster in the workplace where workers will see them.
• Not retaliate against any worker for using their rights under the law.

TABLE 13.2 Employee OSHA Rights

Employee OSHA Rights
• Working conditions that do not post a risk of serious harm.
• Receive information and training (in a language workers can understand) about chemical and other hazards, methods to prevent harm, and OSHA standards that apply to their workplace.
• Review records of work-related injuries and illnesses.
• Get copies of test results done to find and measure hazards in the workplace.
• File a complaint asking OSHA to inspect their workplace if they believe there is a serious hazard or that their employer is not following OSHA rules. When requested, OSHA will keep all identities confidential.
• Use their rights under the law without retaliation. If an employee is fired, demoted, transferred or retaliated against in any way for using their rights under the law, they can file a complaint with OSHA. This complaint must be filed within thirty days of the alleged retaliation.

OSHA standards are rules that describe the methods employers are legally required to follow to protect their workers from hazards.[12] OSHA standards are developed through an extensive process that includes public engagement, notice, and comment. Before a standard can be implemented, OSHA must show that a significant risk to workers exists and that there are feasible measures employers can take to protect their workers. Figure 13.1 shows the OSHA standards which are most commonly violated by employers.

OSHA standards

Rules that describe the methods employers are legally required to follow to protect their workers from hazards.

FIGURE 13.1 OSHA: Top Ten Most-Cited Violations of Standards

Fall protection, construction

Hazard communication standard, general industry

Scaffolding, general requirements, construction

Control of hazardous energy (lockout/tagout), general industry

Respiratory protection, general industry

Ladders, construction

Powered industrial trucks, general industry

Fall protection–training requirements

Machinery and machine guarding, general requirements

Eye and face protection

Source: OSHA

OSHA requires covered employers with ten or more employees to keep a record of work-related injuries or illnesses, although minor injuries requiring first aid only do not need to be reported. OSHA defines a reportable injury or illness as:[13]

- Any work-related fatality.
- Any work-related injury or illness that results in loss of consciousness, days away from work, restricted work, or transfer to another job.
- Any work-related injury or illness requiring medical treatment beyond first aid.
- Any work-related diagnosed case of cancer, chronic irreversible diseases, fractured or cracked bones or teeth, and punctured eardrums.
- In addition, there are special recording criteria for work-related cases involving: needlesticks and sharps injuries, medical removal, hearing loss, and tuberculosis.

Injury and illness records must be maintained at the worksite for a minimum of five years. There are three major OSHA forms with which employers should be familiar:

- **OSHA Form 300.** Log of Work-related Injuries and Illnesses (commonly referred to as the OSHA log, and must be maintained at the worksite). See Figure 13.2 for an example.

- **OSHA Form 300A.** Summary of Work-related Injuries and Illnesses (an annual summary which must be completed between February and April of each year and made available to employees).

- **OSHA Form 301.** Injury and Illness Accident Report (used to report reportable incidents to OSHA).

FIGURE 13.2 OSHA Form 300

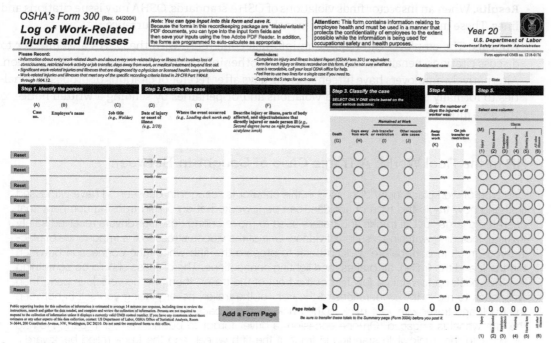

Source: OSHA, https://www.osha.gov/recordkeeping/osha-rkforms-winstr_fillable.pdf.

OSHA standards and regulations are enforced through a combination of reporting, inspections, investigations, citations, and fines. OSHA normally conducts inspections without advance notice, although employers have the right to require OSHA compliance officers to obtain an inspection warrant before entering the worksite. OSHA seeks to focus its inspection resources on the most hazardous workplaces in the following order of priority:[14]

1. Imminent danger situations.

2. Severe injuries and illnesses based on OSHA reports (Forms 300A and 301).

3. Worker complaints.

4. Referrals of hazards from other federal, state, or local agencies, individuals, organizations, or the media.

5. Targeted inspections aimed at high-hazard industries or individual workplaces.

6. Follow-up inspections.

It is helpful for HR and line managers to know what will occur during an OSHA inspection. For lower-priority hazards, OSHA may call the employer to discuss safety and health concerns. The employer then has five days to respond in writing, identifying any problems found and corrective action taken. When OSHA conducts an onsite investigation, the following steps will occur:[15]

- **Presentation of credentials.** The onsite inspection begins with the presentation of the compliance officer's credentials.

- **Opening conference.** The compliance officer will explain why OSHA selected the workplace for inspection and describe the inspection process. The employer then selects a representative to accompany the compliance officer during the inspection. An authorized employee representative, if any, also has the right to accompany the inspector.

- **Walkaround.** The compliance officer and the representatives will walk through the portions of the workplace covered by the inspection, inspecting for hazards. The compliance officer will also review worksite injury and illness records and may point out some apparent violations that can be corrected immediately.

- **Closing conference.** The compliance officer holds a closing conference with the employer and employee representatives to discuss the findings and possible courses of action an employer might take, including the right to contest citations and proposed penalties.

- **Results.** When an inspector finds violations of OSHA standards, OSHA may issue citations and fines. These must be issued within six months of the violation's occurrence.

- **Appeals.** The employer can request an informal conference with the OSHA area director to discuss citations, penalties, abatement dates, or other information pertinent to the inspection. Alternatively, employers have fifteen working days after receipt of citations or proposed penalties to formally contest the alleged violations and/or penalties by sending a written notice to the area director.

HR in the Real World: A Tragic Case of Caught-In/Between

One type of workplace injury discussed in this chapter is "caught-in/between." I have witnessed firsthand how tragic this type of accident can be. I worked at an oilfield trucking company that operated a large fleet of trucks and trailers used to move drilling rigs. Our drivers received safety training, including watching a series of videos. One of the videos stressed the importance of placing your truck in park before walking back to prepare the fifth wheel (the connection between the truck and the trailer), air brakes, and lighting connections. The process should go something like this: back up to within a few feet of the front of the trailer, then put the vehicle in park, then walk back to make the preparations at the front of the trailer, never placing yourself in between the truck and trailer with your back to the truck, then get back into the vehicle and back up until the fifth wheel is engaged. On one occasion, a driver forgot to put his vehicle in park. He had his back to the truck while standing in front of the fifth wheel, and the truck rolled backwards, pinning him against the fifth wheel and causing his death. Perhaps the worst part of this is that the driver's father was the terminal manager and happened to be looking out the window when this happened and witnessed the entire event. It is a tragic reminder that safety training is not enough. Companies need to create a culture of safety, where it is always on employees' minds.

The National Institute for Occupational Safety and Health

The National Institute for Occupational Safety and Health (NIOSH)

A federal government agency that conducts research and makes recommendations for the prevention of work-related injury and illnesses.

The National Institute for Occupational Safety and Health (NIOSH) is a federal government agency that conducts research and makes recommendations for the prevention of work-related injuries and illnesses. NIOSH was established by the OSH of 1970, and is part of the U.S. Centers for Disease Control and Prevention (CDC), under the U.S. Department of Health and Human Services. NIOSH has a mandate to "assure every man and woman in the Nation safe and healthful working conditions and to preserve our human resources."[16] NIOSH employs over 1,300 experts in fields including medicine, nursing, industrial hygiene, safety, psychology, chemistry, and epidemiology.

NIOSH research is primarily driven by the **National Occupational Research Agenda (NORA)**. The NORA research priorities are influenced by:[17]

- The number of workers at risk for a particular injury or illness.
- The seriousness of a hazard or problem.
- The chance that new data or approaches can make a difference.

National Occupational Research Agenda (NORA)

A partnership program developed by NIOSH to stimulate innovative research and improve workplace practices.

Creating a Culture of Safety

Up to this point in the chapter, one might realize that the focus has been on compliance with government regulations, and research and resources provided by the government to prevent workplace injury and illnesses. But there is an important aspect of workplace safety that HR professionals should be focused on, and it is probably more important than complying with OSHA regulations. What we are referring to here is the importance of creating a culture of safety.

HR Talk: Dr. Louis Carfagno

Adjunct Professor

Embry-Riddle Aeronautical University

As a human resources professional, it is paramount to understand safety culture and loss prevention. The hallmark of the most effective safety programs is the belief that it is always better to prevent an incident than to investigate an accident. In pursuit of this goal, successful HR managers stay on top of safety and loss prevention data. They typically track key data on a regular basis, often by using an informational dashboard. It is important to note that:

- Health and safety are usually the responsibility of an organization's human resources department. Therefore, a human resources professional must understand and be willing to lead on matters of health, safety, and the work environment. To be successful, the HR professional must also enlist the assistance and secure the cooperation of all supervisors, managers, and employees within the organization to achieve a common safety goal.
- The HR professional should promote a safe work environment that helps prevent accidents and incidents within the organization. As a result the HR partner and safety manager in particular need to work together in promoting a positive, safety-first environment.
- Data analytics provide a picture of both lagging and leading safety indicators. Lagging safety indicators include injuries in the workplace, accidents, employee lost time and days away from work. On the other hand, leading safety indicators include safety meetings, programs, and awareness just to name a few.

Effectively reducing workplace injuries and illnesses is about being proactive instead of reactive. To accomplish the key goal of injury reduction, one of the major challenges includes creating a positive safety culture that holds all employees accountable for their actions. While managers must respond to negative safety incidents, at the same time they should also be mindful about developing strategies that encourage positive safety behavior. For example, rewarding employees when they are "caught in the act" of doing the right thing from a safety perspective can be an effective way to encourage desired behaviors. Whatever strategies they employ, HR professionals should always keep in mind that an organization must comply with OSHA rules and regulations when implementing plans to improve operations safety.

From the overall organization's standpoint, increases in safety incidents can significantly affect worker productivity and return on investment in the business (ROI). Increases in total recordable injuries can negatively impact employee motivation and fear of being hurt on the job can become a significant distraction for workers. Consequently, continuous improvement plans should not only address quality, but they also need to take safety into account because quality and safety are interconnected.

A culture of safety should be driven by the senior executives and should permeate every level of the organization. Leaders create culture, culture shapes attitudes and behaviors, and attitudes and behaviors influence outcomes.[18] The following leadership strategies can help to develop and sustain a culture of safety:

1. **Vision.** Establish a compelling vision for safety that emphasizes the value of the organization's human resources as opposed to just compliance with government regulations.

2. **Measurement.** Create tangible metrics to measure safety and encourage reporting of incidents.

3. **Trust, respect, and inclusion.** Establish trust and respect with all employees and lead by example. This is critical to creating an environment that emphasizes an awareness of safety and can lead to conversations about injury or illness events, including what happened, why it happened, and how it can be prevented in the future.

4. **Accountability.** Include metrics for workplace injury and illness in the performance management metrics for every level of leadership in the organization. But don't take this too far. Fear of discipline or reprimand can lead to a culture in which people are afraid to report hazards, or even worse, cover up safety incidents.

5. **Reward and recognition.** Provide incentives for departments that meet or exceed safety metrics. Encourage all employees to identify and correct safety hazards. Celebrate safety successes.

6. **Development.** Provide training and development opportunities so that employees understand the best methods for preventing injury or illness.

Forklift accidents are so common that the Industrial Truck Association sponsors an annual National Forklift Safety Day.

Source: © Shutterstock, Inc.

In addition to OSHA, some states also have an agency designated to regulate occupational health and safety. In 2017, maintenance worker Phillip Lee Terry was crushed to death by a forklift while working at an Amazon warehouse in Plainfield, Indiana. A state investigator found that Amazon was at fault, cited four major safety violations, and fined the company $28,000. State officials later overturned the citations, which some claim was because the state of Indiana was bidding for Amazon's HQ2 site.[19] However, John Stallone, the state's investigator on the case, reported that during the site inspection, he quickly found the problem. A tall pole, lying just feet away, should have been used to prop up the forklift during maintenance. In a recording he made of the inspection, Stallone asked an Amazon manager whether there was any written documentation of Terry being trained on that. "No sir," the supervisor says on the recording. He told Stallone that Terry had been informally trained by a co-worker. Stallone interviewed a co-worker of Terry's, who put the blame on Amazon's safety culture coming in second to production demands. "The safety issues I've brought up have been dismissed and not dealt with...there's no training, there's no saftey, its 'Ger 'er done.'"[20]

Understanding What Safety Culture Is

The role that safety culture plays in identifying and mitigating risk of injury in the workplace.

View the video online at: http://www.youtube.com/embed/wNdJHmWyPiI?rel=0

HR Talk: Wendy Padgett

Safety and Health Director

Southeastern Chapter, National Safety Council

Safety can have both a positive and negative impact on a company. If a company has a positive safety culture, then employee retention is strong, while a negative safety culture will lead to massive turnover because injuries and illness numbers will be high. Safety of employees is a paramount function of every employer, and keeping fellow employees safe is a vital responsibility of everyone in the organization, starting at the top. A strong commitment to safety also has a direct impact on productivity. When an employee feels safe, he or she has more time and attention to focus on work, thereby increasing the employer's return on investment and the company's overall wellbeing. Companies can track safety effectiveness by comparing metrics with other companies of similar size and composition, or internally though satisfaction surveys. When a company shows it cares about its employees by positive activities such as asking their opinions, they will often receive a large amount of information in response. While it can be a challenge to organize such data, it is important for companies to evaluate that information and act on it. If employees make an effort to provide input and nothing is done with it, they will become less invested in the company and its culture. Soliciting and implementing change based on feedback is key to safety culture change and improvement.

The first step in creating and maintaining a culture of safety is management commitment. Management must observe the same policies and procedures everyone else are asked to follow. Without management's clear commitment to safety, a culture of safety is unlikely to result. The next step in establishing a culture of safety is employee involvement. Without employees' broad-based involvement, the goal of establishing a safe culture it will also fail. Employees need to feel like they belong to the culture, they are part of a mission or larger purpose, and their voices matter. After all, they are the ones doing the work: Get them involved in the hazard identification process, facility inspections, forming safety teams, and the policy rewrite process. They will perceive the company cares about them, will be more likely to follow guidance, and more inclined to help change the culture for the better. Cultural change may take a while. In fact, some sources estimate the process can take up to seven years. Therefore, it is important to get off to a good start when implementing or improving a culture of safety. False starts or the need to backtrack will only lengthen the change process. Start with management commitment to change, involve employees, solicit employee feedback, and act upon the input. Finding what works and what does not work as a team is the key to building a safer and more productive work environment for everyone.

Key Takeaways

- The Occupational Safety and Health Act (OSH) was passed by Congress in 1970 to assure safe and healthful working conditions for working men and women and to authorize enforcement of the standards developed under the act.
- The Occupational Safety and Health Administration (OSHA) is part of the Department of Labor and covers most private-sector employers and their workers, in addition to some public-sector employers in the fifty states and some other federal jurisdictions.
- OSHA standards are rules that describe the methods employers are legally required to follow to protect their workers from hazards.
- OSHA standards and regulations are enforced through a combination of reporting, inspections, investigations, citations, and fines.
- OSHA requires covered employers with ten or more employees to keep a record of work-related injuries or illnesses, although minor injuries requiring first aid only do not need to be reported.
- Injury and illness records must be maintained at the worksite for a minimum of five years.
- The National Institute for Occupational Safety and Health (NIOSH) is a federal government agency that conducts research and makes recommendations for the prevention of work-related injury and illnesses.
- NIOSH is part of the U.S. Centers for Disease Control and Prevention (CDC), under the U.S. Department of Health and Human Services, and has a mandate to assure every man and woman in the nation safe and healthful working conditions and to preserve our human resources.
- NIOSH research is primarily driven by the National Occupational Research Agenda (NORA).
- A culture of safety should be driven by the senior executives and should permeate every level of the organization.

What Do *You* Think?

1. Were you aware of OSHA, employer responsibilities, and employee rights?
2. Did any of the facts about workplace safety surprise you? Which ones, and why?
3. Have you or someone you know been injured or contracted an occupational disease? Did the employer handle the situation in accordance with OSHA regulations?

13.3 Employee Health

Learning Objectives

1. Explain the importance of employee health and wellness.
2. Identify the major types of cumulative trauma disorders.
3. Recognize the major types of occupational diseases and their causes.
4. Describe the types of personal protective equipment employers should have available for their workers.

Why Is Employee Health and Wellness so Important?

If you owned a delivery company, then you would probably have a preventive maintenance program for your vehicles to make sure they are in good working order and to reduce the chances of having a vehicle out of service for expensive repairs. Or if you owned a manufacturing company, then you would take the same approach with the equipment in your plant. Most manufacturing companies have maintenance technicians who perform preventive maintenance and then diagnose and repair machines when the machines are not working properly. We can extend this argument to the organization's most important asset, which of course are the human resources.

We can make a strong financial business case for promoting employee health and wellness because companies will realize cost savings in regard to health insurance premiums and also higher productivity. But unlike machinery, we can also make a strong moral or ethical case that providing a healthy work environment and helping employees to live healthier lifestyles is just the right thing to do. The World Health Organization identifies several benefits to workplace health promotion for the organization and the employee, as listed in Table 13.3.[21]

TABLE 13.3 Benefits of Workplace Health Promotion

For the Organization	For the Employee
A positive and caring image	Reduced stress
Improved employee morale	Increased job satisfaction
Reduced turnover	Improved health
Reduced absenteeism	Increased skills for health protection
Increased productivity	Improved sense of well-being
Lower healthcare/insurance costs	Enhanced self-esteem
Lower risk of fines and litigation	Improved morale

The emphasis of employee health initiatives is sometimes on a single illness or risk (for example, cumulative trauma disorders or exposure to hazardous substances). But there is increasing awareness of the benefits of focusing on a more comprehensive approach to employee health. Similar to the approach of developing a culture of safety, employee health should be viewed not just from the perspective of reducing risk or cost as the result of a specific illness, but by creating a culture that values and promotes employee wellness. In this section, we will first explore several of the most common workplace health risks, and then how organizations can protect employees.

Restaurants have a responsibility to protect not only customers, but also employees.

Source: © Shutterstock, Inc.

Cumulative Trauma Disorders

cumulative trauma disorder (CTD)

The excessive wear and tear on tendons, muscles, and sensitive nerve tissue caused by continuous use over an extended period of time.

musculoskeletal disorders (MSDs)

Injuries and disorders that affect the human body's movement or musculoskeletal system (i.e., muscles, tendons, ligaments, nerves, discs, etc.)

repetitive stress injuries (RSIs)

Occur due to performing the same motions over and over, and are exacerbated by improper positioning, posture, or workstations.

ergonomics

The science of designing and arranging work areas so that people and things interact efficiently and safely.

A **cumulative trauma disorder (CTD)** is the excessive wear and tear on tendons, muscles, and sensitive nerve tissue caused by continuous use over an extended period of time. CTDs often develop from improper work positioning, repetitive motions, or use of force.[22] CTDs are considered **musculoskeletal disorders (MSDs)**. OSHA estimates that work-related MSDs in the U.S. account for over 600,000 injuries and illnesses each year, and are responsible for 34% of all lost workdays.[23] They account for one of every three dollars spent on workers' compensation, and it is estimated that employers spend as much as $20 billion annually on direct costs and as much as five times that much on indirect costs such as hiring and training replacement workers.[24] The workplace environment, repeating the same task with little variability, decreased time for rest, and an increase in expectations are all major factors in developing CTDs.[25]

Some of the most common CTDs are **repetitive stress injuries (RSIs)**. These occur due to performing the same motions over and over, and are exacerbated by improper positioning, posture, or workstations. Some of the most common and well-known types of RSIs are carpal tunnel syndrome and tendonitis.

CTDs are usually caused by a combination of factors, including:[26]

- Repetitive motions.
- Pulling, pushing, lifting, and gripping.
- Awkward posture or body positions that are unnatural resting positions.
- Holding the same body position without moving or reseting for long periods.
- Mechanical compression of soft tissues in the hand against hard edges (such as holding a hammer).
- Fast movement of body parts (such as swinging of arms).
- Vibration, especially in cold weather (such as holding vibrating tools).
- Mental stress that can cause muscles to tighten and restrict blood flow.
- Insufficient recovery time such as rest breaks or days off.

One of the most effective approaches to reducing the occurrence of CTDs is to educate employees on proper posture and positioning and to design ergonomic workstations. **Ergonomics** is the science of designing and arranging work areas so that people and things interact efficiently and safely. Employers are responsible for providing a safe and healthful workforce for their workers. By applying ergonomic principles, the number and severity of MSDs from physical overexertion and RSIs from repetitive motions, and their associated costs, can be substantially reduced by applying ergonomic principles.[27]

Implementing an ergonomic process is especially effective in reducing the risk of developing MSDs and RSIs in high-risk industries such as office jobs, construction, manufacturing, food processing, healthcare, and transportation. The following are elements of an ergonomic process:[28]

- **Provide management support.** A strong commitment by management is critical. Management should define clear goals and objectives for the ergonomic process.
- **Involve workers.** They should be involved in worksite assessments, solution development, and implementation.
- **Provide training.** This ensures that workers are aware of ergonomics and its benefits.
- **Identify problems.** Identify and assess ergonomic problems in the workplace before they result in MSDs.
- **Encourage early reporting of CTD symptoms.** Early reporting can help prevent or reduce the progressions of symptoms, the development of serious injuries, and subsequent lost-time claims.

- **Implement solutions.** There are many possible solutions to reduce, control, or eliminate workplace CTDs.

- **Evaluate progress.** Establish evaluations and corrective action procedures to assess the effectiveness of the ergonomic process and to ensure its continuous improvement and long-term success.

Occupational Diseases

An **occupational disease** is any illness contracted primarily as a result of exposure to risk factors arising from work activity. The opening case in this chapter focuses on a specific type of occupational disease, pleural mesothelioma. The most common type of occupational disease is airway diseases, including mesothelioma, asthma, and chronic obstructive pulmonary disease (COPD).[29] Almost 30% of adult asthma and COPD cases in the U.S. are attributed to occupational exposure to airway irritants, and over twenty million U.S. workers are exposed to substances that can cause airway diseases.[30] The second most-frequent occupational disease is skin irritations. Other common types of occupational diseases are hearing loss, infectious diseases (e.g., pneumonia, tuberculosis, hepatitis, etc.), low back disorders, traumatic injuries, and reproductive abnormalities.

Occupational diseases are often caused by chemical hazards, noise, vibration, and extreme temperature.[31] They are classified into three levels: annoying, harmful, and dangerous, based on the nature and intensity of the disease. Workers in practically every occupation are exposed to some level of risk for occupational disease. For example, a machinist might be exposed to metal fumes, which have been proven to be related to cases of pneumonia.[32] A healthcare worker might develop a skin irritation due to an allergic reaction to the latex in examination gloves. Or a social worker could be exposed to an infectious disease during a home visit to a client.

occupational disease

Any illness contracted primarily as a result of exposure to risk factors arising from work activity.

Protection

One important point to emphasize is that organizations are responsible for exposure of employees to risk factors and should take preventive measures such as **personal protective equipment (PPE)**. This is equipment worn to minimize exposure to hazards that cause serious workplace injuries and illnesses. Appropriate PPE may include items such as gloves, safety glasses, steel-toe boots, earplugs or muffs, hard hats, masks, respirators, coveralls, safety vests, or full body suits.

The COVID-19 crisis in 2020 brought new awareness to the need to protect employees from infectious diseases. Healthcare workers were used to wearing PPE, but the demands on the system because of the high number of patients strained the supply chain, causing a shortage of PPE. The primary shortages occurred with N95 masks, gowns, and face shields. The CDC provides optimization strategies for PPE when supplies are running low or absent.[33] Contingency strategies can help stretch PPE supplies when shortages are anticipated. The CDC recommends the following contingency strategies for healthcare organizations:[34]

personal protective equipment (PPE)

Equipment worn to minimize exposure to hazards that cause serious workplace injuries and illnesses.

- Maximize use of engineering controls, such as barriers and maintained ventilation systems, and administrative controls, such as altering work practices to minimize patient contact.

- Cancel elective and nonurgent procedures and appointments.

- Reserve PPE for healthcare professionals and replace PPE normally used for source control with other barrier precautions, such as tissues.

- Use reusable PPE that can be reprocessed.

- Use PPE beyond the manufacturer-designated shelf life for training.

- Consider allowing healthcare professionals to extend use of respirators, face masks, and eye protection beyond a single patient contact.
- As PPE becomes more available, promptly resume standard practices.

The CDC issued new guidelines for protective gear for healthcare workers, as illustrated in Figure 13.3.

FIGURE 13.3 New CDC Guidelines for PPE for Health Workers

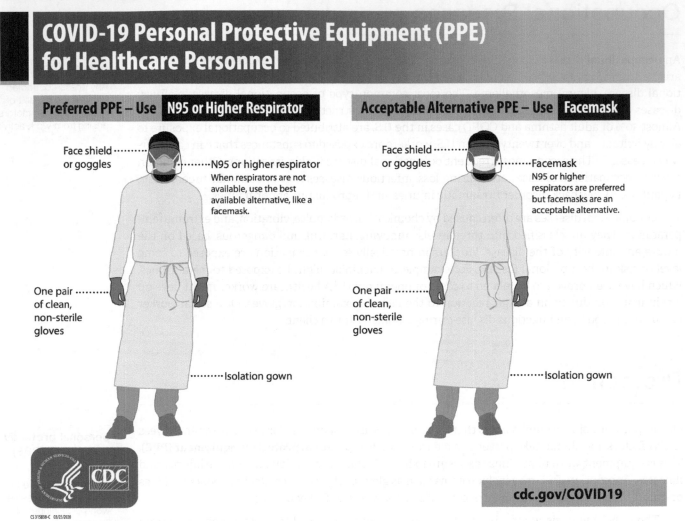

Source: CDC, https://www.cdc.gov/coronavirus/2019-ncov/hcp/using-ppe.html.

Remember that it is not just healthcare workers who need PPE to protect themselves from exposure to infectious diseases. First responders, delivery drivers, and retail workers are all in positions of high-risk exposure. In 2020, the estate of a Walmart worker who died of COVID-19 sued the retailer, alleging it failed to provide workers with protective masks and gloves, failed to suitably disinfect the store, and failed to be clear with workers about the risks they faced.[35] Wando Evans, a fifty-one-year-old man who was a Walmart associate for fifteen years, died from exposure to COVID-19, and four days later, a co-worker at the same store died from complications of the virus.

In addition to the PPE mentioned above, during a pandemic, employers should consider sneeze guards to protect cashiers, closing overnight to disinfect the store, using one-way aisles, limiting the number of shoppers inside a store at one time, and maintaining six feet of social distancing between customers and employees and among the employees. **Social distancing** is the practice of maintaining a greater-than-usual physical distance from other people or of avoiding direct contact with people in public places during the outbreak of a contagious disease, to minimize exposure and reduce the transmission of infection.

social distancing

The practice of maintaining a greater-than-usual physical distance from other people or of avoiding direct contact with people in public places during the outbreak of a contagious disease to minimize exposure and reduce the transmission of infection.

Key Takeaways

- We can make a strong financial business case for promoting employee health and wellness because companies will have cost savings in regard to health insurance premiums and also higher productivity. But we can also make a strong moral or ethical case that providing a healthy work environment, and helping employees to live healthier lifestyles is just the right thing to do.

- A cumulative trauma disorder (CTD) is the excessive wear and tear on tendons, muscles, and sensitive nerve tissue caused by continuous use over an extended period of time. CTDs often develop from improper work positioning, repetitive motions, or use of force.

- Some of the most common CTDs are repetitive stress injuries (RSIs). These occur due to performing the same motions over and over and are exacerbated by improper positioning, posture, or workstations.

- Ergonomics is the science of designing and arranging work areas so that people and things interact efficiently and safely.

- An occupational disease is any illness contracted primarily as a result of exposure to risk factors arising from work activity. The most common type of occupational disease is airway disease, including asthma and chronic obstructive pulmonary disease (COPD), followed by skin irritations.

What Do *You* Think?

1. Have you worked for, or know a company, that has exceptionally good health and wellness initiatives? What are they doing right?
2. Can you think of other steps companies could implement to reduce CTDs and RSIs like carpal tunnel syndrome?
3. Think of one of your current or former jobs. Was the workstation ergonomically designed? Did you have symptoms or MSD or RSI after a long shift?
4. What PPE should you have available for emergencies in the workplace?

13.4 Workplace Security

Learning Objectives

1. Recognize the threats posed by various types of workplace violence.
2. Describe the elements of an emergency preparedness plan.
3. Identify the major types of threats to cybersecurity along with preventive actions.

Workplace Violence

On February 15, 2019, five employees were shot and killed at a warehouse in Aurora, Illinois, by a co-worker who had just been fired. On May 31, 2019, a city engineer resigned from his job and then shot and killed twelve people in Virginia Beach, Virginia. The fifteen-year employee emailed his resignation letter and then began firing indiscriminately at victims on three floors of a municipal building.[36]

On May 31, 2019, a city engineer resigned from his job and then shot and killed twelve people in Virginia Beach, Virginia. The fifteen-year employee emailed his resignation letter and then began firing indiscriminately at victims on three floors of a municipal building.[37]

Every workplace, no matter how safe the environment may seem, is susceptible to security threats. Whether it is a manufacturing plant, retail store, office building, or any other type of facility, security issues are of increasing concern.

It is tempting to think that this would never happen at your workplace. But that kind of attitude can lead to complacency and unpreparedness in the event of a threat. Let's define what we mean by a threat. Workplace security threats include acts of violence, cyberattacks, weather events, fires, earthquakes, and any other event that has the potential to harm employees and customers, or anyone else in a facility.

workplace violence

Any act or threat of physical violence, harassment, intimidation, or other threatening disruptive behaviors that occur at the worksite.

About two million Americans a year are victims of **workplace violence**.[38] Workplace violence is any act or threat of physical violence, harassment, intimidation, or other threatening disruptive behaviors that occur at the worksite. It can occur inside or outside the workplace and can range from threats to verbal abuse, physical assaults, or homicide (one of the leading causes of job-related deaths).[39] Some workers are at more risk, including workers who exchange money with customers, delivery drivers, those who work alone or during late night or early morning hours, those who work in high crime areas, workers who enter homes such as healthcare and social workers, and taxi drivers. But every organization should take the appropriate steps to prevent violent events and develop policies and procedures for how to react when things go wrong. Each employee, especially those at high risk, should undergo training on how to reduce the likelihood of becoming a victim of workplace violence. Research indicates that prevention behaviors reduce the exposure to violent workplace events.[40]

Workforce bullying can include gossip and mocking among co-workers.

Source: © Shutterstock, Inc.

workforce bullying

Repeated mistreatment of an employee by one or more other employees, abusive conduct that is threatening, humiliating or intimidating, work sabotage, or verbal abuse.

Workplace violence also includes **workforce bullying**, which is defined by the Workforce Bullying Institute (WBI) as repeated mistreatment of an employee by one or more employees, abusive conduct that is threatening, humiliating or intimidating, work sabotage, or verbal abuse.[41] A 2017 WBI survey reported that 61% of Americans are aware of bullying in their workplace, and 61% of bullying incidences were perpetrated by bosses.

Is workplace violence a probability at any one place of employment? Probably not, but it is a possibility. Therefore, HR managers should take the necessary precautions to ensure that employees are protected as much as possible. OSHA recommends the following steps that employers should take to protect employees:[42]

- **Secure the workplace.** Where appropriate to the business, install video surveillance, extra lighting, and alarm systems, and minimize access by outsiders through identification badges, electronic keys, and guards.
- **Provide drop safes to limit the amount of cash on hand.** Keep only a minimal amount of cash in registers during late-night or early-morning hours.
- **Equip field staff with cellular phones and handheld alarms or noise devices,** and require them to prepare a daily work plan and keep a contact person informed of their location throughout the day.

- **Instruct employees not to enter any location where they feel unsafe.** Use a buddy system or provide an escort or police assistance in potentially dangerous situations (such as servicing an ATM machine).

- **Develop policies and procedures covering visits by home-healthcare providers.** Address the conduct of home visits, the presence of others in the home during visits, and the worker's right to refuse to provide services in a clearly hazardous situation.

- **Adopt a zero-tolerance policy for bullying in the workplace.** Educate employees so they know what behaviors constitute bullying and how to report it.

Emergency Procedures

Effective emergency procedures that support the people who have to detect, diagnose, and respond to hazardous situations can reduce the likelihood that minor incidents will escalate.[43] Every organization should conduct an all-threats assessment, which examines how prepared they are to respond effectively to any type of threat, from a weather-related event to an active shooter. Figure 13.4 illustrates how encompassing an all-threats assessment should be.

FIGURE 13.4 All-Threats Emergency Preparedness Plan

At a minimum, an emergency action plan should include the following:[44]

- A preferred method for reporting fires and other emergencies.

- An evacuation policy and procedure, including emergency escape procedures and route assignments such as floor plans, workplace maps, safe/refuge areas, and muster points.

- Names, titles, departments, and telephone numbers of all employees and emergency contact information.

- Procedures for employees who remain to perform or shut down critical plant operations.

- Rescue and medical duties for any workers designated to perform them.

- Location of fire extinguishers and other emergency aid such as eyewash and body wash stations.
- Designated employee(s) to be emergency coordinator(s) to include coordinating with outside emergency services.
- Employees designated to assist in emergency evacuation procedures, and trained in the complete workplace layout, alternative escape routes, and evacuation of employees who have disabilities.
- Plans for employees who are able to do so to work remotely.
- Pandemic response plans, including disinfection of workspaces, PPE supplies, and social distancing procedures.

When a natural disaster occurs, whether a wildfire, an earthquake, a flood, or a hurricane, company leaders should ask themselves two questions: "Are our people ok?" and "How can we make their lives easier once it's done?" This is according to Marie Macdonald, director of human resources at Wilmington, North Carolina–based CastleBranch when Hurricane Florence hit.[45] Advance planning and preparation are the keys to handling any emergency situation. At grocery store chain Publix, a cross-functional emergency response team, which includes HR, prepares for hurricanes, tornadoes, and winter storms. Each department in an organization should have its own disaster response plan, says Heather Deyrieux, manager of workforce planning for Sarasota County, Florida.[46] She suggests that remote work may be an option for employees during a natural disaster or pandemic. Another option is that a company might want to establish temporary operations centers in other locations. When mudslides hit Ventura County, California, in 2018, closing down highways, one hospital used boats and an airport shuttle to get its employees to work.

Cybersecurity

cybersecurity

The practice of defending computers, servers, mobile devices, electronic systems, networks, and data from unauthorized use or malicious attacks.

A discussion of workplace security would not be complete without considering technological threats. **Cybersecurity** is the practice of defending computers, servers, mobile devices, electronic systems, networks, and data from unauthorized use or malicious attacks. You may wonder why this content is included in an HR textbook, as opposed to an MIS course. The reason is that many of the risks associated with cybersecurity have to do with people's habits and behaviors, not just technology. Every employee with access to a company computer or mobile or other connected device is the front-line of protection to prevent cyberattacks. A company's data is only as secure as its weakest link, so it is imperative that each employee receives cybersecurity training. Cyberattacks are a big business, as illustrated by Table 13.4.

TABLE 13.4 Largest Corporate Cyberattacks 2016 to 2018

Company	Date	Number of Accounts Hacked
Marriott	2018	500 million
Adult FriendFinder	2016	412 million
MySpace	2016	360 million
Under Armour	2018	150 million
Equifax	2017	145.5 million
MyHeritage	2017	92 million
Uber	2016	57 million
Facebook	2017	50 million

One common cyberattack method is **ransomware**. This occurs when malicious software infects a computer system and blocks users from accessing it until a sum of money is paid (i.e., the ransom). Ransomware attacks in the first half of 2019 were up by 77% over the previous year.[47] But it's not just large corporations that are at risk. Roughly half of all ransomware attacks are targeted at small businesses because they tend to have less protection against computer hacking.[48] It's also not just businesses that are at risk. In September 2019, the Flagstaff, Arizona, school district cancelled classes and childcare due to a ransomware attack that made it impossible to remain open since so many systems and procedures required to operate normally were internet-based.[49] The closing impacted 6,500 students and more than 300 teachers.

> **ransomware**
>
> Malicious software that infects a computer system and blocks users from accessing it until a sum of money is paid.

The following ten cybersecurity best practices will help employees to protect company data:[50]

1. **Protect your data.** Just as you protect your Social Security number and bank account information, treat company data with the same degree of caution and protection.

2. **Avoid pop-ups, unknown emails, and links.** Beware of phishing, which is a fraudulent practice of sending emails purporting to be from reputable companies in order to induce individuals to reveal company or personal information.

3. **Use strong password protection and authentication.** A strong password contains at least ten characters and includes numbers, symbols, and capital and lowercase letters. Require employees to change their passwords on a regular basis.

4. **Connect to secure Wi-Fi.** Office Wi-Fi networks should be secure, encrypted, and hidden. When working remotely, employees should only access company electronic systems via a virtual private network (VPN).

5. **Enable firewall protection at work and at home.** Firewalls prevent unauthorized users from accessing websites, email services, and other electronic sources of information.

6. **Invest in security systems.** Keep antivirus and malware protection up to date.

7. **Install security software updates and back up your files.** Keep security software, web browsers, and operating systems updated.

8. **Talk to your IT department.** Report any security warnings from your security software to IT, and also report any phishing attempts. When you receive an email from your IT department, be sure it is actually your IT department. A common phishing scheme is to send fraudulent emails pretending to be your IT department to try to trick you into installing updates, which are actually malware.

9. **Employ third-party controls.** Monitor any third parties that might have access to company electronic systems or data, such as consultants and vendors.

10. **Embrace education and training.** Provide regular training for employees because the cybersecurity field is rapidly changing, and new threats are continually being introduced. For example, smartwatches have recently been hacked to gain access to company data.

In addition to these practices, companies should develop policies on using personal devices, including laptops, tablets, and smartphones. Employee behaviors can expose a company to cyberattack or cybertheft when personal devices are used for work purposes. For example, if an employee uses their smartphone to access company email or other files, it increases the risk of someone being able to hack into the company data.

Talent Analytics

Most safety professionals track a wide variety of data about their organizations and workforce. This may include individual employee injuries, accidents, and absences, along with aggregate data for each location or operation. They also keep a record of substances used in company operations and information relating to occupational safety and health for each of these substances (referred to as Material Safety Data Sheets, or MSDSs). One reason for tracking data is to comply with reporting requirements of OSHA and other agencies. However, data analysis can contribute to developing a culture of safety by going beyond simply using data for compliance purposes. Data analytics can prove invaluable as professionals seek the best safety measures and improvements to procedures and processes for their organization.

There are two types of insight provided by these systems. One data type is "lagging indicators" which explains events that happened after the fact. If an organization tracks how many lost-time injuries have occurred and which ones required medical attention, this of lagging data. This is data that lags the actual events, and reflects what has already happened and cannot be changed. For example, assume that an organization had 55 lost time incidences among its 600 delivery drivers in the past year, and 42 of those were lower back injuries due to lifting heavy objects. This is lagging data because it reports data after the fact.

The second type of safety data analysis is "predictive". It makes more sense to use data to prevent future accidents or injuries whenever possible. Predictive analysis is based on cause and effect or if one thing happens, another is likely to be a result. Professionals take a large number of observations and incidents and analyze that data. They may then be able to predict future safety incidences and take measures to prevent. This also enables them to discover factors not before considered. For example, an organization could use the data regarding lower back injuries to predict that among its 600 delivery drivers, 9.1% of them will lose time in the next year due to an injury, and 76% of those injuries will be lower back issues from heavy lifting. The organization can then use this data to design preventive measures to reduce injuries, such as training in proper lifting procedures and providing workers with back braces.

Accidents can not always be avoided, even by organizations with perfect or near-perfect safety records. Worker, as well as equipment, failures can happen at any time and may contribute to a safety incident. Predictive analysis may help to prevent such occurrences by enabling safety professionals to see behavioral patterns that could possibly be contributing to safety incidents.

Key Takeaways

- Every workplace, no matter how safe the environment may seem, is susceptible to security threats.
- About two million Americans a year are victims of workplace violence.
  Workplace violence is any act or threat of physical violence, harassment, intimidation, or other threatening disruptive behavior that occurs at the worksite.
- Workplace violence also includes workforce bullying, which is defined by the Workforce Bullying Institute (WBI) as repeated mistreatment of an employee by one or more employees, abusive conduct that is threatening, humiliating or intimidating, work sabotage, or verbal abuse.
- Effective emergency procedures that support the people who have to detect, diagnose, and respond to hazardous situations can reduce the likelihood that minor incidents will escalate.
- Every organization should conduct an all-threats assessment, which examines how prepared they are to respond effectively to any type of threat, from a weather-related event to an active shooter.
- Cybersecurity is the practice of defending computers, servers, mobile devices, electronic systems, networks, and data from unauthorized use or malicious attacks.
- Ransomware is malicious software that infects a computer system and blocks users from accessing it until a sum of money is paid (i.e., the ransom).
- Roughly half of all ransomware attacks are targeted at small businesses because they tend to have less protection against computer hacking.

What Do *You* Think?

1. How secure is your workplace or school? Have they taken steps to prepare employees and students in the event of violence or other type of emergency?

2. Have you or someone you know been bullied at work? How was it handled?

3. What steps have you taken to protect your own data against cyberattacks?

13.5 Conclusion

The chapter began by reviewing federal legislation and regulations governing workplace health and safety, including guidelines for compliance. Strategies for creating a culture of safety were also explored. Then employee health issues such as cumulative trauma disorders and exposure to toxic chemicals were examined. The chapter closed with a discussion of emergency preparedness including pandemics and workplace security awareness.

Theory-into-Practice (TIP) Exercises

1. Using the OSHA website (under resource number one), identify the OSHA standards that apply to a job (at either your current or a former employer) and the training requirements for each standard. Then develop an outline for a safety program for these positions.

2. A work environment that is not ergonomic can lead to increased absenteeism and lower productivity. Working individually or in teams, identify steps that employers can take to reduce the incidences of cumulative trauma disorders. Which of these can you apply to your own study or work area?

3. Conduct a security assessment for your place of work, school, or home. Then write your answers to the following questions:

   a. How safe do you feel at work, school, or home?

   b. Do you and others know how to respond in the event of an emergency?

   c. Are you prepared for an emergency that occurs while you are commuting?

   d. Do you have an emergency preparedness plan?

Then, using Ready.gov (see resource number four), develop a personal emergency plan.

Case Study: Minimizing Workplace Violence

Source: © Shutterstock, Inc.

Workplace violence is on the rise throughout the U.S. One example is an incident that occurred in Aurora, Illinois, on February 15, 2019. Gary Martin of Mueller Water Products in Aurora opened fire on co-workers. Before he did this, earlier that day, he told a co-worker that he was worried he would be terminated for a safety infraction that occurred a few days prior. While venting, Mr. Martin threatened to kill everyone if fired. The co-worker also knew that he kept a gun in his vehicle. The co-worker did not take the threat seriously and failed to report the incident to management.

Later that day, Mr. Martin was called into the HR manager's office, which he attended armed with his 40-caliber revolver (unbeknownst to the others attending the meeting). He was terminated due to the safety infraction and immediately began shooting. The result was that five employees were killed and another injured. Five police officers were also wounded before officers shot and killed Martin. It was later discovered that Martin had a criminal record and had committed aggravated assault in 1995. Mueller did a background check on Martin before hiring him, but somehow the information never made it to those in charge of hiring. There were some safety procedures in place for an active shooter situation and employees followed these by deactivating their access cards and locking down as soon as the shooting started. There were also security cameras outside but not inside the building.[51]

Police Identify Gary Martin as Suspect in Deadly Aurora, Illinois, Workplace Shooting

At least five civilians are dead and five police officers injured after a shooter opened fire at an Aurora, Illinois, manufacturing company. Police identified the suspect as Gary Martin. He was found dead at the scene. CBS News correspondent Adriana Diaz and former Chicago police officer Dimitri Roberts join Nikki Battiste.

View the video online at: http://www.youtube.com/embed/uIMI0fmZT78?rel=0

Case Discussion Questions

1. What are some specific measures Mueller Water Products of Aurora might have taken to minimize or avoid the incident on February 15, 2019?

2. Does your place of employment or college have safety measures in place in case of an active shooter? If so, do you think they are adequate?

3. Some companies are training employees to watch for and report "red flags" or warning signs in other employees. Do you think this is a good idea? What are some disadvantages to this sort of training?

Resources

1. **Occupational Safety and Health Administration.** The official website of OSHA, which includes OSHA standards, training requirements by standard, reporting tools, training resources, and other information to help organizations create a safer workplace.

   https://www.osha.gov/

2. **National Institute for Occupational Safety and Health.** The official website of NIOSH, which provides information on research programs, publications, data and statistics, and training resources to help prevent occupational diseases.

   https://www.cdc.gov/niosh/index.htm

3. **Alliance for a Healthier Generation.** Resources for employee wellness, including physical activity, nutrition, health education, and workplace health promotion.

https://www.healthiergeneration.org/resources/employee-wellness

4. **Ready.gov.** The official website of the U.S. Department of Homeland Security, including resources for creating emergency plans for individuals, families, and commuters.

https://www.ready.gov/plan

Endnotes

1. Case written by Crews, P. (2020). Adapted from Smart, S. (2019). *Occupational asbestos exposure*. Pleural Mesothelioma Center. Retrieved from https://www.pleuralmesothelioma.com/occupations/; Mesothelioma Justice Network. *Asbestos in schools*. Retrieved April 9, 2020 from https://www.asbestos.net/occupations/work-sites/schools/

2. National Safety Council. *Workplace injuries*. Retrieved April 9, 2020 from https://www.nsc.org/work-safety/tools-resources/infographics/workplace-injuries

3. Ibid.

4. Bureau of Labor Statistics. (2017). *Census of fatal occupational injuries summary*, 2017. Retrieved from https://www.bls.gov/news.release/cfoi.nr0.htm

5. Ibid.

6. Meza, S. (2018). Deaths at work: Truck drivers had the highest number of fatal injuries compared to any other job. *Newsweek*. Retrieved from https://www.newsweek.com/truck-drivers-workplace-fatalities-rate-fatal-injuries-771920

7. National Safety Council. *Workplace injuries*. Retrieved April 9, 2020 from https://www.nsc.org/work-safety/tools-resources/infographics/workplace-injuries

8. Occupational Safety and Health Administration. *OSH of 1970*. Retrieved April 9, 2020 from https://www.osha.gov/laws-regs/oshact/completeoshact

9. United States Department of Labor. *About OSHA*. Retrieved April 9, 2020 from https://www.osha.gov/aboutosha

10. Ibid.

11. Occupational Safety and Health Administration. *At-a-glance OSHA*. Retrieved April 9, 2020 from https://www.osha.gov/Publications/3439at-a-glance.pdf

12. Ibid.

13. United States Department of Labor. *OSHA injury and illness recordkeeping and reporting requirements*. Retrieved October 30, 2019 from https://www.osha.gov/recordkeeping/

14. U.S. Occupational Safety and Health Administration. *OSHA fact sheet: Occupational Safety and Health Administration (OSHA) inspections*. Retrieved April 10, 2020 from https://www.osha.gov/OshDoc/data_General_Facts/factsheet-inspections.pdf

15. Ibid.

16. Centers for Disease Control and Prevention. *About NIOSH*. Retrieved April 9, 2020 from https://www.cdc.gov/niosh/about/default.html

17. Centers for Disease Control and Prevention. *National Occupational Research Agenda (NORA)*. Retrieved April 9, 2020 from https://www.cdc.gov/nora/comment/agendas/default.html

18. Tosti, L. (2018). Creating a culture of safety. *Occupational Health & Safety*, 87(7), 90.

19. Darby. L. (2019). After an Amazon worker was crushed to death by a forklift, regulators helped cover it up. *GQ*. Retrieved from https://www.gq.com/story/amazon-indiana-hq2-employee-death

20. Evans, Will. (2019, November 25). "Behind the Smiles: Amazon's internal injury records expose the true toll of its relentless drive for speed." Reveal. Retrieved from: https://revealnews.org/article/behind-the-smiles/. Original witness statement can be found on the Indiana Department of Labor website: https://www.documentcloud.org/documents/6553899-IND5-Witness-Statement.html.

21. World Health Organization. *Workplace health promotion*. Retrieved April 9, 2020 from https://www.who.int/occupational_health/topics/workplace/en/index1.html

22. Cumulative trauma disorder. *Safety and Health Magazine*. Retrieved April 9, 2020 from https://www.safetyandhealthmagazine.com/articles/cumulative-trauma-disorder

23. Occupational Health and Safety Administration. *Prevention of work-related musculoskeletal disorders*. Retrieved April 9, 2020 from https://www.osha.gov/pls/oshaweb/owadisp.show_document?p_id=4481&p_table=UNIFIED_AGENDA

24. Ibid.

25. Iqbal, Z.A.A., & Alghadir, A.H.H. (2017). Cumulative trauma disorders: A review. *Journal of Back and Musculoskeletal Rehabilitation* 30.4 (2017): 663-66.

26. Schmidleer, C. (2018). Guide to cumulative trauma disorders (CTDs). *Health Pages*. Retrieved from https://www.healthpages.org/health-a-z/guide-cumulative-trauma-disorders/

27. U.S. Occupational and Safety and Health Administration. *Ergonomics*. Retrieved April 10, 2020 from https://www.osha.gov/SLTC/ergonomics/

28. Ibid.

29. Centers for Disease Control and Prevention. *National occupational research agenda*. Retrieved April 9, 2020 from https://www.cdc.gov/niosh/docs/96-115/diseas.html

30. Ibid.

31. Skowron, J., & Czerczak, S. (2015). Rules and recent trends for setting health-based occupational exposure limits for chemicals. *International Journal of Occupational Medicine and Environmental Health, 28*(2), 243-252.

32. Torén, K., Qvarfordt, I., Bergdahl, I., & Järvholm, B. (2011). Increased mortality from infectious pneumonia after occupational exposure to inorganic dust, metal fumes and chemicals. *Thorax, 66*(11), 992-996.

33. Centers for Disease Control and Prevention. *Strategies to optimize the supply of PPE and equipment*. Retrieved April 10, 2020 from https://www.cdc.gov/coronavirus/2019-ncov/hcp/ppe-strategy/index.html

34. Ibid.

35. Keshner, A. (2020). Walmart hit with wrongful-death lawsuit by estate of worker who dies of coronavirus. *MarketWatch*. Retrieved from https://www.marketwatch.com/story/walmart-hit-with-wrongful-death-lawsuit-by-estate-of-worker-who-died-of-coronavirus-2020-04-06?mod=home-page

36. Ahearn, T. (2019). Virginia Beach office shooter resigned on day of attack in latest case of workplace violence. *ESR News Blog*. Retrieved from https://www.esrcheck.com/wordpress/2019/06/06/virginia-beach-workplace-violence/.

37. Ahearn, T. (2019). Virginia Beach office shooter resigned on day of attack in latest case of workplace violence. *ESR News Blog*. Retrieved from https://www.esrcheck.com/wordpress/2019/06/06/virginia-beach-workplace-violence/.

38. Occupational Safety and Health Administration. *OSHA fact sheet: Workplace violence*. Retrieved April 9, 2020 from https://www.osha.gov/OshDoc/data_General_Facts/factsheet-workplace-violence.pdf

39. Ibid.

40. Gadegaard, C., Andersen, L., & Hogh, A. (2018). Effects of violence prevention behavior on exposure to workplace violence and threats: A follow-up study. *Journal of Interpersonal Violence, 33*(7), 1096-1117.

41. Workforce Bullying Institute. (2017). *2017 WBI U.S. workplace bullying survey*. Retrieved from https://www.workplacebullying.org/wbiresearch/wbi-2017-survey/

42. Adapted from Occupational Safety and Health Administration. *OSHA fact sheet: Workplace violence*. Retrieved April 9, 2020 from https://www.osha.gov/OshDoc/data_General_Facts/factsheet-workplace-violence.pdf

43. Emergency procedures. (2017). *Loss Prevention Bulletin*, 254.

44. Adapted from Workplace emergency management. (2008). *The National Provisioner, 222*(5), 10,12.

45. Lakidka, S. (2019). Better safe than sorry. *HR Magazine*, 64(4), 63-69.

46. Ibid.

47. Sussman, B. (2019). Cybersecurity report: 2 types of attacks are surging. *Seguro Group Inc*. Retrieved from https://www.secureworldexpo.com/industry-news/cybersecurity-attacks-that-are-surging-now

48. Powell, M. (2019). 11 eye opening cybersecurity statistics for 2019. *CPO Magazine*. Retrieved from https://www.cpomagazine.com/cyber-security/11-eye-opening-cyber-security-statistics-for-2019/

49. Sussman, B. (2019). Ransomware attack: District suddenly cancels school and childcare for thousands. *Secure World*. Retrieved from https://www.secureworldexpo.com/industry-news/ransomware-attack-cancels-school-2019

50. Adapted from Johansen, A. 10 cybersecurity best practices that every employee should know. *Norton*. Retrieved April 9, 2020 from https://us.norton.com/internetsecurity-how-to-cyber-security-best-prac-tices-for-employees.html

51. Case written by Crews, P. (2020). Adapted from Associated Press. (2019). *The latest: CEO: Gunman passed background check when hired*. Retrieved from https://apnews.com/61076852fb264d3aaac62f87411066c8

CHAPTER 14
Global HRM

Learning Objectives

After reading this chapter, you should be able to do the following:

1. Describe the risks and multicultural challenges of global human resource management (GHRM).
2. Identify the challenges of recruitment and selection in GHRM.
3. Discuss the importance of talent development for expatriates.
4. Recognize the factors that influence performance management and labor relations in GHRM.

Recruiting, managing, and retaining human resources at a firm with extensive global operations is especially challenging. The HR functions are similar in some ways to those of domestic companies, such as recruitment, selection, talent development, performance management, and compensation. However, each of these areas has unique issues and legal requirements when engaged in international operations.

This chapter explores the cultural context of global human resource management (GHRM). The various types of multinational organizations, the risks involved in international business, and global multicultural challenges are discussed. The unique challenges of recruiting, training, compensating, and managing various types of global employees will be addressed. Recruitment, selection, talent development, and performance management are each examined. The chapter concludes with a review of international labor standards and international labor organizations.

14.1 Toyota Goes to the Hills of West Virginia

Source: OleksSH / Shutterstock.com

When Toyota wanted to build a plant in Buffalo, West Virginia, many in the community were excited that there would soon be more jobs in the small town of around 1,200. However, there was a need for skilled workers, and very few had the necessary training, nor could they afford to go to school to get it. This is a common problem as foreign companies move to more rural areas in the U.S.

However in 2012, Toyota and Bridgemont Community and Technical College formed a partnership to rectify the problem. They created an advanced manufacturing technician program that would prepare students for careers in a modern manufacturing environment. The students spend two days a week in the classroom learning the fundamentals and technical skills and three days a week on the job, learning the manufacturing processes while earning a paycheck.

Three years after announcing the program, the Buffalo engine and transmission plant now employs its first set of graduates, complete with their associate degrees in applied science. These graduates are trained to work on over one hundred robots and large pieces of equipment. When someone has an issue with a piece of equipment, they call on one of the new technicians to step in and repair the problem.

The graduates had various reasons for entering the program. Some preferred hands-on learning, rather than sitting in a classroom five days a week. Some needed the paycheck while in training. Most were in need of training and work that were close to home. One of the participants stated that being able to get a two-year degree while receiving all of the many hands-on experiences at the plant was unmatched anywhere else.

The tuition at Bridgemont was $1,950 per semester, and the students earned $17.78 an hour in the plant. This meant they could earn around $40,000 for the duration of training. They just had to maintain a C average in order to stay in the program.

With around 600,000 openings in advanced manufacturing technical positions around the country, more programs like the one in West Virginia are being developed. Kentucky was the first state to start such a program with Toyota, with West Virginia being the second. Because of its success and the high demand, other employers in the Buffalo area are planning to partner with Bridgemont to create other similar training programs.[1]

 Toyota Motor Manufacturing WV (TMMWV)

TMMWV manufactures four-cylinder and V6 engines for their plants in Indiana and Canada. The West Virginia plant also produces automatic transmissions and gears for plants in Kentucky, Indiana, and Canada.

View the video online at: http://www.youtube.com/embed/dd2Uv1oA39A?rel=0

Case Discussion Questions

1. What motivates a large foreign company like Toyota to locate a manufacturing plant in a rural area?
2. Can you think of other ways to attract, select, and train new recruits? Also, what are some different ways to compensate and manage the new employees?
3. What are the risks for Toyota associated with this manufacturing strategy?

14.2 The Environment of Global Human Resource Management (GHRM)

Learning Objectives

1. Identify the various types of multinational organizations.

2. Recognize the four major types of risk in international business.
3. Describe the multicultural challenges involved in GHRM.

Types of Multinational Organizations

The opening case focuses on how Toyota uses workers in the U.S. to manufacture some of its vehicles. Recruitment, training, and compensation are just a few of the challenges in GHRM. Before we examine how global HR practices differ from U.S. operations, let's discuss who participates in international operations, what motivates them, the risks and challenges involved, and the key tasks of GHRM.

Small and medium-sized enterprises (SMEs), like this organic soap shop, account for half of all jobs worldwide.

Source: © Shutterstock, Inc.

What types of organizations have employees in multiple countries? Our discussion of Global HRM in this chapter applies to the following types of firms:

- **Multinational enterprises (MNEs).** An organization operating in several countries but managed from one (home) country. Generally, any organization that derives a quarter of its revenue from operations outside of its home country is considered a multinational enterprise.[2]

- **Small and medium-sized enterprises (SMEs)**. The definition of SMEs differs by country. For example, in the European Union (EU), a business with fewer than two hundred fifty employees is considered an SME, while in the United States, an SME has fewer than five hundred employees.[3] Yet in most countries, they constitute about 90% of all existing firms and more than 50% of employment worldwide, and are increasingly engaged in GHRM.[4]

- **Born-global firms.** Business organizations that, from inception, seek to derive significant competitive advantage from the use of resources and the sale of outputs in multiple countries.[5]

- **Nongovernmental organizations.** Nonprofit organizations that pursue special causes and serve as advocates for social issues, education, politics, and research across borders.

What motivates organizations to go international? The reasons can be grouped into five categories:

1. **Extend the life cycle of products**. When a domestic market has become saturated and little additional market growth exists, then firms might expand internationally to take advantage of untapped market potential and new customers. For example, Fremantle is a multinational television company based in London that exported its Britain's Got Talent show to the United States where it aired as America's Got Talent. There are now 71 local versions of Got Talent across Europe, Asia Pacific, the Middle-East, Africa, and the Americas. Starbucks has expanded from its founding in Seattle to locations in 78 countries.

2. **Achieve cost savings through sourcing and production**. For example, Ford Motor Company expanded into Brazil between the 1920's and 1940's to supply Ford's demand for rubber.

3. **Lessen negative public relations by creating domestic jobs**. For example, Toyota, Honda, Mercedes-Benz, Mazda, Mitsubishi, and Subaru are among the foreign automotive manufacturers that now operate plants in the U.S.

4. **Lower cost of production**. Some manufacturers open plants in countries where the labor cost is lower than their home country. Companies also relocate white collar jobs such as customer service and computer programming to lower wage countries. For example, IBM now employs more workers in India than it does in the United States, and almost half of Cisco Systems workforce consists of overseas workers.[6]

5. **Improve innovation, products, and services**. Some firms will engage in collaboration with firms in other countries to learn from each other. For example, Toyota entered into a joint venture with General Motors in the 1980's to manufacture light cars and trucks, called New United Motor Manufacturing, Inc. (or NUMMI). GM was hoping to improve quality and efficiency by learning about the Toyota Production System and Toyota was looking to make its first inroad into manufacturing in the U.S.[7]

Risk of International Business

International business and trade are centuries old. The picture represents a caravanserai along the Silk Road, which ran from Asia Minor (modern day Turkey) to the Far East, and was used by Marco Polo, among others.

International trade has always involved risks, and especially human risks. Along the Silk Road, caravanserais were developed as overnight stops for travelers. They typically included rooms, stalls for camels, bathing facilities, a vet, evening entertainment, and a prayer room. However, while offering the traveler these conveniences, one primary purpose of caravanserais was to provide safe shelter to mitigate the risk of theft and piracy along the Silk Road. Today, although the transportation modes have changed, the risks of piracy still exist.

While the types of risk have changed from the days of the Silk Road, there are still many challenges when firms venture abroad. Firms encounter four major types of risk when they venture abroad: cross-cultural, country, currency, and commercial. Let's take a look at each of these risks more closely.

Cross-Cultural Risk

cross-cultural risk

Arises from differences in business practices, communication styles, and many aspects of human behavior.

Cross-cultural risk arises from differences in business practices, communication styles, and many aspects of human behavior. Cross-cultural risk can be considered in four different domains that impact business and GHRM.

- **Cultural differences.** Risks arise from differences in language, lifestyle, attitudes, customs, and religion, where a cultural miscommunication jeopardizes a culturally valued mind-set or behavior.[8]
- **Negotiation patterns.** Negotiations are required in many types of business transactions but differ in how they are conducted. Errors in understanding these styles can undermine business relations.[9]
- **Decision-making styles.** Managers constantly make decisions about the operations and future direction of the firm.
- **Ethical practices.** Standards of right and wrong vary considerably around the world.[10]

Country Risk

Country risk (also known as political risk) refers to the potentially adverse effects on company operations and profitability caused by developments in the political, legal, and economic environments in a foreign country. Country risk also includes the possibility of foreign government intervention in firms' business activities by restricting access to markets, imposing bureaucratic procedures, and limiting the amount of income that firms can bring home from foreign operations. For example, Singapore and Ireland are characterized by substantial economic freedom—that is, a fairly liberal economic environment. By contrast, the Chinese and Russian governments regularly intervene in business affairs.

Critical legal dimensions that potentially hinder company operations and performance include property rights, intellectual property protection, product liability, and taxation policies. Potentially harmful economic conditions such as high inflation, national debt, and unbalanced international trade can also result in negative financial results for the firm.

country risk

Refers to the potentially adverse effects on company operations and profitability caused by developments in the political, legal, and economic environments in a foreign country.

Currency Risk

Currency risk (also known as financial risk) refers to the risk of adverse fluctuations in exchange rates. Currency risk arises because international transactions are often conducted in more than one national currency. When currencies fluctuate significantly, the value of the firm's earnings can be reduced.[11] For example, when Caterpillar exports heavy construction equipment to Japan, it is normally paid in Japanese yen. If Caterpillar receives fewer yen than it anticipated when they deliver equipment to Japan, its profits will be lower than expected. Inflation and other harmful economic conditions experienced in one country may have immediate consequences for exchange rates as prices of products rise unexpectedly, resulting in lower profit margins for firms purchasing these products.

currency risk

Refers to the risk of adverse fluctuations in exchange rates.

Commercial Risk

Commercial risk refers to the firm's potential loss or failure from poorly developed or executed business strategies, tactics, or procedures.[12] Managers may make poor choices in such areas as the selection of business partners, timing of market entry, pricing, creation of product features, and promotional themes. While such failures also exist in domestic business, the consequences are usually more costly when committed abroad. For example, in domestic business a company may terminate a poorly performing distributor simply with advance notice. In foreign markets, however, terminating business partners can be costly due to regulations that protect local firms. Marketing inferior or harmful products, falling short of customer expectations, or failing to provide adequate customer service may damage the firm's reputation and profitability.

As you consider these challenges, and how organizations might mitigate these risks, think of them in the context of the key tasks of GHRM, as described in Table 14.1.

commercial risk

Refers to the firm's potential loss or failure from poorly developed or executed business strategies, tactics, or procedures.

TABLE 14.1 Key Tasks of GHRM

Key Tasks of GHRM	
Global staffing policy	Activities directed at recruiting, selecting, and placing employees.
Preparation and training of global employees	Onboarding, training and development, and preparing employees for expatriation and repatriation.

Key Tasks of GHRM	
Global performance management	Appraisal, feedback, and coaching for performance improvement.
Compensation of global staff	Design and administration of salary and benefits packages that can vary greatly from country to country.
Global labor relations	Managing relations with unions and the collective bargaining process.
Diversity in the global workforce	The challenges of differences in country cultures, religion, business etiquette, and attitudes toward women and minorities.

Global Multicultural Challenges

To become effective in managing global diversity, it is imperative that you become a student of culture. If you are not already doing this, you should develop habits that will help you to continually become more culturally aware. These habits would include reading, attending cultural events, traveling, and using other means to intentionally place yourself in new environments.

Did you know there are 195 countries, and over 7,000 languages in the world?

Source: © Shutterstock, Inc.

As you explore other cultures, consider the following:

- Great portions of Western culture come from non-Western cultures.
- The role of religion is a significant factor in the worldview of most cultures.
- Survival and the desire to protect the homeland have shaped the values and worldview of many cultures.
- No country or cultural group is dominant permanently.

Persistent differences among cultures are due to their histories as well as their geographic environments. In today's world, different cultural groups cannot remain isolated if they are to compete economically for a livelihood. They need to have, and be able to use, knowledge of other cultures.

Biases can be removed by education. In other words, the more you learn about different cultures, the more aware you are of why they view the world the way they do. This awareness will help counter the natural tendency to stereotype other cultures based on secondhand information, whether that is from the media or another source. Thus, the first step to improve your ability to be effective in cross-cultural communication is self-awareness, and the next step is becoming more aware of the views and values of others. There is no substitute for personal experience when it comes to learning about different cultures.

The following joke is told among Europeans: What do you call someone who speaks two languages? (bilingual); What do you call someone who speaks three languages? (trilingual); What do you call someone who speaks only one language? (an American!). Working in another culture poses significant challenges for employees, the HR department, and the managers of the employees who are involved.

Some of the challenges in expatriate management are obvious: adapting to different social customs, food, dress, etc. In addition to this type of cultural and social adaptation, the employee might need to learn a different management style or a different negotiation style. Communication norms might also be different. For example, ideas about personal space differ from one country to the next. In Middle Eastern and Latin American countries, it would be normal to stand within twelve inches of another person when talking. In the United States, that would be considered an invasion of personal space. The normal distance between individuals in a business conversation in the U.S. would be two to four feet. Consider the examples in Table 14.2 of how communication (verbal and nonverbal) differs from one culture to another:

TABLE 14.2 Communication Differences Across Cultures

Communication Differences Across Cultures	
Calling a Waiter	In the United States, a common way to call a waiter is to point upward with the forefinger. In Asia, a raised forefinger is used to call a dog of other animal. To get the attention of a Japanese waiter, extend the arm upward, palm down, and flutter the fingers. In Africa, knock on the table. In the Middle East, clap your hands.
Insults	In Arab countries, showing the soles of your shoes is an insult. Also, an Arab may insult a person by holding a hand in front of the person's face.
A-Okay Gesture	In the United States, using the index fingers and the thumb to form an "o" while extending the rest of the fingers is a gesture meaning "okay" or "fine with me." In Japan, however, the same gesture means money. Nodding your head in agreement if a Japanese person uses this sign during your discussion could mean you are expected to offer compensation. And in Brazil, the same gesture is considered a seductive sign to a woman and an insult to a man.
Eye Contact	In Western and Arab cultures, prolonged eye contact with a person is acceptable. In Japan, on the other hand, holding the gaze of another is considered rude. The Japanese generally focus on a person's neck or tie knot.
Handshake and Touching	In most countries, the handshake is an acceptable form of greeting (unless the COVID-19 virus causes a permanent culture change in this regard). In the Middle East and other Islamic countries, however, the left hand is considered the toilet hand and is thought to be unclean. Only the right hand should be used for touching.
Scratching the Head	In most Western countries, scratching the head is interpreted as a lack of understanding or noncomprehension. To the Japanese, it means anger.

Communication Differences Across Cultures	
Indicating "No"	In most parts of the world, shaking the head left and right is the common way to say "no." But among the Arabs, and in parts of Greece, Bulgaria, and Turkey, a person says "no" by tossing the head to the side, sometimes clicking the tongue at the same time. In Japan, "no" can also be said by moving the right hand back and forth. Also, someone in Japan may be reluctant to say the word "no." They might instead say something like "It is a difficult decision," which can mean the same thing as saying "no."
Agreement	In addition to saying "yes," Africans might hold an open palm perpendicular to the ground and pound it with the other fist to emphasize "agreed." Arabs will clap their hands together, forefingers pointed outward, to indicate agreement.

There are also differences in attitudes about time. Some cultures are very time-conscious. Included in this group are the United States, Canada, and Northern Europe. Business appointments are held on time, and it would be considered rude to be late. Business negotiations move rapidly, and the emphasis is on "closing the deal." In the Middle East, Africa, Central America, and South America, business negotiations move much more slowly, and the emphasis is on building trust and relationships, rather than closing a deal. It would not be considered rude to be thirty minutes (or more) late for a meeting (or maybe not show at all if something else came up).

There are differences in how organizational decisions are made from one culture to another. Some cultures are centralized, in which decisions are made only by top-level managers. Other cultures tend to be decentralized, and decisions are made more quickly and by lower-level managers. Still another difference is in hiring methods. In the U.S., we normally hire based on qualifications. In many countries, it is more normal to hire based on personal relationships (who you know), or in some cases one has to pay a fee (i.e., bribe). These are just a few of the challenges faced by employees accepting out-of-country assignments. These challenges have implications for the training given to employees before they are sent to another country to work.

 ### Cross-Cultural Management

This video describes the 3R approach to working effectively in a cross-cultural environment. The 3Rs consist of (1) Recognizing cross-cultural differences, (2) Respecting differences, and (3) Reconciling differences.

View the video online at: http://www.youtube.com/embed/rJ4lbhXrqnc?rel=0

HR in the Real World: The Case of the Over-Worked American

I was once on a train in Europe talking with a gentleman in the seat next to me. When he found out I was from the U.S., he said: "There is something that I just don't understand about you Americans. Why do you work all the time?!"

On another occasion, also on a train in Europe, I had a conversation with a woman about how early we had to get up to catch the train. I commented that I was usually up early anyway, so it wasn't much of an inconvenience. She said: "Oh, that's right! You Americans get up at 5 am so you can rush off to work! You should learn to enjoy life."

I have heard similar comments in most of the thirty-one countries that I have visited, lived in, or worked in. While working for six months in Salzburg, Austria, I noticed that people would be off work by 4 or 5 in the afternoon, and then would be walking their dog, playing with kids in a park, or perhaps sitting at a café having a pastry and a coffee. It is important when managing a global workforce to be aware that work plays a much less important role in their lives than it does for many Americans, and they value their leisure time.

Key Takeaways

- A multinational enterprise (MNE) is an organization operating in several countries but with management from one (home) country. Generally, any organization that derives a quarter of its revenue from operations outside of its home country is considered a multinational enterprise.
- Small and medium-sized enterprises (SMEs) constitute about 90% of all existing firms and more than 50% of employment worldwide, and are increasingly engaged in global HRM.
- Born-global firms are business organizations that, from inception, seek to derive significant competitive advantage from the use of resources and the sale of outputs in multiple countries.
- Cross-cultural risk arises from differences in business practices, communication styles, and many aspects of human behavior.
- Country risk (also known as political risk) refers to the potentially adverse effects on company operations and profitability caused by developments in the political, legal, and economic environments in a foreign country.
- Currency risk (also known as financial risk) refers to the risk of adverse fluctuations in exchange rates.
- Commercial risk refers to the firm's potential loss or failure from poorly developed or executed business strategies, tactics, or procedures.

What Do *You* Think?

1. Would you consider taking an expatriate assignment? Why or why not?
2. After reading about the differences in other cultures, which might be the most difficult for you to work in?

14.3 Staffing Multinational Organizations

Learning Objectives

1. Identify the three types of employees in multinational organizations.
2. Describe methods to effectively recruit global employees.
3. Explain the criteria for selecting employees for expatriate assignments.
4. Describe the most common approaches for compensating global employees.

Types of Multinational Employees

expatriates

Employees from the home (or parent) country who are working and temporarily residing in another country. Also referred to as parent-country nationals (PCNs).

host-country nationals (HCNs)

Employees who are natives of the host country.

third-country nationals (TCNs)

Employees who are natives of a country other than the home country or the host country.

When deciding how to staff operations in another country, there are three basic choices:

1. **Expatriates (PCNs).** Also referred to as parent-country nationals; employees from the home (or parent) country who are working and temporarily residing in another country.
2. **Host-country nationals (HCNs).** Employees who are natives of the host country.
3. **Third-country nationals (TCNs).** Employees who are natives of a country other than the home country or the host country.

Table 14.3 summarizes the advantages and disadvantages of each approach.

TABLE 14.3 Advantages and Disadvantages of Types of Multinational Employees

Advantages and Disadvantages of Types of Multinational Employees	
Expatriates (PCNs)	**Advantages** • They know the company, possess product/service knowledge, and are already familiar with internal company procedures. • Gives the company greater control (since the employee understands "how things are done" in the organization). • Provides valuable experience for the employee. **Disadvantages** • Cost and time involved in training (cultural preparation). • High failure rate (when an employee terminates an assignment early). The failure rate for U.S. expatriates can be as high as 40%. In other words, almost half return to the U.S. before the assignment is completed. The number-one cause of early return is spousal adjustment, primarily due to the inability to adapt to culture shock.
Host-Country Nationals (HCNs)	**Advantages** • Possess knowledge of the local culture and business customs. • Understand the local political and legal structure. • Less costly than using an expatriate (lower training costs, relocation expenses). • May already have valuable business contacts (particularly if this is a sales/marketing or business development position). **Disadvantages** • Not familiar with the company, product/services, internal procedures, etc. • May need managerial training (organizational administration, decision-making, etc.)
Third-Country Nationals (TCNs)	**Advantages** • International perspective. • Multicultural skills (multilinguistic, etc.); able to adapt quickly to other cultures. • Mobile (do not experience as high a failure rate; spousal adjustment less of a problem). **Disadvantages** • Costly to relocate. • Usually are paid premium salaries. • Are in demand and highly recruited by other companies.

Most multinational organizations will use a mix of these three types of employees. For example, a U.S. organization might use expatriates for management and supervisory positions because they are familiar with the culture, policies, and procedures of the organization. But they might use host-country nationals for positions involving production, customer service, or sales. Typically, TCNs are employed when a company has a few foreign operations and decides to open yet another.[13] But regardless of the mix of employees, managing the in-country workforce means becoming familiar with the employment laws and the culture and protocols regarding recruitment and selection. Figure 14.1 gives a few examples of how HR differs by country.

FIGURE 14.1 HR Differences by Country

How HR Differs by Country

Did you know...

- Self-employment is not permitted in China.
- The U.S. and Papua New Guinea are the only two countries in the world that do not have laws guaranteeing paid maternity leave.
- Employers in Germany are now required to give 50% of seats on supervisory boards to women.
- In Brazil, an employee's regular salary increases by one-third during their annual leave.
- In Italy, employers with over fifty employees must meet a disability quota of 7% of the workforce.
- Employees in Spain and Italy are entitled to fifteen days paid leave when they marry.
- In many African nations, it is unlawful to have company policies that prohibit discrimination against gays, because being gay is itself illegal.
- In France, an employment contract must always be written in French.
- In France, individual redundancy is a complex matter, which may only be carried out if strict procedures are followed. (A note of explanation: Many countries use the term "redundancy" to refer to being laid off).
- If a German company has five or more employees, then the employees have a right to establish a works council.
- If a company is registered in Germany with five hundred or more employees, it must have a two-tier board. One-third of the directors of the upper "supervisory" tier must be elected by the German workforce.
- In Italy, annual holiday entitlement must be carefully monitored, because the right to a paid vacation is written into the constitution.
- In the Netherlands, companies with one hundred or more employees are required to produce an annual working conditions report and plan.
- In Mexico, the constitution establishes a maximum of eight hours for shift workers, seven hours for the night shift, and a maximum of nine hours of overtime per week. For every six days of work, Mexico's workers must have one day off.

These are just a few examples of how HR laws and protocols differ among countries. Europe is composed of over fifty different countries, each with its own legal framework and employment laws. Those that are part of the European Union are also subject to EU legislation, which imposes a set of common core requirements on national laws. Operating a single HR policy across several countries without taking national differences into account could expose a company to substantial compliance violations.

Another difference in European employment law versus U.S. employment law is the fact that in the U.S., fewer aspects of the employment relationship are regulated.[14] For example, the U.S. is one of the few countries that does not have federally mandatory vacation laws. In Europe there are laws that relate to employee benefits, caps on hours worked, vacation allowances, holidays, sick leave, maternity/paternity leave, written employment contracts, and more. All European countries obligate employers to offer at least twenty days of paid leave; some require thirty or more. Of course, the U.S. does have a few laws, such as the Family and Medical Leave (FMLA), HIPAA, and the FLSA, but these only provide minimal benefits in comparison to European employment law requirements.

By European standards—and even Latin American and African and Asian standards—the Family and Medical Leave Act is stingy because it doesn't give any paid leave. The people who go on maternity leave or on FMLA leave don't have a legal right to get paid. All we're doing in the U.S. is holding open their job until they return. By European standards, that's laughable. Think of the culture shock that Europeans experience who move to the U.S. for employment.

European Union member states such as Switzerland and Germany legislatively limit weekly working hours to forty-five and thirty-five hours, respectively. The Dutch have one of the shortest average workweeks, averaging just over thirty hours.[15] The U.S. has the longest annual average working hours at 1,880 hours. There is a European Union directive that requires written employment agreements or statements of terms and conditions of employment. They are referred to as "Statements of Employment Particulars." In short, employers in Europe have to give everybody a written agreement that covers the list of topics like the place of work, pay rate, title, office hours, etc. The agreement has to be in writing and can't be changed without consent from the employee.

Don't assume that you can hire and fire. Foreign labor laws generally provide much more protection for workers than labor laws in the states. Management approaches such as "employment at will" can rarely be applied in other countries. This is especially the case with employee dismissal, because employment protection laws are generally much tougher in Europe than in the U.S. For example, top executives at Thyssenkrupp, a multinational industrial conglomerate based in Germany, decided to eliminate six thousand jobs in 2019. However, they were not able to act quickly because they had to consult with local works councils first and honor layoff-notice periods contained in employment contracts.[16] By contrast, about the same time, Kentucky coal miners arrived at work one Monday morning to discover that their employer, Blackjewel, had filed for bankruptcy and their jobs had disappeared.[17] After the miners' paychecks bounced, they blocked coal trains for weeks in protest.

In general, the employment-at-will doctrine that is so prevalent in U.S. businesses does not exist overseas. Many countries in South America, Southeast Asia, and Europe require that you have a specific reason for firing someone. In the European Union, for example, layoffs must be negotiated with worker representatives and approved by the appropriate government authority. In Malaysia, you must use the last-in, first-out rule if you are restructuring. Some countries legally require you to work with underperforming employees. Firing workers for any reason is almost impossible in several Southeast Asian countries, such as Indonesia and Vietnam.

Four Ways to Recruit Internationally

The basic recruiting concepts for international assignments are similar to those discussed in Chapter 5. However, the following four can yield results when hiring globally:

1. **Do your homework.** Before recruiting candidates from other countries, research the laws regarding work permits and visas. Make sure you understand the steps to ensure any worker recruited internationally will legally be able to work for your business, as soon as you need them and where you need them. Most countries take their work immigration laws very seriously, partly for economic reasons (when an immigrant is hired, then that is a job that does not go to a citizen of the country), and partly for national security reasons.

2. **Rethink your social media strategy.** Facebook, Twitter, and LinkedIn are not the dominant social media sites in every country. To interact with potential candidates in the countries you are targeting, find out which social sites are the most popular there among the types of employees you seek. For instance, in Russia and Eastern Europe, Vkontakte has long been a social media leader and is sometimes called "the Russian Facebook." In Asia, social media sites QQ, QZone, Google+, and WeChat all rank higher than Twitter or LinkedIn in of number of users.

3. **Focus on women.** In many developing countries, educated, skilled, and ambitious women are often overlooked, according to economist Sylvia Ann Hewlett, co-author of *Winning the War for Talent in Emerging Markets: Why Women Are the Solution.*[18] Globally, 55% of college graduates are now female, and many highly qualified women consider themselves very ambitious, according to Hewlett. These women, who may be overlooked by local companies, represent talented potential candidates for growing international companies eager to establish a presence in emerging markets.

4. **Expand your circle.** Many North American companies interested in recruiting internationally are focused on the leading emerging economies. But business continues to become more global as more countries continue to develop. Recruiters should keep abreast of additional emerging economies, and seek qualified candidates from these others. For example, newly emerging markets include Bangladesh, Egypt, Indonesia, Iran, Mexico, Nigeria, Pakistan, the Philippines, Turkey, and Vietnam.

Talent Analytics

When recruiting individuals for international assignments, the compensation structure should reflect the difference in taxes and living expenses between their home country and the country to which they are being assigned.

This graphic compares the highest personal income tax rate in various countries:

Source: Trading Economics

A cost-of-living calculator can also be used to compare different cities. The following link compares the cost of living between cities: https://www.expatistan.com/cost-of-living/comparison/dallas/london.

For example, if you are transferring an employee from Dallas, Texas, to London, England, the cost-of-living calculator reveals the following:

- Food –6%
- Housing +37%
- Clothes +25%
- Transportation +125%
- Personal Care –23%
- Entertainment +11%
- Overall Cost of Living +40%

Thus, the employee will need 40% higher compensation in London to maintain the same lifestyle they enjoyed in Dallas.

Selection Criteria

There are three major criteria in selecting an employee for an expatriate assignment.

1. **Cultural adaptability.** Has the employee been exposed to diverse cultures before? The more cross-cultural experience a person has had (specifically, experience in social interactions), the better their ability to adapt will be.[19]

2. **Communication skills.** Does the employee already possess the necessary foreign language skills? If not, does the employee have some knowledge of another foreign language? Employ-

ees who already know one foreign language generally have an easier time learning another than someone who has never studied foreign languages. Also, employees who have significant foreign travel experience have probably developed more cross-cultural communication skills than employees who have not. Some research also indicates that extroverts have an easier time adjusting in other cultures.[20]

3. **Family status.** Employees without families will most likely have the easiest time adjusting. This does not imply that employees with families should be excluded from consideration, but it is a concern that should be thought about when selecting someone for an expatriate assignment. Families who have lived or traveled abroad will have an easier time adjusting to a foreign assignment.

Whether deciding to staff multinational positions with expatriates, HCNs, or TCNs, there are some common characteristics that facilitate international effectiveness:

- **Technical competence.** Must have adequate managerial and technical capabilities.
- **Self-reliance.** Entrepreneurial, proactive mind-set, ability to function with considerable independence and limited support from headquarters.
- **Adaptability.** Ability to adjust to foreign cultures, cultural empathy, flexibility, diplomacy, and a positive attitude
- **Interpersonal skills.** Ability to build relationships is key.
- **Leadership ability.** Must view change positively and proactively manage opportunities and threats.
- **Physical and emotional health.** Must handle stresses of living abroad.
- **Spouse/dependents.** Are they prepared for living abroad and able to adapt and handle culture shock?

Compensation

Much of what you learned about compensation in Chapter 9 applies to GHRM. For example, you still need a compensation philosophy, a compensation plan, and an understanding of equity and expectancy theory. Job evaluation systems can also be useful in establishing rates of pay for international employees. However, there are factors in GHRM that make compensation decisions more challenging. There are differences in cost of living and taxation between countries. Some countries have higher levels of mandated benefits and other variations in employment laws.

Fluctuations in the value of currencies between the home country and the host country need to be considered. For example, in April of 2020, the U.S. dollar was trading at $.80 on the British pound sterling. Therefore, a U.S.-based employee working in Great Britain, who is paid in dollars, will realize only $.80 in purchasing power for that dollar. Would you take an assignment in England, knowing that you would lose 20% of your purchasing power? Probably not, but you might be enticed to take the assignment if your employer offered additional compensation to offset the exchange rate. An expatriate might also have additional expenses they would not incur at home, such as private schooling or security.

A detailed explanation of global compensation plans is left to textbooks on international human resource management. Here, we will just overview four common approaches to global compensation plans:

Balance Sheet Approach

The **balance sheet approach** to global compensation is a system designed to equalize the purchasing power of employees living abroad. This method uses the home country as a reference point, and then adjusts the compensation to account for cost differences. The home country salary is the base, and then the employee typically receives allowances for items such as higher housing cost, currency exchange losses, or higher tax rates. The approach is appropriate for expatriates who are eventually expected to return to their home country. Compensation is usually based upon the home country currency, and retirement benefits are based upon home country laws.

> **balance sheet approach**
>
> A global compensation system designed to equalize the purchasing power of employees living abroad.

Local-Plus Approach

The **local-plus approach** pays employees based upon the salary structure of the host country plus additional compensation for expenses incurred by employees. This is in contrast to the balance sheet approach in which the base salary is the home country structure. The "plus" in local-plus refers to items such as housing, transportation, dependents' education, or higher tax rates. One advantage of the local-plus approach is that it keeps salaries of international employees on par with their local colleagues, thereby maintaining internal equity. For example, if a U.S. company sends a manager to work at its facility in China, where salaries are typically lower than the U.S., the balance sheet approach would provide much higher compensation for the U.S.-based employee than his or her counterparts in China, which may cause resentment and perceptions of inequity. In fact, this is one of the major criticisms of the balance sheet approach, in that rewards need to be perceived as fair to be motivating.[21] AstraZeneca's head of global mobility developed a "Total Rewards" package, which was tailored specifically for the country or region to which the employee was being sent. One example is that people working in South America get "today money" with high base salaries rather than pension plans. Those working in the West typically have a lower base pay because it is easier to offer a broader range of benefits.[22]

> **local-plus approach**
>
> Pays employees based upon the salary structure of the host country plus additional compensation for expenses incurred by employees.

Global Market Approach

The **global market approach** pays employees based upon an equivalent compensation scale, regardless of their home country. This approach is appropriate for a multinational enterprise in which employees from different countries are expected to move to more than one country during their career. For example, Toyota operates sixty-nine manufacturing companies in twenty-seven countries excluding Japan.[23] Many executives will work in multiple countries as part of their career development. The intent of this approach is to pay employees based on an international scale, with allowances for additional expenses. An international basket of goods and services would be used for all employees regardless of their home country.[24] Thus, it is similar to the local-plus approach in terms of the allowances, but it is different in that an international standard is established for the base pay rather than using a local standard. The global market approach creates a consistent pay structure across international assignments, but it may require greater administrative effort.

> **global market approach**
>
> Pays employees based upon an equivalent compensation scale, regardless of their home country.

Tetra Pak Global Resources is a food processing and packaging solutions company with 240,000 employees around the world. When employees are assigned to work in other countries, their base salary is a blend of the company's top seven markets, and the base salary structure and target incentive is the same for everyone, although the incentive does vary depending on the level and location. They also receive an offshore pension. "That gives us a common basis for the expats, and the philosophy behind it is that they will always know what they will be earning," says Adrian Moule, director of the Global Mobility Centre of Expertise at Tetra Pak. They are also given location allowances and cost of living adjustments.[25]

Split-pay Approach

split-pay approach

Pays a portion of compensation in host-country currency and a portion in home-country currency.

The **split-pay approach** pays a portion of compensation in host country currency and a portion in home country currency. Typically, the spendable income (compensation spent in the host country, such as living expenses) is paid in host country currency. Other compensation is paid in the home country currency. This approach can help to ensure that compensation complies with local requirements and allows the employee more flexibility in paying obligations in both their home and host countries. It also offers financial stability in host countries with an unstable currency by allocating a larger percentage of compensation in the home country currency.

Key Takeaways

- Expatriates (also referred to as parent-country nationals, PCNs) are employees from the home (or parent) country who are working and temporarily residing in another country.
- Host-country nationals (HCNs) are employees who are natives of the host country.
- Third-country nationals (TCNs) are employees who are natives of a country other than the home country or the host country.
- A major difference in European employment law versus U.S. employment law is the fact that in the U.S., fewer aspects of the employment relationship are regulated.
- Before recruiting candidates from other countries, research the laws regarding work permits and visas.
- Facebook, Twitter, and LinkedIn are not the dominant social media sites in every country.
- In many developing countries, educated, skilled, and ambitious women are often overlooked.
- The three major criteria in selecting an employee for an expatriate assignment are cultural adaptability, communication skills, and family status.
- The balance sheet approach to global compensation is a system designed to equalize the purchasing power of employees living abroad.
- The local-plus approach pays employees based upon the salary structure of the host country plus additional compensation for expenses incurred by employees.
- The global market approach pays employees based upon an equivalent compensation scale, regardless of their home country.
- The split-pay approach pays a portion of compensation in host country currency and a portion in home country currency.

What Do *You* Think?

1. As a global human resource manager, what steps would you take to prepare an employee for a job in another country?
2. If you were making multinational staffing decisions, which approach do you think would be the best overall: hiring expatriates, HCNs, or TCNs?
3. Given that U.S. companies usually require longer work days and fewer days of paid leave, how might you use this information to recruit people for expatriate assignments?
4. When considering the selection criteria, which would you put more emphasis on? Why?
5. If you accepted an international assignment, which pay structure would you prefer?

14.4 Talent Development in GHRM

Learning Objectives

1. Identify the major causes of expatriate success and failure.
2. Describe the stages of culture shock.
3. Consider the types of training programs that will benefit expatriates.

Expatriate Success and Failure

We previously said that an expatriate is an employee from the home (or parent) country who is working and temporarily residing in another country. The key word here is "residing." Someone who is on a short-term assignment of perhaps a week to a month or two, and is living in a hotel, is not normally considered an expatriate. Typically, an expatriate assignment is three months to many years.

The most significant risk of using expatriates to fill positions is the possibility of expatriate assignment failure, which is the premature return of an expatriate due to an inability to perform well abroad. Expatriate assignment failure is costly to a firm due to lost productivity and relocation costs, and costly to the expatriates themselves due to family stress and career disruption. Failure is unfortunately very common in expatriates, with as much as 40% of assignments ending in failure and early return.[26] Of those failures, 28% are due to the inability of the family to adapt, and 28% are due to the inability of the employee to adapt. The number-one reason for expatriate assignment failure is the inability of the spouse and/or children to be able to deal with culture shock.[27]

Culture Shock

Culture shock is a phenomenon experienced by people who move across cultures and into a new environment that requires many adjustments in a relatively short period of time.[28] Culture shock challenges people's frames of reference to such an extent that their sense of self, especially in terms of nationality, can come into question. People, in effect, experience a shock reaction to new cultural experiences that cause psychological disorientation because they misunderstand or do not recognize important cues.

culture shock

A phenomenon experienced by people who move across cultures and into a new environment that requires many adjustments in a relatively short period of time.

Unfamiliar foods are one aspect of culture shock experienced by expatriates, like chicken feet soup, a delicacy in some Asian countries.

Source: © Shutterstock, Inc.

It is also helpful for expatriates to become familiar with the stages of culture shock. When someone experiences a new culture for an extended period of time (for example, spending a couple of months or longer in a different place), then typically four stages are experienced. They are described here and illustrated in Figure 14.2:

Stage One: The Honeymoon. In this stage, there is a feeling of excitement about all of the new experiences.

Stage Two: Irritation. In this stage, the newness has started to wear off, and there might be feelings of irritation or annoyance, or longing for things the way they used to be. It typically is a time of stress.

Stage Three: Gradual Adjustment. One starts to become able to read verbal cues and begins dealing with things that seemed like an annoyance before, with logical reasoning ("Oh, I see why they do it that way here now"), or even humor (maybe not totally understanding it, but being able to laugh about it).

Stage Four: Feeling at Home. The new culture is starting to feel like home, and a sense of belonging starts to occur. One no longer feels out of their comfort zone.

FIGURE 14.2 The Stages of Culture Shock

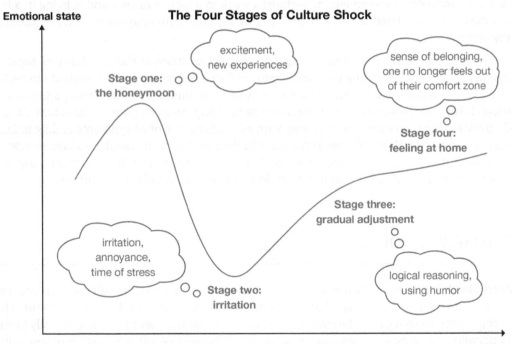

One key in reducing the failure rate for expatriate assignments is to be sure that adequate training and development are extended not only to the employee, but to any family members who are moving also. Returning home is often called repatriation. Sometimes employees and their families experience reverse culture shock when they return to the U.S., and they need to be prepared for that.

Expatriate Training

Proper training is crucial to expatriate success.[29] It is also important to recognize that training should happen not only prior to the assignment, but during and after as well. Table 14.4 summarizes some approaches that can help expatriates to be successful at each stage of their assignment.

TABLE 14.4 Talent Development for Expatriates

Talent Development for Expatriates	
Before They Go	• Develop a clear set of objectives and expectations. • Make sure that selection procedures are valid. Know the predictive factors for success and use these in making the selection. • Provide language and cultural training for the employee and the family. • Offer counseling and career assistance for the spouse. • Establish career planning systems that reward international assignments.
While They Are Away	• Jointly establish a competency-based developmental plan. • Identify mentors who can be a liaison and support person from home. • Establish networking and coaching connections with other in-country employees. • Keep communications open so that the expatriate is kept aware of events at the home country location. • Arrange for frequent visits back home (for the employee and family).
When They Come Back Home	• Throw a welcome-home party. • Offer counseling to ease the transition. • Arrange conferences and presentations to ensure that knowledge and skills acquired away from home are identified and disseminated. • Get feedback from the employee and the family about how well the organization handled the expatriation and repatriation process.

Key Takeaways

- An expatriate is an employee from the home (or parent) country who is working and temporarily residing in another country.
- Expatriate assignment failure is costly to a firm due to lost productivity and relocation costs, and costly to the expatriates themselves due to family stress and career disruption. Failure

is unfortunately very common in expatriates, with up to 40% of assignments ending in failure and early return.

- Culture shock is a phenomenon experienced by people who move across cultures and into a new environment that requires many adjustments in a relatively short period of time.
- Culture shock challenges people's frames of reference to such an extent that their sense of self, especially in terms of nationality, can come into question.
- Proper training is crucial to expatriate success.
- It is also important to recognize that training should happen not only prior to the assignment, but during and after as well.

What Do *You* Think?

1. Have you ever experienced culture shock? What steps did you take to help you adapt?
2. As a global human resource manager, what steps would you take to prepare an employee for a job in another country?
3. What are some ways that a company can help with spousal adjustment or the adjustment of children?
4. What do you think might be the most challenging part of repatriation for someone who has been away from home for three years or more?

14.5 Performance Management and Labor Relations in GHRM

Learning Objectives

1. Distinguish between performance management in the U.S. and other countries.
2. Identify the ways in which performance appraisal is conducted in other cultures.
3. Recognize the impact of international labor organizations and framework agreements.

Performance Management in Other Countries

international performance management (IPM)

A strategic process that enables the multinational corporation to evaluate and improve individual, subsidiary unit, and corporate performance against clearly defined, preset objectives.

International performance management (IPM) is a strategic process that enables the multinational corporation to evaluate and improve individual, subsidiary unit, and corporate performance against clearly defined, preset objectives. Effective IPM creates an incentive system that can ensure international employees and overseas subsidiaries are acting in accordance with the home company's interests. But before we examine IPM further, let's do a little review of some of the basic concepts in performance appraisal.

An effective performance management system focuses on identifying, measuring, and dealing with employee performance. Key aspects of performance management include:

- How organizational strategies are linked to a performance management system.

- Establishing a legally defensible and effective performance appraisal system.
- How to address performance problems and concerns with individuals.

Performance management is a key component in managing any business, as you learned in Chapter 8. It allows a company to measure how well it has traveled along its planned pathway, to check whether resources are being utilized effectively, and what risks must be dealt with. It also motivates personnel to keep focused on desired goals and helps identify training needs.

Although establishing performance criteria is a difficult task because of the many differences in international environments, equitable productivity standards that are applicable to manufacturing and service industries will need to be determined within each foreign subsidiary. Performance criteria and goals are best established by combining the values and norms of each local environment with the home office's performance standards. An individual country profile should be developed and should reflect the foreign subsidiary's environment. This profile should be used to review any factors that may have an effect on the expatriate employee's performance. Such factors include language, culture, politics, labor relations, economy, government, control, and communication.

Once any underlying factors that may affect an expatriate employee's performance have been determined, the information should be used to group together the organization's multinational subsidiaries into country clusters on the basis of similarities among each country's environmental factors. Critical professional profiles for each expatriate employee should be compared against others within that country cluster to ensure that proper performance measurement criteria are, in fact, being used when appraising individual employees who have been placed on international assignments.

International performance management is most effective if it avoids a number of common pitfalls. These are:

- Linking of appraisal too directly and rigidly to pay reviews or promotion.
- Encouragement of risk avoidance.
- Stifling of innovation.
- Promotion of a blame culture.
- Insensitivity to an individual's cultural and personal circumstances.
- Infringement of antidiscrimination laws and company policies.

Performance Appraisal Across Cultures

The Organisation for Economic Co-operation and Development (OECD) defines performance appraisal as "Assessment against a set of predetermined criteria of the efficiency and effectiveness with which an individual fulfils an agreed set of tasks. Such appraisals are frequently used in assessing whether managers should qualify for pay increases or promotion."[30] Performance appraisal involves a structured process for both evaluating an employee's past performance and setting future targets/timetables.

Failed international assignments can be extremely costly to an organization. A consistent and detailed assessment of an expatriate employee's performance, as well as appraisal of the operation as a whole, is critical to the success of an international assignment. Issues such as the criteria and timing of performance reviews, raises, and bonuses should be discussed and agreed on before the employees are selected and placed on international assignments.

Although appraising the performance of an expatriate employee is just as important as appraising the performance of employees hired for domestic assignments, each international assignment is different and unique unto itself. A general rule in appraising expatriate employees is that each international office should use a different appraisal system. Employers should not take a performance appraisal system that was designed for appraising domestic employees and try to modify it for use with expatriate employees because many variables (e.g., cultural environment and mind-set, task criteria, business protocols) need to be understood and taken into consideration when assessing an expatriate employee's performance.

Generally, self-evaluation methods are less common in Europe than in the U.S., and few companies use peers or customers as inputs to the appraisal process. Performance is generally linked in some way to pay reviews or promotional decisions, although in Sweden—which has the highest incidence of performance appraisal in Europe—the link is particularly weak. In Hungary, performance is linked to pay determination rather than training and development, while in Romania strong cultural sensitivities to negative feedback severely limit the use of appraisals as a performance management tool. In Russia, there remains a reluctance to place too much weight on individual accountability, and therefore employees are evaluated more on team and company performance than their separate contribution to goal achievement.

HR Talk: Evelyn Walter, GHPR, SHRM-SCP

Executive Director, HR North America

Cummins, Inc.

It is important that we align our HR objectives with the strategy of the company. At Cummins, we do accomplish this by using a goal tree structure which cascades through the organization. The organization focuses on just three to five goals at a time, at least two of which are people-related.

In 2013, Cummins announced an acquisition of all sixteen of the privately owned distributor businesses throughout North America. The transition of those businesses into Cummins, Inc., has taken place over the past four years, and was completed in 2018 with the final acquisition of our Canadian businesses. Moving nine thousand employees from sixteen individually owned companies in two different countries into a *Fortune* 200 company comes with a lot of promise and much hard work.

Some of our HR challenges are the hourly workforce strategy (span of control, how to onboard hourly employees in remote locations) and creating the "Right Environment" culture. For Cummins, the right environment means that employees feel like they are treated well, are engaged, not overly fatigued, and healthy. We pay attention to the physical and mental well-being of our employees. Our code of conduct outlines how we expect our employees to be treated, and how they should treat others. We also emphasize career growth and rewards. But we also have to balance this with cost efficiency, which sometimes leads to difficult questions.

Labor Relations in GHRM

The first moves toward international labor conventions date back to the beginning of the nineteenth century. In the second half of the nineteenth century, the idea was first taken up by private associations. Thereafter, a number of proposals to promote international regulation of labor matters were made in the French and German parliaments. The first official initiative came from Switzerland—where, following proposals made in 1876 and 1881, and in consultation with other European countries, the Swiss government suggested convening a conference on the matter in Bern in May 1890.

The establishment of an International Association for the Legal Protection of Workers, the seat of which was in Basel, was followed by a congress held in Brussels in 1897.[31] The activity of this private organization led the Swiss government to convene international conferences in 1905 and 1906 in Bern, where the first two international labor conventions were adopted. One of these related to the prohibition of night work for women in industrial employment, and the other to the prohibition of the use of white phosphorus in the manufacture of matches.

During World War I, the trade union organizations of both sides, as well as those of neutral countries, insisted that their voice be heard at the time of the settlement of peace, and that the peace treaties contain clauses for improving the condition of workers. The peace conference entrusted the examination of this question to a special group known as the Commission on International Labour Legislation. The work of the commission led to the inclusion in the Treaty of Versailles and the other peace treaties of Part XIII, which dealt with labor matters. This section of the treaties provided for the establishment of an International Labour Organization (ILO), which might adopt conventions and recommendations in this field.[32] Conventions would be binding only on those states which ratified them.

In October 1919, the International Labour Conference met in Washington to adopt the first conventions and to appoint a governing body. Since then, the International Labour Conference has met regularly once a year, except during the World War II.

At the end of the World War II, the International Labour Conference adopted in May 1944, in Philadelphia, a declaration which defined again the aims and purposes of the organization. This declaration affirmed, in particular:[33]

- That labor is not a commodity.
- That freedom of expression and of association are essential to sustained progress.
- That poverty anywhere constitutes a danger to prosperity everywhere.
- That the "war against want" requires to be carried on with unrelenting vigor within each nation, and by continuous and concerted international effort in which the representatives of workers and employers, enjoying equal status with those of governments, join with them in free discussion and democratic decision with a view to the promotion of the common welfare.

The declaration affirmed that all human beings, irrespective of race, creed, or sex, have the right to pursue both their material well-being and their spiritual development in conditions of freedom and dignity, of economic security, and equal opportunity. The declaration then defined a number of specific objectives, as shown in Figure 14.3.

FIGURE 14.3 Objectives of the Declaration of Philadelphia: International Labour Conference

- Full employment and the raising of living standards;

- Facilities of training policies in regard to wages, hours of work and other conditions of work calculated to ensure a just share of the fruits of progress to all;

- The effective recognition of the right of collective bargaining;

- The co-operation of management and labor in the continuous improvement of productive efficiency; and

- The collaboration of workers and employer in the preparation and application of social and economic measures, the extension of social security measures to provide a basic income to all in need of such protection, and comprehensive medical care, etc.

Source: Adapted from "ILO Declaration of Philadelphia: Declaration concerning the aims and purposes of the International Labour Organisation." Retrieved from: https://www.ilo.org/legacy/english/inwork/cb-policy-guide/declarationofPhiladelphia1944.pdf.

international framework agreements (IFAs)

Voluntary labor agreements negotiated between a GUF and an MNE in order to establish an ongoing relationship between the parties, and ensure that the company respects the same standards in all the countries where it operates.

Because of increasing globalization of business operations and concerns about global respect for fundamental labor rights, unions and employers have responded by augmenting their cross-border collaborative activities, specifically through the signing of **international framework agreements (IFAs)** between global union federations (GUFs) and MNEs.[34] IFAs are voluntary labor agreements negotiated between a GUF and an MNE in order to establish an ongoing relationship between the parties, and ensure that the company respects the same standards in all the countries where it operates. This pattern of transnational labor relations has gained ground lately, as evidenced by the increasing number of IFAs being concluded since 2000.[35] Although IFAs are not collective bargaining agreements in the same sense as agreements reached at the national or local levels, they do provide a framework to encourage union recognition and bargaining.[36]

Key Takeaways

- International performance management (IPM) is a strategic process that enables the multinational corporation to evaluate and improve individual, subsidiary unit, and corporate performance against clearly defined, preset objectives.
- Effective IPM creates an incentive system that can assure that international employees and overseas subsidiaries are acting in accordance with the home company's interests.
- Failed international assignments can be extremely costly to an organization. A consistent and detailed assessment of an expatriate employee's performance, as well as appraisal of the operation as a whole, is critical to the success of an international assignment.
- Although appraising the performance of an expatriate employee is just as important as appraising the performance of employees hired for domestic assignments, each international assignment is different and unique unto itself.
- The first moves toward international labor conventions date back to the beginning of the nineteenth century, when the idea was first taken up by private associations.
- During World War I, the trade union organizations of both sides, as well as those of neutral countries, insisted that their voice be heard at the time of the settlement of peace, and that the peace treaties contain clauses for improving the condition of workers.
- In October 1919, the International Labour Conference met in Washington to adopt the first conventions and to appoint a governing body. Since then, the International Labour Conference has met regularly, in general once a year, except during the World War II.
- Because of increasing globalization of business operations and concerns about global respect for fundamental labor rights, unions and employers have responded by augmenting their cross-border collaborative activities, specifically through the signing of international framework agreements (IFAs) between global union federations (GUFs) and MNEs.
- IFAs are voluntary labor agreements negotiated between a GUF and an MNE in order to establish an ongoing relationship between the parties and ensure that the company respects the same standards in all the countries where it operates.

What Do *You* Think?

1. Do you think the U.S. has stronger or weaker performance appraisal systems than other countries?
2. Should expatriates be involved in setting their performance objectives and in designing the performance appraisal methods?
3. What might be the result if you used the home country performance management processes for all expatriates, regardless of the country they were working in?
4. Why is it important to be familiar with how labor relations have evolved in other countries?
5. Do you agree with all aspects of the Philadelphia Declaration of the International Labour Conference?

14.6 Conclusion

This chapter explored the cultural context of global human resource management (GHRM). The various types of multinational organizations, the risks involved in international business, and global multicultural challenges were discussed. The unique challenges of recruiting, training, compensating, and managing various types of global employees were addressed.

Theory-into-Practice (TIP) Exercises

1. Describe a time in which you experienced culture shock. If you have traveled or lived in another country, then please share international examples. However, even if you have never been out of the country, everyone in the class has still experienced some form of culture shock. Perhaps it was traveling in the U.S., or starting a new job, or even starting college. Describe how you felt, what was different in the new environment, and what social cues you had to learn. Then exchange these experiences and perceptions with one of more of your classmates.

2. Choose a country to conduct a comparative HR analysis with the United States. Research the HR practices there and prepare a summary that identifies the similarities and differences in employment law, recruitment, selection, talent development, compensation and benefits, and performance management.

3. Form a group of three to four students. Then each student should interview one person from a different country about their cultural differences from the United States in regard to meta-communication. Share your results with each other, and practice speaking with each other using the different styles of communication.

Case Study: The Long Arm of the IRS

Source: © Shutterstock, Inc.

It's no secret that U.S. expats are very frustrated and angry over FATCA's, the Foreign Account Tax Compliance Act, impact on their life abroad. It was created to prevent tax evasion. FATCA requires employees to file yet another form to the IRS stating specified foreign financial assets. Expat tax filing is already complicated, and the resulting banking problems have wreaked havoc on their lives. They have had enough, and they are taking the IRS to court.

In addition to individual filing requirements, banks are required to report on the accounts of their American clients. If they do not comply, the IRS will withhold 30% of the expats' payments. This can be crippling for the banks, and many are simply choosing not to work with U.S. expats. *The Wall Street Journal* states that 16% of expats have lost their bank accounts, mortgages, and other financial services in their host country and 22.5% are unable to open savings or retirement accounts. Many employees have lost promotions or start-up opportunities because foreign companies want to avoid the higher compliance costs of working with the Americans and opening up their books to the IRS.

The expatriates who filed the lawsuit against the IRS claim that FATCA invades their privacy and unfairly discriminates against those living overseas. They also state that the regulations set forth in FATCA impose a "guilty-until-proven-innocent" approach to Americans living abroad. Senator Rand Paul has stated that FATCA's reach has gone too far and ignored Congress. He is leading the charge to repeal the act. The U.S. government has thus far stated that the plaintiffs have no standing in this case because they have not suffered sufficient injury or damage.[37]

 FATCA Explained: The New Tax Law for U.S. Citizens Abroad

The Foreign Account Tax Compliance Act—FATCA—identifies U.S. citizens living abroad in order to impose tax payments.

View the video online at: http://www.youtube.com/embed/appsjRuXwZs?rel=0

Case Discussion Questions

1. Do you agree with the expats' case against the IRS? Why or why not?
2. Would these issues cause you to reconsider working in a foreign country?
3. As a global HR manager, what could you do to prepare an employee who is going to work in a foreign country for this problem?

Resources

1. **FedEE Global.** Website of The Federation of International Employers, an international HR support organization for multinational employers.

   https://www.fedee.com

2. **CIA World Fact Book.** Profiles of countries provided by the CIA. Provides information on the history, people and society, government, economy, energy, geography, communications, transportation, military, and other issues.

   https://www.cia.gov/the-world-factbook/

3. **International Labour Organization.** The labor agency of the United Nations that focuses on labor practices across international boundaries. Includes publications, research, labor standards, statistics, and databases.

   https://www.ilo.org/global/research/lang--en/index.htm

4. **Bureau of International Labor Affairs.** An agency of the U.S. Department of Labor which assists in formulating international economic, trade, and immigration policies affecting American workers.

   https://www.dol.gov/agencies/ilab

Endnotes

1. Case written by Crews, P. (2020). Adapted from Hunt, J. (2015). Toyota plant program trains, pays aspiring employees still in school. *Charleston Gazette-Mail*. Retrieved from https://www.wvgazettemail.com/business/toyota-plant-program-trains-pays-aspiring-employees-still-in-school/article_3c8d63be-53bd-571e-b072-92054b7bd000.html

2. Multinational Corporation. *Business Dictionary*. Retrieved April 9, 2020 from http://www.businessdictionary.com/definition/multinational-corporation-MNC.html

3. SME definition. *thebalance small business*. Retrieved April 9, 2020 from https://www.thebalancesmb.com/sme-small-to-medium-enterprise-definition-2947962

4. The World Bank. *Small and medium enterprises (SMES)*. Retrieved April 9, 2020 from https://www.worldbank.org/en/topic/smefinance

5. Baronchelli, G., & Cassia, F. (2014). Exploring the antecedents of born-global companies' international development. *International Entrepreneurship and Management Journal, 10*(1), 67-79.

6. Stewart, M. (2021). Which five companies do the most overseas manufacturing? ITI. Retrieved January 24, 2021 from https://www.itimanufacturing.com/five-companies-overseas-manufacturing/

7. Gomes-Casseres, B. (2009). Nummi: What Toyota learned and GM didn't. Harvard Business Review. Retrieved January 24, 2021 from https://hbr.org/2009/09/nummi-what-toyota-learned

8. *Cultural challenges in managing international projects*. (2014). AMACOM, Publishing Division of the American Management Association.

9. Mauri, A. (2012). Cultural differences in the strategy of the negotiation between France and Italy: The approach of the interlocutor. *Studii De Stiinta Si Cultura, VIII*(4 (31), 93-104.

10. McMurray, A., & Scott, D. (2013). Work values ethic, GNP per capita and country of birth relationships. *Journal of Business Ethics, 116*(3), 655-666.

11. Richmond, R. (2019). Trade Network Centrality and Currency Risk Premia. *Journal of Finance, 74*(3), 1315-1361.

12. Gervais, A. (2018). Uncertainty, risk aversion and international trade. *Journal of International Economics, 115*, 145-158.

13. Reynolds, C. (1997). Strategic employment of third country nationals: Keys to sustaining the transformation of HR functions. *Human Resource Planning, 20*(1), 33-93.

14. Barbieri, P. (2016). Introduction to the Special Section: Employment Protection Legislation and Labour Markets in Europe. *European Sociological Review, 32*(4), 469-470.

15. This country works the longest hours in Europe. (2018). *World Economic Forum*. Retrieved from https://www.weforum.org/agenda/2018/02/greeks-work-longest-hours-in-europe/

16. Brin, D.W. (2020). Smoother sailing. *HR Magazine, 65*(1), 75-81.

17. Ibid.

18. Hewlett, S.A., & Rashid, R. (2011). *Winning the war for talent in emerging markets: Why women are the solution*. Brighton, Mass.: Harvard Business Review Press.

19. Chang, W., Yuan, Y., & Chuang, Y. (2013). The relationship between international experience and cross-cultural adaptability. *International Journal of Intercultural Relations, 37*(2), 268-273.

20. Gupta, R., Banerjee, P., & Gaur, J. (2012). Exploring the role of the spouse in expatriate failure: A grounded theory-based investigation of expatriate spouse adjustment issues from India. *The International Journal of Human Resource Management, 23*(17), 3559-3577.

21. Bonache, J., & Zárraga-Oberty, C. (2017). The traditional approach to compensating global mobility: Criticisms and alternatives. *The International Journal of Human Resource Management: Annual Review, 28*(1), 149-169.

22. Expatriate management policy trends. *Mercer*. Retrieved April 15, 2020 from https://mobilityexchange.mercer.com/Insights/article/Expatriate-Management-Policy-Trends

23. Toyota. *Toyota in the world*. Retrieved April 14, 2020 from https://www.toyotauk.com/about-toyota/

24. Bonache, J., & Stirpe, L. (2012). Compensating global employees. In G. K. Stahl, I. Björkman, & S. Morris (Eds.), *Handbook of research in international human resource management* (2nd ed., pp. 162–182). Cheltenham, U.K.: Edward Elgar Publishing.

25. Expatriate management policy trends. *Mercer*. Retrieved April 15, 2020 from https://mobilityexchange.mercer.com/Insights/article/Expatriate-Management-Policy-Trends

26. Aiken, D. E. (2013). Collaboration experiences and expatriate assignment success (Order No. 3598868). Available from ProQuest Dissertations & Theses Global.

27. Ibid.

28. Qun, W., Syihabuddin, S., Mulyati, Y., & Damalanti, V.D. (2018). Perceiving and dealing with culture shock: The study of Chinese-Indonesian language students. *International Journal of Education, 11*(1), 18-26.

29. Shay, J., & Tracey, J. (1997). Expatriate Managers: Reasons for Failure and Implications for Training. *Cornell Hotel and Restaurant Administration Quarterly, 38*(1), 30-35.

30. OECD. *Performance appraisal*. Retrieved April 10, 2020 from https://stats.oecd.org/glossary/detail.asp?ID=4799

31. International Association for the Legal Protection of Workers 1901. *UIA*. Retrieved October 29, 2019 from https://uia.org/s/or/en/1100037634

32. International Labour Organization. *History of the ILO*. Retrieved from https://www.ilo.org/global/about-the-ilo/history/lang--en/index.htm

33. Lee, E. (1994). The Declaration of Philadelphia: Retrospect and prospect. *International Labour Review, 133*(4), 467-484.

34. Luterbacher, U., Prosser, A., & Papadakis, K. (2017). An emerging transnational industrial relations? Exploring the prospects for cross-border labour bargaining. *International Labour Review, 156*(3-4), 307-343.

35. Ibid.

36. International Conference of Free Trade Unions. (2004). *A trade union guide to globalization*. Brussels, Belgium.

37. Case Written by Crews, P. (2020). Adapted from U.S. expats taking FATCA matter into their own hands. *Greenback Expat Tax Services*. Retrieved March 16, 2020 from https://www.greenbacktaxservices.com/blog/us-expats-taking-fatca-matters-into-own-hands/.

Index